Vernacular Law

Custom was fundamental to medieval legal practice. Whether in a property dispute or a trial for murder, the aggrieved and accused would go to the lay court, where cases were resolved according to custom. What custom meant, however, went through a radical shift in the medieval period. Between the twelfth and thirteenth centuries, custom went from being a largely oral and performed practice to one that was also conceptualized in writing. Based on French lawbooks known as *coutumiers*, Ada Maria Kuskowski traces the repercussions of this transformation – which saw oral customs come to be expressed as bodies of written rules and the language of law shift from elite Latin to the common vernacular – on the cultural world of law. *Vernacular Law* offers a fresh understanding of the formation of a new field of knowledge: authors combined ideas, experience, and critical thought to write lawbooks that made disparate customs into the field known as customary law.

Ada Maria Kuskowski is Assistant Professor of History at the University of Pennsylvania. Her interdisciplinary approach weaves together history, law, and literary approaches to understand how legal cultures developed in Europe. This is her first book.

See the Studies in Legal History series website at
http://studiesinlegalhistory.org/

Studies in Legal History

EDITORS

Lisa Ford, University of New South Wales
Michael Lobban, London School of Economics and Political Science
Thomas McSweeney, William & Mary Law School
Reuel Schiller, University of California, Hastings College of the Law
Taisu Zhang, Yale Law School

Other books in the series:

E. Claire Cage, *The Science of Proof: Forensic Medicine in Modern France*
Kristin A. Olbertson, *The Dreadful Word: Speech Crime and Polite Gentlemen in Massachusetts, 1690–1776*
Edgardo Pérez Morales, *Unraveling Abolition: Legal Culture and Slave Emancipation in Colombia*
Lyndsay Campbell, *Truth and Privilege: Libel Law in Massachusetts and Nova Scotia, 1820–1840*
Sara M. Butler, *Pain, Penance, and Protest: Peine Forte et Dure in Medieval England*
Michael Lobban, *Imperial Incarceration: Detention without Trial in the Making of British Colonial Africa*
Stefan Jurasinski and Lisi Oliver, *The Laws of Alfred: The* Domboc *and the Making of Anglo-Saxon Law*
Sascha Auerbach, *Armed with Sword and Scales: Law, Culture, and Local Courtrooms in London, 1860–1913*

Alejandro de La Fuente and Ariela J. Gross, *Becoming Free, Becoming Black: Race, Freedom, and the Law in Cuba, Virginia, and Louisiana*

Elizabeth Papp Kamali, *Felony and the Guilty Mind in Medieval England*

Jessica K. Lowe, *Murder in the Shenandoah: Making Law Sovereign in Revolutionary Virginia*

Michael A. Schoeppner, *Moral Contagion: Black Atlantic Sailors, Citizenship, and Diplomacy in Antebellum America*

Sam Erman, *Almost Citizens: Puerto Rico, the U.S. Constitution, and Empire*

Martha S. Jones, *Birthright Citizens: A History of Race and Rights in Antebellum America*

Julia Moses, *The First Modern Risk: Workplace Accidents and the Origins of European Social States*

Cynthia Nicoletti, *Secession on Trial: The Treason Prosecution of Jefferson Davis*

Edward James Kolla, *Sovereignty, International Law, and the French Revolution*

Assaf Likhovski, *Tax Law and Social Norms in Mandatory Palestine and Israel*

Robert W. Gordon, *Taming the Past: Essays on Law and History and History in Law*

Paul Garfinkel, *Criminal Law in Liberal and Fascist Italy*

Michelle A. McKinley, *Fractional Freedoms: Slavery, Intimacy, and Legal Mobilization in Colonial Lima, 1600–1700*

Karen M. Tani, *States of Dependency: Welfare, Rights, and American Governance, 1935–1972*

Stefan Jurasinski, *The Old English Penitentials and Anglo-Saxon Law*

Felice Batlan, *Women and Justice for the Poor: A History of Legal Aid, 1863–1945*

Sophia Z. Lee, *The Workplace Constitution from the New Deal to the New Right*

Mitra Sharafi, *Law and Identity in Colonial South Asia: Parsi Legal Culture, 1772–1947*

Michael A. Livingston, *The Fascists and the Jews of Italy: Mussolini's Race Laws, 1938–1943*

Vernacular Law

Writing and the Reinvention of Customary Law in Medieval France

ADA MARIA KUSKOWSKI

University of Pennsylvania

CAMBRIDGE
UNIVERSITY PRESS

CAMBRIDGE
UNIVERSITY PRESS

Shaftesbury Road, Cambridge CB2 8EA, United Kingdom

One Liberty Plaza, 20th Floor, New York, NY 10006, USA

477 Williamstown Road, Port Melbourne, VIC 3207, Australia

314–321, 3rd Floor, Plot 3, Splendor Forum, Jasola District Centre, New Delhi – 110025, India

103 Penang Road, #05–06/07, Visioncrest Commercial, Singapore 238467

Cambridge University Press is part of Cambridge University Press & Assessment, a department of the University of Cambridge.

We share the University's mission to contribute to society through the pursuit of education, learning and research at the highest international levels of excellence.

www.cambridge.org
Information on this title: www.cambridge.org/9781009217880

DOI: 10.1017/9781009217873

First published 2023
First paperback edition 2024

A catalogue record for this publication is available from the British Library

ISBN   978-1-009-21789-7   Hardback
ISBN   978-1-009-21788-0   Paperback

For my parents, Magda and Tadeusz, my sister Ania and grandmother Bożena

Contents

Figures

Acknowledgments

It was in studying common law and civil law simultaneously at McGill that I started seeing law not simply as a set of rules but a product of history, culture, and happenstance. I then found myself drawn in graduate school to questions of how foundational legal ideas develop, how issues in disputes come to be expressed in terms of rules, and other backstories of the written rules that regulate our lives. I first discovered the texts at the heart of this study on a rather dusty portion of a library shelf while in law school at McGill University. Little did I know then that I would look to them for answers, or how long they would be my companions.

The writing and completion of this book was only possible because of the support of many people and institutions along my academic trajectory. What is good in this book has its origins in teachers and friends who were models of avid curiosity, deep thinking, intellectual creativity, and scholarly generosity.

Foremost, this is true of my dissertation committee to whom I owe great thanks for their mentorship, wisdom, kindness, and support. Paul Hyams, my wonderful graduate advisor, and my marvellous graduate mentors, Bernadette Meyler, Duane Corpis, and Eric Rebillard, put in years of discussion, advice, reading, and commentary that have enriched my thought and work in ways that are sure to resound throughout my scholarly career. I will forever admire them and be grateful to them for their intellectual curiosity and great generosity of spirt, intellect, and time.

I also owe great thanks to my wonderful series editor, Michael Lobban, who read the dissertation that led to this book, saw something in it, and guided me and my work through the publication process. I am also grateful to the anonymous reviewers who helped me see various aspects of this project in new ways, whose comments were all indeed 'essential', and who helped me refine my thinking and polish this book. I am also very grateful to the staff at Cambridge University Press, especially Cecelia Cancellaro, for ushering this project to completion notably through the vicissitudes of the pandemic.

Many debts were accrued along the way. They begin long ago in my undergraduate studies at McGill University, where I fell in love with history in the classrooms of Andrew Sherwood and Elizabeth DePalma Digeser. I was fortunate in law school to have generous mentors – Blaine Baker, Nicholas Kasirer, Daniel Jutras, and Daniel Boyer – who encouraged me to pursue legal history in various research projects.

At Cornell, I benefited from the incredible communities of the History Department and Medieval Studies. I am especially grateful for the terrific feedback my work received in the European History Colloquium and in the writing group I had with Thomas McSweeney, Abigail Fisher, and Guillaume Ratel. I found joy in discussing ideas and the support of great friendship in Marie Muschalek, Claudine Ang, Mari Crabtree, Ryan Plumley, Taran Kang, Yael Manes, and Eliza Buhrer. While at Cornell, my research was supported by the Theodor Mommsen Fellowship, Mario Einaudi International Research Grant, Michele Sicca Pre-Dissertation Research Grant, and Sage Fellowship.

I had several intellectual homes after graduate school where I incurred more debts of gratitude. I was a Visiting Scholar with the Quebec Research Centre of Private and Comparative Law at McGill University's Faculty of Law, thanks to the Wainwright Fund Research Grant, where in addition to those named above I also owe thanks to Lionel Smith, Tina Piper, and Mark Antaki. I am also very grateful to Daniel Hulsebosch and Bill Nelson for their mentorship while I held the Samuel I. Golieb Fellowship in Legal History and participated in the dynamic legal-history community at NYU School of Law. While I was a Postdoctoral Fellow in Law and Society at the University of Wisconsin-Madison Law School, I had the great fortune of the mentorship of Karl Shoemaker, Mitra Sharafi, and Howard Erlanger. I also had the support of the Mellon Summer Institute Grant to learn palaeography at Newberry Library at this time.

My first teaching position was at Southern Methodist University where I held the Jeremy duQuesnay Adams Centennial Professorship in Western European Medieval History in the History Department. Words cannot express the gratitude and affection I hold for Jeremy duQuesnay Adams and Bonnie Wheeler, who were models of extraordinary generosity, dynamism, and love of everything medieval. I am also so grateful to have had the support of Kathleen Wellman, Melissa Barden Dowling, Erin R. Hochman, Jill Kelly, Maxime Foerster, Alexandra Letvin, Daniel Sledge, and Benjamin Brand during my time in Dallas. While at SMU, my work was supported by the University Research Council Travel Grant.

I have benefited from singularly rich and vibrant intellectual communities in my time at the University of Pennsylvania. First, I would like to thank my faculty mentors Sarah Barringer Gordon and Antonio Feros, as well as my colleagues in the History Department generally, and notably Marcy Norton, Anne Moyer, Margo Todd, Beth Wenger, Sophie Rosenfeld, Peter Holquist, Amy Offner, Oscar Aguirre-Mandujano, Alex Chase-Levenson, Anne Berg, and Melissa Teixeira.

Penn also has a marvellous community of medieval scholars, and I am grateful to them all for the rich programming and dynamic community, as well as for extremely helpful discussions of my work and for letting me learn from theirs. Mary Channen Caldwell and Sarah Guérin have been my sisters-in-arms, who read most of the chapters in this book and provided invaluable insights. I would also particularly like to thank Emily Steiner, Julia Verkholantsev, Elly Truitt, Talya Fishman, Jerry Singerman, Kevin Brownlee, Rita Copeland, and David Wallace, who have been mentors, models, and friends in various ways.

My work has also greatly benefited from feedback from the legal history group at Penn led by Sally Gordon, Sophia Lee, Serena Mayeri, and Karen Tani, to whom I am grateful also for inviting medieval legal historians to the Legal History Workshop. I would also like to express my gratitude to my colleagues at the Kislac Center, Schoenberg Institute for Manuscript Studies, Steven Miller Conservation Laboratory, and others – notably Mitch Frass, Nicholas Herman, Lynn Ransom, Will Noel, and John Pollack. While at Penn, my work has benefited from the support of the School of Arts and Sciences Research Opportunity Grant and the University Research Foundation Grant.

Illuminating conversations from conferences and gatherings large and small have woven their way through my thoughts on medieval or legal history in various ways. While too many to mention here, I notably thank Ron Akehurst, Peggy Brown, Don Maddox, Jody Enders, Tom Green, Elizabeth Kamali, Rowan Dorin, Laurie Wood, Laura Wangerin, and Meg Leja. I am also especially grateful for the friendship of Glenda Goodman, Sarah Reidell, Martin Labuda, and Kasia Biniecki.

Through all this, special thanks are due to Karl Shoemaker, Sarah McDougall, Brigitte Bedos-Rezak, and Adam Kosto for their comments, suggestions, and encouragement over the years.

On a more personal note, I am so grateful to and for Dan Goldner, for his love and constant support, and for making life more beautiful; to Barbara Goldner for graciously donating her time for childcare as the finish line loomed, and to Addison and little Lev, born as the final revisions for this book were underway, for making it a happy home.

Along this journey, from my undergraduate studies to this moment, my family have given me indefatigable love, encouragement, inspiration, and strength. In many ways, this project began in 'chateau Douglas', where there was a thirst for knowledge, love of books, and joy of storytelling. This book would not have been possible without my parents, Magda and Tadeusz, my sister Ania and grandmother Bożena, and I dedicate this book to them.

A Note on the Text

I have drawn on earlier publications in this book, namely 'The Development of Written Custom in England and in France: A Comparative Perspective' in *Law, Justice, and Governance, New Views on Medieval English Constitutionalism*, ed. Richard Kaeuper (Leiden: Brill, 2013) and 'The Time of Custom and the Medieval Myth of Ancient Customary Law' (in press). The final chapter significantly reproduces 'Inventing Legal Space: From Regional Custom to Common Law in the *Coutumiers* of Medieval France' in *Space in the Medieval West Places, Territories, and Imagined Geographies*, ed. Meredith Cohen and Fanny Madeleine (Ashgate, June 2014) 133–55, with some revisions. I have also drawn upon my dissertation, 'Writing Custom: Juristic Imagination and the Composition of Customary Law in Thirteenth-Century France' (PhD diss., Cornell University, 2013).

I have expanded my views on vernacular writing and law beyond the subject of this book in articles that might interest the readers of this book: '*Lingua Franca Legalis*? A French Vernacular Legal Culture from England to the Levant', special issue, *Reading Medieval Studies*, 40 (2014), 140–58; and 'Translating Justinian: Language, Translation and Repurposing Roman Law in the Middle Ages' in *Law and Language in the Middle Ages*, ed. Matthew W. McHaffie, Jenny Bentham, and Helle Vogt, pp. 30–51 (Leiden: Brill, 2018).

I have generally provided translations of primary sources in the main text and have typically supplied the original texts in Old French or Latin in the footnotes when the original language is important to the arguments I develop. While I have usually used my own translations, I consulted F. R. P. Akehurst's invaluable English translations of Philippe de Beaumanoir's *Coutumes de Beauvaisis* and of the *Établissements de*

Saint Louis, and these were a fantastic resource. While I also consulted Judith Everard's French and Latin edition and English translation of the *Grand coutumier de Normandie*, I have generally relied on Ernest-Joseph Tardif's edition of the Latin text as it best reflects the thirteenth-century version of the text. I refer to manuscripts by their letter in critical editions wherever applicable.

Lastly, because this study treats the thirteenth-century *coutumiers* as a group, it does not purport or aim to provide an exhaustive taxonomic study as would be possible if focusing on a sole text or author. This means that I generally proceed by way of illustrative example rather than providing a typology of each issue in each of my central texts. Where questions are left unanswered, I hope to leave fertile ground for future research.

INTRODUCTION

Vernacular Writing and the Transformation
of Customary Law in Medieval France

'No one before me ever undertook this thing, such that I have a model',
wrote Pierre de Fontaines around 1253 in the preface to his *Conseil à
un ami*.[1] Pierre had written the *Conseil* in response to the pleas of an
unnamed friend who wanted his son to study the laws, customs, and
practices of the secular courts in his region of Vermandois, which was
just north-east of Paris, lying between Flanders and Champagne.[2] This
young man was to succeed his father and govern his lands. Upon
inheriting, he would have to become a legal actor: he would have to
provide justice to his subjects, keep his lands according to appropriate
laws and customs, likely represent himself in court, and provide good
advice to his friends.[3]

There was no easy way to learn these subjects, which together
constituted the sorts of knowledge necessary to understand the legal
culture of secular courts and to navigate them successfully. Procedural
manuals had been written in the twelfth century to clarify, establish,
and demystify the legal process in the Church courts, complementing
an already rich body of rules that formed its substantive law.[4]

---

[1] 'nus n'enprist onques devant moi ceste chose, dont jaie examplaire' (Pierre de
Fontaines, *Le Conseil de Pierre de Fontaines*, 1.3; hereafter Pierre de Fontaines,
Conseil). An exemplar widely meant an example or model as well as a copy of a book.
[2] 'voudriez qu'il s'estudiast ès lois et ès costumes du païs dont it est, et en usage en cort
laie' (*ibid.*, 1.2).
[3] These are the skills the entreating friend hoped his son would acquire from Pierre's
book (*ibid.*, 1.2).
[4] Linda Fowler-Magerl, *'Ordines iudiciarii' and 'Libelli De ordine iudiciorum'*.

However, none of this existed for secular courts. Pierre's friend's son would have to attend court sessions, watch, observe, and try to remember as much as he could. He could learn from his father. He could ask for advice from friends and administrators. He might familiarize himself with the family's documents, affirming their rights and attesting to transactions. Ultimately, it would take him much time and effort to get a good handle on how he should run his own court for his vassals and the residents of his land, as was his duty as a lord, and how to navigate others. For this reason, his father implored Pierre 'so many times' to compose a written text that his son could use to learn how to become a legal actor.[5]

Pierre was a native of Vermandois. He owned lands there, arbitrated disputes in the area, and worked in the court of Mahaut d'Artois in a legal and administrative capacity.[6] He made enough of a name for himself to become the royal justice for Vermandois in 1253, an appointment that did not last the year before he went off to work for the royal Parliament in Paris.[7] At some point in this career, he wrote his *Conseil*, and the book makes clear that he was a man of both experience and learning.[8] He was comfortable with the discursive tools of rhetoric, opening his book with the common trope of a humble author with a great task.[9] The book was framed as a scholastic dialogue, and the textual sources he quoted at length

[5] 'vos m'avez tantes fois proié et requis' (Pierre de Fontaines, *Conseil*, 1.1), 'de ce m'avez vos requis, et requerez que je li face un escrit selonc les us et costumes de Vermandois et d'autres corz laies' (*ibid.*, 1.2).

[6] Quentin Griffiths, 'Les origines et la carrière de Pierre de Fontaines, Jurisconsulte de Saint Louis', 549.

[7] *Ibid.*

[8] We know very little about Pierre's early career before he entered royal service. The *Conseil* is commonly dated 'around 1253' because Pierre had official judicial functions as a royal justice in Vermandois in 1253. We do not know whether Pierre conceded to his friend's request and wrote the text when his career as royal justice of Vermandois was taking off or once he had become a man of the king and it had reached its summit.

[9] This was the *captatio benevolentiae*, a rhetorical tool developed in classical Roman rhetoric. It was common a trope in medieval prefaces to works on diverse subjects meant to gain the sympathies of an audience by showing the importance of a text without overpraising the author. Rhetoric was part of the education of any schoolboy. It could certainly be an asset in the courtroom; a couple of decades after Pierre, William Durand advised lawyers pleading in ecclesiastical courts to gain the judge's favor with 'immoderately unctuous' praise (James A. Brundage, *The Medieval Origins of the Legal Profession*, p. 427).

were books of late antique Roman law, the form of law one could study at university alongside ecclesiastical law.

Yet despite his experience and learning, Pierre's task felt new and unfamiliar to him. How exactly should he compose a work on a subject without a model indicating how to construct a coherent account of customary law, let alone a genre? Without examples to follow, Pierre had to engage in the creative act of choosing which of his myriad observations and experiences to draw upon, which abstract and substantive ideas from his studies to use, and how to write about all of these things.

Adding to the difficulty was the fact that Pierre was expanding access to the study of law to a new audience – laymen, like his addressee – and so he composed the *Conseil* in their vernacular rather than Latin, the general language of legal writing.[10] Unlike clerics and scholars who spent years in Latinate study, 'the mind of a layman cannot spend much time studying such things'.[11] Addressing those 'who wish to learn how to administer justice and hold land', and eschewing 'hard or obscure or long words', Pierre decided that the best approach would be to write with brevity, simplicity, and clarity.[12]

This book tells the story of Pierre and similar authors in northern France who composed the lawbooks, known as *coutumiers* in the French legal tradition, that shaped customary law into a field of knowledge. 'Customary law' typically refers to a type of rule made in practice, and in the courts, by the community, which can include 'the people' in some form, lords and kings, or lawyers and judges.[13]

---

[10] Laymen and the knightly class played an active role in the development of vernacular literature and writing more generally (Martin Aurell, *Le chevalier lettré*.).

[11] Pierre de Fontaines, *Conseil*, 1.2.   [12] Pierre de Fontaines, 1.2.

[13] 'Customary law' can mean significantly different things depending on time, place, and context. For the medieval Latin European West, 'customary law' generally refers to legal rules that are created out of community practice. It can designate the legal rules of both dominant and minority or subjugated populations. Looking beyond the medieval period, its meaning can range from Western European law during the Middle Ages before it was professionalized, to the laws of colonies as opposed to the laws of their metropoles, forms of indigenous law rather than the law of the colonial order, or a form of legal-political rhetoric of the post-colonial order (Jacques Vanderlinden, 'Here, there and everywhere... or nowhere?', p. 143). Customary law holds an important place in modern law, but it tends to be underrecognized outside of international law (Gary Brown and Keira Poellet, 'Traditional and Modern Approaches to Customary International Law', 757). Instead, in contemporary society, customary law is most often identified with the law of so-called 'primitive',

Customs concerning specific rules of property, succession, and other subjects certainly emerged out of this oral practice. *Coutumier* authors, however, both known and anonymous, successfully crafted customary law into an expository genre of writing, and these expositions are an excellent starting point for understanding the legal culture of later medieval France.

**

If what Pierre accomplished – compiling and systematizing disparate rules of custom into a body of coherent law – seems like a natural way to package customary law, it is because he and other *coutumier* authors gave it the form that is familiar and even obvious to us today. Pierre reminds us that it was no obvious thing to decide how to write customary law. Pierre was not actually the first author of a written customary law as his comment implied. Comparable texts had been and were being written elsewhere in Europe and a couple closer to home in northern France, and indeed the textualization of legal ideas was not restricted to Christian communities.[14] Pierre was thus participating in a wider cultural movement that began around the twelfth century, in which lay court practices and ideas about law were gathered and crafted into bodies of written rules.

The 'classical age' of the *coutumiers* stretches from the twelfth century, when this form of lawbook began, to the fifteenth, when the French king demanded that every region compose one official version of its custom.[15] The historiography of the *coutumiers* is incredibly rich but missing a larger view: there is no large-scale work devoted specifically to the northern French or French *coutumiers* as a whole. They appear variously as part of histories of French law, within larger histories of custom and its lawbooks in Europe, or in a multitude of articles on a specific text or legal subject.[16] This book focuses on what

---

traditional, subaltern, or preliterate peoples (David J. Bederman, *Custom as a Source of Law*, pp. 3–15). All of these meanings of customary law bear some connection to Roman categories of legal order – where 'custom' and 'law' together described 'civil law,' a law proper to a people, as opposed to natural law and the law of nations.

[14] Talya Fishman, *Becoming the People of the Talmud.*

[15] Van Dievoet, *Les coutumiers, les styles, les formulaires*, p. 22.

[16] As a genre of writing, the Northern French *coutumiers* are part of Guido van Dievoet's typology of *coutumiers* written across Europe from the twelfth to fifteenth centuries (Van Dievoet, *Les coutumiers, les styles, les formulaires*). The collected works of Paul Ourliac, Jean Yver, André Gouron, and Robert Jacob are foundational

I call 'the first *coutumiers*'. These are the earliest *coutumiers* of northern France, which were composed from the mid-thirteenth century to the first years of the fourteenth.[17] This group of texts includes the *Très ancien coutumier de Normandie* (early thirteenth century with later additions); the *Coutumes d'Anjou et du Maine* (1246); Pierre de Fontaines' *Conseil à un ami* (1253); *Summa de legibus Normannie* (between 1254 and 1258); the *Livre de justice et de plet* (ca. 1260); the *Établissements de Saint Louis* (1272 or 1273); the *Livre des constitutions demenées el Chastelet de Paris* (between 1279 and 1282); Philippe de Beaumanoir's *Coutumes de Beauvaisis* (1283); the *Ancien coutumier de Champagne* (ca. 1295); *Ancien coutumier de Bourgogne* (end of thirteenth century); and the *Coutumier d'Artois* (between 1283 and 1302).[18] Generally, the

reading for understanding these texts. F. R. P. Akehurst's important English translations and studies illuminate not only the meaning but also the courtly context of customary law. The *coutumiers* appear in Yvonne Bongert's analysis of the practice of the lay courts between the tenth and thirteenth centuries, and in Esther Cohen's sociocultural analysis of law and legal practice in the later Middle Ages (Bongert, *Recherches sur les cours laïques de Xe au XIIIe siècle*; Cohen, *The Crossroads of Justice: Law and Culture in Late Medieval France*). John Gilissen provides an analysis of the concept of custom in the European Middle Ages that includes a discussion the *coutumiers* (Gilissen, *La coutume*). The *coutumiers* are an important part of various introductions to French legal history or the history of French private law. Other essential works on the history of custom in Europe include the Jean Bodin Society's series of volumes entitled *La Coutume = Custom*, notably the one devoted to the medieval period edited by John Gilissen, and the wonderful volume on custom edited by Per Andersen and Mia Münster-Swendsen (Gilissen, *La Coutume = Custom*, vol. 2, *Europe occidentale médiévale et moderne*; Andersen and Münster-Swendsen, *Custom: The Development and Use of a Legal Concept in the Middle Ages*). There are many scholars who have studied custom in the general area of Northern France, too many to list here. The reader can refer to the bibliography, looking out notably (but certainly not exclusively) for articles and books by Fredric Cheyette, Jean Gaudemet, Gerard Giordanengo, Dirk Heirbaut, Jean Hilaire, Emily Kadens, Jacques Krynen, Laurent Mayali, and Laurent Waelkens.

[17] The traditional manner in which medieval French law is described is through the distinction between the North of France as the land of customary law (*pays de droit coutumier*), where oral customary law reigned, and the South of France as the land of written law (*pays de droit écrit*), where law was written and Roman. Although specialists have long emphasized that the former made use of Roman law while the latter also relied on custom, this distinction is still commonly repeated. Those terms are used in medieval sources with a rhetorical purpose that needs additional study.

[18] I exclude the *Livre Roisin*, which describes the customs of the city of Lille, from my analysis of the first *coutumiers* because it is an early theorization of municipal law, and its urban context and thus political and legal culture are significantly different. I draw upon but do not focus on the *Livre de Justice et de Plet* (ca. 1260). This text is

coutumiers of the classical age have been defined as works penned by a *patricien* (someone elite or privileged, a judge, a municipal official, a lawyer), who principally treats local or regional law, written in a 'popular' style, often in regional vernaculars.[19]

My approach to these *coutumiers* departs from assumptions in existing scholarship in two critical respects. Scholars tend to emphasize the regional and purely private, 'unofficial' character of the *coutumiers*, as well as the importance of distinguishing them from the learned law studied and composed by canonist and Romanist jurists.[20] These two points, while correct, tend to suggest that all redactors of custom did the same thing; namely, simply to transcribe custom. But when taken as a whole, we can see that the first *coutumiers* each tell a unique story about what it meant to take various elements – live legal practice, observation, opinion, texts recording specific transactions or specific cases, and some learning – and turn these into a largely coherent interpretation of customary law. Instead of copyists who transcribed legal practice, those who composed *coutumiers* were authors who made

---

usually included as part of the Northern French *coutumiers* but it is largely a translation of Roman law with medieval cases inserted as examples. It stretches the meaningfulness of the category of '*coutumier*,' though in doing so it does form an important contrast to other contemporary *coutumiers* and tells an important story about how one person (we have one manuscript), likely someone associated with the university of Orléans, imagined thirteenth-century legal life within a Roman law framework. I do include the *Livre des constitutions demenées el Chastelet de Paris*, which is often overlooked, but is an early theorization of the *coutume de France* (i.e. the royal domain). The *Ancien coutumier de Bourgogne* is the least studied of this group. The title was given to the text in the nineteenth century, but from the incipit it should be the *Usages of Bourgogne*. The date is drawn from the earliest manuscripts, which are from the late thirteenth century (M. Petitjean, 'La coutume de Bourgogne. Des coutumiers officieux à la coutume officielle', p. 14). It may very well be an earlier text. Some provisions seem to go back to the late twelfth or early thirteenth century (André Castaldo and Yves Mausen, *Introduction historique au droit*, s. 445). Where there are ambiguities, the dates of the *coutumiers* listed here are discussed in the brief descriptions of the *coutumiers* near the end of Chapter 1 in 'Brief Descriptions of the "First" *Coutumiers*'.

[19] Van Dievoet, *Les coutumiers, les styles, les formulaires*, p.14.

[20] The line between private and unofficial and public and official for van Dievoet is the legislative intent expressed in the text, not consistent enforcement or other forms of more direct link between text and practice. So in official redactions, he includes the *leges barbarorum*, the *fureos*, the *statuta* of Northern Italian cities, some Scandinavian lawbooks (*ibid.*). Emphasis on the *coutumiers* as 'private redactions' and 'private customals' is a common thread in modern scholarship (Cohen, *Crossroads of Justice*, pp. 30–1). It is not a distinction found in the *coutumiers*.

individual and idiosyncratic choices in how they wrote about custom, some without available models or prototypes. While the *coutumiers* authors hold an important place in French legal history, there is sometimes a tacit resistance to thinking of them as jurists, with the exception of Philippe de Beaumanoir and sometimes Pierre de Fontaines. It is certainly the case for the anonymous authors and thus the majority. Tellingly, a recent volume on the *Great Christian Jurists in French History* includes no *coutumier* author in these ranks.[21]

Coutumier authors deserve to be recognized as jurists.[22] The texts and *techne* of *coutumier* authors differed, of course, from those of Roman and canon law scholars in substance as well as style, the latter with their voluminous Latinate texts and apparatus, formal modes of citation, and scholarly erudition. *Coutumier* authors generally wrote shorter texts in the vernacular for a lay audience that operated in lay courts – they aspired not to complexity but brevity and clarity. Even so, they were persons with an expert legal knowledge, who analysed and offered their commentary on law. I argue in these chapters that their dynamic engagement with a variety of legal ideas from different milieus and the inventive approach they had to have to shape individual customs into holistic bodies of customary law are evidence of expansive juristic minds.

Through these efforts, *coutumier* authors created a form of 'learned law' for the lay jurisdiction. Learned law normally refers to Roman and canon law as these branches of knowledge grew and developed in the university context, with the specific modes of 'teaching, writing, disputing, and questioning' used there.[23] My book considers *coutumiers* alongside books of Roman and canon law as a form of learned law but one whose learning was quintessentially different

---

[21] The recent book of this title has chapters on Ivo of Chartres, Stephen of Tournai, Guillaume Durand, Jacques de Revigny, and Pierre de Belleperche to represent the jurists of the Middle Ages (Olivier Descamps and Rafael Domingo, *Great Christian Jurists in French History*). While such a volume has to be selective, it really should have a chapter on Philippe de Beaumanoir and, arguably, on 'anonymous' as an author.

[22] The transition from diffuse and undifferentiated to professional customary law has almost exclusively been studied in relation to the rise and development of Roman law studies and their diffusion (Susan Reynolds, 'The Emergence of Professional Law in the Long Twelfth Century', 351).

[23] Kenneth Pennington, 'Learned Law, *Droit Savant, Gelehrtes Recht* ', 206.

because it consisted of a lay, vernacular law for the secular courts. The vernacular law composed by *coutumier* authors made customary law into a body of knowledge in its own right, with its own modes of writing, thinking, performing, and arguing. The composition of customary law should be seen neither in opposition to learned law nor as its lesser derivative but as a wholly different endeavour in the formation of legal knowledge.

The 'unofficial' *coutumiers* – those composed before the mid-fifteenth century, when the French king called for each region to write a conclusive and official version of its customs – tend to be treated together and as essentially alike. However, it meant something very different for Pierre de Fontaines to conceive of how to compose his *Conseil* in the mid-thirteenth century without a model than for Jean Boutillier to write his *Somme rural* near the end of the fourteenth century on the heels of many earlier prototypes. Also, the century and a half or so between the two texts saw many fundamental changes in the administrative, legal, and political culture of France. Treating the first *coutumiers* as a discrete set permits us to appreciate what made these texts so innovative and important. They illuminate the writing of custom at its genesis, when *coutumier* authors had to imagine how to create original texts that provided a comprehensive narrative for the customs of the secular courts, before seeing a model or before there was a written tradition showing how to complete the task. In this way, we can glean the evolutionary steps of customary law, distinguishing between the first writing of custom and the written tradition of customary law that developed out of these first texts by the fourteenth century.[24]

---

[24] The vast changes in legal culture and court practice that occurred in the four centuries of the 'classical age' of the *coutumier* are well known. While this fact is commonly mentioned, it is often not reflected in actual analysis of the *coutumiers* and the customs they describe. It is not uncommon to find scholars talking about customary law by lumping thirteenth-century *coutumiers* together with ones from the late fourteenth century (ex. describing an aspect of custom using the *Établissements* together with Jacques d'Ableiges' *Grand coutumier* though there is a century between them) or explaining something in thirteenth-century *coutumiers* by using texts or cases from the fourteenth or fifteenth centuries. This collapses the differences between them and makes it difficult to track change over time. This is the case for Van Dievoet's typology. Though it is a useful and important study, it is divided thematically with analysis skipping back and forth between centuries. While he consistently provides dates, he moves around so much in time that it is difficult to have a clear

As regards the second scholarly assumption, it is certainly true that the *coutumiers* were unofficial and private compositions, in the sense that they were not legislation promulgated by a sovereign. The designation of these texts as private or unofficial belies the nature of the courts in thirteenth-century northern France, which themselves referred preponderantly to custom rather than legislation.[25] Indeed, while the practice of legislating kept increasing throughout the thirteenth century, legislation alone offers a significantly incomplete view of the legal culture of northern France.[26] The binding nature of law in the customary legal culture of the period was not the monopoly of the state or of formal enactments, as shown by the importance of custom and the popularity of Roman law. In other words, unofficial and influential were certainly not mutually exclusive.

**

Authors of *coutumiers* wrote about custom, but what did that mean? It was custom – and not legislation or regulation, although these things existed – that animated legal life in medieval France. Customary law defined the legal practices of the medieval period but, even within this period, the term referred to significantly different forms of legal culture. Roughly the first half of the medieval period – around the end of the fifth century to the beginning of the eleventh – is understood

picture of the stages of development of the *coutumiers* between the twelfth and fifteenth centuries and the relationship between these and more general changes in legal culture. This slippage is common in the treatment of the *coutumiers*, and dates are not always included, so the reader may not be aware of it. This practice is at least partially due to the richness of documentation from the fourteenth century onward. Professionalization and specialization led to a vast expansion in record keeping, not only in the number of judicial proceedings recorded but also in the detail of information about legal arguments and witnesses' testimony. Using these to understand an earlier period whose records are less forthcoming if done must be explained. Another reason is the periodization of the *coutumiers* themselves. The unofficial private works of the thirteenth through the mid-fifteenth centuries are grouped together and distinguished from the official legislated redactions from 1454 onward, giving the former an illusion of sameness. Lastly, an underlying assumption about the unchanging stability of custom and the fixity of written custom is likely shaping how this history is written.

[25] While true, this classifies the *coutumiers* using categories that were not meaningful until later. These categories are awkward for much of the Middle Ages and better fit the centralizing state of the fifteenth century onward, the period where the distinction between official and unofficial starts to matter, where 'unofficial' starts to seem insufficient, and where the crown asks for official texts to be composed.

[26] Gérard Giordanengo, 'Le pouvoir législatif du roi de France (XI–XIIIe siècles)'.

as an age of customary law.[27] People spoke of 'law', but the things encompassed by that term were often all but indistinguishable from other forms of obligation; courts were comparatively unprofessionalized; and the resolution of disputes was often more of a negotiation aimed at peace rather than the selection of a winner and loser according to an established set of rules.

The term custom (*consuetudo*) proliferated in the tenth and eleventh centuries, as local and regional lords in the area that became France claimed political and legal powers held by the Carolingian king.[28] Criminal and policing functions became part of seigneurial jurisdiction. Local and regional lords and their courts became the site of justice and 'custom' typically designated the rights of lords and the exactions they could impose.

At this time communities resolved disputes through negotiation and mediation, political wrangling, or according to a collective sense of what seemed right. The main 'legal' documents produced were charters and brief texts that testified to contracts and transactions or that granted rights, often in land. Developed notions of law based on nuanced categories underlay these terse accounts of what was agreed upon or what happened, but rarely do these documents express legal principles and frameworks.[29] Norms thus existed and left traces in grants; individual agreements; and the occasional, more or less laconic piece of legislation but were not articulated descriptively in comprehensive form.[30]

---

[27] This at one time was described as an 'age without jurists' (Manlio Bellomo, *The Common Legal Past of Europe*, p. 34), and, 'if there were "jurists" in Western Europe, they were capable of little more than knowing how to read, comprehending what they read as best they could. They did not bother to weed out what they did not understand; nor did they take the trouble to reflect on the materials they handled or to wonder whether anthology could become law' (*ibid.*, p. 36). Implicit here was a definition of jurist and what counted as legal thinking, and thus what deserved to be counted as legal history. The period looks different and less lacking when historians inquire into modes of governance and nature of dispute resolution (see Janet Nelson, *The Frankish World*; Geoffrey Koziol, *Begging Pardon and Favor*; Warren C. Brown, *Violence in Medieval Europe*).

[28] J.-F. Lemarignier, 'La dislocation du "pagus" et le problème *des* "consuetudines" (Xe–XIe siècles)', pp. 401–10.

[29] See Stephen D. White, 'Inheritances and Legal Arguments in Western France, 1050–1150'; John G. H. Hudson, 'Court Cases and Legal Arguments in England'; Matthew W. McHaffie, 'Law and Violence in Eleventh-Century France'.

[30] Reynolds, *Kingdoms and Communities*, pp. 14–17.

This began to change around the twelfth century, with the composition throughout Europe of anonymous and authored texts that described custom holistically. Northern French *coutumiers* were part of a unique flurry of legal writing. These lawbooks were written at roughly a similar time for regions geographically proximate and with relatively similar politics and culture. This distinguishes the *coutumiers* from the Latin lawbooks that described laws and customs of the royal courts of England, and from the vernacular *Siete partidas* composed for Alfonso X of Castile, and indeed even from the vernacular *Sachsenspiegel* ('Mirror of the Saxons'). Unlike these lawbooks, the first *coutumiers* formed a unique group of texts. Instead of offering one representative text for a specific time and place, the *coutumiers* of northern France provide a variety of approaches and perspective at a similar time and place. Because of this, they invite a different perspective on the formative moment when customary law was first shaped into written text: they show that customary law, despite overlapping elements, could be imagined in different ways in roughly similar contexts. In this respect, the process is better described as legal authorship rather than transcription. This also shows that, though often imperceptible, individual agency and choice could have an important role in shaping customary law.

The efflorescence of writing of the twelfth and early thirteenth century, both Latin and vernacular, was not limited to the scholarly or literary but also included the administrative and legal. A growing multitude of charters recorded everyday transactions, individual privileges, rights and freedoms of communities, and the resolution of disputes either through peace agreements or court decisions. Increasing regulation affected all sorts of associations, including merchant and craft guilds. The powers and jurisdiction of lay lordship were being negotiated and became more clearly defined in relation to the church and its courts. Methods of proof shifted, and inquests, where proof was obtained by inquiry, became more important judicially as 'irrational' procedures such as the ordeal gradually became obsolete.[31] Ad hoc courts professionalized, as did some of their personnel. Some acquired their legal knowledge by frequenting the courts or participating in cases; some by working in the chancery;

---

[31] Robert Bartlett, *Trial by Fire and Water*.

and others by attending university and studying Roman law, canon law, or both. Generally, law was experienced as a multiplicity of jurisdictions, and this experience also depended on one's status. Not only was there more legal writing in this period, but it also witnessed important transformations of ideas and practices.

By the mid-thirteenth century, when Pierre was puzzling through how to compose his book, 'custom' was a commonly used but nonetheless somewhat elusive term. Very generally, it designated a legal rule drawn from community practice. The rules and procedures of local and regional secular courts were referred to as custom (*consuetudo*, *coutume*) or usage (*usus*, *usage*), and connected to this, custom also designated the norms of territorial lordship and lordly exactions. Customary law in the thirteenth century generally refers to the form of law used and cited in lay courts as opposed to ecclesiastical courts. Even here, however, customary law, Simon Teuscher writes, could 'most easily be described *ex negativo* as the totality of rules that were neither defined by Roman and canonical law – the *ius commune* – nor enacted by established authorities'.[32]

Even in the second half of the thirteenth century, when most *coutumiers* were written, their authors were describing custom in a society whose legal culture was undergoing rapid and fundamental change. While it is expedient to speak of 'France' here, the idea, the physical territory, and the power of kings were still in flux. Conquests and acquisitions in the thirteenth century began to give 'France' its recognizable modern shape.[33] Likewise, while I refer to 'French' to speak generally of the vernacular, medieval France was multilingual. The languages of the North were known as *langue d'oil* and the South as *langue d'oc*, both of which were composed of a diversity of regional

---

[32] Simon Teuscher, *Lord's Rights and Peasant Stories*, p. 16. Even once distinguished from learned laws, custom remained ambiguous: 'In point of fact, it included norms that not only varied from place to place but also were not necessarily regarded as part of a unified system in a given place' (*ibid.*).

[33] Jean Dunbabin, 'The Political World of France', pp. 24–27. The South of France came under effective power of the French crown in the aftermath of the Albigensian Crusade. The Statute of Pamiers (1212), Simon de Montfort's new charter for the conquered South, contains an early reference to the 'custom of France' (the royal domain) in the area around Paris. Southern resistance to northern expansionism continued, despite repressive tactics, and the Hundred Years' War was also a famed theatre of contestation until the end of the conflict in 1453.

dialects.[34] North and South were not only important political, linguistic, and cultural zones. They also influence how we understand law in medieval France and the place of custom in it: the North of France is described as the *pays de coutume* (the land of custom) and the South as the *pays de droit écrit* (the land of written law, or Roman law). These designations do appear in thirteenth-century sources, but the stark difference between a 'Germanic' customary North and a Romanized South is overemphasized.[35] In the South, it is true that the Roman law of the Theodosian Code (438) survived through Alaric's *Breviary* (506) and, in the twelfth century, Justinian's *Corpus iuris civilis* (529–534) spread in the region and deeply influenced legal practice.[36] However, while both Louis IX and Philip the Fair made clear that Roman law had authority in the South, this authority derived from its quality as custom.[37] Conversely, Roman law also spread in the northern 'land of custom' – and in fact some of the first *coutumiers* are excellent examples of its popularity in the north – but local custom had greater authoritative weight. (The distinction between the two *pays* would become extremely politicized in the sixteenth century, when jurists debated whether the 'common law of France' emerged from old French custom or from the Roman law tradition that reached back to antiquity.)

Since the *coutumiers* were written for areas within the royal domain, they show the nature of royal jurisdiction in the region vis-à-vis custom in two ways: the jurisdiction of royal justices, and discussions of the appeal to the crown. Justices known as *baillis* or *sénéchaux* were chief financial, administrative and legal agents of the crown in the royal domain and in the regions. The king and lay lords without formal training or studies had long been involved in areas of law and governance, but especially through the latter half of the thirteenth century, this would increasingly become the purview of career administrators, many of whom had degrees in Roman or canon law by the end of the century. Royal power also grew in the regions as kings

---

[34] David Potter, introduction to *France in the Later Middle Ages*, p. 3.

[35] Jean Hilaire, *La vie du droit*, pp. 105–83.

[36] Antonio Padoa Schioppa, *A History of Law in Europe: From the Early Middle Ages to the Twentieth Century*, p. 185.

[37] C. Ginoulhiac, 'Cours de droit coutumier français dans ses rapports avec notre droit actuel', 70–1; Padoa Schioppa, *A History of Law in Europe*, p. 185.

took on the role of protectors of custom. The development of the appellate function was also key to extending royal power into the regions, as the aggrieved could appeal to the crown if their lords did not give them their day in court or issued an incorrect judgment.[38]

Kings began issuing what can properly be referred to as legislation around the mid-thirteenth century, although ultimately the ruler's duty was 'to impose respect for custom rather than legislate'.[39] Hence, the idea of 'custom' could be deployed in political discourse both as an assertion of local or regional identity and an affirmation of royal power: local custom could be asserted against the encroachment of royal rights and jurisdiction, but it could also affirm royal power when the king was asked to help protect or confirm local custom or when that custom was upheld upon appeal in his courts. While French historiography has emphasized a conflict-driven narrative of state-formation, recent suggestions also point to a process of 'discursive cooperation' where the development of centralizing institutional government went hand in hand with the growth of regional aristocratic identity.[40] In the *coutumiers*, we find assertions of the customs of Champagne or the customs of Vermandois, but we also see the development of a 'common law' of the kingdom of France that transcended these regional delimitations.

Medieval sources commonly referred to the king's 'sovereignty' but it looked more like what today we would describe as 'suzerainty', where royal control co-existed with general regional autonomy. As Philippe de Beaumanoir noted in his *coutumier* in the 1280s, it was both the case that 'the king is sovereign over all and has, as his right, the general care of his whole kingdom' and that 'each baron is sovereign in his barony'.[41] Later medieval France is certainly characterized by the

---

[38] Cohen, *Crossroads of Justice*, pp. 39ff.   [39] *Ibid.*, p. 36, 41.

[40] Alice Taylor, 'Formalising Aristocratic Power in Royal Acta in Late Twelfth- and Early Thirteenth-Century France and Scotland', pp. 35ff. This is not to deny that conflict occurred but that increasing royal domination and aristocratic resistance provide insufficient explanation for the transformations of the twelfth and early thirteenth centuries. New forms of consolidation of royal power created a new 'common vocabulary of legible aristocratic power', where assertions of regional or aristocratic power were not necessarily conflictual but could also be part of royal consolidation and centralization (*ibid.*, p. 62).

[41] 'Li rois est souverains par-dessus tous et a de son droit la general garde de tout son roiaume' and 'chascuns barons est souverains en sa baronie' (Beaumanoir, *Coutumes de Beauvaisis*, XXXIV.1043) This passage is commonly quoted in discussions of medieval ideas of sovereignty. Barons and counts were just as 'sovereign' as kings

growth of royal power.[42] But the region and its custom remained a formidable political entity, leading to the great fiefs and principalities of the fifteenth century, even as the power of kings expanded.[43] Indeed, changes in genre and vernacular writing can be especially revealing of such tensions.[44]

**

Out of shifting meanings and uses of custom, *coutumier* authors crafted a written customary law. This book advances three main arguments about these lay jurists. The first is that *coutumier* authors created a vernacular written law that contributed something new, different, and fundamentally important to lay legal culture specifically and legal culture generally. By 'vernacular law', I mean both a shift in language as well as a distinct approach to forum, audience, and hermeneutics that changed the world of law. By the mid-thirteenth century, there was a general consensus among *coutumier* authors in northern France that the vernacular was preponderantly the language of choice and vehicle of expression for customary law.[45] *Coutumier* authors were not primarily writing for the educated who conducted their intellectual lives in Latin and whose training in rhetoric had introduced them to Roman legal thought through Isidore of Seville, Cicero, and Quintilian. Some among these educated ranks would continue their studies beyond the roughly six years it took to gain a Master of Arts at one of the higher faculties: Law, Medicine, or Theology. The study of law could consist of the study of Roman law, canon law, or both. Legal practice, however, functioned in the vernacular, and now it had a vernacular form of written legal thought to match.[46]

---

but with an important exception. Royal sovereignty was different, Beaumanoir explained, because below the king there was no one who could refuse to be summoned before the king's court for appeals of default of judgment or false judgment or in cases where the king himself was implicated (*ibid.*).

[42] For broad views of the development of Capetian power and historiographical trends in the field, see William Chester Jordan, 'The Capetians from the Death of Philip II to Philip IV'.

[43] Potter, introduction to *France in the Later Middle Ages*, pp. 6–7.

[44] See Gabrielle M. Spiegel, *Romancing the Past*.

[45] Outside of the Norman *coutumiers*, these were all written in French.

[46] While language serves as the basis of any expression of law, relatively little has been written about language and the lawbook in France. Van Dievoet has a short section listing the European *coutumiers* that were written in vernacular languages without discussing the implications of this. The exception is Serge Lusignan's seminal comparative study of 'the language of kings' in France and England (Lusignan, *La langue des rois au Moyen*

This shift in the language of law, of course, did not completely
displace established institutional culture.[47] Latin was the language
of text and instruction at the university – a language that united
students who had assembled from different parts of Europe.[48] No
one who wrote Latin from the eighth century onward could do so
without a conscious endeavour to acquire the language through
study and perseverance.[49] Learning Latin was a rite of passage for
learned men that bonded them in the rarefied culture and small elite
club of *latinitas* and signalled their social positions.[50] Language was
an agent of delimitation and social exclusion as much as
understanding and social connection. Latin brought elite
intellectuals together but excluded those who did not understand
the language.

The sophisticated Latin legal language of the universities, based on
the *auctoritas* of ancient Roman texts, had provided a way of accessing,
knowing, and expressing legal truth on the continent.[51] Beyond this,
language itself is a representation of symbolic power.[52] The addition of
the vernacular as a language of law was a '*bouleversement culturel*',
a true cultural upheaval.[53]

Aside from the earliest examples from Normandy, *coutumier*
authors from northern France all wrote in French vernaculars.

Âge). Lusignan examined the shifting relationship between the vernacular and Latin in
these royal courts and their chanceries through the high and late Middle Ages. The
medieval development of the vernacular as a written language of law has mostly come
out of the field of diplomatics, the records of legal practice (see *ibid.*, pp. 45ff). While legal
translation in France has received important attention recently, there is no larger account
of it for the medieval period, neither as a vernacular language movement nor as
a phenomenon in legal history. French legal translations are included in the monumental
Claudio Galgerisi (ed.), *Translations médiévales*, vol. 2. For specific studies, see for
instance, Leena Löfstedt, *Gratiani decretum*; Willy van Hoecke, notably 'La "première
reception" du droit romain'; Hans van de Wouw, 'Quelques remarques sur les versions
françaises médiévales'; Claire-Hélène Lavigne, 'La traduction en vers des *Institutes* de
Justinien 1er'; Hélène Biu, 'La *Somme Acé*'; Kuskowski, 'Translating Justinian'.

[47] Sebastian Sobecki, *Unwritten Verities*, p. 12.
[48] Robert S. Rait, *Life in the Medieval University*, p. 133.
[49] Carin Ruff, 'Latin as an Acquired Language'.
[50] Ruth Mazzo Karras, *From Boys to Men*, p. 94.
[51] The laws of early-medieval England were written in the vernacular and are a well-
known exception.
[52] See generally Pierre Bourdieu, *Language and Symbolic Power*; Patrick J. Geary,
Language and Power in the Early Middle Ages.
[53] Lusignan, *La langue des rois au Moyen Âge*, p. 254.

Those who composed this vernacular law likely read Latin, and several of them evince familiarity with aspects of Roman or canon law. Many *coutumiers* reveal unmistakable scholastic, Romanist, or canonist resonances, the extent and nature of which vary in each text, from tacit expression to explicit citation.

However, scholarship has overestimated the extent to which *coutumiers* were patterned or modelled after Roman law and, more specifically, the *Corpus iuris civilis*. I suggest in this book that even those *coutumier* authors who most relied on Roman law so dramatically repurposed it that their efforts cannot accurately be characterized as a form of modelling or imitation.

In the most direct, practical terms, the vernacularization of law expanded the place of non-Latin languages in the field. The vernacular gained new terms to capture concepts that were either developing out of practice or imported from the Latin terminology of learned law. The lexical range of the vernacular expanded, and it also increasingly developed a specifically legal register of language – a specialized legal jargon – that overlapped with but was not always the same as ordinary language. To think of custom in the vernacular, however, meant much more than the replacement of Latin words with French ones, or the development of a technical vocabulary. The development of the vernacular as a written language was crucial for the development of customary law, and this legal change cannot be separated from cultural change. Lay people, who had long held court and participated in judicial processes, gained a new way to interact with legal ideas, a new ability to shape or be shaped by them, and a new capacity to exchange and transmit them. And so, vernacular law extended beyond the courts to become an erudite vernacular form of knowledge, constructed and written by lay thinkers.

I use 'vernacular law' to designate both the shift in language and culture. This law spanned the various subjects that constituted custom, from transactions to pleading in court; it was written with clarity and brevity, to help a lay audience think in terms of categories of law and argumentation; it taught lay people how to interpret information and craft it into normative statements and legal lines of reasoning; in a general sense, it taught them how to 'think like a lawyer'.

**

My second argument is that the importance of the *coutumiers* went far beyond the content of their specific rules and procedures. Indeed, they created a discourse and tradition for thinking about custom. With this framework, *coutumier* authors taught their readers and listeners ways of thinking, knowing, and arguing that would empower them in diverse roles in the secular courts.

To the mass of charters describing individual agreements, imaginative descriptions of trials, nascent records of court proceedings, and intermittent legislation, *coutumier* authors added coherent, holistic accounts of custom. In other words, *coutumier* authors shaped a conceptual law – a law based on explicit, generalized rules, procedures, and practices. In so doing, they created a new way of understanding customary law and fundamentally transformed it. Drawing on a wide array of experiences and thought, *coutumier* authors created the broader conventions through which we have come to understand custom.

Each *coutumier* author had to puzzle through how to write a book on lay court customs around diverse subjects as the treatment of murder, land reclamation, wardship, inheritance, arbitration, court procedure, property claims, descriptions of capital crimes, matters of jurisdiction, appeals, and judicial ethics. They had to think about how to contextualize their work in the preface or front matter and decide which practices and themes to include or exclude. They had to find a way to investigate and account for subjects and issues they had not seen in practice, read about in books, or been taught in some way. They had to select sources and authorities to use and decide how they would incorporate their ideas and reference them in their texts. That no two *coutumier* authors arrived at the exact same conclusions shows the subjective element in composing a text of customary law.

Previously, all of the subjects covered in *coutumiers* had been dispersed throughout individual records, memories, and opinions. Pierre and his colleagues gathered, labelled, and organized them. And in this sense the *coutumiers* narrated the law because they created essential groundwork for the written expression of legal custom in the vernacular. Narrativity in law has received a great deal of attention from scholars, but usually in cases that involve the 'fictions in the archives', as Natalie Zemon Davis describes it; the drama of the trial; or cases that explicitly involve a lot of storytelling.[54] Lawbooks create narrative in more subtle ways but thinking about how they do so reveals how they created something that looked like, and became, legal reality. The *coutumier* is a wonderful example of how, as Lawrence Rosen writes, 'legal systems create facts in order to treat them as facts'.[55] Even texts that present themselves as lists of facts, such as the annal, create narrative.[56] Likewise, while the *coutumiers* may look like simple compilations of rules and procedures, they also created narratives, this book argues, and these narratives give us a holistic picture of 'customary law'.

**

My third argument, following logically from the last, is that the writing of custom was not a simple transcription of tradition that existed in community consciousness. Instead, it was an authorial act of composition that was individual, intentional, innovative, and creative. *Coutumier* authors were doing something more ambitious, novel, and groundbreaking than the scholarship usually assumes. For a medieval society reputed for interpreting change as a continuation of tradition, Pierre's claim of innovation might have sounded startling, and especially so since his subject was the customary law of secular courts, a law seemingly synonymous with tradition and replication of the past. Medieval customary law has been understood by scholars to be backward- and not forward-looking, at least in pretence: customary law purveyed the myth that it was ancient or originated from a time beyond memory, a form of 'invention of tradition', purportedly whereby innovation is construed as a preservation of 'old law'.[57] Medieval law purportedly drew on communal memory and, in such a narrative, there is no space for the efforts of individual – let alone innovative – authors.

Arguing against this view of medieval law, I contend that those who authored texts such as the *coutumiers*, as well as those who adjusted the texts in subsequent manuscript versions, were makers of customary

---

[54] Natalie Zemon Davis, *Fiction in the Archives*.

[55] Lawrence Rosen, *Law as Culture*, p. 68.

[56] Hayden White, 'The Value of Narrativity in the Representation of Reality'.

[57] M. T. Clanchy, 'Remembering the Past and the Good Old Law', E. J. Hobsbawm and T. O Ranger, *The Invention of Tradition*. I develop my views on this idea that innovation had to be construed as a preservation of tradition in a forthcoming article titled 'The Time of Custom and Medieval Myth of Ancient Customary Law'.

law. Unlike legislation, which is enacted by a governing body, custom comes from multiple places and is made in multiple ways. It may come from allegations undisputed or disputed and resolved, repetition in practice, a communal notion of what should be done, testimony about what has been done, court judgment, or conventions surrounding records of transactions. Inscription – the addition of written text to an oral culture – is itself a pivotal moment in the history of law and legal practice.[58] But *coutumier* authors did more than inscribe; rather, they composed. They selected the tone of the text and its subjects, formulated narratives, and chose how to combine experience, memory, and learning. The substance of the text included all sorts of customs – old, new, current, good, and bad – about which authors wrote their own opinions. These texts created the perception that medieval customary law was a body of law with clear rules and a coherent logic that could be known and understood. In other words, these figures were true authors rather than transcribers.

Authorship has not been an important part of the history of the *coutumiers*. The composition of custom is usually described impersonally as '*la mise en écrit*', or 'the putting into writing'. Described in this way, the story of the *coutumier* is one about a static and fixed custom that is simply transferred into a different medium. Indeed, modern

---

[58] The rise of written records in law has seen much attention from scholars. The shift from 'memory to written record' was the subject of Michael Clanchy's far-reaching study of the growth of literacy and record-keeping in post-conquest England (Clanchy, *From Memory to Written Record*). Following Walter Ong and Eric Havelock, scholars have placed the textualization of law within a narrative of the shift from orality to literacy (Ong, *Orality and Literacy*; Havelock, *The Muse Learns to Write*. See for instance, Brian Stock, *The Implications of Literacy*; Brenda Danet and Bryna Bogoch, 'From Oral Ceremony to Written Document'; Innes, 'Memory, Orality and Literacy in an Early Medieval Society'; Maria Dobozy, 'From Oral Custom to Written Law'; Geary, 'Oblivion between Orality and Textuality'; Paul Hyams, 'Orality and Literacy in the Age of Angevin Law Reforms'; Teuscher, *Lords' Rights and Peasant Stories*). Oral forms continued even when law was textualized, which could include much performative speech or give a performative valence to text itself (Marco Mostert and P. S. Barnwell (eds.), *Medieval Legal Process*; Koziol, *The Politics of Memory and Identity*). The simultaneousness of oral and written legal culture is especially well illuminated by Simon Teuscher in his study of witness testimony and its relationship to the Swiss *Weistümer*, which he sees as an aspect of lordship and the creation of bureaucrats rather than a custom that developed locally and organically (Teuscher, *Lord's Rights and Peasant Stories*). Teuscher's work shows, among other things, that there was no simple transition from oral to writing, but a complex interrelationship that is particular to its contexts.

assumptions about the inflexibility of the *coutumiers* have led to descriptions of their formalism, namely, a rigid adherence to specific formulaic words and procedural forms and a focus on technicality.[59] And yet, as we will see, the manuscript tradition of the *coutumiers* – each manuscript copy of the text with its emendations, deletions, and additions – shows that written custom continued to be a living law, continuously adjusted and sometimes transformed in, and through, its rewriting.

The manuscript tradition of the *coutumier* is key to understanding the place of writing in a customary legal culture. The writing and ongoing revisions of vernacular law, as conveyed in *coutumiers*, reveals something very important about how written texts were assimilated into a legal culture that remained oral to a large extent. *Coutumiers* were written before an understanding of legal text as fixed predominated, and they invite us to think about two questions central to this book: what is the place of text in a customary legal culture that had just begun to use it, and how does law work in a culture that does not think in terms of fixed legal text?

While individual authors of *coutumiers* such as Pierre de Fontaines and Philippe de Beaumanoir have been studied extensively, the larger meaning and implications of authorship have not. This might be partially because the choice of anonymity made by most of the authors does not lead to the analysis of specific individuals (only two *coutumier* authors studied in this book chose to reveal their identity) and partially because questions of authorship and style might be considered the domain of the literary scholar rather than the legal historian. The neglect of authorship might also have something to do with the theory that medieval customary law had only aggregate authors: it was created through repetitive practice by 'the people'. Yet an additional and complementary understanding of customary law emerges when we focus on the authorship of written custom. Here, we can see how

---

[59] Bongert, *Recherches sur les cours laïques*, p. 183. Bongert used charters to show flexibility but left the perception that it was the *coutumiers*, rather than how modern scholars talk about them, that created the impressions of inflexibility and formalism. Thus the *coutumiers* are still seen as describing a formalist practice and as responsible for scholars' wrongful understanding of practice as formalist (see Chapter 7).

customary law was filtered through the mind of each individual author who crafted, refined, and shaped it.[60]

The *coutumiers* should interest legal historians, and so too should they interest literary scholars, because they show us an as-yet unestablished genre in formation. Each text expressed one legitimate way in which a thirteenth-century author could conceive of customary law as a unit with particular characteristics. Indeed, authors differed significantly in how they chose to handle their common subject matter and common goal of giving custom written expression as a coherent entity.

Even *coutumier* authors who were working with copies of earlier *coutumiers* (we know this because these authors copied sections into their own texts), chose not to replicate exactly the form of the earlier text but instead improvised, innovated, and used authorial discretion and latitude. Authors made individual contributions to the process of shaping custom into a distinct body of knowledge. For example, some relied more on declarations of custom, some described custom through cases, others quoted selections from Roman law, others looked to canon law, and some eclectically used several sources. Together they forged a new field of legal knowledge. These individual authors, who decided what procedures and practices counted as custom, determined how to give them written form, described them as general rules, and inscribed them as bodies of law, were creators of customary law just as much as the communal and oral traditions typically considered the domain of custom.

Each *coutumier* was a witness to customary law in northern France in the thirteenth century, in the sense that witnesses have a personal immediate experience and in the sense that witnesses have subjective experiences that are not all identical. Every subsequent copy also offers an idiosyncratic perspective on customary law. For this reason, the *coutumiers* are useful not only because they demonstrate customary norms but also because they are a gateway into the creative mentalities of written customary law.

This brings us back to Pierre de Fontaines' assertion of innovation and originality. Pierre was familiar with other legal writing and openly

---

[60] In this sense, the *coutumiers* contribute to an ongoing discussion of medieval subjectivity and individual agency (see Brigitte Bedos-Rezak, 'Medieval Identity: A Sign and a Concept'; Bedos-Rezak and Dominique Iogna-Prat, eds. *L'individu au moyen âge*; Ionu Epurescu-Pascovici, *Human Agency in Medieval Society, 1100-1450*).

incorporated lengthy quotations from Justinian's *Code* into his *Conseil*. Pierre was educated, and doubtless his education transformed how he thought, but scholars still need to examine exactly what that meant. For all the continued scholarly focus on the influence of Roman law on the *coutumiers*, it is notable that Pierre used Roman law as a source but understood himself to be creating something different – something he had not seen before. This book argues that Pierre's self-perception was correct. Roman law was not a model – it was a platform to innovate something connected to it and yet fundamentally new.[61]

Pierre followed his comment about the unprecedented nature of his written work with an exhortation that future readers improve his text.[62] Pierre knew that he was inventing an original and creating a model – a palimpsest – that others would work with, and revise. He did not expect his written version of custom to be the final word – a transcription of an oral tradition, frozen and immutable – but rather perceived both his *coutumier* and the custom it contained as moments in a fluid, continuous process of creation. This is not to say that all custom constantly underwent drastic change because it did not. Rather, the *coutumiers* show an awareness that – whether because of future need, contestation, more specific definition, changing opinion, or rewriting – it always had the potential to change.

***

This book is divided into three parts. The first part contextualizes the *coutumiers* and their authors in the legal landscape of thirteenth-century northern France in three ways. I contextualize them within the struggle to define custom from late antiquity up to the time of the

---

[61] In this sense, customary law is a space in which to explore ideas of newness in the medieval period, where 'new combines with tradition, innovation with repetition' (Patricia Clare Ingham, *The Medieval New*, p. 17).

[62] Specifically, he addresses those who will see the written version of the text and asks them to excuse him for three reasons: because no one undertook such a thing and so there is no model, because customs are corrupted and differ between castellanies, and because to have everything in memory and not to err belongs to God. Then he encouraged readers to change the text: 'And it is very pleasing to me that they add their amendments, if they feel it is useful' (*et molt me plest que il i mettent lor amendement, s'il voient que mestier en soit*; Pierre de Fontaines, *Conseil*, preface). This sort of invitation was not uncommon, and it is worth noting how welcoming and positive he is about the idea.

first *coutumiers* and discuss precedents for written secular law before the *coutumiers* (Chapter 1). I then examine the predominant choice of the first *coutumier* authors to write in the vernacular and, to the extent that they can be discerned, their perceptions of laymen who participated in lay courts (Chapter 2).

Unwritten law, or *ius non scriptum*, was a prominent definition of custom in the later medieval period developed especially in learned circles. Though 'written custom' should be a contradiction, this was unevenly perceived. Unlike the authors of the *Bracton* treatise in England, for instance, the *coutumier* authors did not seek to understand or legitimate their writing of custom within this learned framework.[63] Those *coutumier* authors who addressed the question of writtenness viewed the idea of 'written custom' as unproblematic. Instead, they saw writtenness and its lack through a practical lens, as an aspect of custom's potential to be retained in memory. This does not mean they viewed written custom as 'fixed'. Writing in a time of fundamental legal change, they understood that even the custom expressed in written text was mutable. While writing custom could help to keep it in memory, it was potentially changeable in future versions of the text (Chapter 3).

The second part extends the argument about the development of vernacular law by looking at issues of jurisdiction and authority. The *coutumiers* expose real anxieties about the boundaries of power. Expressed either tacitly or explicitly, these anxieties appeared in concerns over jurisdiction, and especially ecclesiastical jurisdiction (Chapter 4). In contrast to legal histories that usually approach the issue of authority in written custom by examining the reliance on and influence of Roman law, I look instead at Roman law within the general use of sources and their associated citation practices in order see what the authors of customary law themselves counted as authorities (Chapter 5). Roman law was certainly an important source for some *coutumiers*, but rather than treat it reverentially as an authority, their authors used Roman law to build something new, lay, customary, and vernacular. The question, then, is not so much about the influence of

---

[63] For an important reassessment of the relationship between *Bracton* and Roman law, see Thomas J. McSweeney, *Priests of the Law: Roman Law and the Making of the Common Law's First Professionals*.

Roman law as it is about the agency of *coutumier* authors who customized something different out of this as well as other sources.

As the third part of this book contends, 'vernacular law' was not only law expressed in a vernacular language but also a distinct conceptualization of law that itself created new possibilities for legal thought. The three final chapters explore these possibilities. I begin with the relationship between the *coutumiers* as texts that describe custom and custom as it is reflected in other remaining records of practice (Chapter 6). I demonstrate how the *coutumiers* represent practice differently from other contemporary records of practice and how, in part, their authors used what they saw in practice to extract principles and articulate norms. By offering this form of generalization, the *coutumier* authors helped transform 'custom' into 'customary law'.

I argue that the goal of these legal texts was to change patterns of thought and teach lay people a set of ideas and skills that would permit them to perform convincingly in lay court (Chapter 7). The last chapter then examines the larger effect of written custom on legal culture. The new technology of writing combined with the social choice of the vernacular permitted customary legal ideas to be transmitted and shared outside their local setting. This increased circulation of ideas was a component setting the stage for the development of a French 'common law' (Chapter 8).

Vernacular Law offers a new account of the formation of customary law. It shows that customary law was not only the product of mass social forces expressed in popular practices but also the product of individual thought, innovation and craft. The lay thinkers who composed custom took these practices and articulated them as rules, and moreover as coherent bodies of rules. They thus transformed social practices into a field of knowledge known as customary law.

PART I

WRITTEN CUSTOM AND THE FORMATION OF VERNACULAR LAW

What Is Custom? Concept and Literary Practice

If the *coutumiers* were written as a response to a specific question, then surely that question was 'What is custom?' Its substance was obvious in some ways and not in others. Custom could refer to a wide range of personal and social habits. The *coutumier* authors were writing in response to a question about custom as a form of law, about practices and rules that were understood to have gained legal force.[1] Despite this specification, the question could still be answered in multiple ways – both implicitly by choosing which set of individual customs counted as 'the custom' of a particular place and in choosing how to discuss them, as well as explicitly through attempts to define the term itself.[2] Indeed, *coutumier* authors were not the only ones tackling

---

[1] In the Middle Ages as today, 'custom' could denote a convention, tradition, or usage with the general sense of a behaviour or procedure practised and accepted by a particular individual, society or community ('custom, n. and adj.', *OED Online*, Oxford University Press, March 2020, www.oed.com/view/Entry/46306 (accessed 30 April 2020)). The term also has a juridical valence. The modern dictionary definition, drawn directly from late-antique Roman jurists, described this juridical custom as a usage established by long continuance to have the force of law (*ibid.*). English language scholarship tends to describe it as a source of law while French-language scholarship tends to describe it as a type of law.

[2] The core question of 'what is custom?' overlapped with another, 'what are the customs?' A primary aim of these texts was certainly to specify particular rules and procedures. In choosing which rules and which procedures to group together and how to present them, each *coutumier* author offered their own understanding of the contours and substance of custom. Each text thus implicitly presented a vision of what custom was, even where the term was not defined or this was not explicitly stated as a goal of the text.

the question. As they embarked on the task of defining custom and figuring out how to write about it, communities of canonists and Roman lawyers had already started wrestling with the notion of custom and continued to do so throughout the thirteenth century.

Each of these communities approached custom in overlapping yet distinct ways because of different interests, source material, and practical concerns. Jurists who studied Roman law tried to make sense of custom by theorizing its definition as well as its applicability through the notion of proof. Meanwhile, medieval ecclesiastics and canon lawyers sought to understand the place of custom in the framework of the church.

These different communities have given rise to different modern fields of study, and histories of custom in these fields have different starting points and emphasis. The history of custom in Roman law might touch on a Greek legacy but normally begins with Cicero and then turns to imperial jurists and codes of late antiquity. It often elides the early medieval period before looking to the Roman law revival and the robust juristic commentary practices on custom that developed thereafter. The history of custom in canon law normally begins with biblical notions of custom (usually with the New Testament), and then turns to the bishops of antiquity and the continuity of the tradition in the early medieval period, before looking to the great books and pronouncements on the subject in the central and high Middle Ages.

The history of custom in secular law, for northern France, generally divides into two periods. One covers the early Middle Ages to the end of the eleventh century, understood as a period of customary law because legal practice was not professionalized and notions of law blurred with other forms of moral imperative.[3] The next phase of this history begins around the twelfth century, when custom came to describe the primary norm of common transactions and lay lordships. Sources on the practice of the lay courts thus began to emphasize a consistency with practice, with 'usage' or 'custom', as justification for following a certain rule or procedure rather than, for instance, justifying it with an official act of lawmaking by a specified authority.

Some scholars describe this as the 'crystallization' of custom, by which individual customs that usually expressed a lordly exaction

[3] Reynolds, *Kingdoms and Communities*, p. 14.

coalesced into rules or procedures tied to a specific lordship and were labelled by contemporaries as usages or customs.[4] They see crystallization in expressions that appeared in charters recording various transactions that tied custom to territorial lordship – ones such as '*secundum consuetudinem partrie*' or '*ad usus et consuetudines Normanniae*', where the particular rule or procedure followed the custom of the land or accorded with its usages and customs.[5] Other scholars describe the 'emergence' of custom, which is similar language for a different idea. By this interpretation, local or regional custom materialized under the influence of Roman law, which enjoyed an intellectual renaissance in twelfth-century universities and provided a new vocabulary, new legal categories and methods, and a new framework for understanding legal life.[6] Lastly, the appearance of the *coutumiers* is also explained by the history of literate practices: as orality

---

[4] The '*cristallisation coutumière*', the shift from the mores of a people to the usages and customs of a specific lordship (e.g. a duchy or a county), in southern France is described as occurring between the fifth and twelfth centuries – so the *mos Burgundiorum* from around the year 1000 shifted to the *bons us et coutumes* of the lordship of the area (Lauranson-Rosaz, 'Des "mauvaises coutumes" aux "bonnes coutumes"', p. 51). Such explicit references to custom only started to become common in northern France in the early thirteenth century: the *Statute of Pamiers* (1212) contains an early mention of custom and usage of France around Paris, while the customs of Champagne, Poitou and Flanders are explicitly referred to around the 1220s onward (Paul Ourliac and Jean-Louis Gazzaniga, *Histoire de droit privé français*, p. 66). While we in retrospect can identify patterns that indicate consistent use of certain practices, these were not labelled as custom or explicitly articulated. For example, John Baldwin writes that patrilineal succession in the Paris region was apparent in practice at the beginning of the reign of Philip Augustus (1180–1223), but it had virtually no express written formulation at that time and that references to 'customs' (*consuetudines*) were exceedingly rare in ecclesiastical charters even in the first couple of decades of the thirteenth century (Baldwin, *Knights, Lords, and Ladies in Search of Aristocrats in the Paris Region*, pp. 65–6).

[5] Jean Yver, 'Les caractères originaux', pp. 2ff; Olivier Guillot, 'Sur la naissance de la coutume en Anjou au XIe siècle'. The Norman customs have been especially studied in this regard because of the earlier development of strong ducal power in the region between the eleventh and twelfth centuries (Gilduin Davy, 'Les chartes ducales, miroir du droit coutumier normand?', 202–5; Mark Hagger, 'Secular Law and Custom in Ducal Normandy').

[6] André Gouron argued over thirty years ago that it was artificial to treat canon-law, Roman-law, and secular-law communities as though they were undergoing isolated developments, and much of his work has been devoted to showing that customary law developed under the influence of Romano-canonical law (Gouron, 'La coutume en France au Moyen Âge', p. 194). In his words: 'Sans renaissance des droits "universitaires", point de coutume' (*ibid.*, p. 205). See also Gouron, 'Aux origines de l'émergence du droit'.

shifted to literacy, these histories argue, oral legal practices were transferred into the written lawbook.[7]

I begin in a different place from these studies, with concepts and texts. This chapter provides a history of the idea of custom and of texts about lay legal life that predate the *coutumiers*. The first part of the chapter examines the struggle to define custom from late antiquity to the time of the *coutumiers*. It shows that the conceptualization and definition of custom in its legal dimension was no obvious thing: common definitional elements existed, but debate and a lack of consensus around the definition of custom would continue through the thirteenth century onward.

I speak here of Roman and canon law communities not to assess their influence on the *coutumiers* but to show the intellectual churn around the concept of custom.[8] The *coutumiers* were composed at a time when the question 'What is custom?' sparked lively debate. Academic communities discussed how to prove individual customs and how to define the term generally. Definitions that later proved marginal, unpopular, or fleeting are as important as the ones that left a lasting imprint in legal thought because together these all show the breadth of ideas about custom in the twelfth and thirteenth centuries. My goal is to shift the discussion from the well-worn analysis of 'influence' towards different community cultures of customary law in Romanist, canonist, and secular circles.

The second part of the chapter briefly examines custom as a subject of literary practice. It begins by considering where and how secular practice was written about in the period before the first *coutumiers* and ends with brief descriptions of each of the *coutumiers* at the heart of this study. My first goal is to place the *coutumiers* not just in the history of the lawbook, as has been done before, but more generally in the history of descriptive or expository writing about secular law.[9] This shift in approach reveals a long interest in and desire for the written exposition of secular law and permits the inclusion of theological and monastic writings that do not get meaningful attention in the history of

[7] Stock, *The Implications of Literacy*, p. 56; Clanchy, *From Memory to Written Record*, p. 29ff; Cohen, *Crossroads of Justice*, pp. 5ff.
[8] The idea of influence is discussed in Chapter 5.
[9] The relationship between the *coutumiers* and acts of practice (such as transactional documents and court records) is treated in Chapter 6.

the *coutumiers*. My second goal is to provide descriptions of the *coutumiers* of thirteenth-century northern France in order to show that, notwithstanding obvious and important commonalities, each text actually showcases a unique approach to writing custom. This reveals the importance of authorial approach and an element of subjectivity inherent to the contents of the *coutumiers*. It adds a key element to the current background narratives of the *coutumiers*, which focus on how individual practices and rules were identified as territorial customs, the pre-eminent influence of Roman law, and the shift from oral to written form. Also, some *coutumiers* are better known and more studied than others, so the descriptions in this chapter permit the group to be viewed as a whole.

Custom and Law in Late-Antique Juristic Thought

Dictionary definitions of custom might seem obvious or natural, but they are the product of a long history. The Roman law of late antiquity played a fundamental role in the history of custom as a form of law in the European Latin West. Its language and categorization had such an impact that modern definitions derived from them still follow them closely. This history shows how the definition of custom developed in contrast to developing notions of law, especially legislation, and that custom is not a static notion but one that changed over time. The jurists of late Roman antiquity, just as later medieval thinkers, found it difficult to choose precisely when and how certain practices came to be obligatory. What tipped the scales from habitual practice to law? Why should unlegislated norms be enforced? A look at the late Roman legal tradition helps illuminate what medieval Romanists constructed out of that tradition as well as the *coutumier* authors' quite different understanding of custom.

We know about Roman views on custom from the writings of orators and jurists. Orators, advocates who did the pleading in court, commonly used arguments from custom in litigation, drawing variously on the wide range of terms for custom: *consuetudo, usus, mos*.[10] Cicero (106–43 BCE), in *De Inventione*, was already defining

---

[10] Caroline Humfress, 'Law and Custom under Rome', p. 24.

custom according to what would become its classic attributes: 'what age has approved by the will of all in the absence of statute'.[11]

The classical jurists (fl. first to third century CE) developed a more technical interest in custom as they sought to account for unlegislated aspects of the civil law, reframing the political ideals of *mos maiorum* (ancestral custom, or the way of the ancestors) into an explanation for contemporary legal practices and institutions.[12] For them, custom with the appropriate sedimentary layers of age accrued into something like law.[13] The second-century jurist Julian (Salvianus Julianus), for instance, explained that 'age-encrusted custom [*inveterata consuetudo*] is not undeservedly held as law [*pro lege*], and this is a kind of Law [*ius*] which is said to be established by habit [*mos*]'.[14] The third-century jurist Modestinus echoed this sedimentary aspect of custom but saw it as a source of law rather than a form of law: 'every rule of Law [*ius*] is either made by agreement, or established by necessity, or solidified [*firmavit*] by custom [*consuetudo*]'.[15]

Classical jurists saw custom as a practice or factual circumstance that acquired legal force through recognition by statute, imperial rescript, magistrate's edict, or the consistent opinion of jurists.[16] For instance, if statute law was ambiguous, Septimus Severus (r. 193–211)

---

[11] Peter Stein, 'Custom in Roman and Medieval Civil Law', 337.

[12] José Luis Alonso, 'The Status of Peregrine Law in Egypt', 370–1.

[13] The *Corpus iuris civilis* was composed by sixth-century jurists at the behest of Emperor Justinian and issued between 529 and 534 CE. The *Institutes*, the introductory textbook of Roman law, was a new composition. The other parts of the *Corpus* were composed by cutting and pasting earlier sources together. While this preserved the earlier sources, it also presented them altered: the *Digest* contains removed and decontextualized passages taken from the works of jurists rearranged and collated according to its own subject matter divisions, and the *Code* contains removed and decontextualized passages drawn from imperial rescripts that are rearranged and collated in a similar manner. The *Novels* is an addendum of new law issued after 534. I present ideas about custom here in chronological order so that the evolution of thinking about custom in late antiquity might be seen more clearly.

[14] 'Inveterata consuetudo pro lege non immerito custoditur, et hoc est ius quod dicitur moribus constitutum', Justinian, *Digest* 1.3.32. There is a difficulty in translation because English uses the term law for both statute/legislation and larger notions of right and justice, unlike Latin which differentiates *lex* as statute/legislation and *ius* as right and justice (as do many continental languages). To distinguish the latter in English Law is written with a capital 'L'.

[15] 'Ergo omne ius aut consensus fecit aut necessitas constituit aut firmavit consuetudo', Justinian, *Digest* 1.3.40.

[16] Stein, 'Custom in Roman and Medieval Civil Law', 338.

indicated that it ought to be interpreted through custom or an unbroken pattern of similar judicial decisions.[17] Unlike later medieval jurists, they were not particularly interested in elaborating a theory of customary law as a form of legal obligation in its own right but rather in understanding how to use custom in specific legal contexts, most notably, provincial contexts.[18] Even references to geographically specific custom seem to indicate less a fixed, longstanding, and established custom than a dynamic interest in how the concept could be deployed in legal argumentation.[19]

Juristic writings and imperial rescripts from the late third and fourth century show that the nature of custom continued to be unsettled and opinions on the subject contradictory. Hermogenian, a jurist under Diocletian (r. 284–305), emphasized length of time in his characterization of custom while pushing its theory a little further: 'we also keep to those rules that have been sanctioned by long custom [*longa consuetudine*] and observed over many years [*per annos plurimos observata*]; we keep to them as being a tacit agreement of the citizen, no less than we keep to written rules of law'.[20] Custom still had to be long, but he clarified 'long' as several years. Longevity, however, was not sufficient to elevate custom to the same force as law: it also had to have been observed through time.[21] That this gave custom the force of law was not necessarily the received

---

[17] David J. Bederman, *Custom as a Source of Law*, p. 19; Justinian, *Digest* 1.3.38.
[18] Humfress, 'Law and Custom under Rome', pp. 25, 47. Custom created a category of law or legal thinking for very specific contexts, notably provincial contexts (*ibid.* pp. 26ff). In 224, Emperor Severus Alexander made it the duty of the provincial governor to follow local custom in local disputes (Justinian, *Code* 8.52.1). As he explained, 'preexisting custom [*consuetudo praecedens*] and the reasons that gave rise to it should be upheld, and the provincial governor will make it his business to prevent anything being done contrary to longstanding custom' ('*Nam et consuetudo praecedens et ratio quae consuetudinem suasit custodienda est, et ne quid contra longam consuetudinem fiat, ad sollicitudinem suam revocabit praeses provinciae*'; Justinian, *Code* 8.52.1). This may be the problem Ulpian (ca. 170–223) sought to address in his Duties of a Proconsul, when he noted that the first line of inquiry to be pursued when someone alleged a custom in court was whether it had previously been upheld in contentious proceedings (Justinian, *Digest* 1.3.34).
[19] Humfress, 'Law and Custom under Rome', p. 30.
[20] '*Sed et ea, quae longa consuetudine comprobata sunt ac per annos plurimos observata, velut tacita civium conventio non minus quam ea quae scripta sunt iura servantur*' (Justinian, *Digest* 1.3.35).
[21] The jurist Paul mentioned the principle of approval earlier, but in a manner that might be deemed more descriptive than constitutive: 'This kind of law is held to be of

view, as can be seen in Constantine's (r. 306–37) statement that longstanding (*longaevi*) custom (*consuetudo*) and usage (*usus*) were 'of not insignificant authority' but that they did not contravene reason or law (*lex*).[22]

Custom achieved firmer standing as a legal norm in itself, one distinct from general habitual action, with the post-classical jurists from about the fourth century onward. Notably, jurists of the pre-eminent law school of the late-antique Roman world at Beirut tended to equate custom with law.[23] In fact, it was at this time that jurists are thought to have developed the theory of desuetude: the abrogation of custom by inaction or silent agreement over time.[24]

Christian theology had also been developing a doctrine of custom. This doctrine first appears in the writings of Tertullian (ca. 160–240), who justified the authority of custom for the church by looking to secular law, which turned to custom in the absence of law.[25] However, he wrote that custom should only be granted by this authority if it was reasonable and conformed to Christian truth.[26] Custom and truth were not necessarily comfortable allies. It was the same Tertullian who first noted that Christ had called himself 'the Truth' and not 'the Custom', a dictum that would have traction in the medieval period.[27]

Indeed, custom came to be linked to resistance to truth, and thus to heresy.[28] While arguments from custom were made at church councils,

---

particularly great authority, because approval of it has been so great that it has never been necessary to reduce it to writing' (Justinian, *Digest* 1.3.36).

[22] 'Consuetudinis usuque longaevi non vilis auctoritas est …' (Justinian, *Code* 8.52.2).

[23] Stein, 'Custom in Roman and Medieval Civil Law', 339.

[24] As Peter Stein notes, a post-classical addition was probably made to Julian's text that mentioned desuetude, though the notion that some early statutory rules had lost force *per desuetudinem* did exist in Gaius' *Institutes* (Stein, 'Custom in Roman and Medieval Civil Law', 339).

[25] '*Consuetudo etiam in civilibus rebus pro lege suscipitur cum deficit lege*' (Tertullian, *De corona*, IV.6 in Jean Gaudemet, 'La coutume en droit canonique', p. 44).

[26] Gaudemet, 'La coutume en droit canonique', p. 44.   [27] *Ibid.*

[28] Ancient custom was a problem for the early church. Tertullian stated that heresy was condemned not for being novelty but for being contrary to truth, and everything contrary to truth is heresy, even ancient custom ('*Sed dominus noster Christus veritatem se non consuetudinem cognominavit. Hersim on tam novitas quam veritas revincit. Quodcumque adversus veritatem sapit, hoc erit heresis, etiam vetus consuetudo*'; Tertullian, *De virginitatis velandis*, 1.2 in René Wehrlé, *De la coutume dans le droit canonique*, p. 47. Cyprian (ca. 200–58) invoked the dictum of Christ as Truth and not Custom in his discussion of the contentious issue of the rebaptism of heretics (*ibid.*, pp. 50ff; Gaudemet, 'La coutume en droit canonique', p. 45). Later, Theodoret

these could be invalidated by allegations that the custom in question went against reason.[29] Basil (ca. 330–79) described custom as having force of law.[30] Augustine (354–430) held that where Holy Scripture had left uncertainties, the custom of the people of God or the institutions of the ancestors should be held as law.[31] Myriad practices, rituals, and ceremonies were fine if they did not contravene 'true doctrine' or 'sound morality' and led towards a better life.[32] However, practices not contained in Scripture, established by councils, or reinforced by the custom of the universal church – practices that varied enormously by place and habit – should be unhesitatingly ended when the reasons for them were no longer perceptible.[33] We can see here a tension around the idea of custom in Christian thinking, one that did not seem to be a preoccupation in the work of jurists. The latter were less interested in judging customs as good or bad than the former, but, this judgement aside, Christian thinkers and jurists deployed very similar if not identical definitions of custom.

The *Theodosian Code* (438) placed a new onus on custom by reserving an entire section for the subject of customary law, titled 'Longstanding Custom' (*De longa consuetudine*), although it was buried at the end of the fifth book of the *Code* and contained only one provision: 'To insist upon things established of old [*veteribus institutis*] is the discipline of future times. Therefore, when nothing that is in the public interest interferes, practices which have long been observed [*quae diu servata sunt*] shall remain valid.'[34] This went

of Cyrrhus (ca. 393–ca. 457) exhorted pagans to convert to Christianity and so to choose truth over the customs of their ancestors and the mores of their country (Wehrlé, *De la coutume dans le droit canonique*, p. 64).
[29] For church councils, see Wehrlé, *De la coutume dans le droit canonique*, pp. 54ff and Gaudemet, 'La coutume en droit canonique', p. 46.
[30] Wehrlé, *De la coutume dans le droit canonique*, pp. 56ff.
[31] 'In his enim rebus de quibus nihil certi statuit Scriptura divina, mos populi dei, vel instituta maorum pro lege tenenda sunt' (Augustine in Wehrlé, *De la coutume dans le droit canonique*, p. 60).
[32] Augustine of Hippo, 'Letter 55 (A.D. 400)' trans. Cunningham, chap. 18.34 (accessed 30 April 2020).
[33] *Ibid.*, chap. 19.35.
[34] 'venientium est temporum disciplina, instare veteribus institutis. ideoque quam nihil per causam publicam intervenit, quae diu servata sunt, permanebunt. dat. iv. kal. mart. constantinopoli, iuliano a. iv. et sallustio coss', *Theodosian Code* 5.20.1. (equivalent to Alaric's *Breviary* 5.12 and Justinian's *Code* 8.52). 'Veteribus institutis'

beyond earlier statements, as it made practices that have been observed over a long period of time legally valid as long as they were not against the public interest. Emperors Leo and Anthemius went beyond this in 469, stating that 'Custom, approved of old and tenaciously adhered to [*antiquitus probate et servata tenaciter consuetudo*], also imitates and upholds the statutes themselves.'[35]

By the time of the great compilation of the *Corpus iuris civilis*, completed between 529 and 534, the authority of custom did not sound too different from that of legislation. The introductory handbook for students, the *Institutes*, stated clearly that 'long-standing custom [*diuturni mores*] founded on the consent of those who follow it is just like legislation'.[36] Custom shared a title with laws and decrees of the senate (*senatus consulta*) in the *Digest* and an independent title in the *Code* detailing how long custom should be understood, '*Quae sit longa consuetudo*'.[37]

The definitions and debates of jurists and theologians of the Roman world had a great impact on understandings of custom in the Middle Ages. The technical language of this custom had not been definitively set, and the boundaries between the various words for custom, *consuetudo*, *mos*, and *usus*, were rather blurry. However, the lexical and rhetorical concepts of custom described here would be deployed and redeployed throughout the medieval period. Late-antique Christian thought established a tension between truth and custom, an uneasiness about how to negotiate unity and diversity, and an emphasis on the subservience of custom to reason. Late-antique

---

is sometimes translated as 'ancient customs', and it could include these but seems originally to have been wider in meaning, including other types of old law. *Institutum* can mean anything from custom to principle, decree, intention, institution, habit, or plan. This is the one and only provision placed under *Theodosian Code*'s heading of 'Longstanding Custom', but it is itself vague. What is interesting is that Alaric's Breviary, promulgated in 506 under the Visigothic king Alaric II, summarized that statement in the interpretation in terms of *consuetudo* and *lex*: 'Long established custom [*longa consuetudo*] shall be observed as law [*pro lege servabitur*] when it does not interfere with the public welfare [*interpretatio. longa consuetudo, quae utilitatibus publicis non impedit, pro lege servabitur*]' (*Theodosian Code* 5.20.1, equivalent to *Breviary* 5.12).

[35] '*Leges quoque ipsas antiquitus probate et servata tenaciter consuetudo imitator ac retinet*' (Justinian, *Code* 8.52.3).

[36] Justinian, *Institutes* 1.2.9.

[37] Alonso, 'The Status of Peregrine Law in Egypt', 379. See Justinian, *Digest* 1.3.32ff, *Code* 8.52.

jurists' categorizations and descriptions of custom – as longstanding, unwritten, assumed to express the tacit consent of 'the people', sometimes the rival of *lex* (law) and sometimes its interpreter – provided medieval thinkers with a set of resources from which to construct their own theories of custom.[38]

Defining Custom in Medieval Canon Law and Roman Law

The terminology and classification of legal norms found in late-antique Roman legal texts were not at the forefront of legal thought in the early Middle Ages. The exception to this was Isidore of Seville (ca. 560–636), who echoed Roman definitions in the fifth chapter of his *Etymologies*, the first half of which was devoted to laws and was essentially a very brief abridgement of the key ideas of Roman law. Isidore, like his Roman predecessors, pitted custom against law (*lex*), describing it variously as 'usage tested by age'; unwritten law, although it was immaterial whether it was written or unwritten; and a longstanding and common usage drawn from mores, taken as law in the absence of law.[39]

The early Middle Ages is known as an age of customary law. At the same time, those who composed the early medieval laws, once known as barbarian laws, described the texts as laws or legislation.[40] Defining custom and separating it from law was not a preoccupation in these

---

[38] David Ibbetson, 'Custom in Medieval Law', p. 152; Jacob, 'Les coutumiers du XIIIe siècle ont-ils connu la coutume?, pp. 103–20.

[39] '1 *Ius generale nomen est, lex autem iuris est species. Ius autem dictum, quia iustum est. Omne autem ius legibus et moribus constat. 2 Lex est constitutio scripta. Mos est vetustate probata consuetudo, sive lex non scripta. Nam lex a legendo vocata, quia scripta est. 3 Mos autem longa consuetudo est de moribus tracta tantundem. Consuetudo autem est ius quoddam moribus institutum, quod pro lege suscipitur, cum deficit lex: nec differt scriptura an ratione consistat, quando et legem ratio commendet. 4 Porro si ratione lex constat, lex erit omne iam quod ratione constiterit, dumtaxat quod religioni congruat, quod disciplinae conveniat, quod saluti proficiat. Vocata autem consuetudo, quia in communi est usu*' (Isidore of Seville, *Etymologia*, 5.3. 1–4: LacusCurtius, https://bit.ly/3PRywe8 (accessed 28 April 2020)). The distinction between written and unwritten in this definition is discussed in Chapter 3.

[40] These texts fit Roman or Isidorian definitions of law as written statute but do not fit modern perceptions of law's relationship to applicability and enforcement. Scholars have been moving away from the idea that a Germanic *Volksrecht* survived via the principle of personality of law to be redacted centuries later and have come to see these texts as the result of various expediencies of their particular moment.

texts, which are best known for listing compensation payments for specific infractions. The *Lex Baiuvariorum*, or Bavarian Laws (mid-eighth century), was an exception within this group in that it reflected uniquely on Roman categories of law and custom. While the prologue traces the Bavarian laws back to Merovingian times, the text in the form we know was a product of Carolingian scriptoria and reflects ideologies of these latter times.

The preface of the Bavarian Laws argued that the text itself was legitimate law. The first two-thirds of the preface was drawn directly from Isidore of Seville's *Etymologies* with some small but important changes. The text began with a genealogy of lawmakers, from Moses to the Greeks to the Twelve Tables to codification by emperor Theodosius (429–34). Rather than ending with the *Theodosian Code* as did Isidore, the Bavarian Laws then noted that a new age began after the *Code*, one where 'each people selected their own law from customary practice'.[41]

The preface next incorporated Isidore's definitions of law and custom but fashioned these into an argument in favour of law. After noting that custom was a type of law, the preface stated that Theoderich, king of the Franks, asked men learned in 'ancient laws' to write the 'laws' of the Franks, Alamans, and Bavarians, keeping what was necessary and discarding the rest.[42] The prologue referred to those norms as 'law' and afterwards differentiated them from 'custom', making this a term associated with a pagan past.[43] Echoing late-antique theologians who opposed heretical custom to Christian truth, the text explained that pagan 'customs' were displaced by 'Christian law'.[44] The preface to the Bavarian laws was clear: it was significant to

---

[41] 'Deinde unaquaque gens propriam sibi ex consuetudine elegerunt legem' (*Leges Baiwariorum*, ed. von Schwind, preface (accessed 28 April 2020), p. 258).

[42] *Ibid.* The prologue's emphasis on the legitimacy of Merovingian rulers, beginning with Clovis' son Theuderic, indicated opposition to Carolingian reforms of Frankish policy but also legitimized laws through ethnicity (Helmut Reimitz, *History, Frankish Identity and the Framing of Western Ethnicity, 550–850*, p. 329).

[43] The text also refers to Theodorich's personal custom (*secundum consuetudinem suam*) in the same sentence (*Leges Baiwariorum*, preface, p. 259).

[44] '*Et quae erant secundum consuetudinem paganorum mutavit secundum legem christianorum. Et quicquid Theodericus rex propter vetustissimam paganorum consuetudinem emendare non potuit, post haec Hildebertus rex inchoavit, sed Lotharius rex perfecit. [...] omnia vetera legum in melius transtulit et unicuique genti scriptam tradidit, quae usque hodie preserverant*' (*ibid.*).

have a written law, one that reflected Christian law, rather than *consuetudines*, which here were now relegated to pagan customs.[45] Roman law via Isidore's *Etymologies* combined here with a theological tradition that understood custom as a valid norm but also associated it with wrong forms of religious thought, whether pagan or heretical.

Only later, in the twelfth century, however, did a real distinction between law and custom gain traction once again in Christendom.[46] Before then, there were certainly norms and legislation, but these were generally not taxonomized or articulated as a body of rules. Rather, they infused specific grants, individual agreements, and occasional though rare legislation.[47] While there were courts and while there was dispute resolution, the world of law was not based on a professional practice and often blurred law and morality, principle and specific instance, and law and fact.[48]

For legal historians of France, this raises the question of when and how law as a concrete category 'emerged' from all of this.[49] Answers tend to point to the rebuilding of 'public' power and the study of Roman law at universities. This question, and the answers, are partly connected to the debate over the extent to which order fell apart in the post-Carolingian West and thus the extent to which domination and violence had supplanted law and the extent to which the ability to think theoretically about law could continue in a world where public governmental institutions had been displaced by banal rights and exactions. The answer is also partially connected to whether, if we accept a world of domination and fines, we accept the university study

---

[45] Patrick Wormald noted that the *Lex Salica* was a basic inspiration for the Bavarian Laws (and others), but effort was made to convey Bavarian custom (Wormald, *The Making of English Law: King Alfred to the Twelfth Century*, vol. 1, *Legislation and Its Limits*, p. 44). The Franks, he noted, were less interested in creating a law for their subject peoples to use than in 'coaching them in the value of having written law' (*ibid.*). He thus emphasized the importance of written legislation for the text, but it also offers an important view on the tension between *lex* and *consuetudo* that builds on a Roman legacy but combines it with Christian thought.

[46] Reynolds, *Kingdoms and Communities*, p.16; Gouron, 'La coutume en France au Moyen Âge', p. 200.

[47] Reynolds, *Kingdoms and Communities*, pp. 14–17, Gilissen, *La coutume*, p. 52.

[48] Reynolds, *Kingdoms and Communities*, p. 14.

[49] See for instance, Jacques Ellul, 'Le problème de l'émergence du droit'; Gouron, 'Aux origines de l'émergence du droit'; Lemarignier, 'La dislocation du "pagus"'.

of Roman and canon law as the necessary condition for a return to legal theory. Those scholars who emphasize the study of Roman law at universities as an explanation generally hold one of the following two positions. The maximalist viewpoint claims that the very use of the term *consuetudo* (as opposed to other normative terms) was itself an indication that an author was not only using the categories of learned law but, beyond that, also signalling their desire to be understood as a branch of learned law.[50] Others more moderately argue that the idea of custom as a category of law resulted from the influence of university study of Roman and canon legal texts.[51]

The predominant definition of *consuetudines* in France in the eleventh century was customary dues, or exactions – the rights and duties owed to a lord, usually translated into monies or services to be paid or done for various obligations or privileges.[52] Yet this was not the sole use of the term. There was some continuity in the notion of *consuetudo* as norm from the sixth to the twelfth centuries, alongside uses of the term that ranged from various forms of habit to exaction.[53] *Consuetudo* was used between the eighth and eleventh centuries on its own but also collocated with law. That is evident in the *Lex Baiuvariorum*. We can also see it in the Carolingian formula 'law and custom demands...'.[54] Abbo of Fleury (ca. 945–1004) invoked the concept of custom in his *Collectio Canonum*, a definition he took from Cicero.[55] Abbo quoted Cicero's definition of custom but shifted its focus from natural law to civil law, reorienting the source for his own purposes.[56] References to custom as exaction abound in early

---

[50] Kroeschell in Teuscher, *Lords' Rights and Peasant Stories*, p. 7.

[51] Robert Jacob, 'Les coutumiers du XIIIe siècle'.

[52] See Olivier Guillot, '*Consuetudines, consuetudo*'; Reynolds, *Kingdoms and Communities*, p. 17; Gilissen, *La coutume*, p. 23. Gilissen describes the various meanings the word 'custom' could have (*ibid.*).

[53] See Jean-Louis Thireau, 'La territorialité des coutumes au Moyen Âge', pp. 453–4.

[54] '*lex et consuetudo exposcit ...*' (*ibid.*, 455).

[55] For Abbo the contrast is between *lex* and *mos* (defined as *consuetudo vetustate probata*), and written and unwritten law (Mostert, *The Political Theology of Abbo of Fleury*, p. 110). See Chapter 3 for more on this subject. Cicero's definition: '*Consuetudine autem ius esse putatur id quod voluntate omnium sine lege vetustas comprobarit*' (Cicero, *De inventione; De optimo genere oratorum; Topica*, trans. Hubbell, 2.22.67).

[56] Mostert, *The Political Theology of Abbo of Fleury*, p. 68.

eleventh-century sources, but instances of custom as norm also persisted.[57]

The desire to further develop the concept of custom can be seen in glimpses before the Roman revival. While the phrases *jus consuetudinarium* and *lex consuetudinaria* did not appear in Roman legal texts and had long been attributed to the legal renaissance of the twelfth century, they have been traced back earlier to eleventh-century texts in northern France and Germany, before Justinianic learning spread to that area.[58] While not frequent, these expressions do point to the existence of the concept of a 'customary law', though one that largely designated fiscal dues or privileges.[59] It was at the very end of the twelfth century, in large measure due to canonists and Romanists trying to understand the nature of custom, that these expressions began to designate a broader customary law in opposition to *jus scriptum* and *jus ecclesiasticum.*[60] Thus, a notion of and vocabulary for 'customary law' as a body of law existed though only later came to designate the norms of particular jurisdictions.

In other words, the meaning of the term *consuetudo* as norm or the idea that it could designate a body of rules were not completely lost or absent and then rediscovered or created apace with the 'rediscovery' of Roman law in the later eleventh century. Nonetheless, the renewed study of Roman law is indeed vitally important to this history. Without a doubt, the popularization of Roman law categories discussed above, the development of these categories by medieval authors, and their dissemination by university-trained graduates led to their diffusion and, by the thirteenth century, their ubiquity.

And indeed, it was canonists who first dusted off older ideas about custom to wage new political battles.[61] Famously, Pope Gregory VII

---

[57] The uses of the term *consuetudo* in the *Theodosian Code* often referred to public administrative practices related to fiscal issues and some treated *exactions* specifically, making the link to seignorial exactions less of a stretch than it may seem (Franck Roumy, '*Lex consuetudinaria, Jus consuetudinarium*', 287–8).

[58] See Roumy, '*Lex consuetudinaria, Jus consuetudinarium*'.   [59] *Ibid.*, 262ff, 288.

[60] *Ibid.*, 290. These three overlapped in practice as it was common for bishops to hold land and rights in the same way that secular lords did, and the boundaries were not always easily discernable. Different subject matter jurisdiction could give them claims in the same issue for different reasons (Amelia J. Uelmen, 'A View of the Legal Profession', 1520).

[61] It is somewhat artificial to divide the canonists and Romanists as these communities have much overlap and often grappled with similar ideas and categories. However,

(1021–85) revitalized the late-antique dictum that Christ had identified himself as the truth and not the custom and utilized it in the effort to wrest the church from secular control.[62] In his words, 'any custom, no matter how old and no matter how widespread, must certainly be considered secondary to truth and a usage that is contrary to truth must be abolished'.[63] In this way, a succession of popes curtailed the importance of custom as a form of law in canon law, changing it from an autonomous form of law to one that was subject to *aequitas canonica*.[64]

Canonical collections also touched on the subject of custom. Generally, the canonists of the twelfth century agreed that the diversity of customs was not a threat to the unity of the church; that truth vanquished custom; and that law superseded a custom that was contrary to it, but custom that confirmed law should be approved.[65] From Ivo of Chartres to Gratian's *Decretum*, emphasis was placed on custom that conformed to reason.[66] Gratian opened his *Decretum* by saying that the human race was 'ruled by two things, namely, natural law and customs [*iure et moribus*]'.[67] Gratian took up Isidore's definition, noting that *consuetudo*-custom was a form of law established by common usage, recognized as legislation in the absence of the same, and confirmable by writing or reason.[68] He did not make the difference between *mos* and *consuetudo* entirely clear.[69] Beyond that, he also seems to collapse the difference between custom and legislation.[70]

---

there were also notable differences, and to make these evident, I discuss them separately, first the canonists and then the Romanists.

[62] Wehrlé, *De la coutume dans le droit canonique*, p. 81.

[63] '*Et certe (ut beati Cypriani utamur sententia) quaelibet consuetudo, quantumvis vetusta, quantumvis vulgata veritati omnimodo est postponenda et usus qui veritati est contrarius, est abolendus*', Gregory VII in W. J. Zwalve, *Law & Equity*, p. 24.

[64] Zwalve, *Law & Equity*, pp. 23–4.

[65] Wehrlé, *De la coutume dans le droit canonique*, p. 84.

[66] Jacques Krynen, 'Entre science juridique et dirigisme', §11.

[67] '*Humanum genus duobus regitur, naturali videlicet iure et moribus*', Gratian, *Decretum*, D. 1. He continued, 'All ordinances are divine or human. Divine ordinances are determined by nature, human ordinances by usages; and thus the latter vary since different things please different people.' ('*Omnes leges aut divine sunt aut humane. Divine natura, humane moribus constant. Ideoque hee discrepant, quoniam alie aliis gentibus placent*', ibid., D 1.1.1).

[68] *Ibid.*, D. 1 c.5.

[69] '*Mos autem longa consuetudo est de moribus tracta tantumdem*' (*ibid.*, D. 1 c.4).

[70] He did so when he said that 'in part, custom has been collected in writing, and, in part, it is preserved only in the usages of its followers. What is put into writing is called

Gratian also described a genealogy for the origins of customary law, one that placed the creation of custom after the creation of natural law, when human beings began to live together.[71] He explained that it nearly disappeared with the Great Flood and reappeared in the time of Nimrod, at the moment when he along with some others began oppressing people, who then foolishly submitted to him.[72] In its ecclesiastical origin fictions, custom was associated with lordly dominance and oppression.

The thirteenth century was characterized by a tremendous proliferation of decretals, papal decrees on issues of canon law, and conciliar legislation. As the authority of the papacy expanded, custom increasingly came to be identified with the voice of dissent. This can be seen in the Third Lateran Council (1179), the main goals of which were to address the problem of schism and the dispute between the pope and the Holy Roman emperor. Canon 16 explicitly confirmed the authority of the majority vote against those who made arguments from *consuetudo*.[73] Arguments based on custom were described as linked to individual will rather than reason, and custom was not to be upheld unless supported by reason and in accord with sacred decrees.[74] This solidified that reason as a general category overrode custom.[75]

In the history of custom, the Fourth Lateran Council (1215) is normally cited for prohibiting clerical participation in judicial rituals that involved the 'judgment of God' – ordeal and judicial duel – and thus pushing secular jurisdictions towards the so-called rational procedure of the inquest.[76] Importantly, however, it also included an

---

enactment or law, while what is not collected in writing is called by the general term custom' (*ibid.*, D. 1 c.5). More on this in Chapter 5.

[71] '*Jus vero consuetudinis post naturalam legem oxordium habuit, ex quo homines convenientes in unum ceperunt simul habitare*' (Gratian, *Decretum* D. 6 c.3 §2).

[72] ' … *postea a tempore Nemroth reparatum sive potius immutatum existimatur cum ipse simul cum aliis alios cepit opprimere; alii sua imbecilitate eorum ditioni ceperunt esse subjecti*' (*ibid.*).

[73] Paul Valliere, *Conciliarism*, p. 127.

[74] The Third Lateran Council, Canon 16, www.papalencyclicals.net/councils/ecum11 .htm (accessed 27 May 2020).

[75] Valliere, *Conciliarism*, pp. 127–8. Third Lateran Council, Canon 16.

[76] Of course, this prohibition was implemented at different paces by different jurisdictions and the non-sacral nature of the judicial duel gave it a much longer life post-ban than other forms of ordeal (Bartlett, *Trial by Fire and Water*, pp. 122, 127ff). The Fourth Lateran Council regulated an inquisitorial procedure that was already in use in church courts (see Pennington, 'The Fourth Lateran Council').

affirmation of the separation between ecclesiastical and secular jurisdiction:[77]

Canon 42. Clerics and laity are not to usurp each other's rights. Just as we desire lay people not to usurp the rights of clerics, so we ought to wish clerics not to lay claim to the rights of the laity. We therefore forbid every cleric henceforth to extend his jurisdiction, under pretext of ecclesiastical freedom, to the prejudice of secular justice. Rather, let him be satisfied with the written constitutions and customs hitherto approved, so that the things of Caesar may be rendered unto Caesar, and the things of God may be rendered unto God by a right distribution.

The importance of Canon 42 is less a matter of novelty than of emphasis: it shows that the contestation of jurisdictional boundaries was an important issue from both ecclesiastical and secular perspectives. It speaks to why jurisdictional issues were such a common theme throughout the thirteenth century, as evidenced in legal texts ranging from the Fourth Lateran Council to the cases before the French royal court in and before the *Olim*, as well as in the *coutumiers*, as we shall see.

   Beyond this, the canons show the importance of the rhetoric of custom to the church. It could be used to diminish particular local rites that may seem uncomfortably foreign, for instance, the customs and rites of the Greeks (Canon 4). At the same time, these rites were often to be accommodated: bishops had to provide celebrants of divine services for multicultural communities 'having one faith but different rites and customs' and languages (Canon 9). Various canons also reveal custom to be a common base of counterargument or protest.[78] The worst of these may be defences of simony based 'on the grounds of long-established custom', which 'should rather be termed a corruption'

---

[77] Fourth Lateran Council, www.papalencyclicals.net/councils/ecum12-2.htm (accessed 16 June 2020). For Latin: Antonio García y García, ed., *Constitutiones Concilii quarti Lateranensis*. This canon repeats nearly verbatim the words of a letter Innocent III likely sent to Bishop Peter des Roches, showing how the drafters of the Lateran canons borrowed from earlier papal decretals or, one might say, how they linked principles and practice (Pennington, 'The Fourth Lateran Council', pp. 17ff).

[78] For instance, it designated a method of protest against punishment for offenses, and canon 7 had to specify that prelates should correct their subjects' offenses and 'no custom or appeal can impede the execution of their decision, unless they go beyond the form which is observed in such matters' (Fourth Lateran Council, Canon 7, www .papalencyclicals.net/councils/ecum12-2.htm (accessed 16 June 2020)).

than custom (Canon 63). Custom whose observance led to mortal sin had to be disregarded, and rights were subject to good faith.[79] While some particular or regional customs had a neutral or positive valence, other regional customs had to be suppressed.[80]

Martial customs are one example of the tension between and co-existence of universalism and regionalism in canon law, whereby regional custom could continue even within an increasingly unitary church.[81] While scholars tend to associate the regionalism of custom with secular law, especially in France, we can also see its importance for the church. It not only referred to minority or foreign practices but also to much broader regional trends: *consuetudo romanae ecclesiae* and *consuetudo generalis Gallicanae ecclesiae*.[82]

The term *consuetudo* was used frequently in the *Decretals* of Gregory IX (1234), also known as *Liber Extra*, composed by Raymond of Peñafort for the pope. *Mos* and *usus* fell by the wayside, and *consuetudo* was the term for a legal form of custom, as opposed to other types of habit or use, though it continued to designate exactions as well.[83] While the great authority of custom was acknowledged, it was not authoritative enough to set aside natural law and could only set aside positive law if it was reasonable and established legitimately by the passage of time.[84]

---

[79] This was said in the context of Canon 41, concerning prescription, which stated that 'since in general any constitution or custom which cannot be observed without mortal sin is to be disregarded, we therefore define by this synodal judgment that no prescription, whether canonical or civil, is valid without good faith'. Also, one could not gain a right through prescription if one knew it belonged to someone else.

[80] Neutral or positive customs: Cistercian custom (Canon 12), extension of special regional custom of publicly announcing bans of marriage to other regions (Canon 51), praiseworthy custom of not demanding payment for funerary rites (Canon 66). Negative customs: regional custom concerning clerical marriage (Canon 14), vicious custom of patrons and bishops collecting incomes from churches that should go to priests (Canon 32), regional custom concerning absolution of excommunication upon payment of a monetary fine (Canon 49).

[81] Korpiola, 'Regional Variations in Matrimonial Law', pp. 1–20, esp. 5ff.

[82] Terms used in canonists' discussions of marriage (see for instance, Lefebvre-Teillard, *Autour de l'enfant*, p. 14).

[83] Wehrlé, *De la coutume dans le droit canonique*, p. 100.

[84] Zwalve, *Law & Equity*, p. 24. 'Licet etiam longaevae consuetudinis non sit vilis auctoritas: non ontradic usuquedeo valitura, ut vel iuri ontradi debeat praeiudicium generare, nisi fuerit rationabilis et legitime sit praescripta' (X. 1.4.11 in *ibid.*, n. 31).

Henry of Segusio (ca. 1200–71), known as Hostiensis, synthesized this foment of ideas though, importantly, did not finalize it. His innovation was to bring together various elements used to define custom: 'Custom is a rational usage prescribed or hardened by an appropriate amount of time, not interrupted by any contrary act, introduced by two acts or by contrary judgment or by something that no longer exists in memory; a usage approved by those who make use of it.'[85] He had much to say about what exactly each of these elements meant: what could make a custom reasonable or unreasonable; how much time it takes to form a custom, which he relates to the very similar concept of prescription; the number of acts (i.e. cases) it takes to introduce a custom, and so on.[86]

Beyond definition, he was also interested in how custom was proven. That there was disagreement on the subject is clear from his detailing of various views on the question held by different jurists, with whom he disagreed.[87] He proposed the following methods, each of which he presented with much qualification and potential sources of vitiation.[88] The people or the sovereign introduced an unwritten custom over an extended time period. Two judgments made according to the alleged custom over a long duration of time introduced a custom if there were no contradictory judgments. A custom was introduced by a contradictory judgment.[89] A custom was introduced if the practice was so old and widespread that no one did anything else.

This process of defining custom continued in the thirteenth century, notably by Thomas Aquinas, and in the fourteenth century by more

---

[85] 'Consuetudo est usus rationabilis competenti tempore praescriptus vel firmatus; nullo actu contrario interruptus, binario actu seu contradictorio judicio vel quod non extet memoria, inductus, usuque communi utentium comprobatus' (Summa Hostientis (Venice, 1498) in Wehrlé, *De la coutume dans le droit canonique*, p. 155).

[86] *Ibid.*, pp. 155–63. See also his discussion of customary aids, which tap into these categories (Elizabeth A. Brown, *Customary Aids and Royal Finance*, pp. 36ff, esp. 39).

[87] Wehrlé, *De la coutume dans le droit canonique*, pp. 163–87.   [88] *Ibid.*, pp. 164–8.

[89] We saw earlier that Ulpian referred to contrary judgments. It is likely that such contrary judgments occurred in cases where at least two conflicting customs were proposed and the judgment affirmed one over the other(s). This position was not generally accepted. According to Hostiensis, 'certain jurists' disagreed, saying that the custom affirmed in this situation should only be maintained outside of that particular case if it can be proved that the judge intended for it to be used again (i.e. intended to create a precedent; *ibid.*, p. 167).

professors, popes, councils, and synods. Ideas, definitions, and modes of proof relating to custom were in a continuous process of appraisal and reappraisal in the canonistic communities of the thirteenth century and beyond.

This was also the case for medieval Roman jurists who, like their late-antique counterparts, had many different opinions about custom. Many of these opinions developed alongside canonistic developments with clear similarities, as both were erected on late-antique Roman law, although with somewhat different concerns, as well. For Irnerius (d. ca. 1125), custom was an unwritten law (*ius non scriptum*) that went beyond the memory of man, but it was an opinion and not something that could be known.[90] In the second half of the twelfth century, Roman lawyers had developed a definition of custom as *ius non scriptum moribus populi diuturnis inductum*: an unwritten law created by social habit and the passage of significant time.[91] This definition was found in the work of Placentius and proved popular afterwards, including with Azo (d. ca.1220) who used it verbatim in his *Summa Codicis* in the early thirteenth century.[92]

It was not enough for Azo to define custom, however – he wanted to bring some precision to the concept. Late-antique Roman sources, he said, only provided obscure answers to what, exactly, constituted a long custom. In fact, there were also many different contemporary scholarly opinions on the subject. For Azo, a long (*longa*) custom was ten or twenty years old, a very old one was thirty years old (*longissimo tempore*), and a custom of great age (*longaeva*) was forty years old or more.[93] He compared custom to prescription, which was deemed *longa* when it lasted ten years.[94] Some jurists said that a long custom is one whose introduction does not exist in memory, but Azo responded in no uncertain terms, 'That does not please me.'[95]

[90] William E. Brynteson, 'Roman Law and Legislation in the Middle Ages', 432.
[91] This appears in the work of Placentinus and is repeated in Azo's *Summa Codicis* (Mayali, 'La coutume dans la doctrine romaniste au Moyen Âge', p. 15).
[92] *Ibid.* The date of Azo's death is uncertain and may have been after 1230 (Bellomo, *The Common Legal Past of Europe*, p. 167).
[93] Mayali, 'La coutume dans la doctrine romaniste au Moyen Âge', p. 15. I discuss these times more later.
[94] *Ibid.*
[95] 'Quidam esse tamen dicunt eam esse longam cujus non extat memoria. [...] Quod non placet' (*ibid.*).

Azo identified three methods to determine whether a custom had
been introduced: if it was received without contradiction, without
petitions of complaint against it, and if upon contradiction it was
judged by the court to be custom.[96] While it was generally agreed
that once did not a custom make, opinions differed widely beyond
that as to how many times or how much time it took to generate
custom.

Azo also defined custom in a way that likened it to nature rather
than law: 'The word custom signifies a common habit and we also say
that, in a different definition, custom is "other" nature.'[97] This
dichotomy between nature and custom went back to the pre-
Socratics in Western thought, beginning with the distinction between
nature (*physis*) and man-made law (*nomos*).[98] But it was Aristotle who
distinguished between a primary and secondary nature, the latter being
custom (*ethos*), which approached or took the place of nature.[99] He
described the link between repetition and permanence that animated
the notion of custom in his *Rhetoric*: 'that which has become habitual
becomes as if it were natural; for the distance between "often" and
"always" is not great, and nature belongs to the idea of "always," and
custom to that of "often"'.[100] This idea of custom as 'other' or 'second'
nature proved popular among medieval jurists, as a gloss by Accursius

---

[96] '*Ex quibus dignoscitur esse inducta? Et quidam ex tribus ontradic. Primum est, quia
sic est obtentum sine ontradiction. Secundem quia libelli quaerimoniarum de re tali
non recipiebantur. Tertium, si cum contradiceretur non esse consuetudinem, ontradic ontradiction judicatum est esse consuetudinem*' (Azo, *Summa Codicis*, 8.53.1, in
R. W. Carlyle and A. J. Carlyle, *A History of Mediaeval Political Theory in the West*,
vol. 2, p. 54).

[97] '*Diciturque consuetudo, quasi communis assuetudo: et alias dicitur consuetuso, et in
alia significatione, altera natura*', *Summa Azonis* (Lyon, 1564) in Wehrlé, *De la
coutume dans le droit canonique*, p. 139. Donald Kelly translates *aletera natura*
as second nature because that is how it was referred to by the early modern authors
who were the focus of his study. I translate it here more literally as 'other nature'
because *altera natura* to me seems to imply an equal or almost equal standing with
nature, as in Aristotle's *Rhetoric*. It was later that early modern authors created
a hierarchy by distinguishing a primary law of nature (*ius naturale primarium* or
primaevum) and a secondary law of nature (*ius natural secundarium*) rooted in
convention and utility (Donald R. Kelley, '"Second Nature"', p. 134).

[98] Kelley, '"Second Nature"', p. 131.   [99] *Ibid*.

[100] *Ibid*. Note also the Aristotelian formula of 'twice makes a custom' (*ibid*., p. 135).
This was echoed in the base number of repetitions for the creation of a custom by
some medieval jurists.

confirms, and was even more important later, in early modern conceptions of custom.[101]

While enormously influential, Azo's *Summa* was by no means the last word on custom, and jurists continued to debate definitions, status, and proof throughout the thirteenth century and into the next. One of the difficulties, for instance, was distinguishing the different custom terms – *consuetudo, mos,* and *usus* – from each other. For his part, Accurisius effectively collapsed the difference between *usus* and *consuetudo* in his *Glossa ordinaria* (ca. 1230).[102] And what was custom's relationship to law? Some jurists emphasized its subsidiary role, while Accursius placed custom above law by declaring that 'custom abolishes law'.[103]

There was also a question about who generated custom – the people or the prince, or both. Roman jurists began to discuss custom in terms of consent and the will of the people. They found in Roman law descriptions of the legislative right of the people: 'What pleases the prince has the force of law, by the Regal Act relating to his sovereign power, the people conferred on him its whole sovereignty and authority.'[104] The Romanist interpretation was that the prince had a delegated power in the form of legislation and that the people reserved some of this law-making power in the form of custom.[105]

---

[101] 'id est consuetudo, quae est altera natura', The Ordinary Gloss on *Digest* XIV, vi, 1, v. *natura* in Brynteson, 'Roman Law and Legislation in the Middle Ages', 433.

[102] Mayali, 'La coutume dans la doctrine romaniste au Moyen Âge', p. 17.

[103] '*Consuetudo vincit legem*' in Kelley, '"Second Nature"', p. 136. Later, in the fourteenth century, Baldus (1327–1400) adjusted this to 'later custom annuls earlier law'(*ibid.*).

[104] '*Sed et quod principi placuit, legis habet vigorem, cum lege regia, quae de imperio euis lata est, populus ei et in eum omne suum imperium et potestatem "concessit"*' (Justinian, *Institutes* 1.2.6). This statement appears in the context of an explanation of the different types of law. Law comes in two forms, written and unwritten, and 'written law includes acts, plebeian statutes, resolutions of the senate, imperial pronouncements, magistrates' edicts, and answers given by jurists' (*ibid.*, 1.2.3). What then did the emperor get when the plentitude of power of the 'people' was transferred to him? The *Institutes* clarified that 'Plebeians and people differ as species and genus. "The people" is a citizen-body including the patricians and senators. "The plebeians" is the same minus the patricians and senators' (*ibid.*, 1.2.4). The 'people' was a corporate political entity, whose legislative power the emperor received. But written law could still be produced by plebeian statute or resolution of the senate.

[105] Mayali, 'La coutume dans la doctrine romaniste au Moyen Âge'.

Though they expressed it differently, canonists also understood this passage as an affirmation of a legislative right of the people.[106]

But who counted as 'the people'? Generally, this meant the *populus christianus*, and not those of other faiths living in the Latin West, and could refer to any sort of community, small or large, that adhered to a particular custom.[107] 'The people' was reduced further to those with full legal capacity, sometimes to the exclusion of those considered ignorant.[108] Beyond that, 'the people' was an abstraction that could be represented by ten individuals.[109] While on the surface, placing the custom of the people above the law of the prince may sound radical, the voice of the 'people' was often that of the judiciary, jurists, or high-status people, lay and ecclesiastical.

The ideas of two jurists from the law school of Orleans exemplify the foment of ideas as well as different interpretations generated by Romanists at the time the first *coutumiers* were being written.[110] For Jacques de Revigny (ca. 1230–96) custom did not have to be unwritten,

---

[106] Gratian used the same portion of the *Institutes* to say that 'an ordinance is an enactment by the people, by which the plebeians together with those greater by birth have established something' (Gratian, *Decretum*, D. 2 c.1). This quite consensual sounding description is made a relic of the past in the Ordinary Gloss, which expanded on the term 'people': 'At one time the people made ordinances, but today they do not because they transferred this power to the emperor. *Institutes* 1.2.6. Or, it may be said that today the people may still do so, and that in that text "transferred" means "conceded"' (Gratian, *Decretum*, D. 2 c.1g).

[107] From empire to kingdom, region, village, guild, monastic community, or other forms of groups (*ibid.*).

[108] Later, in the fourteenth century, Bartolus explained that those excluded were those who had lost their senses (*ements et furiosos*), women, minors and sometimes *rustici* because of their ignorance (Mayali, 'La coutume dans la doctrine romaniste au Moyen Âge', p. 22). As we will see later, *rustici* simply meant lay people to some Romanists.

[109] This notion can be seen in the gloss to Gratian's comment that customary law was almost extinct after the biblical flood because of the scarcity of people. The Ordinary Gloss explained that customary law did not end, nor could it begin, because at first there were just seven people, but at least ten people were needed to form a community (Gratian, *Decretum*, D. 6 c.3 §2b). Later, this becomes a dictum: '*Decem faciunt populum*' (Kelley, "Second Nature"', p. 136).

[110] The bull *Super specula* prohibited the teaching of Roman law in Paris in 1219 and displaced its teaching to Orléans, where we can speak of a law school from 1235 onward, and Jacques de Revigny was one of its great professors (Waelkens, 'La théorie de la coutume à l'école de droit d'Orléans'). For more on Jacques de Revigny and Pierre de Belleperche, see articles by Paul J. du Plessis and Yves Mausen in Olivier Descamps and Rafael Domingo, *Great Christian Jurists in French History*, chapters 4 and 5.

but for Pierre Belleperche (ca. 1230–1308) unwrittenness was one of its essential characteristics.[111] Previously, usage had seemed to generate *consuetudo*, but Jacques de Revigny saw the consent of the people, whether explicit or implicit, as the special ingredient.[112] Pierre de Belleperche added to implicit or explicit consent the passage of time.[113] If statute and custom dealt with the same issue, then Jacques felt the older of the two should be followed, while Pierre felt the court could choose either one.[114]

Both the Bolognese and Orleanais doctors agreed that judicial precedent was one way of establishing custom but was not necessary to its formation. Judicial precedent had probative value for them in that it could be used to indicate popular consent, and, indeed, the notion of judicial precedent as constitutive of custom would become generally accepted by scholars only at the end of the Middle Ages.[115]

The fourteenth century was a watershed in the history of custom, notably in its relation to 'the people'. Bartolus (1313–57) ultimately went back to Isidore's definition that custom was a form of law (*ius*) instituted by habit (*moribus institutum*), which is seen as legislation (*lege*).[116] However, he refined this by describing 'tacit consent' as the proximate or efficient cause of *consuetudo*, relegating *usus* and *mos* to 'remote causes'.[117] For Bartolus, 'custom represents the will of the people'.[118] He would also submit custom to the inquisitorial rule of proof by two witnesses.[119] The idea of 'the people' only became meaningfully concrete later: Bartolus' student Baldus (1327–1400) understood the *populus* as a legal personality, one filtered through the idea of the corporation (*universitas*).[120] While the corporate

---

[111] Waelkens, 'La théorie de la coutume à l'école de droit d'Orléans', p. 35, *La théorie de la coutume chez Jacques de Révigny*, pp. 119ff, 206ff, 212.

[112] Mayali, 'La coutume dans la doctrine romaniste au Moyen Âge', p. 20.

[113] 'Usus non est causa consuetudinis, sed tacita voluntas populi' (*ibid.*, p. 21).

[114] Waelkens, 'La théorie de la coutume à l'école de droit d'Orléans', p. 35.

[115] *Ibid.*, pp. 35–6.

[116] *Ibid.* Bartolus' definition: '*consuetudo est jus quoddam moribus institutum, quod pro lege suscipitur*' (Mayali, 'La coutume dans la doctrine romaniste au Moyen Âge', p. 16).

[117] *Ibid.*, pp. 20–1.   [118] 'Kelley, "Second Nature"', p. 136.

[119] For Bartolus, disputed custom was proved by the testimony of two witnesses from the community in question or by such great notoriety that it should be under judicial notice (Bederman, *Custom as a Source of Law*, p. 24).

[120] Joseph Canning, *The Political Thought of Baldus De Ubaldis*, p. 189.

nature of the 'the people' cannot be assumed for the period before Baldus, it was certainly a key development for ideas of popular sovereignty and of a rhetoric of custom as a form of resistance that would develop in early modern Europe and beyond.[121]

There is no doubt that aspects of definitions of custom and ideas about its proof in canon law and Roman law made their way into the *coutumiers* – texts that occupy a space somewhere between legal practice and academic thought. They also made their way into practice itself, with the ever-increasing number of law school graduates entering the judiciary as the thirteenth century gave way to the fourteenth. This is well known, but I want to emphasize that despite the impression of static immutability that accompanies the notion of custom as tradition and repetition, the concept of custom was itself not only mutable but also debated. It varied between communities as well as within communities. At the time the *coutumier* authors composed their texts, many different voices offered many different opinions about what custom was, how it was made, and how it could be recognized. The capaciousness of *consuetudo* continued far beyond this time. From the glossators to elite canonists of the fifteenth century, scholars continued to struggle when they tried to describe the difference between *consuetudo* as exaction and as norm.[122] Even after many centuries of defining, parsing, and interpreting, Jason of Mayno (1435–1519) would still describe the question of custom as profound and ambiguous.[123]

The variety of ideas about custom in learned communities testify to its enduring conceptual haziness. Definitions abandoned are as important as definitions embraced and lastingly popular because, together, they attest to a society that continued to grapple with the perplexing question of what, exactly, custom was and how, exactly, it could be identified.

It was the great preoccupation of medieval canonists and Romanists to domesticate custom with words. Thinkers constructed methods of proof, attempting to make custom tangible and knowable based on their definitions. The lexical history of the term thus cannot be

[121] See generally, Daniel Lee, *Popular Sovereignty in Early Modern Constitutional Thought*; E. P. Thompson, *Customs in Common*.
[122] Fredric L. Cheyette, 'Custom, Case Law, and Medieval "Constitutionalism"', 382.
[123] Mayali, 'La coutume dans la doctrine romaniste au Moyen Âge', p. 18.

dissociated from ideas about methods of proof, the other preoccupation of learned jurists.

Writing about Secular Legal Practice before the *Coutumiers*

Coutumiers authors wrote about the practice of secular law in northern France because there was no other holistic description of the subject available, at least in written form and likely not in oral form either.[124] To look for written legal ideas about the courts of laymen or associated with lay people before the *coutumiers* means to look through scattered sources, ones that were not necessarily 'legal' and often were not even lay, but ecclesiastical. A brief look at the history of writing secular law in the couple of centuries before the *coutumiers* reveals a desire and attempt to write about lay legal ideas and practice and so give them greater clarity, specificity, and accessibility.

Glimpses of custom, or at least habitual practice, can be found in the multitudes of documents that contained records of transactional law. These sometimes indicate a specific custom, or a pattern can be identified among them that indicates a habitual practice. These are not addressed in this section because the goal here is to examine writings that sought to synthesize ideas about the norms and practices of the courts of lay lords or lay people.[125] This section begins a little before the papal revolution, covers the general efflorescence in written and normative secular law in the twelfth century and ends around the mid-thirteenth century when the *coutumiers* began to be written. I give more space to ecclesiastical writing than is normally done because this receives very little attention as background for the *coutumiers* but is vital to this history.

The era of papal reform and 'rebirth' of Roman law was a great watershed in law, both secular and ecclesiastical.[126] Written record- and document-making increased sharply, leading to new forms of

---

[124] There were of course people who knew the law better than others and were seen as a resource, but northern France does not seem to have had a lawspeaker tradition with the public recitation of law such as in Iceland.

[125] The relationship between charters and the *coutumiers* is discussed in Chapter 6.

[126] See generally, Harold Berman, *Law and Revolution*; Paul Fournier, 'Un tournant de l'histoire du droit'; Bellomo, *The Common Legal Past of Europe*, p. 58.

writing and documentation as well as expanded bureaucracies.[127] However, the demand for legal texts existed before all of this.[128] Even with their heavily oral and ritualistic nature, both secular and ecclesiastical law continued to make use of text in the early Middle Ages.[129] But where exactly could writing about secular law be found in the time leading up to the *coutumiers*?

The correspondence of Fulbert of Chartres (ca. 960–1028) provides a glimpse into different aspects of secular law. Several manuscripts of his letter collection were in fact preserved by others for later legal use.[130] Fulbert indicates which legal texts might be considered of value to a highly educated ecclesiastic around the turn of the millennium. His book chest included a collection of Carolingian capitularies, the collection of capitularies compiled by Ansegisus of Fontanelle, the forged capitularies of 'Benedict Levita' (the pseudonym of the author who purported to continue Ansegius' collection), and the Pseudo-Isidorian Decretals.[131] His familiarity with legal writing extended beyond the cache in his book chest. Notably, he quoted from Roman law in the *Theodosian Code*, which he likely knew from the *Breviary* of Alaric.[132]

---

[127] See generally, Clanchy, *From Memory to Written Record*.

[128] Christof Rolker, *Canon Law and the Letters of Ivo of Chartres*, pp. 85ff.

[129] Bruce C. Brasington, *Order in the Court*, p. 25. Notably, we can find legal literacy not only in charters, formularies, and capitularies, but we can also trace it beyond clerical elites and see its regular use in Frankish government and administration (Rosamond McKitterick, *The Carolingians and the Written Word*; Alice Rio, *Legal Practice and the Written Word in the Early Middle Ages, The Formularies of Angers and Marculf*). Geoffrey Koziol has shown that we cannot not simply see documents like these as straightforward judicial documents issued and guaranteed by a centralized sovereign state, but that there is an incredible richness to the life of these legal texts in terms of both politics and dispute (Koziol, *The Politics of Memory and Identity*). The diplomas he examines demonstrate the dynamic and performative nature of documents that seem like rote and repetitive statements of rights and privileges at first glance (*ibid.*, p. 22ff, 37ff). This was also the case beyond Frankish lands. Ottonian kings also, while not producing much legislation, exercised justice via case-by-case petitions (Laura E. Wangerin, *Kingship and Justice in the Ottonian Empire*, Chap. 5). Law became more sophisticated in practice and the subject of study in places such as Ravenna and Pavia, where we find late-antique Roman law in documents of the tenth century (Simon Corcoran, 'Roman Law in Ravenna', esp. pp. 193ff; Charles M. Radding, *The Origins of Medieval Jurisprudence*).

[130] Rolker, *Canon Law and the Letters of Ivo of Chartres*, p. 55.

[131] Edward Peters, 'Death of the Subdean', p. 58. He likely had abbreviated versions of these texts (Rolker, *Canon Law and the Letters of Ivo of Chartres*, p. 57).

[132] *Ibid.*

Fulbert's famous description of the feudal oath shows lay people demanding the theorization of legal practice. Replying to William V, Count of Poitou and Duke of Aquitaine, he said: 'Asked to write something concerning the form of fealty, I have noted briefly for you on the authority of the books the things which follow.'[133] The resulting mini-tractate on feudal obligations was to have a very long legal history, wending its way into secular law, canon law, and academic law.[134]

Fulbert composed his theorization of fealty in response to a secular lord's desire for concrete written explication of this form of obligation. Fulbert answered not based on observation but on books. Presumably, this was exactly what William wanted, since he himself would have been familiar with instances of fealty in practice. This episode reveals the lay desire to go beyond impressions provided by their own experiences and to seek out a normative – if idealized – statement of these practices. This also shows that we must look for secular law in ecclesiastical writing, as those who study charters of this period well know.

We also must look to collections of canon law that assembled the rules and procedures of the church for early theorization of legal ideas and practice. While their heyday is considered to be the later eleventh century onward, such collections were not only written in the tenth and early eleventh century, but a number were even better organized than later ones.[135] Alongside these collections were numerous unsystematic collections, some of which have been shown to be influential through the eleventh and into the twelfth century.[136]

Burchard of Worms (c. 965–1025) is interesting in this regard because he both composed a collection of canon law and was the instigator of a collection of laws for secular governance. Burchard obtained full control of all justice of the *familia* of Worms from Emperor Henry II with a charter of immunity from interference by

---

[133] 'De forma fidelitatis aliquid scribere monitus, haec vobis quae sequuntur breviter ex librorum auctoritate notavi', Fulbert of Chartres, 'Letter from Bishop Fulbert of Chartres, A.D. 1020', ed. Cheyney, vol 4, no. 3, p. 23.

[134] Pennington, 'Feudal Oath of Fidelity and Homage', p. 93.

[135] Rolker, *Canon Law and the Letters of Ivo of Chartres*, pp. 50–1. Rolker mentions those of Regino of Prüm (d. 915), Abbo of Fleury (d. 1004), and Burchard of Worms (d. 1025) in this regard, noting that that of Burchard became the model for a large number of later collections (*ibid.*).

[136] Rolker, *Canon Law and the Letters of Ivo of Chartres*, p. 59.

local lords in 1014.[137] In his view, these lords had been oppressing the community with their laws and judgments. Burchard therefore had a set of guidelines or precepts composed, known as 'Laws of the *familia* of Worms', and these 'laws', which applied equally to both rich and poor, were to be followed thereafter.[138] A series of rules and prohibitions followed, presented in the language of legislation, which offer a rare insight into crime, property, and family law.[139] Burchard also compiled a practical manual of canon law in his *Decretum* based on principles that unify the canonical tradition that he had identified, as well as examples of the concrete application of these principles.[140]

Burchard's *Decretum* and several other collections of canon law circulated in northern France, influencing the next generation of writers, including Ivo of Chartres (ca. 1040–1115). Unlike Burchard, who separated his canonical collection from laws of general governance that included the laity, Ivo chose to incorporate it.[141] Not only was that an unprecedented move, but the chapter devoted to lay affairs was one of the longest and most elaborate portions of his canonical collection.[142] Additionally, he included a great deal of secular legislation: the *Theodosian Code*, Justinian's *Code*, the *Institutes*, the *Digest*, the *Sententia Pauli*, the *Epitime Juliani*, and Alaric's Breviary, as well as both genuine and forged Carolingian capitularies.[143]

---

[137] Greta Austin, 'Jurisprudence in the Service of Pastoral Care', 931.

[138] 'Lex familiae Wormatiensis' in Lorenz Weinrich, ed., *Quellen zur deutschen Verfassungs-, Wirtschafts- und Sozialgeschichte*, trans. Lane, document 22, www .fordham.edu/halsall/source/lexworms.asp, preface (accessed 31 May 2022). Such texts at this time are better viewed as precepts, warnings, or admonishments (Sara McDougall, *Royal Bastards: The Birth of Illegitimacy*, p. 62). While they seem to present fact, even the definition of marriage was not clear or consistent across texts (*ibid.*).

[139] 'if anyone ... ' or 'This shall be the law of the *familia* ... ' or 'We also establish this ... ' ('Lex familiae Wormatiensis', s. 1, s. 2, s. 19). Many of the provisions punish specific infractions with fines. Some elucidate rules on inheritance or specific aspects of procedure. On one occasion, a custom is specifically abrogated, and the reason is explained: in order to decrease false oaths, the practice of taking oaths to deny and so get out of a debt could be rejected by the lender, who could demand a trial by battle to prove the veracity of his claim (*ibid.*, s. 19).

[140] Greta Austin, *Shaping Church Law Around the Year 1000*, p. 223.

[141] Rolker, *Canon Law and the Letters of Ivo of Chartres*, pp. 177–8.

[142] *Ibid.*, p. 178.

[143] *Ibid.* This was in contrast to Burchard who got what Roman law he had from *Anselmo dedicata* and then obscured the secular origins with some choice alterations (*ibid.*).

The late eleventh century also saw greater assessment of ecclesiastical procedure in writing: while earlier sources only shed a 'faint' light on it, more common references were made to the *ordo iudiciarius* by the 1070s.[144] The writing of French bishops illuminates the development of thought about the *ordo iudiciarius* before it was affected by the diffusion of Roman legal thought from the universities.[145] Indeed, in his letters, Ivo not only included detailed and studied descriptions of procedure but also integrated Roman law into his argument and used it for probative value.[146] The body of works on ecclesiastical procedure only continued to grow afterwards, and, by the twelfth century, much of it heavily incorporated or was based on Roman legal procedure.[147] While this may seem like a straightforward reception, there was actually much debate about procedure, and legists and canonists wrote many, many works treating different aspects of the trial throughout the twelfth and thirteenth centuries.[148]

Monastic communities were also early and prolific compilers of rules and regulations. This went back to the sixth-century rule of Benedict, but from the late tenth century onward, there was a new enthusiasm for monastic rule-making.[149] The writing of liturgical custom began at Cluny around 990, and that text later came to be known as the *consuetudines antiquiores*.[150] Thirty years later, the so-called *Liber Tramitis* began to be written, a text with broader range that included technical matters of administration, policy, and procedure.[151] Around the 1070s, a monk of Cluny named Bernard

---

[144] Brasington, *Order in the Court: Medieval Procedural Treatises in Translation*, p. 20, 31 (see his introduction and first chapter for an excellent analysis of this transition). Sources refer to both the *ordo iudiciarius* and the *ordo iudiciorum* to refer to ecclesiastical procedure, though the latter was more common and other terms were used as well (*ibid.*, xiii).

[145] *Ibid.*, p. 35.　　[146] *Ibid.*, pp. 42–51.

[147] See Fowler-Magerl, '*Ordines iudiciarii*' and '*Libelli de ordine iudiciorum*', pp. 17–28.

[148] *Ibid.*, pp. 34ff.

[149] The texts of various monastic customals are available in K. Hallinger, ed., *Corpus Consuetudinum Monasticarum*.

[150] Gert Melville, *The World of Medieval Monasticism*, pp. 67–8. It seems to be a later practice to refer to these rule-texts as *consuetudines*.

[151] References to the collection appear around 1020, with a first revision after 1033 and second revision between 1050 and 1060 (*ibid.*, p. 68).

composed a new text at the behest of Abbot Hugh I to capture their practice as it had developed and was currently used.[152] Yet another set soon appeared, a little after 1079, by another monk of Cluny, named Ulrich, for William abbot of Hirsau, who wanted to introduce 'customs' to his monastery for the purpose of reform.[153]

These forms of regulatory writing contain important lessons for legal history.[154] English monks, for instance, were developing sophisticated juridical thinking before Roman-law influence, which shows that the development of sophisticated legal thinking was possible as an organic intellectual development and not necessarily the result of influence of university-level Roman law.[155] Indeed, this helps explain why Roman law attracted eager interest. We can see monks, for instance, embracing Roman law. The customs of the abbey of St Gilles, for instance, were compiled in the twelfth century. We have this text in an edited thirteenth-century version, but it is likely that the Roman law, in the form of Justinian's *Code* (probably via the Provençal summa *Lo Codi*) and some of the *Novels*, was already part of the twelfth-century version.[156]

Regulatory writings also flourished in lay contexts. City customs began appearing in the eleventh century, associated with the communal movement. These could be part of a peaceful process or of dramatic founding moments that pitted lords against communities and produced charters in which the rights and responsibilities reflected a new balance of power. These city customs were negotiated rights, like a contract. Galbert of Bruges provided a dramatic account of revolt that led to the founding of a commune and its charter in 1127.[157] This

---

[152] *Ibid.*, pp. 68–9.   [153] *Ibid.*, p. 69.

[154] Monastic communities have been part of this history for their spirit of reform, notably in the context of the Investiture Controversy and papal 'revolution' that created a context for a renewed interest in Roman law and set the stage the birth of a Western legal tradition (Berman, *Law and Revolution*, chaps. 2–3). There has been less recognition of the innovative procedural, normative, and regulatory aspects of monastic writing, with the exception of the work of Alain Boureau.

[155] Alain Boureau showed that new legal consciousness and judicialization could grow organically from extant knowledge and did not necessarily have to be the result of the rediscovery of Roman law (Boureau, 'Droit naturel et abstraction judiciaire', 1464; *La loi du royaume*, pp. 198ff; Boureau also points to the demonstration made by Wickham in *Legge, pratiche e conflitti*).

[156] *Coutumes de St. Gilles*, pp. 24–49.

[157] See Galbert of Bruges, *The Murder of Charles the Good*, trans. Ross.

'little charter of agreement' between the count and the citizen, which he described as 'about the remission of the toll and the ground rent on their houses', was actually the product of radical urban self-assertion.[158]

Beyond this, custom also designated the protections subjects received from their lord and so, in this sense, designated a category of rights.[159] Lords could also make men personally free by granting them *franchisa*, meaning free tenure, and numerous villages and townships paid significant fees for this freedom.[160] Charters of liberties outlined freedoms and rights demanded by and granted to subjects, as well as the powers and obligations of their rulers. The Coronation Charter of Henry I of England, issued around 1100, included such protections and responsibilities, and Magna Carta (1215) became the most famous example. While 'liberty' was primarily an attribute of lordship, litigation action seeking to protect franchises and liberties in the thirteenth century reveals that a notion of individual, personal liberty was also at play.[161]

Charters of municipal rights known in Iberia as *fueros* appeared in the tenth century.[162] Burgos and Castrojeriz received their *fueros* then, and the counts of Castile also made their earliest grants of this kind at this time.[163] Notably, a collection of 'usages' known as the Ustages of Barcelona appeared in Catalonia in the mid-twelfth century, composed during the rule of Count Ramon Berenguer IV of Barcelona (1131–62).[164] It aimed at overriding old Visigothic laws because these were no longer seen as a good fit for current issues. These *ustages* were not described as practices repeated over time – the preface insisted three times that they were decreed – but the description of what was essentially legislation as *ustages* still suggests a conceptual shift.[165]

The recovery and renewed study of Justinian's *Digest* began in the last quarter of the eleventh century.[166] The 'rediscovery' of Roman law

---

[158] *Ibid.*   [159] Reynolds, 'Law and Communities in Western Christendom', 209.
[160] Alan Harding, 'Political Liberty in the Middle Ages', 427.   [161] *Ibid.*, 436–7, 441.
[162] Roger Collins, *Early Medieval Spain*, p. 244.
[163] These are known through later versions (*ibid.*).
[164] *The Ustages of Barcelona*, trans. Kagay, p. 2.
[165] For instance: 'With the approval and counsel of his good men, along with his very prudent and wise wife Almodis, [Lord Ramon Berenguer the Old] issued and decreed the rules of customary law' (*ibid.* s. 2).
[166] Brundage, *The Medieval Origins of the Legal Profession*, p. 78.

through the books of Justinian's *Institutes, Code, Digest,* and *Novels* grew into a fundamental conceptual transformation about what law was and how it should be done. These texts began to be read, studied, and taught and formed the basis of the early university in Bologna around the end of the eleventh century. The enthusiasm for these new legal studies was captured in a letter written around 1127 by a Benedictine monk to his abbot at Saint Victor in Marseille, in which he described crowds of students flocking to Bologna to study law and noted the great benefit this knowledge could have for the monastery in its legal disputes.[167] This was the seed of an intellectual revolution that would ultimately transform legal and political thought in Europe, even though the impact of Roman law on medieval legal practice varied by region and was uneven and diverse.[168]

The impact of ancient Roman jurists on medieval notions of custom was vast.[169] Their definitions and modes of thought gave medieval society a new way of thinking – one might even say a new language – with an expansive vocabulary and a rhetoric based on precision of thought. James Brundage writes that they found new ways to 'frame sophisticated legal arguments, how to manipulate legal categories, how to analyse problems, and how to find solutions to them' that proved to be intellectually exciting but also of practical utility.[170]

That Roman law was seen as having contemporary relevance in its medieval context is evident from the incorporation of a text of secular legal practice into the corpus: the *Libri feudorum.* This was a compilation of treatises of earlier Lombard origin that had been composed layer by layer by various authors in Pavia and Milan and was used as a sort of manual by communal judges and advocates in those cities.[171] In the early thirteenth century, the text was appended to the *Corpus Iuris* by Hugolinus, accrued layers of glosses, and was used in university teaching as well as occasionally in court

---

[167] J. Dufour, G. Giordanengo, and A. Gouron, 'L'attrait des *leges*'. See generally Brundage, *The Medieval Origins of the Legal Profession,* especially chap. 3.

[168] Mayali, 'The Legacy of Roman Law', p. 375.

[169] For introductory histories of the *ius commune,* see Stein, *Roman Law in European History*; Bellomo, *The Common Legal Past of Europe*; R. C. Van Caenegem, *An Historical Introduction to Private Law.*

[170] Brundage, *The Medieval Origins of the Legal Profession,* p. 96.

[171] Magnus Ryan, 'Succession to Fiefs', p. 144. Pillius of Medicina (fl. 1169–1213) gave it its first apparatus of civilian glosses.

practice.[172] It is from this text that, later, lawyers and then historians drew a feudal vocabulary that they then used to describe a 'system' throughout Europe.[173]

Imaginative literature provided an additional forum where lay society could explore ideas of law. The crises of power and of lordship in the twelfth century proved fertile ground for literary narratives that exposed tensions and enabled critiques of the political order as well as of justice and its dispensation.[174] *Raoul de Cambrai* was a commentary on inheritance, lordship, different understandings of the 'fief', and the relationship between vengeance and justice.[175] The trial of Ganleon in the *Song of Roland* explored the responsibilities of men to their lords, notions of treason and felony, and the dispensation of justice. Beyond notions of justice and injustice, romances and *chansons de geste* were permeated with procedural questions, perspectives on punishment, and other juridical themes.[176] These dramatic enactments of law revealed the ethical dimension of society.[177]

Through its themes, language, narrative, and assumptions, imaginative literature showed a society thinking about and questioning its political and normative order. Andreas Capellanus, in

[172] It was then that it was glossed by Accursius, who used Pilius' gloss, and this gloss ended up forming more than half of the Accursian standard gloss. As Ryan explained, 'The technically accurate title by the end of the Middle Ages was the *Decima collatio de feudis*, the tenth and final section of the *Novels* in the vulgate form used at the medieval schools known as the *Authenticum*, but for most of the thirteenth and fourteenth centuries the text could appear just about anywhere in the fifth and "short" volume of the *Corpus iuris* (the *Volumen parvum*) alongside the *Authenticum*, *Institutes* and the last three books of the *Code*, and it went under a variety of titles' (Ryan, 'Succession to Fiefs', p. 144); see also Kathleen Davis, 'Sovereign Subjects, Feudal Law, and the Writing of History', 226.
[173] Reynolds, *Fiefs and Vassals*, p. 6. See her explanation of the nature of the problem (*ibid.*, pp. 1ff). This book, following Elizabeth Brown's groundbreaking article, is devoted to undoing the 'construct of feudalism' as an interpretative framework for the Middle Ages (Elizabeth A. R. Brown, 'The Tyranny of a Construct: Feudalism and Historians of Medieval Europe', 1063–88). Renaissance humanists and lawyers were especially concerned with the origins of the *Book of Fiefs* and its authenticity (Kelley, 'De Origine Feudorum').
[174] Thomas Bisson, *The Crisis of the Twelfth Century*.
[175] Stephen D. White, 'The Discourse of Inheritance in Twelfth-Century France'.
[176] Bernard Ribémont, 'Justice et procédure dans le Tristan de Béroul', 'Le 'crime épique' et sa punition', 'La chanson de geste, une "machine judiciaire"?'
[177] Mary Jane Schenck, 'Reading Law as Literature, Reading Literature as Law'.

On Love (1184/6), developed a complex legal universe complete with illustrative cases and a set of laws.[178] The notion of custom, specifically, was also explored. The various compositions of Chrétien de Troyes mentioned custom on numerous occasions, sometimes a 'custom of the castle' arbitrarily imposed and to be circumvented, sometimes a form of obligatory community behaviour.[179]

Romano-canonical legal thought and methods were brought to bear on the writing of secular law. The *Assizes of Ariano* (also known as the *Assizes of Roger II*) were composed around 1140 by authors familiar with Roman law. This text was unique because no other secular ruler in the early twelfth century had promulgated such a body of law, one that was not only systematically organized but displayed some strong connections to the developing study of Roman law in northern Italy.[180]

The Anglo-Norman world had a long tradition of legal writing from Old English laws to post-Conquest *Leges* – texts that presented themselves as legislation and that foregrounded the early legal literature of English Common Law.[181] The 'first textbook' of English royal law, the *Laws and Customs of England,* known as *Glanvill* because it was once attributed to Ranulf Glanvill, appeared around 1188.[182] It was framed not as assizes or constitutions but as 'laws and customs'.[183] Arguably an 'early, somewhat unusual *coutumier*', Glanvill described the Anglo-French custom that was administered in the king's court by itinerant justices.[184] Soon afterwards, around 1200, the first part of the *Très Ancien Coutumier de Normandie* was composed, and thus the era of the 'first' *coutumiers* began.

---

[178] Andreas Capellanus, *On Love*, trans. Walsh. For more on this, see Peter Goodrich, *Law in the Courts of Love*.

[179] The latter meaning is found in *Yvain* (Donald Maddox, 'Yvain et le sens de la coutume', 2).

[180] Pennington, 'The Birth of the *Ius commune*', 24. See the most recent edition: Ortensio Zecchino, ed., *Le Assise di Ruggiero II*.

[181] See Early English Laws website (https://earlyenglishlaws.ac.uk/).

[182] G. D. G. Hall, trans., *The Treatise on the Laws and Customs of the Realm of England Commonly Called Glanvill*, p. xi. The *Glanvill* author was familiar with Roman legal texts and drew on Justinian's *Institutes* for his preface.

[183] Though this language occurred earlier in the so-called *Leges Willelmi*: 'Cez sunt les leis e les custumes que li reis Will. Grantad al people de Engleterre ... ' ('The (So-Called) Laws of William I' in *The Laws of the Kings of England from Edmund to Henry I. Part Two: William I to Henry I*, p. 252).

[184] Hyams, 'The Common Law and the French Connection', p. 83.

Texts focused on secular law proliferated throughout the European West by the 1230s. The jurists who composed the *Constitutions of Melfi* (or *Liber Augustalis*) for Frederick II in 1231 incorporated more than half of the earlier *Assizes of Ariano* into their *Constitutions*.[185] Eike von Repgow was finishing his German-language *Sachsenspiegel*, or *Saxon Mirror*, by 1235. Various texts of Danish laws – the Laws of Scania, Valdemar's Law of Zealand, Erik's Law of Zealand, the Law of Jutland – were written also in the vernacular between 1150 and 1250.[186] By about 1240, various authors layered their writings to produce the similarly named *Laws and Customs of England*, once attributed solely to Bracton.[187] The *Coutumes d'Anjou et du Maine* was composed in 1246, Pierre de Fontaines' *Conseil* in 1253, and the *Summa de legibus Normannie* was likely composed between 1254 and 1258. At a similar time, the *Siete Partidas* were compiled for Alfonso X of Castile (1252–84).[188]

The writing of the northern French *coutumiers* was deeply associated with the developments described above: the persistent desire for exposition and assessment of practice, the arguments and ideas that animated the lay courts, the foment in ecclesiastical regulatory and procedural writing, the study of Roman law and various types of writing that developed around it, royal and imperial legal literatures, forms of vernacular legal literature (see Chapter 2), and, behind this, the ever-increasing sophistication of legal business in

---

[185] Pennington, 'The Birth of the *Ius commune*', 24.

[186] Ditlev Tamm and Helle Vogt (eds.), *The Danish Medieval Laws*.

[187] Thomas McSweeney has shown how much England was not exceptional but also part of this history. Far from being an inward-looking English text, *Bracton* was intended for an audience that knew its Roman law, indeed the justices who composed the text saw themselves as justices in the Roman model, and the text was written to show that English law too could fit within the framework of the *ius commune* (see McSweeney, *Priests of the Law*); on authorship, see also Paul Brand, 'The Age of Bracton'.

[188] See Jesús D. Rodríguez Velasco's new study which examines the *Siete Partidas* though the aesthetics of lawmaking and as forging an affective relationship between the king and 'the people' (Jesús D. Rodríguez Velasco, *Dead Voice: Law, Philosophy, and Fiction in the Iberian Middle Ages*). Some themes examined here, such as vernacularity and the impact of writtenness, resonate but take on a significant aspect in Castile and would be worth a detailed study. See also, the multi-volume translation, the first of which is *Las Siete Partidas*, vol. 1, *The Medieval Church: The World of Clerics and Laymen (Partida I)*, ed. Robert I. Burns, SJ; trans. Samuel Parsons Scott.

various forms and contexts. The *coutumiers*' discussions of procedure, jurisdiction, and (to some extent) their use of sources certainly situates them in a larger, familiar movement in legal composition throughout Latin Europe.

At the same time, this group is also unique. From the 1240s, at least one new *coutumier* was composed in northern France every decade of the thirteenth century. This shows an exceptional zeal for theorizing the activities of lay courts. This dynamism in legal writing characterized not just the top royal or imperial level but also lower jurisdictions, which speaks to the political background of the texts; namely, the expansion of Capetian power. The regions associated with the first *coutumiers* of northern France became part of the Capetian demesne in one way or another in the thirteenth century, though they were not always under specifically royal control, because of the practice of granting apanages to younger sons. The *coutumiers* thus reflect both local and regional aspects as well as common ones relating to royal jurisdiction.

The 'first' *coutumiers* of northern France were written in a short period of time, in regions that were geographically close, and in a political context that was relatively similar. Beyond this, some of the *coutumier* authors from the later thirteenth century knew the earlier ones.[189] And yet, no two authors constructed their texts in exactly the same way. There were similarities, certainly, but each author elaborated their text uniquely and distinctively. The first *coutumiers* thus show an experimentation with the writing of custom, framing, the use of sources, subject matter, and authorial voice. In other words, they show that there were different ways to think about the question of 'What is custom?' for the secular courts.

The following brief descriptions of the first *coutumiers* illustrate the individual character of each text and provide a general sense of its contents. This is neither meant to be a taxonomy nor to provide an exhaustive list of the contents, sources, and methods of all of the texts. Rather, the descriptions are intended to show the particularity of each text before they are treated as a group in the remainder of this book.

---

[189] Though there are significant differences in exposition, some features of the *coutumier* – vernacularity, the regional aspect of the group, knowledge of earlier texts, and questions of authority – could fruitfully be compared to the Danish laws (see Ditlev Tamm and Helle Vogt (eds.), *The Danish Medieval Laws: The Laws of Scania, Zealand and Jutland*).

The work inherent to composing a comprehensive vision of custom included gathering and assembling information – specific legal facts, rules, or procedures – but also an element of subjectivity and originality. This means that the *coutumiers* afford us a glimpse into the minds of some of the authors who were creating a professionalized customary law in the thirteenth century.

Brief Descriptions of the 'First' *Coutumiers*

Très ancien coutumier de Normandie *(ca. 1200 and ca. 1220)*

Ernest-Josef Tardif, author of the critical editions of the *Très ancien coutumier de Normandie*, described the text as a composite of two works written anonymously: one around 1200 before Normandy was taken by Philip Augustus for the French crown, and the other around 1220.[190] The text comes in both Latin and French versions. Tardif had three incomplete Latin manuscripts and a more complete French manuscript, and thus used the incomplete Latin version filled in with the later French version to construct his critical editions of the texts. However, we now have a new Latin text in a Vatican manuscript that was unknown to Tardif while editing the text, one that is more complete and the basis of a new edition.[191] The *Très ancien coutumier de Normandie* has no prologue, but the new manuscript provides the title of '*Antiqua consuetudo normannie*'. It begins with a discussion of the dukes of Normandy, and the second part begins with an inquest that took place in the reign of Henry II.[192] It has been suggested that the first

---

[190] *Coutumiers de Normandie*, ed. Tardif, vol. 1. See discussion of different possible dates for the earliest text of the *Très ancien coutumier* and their implications in Daniel Power, *The Norman Frontier in the Twelfth and Early Thirteenth Centuries*, p. 170).

[191] I am very grateful to William Eves, who shared his edition and translation of this manuscript with me prior to its publication (Eves, *The Antiqua Consuetudo Normannie*). His transcription of the text of the Vatican manuscript (*Ottobono Latin 2964*) is available online and provides an introduction to the problems of this text, which he explores in detail in his edition of the first part of the text (Eves, *The Earliest Treatise within the Materials Comprising the So-Called Très Ancien Coutumier of Normandy, as found in Vatican Library ms. Ott. Lat. 2964*).

[192] Eves, *The Antiqua Consuetudo Normannie*, p. xix. Eves notes the text may divide further and that the parts may be composite themselves and different elements may have been written at different times.

part is a later text and presents a version of earlier Norman customs
adapted to the needs of the later thirteenth century.[193] The subjects of
the first part include the duties of the duke, excommunication,
inheritance, dower, wardship, land tenure, homicide, punishment, trial
procedure, service, and jurisdiction. The subjects of the second part
include homicide, ecclesiastical liberties, actions to recover
dispossessed land (desseisin), possession, bastardy, minors, dower,
marriage, trial procedure, jurisdiction, warranty, trial by battle, fiefs,
outlaws, gifts of land to the church, and the sale and grants of land. The
earliest manuscripts are from the late thirteenth century, and all the
manuscripts of the *Très Ancien Coutumier de Normandie* also include
the *Grand Coutumier de Normandie*, either in Latin or French.

Coutumes d'Anjou et du Maine *(1246)*

The *Coutumes d'Anjou et du Maine* was composed in French in 1246 by
an anonymous author.[194] We have two manuscripts of the text, one of
which opened with 'These are the customs of Anjou and Maine,' which
gives us the title. The text has no preface to indicate authorial intention or
ideology. It does not often refer to the concept of custom. Rules and
procedures are rather validated '*par droit*', so 'by Law' or 'by Right'. The
contents include a great variety of subjects briefly presented, without
obvious reasoning for the order. *Anjou et Maine* goes back and forth
between substance and procedure. Much of the text envisages different
sorts of problems that different sorts of people might face. The text treats
diverse subjects such as inheritance, dower, jurisdiction, marriage
between classes, theft of animals, guaranteed peace, consorting with
murderers and thieves, co-holding of fiefs, rape, army summons, novel

---

[193] N. Vincent, 'Magna Carta (1215) and the Charte aux Normands (1315)'. See also,
Eves, The *Antiqua Consuetudo Normannie*, p. lvi.'.
[194] Beautemps-Beaupré felt it was not possible to fix an exact date to this text (*Coutumes
d'Anyou et dou Maigne*, ed. Beautemps-Beaupré, p. 40). Viollet argued that it was
composed either in Touraine or in Anjou, and not in Maine, though the legal cultures
of the three were not significant enough to matter (*Les établissements de Saint Louis*,
ed. Viollet, 1:22–23). It must have been composed after May 1246, because it refers
to an ordinance issued then, but before the separation of Touraine and Anjou.
Touraine, Maine, and Anjou were united in the hands of Louis IX in June and
July 1246 but were separated in August – Touraine stayed with the king of France
with the Loudunois, and Maine and Anjou became the *apanage* of Charles, Louis
IX's brother. (*Les établissements de Saint Louis*, ed. Viollet, 1:24).

desseisin, court procedure, heretics, usurers, foreigners, bastards, seizure, quit-rents, excuses for not appearing in court, appeals, mills, gifts, status, issues for commoners, slander, redemption; it ends with lost bees, dower, and judicial battle between brothers and judicial battle fought by champions for the infirm. This text regularly mentions the sorts of things said in court and appropriate responses to them. It does not cite the learned laws, nor does it discuss specific cases. *Anjou et Maine* was used as the basis of Book I of the *Établissements de Saint Louis* some twenty or so years later in the early 1270s.

Le conseil de Pierre de Fontaines (*1253*)

The *Conseil* was written in French by Pierre de Fontaines (see Figure 1.1). Pierre was employed in various courts, notably in the

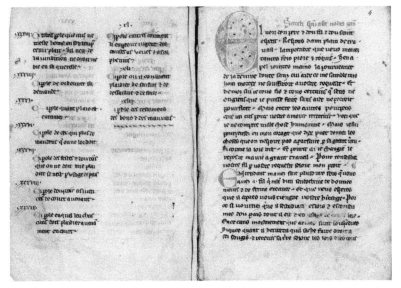

FIGURE 1.1 Pierre de Fontaines' *Conseil*. Some *coutumier* manuscripts contained text without illuminations. This thirteenth-century manuscript of Pierre de Fontaines' *Conseil* was unembellished outside of decorated capitals and section titles written in red ink, which made it easier to locate desired sections of the text. *Coutumier* texts were generally either alone in a manuscript, as in this one, or coupled with other legal texts either composed in French or in French translation. Pierre de Fontaines, *Conseil à un ami*, Bibliothèque nationale de France, ms. fr. 13983, fol. 4v, 5r.

service of Countess Mahaut of Artois (the widow of Louis IX's brother Robert) and then became a royal justice.[195] He began his career in Vermandois, the region commonly associated with this book. He eventually became counsellor to Louis IX.[196] He appeared in Jean de Joinville's *Life of Saint Louis*, where he dispensed justice on the king's behalf under the oak tree in the Bois de Vincennes, and also sat several times in Parliament.[197]

The text is presented as advice written for a friend's son.[198] Scholars have long speculated about the identity of this friend. It is quite commonly claimed that Pierre wrote the text for Philip III at the behest of his father, Louis IX. This view does not seem likely. This is supported by one manuscript from the late thirteenth or fourteenth century.[199] Another manuscript claims the book was written for 'Queen Blanche', Louis IX's mother, while another simply says it was written for a queen of France.[200] Most manuscripts do not specify who the friend or his son were.[201] It seems rather familiar for Pierre to

---

[195] Griffiths, 'Les origines et la carrière de Pierre de Fontaines', 550.

[196] Pierre de Fontaines, *Conseil*.

[197] Pierre Petot, 'Pierre de Fontaines et le droit romain', p. 956.

[198] Pierre de Fontaines, *Conseil*, 1.2.

[199] Bibliothèque nationale de France, ms. fr. 19758 (previous shelfmark Harlay 432). This manuscript, from the late thirteenth or fourteenth century, adds this royal pedigree at the outset of the prologue: 'Ci commence li livres des lois en françois selonc les usages et les coustumes de France que messire Pierres de Fontaines fist pour son ami le roy Phelippe de France et par l'ammonestement au roy Loys son pere, et bien est profitables à touz juges pourvoir' (Henri Klimrath, *Mémoire sur les monumens inédits de l'histoire du droit français au moyen âge*, p. 36). This manuscript refashions text making it specifically useful to a royal heir. Pierre's friend's remark about his hopes that his son will take over his landed inheritance ('vos espérer que après vos tiegne vostre éritage') remains but 'inheritance' is replaced with 'reign' ('vos espérer que après vos tiegne vostre règne'; BnF ms. fr. 19758 *ibid.*).

[200] The former is Bibliothèque nationale de France, ms. fr. 1279, and the latter is the manuscript known as 'Le livre la roine', Bibliothèque nationale de France, ms. fr. 5245. The latter is in a composite manuscript that also includes translated Roman law from the *Institutes* and *Digest* and a translated version of the Norman *Summa de legibus Normannie* (Klimrath, *Mémoire sur les monumens inédits*, p. 35). Henri Klimrath (1807–37), the great nineteenth-century commentator of French customary law, suggested that the 'books of the queen' referred not just to the first text, namely Pierre's *Conseil*, but to the entire vernacular compilation of customary and Roman law texts within the manuscript (*ibid.*, pp. 38–9).

[201] Though the friend seems consistently male, even in the 'livre la roine', where the first title indicates a male friend (*a son ami*) (BnF, ms. fr. 5245, iv.). This makes it more likely that it was not the original composition but copies of the text that were commissioned by a queen. Note that Blanche de Castile died in 1252.

address Louis IX or his son as 'friend', and rather odd not to use the authority of Louis IX, his son, or mother to amplify the prestige of the text if any of these were indeed the original addressee of the text. A manuscript recently sold at auction, claimed by the auction house to be the earliest version, simply began with 'Here speaks [*parole*] my lord Pieres de Fontaines of the rights, and laws and customs of Vermandois'.[202] It is more likely that the association with Louis IX and his mother and son is a later thirteenth-century development associated with the promotion of Louis' memory by his successors.[203]

The text has a pedagogical tone and is written as the teacher's side of a conversation between teacher and student. Pierre had some legal education and incorporated significant portions of a French translation of Roman law into his text, most heavily Justinian's *Code* but also the *Digest*, without citation details. This Roman law is sometimes incorporated into the text and sometimes indicated as the speech of individual Roman emperors. The text treats summons,

---

[202] *Chi parole mon sires Pieres de Fontaines des drois et des lois et des coustumes de Vermandois* (the auction notice has unfortunately been taken down, but a glimpse of the beginning of the manuscript can be found in the auction publicity video here at the 1:20min mark: https://bit.ly/3NPJzCy). The claim that it is the earliest manuscript and original text rests, as far as I can tell, on the identification of the script and illumination as contemporary to the writing of the text, the title of 'parole' which the auction house claims is the original title, the Picard dialect of the text, and the inclusion of passages not extant in other manuscripts (Interencheres, 'Les paroles de Pierre de Fontaines', https://bit.ly/3yay046). These are not decisive. The decorated initial to me seems to be a little more ornate but in the same style and extremely similar to BnF ms. fr. 13983 (formerly Fonds Saint-Germain Harlay MS supp fr. 406), which Marnier dates to the end of the thirteenth century (1280–1300), while the script also seems extremely similar between the two manuscripts (M. A. J. Marnier, introduction to *Le Conseil de Pierre de Fontaines*, p. xxxvii). It is unclear why 'parole' would indicate an original rather than a manuscript variation that reflects the form of the text. The dialect of the text could reflect the language of the author but also of the copyist or recipient and is inconclusive. The inclusion of additional passages does not permit us to say the text is earlier rather than later. Lastly, though the auction house claims that this is the original exemplar composed by Pierre de Fontaines and the one that was offered by Louis IX to his son, it is unclear what in this manuscript permits that claim (Interencheres, 'Les paroles de Pierre de Fontaines'). This manuscript is in private hands, and I have not been able to study it. It is therefore difficult to make any solid claims about it at this time, and I do not include it in my analysis here.

[203] On the memorialization of Louis, see M. Cecilia Gaposchkin, *The Making of Saint Louis: Kingship, Sanctity, and Crusade in the Later Middle Ages*.

continuances, sureties, advocates, judges, minors, contracts, fraud, cases concerning people abroad, arbitration, taverners, judgments, appeals for false judgment, how to structure a complaint and initiate a suit, noting days when suits are not permitted, judges, jurisdiction, different subjects of suits, wills, gifts, and good and bad faith. Pierre notes some, but not many, cases in which he participated.[204] Pierre appraises arguments and ideas but does not provide examples of words to use when pleading or arguing. The goal of the text is to understand how courts work, relevant rules, and connections to Roman law.

Summa de legibus Normannie *(between 1254 and 1258)*

Summa de legibus Normannie in curia laicali was composed by an anonymous author either sometime between 1235 and 1258 or, more narrowly, between 1254 and 1258.[205] The latter date is supported by much more evidence.[206] It was composed first in Latin and then translated

---

[204] For instance, Pierre de Fontaines, *Conseil*, 22.23–4.

[205] *Summa de legibus Normanniae in curia laicali*, in *Coutumiers de Normandie*, ed. Adolphe Tardif, vol.2; *Le Grand Coutumier de Normandie*, ed. William Laurence de Gruchy, trans. Judith Anne Everard. Tardif's edition is a reconstruction of the 'original' Latin version of the text. Everard's edition is based on an edition of the French and Latin texts published in 1539 (reprinted by William Laurence de Gruchy in 1881 because, he said, fifteenth- and sixteenth-century books were becoming rare and expensive). There are thus some differences in the text between this and Tardif's edition, and the chapter numbers do not always correspond. When I refer to the *Summa de legibus Normanniae in curia laicali*, I am referring to Tardif's edition. The manuscripts give this text a variety of names, including *Jura et consuetudines quibus regitur Normannie, Jura et statute Normannie, Cursus Normannie, Liber consuetudinis Normannie, Registrum de judiciis Normannie*, and *Summa de legibus in curia laicali* (*Summa de legibus Normanniae in curia laicali*, in *Coutumiers de Normandie*, ed. Adolphe Tardif, pp. cxl–cxlvi). *Summa de legibus Normanniae in curia laicali* was the title chosen by Tardif because that was the title in seven of his twenty-four manuscripts, which – though not the majority – made it the most common in his corpus (*ibid.*, p. cxliii).

[206] Tardif dated the composition to 1254–58 while Robert Génestal (partially based on work by Robert Génestal) dated it to 1235–58 (*Coutumiers de Normandie*, ed. Tardif, vol. 2, p. cxciv; R. Génestal, 'La formation et le développement de la coutume de Normandie'; Robert Besnier, *La Coutume de Normandie: Histoire Externe*, p. 105). Scholars of Norman law employ both dates (for Tardif's date, see Power, *The Norman Frontier in the Twelfth and Thirteenth Centuries*, p. 185; and for Génestal's date, *see* Davy, 'Les chartes ducales, miroir du droit coutumier normand?', p. 200; François Neveux, 'Le contexte historique de la rédaction des coutumiers normands', p. 18). Tardif provides much more extensive reasoning for his dates. The strongest of these in my view is that the *Summa* replicates the form of

into French prose, and later into French verse as well.[207] It is also referred
to as the *Grand coutumier de Normandie*; this title is sometimes used for
the French text only and sometimes for the Latin text as well. There are
many manuscripts. Tardif used twenty-four manuscripts for his Latin
edition that he grouped into nine families and three principal types:
those with a long and complete text, those that end a little earlier (at
chap. cxxiv), and a third group that ends even earlier (at chap. cxii.4).[208]
The largest number of manuscripts are from the first type, with the longest
text, but the text 'varies so much and offers so little unity' that it is in fact
difficult to see it as the work of one author.[209] Tardif concluded that the
shortest type (ending at chap. cxii) constitutes the earliest version of
the *Summa* to which were added additional texts, some inserted within
the text itself and others appended at the end.[210] Viollet found seventeen
manuscripts of the French version.[211] There is also a French verse
translation of the Latin text composed around 1280.[212] The prose Latin
text has two prefaces, the first of which is concerned with how the book is
organized, and the second with why the author decided to write it. He
explains that his intention was 'to declare the laws and statutes of
Normandy [*jura et instituta Normanniae*]'; that is, the laws and statutes
legislated by Norman princes on the advice of prelates, counts, and
barons.[213] The duke is, of course, the king of France at this point.[214]

---

the oath for *baillis* and royal functionaries that was first enunciated by Louis IX in his
famous ordinance of 1254, and so it must have been written afterwards (*Coutumiers
de Normandie*, ed. Tardif, vol. 2, p. clxxxvii).

[207] *Coutumiers de Normandie*, ed. Tardif, vol. 2, pp. lxv–lxxvii, xciii–xciv, clxxv–
clxxxix.

[208] *Coutumiers de Normandie*, ed. Tardif, vol. 2, pp. x–c (manuscripts and their family
groupings), p. ci. (three principal types). His edition is of the longest of these three
types. Beyond the variation already noted, it also circulated in abridged versions.

[209] *Ibid.*, p. ci. This can be seen in the amount of repetition in those manuscripts, with
some questions treated over and again two or three times (*ibid.*, p. cii). Tardif
distinguishes between the repetitions that are brief and go back to another part of
the text and those that indicate the ideas of another person, such as when the subject
is repeated but views on it are contradictory or where there are doctrinal differences
(*ibid.*, ciii). Considering the difficult manuscript situation, Tardif had to make
difficult choices in establishing a unitary text and in choosing what variants to
include (see *ibid.*, cxliii–cxlvi).

[210] *Ibid.*, p. cix.   [211] Paul Viollet, 'Les Coutumiers de Normandie', p. 67.

[212] *Coutumiers de Normandie*, ed. Tardif, vol. 2, p. cxxxvii.

[213] *Summa de legibus Normanniae in curia laicali*, first and second preface.

[214] While the text consistently refers to the 'duke of Normandy', it also acknowledges
that this position is held by the king of France (*ibid.*, chap. xii).

The text refers to places in western Normandy and may have been written there. It does not reveal much about the identity of the author, who may have been someone named Maucael.[215]

In form, the text is a *summa* – a genre of writing that aimed at synthesizing the entirety of a subject, commonly used in scholastic writing and in the work of canonists and romanists.[216] The author thus takes a scholastic approach, and his tone is expository. It combines substance and procedure throughout. The text begins with basic definitions associated with law and justice, judicial organization, the jurisdiction of the duke, services and dues owed to the duke from his vassals, succession, and forms of tenure. It then moves to the trial and courts: delays, excuses, claims, secular court, the clamour of haro, the assise, the exchequer, complaints, pledges, summons, witnesses, lawyers, and conducting views.[217] Next it returns to suits of specific types and how they are conducted: murder, jurors, assault, breach of truce, suits of women, sanctuary, compurgation, possession, debt, and contracts.[218] It proceeds to claims related to landed inheritance, the

---

[215] The Channel Islands continued using Norman law after the break with Normandy in 1204. There was a Latin copy of the *Summa de legibus Normanniae* in Jersey in the early fourteenth century that was referred to as '*Summa de Maukael*' (see *Coutumiers de Normandie*, ed. Tardif, vol. 2, pp. cc–ccxxxiv; Tardif, *Les auteurs présumés du Grand coutumier de Normandie*; Viollet, 'Les Coutumiers de Normandie', pp. 74ff; Besnier, *La Coutume de Normandie: Histoire* Externe, pp. 106ff; John Le Patourel, 'The Authorship of the Grand Coutumier De Normandie'). Le Patourel summarizes the views of Tardif, Viollet, and Besnier on the subject.

[216] This choice of genre – also that of *Bracton* – suggests a cross-channel legal culture that continued after Normandy was conquered by Philip Augustus, as England and Normandy shared the genre of the *summa* as a way of talking about law (Thomas J. McSweeney, 'Between England and France: A Cross-Channel Legal Culture in the Late Thirteenth Century', pp. 77, 84ff). The Channel Islands broke with Normandy in 1204 and joined England (Le Patourel, 'The Authorship of the Grand Coutumier De Normandie').

[217] The clamour of haro was a particular procedure where by crying out a verbal formula, a plaintiff created an immediate temporary injunction (without judicial sanction) against someone who wrongfully interfered with their property, whereby the latter had to stop this interference until the court resolved the issue.

[218] Sanctuary in its medieval form, Karl Shoemaker explains, protected a wrongdoer who had fled to a church from forcible removal and from corporal and capital punishment, but took different forms and was in constant flux throughout the period (Karl Shoemaker, *Sanctuary and Crime in the Middle Ages, 400-1500*, ix). Compurgation was also known as wager of law or oath helping, this was a way of proving the innocence of the accused via a group of oath-helpers who testified in support of the veracity of the oath of the accused.

shape of the inquest, novel disseisin, mort d'ancestor, dowry, records (both oral and written), advowson, various claims relating to fiefs, records (made orally), proof, compurgation again, judicial duel, and prescription.[219] Sections on specific legal claims generally show the form of the writ one should use. The text rarely mentions oral language to be used at court and refers to no specific cases.[220] It sometimes offers examples or hypotheticals using contemporary medieval names such as Robert and Richard.[221] Roman and canon law are not cited overtly in the text.[222] There is vague Roman influence in that the text very loosely follows the divisions of the Justinian's *Institutes* and employs some Roman law terms.[223] However, more generally, the text gives the impression of a clerical author familiar with scholastic thought and canon law.[224] He also used secular sources, such as Louis IX's

---

[219] Novel desseisin was an action to recover recently dispossessed land. Mort d'ancestor was an action to claim one's landed inheritance upon the death of an ancestor. Advowson was a right of patronage to nominate someone or appoint them for a vacant benefice of the church. Also known as trial by combat or wager of battle, the judicial duel was a method of resolving cases by single combat between accuser and accused (or a representative in case of incapacity). Prescription is the acquisition or loss of a right through use or disuse over time.

[220] Very rarely, the text refers to an act by a specific person, such as a privilege granted by Philip Augustus to prelates (*Summa de legibus Normanniae in curia laicali*, chap. cxi). Everard's edition includes the text of the actual charter as chap. cxii, Tardif does not include it.

[221] This can be seen in Tardif's edition. These names are often Latinized in the 1539 edition published by Everard. Robert and Richard in Tardif are later renamed Titius and Getus in Everard's text (*Summa de legibus Normanniae in curia laicali*, xciii).

[222] After the Middle Ages, the laws and institutions of medieval Normandy became a topos in the rallying cry against the uniformization of law (Gilduin Davy, 'La Normandie, terre de traditions juridiques', 21). The study of Norman lawbooks has tended to attract scholars devoted to an image of Norman law as original, so while an affinity between Norman lawbooks and ideas from the learned laws have been noted, they still need further study (*ibid.*).

[223] This can be seen in the language of property law (McSweeney, 'Between England and France'). Like the *Institutes*, the *Summa* begins with general considerations of justice and then addresses things and then actions, though it skips over persons (*ibid.*, p. 86). The author may have been inspired by Azo for his definitions of law (*ius*) (Viollet, 'Les Coutumiers de Normandie', p. 81). However, his interest in definitions could also have been influenced by Isidore of Seville's *Etymologies*.

[224] The second prologue seems to be inspired by the letter Gregory IX sent with his *Decretals* (1234) to the universities of Paris and Bologna (Viollet, 'Les Coutumiers de Normandie', p. 80). The author's scholastic education seems apparent in the division of the work into distinctions and chapters, in the use of Aristotelian categories and of scholastic terminology (*ibid.*, pp. 80ff). Most strikingly, the author separated law (*ius*) into natural and positive law. The expression 'positive law' was not used in

ordinance from 1254. The author did not make his sources obvious
and rephrased and moulded them for his own purpose.

Li livre de jostice et de plet *(ca. 1260)*

The *Livre de jostice et de plet* was written in French by an anonymous
author around 1260.[225] There is one sole manuscript.[226] The
manuscript begins with Louis IX's great ordinance on the reform of
the kingdom (1254), much of which addressed the royal *baillis*, and
a royal ordinance on trial procedure – the latter also forms the
beginning of the *Établissements de Saint Louis* composed about
a decade later.[227] The text refers to the 'customs of France', meaning
the royal domain, and many times to 'king Louis'.[228] The *Livre de
jostice et de plet* is commonly grouped with the *coutumiers*, but it is an
awkward fit for the corpus because it inserted instances of medieval
customary legal practice into what was mainly a text of Roman law in

---

juristic circles in the mid-thirteenth century but had a continuous tradition in
scholastic scholarship at least since Peter Abelard a century earlier (*ibid.* p. 81;
Stephan Kuttner, 'Sue les origines du terme 'droit positif'').

[225] *Li livre de jostice et de plet*, ed. Rapetti. Rapetti's edition contains about half of the
text and so presents a partial version. Rapetti, drawing on preparatory work by
Henri Klimrath, prioritized the portions of the text that had some relation to
customary law, canon law, or constituted a significant revision of Roman law, and
did not include the portions of the text that were simple translations of Roman law
(*ibid.*, p. li; Graziella Pastore and Frédéric Duval, 'La tradition française de l'"infortiat" et le "Livre de jostice et de plet"', 200n.6). A new edition of the full text edited
by Graziella Pastore (http://elec.enc.sorbonne.fr/josticeetplet/) helpfully indicates
the portions edited by Rapetti in black text and the portions newly edited by
Pastore in blue.

[226] Paris, BnF, ms. fr. 2844.

[227] The title of *Livre de justice et de plet* is drawn from the beginning of the table of
contents, which is at the end of the manuscript. The manuscript begins with the
ordinance of 1254, and so the tone is one of royal pronouncement: 'Lois, par la grace
de Deu roy de France, A toz ceaus qui ceste presente page verront, saluz'. Rapetti
described these ordinances as a preliminary text separate from the *Livre de justice et
de plet* and placed the texts in an appendix (*Li livre de jostice et de plet*, ed. Rapetti,
p. 335). However, the manuscript goes from one text to the other seamlessly, and
these ordinances appear to be introductory matter to the *Livre de justice et de plet*.
The ordinance of 1254 was focused on reforming administration conducted by royal
baillis but also aimed to reform public morality concerning issues such as usury,
blasphemy, prostitution, and gaming (Louis Carolus-Barré, 'La Grande Ordonnance
de Réformation de 1254', p. 181).

[228] *Li livre de jostice et de plet*, ed. Rapetti, p. vii.

translation, while other *coutumiers* that deploy Roman law do the opposite. The text chiefly consists of a French translation of large swathes of Justinian's *Digest*, and its plan follows the *Digest*: it begins with general concepts of law and justice, moves on to legal officers, and turns to trial procedure, judgments, and then legal issues by subject.[229] The author included significant material from canon law, most significantly from the *Decretals* of Gregory IX. He weaves in descriptions of cases, examples and passing references to issues drawn from contemporary society. The names of Roman jurists in the *Digest* are often but not always replaced with those of prominent royal judicial officers of the mid-thirteenth century.[230] Some have argued that the text was the notebook of a student or in some way associated with the University of Orleans, where professors made an effort to integrate Roman law and customary law.[231] Others have argued that it is the work of a royal *bailli*, based on the fact that the judicial officers mentioned by name in the text are preponderantly royal *bailli* and officers of the king.[232] The cases and examples described by the author offer insight into the administration of royal justice, from the cases of butchers and drapers to disputes within and between cities, in the Orléanais, the Gâtinais, Bauvaisis, and the Vexin region of Normandy.[233]

[229] The *Livre de jostice et de plet* is composed of twenty books: books I–X are based on the *Digestum Vetus* (with Book X drawing on the *Decretals* of Gregory IX), books XI–XII are based on the *Infortiatum*, and books XIII–XX are based on the *Digestum Novum* (Pastore and Duval, 'La tradition française de l'infortiat et le Livre de jostice et de plet', pp. 199–200).

[230] The contemporary royal officers named included Jean de Beaumont, Geoffroy de la Chapelle, Étienne de Sancerre, Renaud the bailli of Gisord, Renaud de Tricot. Many of these were senior counselors in the court of Louis IX, whose activities ranged from the 1230s to the late 1250s (see Stein, Henri, 'Conjectures sur l'auteur du 'Livre de jostice et de plet'', pp. 347ff).

[231] Rapetti, *Li livre de jostice et de plet*, p. xxxi; E. M. Meijers, 'L'Université d'Orléans au XIII siècle', pp. 3ff.

[232] Henri Stein, 'Conjectures sur l'auteur du 'Livre de jostice et de plet'', p. 347ff. Stein also argued that Philippe de Rémy, the father of Philippe de Beaumanoir, could have been the author of this text (*ibid.*, p. 372). He provides much circumstantial evidence that is intriguing, but ultimately it is indeed a conjecture as there is no clear direct link. A new prosopography of the individuals mentioned in the *Livre de justice et de plet* is available at http://josticeetplet.huma-num.fr/.

[233] *Li livre de jostice et de plet*, I.iii.5–6, I.v.1ff; for these locations, see Stein, 'Conjectures sur l'auteur du "Livre de jostice et de plet"', p. 372.

Les établissements de Saint Louis *(1272 or 1273)*

The *Établissements de Saint Louis* was a French-language text created by an unknown compiler (see Figure 1.2).[234]

We have over twenty manuscripts of the text, as well as other derivative texts.[235] Beyond this, parts of the text were also copied into or paraphrased in later *coutumiers*.[236] This text is generally identified in manuscripts as a description of regulations (*établissments*) of the king of France for the *châtelet* of Paris and Orleans. The king is commonly unnamed earlier on and the royal aspect is not emphasized until later. The compiler-author created the *Établissements* by putting together two royal ordinances with two earlier texts of customs and then incorporating numerous citations into the text, many of which referred to the Roman law of the *Code* and *Digest* and to the canon law of the *Decretals* of Gregory IX.[237] Three late thirteenth-century manuscripts contain an added prologue that presents the text as an ordinance issued by Louis IX in 1270 (just before his last crusade and death in Tunis), one that he imposed in all the secular courts of the kingdom and within his own domain. This later tradition has Louis IX as proactive originator of the text, which this prologue presents as composed by a commission of 'wise men' and 'good clerks', and makes the text part of his program of reform of law, justice and the judicial and administrative personnel.[238]

Book I begins with the procedure of the Châtelet in Paris, covering judicial duties, proof, jurisdiction, and appeal. It continues with the *Coutume de Touraine et Anjou*, which is heavily based on the *Coutumes d'Anjou et du Maine* described above, and follows the earlier text closely. The contents are about the same, although the compiler *of the Établissements* did make some changes to the text.[239] Book II

---

[234] *Les établissements de Saint Louis*, ed. Viollet; *The Etablissements de Saint Louis*, trans. Akehurst.

[235] *Les établissements de Saint Louis*, ed. Viollet, vol. 1 and vol. 3, respectively.

[236] *Ibid.*, 1:280.

[237] Since we have no copies of the *Établissements* as a whole without the citations, the tradition has been to assume that the person who brought together the earlier component texts and the person who wove in the various citations are the same person.

[238] *Les établissements de Saint Louis*, ed. Viollet, 1:3.

[239] He made some structural changes. He provided more explanatory titles for each section. He sometimes grouped the sections differently (e.g. *Coutumes d'Anjou et du*

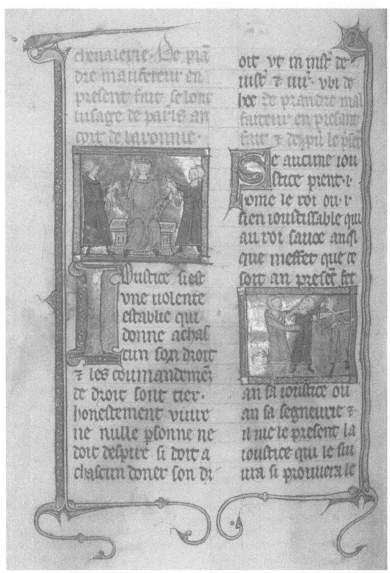

FIGURE 1.2 *Établissments de Saint Louis.* Illuminations in the *coutumiers* captured scenes that reflected the action of the lay courts. Scenes of the judge sitting in judgment and perpetrators being caught were some of the most common throughout the *coutumiers.* In addition to these, this thirteenth-century manuscript of the *Établissments de Saint Louis* includes an image of the judge receiving this book, a witness taking their oath, a trial by battle, a guilty person being punished by hanging, and two relating to homage and fealty. Illuminated *coutumiers* were not so ornately decorated as manuscripts of canon law or Roman law could be. Those *coutumier* manuscripts that were illuminated commonly contained, with a few exceptions, between one and ten images. *Établissments de Saint Louis*, Bibliothèque nationale de France, ms. Fr. 5899, fol. 69v.

contains the court procedure in the baronial courts of the Orleans region. It discusses arrests, requests and complaints, jurisdiction, appeals, summons, duties of advocates, judging, the king's rights, fines, vassal–lord relations, and execution of judgments and ends with complaints to the king against those who come onto one's land armed without right. The manuscripts vary as to the regional attributions of the texts. Both books regularly explain how one should speak to make various sorts of legal claims. The *Établissements* does not refer to specific cases.

Le livre des constitutions demenées el Chastelet de Paris *(between 1279 and 1282)*

This text was written in French by an anonymous author and survives in one known manuscript dating from the beginning of the fourteenth century.[240] The title is drawn from the *explicit*, which labels the text as the 'Book of constitutions carried out in the Châtelet of Paris in all cases'.[241] The *Demenées* is a book for pleaders and 'teaches how one should intend to speak before all judges and especially in lay courts'.[242] Unlike the other *coutumiers* studied here, most of the text concerns trials where non-nobles would be tried before a lone judge (as opposed to a noble tried by peers or appealing to a sovereign).[243] It has a procedural framework that begins with the initial complaint and takes the reader through various aspects of the trial process, though it presents these in a mixed order rather than following the trial from beginning to end. Substantive law is woven into some sections, for

---

Maine s. 19–21 equates to *Établissements* 1.27). Both Viollet and Akehurst bracket what was drawn from *Anjou et Maine*, which shows what was used by the *Établissements* compiler and what he added. Sometimes word changes, even small, change the meaning of the text. For instance, *Anjou et Maine* explains that 'the king cannot impose customs (*coutumes*) in the land of the baron without his consent' (s. 19), while the *Établissements* changes *coutumes* to *ban*, and so states that 'the king cannot issue proclamations in the baron's lands without his consent' (s. 26). The issue of textual variation will be discussed in more detail later in Chapter 7.

[240] *Le livre des constitutions demenées el Chastelet de Paris*, ed. Mortet. Paris, BnF, ms. fr. 19778. The marginal notes are from the end of the fourteenth or the fifteenth century. Mortet is unimpressed with the copyist of the manuscript and notes that there are errors and omissions, but there is no other text to which to compare it.

[241] *Le livre des constitutions demenées el Chastelet de Paris*, ed. Mortet, *explicit*, and Mortet's introduction, p. 7.

[242] *Ibid.*, preface.

[243] Either the judicial officer of a lord or a royal magistrate (*ibid.*, p. 11).

instance, descriptions of types of proof or the nature of custom. Much of the text is devoted to advising pleaders on how to present information and arguments at various stages of a trial and depending on the nature of legal issue. The tone is expository, and explanations are brief. The text makes several references to the 'custom of France', meaning the custom of the royal domain. It draws very little on texts of canon law and Roman law, which are mentioned once each, and does not refer to specific cases. French scholarship refers to highly procedural texts like this one that describe the manner of proceeding in court as a *style* (or *stile*).

Philippe de Beaumanoir, *Coutumes de Beauvaisis* (1283)

This text was written in French by Philippe de Beaumanoir (1247–96) while he was a justice in the County of Clermont in Beauvaisis for Count Robert of Clermont, one of Louis IX's younger sons.[244] Amédée Salmon has fourteen manuscripts for his critical edition.[245] Local to this area, Beaumanoir was made *bailli* of Clermont in 1279 and held the position until 1284.[246] It was while in this post that he composed his *coutumier* and was knighted close to the end of his tenure in Clermont. He then went into royal service as an administrative and judicial officer as *sénéchal* of Poitou (1284–87), *sénéchal* of Saintonge (1287–89), *bailli* of Vermandois (1289–91), *bailli* of Touraine (1291–92), and *bailli* of Senlis (1292–96).[247] He and his father were for some time mistakenly thought to be one person. His father, known as Philippe de Rémy, was a *bailli* in Artois and writer of imaginative literature such as *Jehan et Blonde* and *La Manekine*.[248] Phillipe de

---

[244] Beaumanoir, *Coutumes de Beauvaisis*, ed. Salmon; Beaumanoir, *The Coutumes de Beauvaisis of Philippe De Beaumanoir*, trans. Akehurst.

[245] Beaumanoir, *Coutumes de Beauvaisis*, ed. Salmon, pp. xviii–xxix. He also noted two abridged version (*ibid.*, xxx–xxxii).

[246] Bautier, 'Philippe de Beaumanoir', 6–8. Beaumanoir explains in the first paragraph that he is from the area and speaks of being charged by Robert with upholding the laws and customs of the area as being in the present ('nous sommes de celui païs et [...] nous nous sommes entremis de garder et faire garder les drios et coutumes de ladite contée par la volonté du très haut home et trea noble Robert, fil du roi de France, conte de Clermont ... '; Beaumanoir, *Coutumes de Beauvaisis*, ed. Salmon, prologue s. 1).

[247] Carolus-Barré, 'Origines, milieu familial et carrière de Philippe de Beaumanoir', pp. 29ff.

[248] His father was a *balli* in the Gâtinais region from 1237–50 for count Robert of Artois, brother of Louis IX (*ibid.*, p. 23). Philippe de Beaumanoir inherited some minor lands from his father (*ibid.*, p. 28).

Beaumanoir was his third son, a comital and royal *bailli* as well as a great jurist. His was by far the largest of the first *coutumiers*, with seventy chapters which are each in-depth treatments of a subject. The arc of the text is based on the trial process, beginning with judges, summons, lawyers and complaints, issues of jurisdiction and proof, and ending with judicial battles and judgments. Within this narrative, Beaumanoir treats a variety of subjects at length, including wills, inheritance, minority, illegitimacy, consanguinity, highways, measurements, crimes, novel desseisin, written legal documents, loans, rental, arbitration, property of various types, creditors' remedies, marital maintenance, private war, truces, usury, cases that arise out of bad luck ('misadventure'), and gifts. He discusses the form of written legal documents, from wills to advocate's appointment letters, as well as legal language – how one should make different sorts of claims or statements and their implications. The *Coutumes de Beauvaisis* is written with erudition and has been lauded by later commentators as the most important, best, and most original juridical work of medieval France.[249] Though clearly familiar with ideas from the learned laws, Beaumanoir never cited or quoted texts of Roman law or canon law. Consequently, from the 1840s onward, scholars have debated the nature of his education and his textual sources, variously arguing that at the base of his thinking lay Tancred's *Ordo*, Justinian's *Digest*, other *ordines judiciarii*, or the *Établissements de Saint Louis*.[250] Beaumanoir chose neither to reveal his textual sources nor to borrow their language directly and instead wrote a text whose erudition was evident but presented without debts or ties to outside authority.[251] However, he did refer to practice throughout the text. He made many comparisons between the functioning of lay courts and ecclesiastical courts and cited close to a hundred cases in secular courts that he had either seen, tried himself, or heard about from other counties.[252]

---

[249] F. R. P. Akehurst, introduction to Philippe de Beaumanoir, *The Coutumes de Beauvaisis of Philippe de Beaumanoir*, trans. Akehurst, p. xiii.

[250] Beaumanoir, *Coutumes de Beauvaisis*, ed. Salmon, pp. xvii–xviii. Salmon suggests that these might best be seen, in this context, as texts worth knowing to appreciate the scope and nature of Beaumanoir's work.

[251] *Ibid.*, p. xix.

[252] Beaumanoir, *Coutumes de Beauvaisis*, ed. Salmon; Beaumanoir, *The Coutumes de Beauvaisis of Philippe De Beaumanoir*, trans. Akehurst, p. xxiii.

L'ancien coutumier de Champagne *(ca. 1295)*

The *Ancien coutumier de Champagne* was written in French by an anonymous author around 1295, after Champagne had been incorporated into the royal domain through the marriage of Philip the Fair to Joan of Navarre.[253] This was when the Grands Jours de Troyes, the court of the count of Champagne (who was now also the king), was in transition from one composed of barons to one manned by royal commissioners.[254] Nine known manuscripts of the text survive, the earliest – four of the texts – dating from the fourteenth century. The text begins with an ordinance about the division of inheritance among male children, which was issued in 1224 by Thibaut IV Count of Champagne and King of Navarre with the consent of his nobles. This ordinance gives the text the appearance of legislation, but the rest of the text is an exposition of substantive law. With a few exceptions, each section begins with a substantive rule of law introduced by the locution 'It is custom in Champagne that … ' or 'The manner in which we do things in Champagne is … '.[255] Nearly half of these statements of substantive law were supported with cases, described in varying degrees of detail.[256] The text begins with inheritance, dower, guardianship of minors, escheat, forest law,

---

[253] The text includes cases, the latest of which date to 1295 and give us the approximate date of the text (*L'ancien coutumier de Champagne*, ed. Portejoie, p. 11) Philip and Joan married in 1284, and Philip became king of France in 1285.

[254] *Ibid.*, pp. 4–7. The relationship of Champenois aristocracy to the count changed in 1284: from then on, a bureaucracy made up of outside appointees would liaise with them for a count that no longer resided there (Evergates, *The Aristocracy in the County of Champagne, 1100–1300*, pp. 61, 194).

[255] 'Il est coustume en Champagne que … ' (*L'ancien coutumier de Champagne*, s. 2), 'Encor us'on en Champagne que … ' (s. 5).

[256] *L'ancien coutumier de Champagne*, p. 7. The cases are sometimes very brief and sometimes provide a description of pleadings, parties, forum, judges, and date. These judgments report cases of parties living in the *baillages* of Troyes and Chaumont, it is somewhere in this area that the *coutumiers* must have been written (*ibid.*, p. 11). The judgments themselves are mostly from the Grands Jours de Troyes (both before and after the accession of Philip the Fair), six are from a court of barons that functioned concurrently with the Grand Jours after the latter became dominated by royal personnel, four are judgments of the Parlement of Paris, and a handful cannot be identified (*ibid.*, pp. 7–8). Émile Chénon theorized a primitive text of substantive rules to which the judgments were added later and believed the judgments may have been drawn wholly or in part from a register that he thought was compiled by Guillaume du Châtelet (Chénon, 'Quelques mots sur les deux manuscrits récemment découverts du coutumier de Champagne', 67).

warranty, mortmain, seisin, punishments and fines, marriage between people of different status, and generally includes law relating to the governance of the county.[257] The text does occasionally touch on procedural questions, but reading this text would not be enough to learn court procedure.[258] The substantive law comes in the form of concrete rules and not as an explanation of terminology or abstract principles. It contains no Roman or canon law.

Coutumier d'Artois *(between 1283 and 1302)*

This text was written in French by an anonymous author sometime during the last couple of decades of the thirteenth century or the beginning of the fourteenth.[259] It is preserved in two manuscripts written in different dialects.[260] The text was composed during the rule of Robert II (1250–1302), Count of Artois, grandson of Louis VIII, and nephew of Louis IX.[261] Robert II was an absentee lord, and the county was governed without his presence.[262] Unlike in other regions, the *baillis* of Artois had important duties relating to the administration of justice but did not have their own courts; rather, they called together the men of the

---

[257] Escheat is the reversion of one's property to the crown when one dies without an heir. Seisin is a medieval property concept akin to legal possession, though the equivalence is not nearly that simple (see Ernest Champeaux, *Essai sur la vestitura*).

[258] The procedural law included addresses specific points (for instance, *L'ancien coutumier de Champagne*, s. 33, 34). It cannot have been meant to provide a general overview of trial procedure.

[259] *Coutumier d'Artois*, ed. Tardif.

[260] Paris, BnF, ms. fr. 5249 from the fourteenth century (A); Paris, BnF, ms. fr. 5248 which contains three texts: the *Établissements de Saint Louis*, the *Coutumier d'Artois*, and the *Coutumes notoirement approuvees en la cour de Ponthieu, de Vimeu, de Baillie d'Amiens et en pluseurs autres lieus* (B). The two dialects are Artesian and Picard.

[261] Artois came within royal orbit under Philip Augustus, who claimed it for his son (future Louis VIII) as heir to his mother, Isabelle de Hainaut. Louis VIII made it an apanage for his second surviving son, Robert, who held Artois from Louis IX beginning in 1237 when he came of age. Robert I died on crusade and his widow, Mahaut de Brabant (who married the count of Saint-Pol), served as regent until Robert II came of age in 1265. He ruled until 1302. The fissure between the nobility and the counts of Artois became clear under Robert II's successor, Mahaut d'Artois, incidentally the first in this line to govern in residence. (See Lalou, 'Le comté d'Artois (xiiie–xive siècle)', pp. 23ff.)

[262] Small, 'Artois in the Late Thirteenth Century: A Region Discovering Its Identity?', 201–2.

count who judged in the count's name at the level of the castellany.[263] The *Coutumier d'Artois* author explains in the preface that the text contains the 'customs and usages' of Artois, as they should be and have been practised, part of which conform to the 'written law' of Rome and the church.[264] The text begins with trial procedure – summons, exceptions, delays (essoins) – and then turns to more substantive material on the role of attorneys and jurisdiction of the king, barons, and minor nobles. It then returns to procedure and initiating cases, before coming back to substantive issues of inheritance, succession, and dower. It finishes with appeals, criminal procedures, and the duties of judges. The author used a wide range of sources. He incorporated sections of Pierre de Fontaines' *Conseil* and the *Établissements de Saint Louis* into his text and cites Roman law, Decretals, *ordines iudiciarii* (procedural manuals for canon law), Horace, and the Bible. The author discussed several cases he saw at court himself. The details in these case discussions vary but usually included the court where the proceeding took place, the nature of allegations, and the judgment.[265]

Li usages de Bourgogne (date uncertain, perhaps end thirteenth century)

Li usages de Bourgogne was composed in French by an anonymous author.[266] Recent opinion places the text in the thirteenth century, although dating is difficult: while the extant manuscript is from the late

---

[263] The *bailli* arranged trials, arrested suspects, found witnesses, obtained evidence, but did not act as judges, because the castellany was the center of justice, an anomaly at a time when castellanies were becoming outdated as a unit of political importance in France (*ibid.*, 199). There was no appeal to the count himself and centralized administration in Artois occurred very slowly (*ibid.*, 199–200). However, the *baillis* of the count played a big part in arbitration (see also Maxime de Germiny, *Les lieutenants de Robert II*, pp. 21–2). The subject of arbitration is one of the longest sections of the *coutumier* (*Coutumier d'Artois*, LIII). Artesians could appeal to the Parliament of Paris, which they did from the late 1260s, often in disputes over jurisdiction (Small, 'Artois in the Late Thirteenth Century', 201n.44).

[264] *Coutumier d'Artois*, preface.

[265] The parties to the disputes were mentioned sometimes by name, sometimes by positions (e.g. the *bailli* of a particular place), and at other times generically by 'man' or 'bourgeois'. The author did not provide dates.

[266] *Ancien coutumier de Bourgogne*, ed. A.-J. Marnier and N. Marnier. This title is drawn from the incipit and from the text's continued references to the *us de Borgoigne* as primary norm. Ange Ignace Marnier published it under the title of the *Ancien coutumier de Bourgogne* (*ibid.*).

fourteenth century at the earliest, some provisions seem to go back to the late twelfth or early thirteenth century, and it is possible the text dates to the thirteenth century.[267] The thirteenth-century dating is plausible as the concern of the text is to show the reader how to plead in court using witnesses, and clarifying inquisitorial procedure for lay contexts was certainly a preoccupation of the thirteenth century.[268] Despite the difficulty of dating the text with certainty, I am adding it here – conditionally and pending potential future manuscript discoveries – because it provides an intriguing addition to the corpus and widens the idea of what it meant to write a *coutumier*, although everything said about this text must be taken with the proviso of uncertain dating.

The *Usages de Bourgogne* is an introduction to pleading, and the trial is entirely framed in terms of argumentation. The author thus focuses on explaining the sorts of things one should say in court, the sorts of replies one might get, and the sorts of responses one should make. Despite this similarity to aspects of the *coutumiers* described above, the *Usages de Bourgogne* pays a lot of attention to the preoccupations of rural society. Substantively, the text focuses on the contractual obligations of farmers and wrongs committed by animals.[269] The text begins with how to plead, bring witnesses, types of witness, actions of debt, disagreement among judges, pledges, things purchased at markets and outside markets, lost animals (*betes*), borrowed animals, killing a neighbour's animals, lending animals to others, pigs and other animals that cause damage, how to defend oneself from the charge of being a thief, encroachments on land, delays in paying the *cens*, defences against accusations of treason, defences against accusations of murder, trial by battle, defences women should use if accused of sorcery, defences against accusations of being a leper, and a last incomplete provision on inheritance. The

---

[267] Marnier dates his manuscript to the end of the fourteenth or beginning of the fifteenth century but said that it contained a copy of a more ancient manuscript (*ibid.*, 525). Michel Petitjean states the text is from the late thirteenth century (Petitjean, 'La coutume de Bourgogne. Des coutumiers officieux à la coutume officielle', 14). Castaldo and Mausen note the text contains rules that go back to the thirteenth century if not the late twelfth (Castaldo and Mausen, *Introduction historique au droit*, s. 445).

[268] Of course, this does not bar the text from being later.

[269] Petitjean, 'La coutume de Bourgogne', p. 14.

text is thus generally focused on procedure, though aspects of substance are incorporated, and the text refers to the *us de Borgoigne* and justifications of rules or procedures 'by Law' (*par droit*). The text mentions ecclesiastical courts and treats proof by witnesses but does not cite, quote, or paraphrase texts of Roman law or canon law. Aspects relating to royal justice do not appear in the text.

Additional Note

The *coutumiers* were not the only texts that testified to the energy and experimentation invested in finding a good way to discuss the inchoate stuff of customary law and the business of secular courts. There were shorter texts of various types composed in the thirteenth century on aspects of the lay courts. These tracts do not often appear in recent historiography of the *coutumiers* but are important because they show that the *coutumiers* were part of a broader productive foment surrounding the lay courts and that their authors, while singular for writing more extensive works, were part of an intellectual milieu that was receptive to if not eager for such works. While they are comparatively short, these tracts could be listed with the *coutumiers* because they also deal with cases, abstract rules, or pleading in some way. That I do not include them in my corpus is not a reflection of their importance but of a desire to keep manageable what is already a large source base. It also reflects my view that these texts need their own in-depth study. I provide two examples of these shorter works here, for perspective.

A text known as the *Assises de Normandie* was composed by an anonymous author who was attached in some way to the *baillage* of Caen. It exists both in Latin and French. The title gives the impression that this a formal court record of cases and the author framed it as a record of what he saw at assises: 'The year of the incarnation of the Lord 1234, the Tuesday before the feast of blessed Michael, in the month of April, in Caen. The following Wednesday, I heard what follows in the assise.'[270] However, while the text is based on court judgments rendered between 1234 and 1237 at various Norman

---

[270] 'L'an de l'incarnation du seigneur mil deux cent trente quatre, le mardi avant la fête du bienheureux Mathieu, au mois d'avril, à Caen. Le mercredi suivant j'ai endendu en assise ce qui suit' ('Assises de Normandie au treizième siècle' in Marnier, ed., *Etablissements et coutumes, assises et arrêts de l'échiquier de Normandie*, p. 89).

assises, the case descriptions are extremely brief, and many have no
case at all but are descriptions of abstract principles or procedure.[271]
The author's goal seemed not to be recounting the specifics of
individual trials but writing down the principles he saw at play in
them.[272]

Another example is a tract on the customs of Anjou known today as
the *Compilatio de usibus Andegavie*, to which tradition has given
a Latin title, even though the text was entirely in French.[273] We have
only one manuscript, which also contained the *Établissements de Saint
Louis* and was written in the early fourteenth century.[274] Beautemps-
Beaupré did not find a date for the text but leans towards the later
1270s, while Paul Viollet places it after 1315.[275] The text refers to
usage and right/law (*drois*) of the courts in almost every provision,
starting virtually every provision with 'it is usage that' or 'it is usage
and law that'. The text has no overt citation of Roman or canon law.
The provisions in this text are very short and are forms of rules and
procedures formulated in their most pithy essence, perhaps best
described as customary '*regulae iuris*'.

---

[271] M. L. Delisle, 'Mémoire sur les recueils de jugements rendus', 373. The text covers
assises held in Caen, Bayeux, Falaise, Exmes, and Avranches and cites a handful of
decisions made by the Exchequer of Normandy (*ibid.*). We have one manuscript
from the thirteenth century, three from the fourteenth, one from the fifteenth, and
one from the sixteenth (*ibid.*). Tellingly, the text often accompanied the *Grand
Coutumier de Normandie*.

[272] For example: '*De la dot engagée*. Les héritiers du mari deffunt qui a obligé la dot de
sa femme, sont tenus de la dégager, et de mettre leur propre héritage entre les mains
des créanciers: cela fut jugé pour l'épouse de Philippe de feu Montfort' (*ibid.*).

[273] *Compilatio de usibus et consuetudinibus andegavie* in *Les établissements de Saint
Louis*, ed. Viollet, 3:117ff.

[274] Paris, BnF, ms. fr. 13985. See *Coutumes d'Anyou et dou Maigne*, ed. Beautemps-
Beaupré, p. 44.

[275] *Coutumes d'Anyou et dou Maigne*, ed. Beautemps-Beaupré, pp. 37–8; *Les
établissements de Saint Louis*, ed. Viollet, 3:116. Viollet postulates this date based
on one provision in the text that seemed to refer to an ordinance of 1315. Beautemps-
Beaupré's explanation for the date seems a little more convincing, and the constant
repetition of the word 'usage' rather than 'custom' could suggest an earlier rather
than later date.

2

Composing Customary Law as a Vernacular Law

Clerks have a manner of speaking in Latin that is very pretty; but the lay people who have to plead against them in lay court do not even understand the words that they say in French properly, as much as they may be pretty and appropriate to the pleading. And for this reason, we will discuss in this chapter, in such a manner that lay people can understand it, what is most often said in secular court and what is most necessary.

Philippe de Beaumanoir, *Coutumes de Beauvaisis*[1]

In the passage above, Beaumanoir pitted the cultural universe of lay people against the sophistication of *Latinitas* and the technical French legal vocabulary that resembled it in its obscurity. This community of clerks, which he rendered absurd by its impenetrable and thus pointless erudition, was clearly one that had a presence in secular court and that his audience would recognize but to which it did not belong. Beaumanoir likely had a command of Latin, but the lofty erudition it exuded was an obstacle to him and his readers. It changed the way people thought and spoke, even the way they spoke in their vernacular,

---

[1] 'Les clercs on une maniere a parler mou bele selonc le Latin; mes li lai qui ont a pliedier contre aus en court laie n'entendent pas bien les mos meismes qu'il dient en François, tout soit il bel et convenable au plet. Et pour ce, de ce qui plus souvent est dit en la cour laie et don't plus grant mestiers est, nous traiterons en cest chapitre en tele maniere que li lai puissant entendre' (Beaumanoir, *Coutumes de Beauvaisis*, ed. Salmon, VI.196).

and the aesthetics of the language overshadowed the transmission of meaning.

Implicit in Beaumanoir's statement was a theory of language. He saw that language had the power both to unite and to separate communities. He foreshadowed modern ordinary language philosophy and the simple language movement when he envisioned communication and the conveyance of meaning as the purpose of language. This was also a commentary on legal language, specifically, and its need for specialized jargon that made it difficult to understand, even without linguistic barriers. Less explicitly, Beaumanoir intimated how legal language in the vernacular developed at least partially via clerks who were refining, importing and creating words. Beaumanoir was thus conscious of the role of language in law, and of how that role was changing in his own time.

Language is fundamental to law; indeed, it is difficult to imagine the possibility of law without words or communication. Speech, for instance, is constitutive of the fundamental power to do justice: jurisdiction is literally the ability to speak, to articulate, and to voice the law. The language of law is one of the most important types of language spoken by a community.[2] It creates relationships between people, and between people and things. As Robert Cover has noted, 'law is a resource in signification that enables us to submit, rejoice, struggle, pervert, mock, disgrace, humiliate, or dignify'.[3] With words, one has a marriage, a lord–vassal relationship, or even property – words create a 'mine' and a 'yours'. These concepts are encoded in language in a way that cannot be dissociated from society and culture. Legal concepts, in other words, have a cultural as well as a linguistic specificity.[4] Their expression also has a political valence, as language is a form of symbolic power that both includes and excludes, legitimizes and delegitimizes.[5]

A shift in language necessarily involves a conceptual shift as well as an ideological and cultural one. The thirteenth-century vernacular *coutumiers* of northern France were testimony to such a shift as, outside the Norman texts, *coutumier* authors chose to write in the

---

[2] Berman, *Law and Language*, p. 64.
[3] Robert Cover, 'Nomos and Narrative', p. 100.
[4] Mattila, 'Legal Vocabulary', p. 28.
[5] See generally Bourdieu, *Language and Symbolic Power*.

vernacular instead of in Latin. Hence, they chose not to be part of the cultural and political world of Latinity, a world that rested on a matured ideological role of Latin as the language of authority and tradition, and one that was linked to the prestigious category of *Romanitas*.[6]

The thirteenth century saw the development of a vernacular law, a law written in the language of speech and practice, and on the subject of the speech and practice of lay courts. The vernacular turn in law was thus partially a shift in message and partially a shift in the parties who communicated that message. Written custom made legal ideas available to a new audience and made them something knowable in an erudite way outside of academic circles. This writing of custom as captured in the *coutumiers* was part of a larger, Europe-wide vernacular legal revolution, one that should be recognized alongside the legal revolution in the twelfth century. The *coutumiers* were thus the product of two contemporaneous movements: first, the development of the category of custom as a form of law and the flourishing of legal literature devoted to the subject in many milieus; and second, a flourishing in legal writing devoted to custom in many milieus and a new wave of general vernacular writing that swept Europe.

Cultures of Latinity and Vernacularity

Beaumanoir's valuation of the vernacular followed a line of writers and translators who had made it a written language and a viable alternative to Latin. By the time he was writing, in the early 1280s, vernacular writing was all around him – in epics, romances, songbooks, translations of university texts, and court chanceries. Law courts, chanceries, and aristocratic institutions were making a strategic move to the vernacular as the language of secular power, in a way similar to the clergy's harnessing of the ideological role of

---

[6] For the special function of Latinity in the medieval West, see Nicholas Watson, 'The Idea of Latinity', pp. 124ff. The ideological function of Latin did not extend beyond the Christian West, where Latin was a comparatively impoverished language in the world of learning, leading Roger Bacon to complain that translators could not find enough vocabulary in Latin to translate properly from Arabic (see Szpiech, 'Latin as a Language of Authoritative Tradition', p. 67).

Latin.[7] However, the expansion of the vernacular into the written culture of these was slow, gradual, and not inevitable.[8] The use of the vernacular was not normalized in these spaces until the fourteenth century in France and occurred first in princely chanceries and later in the royal chancery.[9]

Latin had long been understood as having a universalizing tendency. From antiquity, Latin culture and its language would imagine itself as 'powerful beyond all competitors'.[10] In the medieval period, Guillaume Durand (d. 1296) succinctly summarized the cultural imperialism of Latin in his explanation of the trinity of languages in which to worship God: 'Thus God is praised in three languages, namely Hebrew, which by law is the mother of all languages; Greek, which is the teacher; and Latin, which is the empress, on account of the dominion of the Roman empire and of the Papacy.'[11]

In turn, this perceived universality of Latin was contrasted to the confused multiplicity of other tongues, cast as 'vulgar', 'rustic', or 'barbaric'.[12] The topos of comparative impoverishment in antiquity was that of an inferior Latin in comparison to a noble Greek.[13] In the Middle Ages, this was transposed to the relationship between the inferior vernacular and noble Latin.[14] Giles of Rome in his *De regimine principum*, written for Philip IV around 1280, expresses this clearly when he observed that Latin was invented because the vulgar tongue could not perfectly express philosophical matters, so philosophers 'invented for themselves an idiom effectively their own, which is called Latin, or the lettered idiom, which they made so broad

---

[7] Geary, *Language and Power in the Early Middle Ages*, p. 58 and chap. 3 generally.

[8] *Ibid.*, p. 56.

[9] Lusignan, *La langue des rois au Moyen Âge*, p. 112 (chap. 3 generally). French kings start paying a lot of attention to the linguistic policy of their court: it is still fundamentally Latin until the death of Philip V in 1322; French dominates in the reign of Philip VI, though there is some back and forth before the great ordinances of the sixteenth century (*ibid.*, pp. 112ff). This can be seen after 1305 in Chancery records and after 1375 in the registers of Parliament (Claude Gauvard, 'La justice du roi de France et le latin à la fin du Moyen Âge', p. 33).

[10] Joseph Farrell, *Latin Language*, p. 5. In fact, Latin was gendered masculine as paternal speech while the vernacular was gendered feminine as maternal tongue (*ibid.*, p. 52). For more on Latin as *patria lingua* and the vernacular as *materno sermone*, see Szpiech, 'Latin as a Language of Authoritative Tradition'.

[11] 'et latina, que imperatrix est propter Romani dominium imperii, et papatus' (Szpiech, 'Latin as a Language of Authoritative Tradition', p. 65).

[12] Farrell, *Latin Language*, pp. 4–5.   [13] *Ibid.*, p. 28.   [14] *Ibid.*

and copious that they could adequately express all their meanings through it'.[15] Latin, a contender in the search for the perfect language described by Umberto Eco, was, for Giles, a language for philosophers to express all meanings.

While Latin facilitated communication, ably expressed ideas, and created community, from the outside the use of Latin as well as the tendency towards abstraction and technical terms isolated the scholar from laymen. One of the consequences of the development of scholastic intellectuals was the formation of an 'intellectual technocracy'.[16] At the same time, scholars have shown that the medieval university, at least by the thirteenth century, was not an insular ivory tower: just as sermon collections produced in the universities were preached in modified form for lay audiences, significant numbers of university graduates as well as masters obtained gainful employment in administration.[17]

Only an extreme minority still used Latin as a language of communication at the end of the Middle Ages.[18] Even by the end of the thirteenth century, it was primarily the church that still used Latin while the vernacular expanded across many royal, princely, and merchant chanceries of the West, and French had emerged, notably, as a competing language of communication and diplomacy internationally.[19] Indeed, the fairly swift dominance of the vernacular as a language of law beginning in the second half of the thirteenth century could also be seen in Spain, the crusader states, Italy, Germany, and England (first French and then, in the later fourteenth century, English).

The shift in the language of conceptual ideas adds another layer to this. It occurred in the same period as the beginning of vernacular record-keeping and showed that vernacular writing was not just for fixing the memory of facts and events but also for formulating and transmitting wider themes and complex ideas. Those localities that had

---

[15] '*invenerunt sibi quasi proprium idioma, quod dicitur latinum, vel idioma literale: quod constituerunt adeo latum et copiosum, ut per ipsum possent omnes suos conceptus sufficienter exprimere*', Giles of Rome in Nicholas Watson, 'The Idea of Latinity', p. 135.
[16] Jacques Le Goff, *Intellectuals in the Middle Ages*, p. 117.
[17] Adam Jeffrey Davis, *The Holy Bureaucrat*, pp. 12–13.
[18] Geary, 'What Happened to Latin?', 859, 864.   [19] *Ibid.*, 864.

been shaping French into a language of law were simultaneously experiencing a florescence of other types of writing in the vernacular – from literature to historiography – and these must be seen as associated movements.[20]

Written production in the French vernacular was principally in verse form throughout the twelfth century, with the *Song of Roland* as the most famous example. Prose only took off as a medium of writing in the thirteenth century.[21] The great watershed was Villehardouin's history of the Fourth Crusade (ca. 1210), the first vernacular history in French. It was quickly followed by inspiring tales of knighthood such as *Graal* (ca. 1220) and *Lancelot-Graal* (1125–1230) that linked the Holy Land to the mainland and were written in a literary style that reverberated even in the narratives of contemporary charters that were beginning to use the vernacular.[22]

The first half of the thirteenth century also saw translations into French of various subjects originally written in Latin as part of the *translatio studii*, the idea that learning was transferred from Greece through Rome to France. These translations ranged across literature, philosophy, law, medicine, theology, and history and should be seen as a true movement that changed the shape and nature of knowledge. Not all scholarly *auctoritates* were translated. The works that were translated tended to be those used in university teaching and all belonged to the medieval corpus of *auctoritates*.[23] Many of these translations were not direct translations that sought to transmit original meaning but individual products that reshaped and reinterpreted the source text for a new public.[24] Translation was often an act of creation itself that took on a life of its own afterwards. Moral poetry, for instance, was translated from the Latin and then followed by diverse imitations or innovations.[25] An increasingly discerning and literate aristocratic and bourgeois public, wary of ever more fabulous heroic deeds recounted in *chansons de*

---

[20] Lusignan, *La langue des rois*, pp. 60ff.   [21] *Ibid.*, p. 23.   [22] *Ibid.*

[23] Lusignan, *Parler vulgairement*, p. 131.

[24] Jeanette Beer, 'Medieval Translations', p. 729.

[25] Gaston Paris, *La littérature française au Moyen Âge*, p. 150. He cites *Les Droits au clerc de Voudai* as an example of these imitations. This poem appears in one manuscript of the *Établissements de Saint Louis*, where four stanzas from this *Dit* are selected to open the text of the *Coutumes d'Orléans* that form Book II (Book I, or the *Coutumes de Touraine et Anjou*, is completely absent in this manuscript version).

geste, stimulated an appetite for 'true' historical texts in vernacular prose.[26] A range of topics and interests became newly accessible through the vernacular, in different forms and on different themes.

The move to the vernacular developed alongside Latin literary culture. It was propelled by a 'cultural exuberance' energized by a new confidence in and refinement of vernacular culture and language.[27] In the twelfth century, great literary works began to be written in French; in the thirteenth century this literature expanded to include great chronicles such as Primat's *Grandes Chroniques de France* and juridical works like the *coutumiers*; in the fourteenth century this expanded further to massive political works composed in the vernacular that theorized royal power, such as Everart de Trémaugon's *Songe du vergier* (1378).

Beyond that, various works originally written in a vernacular were translated into Latin, such as Marco Polo's travels or the *Coutumes de Beauvaisis*, and even a French Troy romance that the Italian jurist Guido della Colonna (d. after 1287) hoped to make accessible to those who can read 'grammar' – '*qui grammaticam legunt!*'.[28] Guido della Colonna identified Latin with grammar and with a system of language. Dante elucidated this when he wrote the first treatise on the literary use of the vernacular, *De vulgari eloquentia*. Vernacular, he explained, was the language that 'children learn from those around them', without any rules, to be distinguished from what the ancient Romans called 'grammar,' a secondary language only gained through 'the expense of much time and study' – the one is 'natural to us, while the latter is more an artificial creation'.[29] As he explained, a theory of the correct usage of the vernacular is necessary to everyone (even, he noted, to women and children so far as they could understand it).[30] He was writing for this reason – to be of service to the speech of common people.

The first writing in the vernacular was done close to or as part of traditional centres of knowledge – the church and the academy. As is well known, the majority of *litterati* were clerics, so *laicus* acquired the

---

[26] Colin C. Smith, 'The Vernacular', p. 81.
[27] Jan M. Ziolkowski, 'Latin and Vernacular Literature', p. 664.
[28] Beer, 'Medieval Translations', p. 731.
[29] Alighieri Dante, *Literature in the Vernacular*, I.1.
[30] Dante, *Literature in the Vernacular*.

connotation of illiteracy because of the lack of knowledge of Latin –
literate meant clerical, and illiterate meant everyone else.[31] The
relationship between Latin and the vernacular was originally
'symbiotic and convivial', or certainly at the very least 'dialectical'.[32]

Nonetheless, the language of a text would have an effect both on
audience and extent of transmission. Some authors were acutely
conscious of this already in the late-twelfth and early-thirteenth
century, when writing in the vernacular was just beginning to spread.
This is apparent in Walter Map's (ca. 1140–1209) comments to Gerald
of Wales (1147–1223) that:

> your writings are far more praiseworthy and lasting than my words; yet
> because mine are easy to follow and in the vernacular, while yours are in
> Latin, which is understood by fewer folk, I have carried off a reasonable
> reward while you and your distinguished writings have not been adequately
> rewarded; because learned and generous princes have long since vanished from
> the world.[33]

The implication was that sophistication and dissemination were not
necessarily positively correlated, and that writing in the vernacular
could reach many more people and was a desirable and remunerable
skill in princely chanceries or archives. Though there is a sense of
nostalgia for sophisticated esoterica composed in a language only
accessible to the select few, there is no doubt that the wider
dissemination of ideas is tied to a comprehensibility that the
vernacular offers but that Latin cannot.

Perhaps views such as these caused the congenial relationship between
Latin and the vernacular to deteriorate in the thirteenth century.[34] Latin
was transformed from the universal language of communication to the
distrusted language of obfuscation, a thought well captured by Emperor
Rudolf of Hapsburg when he decreed that privileges should be recorded
in the vernacular 'because the difficulty of laymen was giving birth
to errors and great doubts and deceiving laymen'.[35] Indeed, as the

---

[31] Clanchy, *From Memory to Written Record*; Ziolkowski, 'Latin and Vernacular
Literature', p. 660.
[32] Ziolkowski, 'Latin and Vernacular Literature', pp. 658–9; and Gauvard, 'La justice
du roi de France et le latin à la fin du Moyen Âge', pp. 31–53).
[33] Ziolkowski, 'Latin and Vernacular Literature', p. 659.
[34] Ziolkowski, 'Latin and Vernacular Literature', pp. 658–9.
[35] Geary, 'What Happened to Latin?', 863.

next section shows, vernacular moments in legal writing became a veritable vernacular movement by the mid-thirteenth century.[36]

The French language was already fulfilling many types of function, such as being a medium of communication within the family and in civic society, by the thirteenth century and then also became a strong competitor as the language of administration. It was even important to clerks whose grouping into 'nations' at the university level showed the importance of the vernacular as a mode of communication between them.[37] Even at the highest levels of education, then, there was a bilingualism that situated Latin as a second language – albeit aureate and distinguished – specific to learning certain bodies of knowledge, religious, scientific, or otherwise.[38] As for legal writing in texts like the *coutumiers*, Serge Lusignan has noted, Ile-de-France French and Picard were the most popular dialects.[39]

There was also an idea that certain genres would tend to be written in one language or another because they were naturally paired. Raimon Vidal de Besalù (1160–1210), for instance, held that French should be used for romances and pastourelles, while Limousin should be used for verses, *cansos*, and *sirventes*.[40] Dante, on the other hand, explained that the *langue d'oc* was the better language for lyric while the *langue d'oïl* was better for narrative.[41] In a similar manner, there does seem to have been a sense by the mid-thirteenth century – certainly in northern France – that the subject matter of the *coutumiers* was a vernacular one.

Writing Vernacular Law

The *coutumiers* marked lay secular justice as a sphere of vernacular knowledge. Rita Copeland describes how vernacular writing 'authorize[d] itself by taking over the function of academic discourse'.[42]

---

[36] And was certainly not restricted to Christian culture (Kirsten Anne Fudeman, *Vernacular Voices: Language and Identity in Medieval French Jewish Communities*).
[37] Lusignan, *Parler vulgairement*, p. 35.
[38] Lusignan, *Parler vulgairement*.
[39] See Chapter 5.   [40] Ziolkowski, 'Latin and Vernacular Literature', p. 668.
[41] Dante, *Literature in the Vernacular*, X; Ziolkowski, 'Latin and Vernacular Literature', p. 668. He says this in the context of not wanting to choose a best or favourite French dialect, and then turns to an analysis of Italian vernaculars (Dante, *Literature in the Vernacular*, X).
[42] Rita Copeland, *Rhetoric, Hermeneutics, and Translation*, p. 8.

The *coutumiers* were self-authorizing works in the field of law. They participated in the construction of 'vernacular legality', where the vernacular was used self-consciously to explore a previously Latinate realm of authoritative and specialized legal knowledge and practice.[43] The *coutumiers* embody this self-conscious vernacularization of knowledge and self-authorization of a discourse of power.

The *coutumiers* were not the oldest vernacular law but – as a group – they were emblematic of the cultural shift and arguably its best representatives. Earlier lawbooks both in the vernacular and in Latin were close thematic and geographic kin to the vernacular *coutumiers*. However, after the author of the *Coutumes d'Anjou et du Maine* and Pierre de Fontaines wrote about the practice of lay courts in the vernacular, other *coutumier* authors in northern France continued to write in the vernacular. They consistently chose the French vernacular for texts that described the rules and procedures of the secular courts in the thirteenth century, and even the earlier treatises were soon translated into vernacular form.[44]

The oldest 'legal' text written in French was found in the record of the oaths exchanged by Louis the Pious' sons at Strasbourg in 842. This was an early appearance of the vernacular in France, although it was not without precedent, as kings in England had already composed laws in Old English.[45] However, it was really from the end of the eleventh

---

[43] Bruce Holsinger, 'Vernacular Legality', p. 157. Holsinger concentrates on spheres of legal knowing outside 'official legal culture' here, but this idea easily extends to official spheres.

[44] See Ada Maria Kuskowski, '*Lingua Franca Legalis*?'. In the fourteenth century, furthermore, the *coutumiers* continued to be written in French, while treatises on some more specialized subjects might be in Latin. The latter is exemplified by procedural tracts, such as Guillaume Dubreuil's *Stylus Curie parliament Franciae* of 1330 (Charles Aubertin, *Histoire de la langue et de la littérature*, p. 501).

[45] Æthelberht's laws for the kingdom of Kent (early seventh century) were the first attempt by a Germanic-speaking people to record laws in their own language, probably more due to local circumstances than to a specific awareness or investment in the vernacular and its possibilities (Stefan Jurasinski and Lisi Oliver, *The Laws of Alfred: The Domboc and the Making of Anglo-Saxon Law*, p. 4). Ine's laws and Alfred's *Domboc*, written in Wessex, were composed in part to be broadcast outside the kingdom, showing that the development of vernacular writing could be associated with an extra-territorial and outward-looking vision (*ibid.*, p. 51). For more on the Old English Laws, see Wormald, *The Making of English Law*; T. B. Lambert, *Law and Order in Anglo-Saxon England*.

century onward that literary production in French experienced an astonishing acceleration, a huge diversification, and an impressive geographical expansion.[46]

Beyond records of practice, legal thought found its vernacular voice when sets of rules for communities started to be written down in French. The first charters in French appeared at the end of the twelfth and beginning of the thirteenth century as part of a movement in the north that began in the north-east in Tournai, Arras, Saint-Omer, and other towns.[47] The *Establissements de Rouen* were composed between 1160 and 1170, and while they intended to describe the organization and nature of the government of Rouen, this set of rules became the basis for many other collections of city customs. The thirteenth-century *Livre Roisin*, often included in the *coutumier* corpus, was in fact a text on the customs of the city of Lille.

There was also a development, formalization, and specialization of diplomatic documents throughout the thirteenth century and beyond.[48] Before this time, public ritual and witness testimony were the domain of legal memory, and charters were memory markers for the rituals that had publicly established an agreement or change in status or fact.[49] Witnesses guaranteed that a charter would be upheld, rather than abstract notions of law.[50] The increase in charter-writing was related to changes in the law of proof, and the changing status of the judicial duel encouraged the placement of greater value on written proof.[51] The Fourth Lateran Council (1215) banned the involvement

[46] Dorothea Kullmann, introduction to Kullmann (ed.), *The Church and Vernacular Literature*, p. 1. Kullmann writes that the first writing in the vernacular must have been done by clerics as they were the ones who were educated to read and write, and the birth of the written vernacular should not automatically be seen as the birth of lay/profane writing, though by the late eleventh century there is a clear movement in lay vernacular writing (*ibid.*, pp. 1–4).

[47] Lusignan, *La langue des rois*, pp. 46–7. That various aspects of public life were finding written expression in the vernacular can also be seen in the development of early vernacular plays at a similar time, see Carol Symes, 'The Appearance of Early Vernacular Plays'; for a brief survey on the general rise of European vernaculars, see Thomas Brunner, 'Le passage aux langues vernaculaires'.

[48] For a description of these, see Robert-Henri Bautier, 'Typologie diplomatique'.

[49] Lusignan, *La langue des rois*, pp. 31ff.

[50] As Steven D. White shows for the *laudatio parentum* (Stephen D. White, *Customs, Kinship and Gifts to Saints*).

[51] *Ibid.*, p. 28.

of priests in the unilateral ordeal, crippling this method of proof and paving the way for its eventual abandonment in favour of inquisitorial procedure.[52] Louis IX's prohibition of the judicial duel in the mid-thirteenth century was purely for the royal domain, and the practice continued to be deeply entrenched in dispute resolution long afterwards; nonetheless, the prohibition of the duel did create opportunities and impetus for the increasing use of written proof alongside orality, performance, and ritual. [53]

Simultaneous to these developments was the first effort to bring academic law outside of the academy. A collection known as *Lo Codi* appeared in the South of France around 1160. It was a product of the new university learning – basically a *summa* of Justinian's Code – but differed from other transmissions of the *ius commune* such as Roger II's *Assises* because it was written in the Provençal vernacular (the desirability of such material in the vernacular is attested by its later translation into French, Castilian, and Catalan).[54] As a liberal rehashing of Roman sources, *Lo Codi* already evinced some aspects of reinvention that would form the basis of vernacular legal writing and its general approach to description, truth, normativity, and authority.

In the 1230s a great age of translation began, and some of the most important authorities found their vernacular voice. The Bible, for instance, was translated into French around 1230.[55] Likewise, the vernacular shift in the language of conceptual law began in earnest. This first occurred in the form of translations from Latin into the vernacular of the various texts of the *Corpus iuris civilis*, Tancred's *Ordo*, Gratian's *Decretum*, and papal decretals.[56]

Translations of Roman Latin legal texts into the vernacular have only just begun to be studied, and the manuscripts do not seem to have

---

[52] Finbarr McAuley, 'Canon Law and the End of the Ordeal', 473ff.

[53] Gauvard, *'De grace especial'*, pp. 172ff. Gauvard notes that Beaumanoir sees the judicial duel as a necessary tool for the great criminal cases. It was not a procedure used only by lay folk but also appeared in thirteenth-century records of the court of the bishop of Paris in cases of murder and rape/abduction (*ibid.*, p. 174).

[54] See for instance André Gouron, 'Du nouveau sur Lo Codi'. Hermann Fitting seems to have published an edition of the text, and F. R. P. Akehurst is currently working on an English translation.

[55] Olivier-Martin, *Les institutes de Justinien en français*, p. xvi, n. 2.

[56] *Li ordinaire de maistre Tancrez*, BnF, ms.fr. 1073; Leena Löfstedt, *Gratiani decretum*.

been systematically catalogued or analysed. The work done thus far has focused on vernacular versions of Justinian's *Institutes* and the Norman *Summa* (both of which were translated into vernacular prose as well as vernacular verse) and Azo's *Summa*.[57] In these initiatives we can see the drive to make sophisticated legal learning more widely accessible.[58] In the vernacular version of Azo's *Summa*, the translator was a person who knew both Latin and the Roman civil law well but used simple language in order to reach potential law students, practitioners with no Latin, or students preparing to study the texts in Latin.[59] The translator of Justinian's *Institutes* into French verse, for example, made explicit that he was translating to provide a vernacular text to make the Latin easier to learn.[60]

Once written, of course, these translations made that knowledge available to anyone with an interest in law and the ability to read or hear the text read aloud, a common way of connecting with texts in this period. All legal translators combined two cultures: the Latin and the vernacular. They navigated between these worlds, disseminating ideas by word of mouth and by vernacular versions of Latin texts. Yet, once translated, the vernacular versions of Roman law no longer belonged to the cultural world of the original Latin texts.[61] They were reoriented as part of a different language and cultural context and were now one type of literature among many being swept into the new and large category of vernacular legal literature. The first *coutumiers* were composed in this context, part of a larger foment in thinking about custom and law in the vernacular.

---

[57] Félix Olivier-Martin, *Les institutes de Justinien en français*; Lavigne, 'La traduction en vers des *Institutes*'; Kuskowski, 'Translating Justinian'; Biu, 'La *Somme Acé*'.
[58] This was a preoccupation for learned jurists, as Gérard Giordanengo noted: 'learned doctrine aims above all at having an influence on contemporary social life' (Giordanengo, 'Les droit savants au Moyen Âge', 446).
[59] See generally Biu, 'La *Somme Acé*', 417ff.
[60] 'A commencier ceste besoigne / Ne met ung enfant de gascogne / Qui m'est baillie a introduyre / Et a ensaigner et a duyre / Et a tenir lay bien soubz pie. / Se il veult garder suvent / Il y pourra asses aprendre / Et plus legierement entendre / Le Latin quant il le verra / Et trouver ce qu'il querra.' (Lavigne, 'La traduction en vers des *Institutes*', 515, ll. 21–32). This hints that students bound for university may not have the best knowledge of Latin and that, before going off to university and studying the text in Latin, it helped to know it in the vernacular, preferably learning it by heart, as facilitated by this verse translation.
[61] Kuskowski, 'Translating Justinian'.

Nonetheless, the first text in this corpus, the *Très ancien coutumier de Normandie*, was most likely composed initially in Latin.[62] The first part of this text was likely written before 1204 and thus reflects a united Anglo-Norman realm and a tradition of Anglo-Norman legal writing.[63] Since the Conquest, this had largely been in Latin with the exception of the *Leis Willelme* (mid-twelfth century).[64] The *Leis Willelme* was written in French and only later in Latin but was part of a series of works referred to as the 'Leges,' which were otherwise written in Latin and presented as the laws of specific English kings.[65] And indeed, the first English lawbooks followed this tradition and focused on royal jurisdiction and Latin writing: *Tractatus de legibus et consuetudinibus Anglie* or 'Glanvill' from the late twelfth century and *De legibus et consuetudinibus Angliæ* or 'Bracton' from a little before the mid-thirteenth.[66] French-language works on the English common law – *Casus Placitorum, Fet Assaver, Brevia Placitata* – appeared in the 1250s and 1260s.[67]

[62] *Coutumiers de Normandie*, ed. Tardif, vol. 1, pp. xc–xciii.
[63] For the dating of the text, see Eves, 'The *Antiqua consuetudo Normannie*, or "Part One" of the *Très Ancien Coutumier of Normandy*'.
[64] Hudson, *The Oxford History of the Laws of England*, vol 2, p. 865. In contrast to thinking and speaking law, which was done in French and English vernaculars (*ibid.*).
[65] *Ibid.*, pp. 869–70.
[66] An initial text was composed in the 1220s and 1230s and revised successively through the 1240s by various royal justices, of which Henry de Bratton was the most significant reviser, writing in the 1250s (Paul Brand, 'The Date and Authorship of Bracton: A Response', 217ff; Hudson, *The Oxford History of the Laws of England*, vol 2, p. 873; see generally, McSweeney, *Priests of the Law*).
[67] Multilingualism in England and the place of French within it has its own particular history. The French vernacular arrived in an England that was already highly multilingual, home to a mix of Latin and Celtic, Germanic, and Scandinavian vernaculars (Thelma S. Fenster and Carolyn P. Collette, *The French of Medieval England*, p. 1). 'Anglo-Norman' conventionally denoted the French language in England in the twelfth and thirteenth centuries – after this the term 'Anglo-French' is used – but these terms reflected more ethno-nationalist projects of the nineteenth and twentieth centuries than historical realities and are better replaced with 'The French of England' (Jocelyn Wogan-Browne et al., 'General Introduction: What's in a Name: The "French" of "England"', p. 1ff). French became a second language in England for a greater portion of its users in a way that resembled Latin; it was notably important in court circles (Lusignan, 'French Language and Contact with English', pp. 19–20). Legal professionals such as judges and lawyers had to have a solid command of French because, while records were kept generally in Latin, the spoken language of legal proceedings was French (Paul Brand, 'The Languages of the Law in Late Medieval England', pp. 63ff). The French of England was exported to various parts of the British Isles: Wales, Ireland, Scotland, and Gascony (Lusignan, 'French

The second part of the *Très ancien coutumier de Normandie* was composed around 1220, also most likely in Latin, and was an expression of Norman law after the French conquest of Normandy.[68] The French translation of the *Très ancient coutumier de Normandie* cannot be definitively dated but likely occurred around the 1230s and, by this time, the two parts of the text were united.[69] In Normandy around this time other short legal compilations were composed at least partially in French, for instance, the *Assises de Normandie*, which recorded judgments but was organized by subject matter and aimed to distill rules, rather than provide accounts of cases.[70]

Coutumiers composed in the French vernacular appeared soon afterwards, starting with the *Coutumes d'Anjou et du Maine* (1246) and Pierre de Fontaines' *Conseil* (1253). The only exception to this was the Norman *Summa de legibus* (1254–1258), which was likely first composed in Latin.[71] The author translated oral aspects of trials

Language and Contact with English', pp. 22ff). Despite the importance of French, it was Latin that dominated English chanceries, which might partially be explained by the clerical composition of the chancery though more likely was a perception of Latin as more solemn and authoritative (Lusignan, *La langue des rois au Moyen Âge*, pp. 186–7).

[68] John W. Baldwin, *The Government of Philip Augustus: Foundations of French Royal Power in the Middle Ages*, p. 226. There is some variation between the Latin and French texts, but the French was largely faithful to the Latin (*see Coutumiers de Normandie*, ed. Tardif, vol. 1, pp. lxxxvii–xc).

[69] *Ibid.*, p. xciv.

[70] The *Assises de Normandie* discusses cases in the manner indicated that were held between 1234 and 1237 in Falaise, Cean, and Rouen, and the *Arrêts de l'Échiquier de Normandie* recorded cases held between 1207 and 1245 in the same places (Marnier, *Établissements et coutumes, assises et arrêts de l'Échiquier de Normandie*). Marnier's edition also includes a thirteenth-century text he calls the *Établissements et coutumes de Normandie au treisième siècle*, and though he does not provide a more specific date, all of these texts were sources for the Norman *Summa de legibus*, so this text must have been written before the latter (*ibid.*, p. xviii). Marnier provides the French texts. Several manuscripts have the *Assises de Normandie* in Latin, which was probably the original language. Léopold Delisle grouped these with other texts in order to bring together all of these early accounts of the workings of the Norman Exchequer under the Capetians ('Mémoire sur les recueils de jugements rendu par l'Échiquier de Normandie' in *Recueil de jugements de l'echiquier de Normandie au XIIIe siècle (1207–1270)*, ed. Delisle, p. 277).

[71] The identity of the original language of the text produced much debate among scholars in the nineteenth century (*ibid.*, pp. cxxxiii–cxl). Ultimately, Latin was generally accepted by scholars as the original langue of the *Summa*. Tardif explained the reasons for a preference for Latin as an original version: a late thirteenth-century

from French into Latin and drew on Latin original texts, such as formulas for writs.[72] There could be several reasons for this choice of Latin. The Norman *Summa* is very different from the two vernacular *coutumiers* that preceded it, and there does not seem to be a connection between them. It was probably less a choice against the vernacular than a choice to follow an established tradition of writing law in Latin. The texts that preceded the *Summa* in Normandy – 'Glanvill' and the two texts that came together as the *Très ancien coutumier* – were also first composed in Latin, which may still have seemed the obvious language to the author for such a work. The choice of Latin could also reflect the administrative practices that developed under the Angevins and continued under the Capetians.[73] Norman cartularies also show that Normandy held on to Latin longer than other areas of France.[74] And as the author seems to have been a cleric with scholastic and legal educations, he was just the sort of person likely to prefer Latin over the vernacular.

verse translation was made based on the Latin text; a particularly beautiful manuscript was made in the city of Rouen in the early fourteenth century containing the Latin text alone; a fifteenth-century glossator refers to the Latin text to resolve controversy; the first printed editions are of the French version but included the Latin text afterwards; lawyers referred to a Latin text in their pleadings in 1558 preceding the reformed custom; and the Latin text has a style and clarity of exposition that Tardif says are characteristic of original works (*ibid.*, p. cxxxiv, cxxxvii–cxl). It is likely in this period that a text would have been written in Latin and then translated into French rather than the other way around. Nonetheless, the fact that the manuscript tradition does not constitute an especially strong case for Latin shows the importance and circulation of the text in both languages.

[72] Viollet, 'Les Coutumiers de Normandie', 87–8.

[73] Records of cases from the Norman Exchequer were kept already in the first decades of the thirteenth century, while French kings only started keeping such records in 1254, and other princely courts later. Léopold Delisle showed where we can see continuity (Delisle, 'Mémoire sur les recueils de jugements rendu par l'Échiquier de Normandie', pp. 247ff, especially pp. 267ff). The sources that preserved these records were not very interested in questions of fact; they mostly elide what actually happened in judicial proceedings, often skip the names of parties, and do not provide much description of procedure – they focused on questions of law (*ibid.*, p. 280). We only have these unofficial records though it is probably the case that official records were kept as well (*ibid.*, p.1).

[74] Lusignan, *La langue des rois au Moyen Âge*, pp. 58–9. Lusignan provides the example of the barony of Bricquebec in the Contentin region, whose first entry in the French vernacular dates from 1269, and the first produced by the lords of Bricquebec from 1280. This is decades later than in other regions (see *ibid.*, pp. 52ff).

The *Livre de Jostice et de Plet* (ca. 1260) was also a vernacular work. It used French translations of the learned laws and tried to bring practice or lived experiences closer to university legal learning. Here, an author who had likely studied both Roman and canon law at Orleans incorporated tens of case descriptions into this text of translated Roman law and the *Decretals* of Gregory IX.[75] The author 'medievalized' his sources, not only translating technical Latin terms into familiar French ones but also redefining them and modifying their context.[76] This 'medievalizing' was comparable to that of 'the matter of Rome', whose writers adapted antique literature and subjects for a medieval audience by treating Alexander the Great and Achilles as medieval knights or by adding tournaments to narratives.[77]

Authors in other milieus were also writing about custom in the vernacular. The *Rolls of Oleron* and other expressions of maritime law were composed in the French vernacular, which was the common language of maritime activity.[78] Louis IX commissioned Etienne Boileau, the provost of Paris, to compile the customs of merchants and artisans of the city, which he did in a text titled the *Livre des Métiers* (ca. 1268).

Vernacular *coutumiers* appeared in Northern France in quick succession. The French translation of the Norman *Summa*, the *Grand coutumier de Normandie*, was likely completed shortly after 1270.[79] The *Établissements de Saint Louis* (1272/3) was followed by *Le livre des constitutions demenées et Chastelet de Paris* (between 1279 and 1282), Philippe de Beaumanoir's *Coutumes de Beauvaisis* (1283), *L'ancien coutumier de Champagne* (ca. 1295), the *Coutumier*

---

[75] Ribémont, 'Compiling and Writing a Legal Treatise in French: *The Livre de Jostice et de Plet*', pp. 133–4.

[76] *Ibid.*, p. 135.   [77] *Ibid.*, p. 141.   [78] Marianne Kowaleski, 'The French of England'.

[79] The French text clearly refers to Louis IX's successor and so indicates that Louis IX was dead at the time (*Coutumiers de Normandie*, ed. Tardif, vol. 2, p. clxxxi). This French text was also presented under several different titles, such as *Les constitutions de Normandie, Les droiz et les usages de Normandie, Livre de droit et des usages de Normandie, Livre de la coutume de Normandie, Livre coutumier de pays et duché de Normandie*, and many manuscripts provide no designation at all (Viollet, 'Les Coutumiers de Normandie', 68).

FIGURE 2.1 The *Summa de legibus normannie*/*Grand coutumier de Normandie* in French verse, often attributed to Guillaume Chapu. The author of the French verse translation of the Norman *Summa* in this manuscript explains near the end of the text (fol. 301r–301v) that he chose to translate into French verse rather than prose so that lawyers could learn the text by heart because rhymed language is easier to learn and more beautiful. This fourteenth-century manuscript was thick (301 folios) but very small (97x60 mm) and could easily be carried around and studied for memorization. *Grand coutumier de Normandie en vers*, Bibliothèque nationale de France, ms. Fr. 14548, fol. 31v.

d'Artois (between 1283 and 1302), and *Li usages de Bourgogne* (end of the thirteenth century). The Norman *Summa*, seen in Figure 2.1, was translated into verse (c. 1280).[80] Justinian's *Institutes rymees*, a French verse translation of the *Institutes*, was composed by a different versifier.[81] Together, the authors of these texts created a powerful 'idea of the vernacular' for the legal sphere.[82]

A type of diglossia thus emerged within legal communities. Multilingual individuals who functioned both in Latin and the vernacular began differentiating between the two languages based on subject matter, function, and context.[83] The written vernacular created a new discourse that was informed by Latin writing and vernacular orality but also departed from them (and likely in turn influenced Latin).[84] The written vernacular was transformed into a grapholect, a 'low'-language dialect 'taken over by writing' different from the oral by virtue of its prestige, expanded lexicon, and ability to express abstraction.[85] Law was thus changing as it developed as a discrete subject matter, in writing, and in the vernacular.

French as a language of law and of power was not limited to the territories of the French kings. The vernacular *lingua franca legalis* had a wide geographical range that spanned from the crusader states to

---

[80] *Ancien Coutumier en vers* in David Hoüard, *Dictionnaire analytique, historique, étymologique, critique et interprétatif de la coutume de Normandie*, vol. 4, *Supplément*, p. 50. This versifier worked from a Latin text, which can be seen in his own assertion of doing so as well as the fact that the verse version includes many passages that are in the Latin version but missing in the French prose version (Viollet, 'Les Coutumiers de Normandie', 113). The verse translation is commonly attributed to Guillaume Cauph following the argument of Paul Viollet, based on the translator identifying his surname as C.A.U.P.H. in some manuscripts (e.g. BnF ms. fr. 14548, fol. 301r). However, there are other theories and none of them is conclusive (see Lavigne, 'La traduction en vers des *Institutes*', pp. 512ff). There are seven known manuscripts of the verse translation (*ibid.*, p. 514). The translated *Summa* in BnF ms. fr. 14548 is preceded by a Rouen calendar; this interest in timekeeping further suggests this manuscript was intended for practical use.

[81] Though composed separately, these two verse translations appear together in one manuscript (Viollet, 'Les coutumiers de Normandie', 112).

[82] Wogan-Browne et al., *The Idea of the Vernacular*, p. 330.

[83] See Ferguson, 'Diglossia'.

[84] Ziolkowski, 'Cultural Diglossia', pp. 206ff.

[85] Walter J. Ong, 'Writing Is a Technology that Restructures Thought', pp. 27–8.

England.[86] Perhaps the internationalism of Latin fostered a similar spirit in the vernacular, or perhaps the lack of regional frontiers with fixed 'national' identities permitted vernaculars to travel far and wide.[87] The scope of the francophone world must also have been a factor. In the second half of the thirteenth century, French was still the language of the nobility in England, and Anglo-Norman was also used for the vernacular legal treatise; for instance, Britton's reinvention of Bracton's vernacular *De legibus*; the anonymous *Fet Assaver*'s introduction to the practice of the lay courts; or the *Court Baron*'s exposition of the practice of baronial courts.[88] Legal texts in the French vernacular also proliferated in the crusader states – written even as the territory was gradually being lost. These texts included Philip of Novara's *Livre en forme de plet*; John of Ibelin's *Assises de Jerusalem*; the various texts grouped as the 'Assises de Jérusalem'; the *Assises of Antioch*, which we only know from Sempad the Constable's Armenian translation; and the *Assises of Romania*.[89]

Between the eleventh and thirteenth century, French – the 'mother tongue' – developed not only as a language of law and a language of power but also as an erudite vernacular, a *lingua franca*, a language of conquest, and, one might say, a colonial language. More attention has been paid, however, to the relationship between law and Anglo-French, the French language in England.[90] This was due to the post-Conquest

---

[86] See Kuskowski, '*Lingua franca legalis?*'. For French vernacular literature at the limits of the French world and what it said generally about cultural and geographic boundaries, see Kinoshita, *Medieval Boundaries*.

[87] Smith, 'The Vernacular', pp. 77–8. National identities would start hardening in the fourteenth century.

[88] *Fet Assaver* in *Four Thirteenth Century Law Tracts*; *The Court Baron*. For more on French as a language of royal law and administration in England, see Lusignan's *La langue des rois au Moyen Âge* and the essays on the use of English in those courts later in the fourteenth century by George E. Woodbine ('The Language of English Law') and W. Marc Ormrod ('The Use of English').

[89] See Auguste-Arthur Beugnot, *Assises de Jérusalem*.

[90] On the terms used to describe French in England, see Wogan-Browne et al., *Language and Culture in Medieval Britain*. Scholars who have worked on the language of law in England have been especially concerned with dating when exactly English began to be used and when it became dominant as a language of law. George Woodbine raised awareness of the issue, though now his ideas have been displaced by Paul Brand who has shown that the languages of law in English courts were primarily Latin and French in the thirteenth and fourteenth centuries, and W. Rothwell who discussed the use of French legal language in Anglo-Norman literature to show that French must have been used in twelfth-century English law courts (Woodbine, 'The Language of English Law'; Paul Brand, 'The Languages of the Law in Late Medieval England'; Rothwell, 'The Trial

survival and revitalization of French as the *lingua franca* of the Angevin Empire, which led to the complicated relationship of the three languages of law in England, namely, Latin, French, and English.[91] The case of England was particular but not exceptional. French was also an important written vernacular and language of power in Italy and the crusader states, where it similarly co-existed with Latin and other vernaculars, making it a legal language that spanned from England to the Levant.[92]

The shift from the use of Latin to the vernacular in practice was gradual and not linear. French as a language of legal record was no doubt in a dialectical relationship with the language of the church; namely, Latin.[93] French administrators, especially in conservative royal chanceries, continued to use Latin as their language of record until the beginning of the fourteenth century, and even as the use of the vernacular spread, it did not replace but took its place alongside Latin.[94]

Nonetheless, from city customs to the translation of Roman and canon law, to the writing of the *coutumiers* and the development of a legal *lingua franca*, we can see that something new and different was happening across Europe. This was not a random series of disconnected events: we can identify a movement – even a revolution – in vernacular law.

By the beginning of the fourteenth century, the vernacular was starting to be seen not only as good enough but, according to some, better than Latin, and its role as the language of the courts partly explains this transformation. The connection of the vernacular to regular speech was what had made it insufficient for Giles of Rome, yet that was precisely what made it superior to Latin for Dante.[95] Not all vernacular speech

Scene in "Lanval"'). On the famous Statute of Pleading of 1362 that required English as the language of oral communication in royal and seigniorial courts, rather than French, see Ormrod, 'The Use of English'; Bevan, 'English Legal Culture'; Bruce O'Brien, 'Translating Technical Terms in Law-Codes'.

[91] O'Brien, *Reversing Babel*, pp. 212–13.

[92] For preliminary thoughts on this wider movement, see Kuskowski, '*Lingua Franca Legalis?*'.

[93] Gauvard, 'La justice du roi de France et le latin à la fin du Moyen Âge', pp. 31–53.

[94] Lusignan, *La langue des rois*, p. 17. Champagne was the first French principality with French chancery records – with a notable surge in the use of the vernacular after the extinction of the direct line of the counts of Champagne in 1274, which was followed by a decade of regency until a young Jeanne de Champagne was married to the Philip who would become King Philip IV the Fair (*ibid.*, pp. 55–6).

[95] Nicholas Watson, 'The Idea of Latinity'.

earned Dante's esteem, and coarse or low-class language was certainly excluded. Dante argued for a superior, illustrious vernacular, one that was clearly a language of power. As Dante explained,

the vernacular with which we are dealing is both exalted by discipline and power and exalts its followers with honor and glory [...] That it is exalted by power is manifest, for what greater power is there than that which can change human hearts, making men do what they would not, and refrain from what they would, as this language has done and still does?[96]

Here, Dante equally could have been describing the language of law. In fact, he was marvelling at the phenomenon captured by John Austin as 'doing things with words' – the ability of language to restrain, compel, and shape human behaviour.[97] Indeed, Dante continued to explain that this illustrious vernacular deserved to be called curial (pertaining to law and justice) because curiality 'is defined as the rule and balance of things that need to be done', the sort of balancing that is 'only found in the highest courts of justice'.[98] His illustrious vernacular, then, is a language of power that resonates in the highest law courts of the land.

The Authors of Law

At the heart of this vernacular legal culture was the lay jurist, someone with expertise in customary law who attended and participated in the lay courts, who may have had knowledge of the development of its

---

[96] 'Et vulgare de quo loquimur et sublimatum est magistratu et potestate, et suos honore sublimat et Gloria [...] Quod autem exaltatum sit potestate, videtur. Et quid maioris potestatis est quam quod humana corda versare potest, ita ut nolentem volentem et volentem nolentem faciat, velut ipsum et fecit et facit?' (Dante, *De vulgari eloquentia* XVII.2, XVII.4; http://www.thelatinlibrary.com/dante/vulgar.shtml).

[97] See John L. Austin, *How to Do Things with Words*.

[98] 'It also deserves to be called curial, since curiality (law and justice) is defined as the rule and balance of things that need to be done; and since the scales necessary for such balancing are only found in the highest courts of justice, hence it comes about that whatever in our actions is well-balanced is called curial. And since this language has been weighed in the most excellent law-courts of Italy, rightly it is called curial' (*Est etiam merito curiale dicendum, quia curialitas nil aliud est quam librata regula eorum que peragenda sunt: et quia statera huiusmodi librationis tantum in excellentissimis curiis esse solet, hinc est quod quicquid in actibus nostris bene libratum est, curiale dicatur. Unde cum istud in excellentissima Ytalorum curia sit libratum, dici curiale meretur*; Dante, *De vulgari eloquentia* XVIII.4).

written texts, and who may have been university educated. Those who wrote the *coutumiers* were part of a literate culture, but they were also men of practice. Their closest antecedents may have been the lawmen of Carolingian France called *scabini* and also known as *boni homines, boni viri, nobiles viri,* 'good men' who were generally local landowners administering local justice (though there were other offices with judicial responsibilities).[99] Customary dispute-resolution practice was more developed in the eleventh and twelfth centuries than scholars have previously assumed.[100] 'Specialism' and experts emerged in the period after 1100, and non-specialists in courts – courts that had previously dealt with politics and finance as much as law – changed into some version of professional experts who specialized in the discrete field of legal knowledge.[101] Customary law was in essence a form of expert knowledge, and the rest of this section will discuss the possible sources of this expertise.[102]

---

[99] E. N. Estey, 'The Scabini and the Local Courts', 122–3. See also Cam, 'Suitors and Scabini'. For the older maximalist narrative, see Ganshof, *Recherches sur les tribunaux de châtellenie*; John P. Dawson, *A History of Lay Judges.* For a more recent corrective, see also Nelson, 'Dispute Settlement in Carolingian West Francia'. The *sacabini* took part in a well-developed system of participatory collective judgement (see *ibid.,* pp. 58–9). The language of *scabini* and *boni homines* was replaced with *fideles* in the mid-tenth century, and, whether or not this meant the same people, there was a group of people who were active participants in and knowledgeable about dispute resolution, even though it was not their primary field of activity. Ganshof had said that the *boni homines* morphed into the *fideles,* and Georges Duby disagreed – for a review of where that debate is now, see François Bougard, 'Genèse et réception du Mâconnais de Georges Duby'. The *scabini* functioned like a sort of grand jury and 'represented the judicial wisdom of the area' (Jennifer R. Davis, *Charlemagne's Practice of Empire,* p. 52). They were one of a host of officials and agents with judicial functions (*ibid.,* pp. 52–3).

[100] Bruno Lemesle, *Conflits et justice au Moyen Âge*; Hagger, 'Secular Law and Custom in Ducal Normandy'.

[101] Reynolds, 'The Emergence of Professional Law in the Long Twelfth Century', 349–50. This article generated a strong reaction about how to define professional law, how it emerged, and the differences in the story of that emergence in different kingdoms, see Piotr Górecki, Charles M. Radding, and Paul Brand, 'Forum: The Emergence of Professional Law'.

[102] Teuscher, *Lords' Rights and Peasant Stories,* pp. 39ff. Teuscher specifically discusses the position of *consuetudinarius,* a type of expert court consultant in customary law, in a later period (fifteenth century) in the Swiss midlands. That customary law could be a form of expert knowledge resonates with the earlier period discussed here.

By the thirteenth century, this form of expert knowledge could have been acquired through several sources. One was regular attendance at the court combined with some stature in the community. Another was royal service: the post of the *bailli*, or royal justice, continuously expanded since the reign of Philip Augustus, notably with Louis IX's mid-thirteenth century reforms.[103] The role of the *bailli* was to conduct the exercise of royal justice on the part of the king. He had jurisdiction over the king's agents and those who reported directly to him as well as over specifically royal matters. After Louis IX's reforms, he also had jurisdiction over local appeals to the crown. The expertise of this group of legal actors of the lay courts at all levels was drawn from observation, experience, and opinion.

The *coutumiers* show that there must also have been a way of developing an expertise in secular law that has not received much attention: an expertise developed through what might be called a middling education combined with a knowledge of court documents and practice. A clerk educated in a cathedral school and immediately drawn into a court chancery, whose Latin was not outstanding but who could read law-related texts and chancery documents, could have the cultural capital necessary to write a *coutumier*. The authors of the *Coutumes d'Anjou et du Maine* and the *Coutumes de Champagne*, for instance, might most closely match this sort of background: the texts generally demonstrate a breadth of knowledge formed through the court milieu, rather than one shaped by Romanists who taught at universities.

It may safely be said that all the *coutumier* authors were people who were involved in pleading at court or had judicial functions. The author of the *Coutumier d'Artois*, for instance, was anonymous but constantly referred to cases that he had seen in court and recounts them in some detail, including the issue, the procedural steps taken, the arguments of the parties, the resolution, and the lesson to be learnt from it all.[104] He had full confidence in his knowledge. For example, he told his audience the rule that if those people who are within the king's jurisdiction commit a crime, they are tried in the place where they

---

[103] In the South of France (though lines were blurred) the post tended to be called *sénéschal* and remained tinged with its military role longer than in the North.
[104] For example, cases in Arras (II.3, III.19, III.34), Dorlens (V.3), and Encre (VI.2).

committed the crime: 'I tell you [this] with certainty'.[105] The author of the *Coutumier d'Artois*, clearly, felt empowered to give the assurance of certainty based on his hotchpotch of learning and court practice.[106]

This author either had an excellent and practised memory that came from being immersed in a specific milieu or had access to written records of the case. It is more difficult to determine for the author of the *Coutumier d'Artois*, but he likely recalled cases from memory since he discussed them by – at most – naming the principal parties and the jurisdiction of the trial.

The author of the *Coutumier de Champagne*, on the other hand, must have had access to written court records. He described some of the cases in a manner that follows the pattern of charters and in such detail that it would be difficult to see how he could do so without drawing on written record. For instance, he illustrated the custom of Champagne about the division of property between older and younger brothers and the guardianship of older brothers over younger ones with a particular case:

This was judged in Chateauvillain in the year IIc IIIIxx and IX (1289) against Guiot, the brother of Perrin d'Arc, who had asked Simon, the brother of the wife of the aforesaid Guiot, for the division of a house. And the aforesaid Simon defended himself and said that he had been apportioned by friends and by justice, and had held it for five years after the wife of the said Guiot had come of age, and for this reason he did not want to respond to the request. It was judged (*rappourté*) that he would never have to respond to the request. Present at the judgment were Messire Miles de Saumur, canon of Chalons, Guillaume Alexandre, the bailli of Chalons, Messire Guillaume, Lord of Julli, Messire Hues Chauderons, Messire Guy his brother, Messire Jehanz de Marat, and Guillaume of the Chastelet.[107]

The author of the *Coutumier de Champagne* described the customs of Champagne in this manner throughout the text, using cases coupled with general expressions of norms ('it is custom in Champagne that ... '). To compose such a text, it was necessary to have a knowledge of court record and practice as well as some experience with writing and composing ideas in writing.

---

[105] *Coutumier d'Artois*, ed. Tardif, XI.10.
[106] For the extent of his learning, see Chapter 5.
[107] *L'ancien coutumier de Champagne*, ed. Portejoie, XVII.

The author of the *Coutumier de Champagne* also provided insight
into the lay people involved in court practice by naming the jurors who
were involved in judging cases. The case above lists several such people.
Miles de Saumur was a canon, an ecclesiastic. Hugues Chauderon
came from an important feudal family that held the seigneuries of
Briaucourt, and also assisted in the Jours de Troyes.[108] Guy
Chauderon featured on the list of vassals during the regency of
Blanche of Artois (1274–5). He assisted in the Jours of the barons
and was in a case himself, pleading with his daughter against her
father-in-law.[109] Jean de Marat is known only as Lord of Marat.
This was a good group of respectable people, or *bonnes gens*,
traditionally involved in dispute resolution and the courts.

Among these men, however, were two others who had held several
appointments to legal positions. Guillaume Alexandre was
a professional justice: he was *bailli* of Troyes (1240–6), of Provins
(1264), of Troyes again (1269), of both Troyes and Provins (1271
and 1273–6), and of Chalons (1289).[110] Guillaume du Châtelet, on
the other hand, had a distinguished career as a man of law: he was *bailli*
of Meaux (1276), of Chaumont (1278), then of Sézanne, again of
Chaumont (1281–3), then of Troyes (1283–4), and again of Sézanne
(1284), where he remained active after his tenure.[111] He sat on the
Grands Jours de Troyes, and in 1285 he even pleaded against Jean de
Joinville, who had been seneschal of Champagne, though he is better
known as a friend and counsellor to Louis IX, as well as his
biographer.[112] Though Guillaume's career was made in Champagne,
he did go to plead before Parliament in 1291 and 1295. The multiple
holdings of similar law-oriented positions showed how some lawmen
gained legal experience in several different regional jurisdictions.

By the end of the thirteenth century, there were men who were
making careers of court practice. Dirk Heirbaut's analysis of the
spokesmen of the Lille court in Flanders corroborates this.[113]
Heirbaut called 'spokesmen' all those who acted as lords, bailiffs,
judges, arbiters, and legal advisers, those 'who were the intellectual
authors of these courts' judgements and, thus, the main creators of

---

[108] *Ibid.*, p. 170n.6.   [109] *Ibid.*, p. 170n.7.   [110] *Ibid.*, p. 169n.4.
[111] *Ibid.*, p. 10n.28.
[112] *Ibid.*, p. 169n.4.
[113] Dirk Heirbaut, 'Who Were the Makers of Customary Law', p. 270.

customary law'.[114] These same sorts of people participated in northern French courts.[115] Just as he noted for the Lille court, those who were active lawmen in the example of Champagne above 'were not just individuals, but rather a community of legal experts'.[116] One way of becoming a lawman was through regular attendance and participation in the courts.

From the twelfth century on, another way of thinking about law created a new constellation of lawmen, very different from those just described. These men gained expert knowledge in law conceptually and completely outside the realm of the practice of secular courts, and they did so through university studies in Roman law, canon law, or both. Around the year 1130, new terminology for new types of legal expertise began to appear – *legisperitus, magister, notarius,* and *casidicus* – starting in the south in cities such as Montpellier, Carcassonne, and Narbonne and slowly, gradually, moving north.[117] The first hints that university-trained legal thinkers had entered the service of French kings appeared at a similar time. Louis VII used the services of a university-trained professional named Mainier once, a man that Pope Alexander III had named *magister* and an anonymous chronicler had named a *jurisperitus* and who was the earliest known product of university legal studies in French royal circles.[118] Philip Augustus also called on some men of learning. One case mentions two 'wise men' (*sapientes homini*) of the king named Master Geoffroy de Poissy and Master Nicolas of Chartres.[119] The only professor of civil law who appeared at the royal court before 1270 was Simon of Paris, but some students of law, such as Eudes de Lorris, had appeared as clerks of the Parlement and were among the colleagues of Pierre de Fontaine, one of the earliest Northern French *coutumier* authors.[120]

---

[114] Heirbaut, 'Who Were the Makers of Customary Law', p. 273.
[115] *Ibid.* See also Heirbaut, 'The Spokesmen in Medieval Courts'.
[116] Heirbaut, 'Who Were the Makers of Customary Law', p. 271.
[117] Marguerite Boulet-Sautel, 'Le droit romain et Philippe August', p. 490.
[118] Boulet-Sautel, 'Le droit romain et Philippe Auguste'.
[119] Boulet-Sautel, 'Le droit romain et Philippe Auguste', p. 490. Boulet-Sautel notes that the title of *magister* likely made these men jurists.
[120] Griffiths, 'Les origines et la carrière de Pierre de Fontaines', 551.

Some *coutumier* authors fall more closely within this type of legal expertise. How squarely they fit within this framework has long been a subject of debate and is analysed in more detail in Chapter 5. It is worth noting here, however, that the manner in which *coutumier* authors acquired this kind of expertise had commonalities but no uniformity. Pierre de Fontaines, the compiler of the *Établissements de Saint Louis*, Philippe de Beaumanoir, and the author of the *Coutumier d'Artois* clearly had some knowledge of Roman and canon law. However, they had various kinds and quantities of that knowledge; they drew on it in different ways, and they ultimately composed texts with significant differences.

From his *Conseil*, all we can tell about Pierre is that he had parts or all of Justinian's *Corpus iuris civilis* in translation and the cultural capital to construct a text in the shape of a scholastic dialogue. The author of the *Établissements* must have had wider knowledge, as he inserted proper academic citations to learned law into earlier texts of customs, though not in a manner that reflected a thoughtful engagement with the learned texts. Philippe de Beaumanoir is a controversial case, and scholars have argued both that he had little knowledge of university law and also that his text is the product of someone who had perfectly imbibed it and internalized its precepts. When both such arguments can be made, the truth probably resides somewhere between the two. The author of the *Coutumier d'Artois* displayed a very broad education. Roman and canon law are often quoted in this text, but this material is very often drawn from other earlier *coutumiers*.

We know more about Pierre de Fontaines and Philippe de Beaumanoir because, unlike other *coutumier* authors, they did not choose anonymity. Their names no doubt provided added *auctoritas* to their texts. Both authors orbited the centres of political power. They worked at the courts of relatives of the king and eventually became royal *bailli*. They started off in satellite, regional locations of power and then became representatives of central power in the regions.

Accrued traditions have shaped and distorted what we know about Pierre – some scholars have wanted to make him noble, and others bourgeois.[121] As Quentin Griffiths has shown, Pierre de Fontaines was

---

[121] *Ibid.*, 544ff.

an ordinary member of the knightly class, just like many other members of Louis IX's parliament.[122] Pierre seems to have been one of the younger sons in a family of minor nobility, and in the records he appears as an acquisitor of land and a rent collector.[123] We do not know Pierre's origins with any certainty, but he began his career in the Vermandois, and the lands he bought and the rents he collected were in the area around Saint Quentin.[124] He was employed at the court of Mahaut de Brabant in Artois, who was the widow of Louis IX's brother Robert of Artois, before he became *bailli* in 1253.[125] In 1252 he was referred to as 'sire', but by 1257 he had become 'chevalier du roi', *dominus Petrus*, *Mgr Pierre*, and then *chevalier* again when he stopped being a *bailli*.[126]

Philippe de Beaumanoir, on the other hand, was the son of a *bailli* and had probably attended court throughout his childhood. The jurist had long been conflated with his father, Philippe de Rémy, but they were recognized to be two separate people and studied in detail in the indispensable research of a colloquium of French scholars in the 1980s.[127] Philippe de Rémy was not only a *bailli* but was also a literary man and composed poetry and popular romances such as *La Manekine* or *Jehan et Blonde*.[128] Philippe de Rémy had been *bailli* in Artois, where Pierre de Fontaines had been *bailli* before him. Indeed, it is possible that Pierre de Fontaines and Philippe de

---

[122] *Ibid.*, 545. As far as we can tell, it seems that his entire fortune was built on his professional revenues, fief-rents, and royal patronage (*ibid.*, 556). Pierre must have died before 1267, when his wife remarried (*ibid.*).

[123] *Ibid.*, 548.

[124] *Ibid.*, 549. Saint Quentin entered the royal domain around the beginning of the thirteenth century.

[125] *Ibid.*, 550. Mahaut d'Artois and her second husband, Guy de Châtillion the count of Saint-Pol, gave Pierre's son Jean a fief-rent of one hundred pounds in 1258, Pierre was already a royal *bailli* by then (*ibid.*).

[126] *Ibid.*, 548, 549. He sits in five suits in Parlement between 1255 and 1261, where he is variously referred to as master, counsellor, and judge (*ibid.*, 553). The one reference to Pierre as *Mgr*, *magister*, the designation of a university professor, raises the question of Pierre's education. We will look at this more closely in Chapter 5.

[127] See the impressively detailed study of all aspects and contexts of Beaumanoir in Philippe Bonnet-La Borderie (ed.), *Actes du colloque international Philippe de Beaumanoir*.

[128] It is the father, and not the son, who may have travelled to England. In *Jehan et Blonde*, Philippe de Rémy displays his solid knowledge of England, its geography, and political system. There is no indication that his son had been there as well.

Beaumanoir crossed paths there and that when growing up Philippe had known about Pierre's book describing the rules of the lay courts. If speculation is correct about Beaumanoir being born in 1250, he would have been thirty-three in 1283 when he finished the *Coutumes de Beauvaisis*, which he wrote while he was a justice in Clermont-en-Beauvaisis for Count Robert (and not while he was royal *bailli,* as is sometimes claimed). His juridical career took off in the royal administration after this, and he was *bailli* in Senlis, Tours, Vermandois, and Touraine and seneschal of Poitou.

All lay jurists were active in the secular courts and wrote for that context. Each brought their own view of how to think about and present the practice in the lay courts based on their own matrix of experience, practice, and learning. One might call them professionals, though there is some debate about when and how to define the emergence of 'professional' men of law.[129] They were certainly professionalized in the sense of having professional qualities and specializing in a specific subject matter for a particular setting. With written text and the theorization it permitted, they made the customary law of the lay courts into a field of knowledge. They thus facilitated specialization and professionalization. They also made this field of knowledge accessible through their linguistic choice, by choosing not the learned clerk and his Latin but lay people and their vernacular. They were the engines of the new vernacular movement in law.

Lay *Subtilité,* or the Audience for Vernacular Law

At the heart of this vernacular law movement was the desire of lay, non-clerical individuals to participate in the conceptual world of law, undergirded by the belief that the vernacular had become sophisticated and subtle enough as a written language to properly express or transmit those ideas. *Subtilité* – that is, skilfulness, a sharp mind, and cunning – differentiated the clerical and learned from the lay and uneducated. Subtlety rested on 'speculative capacity and cleverness in logic and

---

[129] Reynolds, 'The Emergence of Professional Law in the Long Twelfth Century'; Górecki, 'A View from a Distance'; Radding, 'Legal Theory and Practice in Eleventh-Century Italy'; Brand, 'The English Difference'.

dialectic'.[130] It was a capacity of reason and the intellect and indicated the formal complexity of an author or subject.[131] Subtlety was also a particular characteristic of legal argumentation. John of Salisbury complained about the 'vigorous use of legal subtleties' by canon lawyers who were harassing his master Theobald of Canterbury (r. 1138–61) with lawsuits.[132] *Subtilité* ranged from a mark of high intellectual calibre to the pejorative sense of using words for nefarious ends, Renart the Fox, for example, who used his *subtilité* to deceive all the animals from the village to the king's court in the *Roman de Renart*. Whether used for good or evil, subtlety captured the ability to think and speak with intellectual complexity.

Pierre de Corbiac explicitly stated, around 1225, that his encyclopaedia was written in French to make that knowledge available to those for whom it would otherwise be inaccessible but who had the intellectual ability to grasp the ideas:

Whoever wants to hear this narrative,	Qui velt entendre acest romans,
Can listen to it as they can	Si puet entendre acest commans
To the works of God and clerks	Des oeuvres Diu e de clergie
Since I compose for lay people	Car por laie gent romancie
Who are skilful and have good sense,	Qui soutiu sunt et de bon sens
Of which many can be found in my time,	Dont plusiors trova a mon tens,
Who, if they had learned Latin,	Qui se latin apris eussent,
Would have learned many good things,	Maint grant bien apprendre peussent
And, for such people, I set myself	Por itex gens m'entremis
To setting in the vernacular what was in Latin	Que de latin en romans mis
Something good from the understanding of clercs	Des sens de clergue aucuns biens
About which many people know nothing	Dont maintes gens ne sevent riens
So that they could understand in the vernacular	Qu'en romans puissent ce entendre
What they could not learn in Latin.	Que en latin ne puissent aprendre.[133]

---

[130] Francesco Bruni, *Testi e chierici del medioevo*, p. 105.
[131] Caroline Boucher, 'De la *subtilité* en français', pp. 90–1.
[132] Brundage, *The Medieval Origins of the Legal Profession*, p. 215.
[133] Pierre de Corbiac, *Le Tresor de Pierre de Corbiac*, ll. 1–14. This predates Vincent de Beauvais' *Speculum Maius* by twenty years.

Pierre de Corbiac appreciated that there were already many lay
people with no knowledge of Latin who were capable of subtle,
sophisticated thinking (*qui soutiu sunt*). They formed a new market
for previously exclusive learning – an audience for French-language
compendia of all knowledge such as that of Pierre or Brunetto
Latini.[134]

Not all vernacularizers had such a positive view of the intellectual
abilities of their lay audience. John of Antioch, who translated Cicero's
Rhetoric into Old French (1282), explained that he was translating it
for 'those who cannot have this knowledge'.[135] In contrast to Pierre,
however, John assumed a very limited possibility for the sophistication
of his new readership, and so he decided to omit 'subtleties' to make the
text understandable for his new audience.[136] Whatever the translator's
opinion of their audience, the new readership spurred the growth of
new forms of erudition. This new readership asked scholars to write
books, in the vernacular, either providing a topic or providing the
sources to be used.[137] Translations into the vernacular and works

[134] Brunetto Latini, *Li livre dou tresor*. Brunetto Latini was a notary in Italy and, after
the defeat of the Guelphs, in France, before he returned to Florence where he held
high political offices in the 1270s and 1280s. He was Dante's guardian after his
father's death. In the *Divine Comedy*, Dante placed Latini in the Inferno with the
sodomites, although he portrayed him with sympathy. Brunetto Latini wrote his
encyclopedia in French, 'And if anyone asks why this book is written in the vernacular (*romans*), according to the language of the French, since we are Italian, I shall say
it is for two reasons: the one, because we are in France, and the other, because that
language (*parleure*) is more delightful (*delitable*) and more common to all people
(*plus commune à toutes gens*)' (Brunetto Latini, I.1.1). Also, incidentally, a couple of
paragraphs from his *Trésor* appeared in the *Assises de Jérusalem* published by
Thaumassière (*ibid.*, vi).
[135] 'Ici parole de l'argumentacion de logique, por faire la conoistre a ceaus qui cele
science ne peuent savoir' (Boucher, 'De la *subtilité* en français', p. 92).
[136] 'trop seroit soutil chose et longue a dire coment, et top ennuiouse a home qui ne seit
logique', *ibid.*, p. 92. Boucher discusses the history of representation of lay and clerc,
the former sometimes described as 'dialectical idiots' while the latter are sometimes
praised and sometimes decried for their *subtilité* (*ibid.*, p. 261). Gilles de Rome, for
instance, said that the 'lay and vulgar men [. . .] who do not argue in an elaborate and
dialectical manner are called *idiotae dialectici*' (*ibid.*, n.37). Some fourteenth- and
fifteenth-century texts display an emphasis on keeping *subtilités* from the *vulgus*; for
instance, Raoul de Presles noted in the late fourteenth century that some ideas were
trop soutilles et trop dangeureuses and that he would skip over them (*ibid.*, pp. 94,
95). Pierre de Corbiac presents a very different view.
[137] See generally, Holzknecht, *Literary Patronage in the Middle Ages*. For an examination of how the author's role changed with printing, and how even anonymous

originally composed in the language increasingly became available as the thirteenth century wore on.

The art of seeing distinctions, of asking good questions or making good arguments, while originally an attribute of scholars, was growing into a larger social phenomenon. The lay jurists who wrote the *coutumiers* and their target audience – sophisticated enough to be reading or listening to fairly detailed and complex legal information – were one group of lay thinkers who rose out of this context. Scholars were not the audience for the *coutumiers*. As Pierre de Fontaines remarked, 'those who judge disputes in lay courts are not legal scholars (*légistres*), so they cannot treat disputes so subtly (*si soutilment*) as the written word (*la lettre*)'.[138] While *légistre* could be translated as lawyer or legal expert, Pierre used the term in a way that implied bookish learning in law. This bookish learning was one source of legal expertise, and a knowledge of custom in practice formed the other. In a different passage, Pierre explained to his interlocutor that 'the person who told you that you had begun a proceeding merely because you had asked for a counsel day was not a legal scholar (*légistres*) nor was he knowledgeable about the customs of the area'.[139] There were two valid, though distinct, sources of knowledge about law.

While Pierre saw the written word as permitting an added level of subtlety, he also considered it to be a quality the audience for his *Conseil* either had or could have. Pierre commended his interlocutor for his subtle thinking: 'You are asking a subtle question, namely whether I understand the same thing concerning a serf who had bought a free fief, and become a free man'.[140] Pierre even praises him for elevating the conversation: 'I can see that you want to remain in doubt about nothing of which you might be certain; and if you go on asking questions as you have begun, you will cause my thoughts to rise

---

authors tried to assert their authorship through subtle means, see Cynthia Jane Brown, *Poets, Patrons, and Printers*.

[138] The subject matter, Pierre noted, did not call for such a high level of subtlety: 'Cil qui jugent les quereles ès corz laies ne sont mie *légistre*, dont ne pueent-il mie si soutilment treitier les quereles come la letre: mès certes ci n'eust mie grant soutilleté à entendre celui qui fist tel covent, que on lui du x livres chascun an tant comme il vivroit, à payer à Pasques et à la Saint Jehan' (Pierre de Fontaines, *Conseil*, ed. Marnier, XV.33).

[139] Pierre de Fontaines, *Le conseil*, ed. Marnier, XVII.37. [140] *Ibid.*, XIII.23.

to a place and to a subject to which it is unaccustomed'.[141] In the legal context, *subtilité* thus referred not only to good arguments but also to fine distinctions that indicated advanced, sophisticated legal thinking. While this interlocutor could have been a pedagogical fiction, he did represent the lay audience Pierre was instructing with his text. By teaching the audience these subtleties, Pierre was showing them the art of thinking about law with finesse.

This ability to think of legal ideas in a subtle manner rested not only on vernacular writing but also on the development of a specialized language within that vernacular to express legal ideas that exceeded the capacities of ordinary language. Certain 'terms from the general register of ordinary life become "legal" only by repeated use in legal contexts, from which they take on increasingly legal connotations'.[142] William Rothwell examines the language of the trial scene in Marie de France's *Lanval* to show that the French vernacular already had a developed register of legal terms in the 1170s and compiles an index of legal terms from that source and other vernacular literary texts.[143] Clearly, in the period preceding the *coutumiers*, there was a sophisticated vernacular to describe the procedure of the secular courts, a common recognition that there was a certain way of speaking and thinking that applied to this context, one that any lay listener would recognize as they heard *Lanval* read or recounted.

The *coutumiers*, however, were responding to a legal culture distinct from these precursors. As Rothwell notes for the Angevin context, lawbooks contain an 'extensive and highly sophisticated terminology of the law', which was 'the product of many years of semantic development inside a language evolving on many fronts'.[144] Yet lawbooks also go beyond that, offering a pedagogy that must somehow be helpful or even necessary. And lawbooks were helpful or necessary precisely because legal practice was separating from common action, and the language of law was separating from common speech.[145] David Mellinkoff explains that this separation was characterized by the 'frequent use of common words with uncommon meanings', the use of terms of art or formalized

---

[141] *Ibid.*, III.3.   [142] Rothwell, 'The Trial Scene in "Lanval"', 23.
[143] *Ibid.*, 20. As Rothwell notes, it is artificial to separate or differentiate between insular and continental French in this period (*ibid.*, 23).
[144] *Ibid.*, 27.   [145] David Mellinkoff, *The Language of the Law*, p. 11.

words.[146] Lawrence Friedman expands on this when he notes that legal language consists of 'a *vocabulary* of terms used by legal specialists but not understood by the general public; and a legal *style* characterized by the use of words and syntax which the public understands but does not itself employ in living language'.[147] So this is a language that one does not acquire naturally in daily life but that one must acquire through some effort of learning.

Legal practice in the secular courts was transforming into one that involved some specialized knowledge, as indicated in a change made to the *Coutumes d'Anjou et du Maine* of 1246 when the text became the first book of the *Établissements de Saint Louis* around three decades later. The earlier text explained how to properly request an amendment of judgment and told the petitioner to say: 'Sir, it appears to me that this judgment harms me and is not right; and for this reason I request an amendment and that you set a date for me; and have so many good folk show up that they can know whether the revision is appropriate or not.'[148] These 'many good folk', regular people of good standing, were the locus of legal knowledge here. By the 1270s, however, the compiler of the *Établissements* felt the need to add the following words: 'by folk who can and should do this according to the law and usage in the barony'.[149] The locus of legal knowledge was changing from 'many good folk' to 'folk who can'. It was no longer enough to be a man of good reputation or importance – lay practice necessitated special ability and knowledge.

The *coutumiers* emerged at the beginning of this process, when legal language was starting to branch off from ordinary language. While they largely contain ordinary language about secular law, they sometimes also introduced new words for specialized concepts. Though lexical introductions of this type were not numerous and do not appear in all *coutumiers*, they point nonetheless to an expanding legal register of language. This developing language drew both from internal developments within the secular courts themselves and from Roman law or ecclesiastical procedure. Philippe de Beaumanoir, for

---

[146] *Ibid.*   [147] Friedman, 'Law and Its Language', 563.
[148] *Les établissements de Saint Louis*, ed. Viollet, I.85.
[149] 'par gens qui le puissant faire et doient selon lou droit et l'usage de baronie' (*Les établissements de Saint Louis*, ed. Viollet, I.85).

instance, was comfortable in using the Roman concept of property (*propriété*) as well as the vernacular term seisin (*saisine*).[150]

Beaumanoir's chapter on complaints provides the most conspicuous example of language introduction. After teasing clerks for their pretty and appropriate but incomprehensible language and justifying his own use of a simple and clear vernacular, Beaumanoir proceeded to list the contents of the chapter while introducing and explaining certain terms. Many of these were procedural terms from the ecclesiastical courts. Beaumanoir introduced these words in French rather than Latin. For instance, he explained that 'complaints (*demandes*) are called by the clerks *libelles*; and a complaint (*demande*) is the same as a *libelle*'.[151] Then he goes on illuminating the different terminiologies of lay courts and ecclesiastical courts: 'defences (*defenses*) which the clerks call exceptions (*excepcions*)', or the complainant's response to the defence of the accused 'which the clerks call replication (*replicacions*)'.[152] Beaumanoir was teaching his audience the Latinate terms presumably being used in the secular courts and that had become French but were not part of ordinary speech.

Legal language also developed out of the practice of secular law. Beaumanoir noted, for instance, 'we call pleading at the bar (*nous apelons barroier*) the reasons the defendant raises against the complaint as well as for the reasons the complainant uses in his reply to the defendant'.[153] The French vernacular was also developing its own indigenous legal language where specialized terms arose from regular actions and conventions that had developed in the course of practice. Thus was born a new vernacular lay legal *subtilité*.

**

The *coutumiers* sat at the intersection of two major movements that began in the twelfth century and accelerated in the thirteenth: a movement in vernacular writing and a movement in the study, theorization, and writing of law. The shift in language made space

---

[150] See for instance Beaumanoir, *Coutumes de Beauvaisis*, ed. Salmon, VI.197. *Propriété* and *saisine* were not equivalent concepts. Seisin was a complex property concept that denoted juridical possession created through formal processes that conferred just title and, less often, the fact or state of possession (Ernest Champeaux, *Essai sur la vestitura*, pp. 8–9).

[151] Beaumanoir, *Coutumes de Beauvaisis*, ed. Salmon, VI.196.   [152] *Ibid.*   [153] *Ibid.*

for a new form of legal thinking, one deeply connected to earlier forms but one that also fulfilled a new social, political, and symbolic function.

The move to the vernacular in law was thus a conceptual shift both culturally and ideologically. Of course, Latinate law continued to occupy a vast space in legal culture, from the practice of canon law courts to university studies to much record-keeping. However, the law of the lay courts could now be known, theorized, and transmitted to any person who could read or follow as the French was read aloud. It was also a political moment, as this was a valorization of a specific jurisdiction, those who populated it, the manner in which it conducted its business, and custom as its primary norm.

3

Writing a '*ius non scriptum*': Writtenness, Memory, and Change

Laws, or our narratives about law, have a special relationship with writing. The moment of writing transforms law from lore to fact, from memory to record, from ephemeral to inscribed. This moment is commemorated not only in the material inscription in stone, tablets, scrolls, or codices but also in narratives where the writing of law provides a dramatic climax, placing writing at the centre of lawmaking, divine or human. As Justinian's *Institutes* remarked, written law was part of the very foundation of civil society: 'civil laws first came into existence when states began to be founded, magistrates to be created, and laws to be written'.[1]

Roman jurists acknowledged that law existed in both written and unwritten form, a legacy they described as inherited from the Greeks.[2] It was writtenness that separated law from custom. For Hermogenian this was a difference in how legal rules were created and not in authority: 'we also keep to those rules which have been sanctioned by long custom and observed for over very many years, we keep to them as being a tacit agreement of the citizen, no less than we keep to written rules of law'.[3] This distinction between law in writing and law

---

[1] This was in contrast to natural law: 'natural law is clearly the older, having been instituted by nature at the first origin of mankind' (Justinian, *Institutes* 2.1.11).

[2] Justinian, *Institutes* 1.2.3; Justinian, *Digest* 1.1.6.

[3] Justinian, *Digest* 1.3.35. The jurist Julian explained why written statute and unwritten custom should both be binding: 'given that statutes themselves are binding upon us for no other reason [than] that they have been accepted by the judgment of the populace,

without writing became important in the Middle Ages, when *ius scriptum* and *ius non scriptum* shifted from descriptions of the form of law into terms of art. They came to have precise meanings within the legal profession: *ius scriptum* came to designate law, especially learned law, and *ius non scriptum* came to designate custom. When custom was written, however, the latter term became a paradox.

This chapter examines the prominent definition of custom as an unwritten law, or *ius non scriptum*, and the meaning that *coutumier* authors in the thirteenth century attached to writing custom. The attention to the category of writtenness in assessing law and custom depended on intellectual and cultural milieu. The terminology of *ius scriptum* and *ius non scriptum* came primarily from learned circles, which wrestled with the implications of writtenness. If *coutumier* authors had been very invested in these categories, written custom would seem like a contradiction that they somehow would have to explain away. However, *coutumier* authors did not understand custom in this way. The distinction between written and unwritten and between law and custom, so important to the first lawbooks of the English common law, was not a concern for lawbook authors in northern France. Those authors who revealed their thoughts on the impact of writing on custom did it differently – they linked the issue of writtenness to the idea of legal memory.

It is important to note that just as many *coutumier* authors do not remark on writtenness as do. These were notably *coutumiers* authors who were less scholastic and more pragmatic, seeking to directly address the needs of the present. Of those who displayed a sense of legal pastness, their discussions of memory reveal their 'presentist' perception of legal actors and legal practice, one knowingly based on personal opinion and current practice. While contemporary practice was comprised of both old and more recent customs and procedures, the *coutumier* authors describe actors and a practice focused on contemporary use rather than a lionization of the past.

certainly it is fitting that what the populace has approved without any writing shall be binding upon everyone' (Julian in Bederman, *Custom as a Source of Law*, p. 21). Roman jurists had different opinions about the relationship between written and unwritten law (Justinian, *Digest* 1.3.32–41).

Custom as Unwritten Law

Ius scriptum and *ius non scriptum* began as terms that described the form in which law was packaged and, over time, changed to describe different types of law. By the time the *coutumier* authors were writing, these were terms of art among learned legal intellectuals. When and why did writtenness, or the written or unwritten form of law, become important? When did these ideas about the form of law come to be mapped on to different types of norms; in other words, when did the 'written' come to designate law and the 'unwritten' come to designate custom? And, once customary law actually began to be packaged in written form in texts like the *coutumiers*, how was the ostensible paradox of written custom perceived?

The consciousness that there existed two types of law, one written and one unwritten, was described by late-antique Roman jurists as an inheritance from classical Greece.[4] According to their genealogy, *ius scriptum* and *ius non scriptum* originated with the two great superpowers of ancient Greece, Athens, and Sparta. Each city-state defined itself in terms of the form of its law. Athens stood for written law. The city traced its formative moment of law-making to Draco and Solon's codifications, and by the fourth century BCE, within the political sphere, the notion developed of a special relationship between written law, justice, and democracy – the act of writing made law known and accessible and was thus a democratic initiative.[5] Sparta, on the other hand, saw itself as a state of unwritten law. The lawgiver Lycurgus gave Sparta its law, which was so ingrained in each individual Spartan that it did not have to be written.[6] So the unwritten here was not a handicap but an asset, connoting a higher order of legal culture.

These narratives became part of Roman understandings of their own legal history in a number of ways. The narrative of inscription, of a written law that was more certain and therefore better, came from

---

[4] Justinian, *Institutes* 1.2.3; Justinian, *Digest* 1.1.6.

[5] Rosalind Thomas, 'Written in Stone?', 66. Though Sophocles' Antigone shows a different view, one of conflict between the laws of the state and the unwritten laws of the gods, which had the higher moral value (*ibid.*, 65). But this also just showed the extent to which the political ideology of Athens had come to be identified with the written form of law.

[6] Thomas, 'Written in Stone?', generally.

Greece. According to the second-century Roman jurist Pomponius, when the Romans overthrew their kings, the Romans were 'governed by uncertain laws and customs, rather than enacted laws', so they wrote to the various states of Greece for their laws, inscribed them on ivory tablets, and displayed them in the rostra.[7] This was a narrative of progress, where the unwritten was contrasted with and displaced by the written.

In the development of more precise definitions for law by the Roman classical jurists of the second and third centuries CE, unwritten law began to be theorized and then attached specifically to custom. While references to custom occurred earlier, they were generally indistinguishable from the *mos maiorum*, or custom of the ancestors. It was less a legal category than a strong argument made from tradition.[8] In fact, custom was one of several types of unwritten law, as natural law and much of the law of nations were likewise unwritten.

As classical jurists started thinking about the civil law more theoretically, written law became a catch-all term for all sorts of legislation (including the praetor's edict, decrees of the senate, and so on). This written law, however, did not cover all of the rules invoked in legal practice, and the question then became how to think about and describe the rest. Julian, for instance, thought that 'What ought to be held to in those cases where we have no applicable written law is the practice established by customs and usage.'[9] So he set custom and usage against written law, cast custom as subsidiary to law, and then added: 'Ancient custom is not undeservedly cherished as having almost statutory force'.[10] So ancient custom is a type of law, but not as authoritative as statutes or *leges*.

Comparison of custom to written law continued as custom became more important and even comparable to law. A century later, Hermogenian elevated the status of custom, as noted earlier, to be equal to written law. Around the same time, his contemporary Paul

---

[7] 'Exactis deinde regibus lege tribunicia omnes leges hae exoleverunt iterumque coepit populus romanus incerto magis iure et consuetudine aliqua uti quam per latam legem, idque prope viginti annis passus est', Justinian, *Digest* 1.2.2.3–4.

[8] The universal grant of citizenship to all free men within the Roman Empire spurred the jurists to reconsider the nature of Roman civil law, and so Justinian's *Corpus Iuris* replaced the vocabulary of law for local legal rules with the vocabulary of custom (Clifford Ando, *Law, Language, and Empire in the Roman Tradition*, pp. 31–34).

[9] Justinian, *Digest* 1.3.32.   [10] *Ibid.*

deployed the Spartan argument in custom's favour. 'This kind of law', he said, 'is held to be of particularly great authority, because approval of it has been so great that it has never been necessary to reduce it to writing'.[11] To some jurists, the unwritten had the greater authority because it was known and accepted as law even without writing.

The authority of custom grew in the late-antique Roman Empire and, by the sixth century, came to represent the foundational division of civil law. Justinian's *Institutes* explained that Roman civil law was 'divided into two branches; since in its origin it derived from the institutions of two states, namely, Athens, and Sparta', for in Sparta (Lacedaemon), they committed their laws to memory, while in Athens, they observed written laws.[12] The practice that derived its authority from use, time, and popular consent got tied to the notion of unwritten law. This occurred not so much because no custom had ever been committed to writing or because custom was the only type of unwritten law but because 'unwritten' developed as a foil to the technical definition of law as 'written'. Codification only reinforced this definition. The notions of writtenness and unwrittenness, each backed by a noble lineage and a political philosophy, became categories of law that were seemingly opposed but actually complemented each other.

By the time Isidore of Seville was composing his section on laws in his *Etymologies* in the early seventh century, law was for him not only definitionally but even etymologically something that was written. According to Isidore,

> All Law (*ius*) consists of legislation and habit (*legibus et moribus*). Law is written statute. Habit (*mos*) is custom tested by age (*vetustate probata consuetudo*), or unwritten law (*lex non scripta*), for law (*lex*, gen. *legis*) is named from reading (*legere*), because it is written.[13]

---

[11] Justinian, *Digest* 1.3.36.   [12] Justinian, *Institutes* 1.2.10.

[13] 'Omne autem ius legibus et moribus constat. Lex est constitutio scripta. Mos est vetustate probata consuetudo, sive lex non scripta. Nam lex a legendo vocata, quia scripta est. Mos autem longa consuetudo est de moribus tracta tantundem. Consuetudo autem est ius quoddam moribus institutum, quod pro lege suscipitur, cum deficit lex: nec differt scriptura an ratione consistat, quando et legem ratio commendet. Porro si ratione lex constat, lex erit omne iam quod ratione constiterit, dumtaxat quod religioni congruat, quod disciplinae conveniat, quod saluti proficiat. Vocata autem consuetudo, quia in communi est usu' (Isidore of Seville, *The Etymologies*, ed. Lindsay, https://bit.ly/3Mqfrww (accessed 7 June 2022).

The fact of writing, or lack thereof, distinguished categories of law for Isidore. Law (*lex*) was characterized by the fact of writing, as encoded in the word itself according to Isidore's invented etymology, which rooted law as legislation (*lex*) in the act of reading (*legere*). Custom, denoted by both *mos* and *consuetudo* here, is its foil as an unwritten law.

While he emphasized the notion of writtenness at the beginning of the passage, the distinction between law as written and custom as unwritten was not, as has been claimed, 'firmly drawn' by Isidore.[14] He elaborated that custom could either be written or unwritten, thus blurring the boundaries he had just drawn: 'nor does it matter whether it (*consuetudo*) exists in writing or reasoning, since reason also validates law (*legem*)'.[15] While writtenness was a characteristic of law (*lex*), it was not its sole source of legitimation. Reason could validate written or unwritten custom, just as it could validate law. At the beginning of his definition, it seems that Isidore took writtenness to be the prime distinction between custom and law. Ultimately, however, the result was terminological confusion. While Isidore presents the notion of custom as synonymous with unwritten law, he did not see unwrittenness as an essential quality of 'unwritten law'.

Writtenness as a boundary between law and custom waned after Isidore but found a new life in canonistic circles in the tenth century, appearing in the work of Regino of Prüm, Abbo of Fleury, Burchard of Worms, and Ivo of Chartres.[16] In the late tenth century, Abbo of Fleury (ca. 945–1004) referred to *ius scriptum* and *ius non scriptum*.[17] Citing Cicero and Isidore, Abbo explained that '"lex" is the written constitution of princes; "mos," however, is custom sanctioned by age, and not written'.[18] These categories were thus resurfacing,

---

[14] Ibbetson, 'Custom in Medieval Law', p. 154.

[15] Ibbetson, 'Custom in Medieval Law'.

[16] For custom in the ninth and tenth centuries, see Wehrlé, *De la coutume dans le droit canonique*, chapters 8 and 9.

[17] Mostert, *The Political Theology of Abbo of Fleury*, p. 110.

[18] '*Nam lex est principium constitutio scripta; mos vero consuetudo vetustate probate, nec tamen scripta*' (Abbo in Mostert, *The Political Theology of Abbo of Fleury*, p. 111). While Abbo noted that 'men either follow good laws, or good customs', he saw the former as having pre-eminence: 'In the same way that "rex" is said to derive from "regere", thus "lex" from "legere"'. Hence the promulgation of laws is extended to the edicts of kings, and everyone within the limits of their realm follows a Christian order with piety. Custom submits to this. If it is not impeded by public expediency it amounts to law' (*Sicut rex a regendo dicitur, ita et lex a legendo.*

though not through the *Corpus iuris civilis* but, instead, through legal ideas as filtered through other sources.

Indeed, the idea of written law conspicuously made an appearance in an anonymous polemical tract that seems to have been written in 1084, as part of the early days of the Investiture Controversy, a conflict of the later eleventh and twelfth centuries between popes and monarchs over the right to appoint church officials. This tract referred to three types of law: 'natural law, written law and customary law'.[19] This was the earliest use of the expression *ius consuetudinarium* found by Franck Roumy. The text argues for placing the spirit of the law above its letter but does not further parse these categories; nevertheless, it is significant here that human law was divided into categories that contrasted written law with customary law. Ivo of Chartres (ca. 1040–1116) even titled the fourth book of his *Decretum* 'On canonical writing and custom and on the celebration of the council'.[20]

Questions about the difference between law and custom, and their different sources of authority, form, and definition returned to preoccupy jurists in the legal revival from the twelfth century onward.[21] A council in Rouen stated that 'custom that was in opposition to written law could be defended neither by its generality nor by its long use'.[22] Not all agreed with this. Ivo, for instance, argued in favour of an ancient and immutable custom.[23] Whatever the case, this does suggest a resurgence in the contrast between law and custom,

---

Quapropter legum promulgatio regum edictis extenditur, et unusquisque infra sui regni fines imperium christianum pietate exequitur. Cui consuetudo par est; quae si publicis utilitatibus non impedit ipsa pro lege succedit; ibid., p. 110).

[19] '*ut jus naturale, jus scriptum, jus consuetudinarium*' (Roumy, '*Lex consuetudinaria, Jus consuetudinarium*', 269).

[20] 'De scripturis canonicis et consuetudinibus et celebratione concili' (Ivo in Wehrlé, *De la coutume dans le droit canonique*, p. 83).

[21] See Pennington, *The Prince and the Law*, pp. 1off. While 'written law' eventually became a term of art for Roman and canon law, it also reinforced the sovereignty claims of emperors, kings, and princes. This was the case for the early Middle Ages and the written law text, as Patrick Wormald has shown (Wormald, 'Lex Scripta and Verbum Regis'). It was also the case later when arguments for the authority of 'written law' developed alongside political commentary that vested the will of the people within the emperor, such that his will reflected the will of the people.

[22] 'Consuetudo quae scripto juri approbato opponitur, nulla sui generalitate vel temporis prolixitate defenditur' in Wehrlé, *De la coutume dans le droit canonique*, p. 86.

[23] Wehrlé, *De la coutume dans le droit canonique*, pp. 88–7.

between written and unwritten law, and in the perception of the superiority of the former over the latter.

The category of *ius non scriptum*, in contrast, seems to have been an uneasy, atmospheric one among twelfth-century scholars. The glossator Martinus, on the one hand, argued that in case of conflict, the written rule prevailed over the unwritten one.[24] Bulgarus, on the other hand, argued that a reasonable general custom could abrogate law, and John Bassianus added that law did not derive its authority from being written.[25] Meanwhile, the Vacarian gloss maintained that the only difference between custom and law was the written form.[26] Gratian, for one, departed from the Isidorian position. While Isidore said 'it does not matter whether custom is confirmed by writing or by reason', Gratian subverted this definition by explaining that 'this shows that, in part, custom has been collected in writing, and, in part, it is preserved only in the habits (*moribus*) of its followers. What is put in writing is called enactment or Law (*constitutio sive ius vocatur*), while what is not collected in writing is called by the general term "custom" (*que uero in scriptis redacta non est, generali nomine, consuetudo videlicet, appellatur*)'.[27] Gratian, then, implied that writing transformed custom into law.[28] Concomitantly, he made the lack of writing the essential attribute of custom.

This idea did not quite catch on. One gloss (D.1 c.5) refuted this idea explicitly and explained that 'it says that it does not matter whether custom is in writing or by reason alone, that is, determined without writing'.[29] Johannes Teutonicus commented on Gratian's work, circa

---

[24] Stein, 'Custom in Roman and Medieval Civil Law', 340.   [25] *Ibid.*   [26] *Ibid.*, 341.
[27] Gratian, *The Treatise on Laws*, trans. Thompson and Gordley, *dicta Gratiani post* D.1 c.5. The Latin is also the text in the First Recension: '*Cum itaque dicitur: "non differt, utrum consuetudo scriptura, uel ratione consistat," apparet, quod consuetudo partim est redacta in scriptis, partim moribus tantum utentium est reseruata. Quae in scriptis redacta est, constitutio siue ius uocatur; quae uero in scriptis redacta non est, generali nomine, consuetudo uidelicet, appellatur*' (Gratian, *Decretum magistri Gratiani*, https://bit.ly/3mptc4d (accessed 30 March 2020)).
[28] Gratian notes the wide ambit of the term 'custom' by describing it as general; from this definition, it seems it includes all usage that is unwritten. This definition also aligns custom with reason: the custom that is confirmed by reason is the one that is preserved by the usage of its followers. It is not clear how he shifts from *mos*-custom to *consuetudo*-custom in this passage.
[29] Gratian, *The Treatise on Laws*, trans. Thompson and Gordley, D.1 c.5. The clarification in this fragment concerns what is meant when a custom is confirmed by

1215–18, that '"usage" was used for unwritten law; "custom" was used generally for law whether written or unwritten'.[30] Perhaps the most telling testament to the fluid understanding of custom's form in learned communities came from Accursius, who said that city statutes were more similar to legislation than to 'written custom' (*consuetudo scripta*), thereby implicitly acknowledging the category of written custom.[31]

Closer to home, Jacques de Revigny (ca. 1230–96), professor at the University of Orleans for some time in the latter part of the thirteenth century, omitted the notion of *ius non scriptum* from his definition of custom and held that writing was a method of publicity and not an essential characteristic of law, and that its lack was not an essential characteristic of custom.[32] The fact that law was put in written form more commonly than custom was not because one was written and the other unwritten, according to Jacques, but because law was more certain that custom.[33] That this choice, though made with good reason, was not the generally accepted view can be seen in the responses of contemporaries and later scholars.[34]

By the thirteenth century, then, the category of *ius scriptum* was starting to look quite developed, and there was no real debate over the nature of law: it was legislation, it was ordinance, it was the *Corpus iuris civilis* and texts of canon law. Around this time a new elaboration

---

reason – taken here to mean it is determined without writing. The full passage focuses on the nature of custom: 'it says that it does not matter whether custom is in writing or by reason alone, that is, determined without writing, since reason also supports ordinances. In the third section which begins with "Furthermore ... " it says that as an ordinance will be a rule when it is rational, so custom will be an ordinance, that is, will be obeyed like an ordinance, as long as it is rational, congruent with religion, consistent with discipline, and helpful to salvation. It is called custom because it is in common use.' (*ibid.*)

[30] Gratian, *The Treatise on Laws*, trans. Thompson and Gordley, Ioannes Teutonicus, D.1 c.4a.

[31] Canning, *The Political Thought of Baldus de Ubaldis*, p. 96.

[32] Waelkens, *La théorie de la coutume chez Jacques de Révigny*, p. 210. Very little is known about the details of Jacques' life. He studied under Jean de Monchy, Guichard de Langres, and Simon of Paris; he was a professor at the University of Orleans for some time; he went into church service as archdeacon of Toul and then became bishop of Verdun (Paul du Plessis, 'Jacques de Revigny', pp. 72–3).

[33] Waelkens, *La théorie de la coutume chez Jacques de Révigny*, p. 210.

[34] Waelkens notes that this choice should not have been so shocking to contemporaries and later scholars for various reasons (*ibid.*, p. 211). However, the fact that it was is revealing of how Jacques' ideas were received at the time.

appeared: a reference to Roman law as *'ratio scripta'*, or written reason, a term that appeared in the early thirteenth century and took off in the fourteenth.[35]

The form of the text in manuscripts and illuminations provides some insight into the difference between 'written' and 'unwritten' law. To study Roman law at university level was to learn to practise the art of the *ius scriptum*, one that turned around the interpretation and application of the urtext. Glossing practices separated the original text from later changes and commentaries, both visually and intellectually. University lectures on Roman law consisted of the interpretation of the urtext, as depicted in Figure 3.1.

That this was a quintessentially textual form of thought is captured in depictions of law classes that showed the master with an open book before him, surrounded by students sitting at desks with their own books.[36] This contrasted with the first *coutumiers*. Though a number of the *coutumiers* used Roman law, they generally did not replicate its classic form of an urtext surrounded by glosses.[37] They certainly had no 'ordinary' gloss. Illuminations in the *coutumiers* did not depict classroom settings or even several figures holding books.

The imagery in the *coutumiers* suggests the value of the *coutumier* as a book but not as a legal practice in the lay courts that was specifically textual, as in based on written legal texts that were cited and interpreted in court. The manuscripts in Figures 3.2 and 3.3 show customary lawbooks being given to a judge and to the patron who commissioned a copy.[38]

This sort of image depicting the author presenting their book to a dedicatee or patron was common in medieval manuscripts of all types, from literature to medical books to lawbooks. While illuminations in the *coutumiers* depict the texts as a book given to such a central figure, they comparatively infrequently depict other aspects of writing related to the judicial process as can be found in

---

[35] See Alejandro Guzmán, *Ratio scripta*.   [36] McSweeney, *Priests of the Law*, p. 84.

[37] The exceptions to this are few and date to around the turn of the fourteenth century. The Latin version of the Norman *Summa de legibus* in BnF ms. lat. 12883 (see Figure 5.1) does, for instance, have some added glosses. One manuscript of the *Établissments de Saint Louis*, written in the first part of the fourteenth century (BnF ms.fr. 13985), was glossed and in addition contains a text on wills and testaments and the *Compilatio de usibus Andegavie*.

[38] For more on 'Le livre la roine', see the description of Pierre's *Conseil* in Chapter 1.

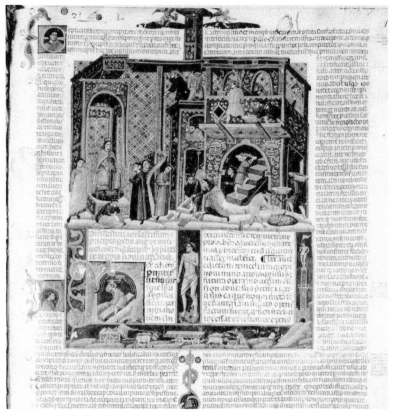

FIGURE 3.1 Roman law and the Urtext. This early fourteenth-century manuscript of Justinian's *Digest* with its Accursian gloss demonstrates the importance of the original foundational text in Roman law thought: it is offset in the middle of the page, surrounded by imagery and then encircled by the gloss. Canon law was subject to similar glossing practices. Texts of Roman and canon law did of course take other forms, but the image of the glossed text does capture the centrality of the urtext in learned intellectual culture. Glossing was a general intellectual practice and was not restricted to the subject of law. Roman law and canon law manuscripts, such as this one made in Bologna, could be decorated with highly ornate, beautiful images such as this one. Justinian, *Digestum novum cum glossis Accursii*, Bibliothèque nationale de France, ms. lat. 14341, fol. 1r.

manuscripts of canon law, such as a clerk recording the proceedings, open books being used, or voluminous documents.[39] Roman law was

[39] For imagery in canon law manuscripts, see Susan L'Engle and Robert Gibbs, *Illuminating the Law: Legal Manuscripts in Cambridge Collections.*

FIGURES 3.2 AND 3.3 Author or copyist offering lawbook to patron or dedicatee. The depiction of authors or copyists, often on bended knee, presenting their text to a patron, friend, or dedicatee is a known iconographic feature of medieval manuscript books. These manuscripts of the *Établissments de Saint Louis* and Pierre de Fontaines' *Conseil* from the last decades of the thirteenth century show texts of customary law being given to a judge and a commissioning queen (Figure 3.2 (left): *Établissments de Saint Louis*. Bibliothèque nationale de France, ms. fr. 5899, fol. 1r; Figure 3.3 (right): 'Le livre la roine'. Bibliothèque nationale de France, ms. fr. 5245).

not only the study of a text but a quintessentially textual form of thought. While the study of a book of customary law was valuable, customary law thinking did not turn around the interpretation, application, or citation of an original, foundational text.

The question then becomes whether or how the categories of *ius scriptum* and *ius non scriptum* affected those who composed texts of customary law and whether they saw the category of *ius non scriptum* as problematic. Some authors perceived it to be a problem and others did not, and this variation shows that there was, as yet, no blanket understanding of custom as *ius non scriptum*. Authors' reactions may have been related to their proximity to and need to be seen as legitimate by scholarly circles that categorized law and custom this way.

Those who composed texts of customary law in England were troubled by how their own writing fitted within this framework. Writing in the late 1180s, the *Glanvill* author reflected that:

Although the laws of England are not written, it does not seem absurd to call them laws [...] For if, merely for lack of writing, they were not deemed to be laws, then surely writing would seem to supply to written laws a force of greater authority than either the justice of him who decrees them or the reason of him who establishes them.[40]

The *Glanvill* author was clearly well aware of definitions of law as *lex scripta* and *ius scriptum*, and custom as *ius non scriptum*. Avoiding the notion of custom altogether, the *Glanvill* author argued that unwritten laws were still, fundamentally, laws.[41]

However, he did object to the idea that an unwritten custom should not be seen as law simply because of its form. He was clearly replying to the idea, if not the accusation, that it was absurd to call custom law. Authority, it was argued here, should come not from the fact of inscription but from the legislator, and specifically from the legislator's justice and reasoning.

This was not a defence of the category of custom or an attempt to show that custom as *ius non scriptum* was equal to law; rather, the goal was to elevate the norms of English courts to the category of law. The text began by designating 'the laws of England' as not written and then argued that despite this they could and should indeed be understood as laws. Perhaps the author purposefully chose to avoid custom-terms such as *mos* or the by now more popular *consuetudo* with this clear focus on framing the contents of the text as law.

The Bracton authors took up this idea but also modified it, placing this discussion squarely within a framework shaped by the law as *ius*

---

[40] '*Leges autem Anglicanas licet non scriptas leges appellari non uideatur absurdam, cum hoc ipsum lex sit "quod principi placet, legis habet uigorem," eas scilicet quas super / dubiis in concilio diffiniendis, procerum quidem consilio et principis accedente auctoritate, constat esse promulgatas. Si enim ob solum scripture defectum leges minime censerentur, maioris proculdubio auctoritatis robur ipsis legibus uideatur accomodare scriptura quam uel decernentis equitas aut ratio statuentis*' (Hall, trans., *Glanvill*, prologue 3).

[41] The Becket conflict lay in the background, where royal lawyers must have been sensitive to the accusation that royal law was something lesser than the *ius non scriptum* of Rome and of canon law (Hyams, 'Orality and Literacy in the Age of Angevin Law Reforms', p. 67).

scriptum and custom as *ius non scriptum*. They altered *Glanvill* as follows:

Though in almost all lands use is made of the laws and written law (*leges* and *ius scriptum*), England alone uses unwritten law and custom (*iure non scripto et consuetudine*). There law (*ius*) derives from nothing written [but] from what usage has approved (*ex non scripto ius venit quod usus comprobavit*). Nevertheless, it will not be absurd to call English laws laws (*leges*), though they are unwritten.[42]

The Bracton authors were concerned with establishing these categories. Drawing on a combination of Justinan's *Institutes*, Azo, and *Glanvill*, the authors opened with the fundamental division of civil law developed by Romanists and canonists. For clarity, they emphasized what fell within those categories by collocating laws and written law (*leges* and *ius scriptum*) and unwritten law and custom (*iure non scripto et consuetudine*).[43] Thomas McSweeney shows that this passage distinguishes what is done in England from Roman and canon law, while at the same time placing English law firmly within those traditions.[44]

The comparative and exceptionalist statement that England alone used unwritten law and custom is a puzzling one from a French perspective because the Bracton text incorporated more Roman law material than any French *coutumier*. Such a statement says more about the authors' view of English law than any truth about law outside of England. The authors display an anxiety about the learned categories of written and unwritten law and what they meant for English law. The English texts show their authors' perceived need to acknowledge the problem of unwrittenness and then to find a way of dismissing it in their introductory content so that the reader could understand why the material within could be described as law even though it had the primary characteristic of custom.

---

[42] '*Cum autem fere in omnibus regionibus utatur legibus et iure scripto, sola Anglia usa est in suis finibus iure non scripto et consuetudine. In ea quidem ex non scripto ius venit quod usus comprobavit. Sed non erit absurdum leges Anglicanas licet non scriptas leges appellare, cum legis vigorem habeat quidquid de consilio et consensu magnatum et rei publicæ communi sponsione, auctoritate regis sive principis præcedente, iuste fuerit definitum et approbatum. Sunt etiam in Anglia consuetudines plures et diversæ secundum diversitatem locorum ...*' (Bracton, *De legibus et consuetudinibus Angliæ*, ed. and trans. Thorne, vol 2, p. 19, bracton.law.harvard.edu /Framed/mframe.htm (accessed 6 July 2018)).

[43] *Ibid.*, 2:19nn.4–9.   [44] McSweeney, *Priests of the Law*, p. 109.

The authors of the northern French vernacular customary lawbooks, however, did not seem to be bothered by these learned categories at all. This is especially notable as there were clearly differences of opinion among the pre-eminent Roman jurists of northern France about whether custom needed to unwritten in order to be custom.[45] They were not concerned with how French law fitted within this framework, nor were they concerned that it could be called *ius non scriptum* and still in fact be *scriptum*.

Even the Latin texts were unconcerned with these categories. The Norman *Summa de legibus* did not address the form of law, instead defining customs as 'mores had from antiquity (*consuetudines vero sunt mores ab antiquitate habiti*), approved by rulers and kept by the people, which delimit of whom [a thing] is or to whom it pertains'.[46] They betrayed no concern about the status of custom vis-à-vis law or written law. In his definition of custom, Philippe de Beaumanoir tried to define 'what is and what should be held as custom', but did not incorporate writing or lack thereof into his definition.[47] Unlike the English texts, the French texts had no anxiety about these learned categorizations or about the apparent contradiction of written custom.

This was the case even in texts that had a familiarity with *ius scriptum* as a term of art. The compiler of the *Établissements de Saint Louis* (ca. 1272) used the expression 'written law' to denote Romano-canonical law; for instance, the text said 'it is written in the Code', 'according to the written law in the Code', 'according to the law written in the Digest', or 'according to written law in the *Decretals*'.[48] However, he also referred to sections written in his own text as 'written,' though he did not designate them as 'written law'. He clearly saw Roman and canon law as written law but was comfortable referring to his own written text without feeling compelled to explain how it fitted within the category of law versus custom or *ius non scriptum*.

[45] Jacques de Revigny, as noted above, was a notable proponent of this view (see Waelkens, *La théorie de la coutume chez Jacques de Révigny*, pp. 208–12).
[46] *Le grand coutumier de Normandie*, ed. de Gruchy, trans. Everard, XI.
[47] Beaumanoir, *Coutumes de Beauvaisis*, ed. Salmon, XXIV.
[48] 'et est escrit ou Code, De edicto divi Adriani tollendo, l. Quamvis quis se filium defunct, etc.' and 'selonc droit escrit ou Code' or 'selonc droit escrit en la Digeste' (*Établissements*, ed. Viollet, Book II.4) or 'selonc droit escrit en Decretales' (*ibid.*, Book I.89).

These categories that came to define law and custom had a history that began in Greek and especially Roman times and developed throughout the medieval period. Law as *ius scriptum* and laws as *leges scriptae* seem to have been unproblematic categories in and of themselves. For those familiar with and invested in these categories, the problem was that custom and customary practice did not automatically or comfortably conform to the learned categories developed to explain their place in the legal universe.

Writtenness, Memory, and Change

This is not to say that the written form was unimportant to the world of the thirteenth-century *coutumiers* but only that its significance lay less in categorizing law and custom in the learned manner and more in its cultural signification.

The *coutumiers* were written partially because historical factors had converged to create the conditions for this writing, but they were also written in a deliberate attempt to grapple with the intense pace of legal change in the second half of the thirteenth century. The lay courts were undergoing fundamental sociocultural change, and the people of the law associated with those courts were intensely aware of it.[49] The vernacular, initially the language of oral communication and then of literature, was rapidly expanding as the language of other spheres of lay activity. And as legal practice was professionalizing and becoming more complicated, the use of writing within the field of law expanded. Rather than an image of stability and changelessness that is so often associated with customary law, some *coutumiers* evince the opposite: a malaise if not overt anxiety about a legal culture that was rapidly transforming.

The very pace of change made memory a preoccupation for some of the *coutumier* authors – those closest to scholastic and university intellectual milieus. For them, memory was important because people did not remember. Just as earlier charters associated records with the preservation of memory, Pierre de Fontaines and Philippe de Beaumanoir both said they wrote about custom in order to aid memory.

---

[49] Cohen, *Crossroads of Justice*, pp. 20ff.

The language of memory is often deployed in the service of social traditionalism and resistance to change, and some aspects of the writing of the *coutumiers* can be interpreted in this light. However, the texts themselves and the opportunities they created were innovative. This ambivalence may not have been an incongruous contradiction. As Mary Carruthers has noted, despite the increasing availability of books, medieval society remained essentially memorial in nature.[50] However, this did not indicate a rote re-enactment of the past: memory was identified 'with creative thinking, learning (invention and recollection), and the ability to make judgments (prudence and wisdom)'.[51] The emphasis on writing to aid memory, then, did not support a rigid and fixed society but rather a society that recognized the creative aspect of the memorial act.

Four *coutumier* authors – Pierre de Fontaines, the author of the Norman *Summa de legibus*, Philippe de Beaumanoir, and the author of the *Coutumier d'Artois* – made explicit statements about why they used the increasingly widespread technology of writing to record custom. These authors saw writing as a support to the frailty of human memory, a topos common to medieval sources. This idea went back to Isidore of Seville, who explained that written letters were created 'in order to remember things. For lest they fly into oblivion, they are bound by letters. For so great is the variety of things that all cannot be learned by hearing, or contained only in memory.'[52] The natural process of memory is to flee, and individual

---

[50] Carruthers, *The Book of Memory*, p. 195.

[51] Carruthers, *The Book of Memory*. Trevor Livelton has noted that while 'memory' is a more common term, he prefers 'recollection' in analysis of modern archives 'to point to the element of choice implicit in the idea. Memory can be involuntary, whereas recollection suggests something more deliberate. As well, *recollection* better embodies the ambiguity in this root meaning between memories that are distinctly personal or subjective and those that have a social or objective quality, simply because they are shared with others' (Livelton, *Archival Theory, Records and the Public*, p. 84n.2). While Livelton is concerned with modern archival theory, his thoughts on 'recollection' apply directly to the issues discussed here. The notion of 're-collecting' may be more apt in the *coutumier* context as well – the authors were deliberately and selectively collecting past notions (customs, usages, procedures) that were scattered and combining them in a new way for their own social context.

[52] '*Usus litterarum repertus propter memoria rerum. Nam ne oblivione fugiant, litteris alligantur. In tanta enim rerum varietate nec disci audiendo poterant omnia, nec memoria contineri*' (Isidore of Seville, *Etymologies*, 1.3.2, in Carruthers, *The Book of Memory*, p. 139).

memories must be strapped down by letters if they are to be retained. Isidore saw writing and memorizing as essentially the same process – 'writing is an activity of remembering, as remembering is writing on the tables of the mind'.[53]

The concern for the preservation of memory spanned various intellectual disciplines and genres of writing during this period. Students of *ars memorativa* included students of law, bureaucratic clerks, and notaries.[54] The invocation of memory had long been commonplace in charters, which cemented claims and recorded moments of agreement, loss, subjugation, victory, munificence, and belonging. For instance, in a charter from 1211 confirming that a new hospital would not be taxed by her or placed under her jurisdiction, Countess Blanche confirmed that 'In order to preserve perpetual memory of this act, I have had this charter drawn up and sealed with my seal'.[55] Despite these sorts of invocations of permanence in charters, Brigitte Bedos-Rezak has shown that they were not necessarily invoked in land disputes and so not always the 'obstacles to oblivion' intimated by the language of memory in the text.[56]

The *coutumiers* that cited ideas of memory – Pierre de Fontaines' *Conseil*, the Norman *Summa de legibus*, Philippe de Beaumanoir's *Coutumes de Beauvaisis*, and the *Coutumier d'Artois* – were also those with the closest intellectual affiliations to scholastic or university legal culture. Other *coutumier* authors did not directly address the role of memory in the body of their texts. The views of the former authors should not be assumed to apply to the latter. The relationship and orientation of memory was fundamentally different in

---

[53] Carruthers, *The Book of Memory*, p. 139. The system of shorthand and abbreviations known as *notaria* was one that was learnt by medieval lawyers and notaries – it was notably prized by John of Salisbury and, as Thomas Bradwardine noted around 1333, learning the notarial art helped attain the 'highest perfection' in the art of memory (*ibid.*, pp. 140–2).

[54] Carruthers, *The Book of Memory*, p. 153.

[55] 'Foundation of the Hospital of La Barre' in Theodore Evergates, *Feudal Society in Medieval France*, pp. 140–1.

[56] Brigitte Bedos-Rezak, *When Ego Was Imago: Signs of Identity in the Middle Ages*, p. 21.

each case, with differing emphases on the past and the passage of time as important contexts for custom.

The *coutumier* authors who did invoke memory clearly felt they belonged to the intellectual tradition that saw writing as an antidote to forgetting. They were moving in the wider literary current of the age, which was not only concerned about forgetting things old or past but also about remembering specific types of information. By specifying their writing as an act of memory, *coutumier* authors who invoked this topos were participating in this established intellectual ecology.

For example, the second preface to the Norman *Summa de legibus* explained that laws and statutes were established through the hard work of the rulers of Normandy (*Normannorum principes*) with the counsel and consent of prelates, counts, barons, and other prudent men. But because of diverse languages and the lapse of pristine memory, these laws and statutes 'might be shut away in the dark prison of oblivion'.[57] So the author decided, 'inspired by the Lord, for the common convenience of everyone', to attempt 'to recall some if not all of them from the darkness of ignorance, so that, deposited in the treasury of writings by my labour, for those as much in the future as in the present, let the role of writings by which lawsuits to come to an end be declared'.[58]

Vernacular *coutumier* authors drew on these familiar topoi, but also expressed specific contemporary reasons for the disappearance of old norms. Pierre's treatment of memory, for instance, included a genuine anxiety about the lay courts. People were not making an effort to try to remember old customs, and they were being corrupted and forgotten:

---

[57] *Coutumiers de Normandie: Textes critiques*, vol. 2, *La Summa de legibus in curia laicali*, prologus, p. 3.

[58] '*per diversas diversiorum linguas vagantia, elapsa pristinorum memoria, in ignorancie ergastulum recluserit oblivio tenebrorum, ad commune commodum singulorum, aspirante Domino, et si non omnia eorum tamen aliqua ab ignorancie tenebris aggrediar revocare, ut in scripturarum thesauro meo sudore deposita futuris ac presentibus ad lites dirimendas litterarum officio declarentur*' (*ibid.*). Everard translates '*litterarum officio*' as 'the form of letters', which indicates the shape or structure of writing, but *officium* in the thirteenth century really seems to indicate more a position or role, notably one that is authoritative or administrative, and I think the text is referring here to the general place of writing in the ending of lawsuits. That said, the French text skips this expression and simplifies this last part to: 'how court proceedings should be brought to an end' ('mon travail soit esclarie par scriptures a ceuls qui sont et qui avenir sont comment li plait doivent estre fine', Bibl. Nat. ms. fr. 5961).

As to the customs of the Vermandois, I am much concerned [*esbahi*]: because *the old customs, which good folk [preudome] used to observe and put into practice in the past are much destroyed and almost all have disappeared* in part because of *baillis* and provosts, who are more concerned with *doing their will* than observing customs: in part by the will of people [ceus] who value more their own opinion than the actions of past generations [*des anciens*]: in part again because of all the rich folk, who have permitted the poor folk to be despoiled, and now the rich are despoiled by the poor, so that the area is almost without customs. *So that everything works by the common opinion* of four or three persons, without an exemplar [*exemplaire*] of a customary law.[59]

We do not find the traditional topoi of memory and forgetting in this passage, whereby humanity appears defenceless against the powerful forces of time and oblivion. Rather, Pierre located the loss of old customs squarely within the field of human agency: it was not that memory naturally faded due to an insuperable force but that customs were disappearing because of human action, human choice, and people's self-assured confidence in their own opinions. In other words, Pierre was describing a wilful forgetting.

Pierre felt that judges were corrupting custom because they made judgments based on their own opinion at the expense of old rules. This anxiety about the use of personal opinion – which we might call judicial discretion – was felt elsewhere at this time. A little earlier, the introduction to *Bracton* stated that this text was written because laws and customs were being misapplied by unlearned judges and were often subject to the will and opinion of the powerful rather than to the 'authority of law' or the 'ancient judgments of just men' – ideas already found in Azo's *Summa Codicis*.[60]

---

[59] 'por ce que les ancienes costumes que li preudome çà en arière soloient [avoir l'habitude de] tenir et user, sont molt anéanties et presque totes failles, partie par bailli et par prévoz, qui plus entendent à lor volonté fère que à user des costumes; partie par la volonté de sens, qui plus s'aert à son avis que a fez des anciens: partie mès presque toz les riches, qui on soufert à despoillier lespovres, et or son par les povres li riches despouitié, et si que li païs est à bien près sanz coutumes' (Pierre de Fontaines, *Conseil*, ed. Marnier, I.3; italic added for emphasis).

[60] 'Since these laws and customs are often misapplied by the unwise and unlearned who ascend the judgment seat before they have learned the laws and stand amid doubts and the confusion of opinions, and frequently subverted by the greater who decide cases according to their own will rather than by the authority of the laws, I, Henry de Bracton, to instruct the lesser judges, if no one else, have turned my mind to the

The treatise writers' anxieties were a response to a world where personal opinion was key in legal thinking. This can be seen in debates beyond northern France, as well, about how trials should be conducted. The discussion of judicial discretion yielded some divergent and contradictory theories among jurists of the *ius commune*.[61] Some argued for close adherence to the two-witness rule, while others argued that more discretion would render punishment more efficient.[62] While the former argument prevailed in law schools, it was the latter – discretion, and personal opinion – that shaped criminal statutes in Italy in the thirteenth and fourteenth centuries.[63] In cases of homicide in England, juries made 'conscientious verdicts' to get the result they desired, instead of producing a verdict that closely followed the law.[64] The problematic contest between older rules and opinion was clearly a preoccupation in diverse legal communities.

The recourse to opinion rather than text was also clear in another passage where Pierre mentioned textualized practice. He was dissatisfied with current legal practice, where 'everything works by the common opinion of four or three persons, without having an exemplar [*exemplaire*] of custom'.[65] Pierre did not refer to an example (*essample*) but to an exemplar, namely, a model or a textual prototype. This meant a written document, and the fact that he expressed frustration that written text was not understood as a reference for court practitioners implied that he felt it should be. Nonetheless, lay jurists were comfortable relying on their group opinion rather than text.

---

ancient judgments of just men [. . .] by the aid of writing to be preserved to posterity forever' (*Cum autem huiusmodi leges et consuetudines per insipientes et minus doctos, qui cathedram iudicandi ascendunt antequam leges didicerint, sæpius trahantur ad abusum, et qui stant in dubiis et in opinionibus et multotiens pervertuntur a maioribus, qui potius proprio arbitrio quam legum auctoritate causas decidunt, ad instructionem saltem minorum ego, Henricus de Brattone, animum erexi ad vetera iudicia iustorum [. . .] scripturæ suffragio perpetuæ memoriæ commendanda . . .*; Bracton, *De legibus et consuetudinibus Angliæ*, ed. and trans. Thorne, 2:19).

[61] See Richard M. Fraher, 'Conviction According to Conscience'.
[62] See *ibid.*, 27.
[63] *Ibid.*   [64] See Thomas Andrew Green, *Verdict According to Conscience*.
[65] 'Si que presque toz va par avis comun de IIII ou de III, sans exemplaire de costume qu'il tiengnent. Et de ces avis avient-il molt souvent que tex pert qui gaagnier devroit' (Pierre de Fontaines, *Conseil*, ed. Marnier, I.3).

Like Pierre, Philippe de Beaumanoir also had the sense that human choice favoured the new instead of the old and that the old was falling into desuetude. He did not repeat Pierre's language of opinion and will but perceived a similar problem, albeit described differently, that Pierre had noted some twenty years earlier. In his prologue, he stated that:

because we see people *acting according to local customs, and forsaking old laws for these customs*, it seems *to us and also to others* that it is good and profitable to *write down and register the customs which are current now, so that they can be observed without change from now on*; because owing to memories which fade and people's life which is short, what is not written down is soon forgotten.[66]

Beaumanoir placed his writing more squarely within traditional concepts of the idea of writing. He used the language of *memoria* within its conventional framework – memories fade, life is short, and the unwritten is forgotten. While a significant group saw custom in terms of the expediency of the present, Beaumanoir belonged to a different community of people who were apprehensive about the fate of old rules – 'it seems to *us and also to others* that it is good and profitable to write down and register the customs' – a community devoted to preserving knowledge and staving off forgetting. The immanence of forgetting can be seen in Beaumanoir's goal to record specifically those customs of his particular moment in time, those that were 'current now' but could change at any moment.[67]

Philippe de Beaumanoir contributed a new idea to the *coutumier* tradition in the passage above: the idea of using writing to condition practice and to create a practice that could become fixed and unchanging. No other northern French *coutumier* made this claim, though the Bracton text had earlier mentioned using the aid of writing to preserve what the author(s) found noteworthy in the

---

[66] 'Mes pour ce que nous veons user selonc coustumes des terres et lessier les anciennes lois pour les coustumes, il m'est avis, et as autres aussi, que teus coustumes qui maintenant sont uses sont bonnes et pourfitables a escrire et a enregistrer si qu'eles soient maintenues sans changier does ores en avant, que, par les memoires qui sont escouloujans et par les vies as gens qui sont courtes, ce qui n'est escrit est tost oublié' (Beaumanoir, *Coutumes de Beauvaisis*, ed. Salmon, prologue s. 7).

[67] Pierre de Fontaines also refers to the usage that is current now 'par l'usage qui or cort' (Pierre de Fontaines, *Conseil*, ed. Marnier, IV.18).

ancient judgement of just men 'to posterity forever'.[68] To use text in
the service of memory was one thing, but Beaumanoir went beyond this
and envisioned the formative role of text: the power of letters to shape
human action.

Beaumanoir does not elaborate on what the idea of fixity might have
meant to him or the contours of possibility that he imagined when he
stated that customs ought to be observed without change. His goal here
seems to have been less to imagine a utopian formalistic society and
more to highlight the speed at which he felt customs to be falling into
desuetude. Beaumanoir makes this point strongly in the conclusion of
the *Coutumes de Beauvaisis*:

And since the truth is that *customs come to an end* because of *young jurors who
do not know the old customs well*, so that in the future the opposite of what we
have put into this book will be observed to happen, we pray to all to excuse us,
for when we wrote the book, *we wrote as far as we could what was enforced or
what should have been done ordinarily* in Beauvais; and the *corruption of the
time* to come should not bring us into ill repute, or be blamed on our book.[69]

Pierre de Fontaines, as we saw earlier, observed that opinion and will
were displacing sources of law that he perceived as more legitimate.
About a quarter of a century later, Beaumanoir attributed the same
phenomenon of displacement to a lack of knowledge of the old
customs, behind which seems to have lurked a lack of desire to
adhere to them.[70] Beaumanoir turned to the idea of writing as an act

---

[68] 'I, Henry de Bracton, to instruct the lesser judges, if no one else, have turned my mind
to the ancient judgments of just men, examining diligently, not without working long
into the night watches, their decisions, consilia and responsa, and have collected
whatever I found therein worthy of note into a summa, putting it in the form of titles
and paragraphs, without prejudice to any better system, by the aid of writing to be
preserved to posterity forever (*scripturæ suffragio perpetuæ memoriæ commendanda*)' (Bracton, *De legibus et consuetudinibus Angliæ*, ed. and trans. Thorne,
II.19).

[69] 'Et comme la verité soit tele que les coustumes se corrompent par les juenes jugeeurs
qui ne sevent pas bien les anciennes coustumes, par quoi l'en voie ou tans a venir le
contraire d'aucune des choses que nous avons mis en cest livre, nous prions a tous que
l'en nous en vueille tenir pour escusé, car ou tans que nous feismes de tout nostre
pouoir nous escrisimes ce qui tenoit et devoit ester fet communement en Beauvoisins:
si ne nous doit pas disfamer ne blasmer nostre livre la corrupcions du tans a venir'
(Beaumanoir, *Coutumes de Beauvaisis*, ed. Salmon, conclusion s. 1982).

[70] The need for judges to be wise and learned is also in Bracton, Azo, and other sources
going back to the Justinianic corpus.

of registration and a medium of fixity, but he seems to have done so because it was the opposite of the reality he was experiencing. Writing, far from shaping action, became the measure of time past, change, and desuetude.

Like Pierre, Beaumanoir betrayed a deep angst about the pace of legal change. Even the fixity of books could not prevent the rapid obsolescence of the ideas within them. This may seem somewhat dramatic and alarmist, but it underscored his own perception of the extent of legal change occurring around him. This was most plainly revealed in the first words of Beaumanoir's work, where he begins his text with the following introductory words: 'Here begins the book of the customs and usages of Beauvais as they were current at the time this book was made, that is to say in the year of our Lord's incarnation 1283'.[71] He indexes custom not to communal memory, nor to his own memory, nor to his lifetime, nor to the tenure of the count of Clermont, nor to the reign of a specific king – all legitimate and common contemporary ways of indexing time. Instead, Beaumanoir's awareness of the pace of change led him to pinpoint the customs he described to a specific year – they were valid in 1283 – and Beaumanoir was accountable for an accurate description of custom for that particular year only. Before this year, some customs and usages may have been different, and likewise, after that date they would also change. This presentness of custom – its contemporary quality and immediacy – also reappeared later in his text, where he clarified that he was discussing 'the custom that there is now', as opposed to the custom that was in force prior to the present moment or that would be in force afterwards.[72] Beaumanoir himself was explicitly *not* writing down custom as handed down through generations, consecrated by age and communal consensus, that is, the developing definition of custom in the universities. Rather, he was recording new and current 'custom' that had replaced old laws in the form that he saw his contemporaries using it.[73]

---

[71] 'Ci commence li livres des coustumes et des usages de Beauvoisins selonc ce qu'il couroit ou tans que cest livres fu fes, c'est assavoir en l'an de l'Incarnacion Nostre Seigneur .M.CC.IIIIxx et trois', Beaumanoir, *Coutumes de Beauvaisis*, ed. Salmon, incipit.

[72] 'mes par la coustume qui maintenant i est' (*ibid.*, XL.1257), 'la coustume qui ore queurt' (*ibid.*, XXXVIII.1133).

[73] Interestingly, he nonetheless defines custom as 'maintained for so long as men can remember without debate' ('maintenue de si long tans comme il puet souvenir a home sans debat'; *ibid.*, s. 683).

The third *coutumier* that overtly linked its efforts to *ars memoriae* was the *Coutumier d'Artois*, which was less philosophical and less sorrowful about the issue of memory and forgetting. The author put the 'laws and customs of the region of the lay court [... in writing] with brevity, because memory is short and things soon gone and this is not enough to remember many things, because new things take away the memory of old ones'.[74] Memory here was envisioned as a finite space. Accordingly, the author took a more pragmatic approach to making things easier to remember by reducing their quantity. Drawing inspiration from the 'good clerk Orasses' (the ancient author Horace), the author concluded this was the best option because 'the hearts of people better retain short words than long ones'.[75] The author's views on memory shaped his presentation of custom: the text contained the most memorable version of custom, a briefer version rather than the most accurate or complete one.

---

[74] 'Et de ce m'avés requis et requires que je fasse un escrit, selonc les loiys et coustumes dou pais de court laie. Et je les ai mis briement, pour ce que memoire est escoulour-gans et chose tost alee, et ce souffist mie a ramenbrer tant de chose, car les nouvieles choses tolent la ramenbrance des vies.' (*Coutumier d'Artois*, ed. Tardif, prologue, s. 4; note this is not in manuscripts A and B). See Carruthers, *The Book of Memory*, p. 146.

[75] 'A cette chose s'accorde Orasses, li bons clers, qui dist: "Quanques tu commanderas, di briement", car li cuer des gens retienent mieus les paroles courtes, que les longhes: ne nuls riens n'est isniele a oir a celui qui est desirrans d'oir, ançois li samble que li isnieletés de le parole est demourance' (*Coutumier d'Artois*, prologue). Note how memory is seen to be located in the heart, rather than other parts of the body. The link between memory and brevity was not new; for instance, Hugh of St Victor noted that 'memory rejoices in brevity'. In fact, it had even appeared in the earlier Castilian *Code of Cuenca*, which also cited Horace as its source: 'Therefore, rejecting the showy circumlocutions of prologues, I cite the phase, "I made an effort to be brief" [Horace, *Epistulae* 2.3.25]' (*The Code of Cuenca*, trans. Powers, prologue). This prologue emphasized utility – the author presented himself as more inclined to utility than to the sweetness of poetry. He also made a note of memory: 'the memory of men is fragile and insufficient for a multitude of things and for this reason one has proceeded with the sagacity to put the laws of legal statute and civil rights in writing' (*ibid.*). The dating of this text is debated. Powers makes a good argument for a twelfth-century date rather than a later one (*ibid.*, pp. 19ff). This does not leave out the possibility of later commentator-copyists adding interpolations into the text, the earliest sample of which we have from the mid-thirteenth century. This may have very well been the case since the prologue, as those who argue for a later date have noted (*ibid.*, p. 19), is composed with a high-handed rhetorical style more consistent with a later date. Contrast this to the *Ustages of Barcelona*, which used the language of issue and decree but did not reflect on the writtenness of the text (*The Ustages of Barcelona*, trans. Kagay, s. 1–2).

The importance of memory in this group of *coutumiers* was a reaction to change and a feeling of loss. By the second half of the thirteenth century, change had accelerated and was easily observable – and, for some, undesirable. Four of our first *coutumiers* of northern France reflect this view, but they do not constitute the majority of the texts. Instead, memory is a non-issue for other *coutumiers*, which communicate their customs assuming their immediacy and contemporary relevance.[76] Even those authors who wrote with a sense of legal commemoration recognized that there was a currency or 'presentness' to custom.

**

The definition and theorization of custom occurred both along with and in contrast to the definition and theorization of law. The history of *lex non scripta* did not run directly parallel to that of *lex scripta*, even as it attached to it, was a reaction to it, and became its foil. *Lex non scripta* and *lex scripta* were learned designations and learned debates, ones that did not neatly overlay customary law as practised in or theorized from the lay courts. From the vantage point of the lay courts, writtenness did provoke anxiety for some, but that anxiety stemmed from the ephemeral nature of custom, even when written. For lay jurists of the secular courts, the fast pace of legal change quickened anxieties about writing, fixity, memory, and forgetting.

A passing comment by Jean de Joinville nicely captures this pace of change. He noted that Louis IX organized things so that, after mass, some members of his entourage, including the Lord of Nesle, the Count of Soissons, and Joinville himself, would go to hear the 'pleas of the gate *(plez de la porte)* that we now call petitions *(requestes)*'.[77] Within his own lifetime, Joinville saw the business of law professionalizing and its terminology changing and specializing. Joinville had been seneschal of Champagne; in fact, his name appeared in a number of cases described in the *Ancien Coutumier de Champagne*. He was sensitive to legal change between the events of his narrative in the 1240s and the

---

[76] Kuskowski, 'The Time of Custom and the Medieval Myth of an Ancient Customary Law' (forthcoming).

[77] Jean de Joinville, *Vie de Saint Louis*, ed. and trans. Monfrin, p. 57. The pleas were called *plets de la porte* because pleas were often held at gateways or doorways, in this case, the entrance of the king's home, but the terminology changed to describe more formally what was being done.

first years of the 1300s when he was writing the *Life* – the same time span when the first vernacular *coutumiers* flourished.[78]

The designation of custom as *lex non scripta* must have been known to those *coutumier* authors familiar with Roman and canon law, at the very least. We might question, then, how or why they had no concern about written custom as a concept. 'Unwritten law' began as a description of the form of law and as a way to distinguish law from custom. Why did *lex non scripta* remain a useful category and an effective way of describing custom even after it was inscribed and physically become a *ius scriptum*?

Perhaps because it described a legal culture where the written text was not treated as a supreme authority, even though all legal writing – Roman law, canon law, texts of customs – could be sources for crafting a good argument from 'custom'. *Lex non scripta* had shifted from describing the form of law to being a technical term for custom, one that better reflected the use of text and place of textual authority in the lay courts and the practice of customary law. Beaumanoir explained this most clearly when, despite his dismay, he could not help but describe custom as essentially an unwritten writing. It was written but did not have the fixity of writing. Ultimately, with writing, it embodied a contradiction: it was a sometimes-written *ius non scriptum*.

---

[78] *Ibid*. The *plets de la porte* must refer approximately to the 1240s; it was in the years before Louis went on crusade in 1248. Jeanne of Navarre had asked Joinville to write Louis IX's life, which was written sometime between her death in 1305 and the text's dedication to Louis IX in 1309. Jean de Joinville lived a remarkably long time, almost one hundred years – from 1224 to 1317.

PART II

POLITICAL AND INTELLECTUAL TENSIONS

4

Uneasy Jurisdictions: Lay and Ecclesiastical Law

The juridical sphere has a political aspect, one that is visible in the *coutumiers* notably in their treatment of the subject of jurisdiction. While jurisdiction literally meant to 'speak the law', its meaning was more specific than that: it was a term of art developed in Roman law for the authority that designates the ability to hold court. It orders power as an authority 'to do justice'; in the words of Bradin Cormack, it 'is the precondition for the juridical as such, for the very capacity of the law to come into effect'.[1]

The *coutumier* authors did not always use the term jurisdiction, but they were consistently interested in its central preoccupation: the boundaries of law and power. The texts all identified themselves as belonging to the lay courts and placed great emphasis on this jurisdictional setting. This was not an inward-looking designation but an oppositional and comparative one. The *coutumiers* belonged to the lay courts as opposed to the other sort – the ecclesiastical courts, with their clerks, Latin, and canon law. The *coutumiers* were designed to theorize, regularize, and professionalize the lay courts to assert the nature and ambit of these in contrast to ecclesiastical courts that had already gone through the same process.

Anne Lefebvre-Teillard observed in 1984 that the place of canon law in the *coutumiers* has largely been ignored, despite the fact that the *coutumiers* referred to and quoted canon law as well as the practice of

---

[1] Bradin Cormack, *A Power to Do Justice*, pp. 1, 3.

ecclesiastical courts relatively often.[2] Aside from her article, however, the place of canon law in the *coutumiers* has received little attention with the exception of an article by Robert Jacob. Jacob steps back from the main controversy embroiling the *coutumiers* in the last few decades; namely, whether references to the term 'common law' (*droit commun*) in the *coutumiers* were references to Roman law or to a notion of a common customary law.[3] Instead, he focuses on the manner in which canon law and ecclesiastical court procedure appeared in Philippe de Beaumanoir's *Coutumes de Beauvaisis*, showing their importance and arguing that canon law was central to the history of the *coutumiers*.[4] Scholarly debate about the *coutumiers*, he argues, should pay attention to the tensions between local church courts and lay courts.[5]

In addition to the importance accorded to canon law, the *coutumiers* reflected lay jurisdiction and made a political argument about it. They aimed to uphold, organize, and further the lay jurisdiction, which meant more broadly that they were intended to strengthen and develop lay lordship. Thomas Bisson defines lordship as including 'personal commands over dependent people who might be peasants in quasi-servile status or knights or vassals having or seeking elite standing; the word also denotes the value or extent of such dependencies (patrimony, *dominium*)'.[6] Lordship and its juridical power, jurisdiction, were relational concepts and involved all levels of power. Scholars such as Jacques Krynen and Albert Rigaudière have rightly emphasized that the development of royal power is important to the history of the *coutumiers*.[7] However, the assertion of royal power was paralleled by an assertion of regional lordship, and the *coutumiers* reflected the centralization and professionalization at various levels of lay power.

This chapter broadly examines the nature of jurisdiction in the *coutumiers*. In this, it in part takes up Jacob's call for an examination of the tension between lay and ecclesiastical courts in these texts.

[2] Lefebvre-Teillard, 'Recherches sur la pénétration du droit canonique'.
[3] Jacob, 'Philippe de Beaumanoir et les clercs'. The question of common law will be treated in Chapter 6.
[4] *Ibid.*   [5] Jacob, 'Philippe de Beaumanoir et les clercs', 163ff.
[6] Thomas N. Bisson, *The Crisis of the Twelfth Century*, p. 3.
[7] See Krynen, *L'empire du roi*; Albert Rigaudière, *Penser et construire l'État*.

However, this tension was one among others discussed in the *coutumiers* about the boundaries of power in the practice of lay justice. This chapter accordingly also investigates jurisdictional tensions more generally in order to understand how the authors of these texts understood and shaped different boundaries of power.

The Wolf, the Fox, the Lion, and the Camel

The *Roman de Renart* provides a rare glimpse of the first contacts between customary legal practice, royal authority, and learned canon law, and thus illuminates early lay attitudes towards *ius commune* learning and, specifically, canon law. Composed between the end of the twelfth and the middle of the thirteenth century, this animal fable about a scoundrel fox and his unwitting victims was one of the most popular tales of the Middle Ages.[8] In France it became so ingrained that Renart's name displaced *groupil* as the word for 'fox', and its wide circulation and numerous vernacular translations attest to its popularity across Europe. The tale narrated a long trial where the eponymous fox anti-hero was tried before the *parlement* of the lion king in response to the serious accusation that he had raped the wolf Isangrin's wife, Hersent. Hersent's perspective and the victim's trauma of sexual violence get little attention in the account of the proceeding. However, this trial did capture an encounter and moment of confrontation between royal justice, ecclesiastical and learned justice, and baronial or feudal justice in the years that preceded the *coutumiers*.

Isangrin the wolf, the narrator tells us, was heavy-hearted and filled with shame because of Hersent's rape by Renart. He thus assembled his friends to ask their counsel about how he could seek vengeance, and they all agreed that he should make a complaint in the king's parliament.[9] Off he went to present the

---

[8] *Le roman de Renart*, ed. Fukumoto, Harano, and Suzuki, trans. Bianciotto. The Renart stories appear in the late twelfth century and the first half of the thirteenth. There are approximately twenty-six surviving tales (of course more may have existed), over half of which were already written by 1205. There are two named authors, Pierre de Saint Cloud and Richard de Lison (of whom we know nothing), and as many as twenty anonymous authors that contributed (*ibid.*, p. 10).

[9] *Ibid.*, 9:15–24. This is an indication of the role of 'legal' procedures in the vengeance economy. As Mary Jane Schenck noted, the gamma family of the manuscript branches gives Hersent a larger role in initiating the trial, making her the one who proposes

plaint to the king and his court. The *Roman* narrator explained that
the king would have preferred to let the matter go, but he saw
Isangrin's tenacity and reluctantly replied that he would be dealt
with 'by judgment and by reason/according to the purview of my
house'.[10] The king did not decide on the judgment himself; instead,
he first asked for expert opinion and then gave the issue to the
animal-peers to resolve.

Seated next to the king was the camel, who was learned, well-
connected, and 'highly prized at court'.[11] The text emphasized this
camel's importance and legal pedigree: he had come from Lombardy to
bring the king the tribute sent from Constantinople, he was a friend of
the pope and a papal legate, and he was very wise and a good legal
expert (*bon legistres*).[12] The king turned to the distinguished camel and
asked his opinion on the case at hand: '"Master," said the king, "if you
have heard of such complaints in your land, like those now heard in my
court, we would truly like to know from you what judgment to deliver
in such a case."'[13] The description of the *auctoritas* of the camel and
the reverence shown to him by the king contrasted starkly with ensuing
events, which were a gleeful parody of the type of *ius commune* legal
expert (*legistre*) represented by the camel. While important and
eminent, the camel replied in a pidgin legalese that mixed French,
Italian, Occitan, and Latin. The camel responded to the king (here
the Latin has been retained while words from other languages have
been underlined to try to convey the bizarre and amusing admixture of
languages):[14]

---

going to Noble's court (Schenck, 'Paulin Paris' Influence', 122). Here, she also notes,
there were two attitudes towards the court in play here: Hersent wanted her husband
to go to court as a way to pursue private vengeance, while her husband and his friends
decide to go to court out of respect for the king's peace and in pursuit of redress
(*ibid.*, 121).
[10] 'Et neporquant s'ert il traitiez / Par jugement et par raison / Selonc l'esgart de ma
meson', *ibid.*, 9:178–81.
[11] 'Mout fu en la cort cher tenu', *ibid.*, 9:183.
[12] 'Li chameus siet joste le roi, / Mout fu en la cort cher tenuz. / De Lombardie estoit
venuz / Por aporter monseigneur Noble / Treü devers Costentinoble. / Le pape l'i avoit
tramis, / Ses legas ert et ses amis. / Mout fu sages et bon legistres', *ibid.*, 9:182–9.
[13] 'Mestre, fait li rois, s'ainz oïstes / En vostre terre tex complaintes / Con a ma cort a l'en fait
maintes, / Bien vodrions de vos aprendre / Quel jugement en en doit rendre', *ibid.*,
9:190–4.
[14] *Ibid.*, 9:195–203.

Quare, sire, *me audite.*	*Quare*, messire, *me audite.*
We find written in a Decretal	Nos trovons en decrez escrite
Legem expressly published	*Legem* express publicate
On matrimony violated.	De matremoine violate.
Firstly he must be examined,	Primes le doiz examinar,
And if he cannot justify himself	Et s'il non se puisse espurgar,
You can afflict him as it pleases you,	Grever le puez si con te place,
He who did such a great wrong.	Que mout grant chose mesface.
Hec is my sentence ...	*Hec* est en la moie sentence ...

The camel had such sophisticated knowledge and worldly background that it did not quite make sense, and he became a bit of a fool. He continued to say – always in his mongrel argot – that if Renart should refuse to undergo a trial, his wealth should be confiscated and he should stoned or burned to death.[15] Even this serious sentence came with comic relief, when the camel ended it by referring to Renart as 'la Renarde' – because fox, *la volpe*, is feminine in Italian – and so turned the miscreant fox into a woman.[16]

The *Roman de Renart*'s dystopian take on medieval society and Isangrin's quest for justice is an emblematic tale of the injustices that can result from the legal process. Renart afterwards used his knowledge of procedure to create delays and a long and protracted process, leaving Isangrin frustrated, justice not served, and society imbalanced. As Richard Kaeuper notes, this tale was composed at a time of intense governmental growth during the reigns of Louis VII, Philip Augustus, and Henry II, and it provides socio-political commentary about some problems troubling society, reactions to how those in power addressed those problems, and the effectiveness of their response.[17] The scene with the camel in addition illustrates a meeting between the different legal cultures of canon law and customary law.

The camel's cameo in the *Roman de Renart*, while humorous, also nicely demonstrated the lay reaction to the learned canonist and his

---

[15] 'S'estar ne velt en la sentence, / Desi que parmaine commune / Universe soue pecune, / De lapidar la corpe ou ardre / De l'aversier de la Renarde', *ibid.*, 9:204–8.

[16] *Ibid.*, 9:208.

[17] Kaeuper, 'The King and the Fox', p. 11. See this article for more on kingship and especially the king's peace in this text.

mode of legal reasoning. The camel was the canon lawyer in finest form – he was known for being very wise and a great jurist, he was not only a legate but also a friend of the pope, he cited the proper section of the proper authoritative text, he pronounced on proper procedure and matched the crime to the appropriate sentence as a good canon lawyer should. The camel was thus bathed in many sorts of *auctoritas*.

The scene also connected justice to Roman law and made an argument for royal power: the camel reminded the king of his duty to dispense justice and make wrongdoers pay for their wrongs, to apply justice and the law as Julius Caesar had, and to not be afraid to apply the full force of royal law and protect his kingdom.[18] The camel, as Kaeuper notes, made a forceful case for interventionist royal power and royal judicial activism.[19] Indeed, the camel suggested that the king's power would be diminished if he did not follow his advice.[20] Many nodes of power supported each other in this interlude: the king, the papacy in the form of the legate, canon law, Roman law as the form of justice administered by Caesar, and Caesar himself as the representative of imperial power.

The camel's speech provides some idea about zones of contact between forms of knowledge, possible methods of transmission and perception of this knowledge. For the camel's cameo to have been funny, the audience must have been familiar with this sort of character. Indeed, it is around the last part of the twelfth century that the first university-trained lawyers begin to appear around the French king.[21] While the scene stressed the ridiculous, there was a sense that this sort of canon lawyer could be present at a trial before the king, a trial outside of ecclesiastical jurisdiction, and that his opinion was considered valuable by virtue of the *auctoritas* supplied by his learning and position.

His absurdity served to highlight the poor rule of the lion king, who invited the foreign fop to sit at his side and to pronounce his opinion, which seemed discordant to the setting in style and delivery. Despite all of this authority and power, the royal deference to the camel was offset

---

[18] *Ibid.*, 9:209–32.   [19] Richard Kaeuper, 'The King and the Fox', p. 14.
[20] Schenck, 'Paulin Paris' Influence', 125.
[21] See especially articles by Boulet-Sautel and Ourliac in Robert-Henri Bautier (ed.), *La France de Philippe Auguste*.

by the irrelevance of his opinion. The camel's speech left his audience with mixed feelings.[22] The king then turned to the peers at court and asked them for a verdict. The peers retreated for deliberations, in which many animal-peers voiced their view on the matter, recounted page after page in great detail. The camel's learned opinion, however, was never once mentioned again.[23] Not one animal claimed they should take the course recommended by the camel, and not one supported or even referred to his opinion. Authority in secular court came from elsewhere.[24] The camel seemed more a feature of royal display than a productive part of the court process.

Mary Jane Schenck has argued that the camel was a comedic interlude in a charged trial.[25] While the camel, she notes, was a legitimate spokesperson for one type of law, which he tried to convince the king would increase his power, his view was ultimately presented as 'silly talk' and dismissed.[26] The scene was indeed funny. For this humour to be meaningful, however, the lay vernacular world would have had to have been familiar with the camel's sort of character: the learned lawyer, with his authorities and foreign connections. This type of individual was not only coming to have a presence in lay courts, but was invited to have a voice in in these courts by the top level of lay authority, the king. The scene is rare narrative testimony to an interaction between legal cultures before the appearance of the first *coutumiers* and suggests one way in which legal ideas could be transmitted from scholars, texts, and centres of learning to the lay courts.

Defining Jurisdiction

As Brigitte Bedoz-Rezak observes of the twelfth and thirteenth centuries, 'both ruling authority – royal, episcopal, or comital – and political ideology brought about the formation of people into collective

---

[22] 'Quant li baron l'orent oï, / Tiex i a qui sont esjoï, / Et tiex qui en sont coroucié', *Le roman de Renart*, ed. Fukumoto, Harano, Suzuki, pp. 233–5.

[23] This despite the fact that some parts of the camel's pronouncements echoed in the discussion of the jury – the idea that the case should be tried and that if found guilty he should be severely punished by the king, whose response would be the litmus test for his kingship, which would be revealed as good or bad depending on his response.

[24] See Chapter 7.   [25] Schenck, 'Paulin Paris' Influence', 125.

[26] Schenck, 'Paulin Paris' Influence'.

groups […] within boundaries textually if not territorially defined'.[27]
As these groups formed, they confronted one another and raised
questions about their relationships and how they interacted and
overlapped. It is well known that throughout the medieval period
any one place had multiple and overlapping legal systems that
included manorial law, feudal law, municipal law, royal law,
merchant law, maritime law, and canon law, each with its own
court.[28] And the ostensibly basic division that organized all of these
was the one between lay and ecclesiastical.

The idea that the world was ruled by two powers, the temporal and
the spiritual, dated far back to Pope Gelasius I, who enunciated it in
a letter in 494. It took on a new life in the Investiture Contest of the
eleventh and twelfth centuries as some boundaries between temporal
and spiritual jurisdiction were worked out. Nonetheless, what
belonged to the ambit of one or the other continued to be debated
and negotiated throughout the thirteenth and fourteenth centuries.
'Lay', as opposed to 'ecclesiastical', in the legal context did not mean
non-religious.[29] One example of judicial responsibility illustrates this:
James Q. Whitman shows how judges were directly responsible to God
and the impetus for judging properly came from their knowledge that
God would ultimately judge them.[30] The *coutumiers* viewed this divine
judgment as a key aspect of the judicial function. Pierre de Fontaines
counselled his audience thus: 'When you are judging, always keep
before the eyes of your heart the One who will reward each of us
according to his works. For you will be judged according to the very
same yardstick, false or true, that you use to measure others.'[31] That all
judges were ultimately responsible to God was echoed in imagery of the

---

[27] Brigitte Bedos-Rezak, 'French Medieval Regions', 154.
[28] Brundage, *Medieval Canon Law*, p. 2.
[29] Joseph Strayer saw in the medieval lay *qua* secular *qua* temporal something of the
    modern separation of powers, where secular also meant non-religious and heralded
    the modern sovereign state (see Strayer, *On the Medieval Origins of the Modern
    State*). Susan Reynolds compellingly described the lay realm as a legitimate sphere of
    thought, activity, and writing that was non-ecclesiastical and non-university (see
    Reynolds, 'Social Mentalities and the Case of Medieval Skepticism'). See also
    Constance Bouchard, 'Community', 1035–6.
[30] James Q. Whitman, *The Origins of Reasonable Doubt*.
[31] Pierre de Fontaines, *Conseil*, ed. Marnier, XXI.1]. Pierre develops this point when he
    states: 'you should know that according to God you do not have complete power over
    your villein; therefore, if you take any of his property except the lawful dues [*droites*

Last Judgment, which could be found both in church and court.[32] After all, the dispensation of justice was a power delegated by God.[33]

Around the mid-thirteenth century onward, these ideas were reinforced by political ideology as it developed in the reign of Louis IX. Louis IX's governmental reforms and administration of justice were shaped, as William Chester Jordan shows, by his deep piety which coalesced into a penitential style of rule after his participation in the unsuccessful seventh crusade.[34] Even before the crusade, the mostly ecclesiastical administrative agents in charge of the great reforming inquests had had been spreading the notion that the king was just and good.[35] The Great Reform Ordinance of 1254 shows Louis' deep commitment to the moral purity of his agents notably in the administration of justice.[36] As his reign progressed, Louis and the men who surrounded him developed a model of salvific governance, one characterized by strident moralism that often entailed a repressive and rather merciless approach in support of Louis' vision of what was right and just.[37] The administration of justice in this period cannot be dissociated from the religious feeling that shaped its agenda.

At the same time, even with these blurred boundaries, the distinction between lay and ecclesiastical remained important because these were designations of legitimate power and of legitimate competency to take specific actions. Each implied a type of person who presided over a type of court that had a type of competency over specific issues or people, provided specific types of sanctions, and followed its own internal logic, rules, and authorities. Traditionally, the church could only impose spiritual sanctions that did not involve

redevances] he owes you, you are taking them against God and to the peril of your soul, like a robber. And when it is said that everything a villein has belongs to his master [*seignor*, 'lord'], it is a truth to be examined: for if they were the master's own, there would be no difference between a serf and a villein [*entre serf et vilein*], but according to our practice there is no other judge but God between you and your villein, as long as he is resident on your land, if he has no other law with respect to you than the common law [*s'il n'a autre lois vers toi que la commune*]' (Pierre de Fontaines, *Conseil*, XXI.8).

[32] See Robert Jacob, *Images de la justice*.   [33] *Ibid.*, pp. 24ff.
[34] See William Chester Jordan, *Louis IX and the Challenge of the Crusade*.
[35] See Marie Dejoux, *Les enquêtes de saint Louis*, especially chap. 8.
[36] Gaposchkin, *The Making of Saint Louis: Kingship, Sanctity, and Crusade in the Later Middle Ages*, pp. 34–5.
[37] Jordan, *Men at the Center*, pp. 101ff.

the spilling of blood, such as penance and excommunication.[38] As the spiritual sword, the church had claims over several areas of legal activity. It had authority over certain groups of people who were considered disadvantaged or quasi-cleric, such as widows, poor people, orphans, and crusaders. It also adjudicated any case involving a cleric, even crimes normally under lay jurisdiction, such as murder or theft. Furthermore, it had authority over transactions deemed to belong to the spiritual realm, such as alms, testaments, or marriage – all which could involve massive transfers of land.

The lay courts had competency generally over other areas of law, which in France they divided into low and high jurisdiction. Low jurisdiction essentially encompassed what we might call today private law and petty crimes, and the sanctions associated with it were monetary penalties, restitution, or minor physical punishment. High jurisdiction encompassed especially heinous crimes such as murder, arson, or rape, and the holder of high jurisdiction could punish the guilty with death. While some *coutumier* authors, including Pierre de Fontaines and Philippe de Beaumanoir, invoked God at the beginning or end of their text, illuminations in the *coutumiers* tended to secular matters and did not often have a religious quality. For instance, the Last Judgement was extremely important to judicial ideology.[39] However, scenes of the Last Judgement in the *coutumiers* – the one in the *Coutumier d'Artois* in Figure 4.1 for example – are not common in the first *coutumiers*. Their illuminations more commonly depicted courtroom scenes or depictions of the concepts or procedures in the text. While religious feeling and policy certainly animated many aspects of the lay courts, this imagery does suggest a conscious separation between spiritual and secular matters.

Still, the specific competency of each jurisdiction was not always clear, and in practice there was no neat or obvious separation between the legal matters covered by lay and sacred jurisdiction.[40] There was such overlap between competencies that while the courts and

---

[38] When the church did need to use some strong-armed persuasion or punishment, they handed over the accused or guilty party to lay authorities, who did the torturing and executing for them, as in the famous example of the inquisition. For an example of the development of legal rules related to the spilling of blood and who these rules protected, see Whitman, *The Origins of Reasonable Doubt*.
[39] Jacob, *Images de la justice*, pp. 65ff.   [40] Cohen, *Crossroads of Justice*, pp. 17ff.

FIGURE 4.1 Judgment in the courtroom and the Last Judgement. This scene from a fourteenth-century manuscript of the *Coutumier d'Artois* depicts a judicial scene in the lower panel, mirrored by a scene of the Last Judgement in the higher panel – a potent reminder to judges that they will be judged as well. This sort of imagery was not common in the *coutumiers* of the thirteenth century, which tended to depict subjects related to lay justice. *Coutumier d'Artois*, Bibliothèque nationale de France, ms.fr. 5249, fol. 44v.

personnel were distinguishable, the specific jurisdiction of each was not always easily recognizable from the other. Clever kings harnessed the imagery of sacral kingship to buttress their own claims, position, and power.[41] This overlap and the resulting confusion caused friction between the two as each side felt the other intruded into its domain.

In the early thirteenth century, lay rulers at local, regional, and royal levels were protesting the expansion of ecclesiastical jurisdiction into traditionally lay affairs.[42] By mid-century, these protests turned into

---

[41] See James Given on Philip IV in this regard: Given, 'Power and Fear in Philip IV's France', 93.
[42] See Richard Keyser, 'Peaceable Power'; Baldwin, *The Government of Philip Augustus*, pp. 318–23; Reynolds, *Kingdoms and Communities*, p. 284.

more concerted actions, such as the one taken in 1246, when many barons swore to punish those who used the church courts for issues related to lay property with fines or imprisonment and to ignore the sanction of excommunication that the church might issue in response.[43] To buttress and develop their jurisdiction, the lay courts also reacted by offering services parallel to those of the ecclesiastical courts and adopting elements of the latter model while simultaneously differentiating themselves from them, all in order to present themselves as a viable alternative to the church courts.

Before the thirteenth century, when individuals in northern France wanted to have an act authenticated and recognized officially by public authority, they would have to use the services of the local episcopal courts known as the *officilités*.[44] As the thirteenth century progressed, however, various lower-level lay jurisdictions began offering the same services through what was known as the *jurisdiction gracieuse*, a notarial service that produced the documents and writings useful to solidify contracts or claims of all sorts by producing a certifiably authentic document. This development of specialized personnel for the creation and validation of documents is another indication of the expanding place of writing in law, as well as of the keen desire of lay courts to keep up with, or preferably outpace, the services of the ecclesiastical courts. In Paris, for instance, this lay *jurisdiction gracieuse* was the predominant source of these acts and practically eliminated the ecclesiastical competition in the fourteenth century.[45]

---

[43] Fournier, *Les officialités au Moyen Âge*, pp. 100–4. Fournier notes how bishops, from the end of the twelfth century onwards, attempted to create some uniformity in direction and authority in areas under their control by creating the *officialités* and delegating authority to them. According to him, one of the pressures that led to the creation of the post was the perceived attempts of potentates to try to take away their rights of jurisdiction. Similar arguments, then, were being deployed on both sides of the issue.

[44] *Ibid.*; Boulet-Sautel, 'Le notaire contre le *Jus civile*', p. 72. Some even had special writing bureaus organized to deliver this service.

[45] *Ibid.* A royal ordinance of 1301 had established on a permanent basis an office of notaries in charge of such writings in the Châtelet (theoretically they were delegates of the Provost of Paris; *ibid.*). France was divided into *tabellionage* or *jurisdiction gracieuse* in the North, and the *notariat* in the South, a division which was reabsorbed in favour of the *notariat* starting in the sixteenth century (Lusignan, *La langue des rois au Moyen Âge*, p. 77).

By the end of the thirteenth and beginning of the fourteenth centuries, the Parlement of Paris had taken on the role of intervening in jurisdictional disputes between church courts, lay regional courts, and royal courts. It was especially attentive to supervising the limits of ecclesiastical jurisdiction as well as what it considered clerical abuse of excommunication and sanctuary, as these directly affected lay jurisdiction, and even began providing alternative procedures in disputes over marriages and wills.[46] This shows both that there was a need to keep policing jurisdictional boundaries and that the central government could arrogate this policing role for itself.

That the *coutumiers* all repeated insistently that they were discussing the customs of the lay courts and not those of another type of court indicates the extent to which jurisdictional disputes preoccupied them.[47] Current scholarship has tended to focus on the relationship between the *coutumiers* and the expansion of royal power, but the deliberate emphasis on the lay court as the arena for the texts' action indicates that the primary competition and foil was the ecclesiastical court. Robert Jacob has importantly emphasized this point for Beaumanoir.[48] Beaumanoir was conscious of his ecclesiastical competition and spent more space than his counterparts discussing the issue of the cases 'whose cognizance belongs to the holy church and [...] which cases belong

---

[46] Harding, *Medieval Law and the Foundations of the State*, p. 169.

[47] The writing of procedural manuals (*ordines iudiciarii*) for the ecclesiastical courts was likely one of the inspirations for the *coutumier* authors to write the rules and procedures of the lay courts. The focus on lay courts that runs through the texts must be a contrast to the church courts. Unlike canon law and customary law, Roman law did not have courts in which it was specifically applied. It was the law taught at universities that, when it came into practice, did so through graduates who had learned to think in a Roman-law manner and adopted its scholastic process as well as notions and categories. Some of these graduates went into the royal administration and brought Roman law notions with them. We see these occasionally in the later thirteenth century, for instance, Pierre de Belleperche, who studied Roman law under Jacques de Revigny at the University of Orleans and then became an advisor to Philip the Fair (r. 1285–1314). Also, it should be noted that in the late thirteenth and the fourteenth centuries, the South of France began identifying itself as the *pays de droit écrit* (the land of written law). It was then that the customary law of the South (shaped by a reception of a summarized Roman law into Visigothic law that bore almost no resemblance to the *Corpus Iuris*) was infused with the Roman law of the universities, largely as a post-Albigensian-Crusade reaction of Southern jurists against the king's customary law.

[48] Jacob, 'Philippe de Beaumanoir et les clercs', 163–88.

to lay court'.[49] Other *coutumier* authors address this question of
jurisdiction more obliquely in their repeated emphasis on the lay
court as their arena. The *coutumier* authors evinced a keen interest
in developing an identity for their courts, one that stood in contrast
to the ecclesiastical courts.

Canon Law in the *Coutumiers*

Around the mid-thirteenth century when the *coutumiers* began to be
written, the place of the camel in lay court had changed significantly.
Once a little ridiculous, the camel-figure was now less exotic and more
familiar, and his decretals even made an appearance first in the lay
courts and then in written theorizations of its procedure in the
coutumiers. *Coutumier* authors either had some knowledge of the
texts of canon law or a good knowledge of the actual functioning of
the ecclesiastical courts, or both. While they cited texts of Roman law
with greater frequency than texts of canon law, both sorts of texts were
used in a similar manner. But canon law also existed outside texts as
part of a live practice in the ecclesiastical courts – a practice that pushed
up against and encroached on the lay sphere. The *coutumiers* thus
show added anxiety about and vigilance towards canon law and
especially its limits vis-à-vis the lay courts.

Pierre de Fontaines finished his *Conseil* in 1253. He copied block
quotations from Justinian's *Institutes*, *Code*, and *Digest* but only
referred to the textual tradition of canon law once. In his section on
judgments, Pierre explained that no judgment ought to be made on
a dispute if both the complaint and a reply have not been heard, unless
the lack of reply resulted in a party holding seisin for a year and a day.
Pierre explained that 'law and decretal, are in accord with this,
I believe'.[50] This was probably a reference to the *Decretals* of
Gregory IX (1234) and the only written text of canon law overtly
cited, even though he seems to have incorporated sections of the
French translation of Tancred's *Ordo* into his work.[51]

---

[49] Beaumanoir, *Coutumes de Beauvaisis*, ed. Salmon, XI.311. He provides an entire
chapter (XI) on the subject.
[50] Pierre de Fontaines, *Conseil*, XXI.12.
[51] Compare Pierre de Fontaines' *Conseil*, chap. 25, sections on litiscontestation, with
Tancred's *Ordo* 1.3 (*De litis contestations*). See the next section of this chapter.

Pierre was keenly interested in jurisdiction. In the same section where he made his one overt reference to canon law text, Pierre made an argument for keeping a clear and separate division between jurisdictions. He provided the following example:

A clerk is trying to redeem because of his kinship some land which one of his relatives has sold, and he prosecutes the suit for a long time in the ecclesiastical court, and without obtaining a judgment he goes to the lay court and sues there. The other party says he does not want to give an answer, because he has held the land without challenge for a year and a day. The clerk says he has not, for he has sued him in the ecclesiastical court. Now you are asking if the time of possession will be in the buyer's favor. And certainly it will; *for a person who is not suing in the proper forum for something is not suing properly.*[52]

Pierre's intransigent approach to proper forum in this case shows anxiety about limits and boundaries, as well as about forum shopping.

He thus took pains to distinguish the practices of the ecclesiastical courts from those of the lay courts. He noted the occasional similarity between the procedure of the lay and ecclesiastical courts but made a point of describing distinctions between procedure or the different terms that could be used for common practice.[53] And as he distinguished the procedure of the court, he also occasionally commented on the culture of the courts. For instance, in describing how to structure a complaint, Pierre noted that 'We do not require or make such great subtleties in forming our complaints as the clerks do.'[54] Subtlety was often a term of praise that denoted intellectual sophistication but in vernacular writing of this period, it could also connote opacity and obfuscation. Like the camel's commentary in the *Roman de Renart*, intellectual sophistication could become too subtle to understand.

Pierre also noted his disagreements with canon law. He devoted an entire chapter to the problem of the crusader who has been away for an extended period of time and the question of what happens to the

---

[52] Pierre de Fontaines, *Conseil*, XVII.9 [emphasis added].

[53] 'And what we have said for us [the secular court] is the same as what clerks do "under protest" except that according to them, the principal party in the case can make a protest; but according to our practice, principal parties have no right to amendment when they themselves do the pleading' (*ibid.*, XII.8).

[54] *Ibid.*, XXIV.1. Beaumanoir makes a similar comparison, with more detail, *Coutumes de Beauvaisis*, p. 196.

property he left behind.[55] He felt that the church provided crusaders with excessive protections. In Pierre's words, 'And certainly, in my opinion, their privileges do not extend so far as is sometimes said, namely that all their affairs are in the protection of Holy Church, and remain the same, and unchallenged from then until their return or their death is known with certainty.'[56] Pierre continued that the practice of the lay courts had often been to return to them the property that was transferred away from them. As he noted, a good judge would carefully weigh all evidence connected to sale or transfer and be sensitive to how difficult it could be for relatives to have a piece of property frozen for years while its lord was off on crusade. Lay jurisdiction could and should be extended in the appropriate case, and here it was a matter of reason and equity.

The compiler of the *Établissements de Saint Louis* included citations to canon law alongside those to Roman law when he reworked his source texts. All of these references to canon law were to the *Decretals* of Gregory IX, which appeared in the text when a particular point in a decretal agreed with the author's point.[57] This compiler was interested in adding citations of canon law that fit within his program.

Beaumanoir devoted an entire chapter to the jurisdiction of the ecclesiastical court, describing these in detail to avoid jurisdictional confusion.[58] He was emphatically clear about the cases where 'the secular courts should be in control, and Holy Church should not get involved'.[59] As Jacob notes, men of law in such small towns as Clermont-en-Beauvaisis must have known each other, talked through ideas and compared their procedures and norms, and attended each other's sessions, whether or not they tolerated each other's work and jurisdiction.[60]

Perhaps because of this proximity, it seems that even justices in both kinds of courts could have a blurry perception of what rules and procedures belonged where – and hence the need for a detailed

---

[55] Pierre de Fontaines, *Conseil*, XVII.14.   [56] *Ibid.*, XVII.14.

[57] 'for the law is in agreement in the *Decretals*, On the homage of a serf, in the chapter Dilectus filius' (*Les établissements de Saint Louis*, ed. Viollet, II.31). This is the scholastic form of citation, which the *Établissements* compiler also follows in his citations of Roman law that he adds to the original text.

[58] Beaumanoir, *Coutumes de Beauvaisis*, ed. Salmon, chap. XI.   [59] *Ibid.*, II.340.

[60] Jacob, 'Philippe de Beaumanoir et les clercs', 163ff.

chapter about jurisdiction to explain and learn the boundaries. Beaumanoir was so knowledgeable about ecclesiastical jurisdiction that at one moment he lost track of his topic and began to address practices specific to the ecclesiastical courts that did not at all relate to the lay courts. Noticing that he did this, he interrupted himself and made a conscious effort to get back on track: 'But when they plead against each other in an ecclesiastical court – we should not speak of that since we intend to speak only of the customs of lay courts'.[61] This was a rare moment that provides an inkling of how hard it was to confine discussion to just one jurisdiction or the other, even for a sophisticated thinker like Beaumanoir who had such a talent for categorization and compartmentalization.[62]

Beaumanoir's suggestion that it was important to try to distinguish the two jurisdictions may be related to some events that transpired while he was *bailli* of Clermont. Of three charters we have contemporaneous with his holding this post, one was a record composed by Roger, priest of Delaincourt, testifying to the reparations made by Beaumanoir as *bailli* of Clermont and his sergeants for abusing their power by violating the church's privilege to offer sanctuary.[63]

Beaumanoir and his men had come armed, along with many people, and violently removed Robin le Quantois – a sergeant suspected of murder and larceny – from the door of the Cistercian abbey of Chaalis against the will of the religious there and threw him in prison.[64] The people of Chaalis complained 'to the king and masters of the court of the shame and villainy and violence of the disseisin of the aforesaid place'.[65] The king and his court judged that the abbey should be reseized of Robin le Quantois.

---

[61] 'Mes quant il pledent li uns a l'autre en court de crestienté, il ne convient ja que nous en parlons pour ce que nous n'entendons a parler fors que des coustumes de la court laie' (Beaumanoir, *Coutumes de Beauvaisis*, ed. Salmon, XXIX.1211).

[62] As we will see in the next section, Beaumanoir introduced the table of contents to his readers as a new and useful tool – another moment that shows the extent to which legal thinking was rapidly changing.

[63] Between the twelfth and fourteenth centuries, canonists increasingly framed sanctuary as a jurisdictional immunity of the church, a territorial privilege that stood against encroachment or intrusion by temporal justice (Karl Shoemaker, *Sanctuary and Crime in the Middle Ages, 400–1500*, pp. 152ff).

[64] 'Pièces justificatives' in Bordier, *Philippe de Remi*, xxiv, p. 130.   [65] *Ibid.*

Roger's record names a staggering seventy-six witnesses who watched as Beaumanoir's sergeants returned Robin to the door of the religious house. A great show was made of the return of Robin. Beaumanoir does not seem to have been there as the record states that 'the *bailli* and aforesaid people reseized the aforesaid place by the hand of Alaimie and Pierre Verjus and other aforesaid sergeants'.[66] These men announced that the man they had seized for the count was being returned by the count and reseized by the abbey – to which Roger responded that it was not actually by order of the count, but 'by order of the king and the masters of the court'.[67] As a symbolic gesture, Robin's hands were placed inside the door, and he was led to the chapel.[68] The majority of the record is the long list of witnesses who saw the reseisin at the door and the chapel. Beaumanoir's sensitive treatment of the boundaries between lay and ecclesiastical jurisdiction may be related to his insensitivity to them, whether mistakenly or on purpose, during his tenure as *bailli*.

Just as it was important to try to distinguish the two jurisdictions, it likewise could be useful to understand how each functioned. Some manuscripts were made specifically with this in mind. Figure 4.2 shows a manuscript containing a French translation of Tancred's *Ordo*, a procedural manual for ecclesiastical courts, as well as the *Coutumes de Champagne*. There is a manuscript that contains Tancred's *Ordo* followed by the *Établissements de Saint Louis* that is so similar that it must have been produced in the same context.[69] These manuscripts were clearly made for people who needed to understand how both courts functioned and who were more comfortable in the vernacular than in Latin.

Anxiety towards the ecclesiastical courts continued from Pierre de Fontaines to Beaumanoir. It is evident in authors' repetitious reminders that they were treating the lay courts, in concerns about jurisdiction and attempts to co-opt it, and even in some mockery of the processes and language of the church courts.

Written Custom and Lay Law

The *coutumiers* sought to reinforce the sphere of lay law. In service of this, they partially constructed their identity in opposition to the foil of canon law and the practice of the ecclesiastical courts. But they

---

[66] *Ibid.*, pp. 130–1.   [67] *Ibid.*, p. 131.   [68] Ibid.   [69] BnF, ms. fr. 1075.

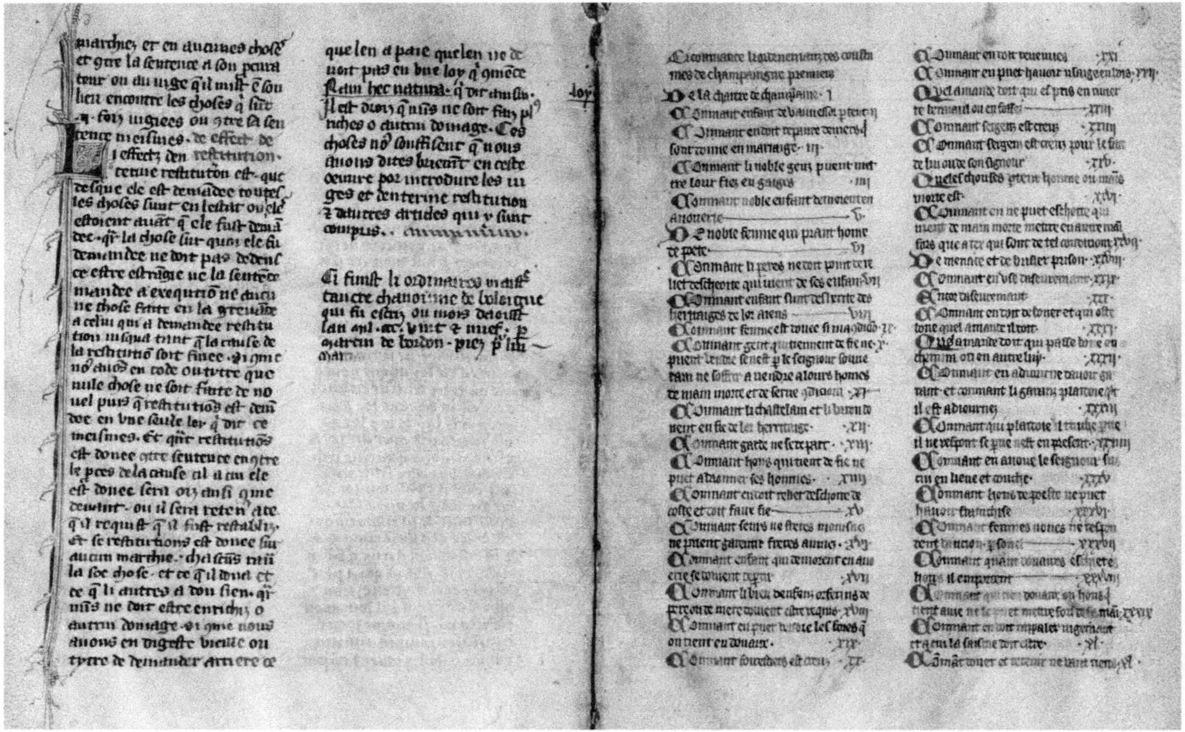

FIGURE 4.2 The end of Tancred's *Ordo* in French translation and the beginning of the *Coutumes de Champagne*. This fourteenth-century manuscript permitted the reader to study the rules and procedures of both the ecclesiastical courts and the lay courts in the French language. *Coutumier* manuscripts often focused on legal texts. This particular manuscript also included a lapidary and a recipe for snake powder after the legal texts. *Ordinaire de Tancrède, Coutumes de Champagne, etc.*, Bibliothèque nationale de France, ms. fr. 25546, fol. 129v and 130r.

also thought out and developed what law and legal practice meant to lay lordship. The texts were focused on relations between the aristocracy, between lords and vassals and peers, between the aristocracy and other classes, and on the aristocracy's legal duties. Hence, they made a political argument in favour of lay jurisdiction.

The *Coutumes d'Anjou et Maine* did not explicitly identify its audience beyond its emphasis on the lay court milieu. Its contents, however, indicated that it was a guidebook for lordship: how to handle different legal situations and clarifications about jurisdiction and the different rules that apply to a person according to their status and gender. While some sections referred to 'any man' (*si aucun homs*), most concerned aristocracy (*gentis homs*) or referred to rules that assumed vassalage or landed lordship.

This lordship theme was clear in Pierre de Fontaines' discussion of audience. Pierre responded in his prologue to an interlocutor who encouraged him to write his text – an interlocutor (whether real or invented) who was a lay lord and desired that his heir would learn from Pierre about lay lordship and how it worked:

> You have made me understand many times that you have a son who is learning good morals and a firm faith very well, and that you hope that he will hold your inheritance after you, and because of this, you want him to study the laws and customs of his country, and the practice [*usage*] of the lay courts, at this time when military operations [*armes*] are suspended, so that when he inherits, he will know how to do justice to his subjects and maintain his land according to the laws and customs of the country, and give advice to his friends when it will be necessary: and you have requested me to do this, and now request that I write him a text according to the practice and the customs of the Vermandois area and of other lay courts.[70]

Pierre, taking up the classic theme that in times of peace good rulers should turn their minds to law, situated his *coutumier* in the context of landed lordship and its content in the context of other lordly virtues. Its practical setting is the administration of justice, the governance of land, and the duties of the governing and the governed.

---

[70] 'un escrit selonc les us et les coutumes de Vermandois et d'autres corz laies' (Pierre de Fontaines, *Conseil*, prologue.2).

The *Établissements* manuscripts of the thirteenth century introduced Book I as addressing the ordinances (*établissements*) that the provosts of Paris and Orleans implemented according to the usage of baronial court. Early fourteenth-century manuscripts had shifted the context to a royal setting, which we will return to later in this chapter. Book II opened by explaining its ambit, which was 'on justice and law (*droit*), and the commandments of law (*droit*), and the office of chivalry and of capturing wrongdoers in the act, and the usage of the *châtelet* in Orléans in baronial court, and on punishing wrongdoers'.[71] Law and justice were not only aristocratic but increasingly wrapped in chivalric virtue.

Philippe de Beaumanoir first frames his *coutumier* in religious terms as part of the duty to 'love our neighbours as ourselves' but then framed it as a sort of guide for princes, where the count 'may be instructed by this book concerning how he should preserve and enforce preservation of the customs of his land in the county of Clermont, so that his vassals and the common people can live in peace under his rule'.[72] The *Coutumier d'Artois* reprised this approach, copying entire sections of Pierre's text, including Pierre's comments about writing at the request of a lord who wanted the text for his son and heir, for the purpose of teaching the customs of the area so that he would be able to uphold these when governing and provide good counsel to others when needed.[73]

On two occasions customary law was framed as comital ordinance. The *Coutumier de Champagne* provided an ordinance of Thibaut of Champagne as the prefatory matter, making the text itself into a comital promulgation backed by a long list of nobles who provided counsel and consented to its contents.[74]

This resembles a later manuscript of the *Établissements* that reframed the text as an ordinance of Louis IX. The *Établissements de Saint Louis* was compiled in 1273 or 1274, but it took an interesting turn in the early fourteenth century, when copyists of three manuscripts (Q, R, and S)

---

[71] *Les établissements de Saint Louis*, ed. Viollet, Book II *implicit* (vol. 2, p. 327). Several manuscripts simply say instead that Book II concerns matters of high justice (*haute justice*).

[72] Beaumanoir, *Coutumes de Beauvaisis*, ed. Salmon, prologue s. 2–3. He continues by adding that the text will provide these people with ammunition against cheaters and litigious types (prologue 0.3).

[73] *Coutumier d'Artois*, ed. Tardif, prologue s. 3.

[74] *L'Ancien Coutumier de Champagne*, ed. Portejoie, s.1.

added a prologue to introduce this *coutumier*. Instead of introducing the text as the customs of Orleans or the Châtelet in Paris, these copyists added a prologue that attributed the text to King Louis IX. This prologue transformed the entire text into a royal ordinance promulgated by Louis IX before he departed on crusade.

The prologue also framed the *Établissements* as the result of an ideologically powerful, if imaginary, process of redaction that coloured the content. This later prologue explained that the *Établissements* was the product of an agreement between different types of lay and ecclesiastical figures, who together had harmonized different types of laws; the text explained, 'and these laws were made after great consultation of wise men and good clerks, through the concordance of laws and canons and decretals, to confirm the good practices and ancient customs, which are adhered to in the kingdom of France'.[75] Whoever composed the prologue transformed the *Établissements* into the product of the distilled wisdom of all jurists and men of law, and the harmony of textual authority of all relevant legal traditions – all under the auspices of the king.

This was obviously an argument rather than fact. The writer of the prologue and subsequent copyists were clearly advocating a harmony of discordant laws and a close relationship between ecclesiastical and lay courts. Though jurisdiction was to remain a point of contention, the prologue writer was correct in the sense that some differences between lay and church courts had faded a little by the turn of the fourteenth century – inquisitorial procedure was accepted by lay courts, the lay authorities now offered the *jurisdiction gracieuse* to parallel the *officialités*, the consolidation of royal power and the spread of royal justices created a structural similarity, and there was now a textual tradition behind secular law as well, such that one could learn and understand it from books as well as practice.

Kings and Custom

A reminder that these texts reflect a professionalization of lay lordship is important because the story of the *coutumiers* has, of late, most commonly been linked to the rise of increasingly powerful kings, who

---

[75] *Les établissements de Saint Louis*, ed. Viollet, prologue added in manuscripts Q (BnF, ms.fr. 5248), R (BnF, ms.fr. 18096), and S (BnF, ms.fr. 13986).

were trying to claim supremacy over a political space in which they had been languishing as figureheads. There is no doubt about the rise of royal power in this period and no doubt about an understanding that kings had to deliver justice. However, there is no evidence that the kings were actually behind the writing of the *coutumiers* or that they even encouraged them to be written.[76] Some of the *coutumiers* were simply testimony to the fact of expansion of royal power while others did something more in being overtly in favour of it. The two known *coutumier* authors were royal *bailli* (though at least one obtained this post after writing his book). Of course, royal power was an important context for the production of the *coutumiers*. However, in the absence of clear evidence of royal impetus – as exists for *Glanvill*, *Bracton*, and the *Siete Partidas* – it is difficult to accept that the texts resulted specifically from royal initiative.

In the territory that was coalescing into 'France', the balance of power between kings and aristocracy was changing in the twelfth century, especially by the end of the century under the reign of Philip Augustus. The French kings of the thirteenth century continued to expand their power over territory and, notably, reclaimed their traditional responsibility over justice and over the legal-political processes of conflict and its resolution. An important body of scholarly literature treats the subject of the expansion of royal power and its relationship to justice.[77]

Theoretically, the essence of the royal function lay in the dispensation of justice, which was part of the king's oath during the coronation. His duty was to make laws for the common good, which his *baillis* then had the duty to uphold.[78] The terminus for a suit was

---

[76] André Castaldo, 'Pouvoir royal, droit savant et droit commun coutumier dans la France du Moyen Âge', 128.

[77] See for instance Krynen, *Idéal du prince et pouvoir royal*; Krynen, *L'empire du roi*; Cheyette, 'La justice et le pouvoir royal'; Guillot, Rigaudière, and Sassier, *Pouvoirs et institutions*; Yves Marie Bercé and Alfred Soman (eds.), *La Justice royale et le parlement de Paris*; Rigaudière, *Penser et construire l'État*; Gauvard, *Violence et ordre public au Moyen Âge*; Silvère Menegaldo and Ribémont (eds.), *Le roi fontaine de justice*; Justine Firnhaber-Baker, *Violence and the State in Languedoc*.

[78] 'Li establissement que li rois fet pour commun pourfit doivent estre fourment gardé par la porveance des baillis' (Beaumanoir, *Coutumes de Beauvaisis*, ed. Salmon, I.51).

the king's court, as there was no appeal beyond it.[79] Law and justice were part of the king's duty to provide a peaceful realm for his subjects.

Jean de Joinville made this duty clear in his *Life of Saint Louis*. He recounted an episode where Hugues de Dignes, aiming to educate the king, sermonized on the Bible and its stories of infidel princes where kingdoms were lost and went from one lordship to another when justice was not rendered (*defaute de droit*).[80] Joinville, who had held judicial functions and was familiar with law, used a technical legal term here – default of justice (*defaute de droit*) – that created grounds for appeal to another authority and gave one legitimate cause to abjure one's lord. But if the king rendered good and swift justice to his subjects, Hugues continued, the good Lord would permit him to keep his kingdom in peace throughout his life. According to Jean de Joinville, the king never forgot this lesson, which was then transmitted to the future Louis X (Philip the Fair's son and Louis IX's grandson) to whom Joinville had dedicated the book.[81] Joinville's message about Louis IX's dedication to justice would have been difficult for his grandson to miss.

Joinville also famously recounted the most celebrated scene of Louis IX providing justice – as he often did after mass – perched under a great oak tree in the Bois de Vincennes.[82] Anyone could come to him there with their petition, without fear of his guards. Louis IX called on Pierre de Fontaines and Geoffroy de Villete and said: 'Deliver judgment for me'.[83] Those who had pleas or petitions were serviced, one by one, by royal justices. The king presided over the administration of justice; he was the fount of justice, but justice itself was delivered by his officers.[84]

Within this duty to deliver justice, the king had a well-known special role as the protector of custom. He could confirm or interpret customs, give exemptions to custom in the form of a privilege, or abolish bad customs.[85] It was his duty to ensure that custom was upheld by

---

[79] This idea is already present in the first years of the thirteenth century: 'il doit envoier les parties a l'ostel le roi, si que la cause i soit terminee' (*Coutumiers de Normandie*, ed. Tardif, vol. 1, 77.1).

[80] Jean de Joinville, *Vie de Saint Louis*, ed. and trans. Monfrin, p. 55.   [81] *Ibid.*, p. 57.

[82] *Ibid.*, p. 59.   [83] 'Delivrez moy ceste partie', *ibid.*, p. 59.

[84] For the religious and penitential underpinnings of Louis IX's interest in justice and judicial and legal reform, see Dejoux, *Les enquêtes de Saint Louis*.

[85] Paul Ourliac, 'Législation, coutumes et coutumiers', p. 476.

others.[86] Indeed, the king's role as protector of custom was a useful pretext to expand his role in the mid-thirteenth-century legal practice with the creation of the appeal. As Pierre de Fontaines made clear, one of the grounds for appealing to the crown for 'false judgment' was a judgment rendered contrary to the customs of the region. In such a situation, Pierre said that one should appeal to the king, whose duty it was 'to preserve the customs of the regions and have them upheld'.[87] The *Coutumier d'Artois* made this a formal aspect of the king's justice by listing 'judgment made against common custom' as a separate ground for appeal to the crown.[88] The development of appeals for denial of justice or false judgment placed the king at the apex of justice in the kingdom. He had gone from figurehead to guarantor, and the *coutumiers* reflected this shift.

This was partially the continuation of an earlier tradition: kings had been confirming small-scale customs, such as city customs, as early as the twelfth century. As they were being redacted, city customs were changed and 'perfected', resulting in some degree of uniformity. Before confirming new city customs, the king had commissions called to investigate the customs and to abrogate from or add to them whenever necessary.[89] As Jacques Krynen notes, the more customs were approved in this manner, the more urban customs were homogenized under the auspices of royal power.[90]

A duty to uphold good customs and abrogate bad ones, as Louis IX advised his son, could be a great source of power, as well as a great responsibility. It was one that had to be tended judiciously. The royal

---

[86] See for instance Beaumanoir, *Coutumes de Beauvaisis*, ed. Salmon, XXIV.683.

[87] 'Mès je lô que cil contre qui tel jugement sont rendu, qu'il dient: "Je ne reçoif, ne ne m'assent à tel jugement qui est contre la costume commune del païs," et voist au roi, à qui les costumes del païs sont à garder et à fère tenir, qui la costume li fera tenir' (Pierre de Fontaines, *Conseil*, XXII.32). He repeats the same sentiment soon afterward: 'Quant aucuns dit que l'en li a fait jugement contre la costume del païs commune, bien afiert au roi, qui les costumes a à garder' (*ibid.*, XXII.33).

[88] 'de defaute de drois, ou de jugement fait contre *commune coustume*, ou de faus jugement' (*Coutumier d'Artois*, ed. Tardif, XI.1; emphasis added). See Chapter 8.

[89] Krynen, 'Entre science juridique et dirigisme', s. 23, http://journals.openedition.org /crm/892 (accessed 8 June 2022).

[90] Krynen, 'Entre science juridique et dirigisme', s. 22. The thirteenth-century customs of Agenais and of Toulouse are the two *causes célèbres* of this royal attention, but according to Krynen this was in fact the norm.

practice of abolishing evil customs was an old one, going back at least to the middle of the eleventh century.[91]

From the time of Saint Louis, the king's role expanded from the protector of custom to a veritable 'censor of custom' through the abrogation of bad custom.[92] Some *coutumiers* defended this royal prerogative. Beaumanoir defended the king's duty to abrogate bad custom for the better when he explained, 'the intention of the law is not to take away others' rights, but to insure that things are done according to reason, and to terminate bad customs and favour the good ones'.[93] This suggests obliquely that some must have thought that this practice did, indeed, take away the rights of others. Albert Rigaudière makes the important argument that even if, considered separately, these royal interventions dealt with relatively minor things, the royal acts that abolished bad customs essentially resulted in a new order that affirmed the power of the state and the king, who was gradually making customary norms conform to those that he himself decreed.[94]

Nonetheless, the power of the French kings continued to be mitigated by the politics of consent, even if the king's need for approval would gradually wane over the thirteenth century. The century that began with Philip Augustus, who could not legislate outside the royal domain without the consent of each of his vassals, ended with Philip the Fair, who had some obligation to consult with his personal counsel (and no longer all his barons) and give weight to its opinion but was not bound by it. It started with a fledgling royal judicial presence in the regions, when Philip Augustus sent out the royal *baillis* to manage things both economic and judicial related to the crown, and ended with a machinery of royal justices with purely judicial functions stationed in the various regions and rotating to avoid corruption.

Jacques Krynen argues that the impetus for writing the *coutumiers* came from the king.[95] He writes that the monarchy was becoming the locus of power and actively engaged in the task of state-building and

---

[91] Guillot, Rigaudière, and Sassier, *Pouvoirs et institutions*, p. 130.
[92] Krynen, *L'empire du roi*, p. 78.
[93] 'l'intencions des establissements n'est pas pour tolir autrui droit, mes pour ce que les choses soient fetes avec reson, et pour les mauveses coustumes abatre et les bonnes amener avant' (Beaumanoir, *Coutumes de Beauvaisis*, ed. Salmon, XLVIII.1496).
[94] Rigaudière, *Penser et construire l'État*, pp. 209–51.
[95] Krynen, *L'empire du roi*, p. 77.

describes these texts as part of royal expansionism whose purpose was to reinforce the power of the crown.[96] This is a tempting thesis, especially because the *coutumiers* were indeed tied entirely to areas that had been annexed or inherited by the crown: Artois came to the French kings in 1191 as Isabelle de Hainault's dowry when she married Philip II in 1180 (sealed with the Treaty of Melun in 1226); Maine (1203) and Anjou (1204) were gained in King John's losses to Philip Augustus; Vermandois passed to the French kings when Eleanor Countess of Vermandois and Valois died without an heir in 1214; Clermont-en-Beauvaisis was purchased by the French crown in 1218; and Champagne was acquired by the French kings in 1284 through the marriage of Jeanne and Philip the Fair. The texts also appear soon after Louis IX's sweeping measures to reorganize law and governance in his kingdom.

It is possible that the *coutumiers* were written to clarify custom after a shift in political power. It is possible that they were written to help the new class of roving *bailli* know the customs of the regions where they were temporarily stationed. It is possible that the directive to write them came from the centre, as it did much later in the fifteenth century when the king issued an ordinance that regional custom had to be officially redacted.

If this was indeed the case, however, one would expect to find more evidence of this genesis in the *coutumiers* themselves. There was a pre-existing tradition of royal custom, after all – Frederick II had the *Liber Augustalis*; the laws and customs of England were written first in *Glanvill* and then in *Bracton*; and Alfonso X of Castile had his *Siete Partidas*. Yet while royal power is clear in a number of *coutumiers*, there is no comparable statement of royal initiative. This is true even in the *Demenées*, where one might expect a real argument for royal power. The closest thing to statement appears in the three early fourteenth-century manuscripts of the *Établissements de Saint Louis* that added the prologue attributing the text to Louis IX, transforming the customs of Paris and Orleans into a royal promulgation. But this prologue was a later addition, a transformation that reflected the nature of royal power as the reign of Philip the Fair matured.

The reason for this is rather prosaic: the *coutumier* authors were seeking to order, theorize, and professionalize the lay courts generally

[96] *Ibid.*

as part of an overall strengthening of lay lordship, in competition with
ecclesiastical courts. The texts were written for principalities that
already felt the strong influence of royal authority and, as such, they
reflect the regional influence of royal power in law. At the same time,
the texts were also cementing power at other levels that scholars
generally overlook: notably, the *coutumiers* were actively building up
the idea of regional power at the expense of local customs.

Custom and Lay Jurisdiction

The emphasis on the *coutumiers* in the development of monarchial and
state power has eclipsed the story they tell about the consolidation of
all levels of power and jurisdiction: monarchic, ducal, comital, and so
on. Custom continued to be identified generally with the juridical
powers of lordship in the thirteenth century.

The *coutumiers* illuminate juridical aspects of lordship in a variety
of ways. *Le livre des constitutions demenées el Chastelet de Paris* was,
along with Beaumanoir, one of the earliest *coutumiers* to provide
a working definition of custom. This text showed that although
custom was becoming professionalized and meant more than
exaction, it was still very much associated with the idea of lordship.
Jean Yver was the first to point this out when he demonstrated that the
customs in the *Très ancien coutumier de Normandie* actually reflected
ducal legislation in Normandy rather than autochthonous norms.[97]

Other *coutumiers* sometimes also suggest a view of custom as an
imposition from above. When the author of the *Demenées el Chastelet
de Paris* speaks of rules, he most commonly speaks of *droit* and *coutume*.
He mentioned 'the custom of the area' but also referred to the 'custom of
France,' of the king's domain, or the 'usage and custom of France'.[98]
Importantly, however, he defined custom as the lord's command:

Custom must be made by the command of the king or count, or bishop, or
royal abbot, or by such person who can make it and must do so; and the custom
must be declared in the area where it exists by any of the above mentioned
lords; and the custom must be kept for precisely the above-said forty years, the

---

[97] Yver, 'Le très ancien coutumier de Normandie'.
[98] 'la coustume du païs' (*Le livre des constitutions demenées*, ed. Mortet, 17), 'as us et
aus coustumes de France' (*ibid.*, 85), 'la coustume de France' (*ibid.*, 12, 30, 40, 86).

custom must not be null or estimated as null by law (or rightfully); and if custom is made in another manner and against it, it is null and estimated as null, nor must it be kept nor maintained by any good judge. [99]

This passage obviously presents a much less romantic view of custom than the zeitgeist of a people or the preservation of ancestral memory. Here, custom was made by those in power, imposed on an area by those in power, and enforced by those in power. Charles Mortet, the editor of the text, was uncomfortable with this definition and deemed it 'inexact'.[100] However, we must assume that the author provided this definition because, to their knowledge, it seemed like the correct one.

The notion of custom as imposed and as an aspect of lordship recalls its history as a lordly exaction. The idea of custom as a toll or fee did not vanish with the expansion of the concept as a general legal norm. The term also continued to define the relations of lordship: the 'customary man' (*home coustumier*) designated men submitted to a lordship and the dues of that lordship – customary man was another term for villein.[101]

According to the author of the *Demenées el Chastelet de Paris*, custom was a rule that was commanded and brought into an area. That this was not an outlier view can be seen in the echo of this definition in a later

[99] 'coustume doit estre faite par commandement de roi ou do conte, ou d'evesque, ou d'abbé royal, ou de tel qui puisse faire et doie; et doit la coustume estre aportée el païs ou elle estre par aucuns des seigneurs desus dis; et doit la coustume estre gardée par prescricion de XL ans dessus dis, la coustume ne doit estre de nulle ne de nulle value par droit; et se coustume est fait autrement et contre, est nulle ne de nulle value, ne ne doit estre gardée ne maintenue par nul bon juge' (*Le livre des constitutions demenées*, ed. Mortet, 41). There is an echo of this in the *Coutumier d'Artois*, which warned that agreements made against law or custom would not be upheld because 'laws and customs were put in the region [*les loys et coustumes mises ou pais*] so we can practise according to them and not against them. And for this reason, lords make their commands and *établissements*, because they want us to preserve them, and not to breach them' (*Coutumier d'Artois*, ed. Tardif, VII.3).

[100] Mortet said the definition was inexact because many customs were not ordered by lords (citing Beaumanoir's mention of popular consensus) and that the author's views must have been coloured by the fact that this author was concerned with the rules followed in lay court where pleaders and practitioners were more likely to apply well-established customs [*coutumes notoires* or *approuvées*] (*Le livre des constitutions demenées*, ed. Mortet, p. 55 n. 2). One might reply that the rules that were challenged at court were less likely to be these than unsettled ones. Outside of Beaumanoir, Mortet cites fourteenth-century texts such as Bouteiller's *Somme rural* and the *Grand coutumier de France*, but it seems better to come at the question from what we know existed before than to view it from what happened afterwards.

[101] Laferrière, *Histoire du droit civil de Rome*, vol. 6, p. 23.

source written for the Parlement of Paris by the brothers Pierre and
Guillaume Maucreux around 1330, which differentiated 'unwritten
law' from 'custom of the region/area [*païs*]'.[102] Unwritten law, said the
two lawyers, was that which was 'confirmed by long usage, or long
customs which are confirmed by the consent of those who use them'.
'Custom of the region', however, was 'no other thing but an ordinance
made for the area by the prince of the land'.[103]

Custom, in these texts, is part of an active top-down policy. This
does not mean that all custom was an imposition, but that custom
could legitimately be created through an imposition, and it would still
be termed custom rather than law.

Creating a 'Regional' Custom

While the *coutumiers* created an image of a unified region, multiplicity
was the hallmark of both medieval lordship and custom. The two were
attached to each other on many overlapping levels and in many
dimensions as well as through many relationships that were constantly
being renegotiated. With the exception of Beaumanoir's *Coutumes de
Beauvaisis*, the *coutumiers* generally ignored the existence of the
multitude of jurisdictions that nested within comital and baronial
jurisdictions. Texts of practice, such as charters that recorded
agreements or disputes, were replete with mentions of local particular
customs that only had currency in a small village or town. The *coutumiers*
discussed issues of jurisdiction and appeals to higher courts, but these
local customs were largely excluded from their narratives.

The reason for this may be that the *coutumiers* were specifically
interested in other types of jurisdictions against which they might have
had some competitive interest. The limits of ecclesiastical jurisdiction

---

[102] 'Droit non escript est ce que lonc usage a conformé ou les longues coustumes qui sont
confermees par le consentement de ceulx qui en usent sont autre cy come lois.
Institutes C. ex non scripto' (Stéphane Pillet ed., '"Les ordonnances de plaidoyer
de bouche et par escript" des frères Maucreux (BnF. ms. fr. 19832)', p. 183). The title
of the text, *Les ordonnances de plaidoyer de bouche et par escript*, translates as
'Ordinances on pleading by mouth and in writing'.
[103] 'Coustume de pays n'est aultre chose que ung establissement mis ou pays de par le
prince de la terre pour aucuns humains besoings pour le profit commun appoyés de
raison garder et approuver notoirement et par escript par le temps de XL ans. Et
souffit qu'elle soit prouvee par XII dignes de foy' (*ibid.*).

and its relationship with royal power were important themes of the texts, along with the duties of lords vis-à-vis their vassals and how their own courts ought to be run.

While the *coutumiers* mentioned people of different status, the texts largely elided the particularities of the customs of various subgroups within their designated territories. In other words, the *coutumier* authors tended to smooth over variation within individual regions. Just as the king was expanding and cementing his jurisdiction, counts and barons were also attempting to cement their jurisdiction over the areas they controlled. Glimpses of these lower jurisdictions in the texts are brief and ephemeral. They can be seen in rare moments when the texts noted exceptions to general rules. One rare instance in the *Établissements de Saint Louis* explained that while there was a general rule that the sons of the king's free men and women were under royal jurisdiction, an exception was made for Sainte Croix and Saint Aignien.[104] The *Établissements* usually did not report these sorts of differences and exceptions, providing a general gloss of uniformity for the customs of Touraine, Anjou, and Orleans. Local customs are rife in charters but barely present in the *coutumiers*.

Only Philippe de Beaumanoir – curiously, the *coutumier* author who wrote about the smallest region – directly acknowledged and commented on variation in local custom within the larger jurisdiction of Beauvaisis. For example, when Beaumanoir detailed the jurisdiction and care of roads, he described the rule from the most general to the most specific jurisdiction. According to common law (*droit commun*), jurisdiction over roads belonged in all ways to the lords, who held their land directly from the king.[105] However, there was a different 'general custom' in Beauvaisis: if one held the land on both sides of the road and one had jurisdiction and lordship in this land, then one had jurisdiction over the part of the road that was on one's land.[106] There were yet finer distinctions: even within small Beauvaisis, there were local exceptions to this general custom, and some people had highway jurisdiction over roads that passed through land other than their own.[107]

---

[104] 'And if he can prove he is the son of the king's free woman or free man, he will remain in the king's jurisdiction, unless he is a man or woman of Sainte Croix or Saint Aignien' (*Les établissements de Saint Louis*, ed. Viollet, 2.31).

[105] Beaumanoir, *Coutumes de Beauvaisis*, ed. Salmon, XXV.721.   [106] *Ibid.*

[107] *Ibid.*, XXV.722.

Exceptions could be made for person or place. For instance, in the county of Clermont, no one could take property from their surety without first making a complaint in court.[108] This was generally true within this county, unless one lived in one of three localities that were the exception to this rule. In the castellany and town of Creil and the localities of Sacy and La Neuville-en-Hez, anyone could simply take their surety's property.[109]

Customs that concerned quantification and measurement, in particular, varied in small localities. Measurement used by tradesmen often varied from place to place. Beaumanoir devoted an entire chapter to an attempt to manage the problem of varying measurement (Chapter XXVI):

because many kinds of merchandise are sold by weight or volume, and especially things which should be delivered by volume, we shall speak in this chapter of volume measurements and of things which cannot be sold except by measurements, and the dangers which lie in buying and selling because the measurements differ from town to town according to the local custom, and we shall speak also of what measurements are used in general according to our custom.[110]

Beaumanoir was making an argument in favor of uniformity. The particular customs of small localities were permitted to persist as long as they did not contradict the customs of the county. On important issues, such as issues relating to land, the policy was uniformity.[111] Just as kings were attempting to cement their control

[108] *Ibid.*, XLIII.1323.   [109] *Ibid.* This must have been bad for business.
[110] *Ibid.*, XXVI.743.
[111] Beaumanoir is clear that on important matters, such as the right of redemption on sold land, there must be unity in the county. As he explains: 'There are some twenty towns in the county where they want to uphold as a custom that when someone buys property, there is an announcement in the parish that such-and-such a property has been sold [and those who want to redeem it should do so within 15 days ...]. But such an announcement and order is not valid, for it is against the general custom of the castellany of Clermont [where you have a whole year to redeem]; and subjects of the count cannot and must not make customs which are contrary to the custom of the castellany which is their chief town. And I have no doubt that if someone in the above-mentioned towns, where such an order was given, tries to redeem a property by the end of the year, he will be able to, if he pursues the suit to a judgment. If the opposite were judged, he would have a good appeal' [*Mes teus cris ne tele maniere de commandement ne vaut riens, car c'est contre la general coustume du chastel de Clermont; ne li sougiet du conte ne pueent ne ne doivent fere coustume contraire a cele du chastel qui est leur chiés*] (*ibid.*, XLIV.1387).

over their kingdom and introduce some level of commonality, there was a real move to create some uniformity within the substrata below.

Variations in local custom within the region must have been an important part of the knowledge necessary for the everyday administration of regional justice. This makes the lack of discussion or notice paid to local customs in most of the *coutumiers* noteworthy. It must have been a purposeful elision, one appropriate to the construction of regional power as opposed to local power, and one that buttressed the position of larger lordships as opposed to smaller units. This elision reveals another aspect of the *coutumier* authors' creativity: they were in effect creating the image of a harmonized 'regional' jurisdiction as well as linking it to the general customs of the lay courts.

**

The fascination with the influence of Roman law and royal power on the *coutumiers* has created a narrative of these texts as shaped by compelling outside forces. The *coutumiers* were indeed responsive to their context but not so passively. While both royal power and Roman law helped shape lay justice as described by *coutumier* authors, these authors' deeper preoccupation lay in the jurisdictional contest between the lay and ecclesiastical courts. They provided lay courts with a body of law, albeit informal because unlegislated, that characterized them and showed them to be competent, organized, and professionalized.

As such they reinforced a firm jurisdictional identity for lay lordship. While the concepts of lay or temporal versus ecclesiastic or spiritual had long existed, the meaning of these in practice was often unclear. The professionalization of the church courts spurred the lay courts to follow suit. As they did, the two courts confronted one another. This confrontation created a need to know which cases, people, procedures and rules belonged to which forum, and how to navigate the boundaries between them.

Jurisdiction at this early developmental stage was truly about forms of power and about who held it. Contests for power can only exist relationally, and jurisdiction was about relationships and boundaries. Cormack defined jurisdiction as 'the administrative principle that orders power as authority by defining the scope of a particular power over a given matter or territory'.[112] The administrative and territorial aspects he emphasized – quintessential aspects of how we define jurisdiction – were in the process of development in the thirteenth century. It was a fruitful time for invented traditions, the sort that nurtured germinal forms of political power.

While the thirteenth-century *coutumiers* were characterized by anxiety towards the ecclesiastical courts, we find a rapprochement by the beginning of the fourteenth century. When customary law began to be written in the *coutumiers*, the initial anxiety and competition was with the personnel, procedure, and jurisdiction of the ecclesiastical courts. It was only as the fourteenth century progressed into the fifteenth and sixteenth that jurists began to fight over the soul of French law and debated whether it was rooted in Roman or customary law. When customary law first developed as a written body of knowledge, however, its politics were directed at the ecclesiastical courts, and its central concern was to create an identity and toolkit for the lay courts in the context of professionalizing lordship.

---

[112] Cormack, *A Power to Do Justice*, p. 3.

5

Roman Law, Authority, and Creative Citation

Coutumier authors are often presented as grappling with the anxiety that their texts were not enough like their powerful predecessors; namely, the tomes produced by Roman lawyers of late antiquity as packaged in the *Corpus iuris civilis* and various texts produced by medieval commentators on Roman law.[1] They have been described as feeling keenly their own inferiority compared to the learned laws and attempting to use these superior learned laws to bolster authority for their own works. Peter Stein, for instance, writes that Philippe de Beaumanoir 'adapted Roman law to quite unroman institutions, to give them greater authority'. By Stein's interpretation, it seems, Beaumanoir felt that both the *coutumier* and general customary law and practice needed buttressing by the greater authority of Roman law.[2]

Authority, and the authority of Roman law specifically, ought to be discussed differently. It is not a simple trajectory by which the learned unidirectionally influenced the unlearned. Modern notions of the medieval use of citations have appreciably shaped our understanding of the relationship between Roman law and the *coutumiers*. The medieval author is often understood as dominated by his or her

---

[1] For Bloom's theory on the 'anxiety of influence', that poets grapple with the anxiety that all their work is influenced by their strong predecessors, see Harold Bloom, *The Anxiety of Influence*.

[2] Stein, *Roman Law in European History*, p. 66.

citations. The difference between modern and medieval citations, in the words of Anthony Grafton, is that

[The modern] historian who cites documents does not cite authorities, as the theologians and lawyers of the Middle Ages and the Renaissance did, but sources. Historical footnotes list not the great writers who sanction a given statement or whose words an author has creatively adapted, but the documents, many or most of them not literary texts at all, which provided its substantive ingredients.[3]

But was medieval scholarship truly confined to authorities or their adaptation, with little interest in building intellectual monuments of its own?

Citation practices, Grafton also notes, are reflections of the culture of erudition to which they belong.[4] As their citation practices indicate, *coutumier* authors approached Roman law and the texts they cited with the fundamental attributes of change, creativity, and innovation. These authors were not citing authorities in the sense that the weight of the reference's influence conditioned the content of the text. The *coutumiers* did not cater to authorities, and authorities did not condition the normative exposition of individual *coutumier* texts. The sources they used were *authoritative* in the sense that they carried a moral weight and an epistemological nobility that bears a certain persuasive gravitas. However, they also used these sources liberally. They were citing sources in order to create their own text and to showcase the erudition of that text.

Harold Bloom wrote that a poet could only overcome his anxiety towards his formidable predecessors and become great by a 'strong misreading' of the earlier texts would permit him to create his own – 'weaker talents idealize; figures of capable imagination appropriate from themselves'.[5] Authors of the first *coutumiers*, written around the second half of the thirteenth century, were such 'figures of capable imagination'. They built up their own texts by collating a variety of sources, which they often subjected to a strong misreading that shaped the sources for their new purpose. Authors could not behave this way towards sources if they slavishly followed

---

[3] Anthony Grafton, *The Footnote*, p. 33.
[4] Grafton, 'Learning, Citation and Authority in Musical Culture before 1600', p. xxi.
[5] Bloom, *The Anxiety of Influence*, p. 5.

them as authorities, but only if they were creators, reshaping sources for a new destiny.

Authority

Roman law is commonly credited with supplying not only the framework for customary law but also the conceptual apparatus by which it could define and form itself: Stein writes, 'the thirteenth century saw attempts in several European countries to set down the local law in writing and in every case those responsible turned to the civil law to provide organizing categories and organizing principles'.[6] The *coutumiers* have often been judged by the extent to which they successfully conformed to this picture – by how ably they incorporated Roman law. This tendency to assume that the learned sway and the less learned or unlearned are swayed is not specific to legal history and derives from general assumptions about authority in the Middle Ages. But scholarship on diglossia and the rise of the vernacular show that medieval approaches to learned authority were more complicated than that. We can see this complexity in attitudes about learned law in vernacular literature that should make us reconsider how we think of authority for customary, vernacular law.

The *Établissements de Saint Louis* is a good example of a legal text whose reputation has been shaped by modern assumptions about authority in the Middle Ages. The *Établissements de Saint Louis* (1272/3) was transcribed, abridged, and adapted – and, with twenty-four manuscripts surviving from the end of the thirteenth and beginning of the fourteenth century alone, it was probably the most popular northern French *coutumier* of the thirteenth and early fourteenth centuries.[7] A text clearly admired in these centuries, the *Établissements de Saint Louis* has elicited rather different responses in modern scholars, ranging from bewilderment to disdain. Already in the

---

[6] Stein, *Roman Law in European History*, p. 64.
[7] '*Établissements de Saint Louis*' in Geneviève Hasenohr and Michel Zink, *Dictionnaire des lettres françaises*, p. 418. Paul Viollet describes these twenty-four manuscripts in detail in his introduction to the critical edition. The manuscripts of the *Établissements* are currently found all over the place: the Archives nationales in Paris, the faculty of medicine at Montpellier, Troyes, the municipal archive in Beauvais, the Vatican, the Royal Library in Stockholm, Munich, and Cheltenham (UK).

eighteenth century, Montesquieu was asking, 'What is this obscure, confused, and ambiguous code?'[8] Montesquieu called into question a text where 'French law is continually mixed with the Roman'.[9] The rather strong aversion to this mixture can also be gleaned in de Valroger's assessment of the text as a *'compilation indigeste'* – an indigestible compilation of Roman law, decretals, and French customs.[10]

This negative impression was rooted in the *Établissements* author's methods of composition and citation and has persisted in more recent evaluations. Giving it the shortest treatment of the *coutumiers* he examines in his article, Jean Gaudemet dismisses the *Établissements de Saint Louis* generally as a work that is ostentatiously doctrinaire and that makes dull and uninteresting use of legal citation. Instead of making constructive use of Roman law to structure the customs, nourish developments, or justify solutions, Gaudemet explains, Roman law appears in this text as a 'pedantic' inclusion that contributes little to the customary law within.[11]

Jean-Philippe Lévy's 1957 article still stands as the primary analytic framework for the *coutumiers*. In this article Lévy appraises the penetration of Roman law into the *coutumiers* along a spectrum, from superficial – somewhat awkwardly inserted quotations – to substantial, where the Roman law animated the writer's spirit and became the unconscious craftsman of the text.[12] The language of penetration, sometimes expressed more softly as 'influence', has long conditioned how we interpret the presence of the learned laws in the *coutumiers*.[13] A sophisticated and powerful Roman law steamrolls through an impressionable, inchoate, and even naïve customary law. As Emanuele Conte has noted, this is part of a continental historiographical tendency inherited from the German Historical

---

[8] Montesquieu, *The Spirit of the Laws*, trans. Nugent, II.38.   [9] *Ibid.*

[10] Viollet, introduction to *Établissements*, ed. Viollet, vol. 1, p. 3. Decretals are papal decrees, or a collection of such decrees.

[11] Gaudemet, 'L'influence des droits savants', p. 175.

[12] See J. P. Lévy, 'La pénétration du droit savant', 1–53. Lévy uses the language of 'penetration' specifically to avoid the language of 'reception', which he does not feel fits this earlier time (*ibid.*, 3).

[13] See for instance, Lefebvre-Teillard, 'Recherches sur la pénétration du droit canonique'; Gaudemet, 'L'influence des droit savants'; Petot, 'Pierre de Fontaines et le droit romain'; Georges Hubrecht, 'Le droit canonique dans le coutumier de Beaumanoir'.

School to 'think of the contrast between customs and Roman law as a confrontation between popular institutions and a superstructure imposed by political and economical power'.[14]

The use of authority in law, however, is often a reimagining of the past to shape a desired present. In the thirteenth century, as today, a vigorous tradition of making creative use of past narratives and past written texts can be seen in the works of lawyers, theologians, and storytellers. As Jacques Le Goff observes for the twelfth century, authoritative texts were materials with which to construct an aesthetic and intellectual creation, an *oeuvre*.[15] Bernard of Chartres (fl. twelfth century) made what is probably the most famous medieval remark about authority when he said that he was sitting on the shoulders of giants, in order that he could see further.[16]

Gilbert of Tournai captured this wave of intellectual optimism, LeGoff notes, when he said that the truth will never be found based on what has already been found – 'those who wrote before us are not our lords but our guides. The truth is open to all, it has not yet been possessed in its entirety.'[17] Alan of Lille also said explicitly that figures of authority had 'wax noses' (*cereum nasum*) which were remoulded by subsequent uses of their authority.[18] Authority was not meant to be faithfully perpetuated. Rather, the process of being used changed that very 'authority'. The notion of authority here was flexible, and we may want to revisit the analytical category of authority if 'authorities' were meant to be changed, built upon, and improved.

Vernacular literary culture also embraced the idea that authority was flexible. Some tales, of course, drew their claims from antiquity, including *Le Chanson de Girart de Rousillon*, which draws on the age of the tale in the first few words: 'Here is a good old song'.[19] Even with ancient and old tales, however, authors still saw themselves as creating

---

[14] Conte, 'Roman Law *vs* Custom in a Changing Society', p. 37.
[15] Le Goff, *Les intellectuels au Moyen Âge*, p. 99.
[16] Bernard of Chartres in Le Goff, *Les intellectuels au Moyen Âge*, p. 99.
[17] 'Jamais nous ne trouverons la vérité, si nous nous contentons de ce qui est déjà trouvé … Ceux qui écrivirent avant nous ne sont pas pour nous des seigneurs mais des guides. La verité est ouverte à tous, elle n'a pas encore été possédée toute entière', Gilbert of Tournai in Le Goff, *Les intellectuels au Moyen Âge*, p. 99.
[18] Rico, '"Auctoritas cereum habet nasum"', p. 28.
[19] *La Chanson de Girart de Rousillion*, trans. Gouiran, I.1.

something distinct in their own versions. Béroul, for instance, criticized his predecessors for getting the story of *Tristan and Iseut* wrong:

The storytellers say that [Tristan and Gouvernal] had Yvain drowned. They are stupid and do not know the story well at all. Béroul preserved the story in his memory. Tristan was too valiant and courtly to kill people of such [low] status.[20]

Béroul verges on literary criticism when he implies that other storytellers simply did not understand Tristan's character adequately to tell the story well – they impute actions to Tristan which he himself could not possibly perform. Based on his knowledge of the story and of Tristan's character, their versions could not be correct. Béroul claimed authority based on a superior memory of the tale, but he also built it on a rejection of earlier tellers of that tale. 'The story' was not a static, closed, or stagnant category.[21] Rather, this looks very much like Alain of Lille's wax nose – a story being shaped and reshaped by different writers. Béroul showed us that there was at the very least a vernacular practice of critique in the twelfth century.

Other authors made overt claims of authority based on novelty. The opening of Jean Renart's *Roman de la rose, ou Guillaume de Dole* makes its entire claim for attention on the basis of the novelty of the narrative and its departure from its predecessors. Jean says in the opening of this work that he is creating something original – it is a 'new thing, so different from the others, and so well woven with pretty verse in some places, that a boor could not but appreciate it. Know this both by faith and by sight: this work surpasses all the others.'[22] According to Jean Renart, then, what is new is not only good but, as in this case, potentially superior.

Clearly, there was a great deal of fluidity and play in medieval relationships to 'authority', and this should inform our interpretation of authority in law. Marguerite Boulet-Sautel, for instance, has shown that

---

[20] 'Li conteor dïent qu'Yvain / Firent nïer, qui sont vilain; / N'en sevent mie bien l'estoire, / Berox l'a mex en sen mémoire, / Trop est Tristan preuz et cortois / A ocirre gens de tes lois' (Béroul, *Tristan et Iseut*, in *Tristan et Iseut*, trans. Lacroix and Walter, ll. 1265–70; my trans.]. Béroul also says that he saw the story in a written version (*ibid.*, ll. 1790).

[21] See generally Simon Gaunt, *Retelling the Tale*.

[22] ' ... *Roman de la rose / qui est une novele chose / et s'est des autres si divers / et brodez, par lieus, de biaus vers / que vilains nel porroit savoir. Ce sachiez de fi et de voir,/ bien a cist les autres passez*' (Renart, *Roman de la rose*, trans. Dufournet, ll. 11–17). Jean Dufournet translates 'novele chose' as 'œuvre originale' (*ibid.*, 71).

Parisian notaries did not necessarily use Roman law all that faithfully during the thirteenth century.[23] Even the gloss, the archetypal form of medieval reverence for the urtext, had moments of creative adaptation.[24] In his introduction to the *Glossa Ordinaria* to Gratian's *Decretum*, for instance, Bartholomaeus Brixiensis explained that he had 'improved as necessary' the apparatus of the *Decretum*.[25] James Gordley notes the liberties that Romanists took with their sources, and this creativity drew serious criticism from some in their community by the fourteenth century.[26] Richardus Malumbra (d.1334), for instance, complained that while they should be sticking to the original text, its gloss, and the opinions of the most respected *doctores*, Roman jurists were turning 'to fables or mak[ing] arguments so logistic and sophistic that they have no truth but only its appearance'.[27] This sort of accusation was of course intended to make the work of others seem unreliable in comparison to his own. That it was an effective form of critique shows that accusations of creativity – though negatively cast here – had traction. In these instances of unfaithful use, improvement, and imaginativeness, we can see some creative reinvention of authority even in those Latinate legal communities that were supposed to be most devoted to their urtexts.

A deeper look at tagging and referencing will help us move away from assumptions about the influence of learned authorities and see how authority generally was constructed.

Citation Practices

Robert Connors explains that the study of citation systems permits us to ask rhetorical, social and stylistic questions, such as 'why these systems evolved and proliferated, what they suggest about authors'

[23] Boulet-Sautel, 'Le notaire contre le *Jus civile*'.
[24] The gloss foregrounds the textual authority – it emphasizes its centrality in a very visual way by framing it. Later, even glosses had trouble keeping focused on *auto-ritates*. Robert Connors has noted that the first use of the endnote that he could find accompanied glossing, in the Rheims New Testament (1582), which used endnote glosses at the end of each chapter of each book of the New Testament (Connors, 'The Rhetoric of Citation Systems', 21). The endnote, then, was invented 'to solve a Catholic rhetorical problem: how do you appear to foreground the scriptural text when you actually have such a massive glossing apparatus to purvey?' (*ibid.*).
[25] Short introduction to the gloss, found before Distinction One (Gratian, *The Treatise on Laws*, trans. Thompson and Gordley, p. 3).
[26] James Gordley, '*Ius Quarens Intellectum*', p. 92.   [27] *Ibid.*, pp. 92–3.

feelings of debt and ownership, how they effect the ways we read and process text and the intentions behind it, and, finally, the effects on reading and writing of social decisions to promote and valorize new citation systems and subsystems'.[28] General citation practices give us a vantage point on the project and also permit us to uncover ideas of reasoning and intellectual belonging that underpinned the *coutumiers*.[29]

The learning and experience conjured in the vernacular *coutumiers* of the thirteenth century shows the range of possibilities for thinking and constructing customary law. This is not to dispute the importance of Roman law or its effect on law beyond the university – undoubtedly it had a profoundly transformative effect on legal life and practice in high medieval Europe.[30] However, the *coutumiers* rely on other sources in addition to Roman and canon law, including custom, usage, previous judgments, common practice in lay court, wisdom from the authors' personal experience, narrative storytelling, moral poetry, and popular wisdom. Some of these sources are not classic 'authorities', and some fall outside of what we might understand as the ambit of law. But they are all references used by the authors of these texts and this constellation of references shows what one could use to create an authoritative account of customary law.

Each *coutumier* constructed its customary law in its own individual manner. In other words, the *coutumiers* are not uniform in the type of sources they use, the extent to which they use sources, and the manner in which they do it. Manuscript versions of a text can also vary. Each one provides us with insight about the relationship between text and authority, court practice and university learning, lay jurists and scholars, and the potential configurations of customary law.

The *Coutumes d'Anjou et du Maine* (1246), one of the earliest *coutumiers*, contained few citations. The few direct references in the text referred to 'custom in the lay courts' or to parts of its own text.[31] It

---

[28] Connors, 'The Rhetoric of Citation Systems', 7.
[29] For a thoughtful consideration of the term 'project', see generally the introduction to Claire Monagle, *The Scholastic Project*.
[30] See for instance Bellomo, *The Common Legal Past of Europe*; Van Caenegem, *An Historical Introduction to Private Law*, trans. Johnston; Stein, *Roman Law in European History*.
[31] '*Telle est la coustume de cort laie ...*' (*Coutumes d'Anjou et du Maine*, §101); '*si comme nous avon dit desus*' (*ibid.*, §145).

did not cite Roman or canon law and focused on explaining impersonally what was currently done or ought to be done in the lay court, giving the impression that the content of the text itself was source and authority.

This changed with Pierre de Fontaines' *Conseil* (1253), which showed a real preoccupation with sourcing its information. Pierre constantly referred to the usage of the courts as well as to Roman law. While Pierre occasionally cited custom (*coutume*), he preferred the language of usage (*usage*) to describe the sources of rules from practice; for example, 'according to the usage of lay courts', 'according to our usage', and 'by reason of our usage'.[32] He mentioned 'the philosopher', Aristotle, as well as the Bible.[33] He only cited canon law once, though he did discuss procedural issues in ecclesiastical courts and was comfortable doing so.[34]

Pierre's *Conseil* incorporated more Roman law than any other, much of it drawn from the *Code*. Significantly, he often referred to Roman law through large block quotations. Some chapters barely made any use of Roman law;[35] other chapters were composed almost entirely of it. In these cases, block quotations could last for pages, with only a couple of paragraphs and a few sentences that explained where custom varied or concurred.[36] At other times, Pierre might incorporate a short quotation. Pierre occasionally noted that he was quoting from the Roman law, and when he did so he referenced either 'written law' or the name of a specific issuing emperor.[37] Pierre provided only this information and nothing more. He did not provide citations in the scholastic manner, where work, book, and chapter were detailed such that the reader could go to the original work and locate the reference.

---

[32] '*par la coutume*' (Pierre de Fontaines, *Conseil*, ed. Marnier, 4.8, see also XIV.15, XV.8), but these are far outweighed by his constant references to usage: '*par usage de cort laie*' (*ibid.*, XI.8), '*selonc notre usage*' (*ibid.*, IX.1) or '*par nostre usage*' (*ibid.*, XII.8), and '*Il est resons par nostre usage ...*' (*ibid.*, XII.2).

[33] '*car li philosophes dit que homs ne puet avoir droiture en soi qui doute mort, périll, essil, ne dolor, ne povreté*' (*ibid.*, XXI.3); '*Cremor de Dieu est li comencemenz de sapience, si come dit l'Escriture*' (*ibid.*, II.2).

[34] See for instance, *ibid.*, IV.15.

[35] See for instance, *ibid.*, XXI. In chapter XXI, nineteen of sixty-eight sections are block quotes of Roman law, which works out to about thirteen pages of Marnier's sixty-five -page chapter (pp. 220–85).

[36] See for instance *ibid.*, XXIX. In Marnier's critical edition, this chapter runs from page 341 to page 359. The size of these block quotes must be emphasized: in these eighteen pages of chapter XXIX, Pierre adds only two paragraphs and five sentences about custom.

[37] For instance, 'La loi escrite dist que' (*ibid.*, XI.7); 'et ce dit lois' (*ibid.*, VII.5); 'Encore dient aucune lois escrites' (*ibid.*, IX.5); 'si come la lois escrite dist ...' (*ibid.*, XI.1), etc.

Pierre did not seem to expect his audience to go and read the original text, and it is quite possible that he did not even take them from the original text but from a secondary source.

The compiler of the *Établissements de Saint Louis* (1272/3) employed a different method, taking smaller portions from a wider range of sources. The *Établissements* referred specifically to the usage of lay courts, baronial court, and the Orleans district.[38] Unlike Pierre, the *Établissements* also commonly adopted the language of custom (*coutume*) to refer to the norms of the lay courts, citing the 'custom of the land', 'custom of the region', and 'the custom of the region and of the land'.[39] In addition, the text referred to four types of written sources: Roman law, canon law, customary law, and royal law. The learned laws were cited both with a reference to the text and in a way that emphasized their quality of writtenness: 'it is written in the Code', 'according to the written law in the Code', 'according to the law written in the *Digest*', or 'according to written law in the *Decretals*'.[40] The *Établissements* also cited other parts of its own text in a formal manner.[41] Book I was copied straight from royal ordinances, though there is no citation that would identify it as such, but other parts of the text referred to royal law directly, such as the rule that 'the king forbids weapons and excursions and novel claims and private wars by his ordinances' or the 'king of France forbids trial by battle by his ordinances'.[42] Some manuscripts included a prologue that introduced the entire text as a royal ordinance, also a form of citation to royal authority.[43]

---

[38] 'selonc l'usage en cort laie' (*Établissements*, ed. Viollet, II.4); 'selonc l'usage de la cort de baronie' (*ibid.*, II.4); 'selonc l'usage d'Orlenois' (*ibid.*, II.21, II.26 ...).

[39] 'par la costume de la terre' (*ibid.*, I.7), 'par la costume dou païs' (*ibid.*, I.102), and 'par la costume dou païs et de la terre' (*ibid.*, II.4).

[40] 'et est escrit ou Code, De edicto divi Adriani tollendo, l. Quamvis quis se filium defunct, etc.' and 'selonc droit escrit ou Code' or 'selonc droit escrit en la Digeste' (*ibid.*, II.4) or 'selonc droit escrit en Decretales' (*ibid.*, I.89).

[41] While the *Établissements* use royal ordinances, which are of course written sources, these are not cited. There is one possible exception where the text does refer to the *establissemenz le roi*, but it is unclear whether this refers to some ordinance or whether this is another place in which the text refers to itself as a source.

[42] 'mes sires li roi deffant les armes et les chevauchiées, par ses establissemenz, et les novels avoeries, et les guerres' (*Établissements*, ed. Viollet, II.38); 'selonc les establissemenz le roi' (*ibid.*, II.4); 'car li rois de France deffant les batailles par ses establissemenz' (*ibid.*, II.11).

[43] Manuscripts Q, R, S. More on this in Chapter 5.

One manuscript of the *Établissements* prefaced the text with a poem that reframed the rules of customary law within as part of a general moral duty.[44] In 1303, the unknown compiler of manuscript N used a selection from a moralistic poem to introduce the body of the text.[45] Manuscript N began by explaining that the text will discuss justice, Law (*droit*), laws (*commendemens de droit*), the duties of knights, the apprehension of wrongdoers in the act, the customary laws of the baronial courts of Orleans, and the punishment of wrongdoers. Then, the compiler selected four stanzas drawn from a sixty-four-stanza moralistic poem, *Des droiz au clerc de Voudoi*, and used these to introduce the *Établissements*:[46]

Ore entendés une chosete	Now hear a little thing
Petite qui est nouvelete	A little thing which is a little new
Que je veuil de droiture dire.	That I want to say about justice.[47]
[…]	[…]
Droiz dit, et j'en sui emparlier,	Law says, and I am its advocate,
Que quiconques est chevaliers	That whoever is a knight
Qu'il ne doit de nelui mesdire.	Must not speak ill of it.
Droiz dit qu'il soit drois conseillers.	Law says that he be an upright counsellor.
Droiz dit qu'il soit drois joutisiers,	Law says that he be an upright judge.
Si qu'en ne le puisse desdire.	So that no one can speak against him.

When the poem ended, the compiler explained that it is for 'these reasons;' namely, the moral propositions about the nature of law in the poem, that he would now speak of justice.[48] The poem's place,

[44] For modern discomfort at the use of poetry as a form of judicial expression, see for instance Rains, 'To Rhyme or Not to Rhyme'.

[45] This was not the only example of poetry meeting law. The Bible, for instance, was put into verse in the thirteenth century. The *Grand coutumier de Normandie*, a translation of the Latin *Summa de legibus Normanniae*, was put into verse near the end of the thirteenth century. The customs of Normandy, first written around 1199/1200, were updated mid-thirteenth century as the *Summa de legibus Normanniae*, which was quickly translated into the vernacular and was versified around 1280.

[46] There are manuscripts of both Manuscript N and of *Des droiz au clerc de Voudoi* in the Beauvaisis archive.

[47] 'Droiture' has a wide range of meanings, from 'in a straight line' or 'directly' to 'uprightness' to 'law, justice and rights', see Greimas, *Dictionnaire de l'ancien français*, p. 185.

[48] 'Por ce, vueil de joutise presentement parler' (*Établissements*, ed. Viollet, II.1).

between the title and the body of the text, affirmed its symbolic dimension.[49] The moral economy expressed in the poem now coloured the *Établissements*, and the text was meant to be read in the light of it.

The main source for *Le livre des constitutions demenées el Chastelet de Paris* (ca. 1279–82) was custom (*coutume*). The specific 'custom of France' or 'custom of France and especially of the court of the Châtelet of Paris' is preferred over the more vague 'custom of the region'.[50] Except for one potential citation of a decretal, which could not be corroborated by Mortet, the *Demenées el Chastelet de Paris* did not cite the learned laws at all, nor do they seem to borrow from it more covertly.[51] On two occasions, the text used an example to illustrate rules.[52] Generally, the text's authority was based on referencing rules and procedure as custom.

Philippe de Beaumanoir's long, sophisticated *Coutumes de Beauvaisis* (1283) made references to a wide array of sources and paid attention to sourcing the information he provided but never explicitly referred to Roman law and did not use scholastic citation methods. He constantly made reference to custom, using a wide range of identifiers: 'current custom', 'our custom', 'the custom of Beauvaisis', 'our custom in Clermont', and 'custom of the lay court'.[53] He cites the king's statutes.[54] He made use of proverbs and legal maxims, and quoted the Bible.[55] He

---

[49] Rémy Cabrillac, *Les Codifications*, p. 245. Cabrillac notes this for the preliminary provisions of modern codes.

[50] *Le livre des constitutions demenées*, ed. Mortet, 'par la coustume de France' §12 (see also §30, 40, 44, 49, 63, 85, 86); 'selonc la coustume de France et especiaument de la court de Chastelet de Paris' (*ibid.*, §44); 'selonc la coustume du païs' (*ibid.*, §17).

[51] *Ibid.*, 11–12, 44n.3.   [52] *Ibid.*, §68, 76.

[53] 'par la coustume qui ore queurt' (Beaumanoir, *Coutumes de Beauvaisis*, ed. Salmon, XXXVIII.1133); 'par la coustume de Beauvoisins' (*ibid.*, IV.137); 'selonc nostre coustume' (*ibid.*, IV.160); 'selonc nostre coustume de Clermont' (*ibid.*, LVIII.1653); 'coustume de la court laie' (*ibid.*, VII.246).

[54] 'par l'establissement nostre roi Phelippe' (*ibid.*, V.176); 'car nouvele dessaisine est nouvel establissement; si doit on suir l'establissement en fere sa demande' (*ibid.*, VI.205); 'Et est l'establissement teus que … ' (*ibid.*, XXXII.986, see also XXXIX.1165).

[55] He described people who lie about the things they sell, and then explained that this was the origin of the expression: 'Merchant or thief' [et pour ce dit on: 'Marcheans ou lerres'] (*ibid.*, XXXI.946); and 'pour ce dit on: "Convenance vaint loi", exceptees les convenances sont fetes pour mauvaises causes' 'C' (*ibid.*, XXXIV.999). The biblical quotation: 'whoever agrees in a bad judgement is required to pay the damages of a person who loses by a false judgement, if he wants to be pardoned by God for the

discussed rules based on decisions made by the consensus of the wise men of the county.[56] He often referred to his own personal opinion about what was right to buttress a rule or procedure and to disagree with others' opinions.[57]

Previous judgments, in a number of guises, were another important source for Beaumanoir. He cited cases over which he himself had presided as *bailli* of Beauvaisis. On one occasion he explained that he was describing the case so that that people would be convinced to act similarly in the future.[58] Here, he was attempting to convince his audience to think in terms of precedent and use an earlier case as a guide for a future decision. He also drew upon judgments from different areas, some that were still in the county of Clermont but not in Beauvaisis, and some from outside altogether.[59] He explained debated issues and noted when there was a judgment on a specific issue as proof of the rule.[60] He even cited cases where his own judgment proved to be wrong, telling his reader that 'you will know that this is true because we will recount a case we saw' that reversed his own actions.[61]

Beaumanoir cited some real cases with real names and dates, expressing his knowledge of practice and court expertise.[62] He

---

offence; and for this reason it was said to judges: "Be careful how you judge, for you will be judged"' (*ibid.*, LXV.1861). This is Matthew 7:2.

[56] 'The council of wise men of the county considered the issue [Il fu regardé par le conseil des sages hommes de la contreé que], [...] And by this it can be seen that anyone [et par ce puet on savoir que chascuns] ... ' (*ibid.*, XV.524).

[57] 'We say yes, provided that ... ' (*ibid.*, V.186); 'we say no [*Nous disons que nenil*]' (*ibid.*, XII.375), 'we say that [*Nous disons que se ... *]' (*ibid.*, XII.376).

[58] *Ibid.*, LVI.1619.

[59] 'It was judged in Creeil, which is part of the county of Clermont, that ... ' (*ibid.*, XIII.442); 'For in Normandy there is a custom in some places that ... ' (*ibid.*, XXXV.1101).

[60] 'and we have to put his in our book because of doubts we have seen [...] and on this issue they requested judgment' (*ibid.*, XII.414) 'It was judged that ... [...] and by this judgment you can see that ... ' (*ibid.*, XII.415).

[61] 'et que ce soit voir vous savrés par ce que nous dirons un cas que nous en veismes ... ' (*ibid.*, XII.372), and he concludes that in this case 'such a gift was permitted by the custom of Beauvais, it was wrongful of us to make a seizure of it for lack of a vassal [*et l'en pouoit tel don fere pare la coustume de Beauvoisins, a tort i metions la main pour defaute d'homme*]' (*ibid.*, XII.373). This language of *seeing* is similar to that in the *Coutumier d'Artois* used to recount the facts of a specific case.

[62] See for instance in Beaumanoir: 'My lord Pierre de Thiverny sued the town of Les Haies, saying that ... ' (*ibid.*, XXIV.689) or 'And we saw a judgment on this matter for the lady of Milly in king's court' (*ibid.*, XIII.454) or 'A woman from La Neuville-en-Hez said to a bourgeois' (*ibid.*, XXXIX.1159), or 'And we saw a judgment on this

commonly also used pedagogical hypotheticals, saying 'let us see ... ',
'if ... ', 'such as if ... ', 'supposing that someone ... '.[63] He often used the
generic 'I' in examples that he introduced by saying 'such as when
I am ... ' or 'such as if I ... '.[64] He often used generic names for these
hypotheticals, most commonly Pierre and Robert. When he needed
a third party he added Guillaume, and when he needed women, he
used Marie and Jehane.[65] Sometimes he designated people by using
generic social status; for instance, when he recounted a case
concerning a knight and a lady, or a suit involving a respectable man
or gentleman.[66] Beaumanoir was diligent in citing a variety of sources
and was descriptively careful and specific. Clearly learned, his lack of
unambiguous, overt reference to Roman law has puzzled scholars (and
will be addressed later in this chapter).

The *Ancien Coutumier de Champagne* (ca. 1295) regularly referred
both to custom and usage.[67] The phrase 'it is custom in Champagne'
appeared constantly in the text.[68] Unlike other *coutumiers*, this text
consistently described specific cases as proof of custom. It provided
specific reference information on the date of the judgment, the location
of the trial, the nature of the issue, the arguments made, and the names

issue at Creil' (*ibid.*, XXXIX.1219). This can be contrast to his narration of
a situation in Lombardy ('I will tell you what happened in Lombardy ... ' (*ibid.*,
XXX.886)) where again he uses no names but is clearly recalling an issue that has
occurred.

[63] '*or veons*' (Beaumanoir, *The Coutumes de Beauvaisis*, trans. Akehurst, p. 46n.2);
'If ... ' (Beaumanoir, *Coutumes de Beauvaisis*, ed. Salmon, VI.220) ; *si comme se ...*
(*ibid.*, VI.224); '*S'il avient qu'aucuns...*" (*ibid.*, XIV.484). See also Beaumanoir, *The
Coutumes de Beauvaisis*, trans. Akehurst, 46n.2.

[64] 'si comme se l'en me demande' (Beaumanoir, *Coutumes de Beauvaisis*, ed. Salmon,
VII.238); 'si comme se je ... ' (*ibid.*, VII.239).

[65] Pierre and Jehan (*ibid.*, II.80), Guillaume (*ibid.*, XXIV.1014), and Marie and Jehane
(*ibid.*, XIV.472). There is good reason to think Beaumanoir would have known of
Pierre de Fontaines' work. And interestingly, when it came to citing examples with
generic names, he changed Pierre de Fontaines' Philippe for Pierre. Perhaps he felt silly
using his own name as a generic name in all his examples. So Robert stayed,
Guillaume was added as a third party, and Philippe became Pierre (can this be
a coincidence?) in his examples.

[66] 'uns chevalier' and 'une dame' (*ibid.*, XII.373), 'preudhons' (*ibid.*, XXIII.680), 'gen-
tius hons' (*ibid.*, XLV.1449).

[67] 'il est coustume en Champane' (*L'ancien coutumier*, ed. Portejoie, II, V, etc.); 'Einsinc
en us'on en Champagne' (*ibid.*, IV, XXV, etc.); 'De droit commun et par le coustume
de Champagne, li sires sous cui il lieve et couche en aura court, se il la requiert' (*ibid.*,
XXXV).

[68] *Ibid.*, II, V, VI, VII, etc.

of jurors who made the judgment. These cases were introduced with the following phrases: 'this was reported in', 'this was proved in', 'this was examined for', 'this was how it was used', or 'the following was judged'.[69] The prime authority in this text was usage or custom, followed closely by the judgment. Royal power was only mentioned by virtue of references to cases decided by the Parlement of Paris.[70] The learned laws were not referenced overtly and do not seem to have had an appreciable impact on the text.

The *Coutumier d'Artois* (between 1283 and 1302) was a more motley composition. It variously cited custom and usage: 'it is the custom of Artois', 'by the custom of Artois and other places', 'by the general custom of the barony', 'by the usage of the lay courts', 'general custom', and mentioned a usage of the *prevostés* of the king that ought to be applied in Artois.[71] The author also cited reason and right.[72] References to the learned law appear often, sometimes generally in claims based on 'written law' and sometimes with references to specific texts of Roman or canon law.[73] This *coutumier* also quoted maxims from the learned laws.[74] Like the *Ancien coutumier de Champagne*, this *coutumier* made frequent references to cases.[75] A large number of these were ones the author had seen in person in various types of court. The author referred to a case he had seen in Heding, another in Biaukaisne, another in the castle at Encre, another in the court of the count in Arras, and one in the king's court at Dorlens.[76] He also included examples that resemble descriptions

[69] 'Ce fu rapourté a' (*ibid.*, XIX), 'Ce fuit esprouvé a' (*ibid.*, XX), 'Ce fu regardé pour' (*ibid.*, LX), 'Ainsi on a usé' (*ibid.*, VI), 'Ce fut jugié' (*ibid.*, XV).

[70] *Ibid.*, XV.

[71] 'par le coustume d'Artoys' (*Coutumier d'Artois*, ed. Tardif, XXI.4); 'par la coustume d'Artois et d'autres lieus' (*ibid.*, V.1); 'par la general coustume de baronie' (*ibid.*, XI.11); 'par l'usage de court laie' (*ibid.*, III.1); 'Car il est generale coustume . . .' (*ibid.*, III.18); 'Je te di qu'il est usages, orendroit, tous generaus par les prevostés le roy – et aussi deveroit il estre en Artois . . .' (*ibid.*, IV.1).

[72] 'Et c'est de raison, et de droit' (*ibid.*, XX.18).

[73] 'Et la lois escrite dist bien que . . .' (*ibid.*, III.16); 'selon droit escrit en le digeste: *de procuratoribus, Lege 3*, et en decretales, *de procuratoribus, C. None juste*' (*ibid.*, III.6). The citation to learned law is uneven, some parts of the text make little use of it, while references veritably explode in chapter on lawyers (*procureurs*), for instance.

[74] 'Et si est de droit escrit: *Jure debet causam admittere, qui tanquam contumax negligit in judicium comparere*' (*ibid.*, III.33, see also XLVII.10).

[75] 'il fut dit par jugement que' (*ibid.*, VI.3).

[76] '.i. plaidiet, que jou en vi a Heding' (*ibid.*, XVIII.4); 'et si vi je a Biaukaisne' (*ibid.*, II.9); 'Si vi je a Encre, ou chastel' (*ibid.*, VI.2); 'Je vi en la cort le conte a Arras' (*ibid.*,

of earlier cases but without the specific details of the trial.[77] He quoted the
ancient poet Horace.[78] He also included quotations of lessons contained
in poetry, in the form of Latin verse. Although unattributed in the
coutumiers, they were drawn from three different *ordines iudiciarii* by
Marinus de Fano, Dino Mugellanus, and an anonymous Italian jurist.[79]
Lastly, on one occasion he quoted the Bible.[80] Lastly, the *Ancien
Coutumier de Bourgogne* often referred to Law (*droit*) and the usage of
Bourgogne, but did not cite any written sources.

This brief inventory of the range of citations used by lay jurists who
composed the *coutumiers* shows that their citation practices
overlapped but were not uniform. This was a juristic community that
was beginning to recognize which sources were fundamental to
understanding the lay courts – custom, usage, earlier cases, and
forms of law drawn from outside the lay courts, such as Roman law,
canon law, the Bible, and moralistic writing in various forms. The
coutumier authors did not see custom as a closed body of knowledge
or one that was completely autonomous from others. A broader
perspective on what constitutes a source and an authority permits us
to appreciate the array of material used and the inventiveness in the
composition of written custom.

Writing Custom and Roman Law

This inventiveness can be seen even more clearly with closer
examination of one example. The *Établissements de Saint Louis*
shows one construction of customary law and illustrates how Roman
law and other sources were put together to create authority for custom.
Paul Viollet pointed out long ago that the references to Roman and
canon law in Book I of the *Établissements* were *post factum*

II.3, III.19); 'Je vi en la court le roy a Dorlens' (*ibid.*, V.3). This jurist was clearly
travelling to and attending the secular courts of many different places.

[77] *Ibid.*, XXII.3. The detailed description of arguments here is coupled with a lack of
names, places, and dates.

[78] 'Orasses, li boins clers, qui dist : "Quanques tu commanderas, di briement"' (*ibid.*,
Prologue.4).

[79] 'si s'ensieut par ces vers: Conditio, sexus, etas, discretion, forma, / Et fortuna, fides: in
testibus ista requires; / Consanguinea partier domestica turba / Et clerus laicos ad se
fugiat, et vice vera' (*ibid.*, L.12, see also LI.6).

[80] 'et il est escrit en l'Evangile: *in ore duorum, vel trium, stet omne verbum*' (*ibid.*, L.19).

insertions.[81] As we have seen, Book I of the *Établissements* was composed of two royal ordinances and an earlier text of the *Coutumes d'Anjou et du Maine* (known as the *Coutumes de Touraine et d'Anjou* in the *Établissements*). These earlier texts were devoid of references to Roman and canon law. The compiler of the *Établissements* took these earlier texts and inserted the citations. The earlier *Coutumes d'Anjou et du Maine*, for instance, is used almost entirely. A few words are changed here and there, but essentially almost nothing is excised from the earlier text.[82]

The change came in the form of additions to the earlier text. The example chosen by Viollet to illustrate this is telling – the earlier provision in *Anjou et Maine* (I add italics here to track the changed portions):

the judge should assign a court date to both parties and take the property under his control until one or the other has gained seisin by judgment. *And if the one who will win seisin by judgment* comes to the lord and tells him …[83]

turns into the following in the *Établissements*:

the judge should assign a court date to both parties and take the property under his control until one or the other has gained seisin by judgment. *And it is written in the Code, Et est escrit ou Code, De ordine cognitionum, l. Si autem negotium, circa medium legis. The latter* comes to the lord and tells him …[84]

The citation to Justinian's Code, complete with directions to locate the actual text, is neatly inserted into a text previously barren of

---

[81] *Établissements*, ed. Viollet, I.80. See also *Coutumes d'Anjou et du Maine*, ed. Beautemps-Beaupré, 21.

[82] On the very few occasions that the text of *Anjou et Maine* is changed, these changes seem to be directly related to political implications. For instance, *Anjou et Maine* claims that 'the king cannot impose customs [*ne puet mestre coutumes*] on the baron's land without his assent' (*Coutumes d'Anjou et du Maine*, ed. Beautemps-Beaupré, §19), while the *Établissements* changes this language to 'the king cannot issue proclamations [*ne puet metre ban*] in the baron's land without his assent' (*Établissements*, ed. Viollet, I.27).

[83] 'La justice doit mestre jor es II parties et tenir la chose en sa main, jusqu'à tant que le quel que soit ait gueaigniée la sesine par droit. *Et si cil qui avra gaingné la sesine par droit* vient au seignor et il li die … ' (*Coutumes d'Anjou et du Maine*, ed. Beautemps-Beaupré, 74; equivalent to *Établissements*, ed. Viollet, I.10).

[84] 'La joustise doit metre jor as II parties et tenir la chose en sa main, jusques à tant que li quiex que soit ait gueaigniée la sesine par droit. *Et est escrit ou Code, De ordine cognitionum, l. Si autem negotium, circa medium legis. Li darreniers* vient au seignor et li die … ' (*Établissements*, ed. Viollet, I.10; I.69).

learned law. The compiler similarly inserted citations to canon law, or more specifically to the *Decretals* of Gregory IX. Viollet also suspected that Book II of the *Établissements*, or *Li Usages d'Orlenois*, was the product of a similar process, but he never found the original reference-less text to prove it.[85]

The process of inserting learned-law references into texts that previously contained none had an important earlier analogue. Roman law was not originally part of Gratian's *Decretum* either.[86] As Anders Winroth shows, there were two recensions of Gratian's text, the earlier one being considerably shorter and with rather poor knowledge of Roman law, as might be expected in the early days of Roman law teaching.[87] Excerpts from the Justinianic corpus were added, by another author, after the original compilation was completed.[88] Winroth describes how these additions were often awkwardly inserted into the text, disrupting the flow of the narrative or argument with barely relevant canons.[89] This observation echoes Gaudemet's that references to Roman and canon law occasionally truncate descriptions or phrases in the *Établissements*.[90]

Both the *Établissements* and the extant texts of the *Decretum* were products of a similar process, whereby different authors over time changed an earlier text, concerned as they were to add references to learned laws. They are part of the same early history of the introduction of Roman law into earlier texts by later authors.

The *Établissements* compiler, however, also added other citations. The insertion, or 'penetration' *qua* influence, of Roman and canon law must be placed in context of all of the insertions made by the compiler. The historiographical focus on 'learned' law has tended to ignore other types of citation that were also added to the earlier texts used to write the *Établissements*. In fact, the compiler also added numerous citations to custom and the practice of the lay courts. While the earlier text of *Anjou and Maine* that he used already contained some references to

[85] *Établissements*, ed. Viollet, I.7. He actually reconstructs this so-called 'primitive' text; it is one of the documents included in his critical edition.
[86] See Anders Winroth, *The Making of Gratian's Decretum*; Winroth, 'The Two Recensions of Gratian's Decretum', 24.
[87] Winroth, *The Making of Gratian's Decretum*, pp. 3–4, 147, 157ff.
[88] *Ibid*., chap. 5, conclusion.
[89] *Ibid*. Winroth, 'The Two Recensions of Gratian's Decretum', 30.
[90] Gaudemet, 'L'influence des droits savants', p. 175.

custom, the compiler of the *Établissements* felt the need to insert more. A very clear example of the various types of citations added by the compiler is provided by a rule that explains what happens when a bastard sells his inheritance. The following rule in *Anjou et Maine* that states that

> if he died without heir and without kinsmen, it would devolve first to the estate from which it was held, and not to the bastard. For a bastard cannot ask for anything by reason of kinship.[91]

became, in the *Établissements*,

> if he died without heir and without kinsmen, it would devolve *to the holder of justice* before it would to the bastard, or to the estate from which it was held; for a bastard cannot ask for anything by reason of kinship, *or for any other reason, because of his inferior condition. And written law is in agreement in the Code, On establishing the heir and what persons may be heirs, in the second law, and in the law Si pater, ect., and in the Digest, On the status of men, in the law Vulgo concepti, etc., and according to the Usage d'Orlenois, in the title On bastards. And the custom of the region agrees.*[92]

On this occasion, the compiler's additions were not restricted to the learned law alone. He also cited a written text of customary law, the *Usages d'Orlenois* (the basis of Book II of the *Établissements*), and added that this accorded with unwritten practice, namely, custom of the region.[93] The compiler's interest in citation, then, was not confined

---

[91] 'Et si il mouraient sanz hair et sanz lingnage, si escherroient avant à la seignorie de qui il tendroint que il ne feroint au bastart. Quar le bastart ne puest riens demander part lingnage' (*Coutumes d'Anjou et du Maine*, ed. Beautemps-Beaupré, 107).

[92] 'Et se il moroient sanz oir et sans lignage, si escherroit il avant à la joutise que au bastart, ou à la seignorie de cui il tendroit; quar bastarz ne puet riens demander ne par lignage, ne par autre raison, par sa mauvaise condicion. Et drois s'i accorde ou Code, De establir oir et quiex persone puet estre oirs, en la seconde loi, et en la loi Si pater, ect., et en la Digeste, De l'estat des homes, en la loi Vulgo concepti, etc., et selonc l'Usage d'Orlenois, ou titre Des bastarz. Et coutume dou païs s'i accorde' (*Établissements*, ed. Viollet, I.102; italic emphasis added]. It should be noted that the property devolves to different people in these two texts – *Anjou et Maine* have this inheritance rejoining the original estate, while the *Établissements* see the land as devolving to the holder of justice.

[93] The rule on bastard inheritance is presented here as fact about customary law. However, Sara McDougall has shown for royal succession that these rules were of a recent vintage. Ideas about legitimate birth framed by Christian marriage law did not begin to coalesce until the late twelfth century, and change itself followed very slowly (McDougall, *Royal Bastards: The Birth of Illegitimacy*, p. 6). This may hint at

to learned law, but also included the custom of the region as well as references to other parts of the *coutumier* itself. The compiler of the *Établissements* did not simply have a preoccupation with the citation of learned law but with citation in general.

This suggests that Roman law could benefit from the extra support provided by custom and customary law, as well as the opposite. The layering of citation upon citation was a hallmark of this compiler's work. Sometimes a section from the *Établissements* was cited in conjunction with the Roman law, such as citations that referred to a chapter of the *Établissements* as well as the *Code* 'and its concordances'.[94] On other occasions custom and the *Decretals* were cited together, and, on others still, Roman law and canon law were cited together.[95] Adding citations to customary law was as important to the compiler as adding references to learned law. Custom certainly was bolstered with citation of Roman and canon law. However, the converse was also true, and Roman and canon law were bolstered with citation of custom and practice.

Strong Misreading and the Birth of the Lay Jurist

Were the *coutumier* authors citing authorities in such a way that the weight of the reference's influence exerted a powerful sway over the content of the text? Or were they citing sources, the ones they used to assemble and develop their own ideas? If the references were made to authorities, then presumably these references would pander to the authorities, and in turn the authorities would condition the textual content of the *coutumiers*. However, not only did the *coutumier*

why the compiler felt the need to marshal so many authorities in support of the rule in the *Établissements*.

[94] 'And if they warrant that the judgment was as he said it was, he should be reimbursed the costs and expenses he spent on the suit, as we said above, in the chapter on Novel Disseisin and according to written law in the Code, *De fructibus et litis expensis, l. Non ignoret* and its concordances' ['*si come nos avons dit desus, ou titre De novele dessaisine, et selonc droit escrit ou Code [...] o ses concordances*'] (*ibid.*, I.96).

[95] When explaining the rules that the property of convicted heretics goes to the baron, the text cites both the Decretals and custom: 'and it is written in the Decretals, at the title "On the meaning of words" in the chapter *Super quibusdam*. And custom is in agreement' ('Et est escrit en Decretales, ou titre *Des significacions de paroles*, ou chapitre *Super quibusdam*. Et costume s'i acorde,' *ibid.*, Book I.90); 'according to written law in the Code, *De foro competent, l. Juris ordinem* and in the Decretals *De dolo et contumacia, capitulo Causam quae* where the matter is discussed' (*ibid.*, I.28).

authors provide 'misinterpreted' citations in the *coutumiers*, but they also noted disagreement between Roman law and custom. In other words, to recall Harold Bloom, the *coutumier* authors were appropriating in order to create and not idolizing something perceived as greater or more authoritative.

Pierre de Fontaines' *Conseil*, one of the earliest *coutumiers*, used more Roman law quotations than did the other *coutumier* authors. His attitude to Roman law provides a good starting point. Pierre indicated on a number of occasions that some rules of practice and Roman law were in harmony: he would describe a usage and note that it conformed to written law, or he quoted from Roman law and then remarked that the rule conformed to usage.[96] These are the two main types of references that Pierre makes. Indeed, according to him, these were the two sources of sound legal advice, and 'advice which does not follow either written law or approved custom is very dangerous'.[97]

Both 'written law' – the term of art for Roman law – and custom were good sources of legal advice.[98] The best possible scenario was when they agreed with one another and, as Pierre has noted, 'We must greatly cherish and firmly uphold the usage which agrees to the written laws, for there is no surer way to judge'.[99] Clearly, for Pierre, current custom that conformed to Roman law was the strongest type of custom.

It appears, however, that his audience did not necessarily agree and had to be convinced. In this dialogical text, Pierre responded to criticisms of his pupil-interlocutor when he explained: 'If you knew what the written laws say on many points which do not disagree with

---

[96] 'Bien s'acorde nostre usage à la loi escrite, qui dit einsi … ' (Pierre de Fontaines, *Conseil*, ed. Marnier, XII.1); 'Et certes nostre usage ne se descorde pas de la loi, qui einsi dist … ' (*ibid.*, XIV.13); 'Bien s'acorde nostres usages à molt d'aides que les lois escrites font as souz-aagiez' (*ibid.*, XIV.8); 'et à ce s'acorde bien une lois … ' (*ibid.*, XIV.9).

[97] 'Car li avis est molt périlleus, qui ne suit ou loi escrite ou coustume aprovée' (*ibid.*, I.3).

[98] The *coutumiers* generally refer to Roman and canon law as 'written law.' The term 'common law' (*droit commun* and variations) was used in other ways in the *coutumiers* (see Chapter 8). This suggests a difference from learned contexts, where – along with *utrumque ius* (one and the other law, both laws) – *ius commune* designated the rules and procedures of Roman-canon law (see for instance, Karl Shoemaker, '"I Have Asked for Nothing except the *Ius Commune*"', pp. 67, 73).

[99] 'Molt doit-en amer l'usage et fermement tenir, qui s'acorde à lois escrites: car plus seurement ne puet nus juger' (*ibid.*, XV.24).

our usage, you would not ask me so often the questions that you do.'[100] Vexed and irritated, Pierre justified his use of Roman law and defended it by saying it conformed to custom and was therefore not irrelevant to his discussion of rules and procedures of lay courts.[101]

Though he had a deep appreciation for late-antique law, Pierre approached it more as a useful pool of knowledge from which to provide additional support for existing custom and to draw ideas for undeveloped areas of law, but he did have a critical approach towards it. He noted occasions on which custom and Roman law diverged and even disagreed.[102] On some occasions he pointed out that written law has some good ideas but did not argue that these good ideas should influence practice. The written law, for instance, placed limits on the length of a trial, which Pierre thought was a very useful thing [*molt profitable chose*], but he then pointed out that, 'nonetheless, our usage does not fix any limits'.[103] On another occasion, he used a series of block quotes from Roman law to discuss the location of trials. In the middle of this long excerpt from Roman law, Pierre interrupted the narrative to explain that a specific point 'is not upheld by our usage'.[104] On other occasions, Pierre came out strongly against a Roman law rule: 'Furthermore, other written laws say that the heir to a pledge must be held to uphold the pledge, however our usage does not consent to this at all.'[105] In other words, the Roman law, though it may contain great ideas, was not authoritative in and of itself. Pierre included citations to the Roman law in his text and discussed where it converged with custom, but when it came to choosing the authority of usage or of Roman law, Pierre dismissed Roman law that did not conform to usage.

---

[100] 'Se tu seusses ce que les lois escrites dient en molt de cas qui ne se descordent pas de nostre usage, tu ne me feisses mie si sovent tels demandes come tu me fes' (*ibid.*, XIV.15).

[101] 'Et por ce voil-je que tu saches que une lois dit qui bien termine ta demande ... ' (*ibid.*, XV.24).

[102] 'car nostre usages met [...] que ne font les lois, qui le metent ... ' (*ibid.*, XV.35).

[103] 'Encore metent les lois escrites terme en finer totes manières de plez, qui est molt profitable chose, si come [... gives examples ...]; nequedent nostre usages n'i met point de terme, mès il i met ordre et qui tex est' (*ibid.*, XXI.7).

[104] 'Ce ne tient pas nostre usages, fors de la meismes cause dont plez est' (*ibid.*, XXIX.5).

[105] 'Encore dient aucune lois escrites, que li oïr au plége soient tenu à plégerie, nequedant nostre usage ne s'i assent mie ... ' (*ibid.*, IX.5).

The *Coutumier d'Artois*, which used Pierre's *Conseil* as one of its sources, followed suit. In discussing agreements made in arbitration, the author of this *coutumier* quoted a paragraph from the *Code* about the role of women in this process, specifically to disagree with it.[106] In the passage the emperor Justinian explains that agreements made by women could be broken at will, even if the woman in question was an employer, and even if she was hearing a dispute between people to whom she had granted freedom.[107] When the author of the *Coutumier d'Artois* closed the quote, he explained:

However, by our usage, women have enough significant [*grigneur*] power to take agreements upon themselves, since they have a voice in judgment along-side the other men of the prince and other nobles, when they are present, and they have landed inheritances for which they give faith and homage to their lord, or when they are [legal] guardians of their children.[108]

The author of the *Coutumier d'Artois* quoted the Roman text to acquaint the reader with the Roman rule and to establish its irrelevance to contemporary legal culture.[109] However, the fact that he bothered to make this point indicates that it was one that required a rebuttal and that there were people at the secular courts making such arguments based on the Roman rule.

Peter Stein notes how medieval learned jurists, such as Bulgarus or Johannes Bassianus, wrestled with what happened if custom contradicted Roman law and tried to solve this problem.[110] The

---

[106] *Coutumier d'Artois*, ed. Tardif, LIV.73–74. The text does not cite a reference, but because it is a quotation from an emperor, it must come from the *Code*.

[107] *Ibid.*, LIV.73. Justinian notes that women should keep in mind their chastity, and the works that nature has granted them and those from which they should keep themselves separate, one of which is making contracts (*ibid.*).

[108] *Ibid.*, LIV.74.

[109] The place, agency, and nature of women could have significant differences in customary law and Roman law. For instance, Nicolas Laurent-Bonne, in his study of gifts between spouses, has shown that Roman jurists treated husbands as potential victims of greedy wives using feminine wiles against them, while French customary law treated wives as the ones needing protection from pressure or demands of their husbands (Laurent-Bonne, *Aux origines de la liberté de disposer entre époux*, pp. 14ff, 47ff).

[110] Stein, *Roman Law in European History*, p. 62. As Stein notes, Bulgarus distinguished between a general custom and a local custom – while the former always prevailed over an earlier law (customary or written), the latter only did if it was introduced knowingly as an abrogation. This distinction between general and local custom comes into customary law later, Jean Boutillier discusses it in his late fourteenth-century *Somme rural*. Martinus felt a custom could only affect an earlier

coutumier authors – even those convinced of the utility of Roman law – clearly felt it was legitimate and unproblematic to disagree with it. As the above examples show, if custom or usage and learned law contradicted each other in the secular courts, then custom prevailed, unproblematically.

It was precisely the devotion of laymen to custom and usage that bothered Jacques de Revigny, professor of law at the university in Orleans. He frequently mentioned these people, calling them either rustics (*rustici*) or laymen (*laici*) interchangeably 'because they do not know (Roman) law nor do they have access to experts. Thus I would call a cleric or priest not learned in law a rustic'.[111] For Revigny only an education in the learned law could provide actual learning – no amount of legal practice or knowledge of the functioning of the courts could do the same. Kees Bezemer identifies as a commonality between Revigny's 'rustics' and 'laymen' their common set of legal standards: they keep arguing that they have done things a specific way since time immemorial.[112] Revigny is clearly responding to a group of people who felt they made strong authoritative arguments based on practice, untroubled by the fact that they did not assign normative value in the same way as Revigny.

While Revigny showed some contempt for lay jurists, his world was tied to theirs. It was clearly important to Revigny to know their arguments and to respond to them. The practice of the *coutumier* authors of mentioning some Roman law rules only to disagree with them finds a parallel practice in Revigny's work. Revigny also occasionally cited custom only to disagree with it because the Roman rule was different. For instance, after explaining the French custom that a daughter who lived with her husband was now under his authority, and not her father's, Revigny noted that 'This is false ... though rustics believe it'.[113] Revigny also rejected the customary time limit of one year and one day for prescription – 'That opinion has lay justice in its favor, yet neither a (Roman) law nor reason'.[114]

---

custom. Johannes Bassianus felt that so long as custom was based on reason (Roman criterion), it is valid, no matter whether it was knowingly introduced as an abrogation (*ibid.*).
[111] Jacques de Revigny cited in Kees Bezemer, *What Jacques Saw*, p. 13.
[112] *Ibid.*   [113] *Ibid.*   [114] *Ibid.*, 14.

Revigny clearly had some knowledge of the customary law of the lay courts. Revigny, like Pierre before him, seemed bothered by lay disinterest in the sophistication and reason of Roman law. Indeed, he noted that laymen rejected advice based on Roman law because they did not think it would work in court.[115] Lay and learned jurists clearly had contact with each other, and their differing values were in a conversation that does not necessarily seem to have been imbalanced. Lay jurists did not lack confidence about their standing in this conversation, just as *coutumier* authors were not responding to Roman law or its learned practitioners from a position of inferiority. Those like Revigny who knew Roman law wanted to make Roman law relevant to practice.

Manuscripts of the *coutumiers* testify to some individual strategies used to bring Roman law thought to the *coutumiers* or to amplify its importance in those texts. In one manuscript of the Latin version of the Norman *Summa de legibus*, we find the note of a later reader adding the Roman law definition of justice in the margin, as depicted in Figure 5.1.

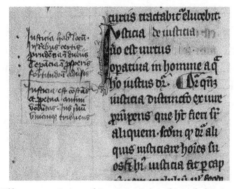

FIGURE 5.1 Different notions of justice. A reader of this manuscript of the Latin text of the *Summa de legibus normanniae*, copied in the early fourteenth century, added the Roman law definition of justice to complement the one presented by the *coutumier*. This reader did not cross out the original definition but was unwilling to let it stand without noting the Roman law definition for himself or future readers of the manuscript. *Coutume de Normandie*, Bibliothèque nationale de France, ms. lat.12883, fol. 14v.

---

[115] *Ibid.* See Bezemer for the story of the townsman who rejects advice based on the *action Publicana* because it would be redundant in court, and other like examples.

The Norman *coutumier* defined justice as 'the virtue operative in man by which man is said to be just'.[116] It was important to someone later to add, offset in the margin, the classic Roman law definition of justice that became so widespread in the medieval period, 'Justice is the constant and perpetual wish to give each his due'.[117] Whether this was a contrast for the sake of comparison or an emendation, what is important is this impulse to add.

For Revigny's rustics as for *coutumier* authors, custom trumped Roman law, and practice trumped the written source. Beyond that, these authors were not simply adding citations to create a concordance, one that would guide the reader to the supra-authority of the learned law. The lay jurists who wrote the *coutumiers* apparently did not feel that they had an obligation to stay true to the rules of the Roman law.

The particular use of citations reinforces this observation. If the purpose of the citation was to create a real dialogue between the *coutumiers* and learned-law texts, then one would expect the *coutumiers* to provide the sort of references that would help the reader find the text cited. However, only Pierre's *Conseil*, the *Établissements*, and the *Coutumier d'Artois* overtly and regularly used Roman law, and even then without homogeneity: the first provided block quotes with no guide to the original text, the second provided citations, and the last did both.

Where Pierre drew on the content of Roman law, the compiler of the *Établissements* found it enough to provide citations without quoting or paraphrasing Roman law texts. The bulk of references to Roman law in Pierre's *Conseil* cited the 'law' or 'written law', followed by or concluding a large block quotation from Roman law provided in the vernacular.[118] It provided little information as to where in the 'written law' the quote could be found. Pierre might note the relevant jurist or issuing emperor, so one could surmise whether the *Digest* (jurist) or *Code* (emperor) was involved, but even so this was not very helpful as a guide to the source text. Pierre, then, conditioned the reader's

---

[116] *Justicia vero est virtus juris operativa in homine a qua homo justus dicitur* (*Summa de legibus normanniae*, I.3). Note the similarity to Isidore of Seville, who said, 'it is called Justice/Law (*ius*) because it is just (*iustus*)' (Isidore of Seville, *Etymologies*, V.3). This dating of the manuscript comes from Ernest-Joseph Tardif (*Coutumiers de Normandie*, ed. Tardif, vol. 2, p. cxcix).

[117] '*Justicia est constans et perpetua voluntas jus suum cuique tribuendi*' (*Digest*, I.I.10).

[118] He only cites canon law on one occasion.

knowledge of the Roman law, selectively choosing passages he decided were appropriate, but did not seem to want or expect the reader to pursue this knowledge further.

Only the compiler of the *Établissements* consistently provided a real and usable roadmap to the original text. He linked the body of the text to sections of the *Code, Digest*, and *Decretals* of Gregory IX. No quote or paraphrase was provided, just the citation as link, and the reader would have to look up the citation to know its specific substance. These citations were sometimes in the vernacular, sometimes in Latin, and sometimes both.

The *Coutumier d'Artois*, which copied text from both Pierre and the *Établissements*, used both of their citation methods. Sometimes, it gave full scholastic references.[119] On other occasions, it cited without this roadmap to the original text, simply referring to the 'law', 'written law', or 'the decretals'; sometimes it agreed with a previous discussion; occasionally it paraphrased a principle.[120] A few times, the author used short quotes from one or the other learned law – most often in the vernacular but a couple of times in Latin.[121] The author did not make an effort to homogenize the citations – to express them all in the scholastic style that would permit them to be a reference tool – or to look them up to turn them into quotations or paraphrases that would give the reader instant access to the text cited. The variation in the *Coutumier d'Artois* was likely the result of the author's replication of the form provided in his sources rather than an indication of authorial selection.

Ultimately, there was no consistent format for references to the learned law in this first phase of *coutumier*-writing. The inclusion of references to the learned laws was likely less an attempt to conform to learned authority, dialogue, or concordance but a selective use of source material in the service of an original text. The philosophy that underlay the uses of the Roman law in the

---

[119] For full scholastic references, see *Coutumier d'Artois*, ed. Tardif, III.6, IX.2–8.

[120] For general citations, see *ibid.*, III.18 and III.34 (general statement that the learned law agrees with a point just laid out, III.16 (paraphrase).

[121] *Ibid.*, III.33 (short quotation from Roman law in Latin) and XI.8–9 (paragraph quotations of Roman law in the vernacular). All of these varieties of citation can be found in one chapter (e.g. Chap.III) and are not a reflection of different parts of the text and different stages of writing. The *Coutumier d'Artois* is quite consistent in this polymorphous approach.

coutumiers seems to have been one of amendment and alteration. Just as Pierre de Fontaines invited future jurists to amend and improve his work, lay jurists wrote, compiled, amended, or excerpted from the *coutumiers* for their own purposes without feeling obliged to replicate or preserve the integrity of the source text. This insouciance towards the original text was not a function of their inability to understand the more complex learned law. Even those, like the compiler of the *Établissements*, who were devoted to making the learned law relevant to a customary context used it selectively to show wider support for customary rules and procedures, rather than in an effort to reproduce it or make customary law confirm to it. To these lay jurists, learned law was important insofar as it could serve custom.

The Sound of Silence

Citations provide intellectual trails. Following them reveals the learning writers chose to showcase, with which they affiliated or identified themselves, or which they felt the need to address or rebut. What sort of learning contributed to the text, and how directly or indirectly was it gained? Why choose not to cite when it was common practice, and what was the meaning of the silence?

The lack of citation by a learned author of a learned text presents a puzzle. Philippe de Beaumanoir's *Coutumes de Beauvaisis*, for example, is notorious for leaving scholars debating these questions because, for all the sophistication of his exposition, he never explicitly referred to Roman law, 'written law', late-antique jurists or emperors, and so on.[122] Beaumanoir has been accused of affecting an ignorance of the learned law.[123] Paul Ourliac doubted whether he knew any Latin and questioned whether he acquired his learned law textually or perhaps from a vernacular translation of an abridged version of one of the Justinianic texts.[124] He has also been seen as

---

[122] See Stein, *Roman Law in European History*, p. 66; Hubrecht, 'Le droit canonique dans le coutumier de Beaumanoir', pp. 580–4; Paul Vinogradoff, *Roman Law in Medieval Europe*, p. 71; Lefebvre-Teillard, 'Recherches sur la pénétration du droit canonique', 66; Ourliac, 'Beaumanoir et les Coutumes de Beauvaisis', pp. 75–9; Jacob, 'Beaumanoir versus Revigny', to name only a very few.

[123] Ourliac, 'Beaumanoir et les Coutumes de Beauvaisis', p. 75.   [124] *Ibid.*, p. 78.

a great Romanist, and the fact that both claims can be made about the same text should at the very least alert us to the ambiguities it presents.

Ourliac has noted that, for one of the top medieval French jurisconsults, Beaumanoir was more part of the world of knights than of schools.[125] That may explain why he chose to write about the secular courts, but he was also learned, truly erudite, and in some capacity a product of the schools, though it is difficult to determine at what level and to what extent. His *coutumier* does not draw on or model Roman law directly. Nonetheless, he must have had contact with learned law as it is difficult to imagine him writing this text without at least some knowledge of canon law and, notably, the procedural manuals drawn up for canon law courts (*ordines iudiciarii*). Clearly, he had a strong knowledge of the procedure of the ecclesiastical courts as well as its specialized terminology, which he explained to the reader on some occasions to distinguish it from, or borrow it for, the secular courts.

Why would such a learned man disguise his learning? Was it, as Jean-Philippe Lévy claims, a case of substantial penetration whereby Beaumanoir had so internalized the Roman law that it had become part of his soul? Was Beaumanoir trying to make a political statement by not referring to the 'written law'? Or, as Robert Jacob has argued, was he emphatically denying the learned law a position within the legal system, possibly in relation to the king's injunction against the use of Roman law in the places where custom applied?[126] If it was a political statement, was it part of a phenomenon described by Anthony Grafton, 'a *damnatio memoriae*, which the circle of interested parties will immediately recognize and decode'?[127]

The notion that Beaumanoir purposefully snubbed citation presupposes that Beaumanoir ought to have cited the learned law. Our review of the range of citation in the *coutumiers*, however, does not suggest that a *coutumier* author in the 1280s would necessarily have felt this obligation. As already mentioned, of the eight *coutumiers* in our group, only three – Pierre de Fontaines' *Conseil*, the *Établissements de Saint Louis*, and the *Coutumier d'Artois* (which copied from Pierre's *Conseil* and the *Établissements*) – referred to the

---

[125] *Ibid.*, p. 79.   [126] Jacob, 'Beaumanoir versus Révigny', p. 244.
[127] Grafton, *The Footnote*, p. 9.

learned law overtly and consistently. The *Livre de Jostice et de Plet* paraphrases without citing. The rest of the *coutumiers* refer to the learned law on a couple of occasions, if at all. If we dispense with the assumption that the *coutumiers* were inferior texts that drew on Roman law to buttress their authority, the lack of citation may not have been a snub after all. *Coutumier* authors did not have an established practice of using or citing Roman law, and Beaumanoir was participating in the lay juristic culture of his time.

Lay Jurists and Roman Law

Ideas from Roman law had infiltrated customary thinking through many pathways. Graduates from law schools were beginning to appear in secular and ecclesiastical administrations. Romano-canonical procedure had also made its way into the royal domain and the royal courts by royal decree and could be used in other jurisdictions if elected. From the beginning of the thirteenth century, Roman and canon law texts and some of their glosses were translated from Latin into the vernacular, making the ideas more accessible to the educated layman. Indeed, they could get their Roman law from vernacular translations of canon law texts – Pierre de Fontaines, for instance, may have used Vacarius' *Liber Pauperum* for his Roman law sources.[128] Personal contact with clerics and ecclesiastical courts allowed for word-of-mouth transmission and experience of learned doctrine.[129] Personal contact with those who alleged Roman law in the secular courts, whether successfully or unsuccessfully, would also acquaint those who attended with some sense of the rules.

Some were more concerned with including Roman or canon law in the *coutumiers* than others. Pierre de Fontaines' *Conseil*, the *Établissements de St Louis*, and the *Coutumier d'Artois* were composed by people concerned with finding a place for Roman law and to a lesser extent

---

[128] Petot, 'Pierre de Fontaines et le droit romain', p. 960. He follows Émile Chénon's suggestion on this.
[129] Jacob, 'Beaumanoir versus Révigny', p. 245. Jacob notes that, when Beaumanoir used vocabulary that was common to canon law, he indicated that he got it from clerics or that he is referring to 'what the clerics call' or 'what they say' (see s. 196, 228, 1191, 1908) (*ibid.*). While this could refer to textual quotations, Jacob interprets it as a reference to orality (p. 245 n. 38).

canon law within the *coutumiers*. Copyists could also have this inclination. For instance, as five (of the twenty-one manuscripts) of the *Établissements de St Louis* show, some manuscript versions of a text might exhibit a greater concern for Roman law than others.

Two manuscripts of the *Établissements* were, for instance, made by or for someone who wanted to emphasize the place of Roman law in this text, one of which can be seen in Figure 5.2.[130] Where other manuscripts offset the titles of the sections by writing them in red ink, these manuscripts also contrasted in red ink those portions of the text that referred to 'written law'. Learned law in these manuscripts was thus given the same visual status and importance

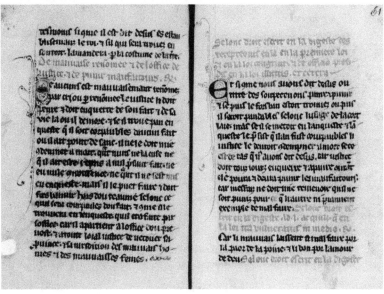

FIGURE 5.2 Red letter law. Manuscripts of the *Établissements de Saint Louis* tended to offset the titles of the sections from the text, often with red ink. This thirteenth-century manuscript of the *Établissements de Saint Louis* was copied with both the titles of the text and portions of the text that refer to 'written law', both Roman and canon law, in red. This small change in visual presentation served to emphasize the importance of Roman law and canon law within the text. *Établissements de Saint Louis*, Bibliothèque nationale de France, ms. fr. 13987, fol. 61r.

---

[130] The other is: Paris, BnF, ms. fr. 5278.

as titles that organized the text, a distinguishing mark that provided emphasis while also making the learned law easier to find.

For either the copyist or the recipient of the manuscript, it was important to emphasize the importance of the 'written law' on an equal level with the titles in the text, and for both to be easily findable. However, demarcation meant to emphasize or differentiate was not necessarily exclusive to learned law. Two other manuscripts where the text was in black ink used a pilcrow symbol (¶) to point out uses of learned law; however, one of these also used this sign to point out *usage*.[131] Another manuscript of the *Établissements*, one of the few that conjoined it to other texts – a vernacular version of Tancred's *Ordo*, a procedural manual for the ecclesiastical courts – followed the usual method of red titles and black text without using red ink for the learned laws but proceeded to identify the nature of the rules by writing 'law', 'decretal', or 'case' in the margins.[132] Thus, these manuscripts specially demarcated usage and cases as well as learned sources of law, which indicates a general interest in citation and categorization that favoured but was not exclusive to Roman or canon law.

More typically, terminology from the Romano-canonical tradition would make its way into the *coutumiers*. We saw Beaumanoir explaining terms of ecclesiastical procedure to his lay audience in Chapter 1. Beaumanoir's *Coutumes de Beauvaisis*, the *Établissements de Saint Louis*, *Demenées el Chastelet de Paris*, and the *Coutumier d'Artois* all include traces of *romanitas* in the form of vocabulary or maxims drawn from the learned law. Beaumanoir, for instance, explained some of the technical vocabulary the secular courts acquired as they professionalized. Arguments made to postpone a complaint, he explained, 'are called dilatory exceptions. To say dilatory exceptions is the same as saying arguments which serve only to delay the suit.'[133] Technical legal vocabulary drawn from Roman and canon law was clearly making its way into the secular courts, and Beaumanoir had to clarify its meaning for his readers because some may not yet be familiar

---

[131] Paris, BnF, ms. fr. 5977 and ms. fr. 18096.   [132] Paris, BnF, ms. fr. 1075.

[133] Beaumanoir, *Coutumes de Beauvaisis*, ed. Salmon, VII.236. He mentions this again in the next section: 'by many other arguments also, which you can recognize by those which are stated above, which are only to delay suits; and they are all called dilatory exceptions' (*ibid.*, VII.237).

with it. He did not suggest that this was a foreign import from Roman into customary law, but a process of diffusion that accompanied professionalization.

A similar reverse process occurred with some maxims drawn from Roman law: they had converted into custom. Take the Roman maxim that 'agreement beats law'. This maxim appears in three of our *coutumiers*, but none cites Roman law.[134] Instead, they understand the maxim as a common contemporary proverb. Pierre de Fontaines said that we know 'according to our usage that agreement beats law'.[135] Philippe de Beaumanoir introduced it with the traditional marker of a proverb 'for this reason we say: "agreement beats law"'.[136] The *Coutumier d'Artois*, furthermore, refers to this maxim as 'a common expression that we say'.[137] This maxim had gone through a process of transmission and adaptation whereby it had lost its *romanitas* and become a common proverb.

Some maxims were adopted but their meaning reinterpreted or adapted for their new context. This was the case with the famous Roman maxim that 'what pleases the prince has the force of law', which appeared both in the *Digest* and in the *Institutes*.[138] Beaumanoir used this well-known Roman law rule for purposes that sixth-century jurists would have found peculiar: he explained that the king could postpone the debts of those joining his army, going on crusade, or going on special business for him, because 'what he pleases to do must be held as law'.[139] Peter Stein takes this example as proof that Beaumanoir was well trained in Roman law and could apply it to un-Roman institutions to lend them greater authority.[140] Albert Rigaudière, in contrast, points out that while the maxim in this

---

[134] '*conventio vincit legem*' (Justinian, *Digest* 16.3.1.6).
[135] 'selonc nostre usage, que covenance loi veint' (Pierre de Fontaines, *Conseil*, ed. Marnier, XV.6).
[136] Though Beaumanoir notes an exception – the rule does not apply if the agreement is made for bad purposes: 'pour ce dit on: "Convenance vaint loi", exceptees les convenances sont fetes pour mauvaises causes' (Beaumanoir, *Coutumes de Beauvaisis*, ed. Salmon, XXXIV.999).
[137] 'Et se te fais je entendant une coumune parole que on dist: convenence loy vaint' (*Coutumier d'Artois*, ed. Tardif, VII.5).
[138] '*Quod principi placuit legis habet vigorem*' (*Digest* 1.4.1; *Institutes* 1.2.6).
[139] 'car ce qu'il li plest a fere doit estre tenu pour loi' (Beaumanoir, *Coutumes de Beauvaisis*, ed. Salmon, XXXV.1103).
[140] Stein, *Roman Law in European History*, p. 66.

context did not recognize its full original ambit, the interpretation was actually the one current among lay jurists of Beaumanoir's time.[141] Lay jurists were developing their own understanding and common community consensus of such maxims.

Roman law belonged to a larger pool of legal knowledge that lay jurists could draw from to understand or validate the present. Theirs was not a systematic approach, because systematization was not their goal. This was an understanding that differed from university *doctores*, who valued the Roman law as a coherent whole. Law professors in the universities, such as Jacques de Revigny, wanted to stay true to the Roman law, understand it as a system, and reason within that system. The *coutumier* authors' work was centred on custom and practice, and they pulled small, highly selective fragments to reinforce or complement their understanding of it.

A History of Roman Law in Customary Law

In essence, lay jurists and university law jurists had different epistemological views of Roman law. The lay jurists' understanding of the epistemology of Roman law may have drawn on a longer tradition of citing the Roman law as a source before its 'rediscovery'. Roman law had not disappeared between the fall of the empire and the twelfth century. While the Justinianic texts had never made it to the former Roman West and were barely known between the seventh and eleventh centuries, the *Novels* known through the *Epitome Juliani* were the one Justinianic book with significant circulation in this period.[142] Some other texts of Roman law were similarly copied, preserved, and used, both in the North and the South of France. The

---

[141] '*Princeps legibus solutes est* (*Digest* 1.3.31) et *Quod principi placuit legis habet vigorem* (*Digest* 1.4.1 et *Institiutes* 1.2.6) à travers trois coutumiers du XIIIe siècle', in Rigaudière, *Penser et construire l'État*, p. 46. Albert Rigaudière tentatively argues, pending work on a greater number of sources (he looks at three *coutumiers* – Pierre de Fontaines' *Conseil*, the *Livre de jostice et de plet*, and Beaumanoir's *Coutumes de Beauvaisis*), that this manner of using this maxim was common in thirteenth-century France, when the expression was used in a very formal and restrained way, which in fact reflected the nature of royal power at the time (*ibid.*, 66).

[142] Radding, 'Reviving Justinian's *Corpus*', p. 36. He also argues that rather than a rediscovery in Bologna, the *Code* was restored to its full length in various centres in Italy as early as the late eleventh century. Pavia, the stronghold of Lombard legal thinking, was an important part of this story.

most important of these were the *Theodosian Code* and the *Breviary of Alaric* (*Lex romana wisigothorum*), which were also known by way of the intermediary of various epitomes and abridged versions, and Book V of Isidore of Seville's *Etymologies* (which circulated independently), as well as various forgeries that made use of Roman law.[143] Roman law was also packaged into collections of quotations of learned wisdom with excerpts, *florilegia* (casebooks), and compilations of references.[144]

Roman law, then, was not only known but also a type of living law, albeit not in the systematic manner that would later develop in the universities. The 'venerable Roman laws promulgated by the princes through divine inspiration' were mentioned in a late ninth-century letter from Pope John VIII to Emperor Louis II, as Gérard Giordanengo notes.[145] Likewise Christof Rolker argues that the lack of sources from before 1050 does not indicate stasis, when the foundation was laid for the rapid developments in the later eleventh century and onward.[146] The most sophisticated writers of the day, such as Burchard of Worms and Ivo of Chartres, did not approach Roman law as a coherent system but as a collection of separable parts. They drew upon Roman legal principles and maxims as well as a variety of other sources, such as patristic works, to construct arguments about rights and responsibilities.[147] Indeed, the various collections of Ivo's letters show that his correspondence was read for its legal content and arranged into casebooks.[148]

Ivo of Chartres' canonical collection, dated before 1095, is a telling example. This collection is composed of 3,760 canons. Of these, 424 chapters are excerpts from secular law, 214 are excerpts from Roman law, and 210 are taken from the capitularies of the kings of France.[149]

---

[143] Gaudemet, 'Le droit romain', 367. See Gaudemet's list of Roman law sources available before the 'rediscovery', 366ff.

[144] Gaudemet, 'Le droit romain', 367.

[145] Giordanengo, 'Le droit romain au temps de la Reforme', 872–3.

[146] See Rolker, *Canon Law and the Letters of Ivo of Chartres*, chap. 2.

[147] Giordanengo notes a number of uses of Roman law: legal principles and formulas such as '*spoliatus ante omnia restituendus*' (Code 5.16.10) were drawn upon, and legal maxims were used in letter writing between luminaries. Importantly, Giordanengo also notes that other sources, such as patristic writings, were are also used in this same manner, as legal maxims (Giordanengo, 'Le droit romain', 876).

[148] Brasington, 'Collections of Bishops' Letters as Legal Florilegia', p. 78.

[149] Giordanengo, 'Le droit romain au temps de la Reforme', 878.

He relied rather heavily on lay law – more so, in fact, than on Roman law. The Roman law used here was mostly drawn from the *Epitome Juliani* and from the Theodosian texts (*Theodosian Code, Sirmondian Constitutions, Breviary of Alaric*) though Justinianic texts were also included, and the royal capitularies were not actually drawn from collections of royal capitularies but from the *Decretum* of Burchard of Worms.[150] Ivo, then, applied citation practices that continued to be used later on. He constructed his canonical collection with a motley group of sources that were authoritative because they contained normative wisdom that could be extracted and adapted.[151]

This use of legal sources explains the popularity of books of quotations and compilations of references, such as the one composed earlier in 868 by Hincmar of Rheims. This pre-'rediscovery' scholarly view of Roman law, as a pool of useful quotations and a repository of rules and ideas that could be excised and reapplied, changed when the Justinianic texts began to be studied as a *corpus*. The scholarly view of the use of Roman law post-'rediscovery', expounded from the universities, came to focus on the coherence of the Roman texts.

The *coutumier* authors who thought it was important to cite Roman law used it following the pre-'rediscovery' tradition. They saw Roman law as a body of knowledge that could be used in the service of the present; their goal was not to reproduce the original meaning or context faithfully. The earlier popularity of books of quotations and abridgements of Roman law also shows that this material was not viewed as a system of laws to be followed but as a type of knowledge to be passed on.

Pierre de Fontaines, for instance, referred to Emperor Antoninius in a domesticated vernacular French form when he explained that 'the emperor Antoine said the following to one woman ... ' that she was disgraced if she was convicted of theft if she knowingly had stolen

---

[150] See Giordanengo, 'Le droit romain au temps de la Reforme'. Giordanengo calls the Theodosian Code, the *leges barbarorum* and the various epitomes that were composed pre-rediscovery the 'old Roman law,' distinguishing it from the 'new Roman law', which was the full set of Justinianic texts that came to be studied in the twelfth century and eventually replaced the old Roman law.

[151] See Giordanengo, 'Le droit romain au temps de la Reforme', 879–80 for more on Ivo's approach to sources, his bias against custom, and for reason and law.

goods.[152] Or he quoted Emperors Gratian and Valerian for the principle that one could not judge in one's own suit, or that 'we must keep our agreements, because written law says: "there is nothing more proper to human faith than to keep that which you agreed to do"'.[153] When he used quotations of the emperors drawn from the *Code*, he approached the emperors as wise scholars or generally wise men from the past who belonged to the same culture and tradition as that of the words they transmitted.

In southern France, of course, Roman law had continued to be living law more directly, not through Justinian's corpus but the *Theodosian Code*, the *leges barbarorum* (especially the *leges wisigothorum*) and various epitomes. This Roman law, however, did not survive in appreciably better shape in the South – the future *pays de droit écrit* – than it did in the North.[154] Paul Ourliac observes that this Roman law was more an idea in communal memory than it was a body of rules, and it was only around the 1250s that Roman law in the form of specific rules (dowry, prescription, etc.) began to be inserted into the custom of the region.[155] Pierre Tisset noted long ago that this new diffusion of Roman law in the South was part of the political aftermath of the Albigensian crusade, whereby the patriciate attached itself to the myth that they had followed Roman law since antiquity to counter rapidly increasing French influence in the area.[156] It is likely, also, that the importance of Roman law for the customs of Toulouse (1296) has also been exaggerated.[157]

Even around the end of the thirteenth and beginning of the fourteenth century, Roman law as it was used in the South was still often in the older customary form and indeed referred to as a form of custom – this is why, in a case in the *Olims* from 1312, the Parlement of

---

[152] 'Li empereres Antoines dist à une feme einsi en une loi … ' (Pierre de Fontaines, *Conseil*, ed. Marnier, XIII.17); 'En une loi dient li empereor Gratiens et Valeriens ansi … ' (*ibid.*, XXIII.3).

[153] 'Bien doit-on garder ce qu'en convenance, car la lois escrite dist qu'il n'est nule riens tant soit covenable a humaine fois, for de garder ce où en convenance' (*ibid.*, XV.1).

[154] Gaudemet, 'Le droit romain', 368.

[155] Ourliac, 'Législation, coutumes et coutumiers', pp. 484–5. Gaudemet sees the insertion of Roman law into the customs of the South beginning even later, in the early fourteenth century (Gaudemet, 'L'influence des droit savants', p. 183).

[156] Pierre Tisset, 'Mythes et réalités du droit écrit'.

[157] Gaudemet, 'L'influence des droit savants', p. 184.

Paris supported the succession claims of a younger daughter against
her older sister, because her father had the right to make her heir,
'following the customs of the land of Rodez which are ruled according
to Roman law'.[158] In fact, Albert Rigaudière has shown that much
fourteenth-century litigation that travelled from the South to the
Parlement in Paris concerned the uncertain question of whether
specific regions were part of the *pays de coutumes* or the *pays de
droit écrit*.[159] If there was such uncertainty, the answer cannot have
been obvious from the substantive content of these *coutumes* and *droit
écrit*. The South developed a new Roman-law identity, one that
eventually became a counterpoint to the custom of the North, but
when and how exactly that happened merits further study.

Developing a Lay Juristic Scholarly Practice

This creative mining of sources was not the *coutumiers*' only approach
to the learned laws, but it does characterize their approach to citation
generally. When one looks at the array of sources in the *coutumiers* and
the authors' idiosyncratic uses of them, it is clear that *coutumier*
authors did not follow their predecessors blindly, be they learned law
or customary texts, even when they copied from them. While these
texts had a common goal – writing the customs and usages of the
secular courts – the manner in which they executed it remained
unique, and no two *coutumiers* follow the exact same form.

　　An example from the *Établissements de Saint Louis* shows us that
the compiler was cobbling together various sources under specific
headings, as seemed fitting. In Book II.4, a section that explained
how to request seisin as the nearest relative or as heir, the compiler
used eight different citations:[160]

And that his reservation is valid is <u>written in the title "On appealing against
a man for murder and treachery</u>." The law says that the heir should be in
possession; and it is <u>written in the Code, De edicto divi Adriani tollendo,</u>

---

[158] *'facere potuerat, secundum consuetudinem terre Ruthenensis que regitur jure
scripto'* (see Rigaudière, 'La royauté', 892).
[159] Rigaudière, 'La royauté', 885–908.
[160] I used italics earlier to designate the compiler's additions to the earlier *Coutumes
d'Anjou et du Maine* in the *Établissements de Saint* Louis, so here I use underlining to
showcase the different citations used by the compiler.

l. Quamvis quis se filium defunct, etc. And the <u>practice of the Orléans</u> district is <u>that</u> the dead man gives seisin to the living [...] And the lord before whom he is requesting the aforesaid things must give him a ruling, in his court, in a judgment, by his liege men, by those who owe him faith, by knights, for the things that are done in the presence of noble persons and the court of the prince are enforceable, according to <u>written law in the Code,</u> "<u>On wills and how a will is executed,</u>" in *lege omnium testamentorum solepnitatem,* at the beginning, etc. [...] and if there is no agreement on the judgment] the lord can give his own judgment, after taking honest counsel, according to <u>written law in the Digest, De re judicata,</u> l. *Inter pares* [...] And if the lord did not do this and was in default, and the default was proved against him, the case would go to the sovereign, and the lord would lose what jurisdiction he had, according to the <u>custom of the area and the district;</u> which is to say the obedience <u>according to king's statutes as contained in the chapter "On appealing against your lord for default of judgment"</u> according to the practice of the Orléans district, in the secular courts.[161]

This selection shows the extent of *collage,* or *bricolage,* that could be marshalled in the composition of a *coutumier.* The compiler patched together a plethora of citations that created a narrative of authority for one rule. Each of these sources was plucked from a different text – the *Établissements* II:21, the *Code* 6.33.2, the practice of the Orléans district, the *Code* 6.23.19, the *Digest* 42.1.38, the custom of the area or district, the king's *établissements* (the royal ordinance that constitutes *Établissements* I.8), and the practice of the Orleans district in secular court. Taking them out of their previous context, the compiler created a new narrative based on a collage of sources.

This small portion of text is characteristic of *coutumier* composition more broadly. The *Coutumier d'Artois,* composed between 1283 and 1302, and possibly chronologically last in our group, seems almost to be a symphony of eclectic sources, used idiosyncratically, and citation.

---

[161] 'Et que retenue li vaille il est escrit ou titre D'apeler home de murtre et de traïson [...] et est escrot ou Code, De edicto divi Adriani tollendo, l. Quamvis se filium defuncti, ect. Et li usages d'Orlenois si est que [...] selonc droit escrit ou Code, Des Testamens et coment testamens est ordonez, in lege Omnium testamentorum solemnitatem, ou comancement ect [...] selonc droit escrit en la Digeste, De re judicata, l. Inter pares [...] par la costume dou païs et de la terre; c'est à savoir l'obeïssance selonc les establissemenz le roi, si com il est contenuz ou titre D'apeler son seignor de defaute de droit, selonc l'usage d'Orlenois, en cort laie' (*Établissements,* ed. Viollet, II.4; bold emphasis added].

This *coutumier* cites custom, usage, reason, right, case references, cases the author had seen with his own eyes, Roman law, canon law, legal maxims, examples, the words of a clerk, Latin verse that is extracted from three *ordines iudiciarii*, and the Bible. Each of these sources constituted authority in some form. The act of bringing them together, however, amounted to the creation of an *oeuvre* – an act that makes use of sources to create something new, rather than a show of devotion to authorities.

The *Ancien coutumier de Champagne*, finished around 1295, was perhaps the most fully engaged in the culture of citation, though not of learned authority of Roman or canon law. It opened with an ordinance by Thibault IV of Champagne (unlike in the *Établissements*, quoted in full and explicitly attributed to the count).[162] Either custom or usage is cited in almost all sections of the text, no matter how strained the tag of local Champenois custom or usage, since several of these customs or usages refer to decisions of the Parlement of Paris.[163]

The *Demenées el Chastelet de Paris* used little citation compared to the other texts described. Its author immediately explained its narrow focus and very practical purpose as a guide to pleading before judges in the Châtelet in Paris and other lay courts; it was very close to a *style*. Most of the text was devoted to the words exchanged in court or procedures that ought to be followed. When it did cite, it drew upon the custom of the area, one decretal, and several times to the custom of France.

While they did not follow authority slavishly, the *coutumier* authors did learn a lesson from the law schools and from the scholastic method:

---

[162] 'il est coustume en Champane' (*L'ancien coutumier*, ed. Portejoie, II); 'Einsinc en us'on en Champagne' (*ibid.*, IV). These expressions seem to be fairly interchangeable and, for the author of this *coutumier*, to mean the same thing.

[163] Some of these cases are reports from the Parlement of Paris, that involved litigation between parties that had little to do with Champagne. See for instance, *L'ancien coutumier*, ed. Portejoie, XL. This section implies that there is a specific, customary way in Champagne in which one appeals a decision of seisin to the king. This specifically Champenois mode of appeal is proven by the example of a case between the duke of Burgundy and some lords of Artois, a case that was judged in Paris. This is a case of royal law, so it is perhaps not surprising that it would be done in a uniform manner and that the word of the Parlement of Paris would be followed. The text, however, opens with 'It is custom in Champagne that … ' and then explains the rule before buttressing the rule with the case.

that the mark of erudition was the general use of citation. Hence, we see a general preoccupation with citation, reason, and justification.

**

Analysis of the *coutumiers* has focused on their relationship with the Roman law, be it through comparison, penetration, or reception. The relationship between Roman law and the *coutumiers* has even been compared by scholars to a colonial process, where Roman law 'colonized' the customary law and became its ultimate authority.[164] While modern scholarship perceives antagonism between customary and Roman law, this is not the picture that emerges in the early *coutumiers*, composed in the thirteenth and the early fourteenth century.

The difference between the citation of authorities and sources is significant. If we think that *coutumier* authors were citing authorities, then it means we think that the weight of the references exerted a powerful sway over the text itself, and that these authors submitted to the ideas of their authorities and shaped their own text to conform to those authorities. In this case, we are discussing a culture of textual and conceptual deference that does not seem to describe accurately the thought world of the *coutumier* authors. On the other hand, if we think they were citing sources, then we think that they possessed the agency to assemble and create their own texts and used other texts in the service of their own legal milieu and culture.

The *coutumiers* used sources in a conscious and self-confident juristic project devoted to theorizing, describing, and creating the dispute resolution customs of the secular courts. Their authors were not servile followers of authority, but Harold Bloom's 'figures of capable imagination' who appropriated material for themselves to create something new.[165] They took what the emperors had said and what the jurists and canonists opined and built up their own texts by selecting and collating sources as they saw fit, subjecting these sources to a 'strong misreading' in order to reshape them for a new purpose.

---

[164] Jacob makes the colonial comparison in passing, see Jacob, 'Les coutumiers du XIIIe siècle'.
[165] Bloom, *The Anxiety of Influence*, p. 5.

PART III

IMPLICATIONS

6

Custom in Lawbooks and Records of Legal Practice

Each *coutumier* indicated that it described custom or usages in some way. Scholars long assumed that these assertions meant that the texts contained straightforward descriptions of legal practice. However, the relation between the *coutumiers* and practice is more complicated, in part due to the fact that *coutumiers* only came to be cited in records of court proceedings at the very end of the thirteenth century and, even then, only rarely. This should not be taken as an indication that these lawbooks were irrelevant, however. It was certainly not a foregone conclusion in the thirteenth century that the practice of the secular courts would become a bookish one – a legal culture based on textual citation and textual interpretation, like the one that had developed in the ecclesiastical courts.

Indeed, legal practice in the courts of northern France revolved around a generalized notion of custom: allegations of the parties made almost exclusive appeal to the notion of 'custom' (*consuetudo*) as the relevant form of applicable law, even in the Parlement of Paris.[1] In other words, courts commonly referred to custom for legal authority

---

[1] Hilaire, 'Coutume et droit écrit au Parlement de Paris', p. 67. Hilaire notes this for the decisions of the Parlement of Paris for the period from the mid-thirteenth century until the beginning of the following century (*ibid.*, p. 65). The Parlement of Paris was the royal court, and many of its members had studied one or both forms of university law by the last decades of the thirteenth century. If there was a court that had an interest in elevating ordinance or law as primary norm above custom, it would have been this one, but it was not the case.

and not ordinance, law, books, or case precedent.[2] This was also the case for transactional records.

Generally, a specific action or procedure was claimed to be 'according to custom', and often the custom of a particular jurisdiction. Unsurprisingly, we sometimes see ideas about custom that are drawn from practice. For instance, when asked in court, a witness might explain that they knew the custom they alleged because they had seen it used, and they might then explain when and by whom. These descriptions were often more factual than normative; for instance, they might take the form of a story about what happened with a particular woman's dower or a particular exercise of jurisdiction.[3]

The difficulty for historians is that invocations of custom were regularly made unaccompanied by information about its source. A claim would be made 'according to the custom' of a particular area or people.[4] Where records provide no additional information, we cannot know whether a *'coutume de Champagne'* was known through experience of practice, based on an assumption or opinion, drawn from memory of elders or a rumour, something that seemed right or appropriate, a rule contested and then confirmed by a court, or an idea drawn from a written text of custom.

Unlike for canon lawyers and Roman lawyers, it was not common practice to cite specific texts in lay courts. Even where we find a correlation between a rule or procedure described in a *coutumier* and in a record of a court case or other legal document, this only

---

[2] This valuation of custom can be seen in Beaumanoir 'we made an ordinance and had it kept as a custom in Clermont in our administration' (Beaumanoir, *Coutumes de Beauvaisis*, ed. Salmon, LVII.1653).

[3] Note that witness statements recounted the customs that they had seen used or that they had used themselves. They do not necessarily tell us where the idea to use them came from in the first place and thus do not exclude books as one of the potential sources for knowing custom and driving use.

[4] The second case recorded in the *Olim* provides an example of emphasis that the usages and customs of the land are being followed, with custom itself as the source without any information as to how the custom was known: '*Inquesta facta super hoc quod in terra Pertici primogenitus petit habere, secundum usus et consuetudines ipsius patrie, de stangnis (2) que debent dividi, quodcunque voluerit, ubicunque eciam sit: Prohatum est quod primogenitus debet habere quodcunque stangnum voluerit, ubicunque sit, secundum consuetudines ipsius terre*' (*Olim,* vol. 1, p. 4, no. 2).

shows correlation and not causation. All of this means that the specific use of these texts in practice can be difficult to gauge from records of practice.

At the same time, the extent of their use in court cases is but one way of thinking about the relationship between the *coutumiers* and legal practice. This chapter looks at this relationship from a different angle and examines when and how *coutumier* authors used experiences or records of practice to construct their understandings of custom.

The *coutumiers* have different approaches to cases. Some refer to no cases (*Summa de legibus Normannie, Coutumes d'Anjou et du Maine, Les établissements de Saint Louis, Le livre des constitutions demenées el Chastelet de Paris, Li usages de Bourgogne*); some refer to only a few (*Très ancien coutumier de Normandie, Le conseil de Pierre de Fontaines*); and some refer to many (Beaumanoir's *Coutumes de Beauvaisis, L'ancien coutumier de Champagne, Coutumier d'Artois*).[5] I focus this chapter on the *coutumier* authors who reveal how they used elements from legal practice, and the conclusions here are not meant to extend to those authors who did not.

At one level, this chapter shows how at least some people were thinking about the court cases they presided over, took part in, witnessed, or heard about. It shows how they were puzzling through the issues these cases presented and what these cases meant generally for others, beyond their specific parameters and parties. On another level, through the *coutumiers*, we can see how individual actors refashioned specific cases and transactions into general principles, and those general principles into a body of customary law. Of course, there is no doubt that custom was developed in transactions, arbitration, and court proceedings. However, as we will see, the *coutumiers* also tell an important story about how 'customs' were transformed into 'customary law'.

Law 'in the Books' and Law 'in Action'

The earliest mention of a *coutumier* in records of judicial proceedings in northern France occurs in a record of the Exchequer of Normandy of

---

[5] *Li livre de jostice et de plet* also includes many cases. I am not including it here because *Li livre de jostice et de plet* splices cases into Roman law, and this chapter focuses on how *coutumier* authors used experiences or records of practice to construct customary norms.

1296.[6] The account mentions that 'the book of customs of Normandy' was examined – all we know is that the book was consulted.[7] We can see that it had some authoritativeness or probative value as it was mentioned as an authority alongside the parties, *bailli*, and counsel of wise people. But there is no other information as to what the judges looked for, what they found, or whether they used it and, if they did, how.

The next is a record of the Norman Exchequer from 1299, where one of the parties alleged that his case was supported by 'the register of customs of Normandy'.[8] This book of customs was probably the *coutumier*, though we cannot be absolutely certain. Such references continued in the fourteenth century: Philip IV ordered the consultation of a 'book or register of the customs or statutes of Normandy' in 1302 and the *Charte aux Normands* (often included in fourteenth-century manuscript versions of the *Grand coutumier de Normandie*) mentioned that a hearth tax known as *fouage* was to be levied according to a 'register of custom of Normandy' in 1315.[9] In a later example, the written text of the *Très ancienne coutume de Bretagne* (possibly written between 1312 and 1325, definitely by 1341) was cited in a case between Charles of Blois and John of Montfort in 1341.[10] The practice of citing books of custom thus occurred occasionally but was still rare in the fourteenth century.

This is not to suggest that northern French legal culture was wanting in the thirteenth century but that the practice of citing lawbooks in judicial proceedings was not one of its features. In

[6] To my knowledge.
[7] '*Auditis rationibus utriusque partis, ballivo eciam audito, inspectis libris consuetudinis Normannie et habito super hoc consilio sapientium, judicatum fuit et per arrestum redditum quod dicta inquesta non fuerat sufficienter examinata quia ...*' (*Arresta Communia Scacarii*, ed. Perrot, p. 122, no. 151). Perrot presents this text in an appendix because it is not present in several manuscripts of the text.
[8] '*In illius brevis prosecutione, idem Petrus, actor, fecit pro unico defectu unicam emendam, per quam emendam, et reus affirmans hoc in regestis consuetudinis Normannie contineri ...*' (*ibid.*, p. 125, no. 153).
[9] '*librum seu registrum dictorum consuetudinum esu statutorum Normannie videri fecimus*' and '*Quod Foagium non faciemus levari, nisi quatenus in registro consuetudinis Normaniae continetur, usu contrario non obstante*' (Power, *The Norman Frontier in the Twelfth and Thirteenth Centuries*, p. 148).
[10] *La très ancienne coutume de Bretagne*, ed. Planiol, p. 6.

fact, it is quite remarkable that the *coutumiers* began to be cited a handful of decades later, around the turn of the fourteenth century, considering that they were neither legislated nor part of a formalized academic curriculum such as canon or Roman law. The beginning of citation in court shows changing attitudes towards written authorities in secular courts and indicates suggestively that at least some *coutumiers* were starting to be such an authority by the turn of the fourteenth century.

While it may not have been practice to cite the *coutumiers* by text and chapter, written custom was understood to have utility. In the words of the jurist Azo, during the earlier part of the thirteenth century, 'The meaning of custom, although it is general and obligatory, does not necessarily have to be rendered in writing, but it can be redacted in writing by reason of desire or utility, in order to conserve its memory'.[11] And by mid-century, Pierre de Fontaines described his book as 'counsel' for a friend's son so that he may know 'the laws and customs in his region and used in lay courts', be it delivering justice to his subjects, governing his lands according to those principles, or providing counsel himself.[12] Guillaume Chapu gave three reasons for translating the originally Latin-language *Grand Coutumier de Normandie* into French verse, the first being 'so that current and future lawyers [*avocats qui sont et seront*]' can 'know the text and its contents by heart faster'.[13] One manuscript of this verse

---

[11] '*Interpretatio consuetudinis, an sit redigenda in scriptis. Consuetudinis autem interpretatio licet generalis sit, et necessaria, non tamen necessario in scriptis redigneda, sed ex voluntate et utilitate ad conservatem memoriae quisque in scriptis redigere potest*' (*Summa Azonis* in Wehrlé, *De la coutume dans le droit canonique*, p. 144).

[12] Pierre de Fontaines, *Conseil*, Preface II, p. 3.

[13] Lavigne, 'La traduction en vers des *Institutes*', 519. Someone, perhaps named Guillaume Chapu, translated the text into verse, likely from the Latin text and not the French-verse version (*ibid.*). The authorship of the verse version is debated – some scholars say the translator was also Richard Annebaut because he translated *Institutes*, and this text and the *Grand coutumier de Normandie* were often coupled together. One manuscript carried the name Bertrand Chalphepie, which led Tardif to believe the translator was the student for whom Richard d'Annebaut translated Justinian's *Institutes*, while Viollet thought it was a certain Guillaume Caulph/Chapu because the epilogue of one manuscript hinted at this name in an anagram. The anagram passage was as follows: 'Qui mon nom vault appercevoir / Par aiguille, & pour me voir / Le sçaura, & le sournom sache / Cil y met C.A.U.P.H.' (Lavigne, 'La traduction en vers des *Institutes*', 513). Lavigne reasonably settles on saying that the text is attributed to Guillaume Chapu.

translation explains that it should be translated into French rhyme because the text was in common use:

> the Norman *coutumier* which
> Is common to all lawyers
> Of the lay courts when it comes
> To addressing their quarrels
> They must have and hold dear. [14]

These are only a few examples, as a more detailed analysis of the authors' purposes in writing the *coutumiers* will follow. However, it is clear that the *coutumiers* were assumed to have practical uses, whether because they recorded one memory of custom, provided counsel as to the nature of custom and its usage in court, or contained specialized learning that could be applied to quarrels. At least for the thirteenth century, practical use was not understood specifically as the citation of *coutumier* text in court, either as custom or proof of custom.

If we cannot find evidence of practical use in direct application proved by citation, we might be tempted to look for it through 'gap analysis'.[15] This methodology consists of the evaluation of the disjunction between 'law in the books' and 'law in action'.[16] It has

---

[14] Harl. 4477.1 (folio 4), this link can be seen in the prologue: 'Si veul le français mestre en rime / Du latin li livre qui me / Semble bon, est que l'on appelle / Le Coutumier normant, que le / Commun de tous les advocas / De la cour loye, quant au cas / De leurs querelles adrechier / Doyvent avoir et prendre chier' (Lavigne, 'La traduction en vers des *Institutes*', 522n.10).

[15] Gap analysis grew out of American sociolegal writing in the 1930s. Its fundamentally instrumentalist conception of law gained real presence in the academy in the United States in the 1960s and 1970s with the rise of the social sciences and their claims of being better interpreters of the truths of society (Austin Sarat, 'Legal Effectiveness and Social Studies of Law', 24–6). It had contemporary relevance and was meant to reveal hypocrisies in the system as a critique and an argument for reform and societal change (G. Edward White, 'From Realism to Critical Legal Studies').

[16] The meaning of these terms is often assumed rather than defined. Loosely, 'law in the books' brings together anything doctrinal that expresses legal principles and is often used synonymously with 'theory'. It groups together texts with significantly different purposes: statements about law from centralized authorities such as legislation, erudite scholarly treatises, and other unofficial types of descriptive accounts of practice. Meanwhile, 'law in action' generally refers to social practices, experiences of individual actors, and empirical analysis of what courts, parties, and lawyers do. It tends to focus on litigation and the judicial process, police and enforcement action, and non-state normative worlds and extrajudicial dispute resolution. The expression is often used synonymously with 'practice'. The methodology takes a variety of forms: a focus on the intent of the lawmaker and whether they really had an interest in

been key in shaping perceptions of lawbooks such as the *coutumiers* because the methodology tacitly assumes that if articulated legal norms and instances of human behaviour diverge, then 'law in the books' and its authors, or the state, have failed or were out of touch.[17] If we rely on this approach alone, however, we might miss how lawbooks were used or understood within their own societies, whose notions of 'practical use' may very well have differed from modern contemporary ones.

Studies of early medieval law have shown that lawbooks were written for different reasons, and even those presented as legislation could have been but were not necessarily enforced on the ground. For instance, instead of assuming that the purpose of legislation was to condition human behaviour according to stated rules and to penalize deviation from those rules, Patrick Wormald asked what exactly was the purpose of legislation for the moment and society that produced it. He asked: 'why did kings make a fraction of contemporary custom "their own", and how was this "of practical use"? *How* did legislation make one "more of a king?"'.[18] He then argues that these '*leges*' did not tell a story about law per se but were part of the ideological trappings of kingship.[19]

---

enforcement, an analysis of modes of implementation and enforcement, or analysis of the gap as a structural feature of a particular system (Hendrik Hartog, 'Pigs and Positivism', 924).

[17] The goal behind finding the extent of the gap was to understand the extent of 'legal effectiveness', which means the extent to which 'law in the books' is reflected in behaviour on the ground, and so the extent to which normative statements condition human behaviour (Sarat, 'Legal Effectiveness and Social Studies of Law', 24; Hartog, 'Pigs and Positivism', 924). The method created a disjunction that it then could not help but keep finding, even in modern societies with highly developed states and legal enforcement mechanisms (Sarat, 'Legal Effectiveness and Social Studies of Law', 27). It also implies that 'real law' lies in what people do and not what legislators or lawbook writers think ought to be done. Marc Galanter noted this should not be a stark binary in his influential article (originally published in 1967) that moved legal history beyond the courtroom and law library to include local interpretations, informal operations and popular legalities: 'law' generally should be 'visualized as a continuum stretching from this official "lawyers' law" at one end to the concrete patterns of regulation which obtain in particular localities at the other' ('The Uses of Law in Indian Studies' in Galanter, *Law and Society in Modern India*, p. 4). The true story of law, or custom in our case here, exists both in official or normative forms of law and its particular lived moments (as well as in the continuum between the two), and neither of these exclusively or more truly tells the story of law; rather, each tells different aspects of that story.

[18] Wormald, '*Lex Scripta* and *Verbum Regis*', p. 3; emphasis in original.

[19] See generally, Wormald, *The Making of English Law*. Wormald's views were more complex than this brief description allows to describe (see Stefan Jurasinski and Lisi

Practical use did not have to lie in the detailing of rules to be imposed, enforced, and cited in lawsuits, but could also be found elsewhere.

Written law, even written legislation, did not necessarily imply a legal culture that revolved around the text of legal norm. Records of lawsuits indicate a textualized legal culture but not a 'codal' one, that is, a legal culture based on a law code, an official text of law issued by an accepted authority that is essential to the legal process and meant to be imposed and enforced.

Wormald noted in the first volume of his magnum opus that 'Much of this volume has dwelt on the apparent failure of the written law to do the job that it would be expected to do'.[20] This expectation was a modern one about the job we assign to law. Expectations of the law in the medieval period cannot be assumed to be the same, and indeed, scholars have been moving away from the view of legislation as symbolic posturing.[21] Wormald's questioning of different expectations and meanings of the law and how it should work for medieval people and modern scholars remains relevant.

Normative legal texts may be idealistic and therefore not directly mirror human behaviour. Instead of seeing this as a flaw, we can seek to imagine what this law meant in a legal system whose primary goal was not to assert a state monopoly on legitimate violence.[22] Tom Lambert has shown how early English laws, though generally not applied in practice, illuminate how the society that produced them conceived of and shaped their social, political, and legal order, and

---

Oliver, *The Laws of Alfred: The Domboc and the Making of Anglo-Saxon Law*, pp. 78ff).

[20] He expected to develop his ideas about how kings were able to dictate to their subjects without the specific enforcement of written law and to show that 'the development of English *law* from Alfred to Cnut and beyond did not run along the tracks that *legislation* marked out, but did run parallel to them' (*ibid.*, p. 483). This second volume was reconstructed as much as it could be from various proposals, papers, outlines, and chapters and is available online: Wormald, *Papers Preparatory to the Making of English Law*, https://bit.ly/3OmGXgf.

[21] A move Wormald himself may have welcomed (see Jurasinski and Oliver, *The Laws of Alfred: The Domboc and the Making of Anglo-Saxon Law*, p. 80). Alice Taylor, for instance, describes written law 'if not as evidence for practice, at least as intimately concerned and connected with it, and as something that might represent and have absorbed the values of a locally based enforcement' (Taylor, 'Lex Scripta and the Problem of Enforcement: Anglo-Saxon, Welsh and Scottish law compared', p. 72).

[22] T. B. Lambert, *Law and Order in Anglo-Saxon England*, pp. 2, 13.

how that order functioned.[23] Even laws that described an idealized form of social relations can be used to understand the ideas of order that undergird society.[24]

Of course, these early medieval *leges* were legislation and official 'state' law.[25] The *coutumiers*, in contrast, were not legislation promulgated by a sovereign as a manifestation of public power. Instead, they were individual attempts to understand and explicate the norms, ideals, and practices of secular courts. And the customary law they discussed was described as useful to practice even though it was not written to be cited and enforced to the letter. This should lead us to wonder how they were viewed and used, and what they can tell us about customary law as a legal culture. In what sense were the *coutumiers* useful at the time they were written? And what could 'practical use' have meant to those 'using' a *coutumier* in the thirteenth century? The articulation of law in terms of general ideas rather than specific issues is vital to understanding how these texts would have been 'practical' in their own time.

Records of Court Proceedings and Conceptual Law

The most obvious use or benefit of the *coutumiers* is that they generalized the workings of secular courts by articulating the rules of these courts. This required effort and ingenuity. Generalization involved moving from particular instance to abstract thought: one must take a specific datum, experience, event, action, or impression and reshape it in different language in a way that extends it to other contexts. This is one means of producing norms.[26] The *coutumier* authors drew out

---

[23] More specifically, 'when laws prescribe practice, they must usually be prescribing practices that made sense in the context of Anglo-Saxon elite understandings of existing legal customs, practices which at least some of those gathered in great assemblies thought they could realistically hope people would adopt' (*ibid.*, p. 16).

[24] See generally Lambert, *Law and Order in Anglo-Saxon England*.

[25] Caroline Humfress offers an important critique of the use of gap analysis even where there is a code meant to dictate practice issued by 'the state' (Humfress, 'Law's Empire', pp. 92–3). She argues for taking an anthropological approach reconstructing late Roman legal practice that includes both legal practice from the perspective of individual actors and different types of formal legal knowledge.

[26] It is different, for instance, from analogical reasoning such as in precedent, which creates patterns between specific instances by showing (or rather, arguing for) sameness or similarity between them. For the main questions and philosophical problems related to this form of reasoning, see Grant Lamond, 'Precedent and Analogy in Legal Reasoning'.

generalizations that articulated the ideas and normative assumptions of those who practised in the courts but who generally did not expressly assert these ideas or assumptions.

While the goal of a *coutumier* author was to generalize, the goal of a record of a court proceeding was to provide an account of one particular dispute. These were radically different goals that demanded different types of information and different forms of thinking. Historians know well that different forms of sources are created for different purposes. Unsurprisingly, then, while both records of practice and the *coutumiers* overlapped in discussing issues of law, their form was distinctive, and they treated the same legal issues very differently.

This can be seen by comparing two inquests concerning high justice and two *coutumier* descriptions of high justice. Our goal is to analyse how generalization as a form of norm creation works, and its practical benefits. An inquest concerning high justice was held in a case between the French king and Gui Mauvoisin in the mid-1230s.[27] The parties were disputing the type of 'justice', here meaning jurisdiction, that Gui claimed in the suburbs of Mantes as well as his claim both to low and high justice in all his lands.[28] An inquest was conducted by two *baillis*, Pierre de Roucy and Jean des Vignes.[29] They called fifty-two witnesses to testify, first, all of those on behalf of the king, then all of those on behalf of Gui.[30]

The record does not indicate how the first witness was directed by the judges or what question or questions he was asked. But it prompted the following answer: 'Robert Patrocin, priest, under oath, said a certain man was captured within the suburbs between Rosny and

[27] This is a case of the royal court before the records of Parlement of Paris started being formally kept in 1254. The Mauvoisin family was the most prominent family in the marches of Francia between Vernon and Mentes (Power, *The Norman Frontier in the Twelfth and Thirteenth Centuries*, p. 254).

[28] Edgar Boutaric, *Actes du Parlement*, p. ccciv, no. 15. The inquest was held by two *baillis*, Jean des Vignes and Pierre de Roucy. The record does not provide an exact date, so Pierre de Roucy's life is used to date this case, which must have taken place before his death sometime in 1236. Mantes was Capetian land on the border with Normandy, thus politically significant, it gained communal status from Louis the Fat in 1110 and grew wealthy (Aristide Guilbert, *Histoire des villes de France*, p. 751). Philip Augustus referred to it as his beloved (*dilectam*) city and made it the seat of great assemblies of the kingdom; it was where he died, and his heart was placed at the Church of Notre Dame in Mentes (*ibid.*).

[29] Boutaric, *Actes du Parlement*, p. ccciv, no. 15.

[30] Musée des Archives nationales, *Documents originaux de l'histoire de France*, p. 132. Boutaric printed a selection of this testimony.

Mantes, because he had stolen one bushel of eels and was taken to Mentes and was hanged there.'[31] When asked when this occurred, he said in the time of King Philip. He added that 'the provost of Lommoye killed a certain priest and was captured in his house and taken to Mentes and the court of the lord king, was dragged through the city of Mentes and hanged. He also said, on his oath, that the justice is the lord king's, as he believed.'[32] From these responses, we can see that the testimony covered three main questions: What had the witness seen that could provide information on the issue of jurisdiction in the area? Who had jurisdiction? And what kind of jurisdiction was it?

Much witness testimony followed. Comparing the specifics might permit us to deduce from the patterns of witness testimony what exactly they thought high justice was or at least what it was in this specific case. However, it might not be easy to decide what element or combination of elements proved high justice. Was the operative information the capture of alleged criminals, the place of capture, the thieving, the nature of the things stolen, the place of judgment, the fact of punishment, the nature of the punishment, or the person punishing?

The court record does not tell us. Witnesses testified to what they knew or had seen as to the exercise of justice. Those conducting the inquest decided who had high justice, but we do not know on what grounds. Nor do we know whether a rule or definition was invoked or the points of debate in their deliberations.

That was one example. A later inquest from around 1250 approached high justice differently. It concerned the rights of high justice in the suburbs of St Vaast, which were contested by the Countess of Artois and the aldermen of Béthune.[33] The first witness,

---

[31] Boutaric, *Actes du Parlement*, p. ccciv, no. 15.

[32] One man, Bernard Boitter, appeared twice, and his testimony was used on behalf of both sides. Listed as the eighth witness on the king's side, he had 'on his oath, said that a certain man had stolen one bushel of eels between Rosny and Mantes and wanted to bring them to Vernon for sale. He was captured and taken to Mentes and placed in prison. Afterwards, he was taken out and placed in the pillory with the bushel around his neck and was dismissed beyond the city' (*ibid.*). He reappeared as the forty-first witness. When asked how he knew that the thief about whom he spoke had stolen the eels between Rosny and Mentes, he said because he heard it said by those who took the thief to Mentes where he saw him held by the duke. When asked how he knew other things that he said in his testimony about the said thief, he responded that he has seen it (Musée des Archives nationales, *Documents originaux de l'histoire de France*, p.132).

[33] Boutaric, *Actes du Parlement*, pp. cccxi–cccxiii, no. 27.

Eustace de Hamel, from the start made the legal claim that 'the people of the count of Artois have used high justice in the suburbs', but as his questioning continued it became clear that the aldermen had exercised high justice there as well.[34]

Society accommodated and lived with what should have been a contradiction – two holders of high justice – but it did not become a contradiction until the moment of contestation, and it is that moment captured in the inquest. Those conducting the inquest had to think not in terms of who was right or wrong but in terms of who had the 'greater right'.[35]

The nature of the high justice in the case was proven by witness testimony of various instances of murder and rape and who had handled them. This was similar to the previous case, but, unlike it, the record of this proceeding also shows us elements of proof to evaluate the legitimacy of an exercise of high justice. Eustace was asked whether 'the alderman used this high justice in open view and with the knowledge of the area, and [whether] they do so because they have the right?'.[36] He replied yes and that they did everything 'openly, in the light of day, and using regular summons'.[37] This gives us a sense of some of the criteria that might have been used to evaluate who had the 'greater right', and thus what might provide greater legitimacy to the exercise of high justice. The information provided in the court record gives us an idea of what high justice was for the purposes of this particular case, but it does not give us a categorical understanding of high justice and its components.

The latter is precisely what the *coutumier* authors provided to the communities of northern France. The *Établissements de Saint Louis*, drawing on a royal ordinance, explained that 'the cases of high justice of barons' were 'treachery, rape, arson, larceny, and all serious crimes

---

[34] *Ibid.*, pp. cccxii–cccxiii.

[35] The question of who had the greater right was not a new one. Philip Augustus appointed his *bailli* Guillaume de la Chapelle to inquire whether the abbey of St Denis or the church of Saint Aignan or Gaucher de Joigny had 'the greater right' over an elm tree ('*Nos autem Guillelmo de Capello, ballivo nostro, dedimus in mandatis ut ipse inquireret quis predictorum in hoc magis juris haberet*', *Recueil des actes de Philippe-Auguste, roi de France*, ed. Berger, vol. 2, p. 251, no. 689). Across the channel, the *Glanvill* treatise as well as writs and plea rolls also spoke of having 'greater right' (McSweeney, 'Between England and France', p. 79).

[36] Boutaric, *Actes du Parlement*, p. cccxiii.   [37] *Ibid.*

where the penalty may include loss of life and limb'.[38] High justice here was defined by categories of acts and the form of punishment. This treats the same subject of high justice but in a very different fashion.

About a decade later, Philippe de Beaumanoir also offered a generic description of high justice, though he chose to describe it a little differently. He included in high justice all cases of serious crime – those 'for which the sentence is and should be death for those found guilty and convicted'. Contrary to the *Établissements*, Beaumanoir did not include larceny as a case of high justice, despite the fact that thieves lost their lives for larceny, 'but all other serious cases (*cas vilain*) are, such as murder, treason, homicide, raping women, damage to property by fire or destruction by night, and all cases which can lead to a wager of battle, and counterfeiting, and consenting to or procuring [such crimes]; and all these offenses are cases in high justice'.[39] Beaumanoir defined high justice by categories of act and the form punishment, as did the *Établissements*, but made a significant change by adding 'consenting to and procuring such crimes' to the list of acts that constituted high justice.

---

[38] 'Ce sont li cas de haute joustise be baronie. En ceste manière ira l'en avent es quereles de traïson, de rat, d'arson, de larrecin, et de touz crimes ou il ait peril de perdre vie ou membre, la ou en faisoit la bataille', *Les Établissements de Saint Louis*, ed. Viollet, I.5. The first nine sections of the *Établissements* are drawn from a royal ordinance that we know largely from the manuscripts of the *Établissements*. The *Établissements* does not say this is a royal ordinance but presents it as the practices of the provosts of Paris (with some variation). This ordinance also appeared as part of the *Livre de Jostice et de Plet*. Beyond this, it appears in one manuscript where it stands independently under the title *C'est la forme de pledier que li rois Loois commanda a garder en France*. The latter contains the same text except s. 9 is cut short and, of course, it does not contain the Roman and canon law additions added by the compiler of *Établissements* (*C'est la forme de pledier que li rois Loois commanda a garder en France*, Vatican City, BAV, Reg. lat. 773). The other texts in Reg. lat. 773 were a *liber provincialis* for the city of Rome and a Latin translation of the *Kyranides*, a text originally in Greek about the healing powers of plants, animals, and stones. Note the similarity between high justice and categories of felony that coalesced in England in the thirteenth century (Elizabeth Papp Kamali, *Felony and the Guilty Mind in Medieval England*, p. 43).

[39] Beaumanoir, *Coutumes de Beauvaisis*, ed. Salmon, LVIII.1642. To this he added nuance by noting that some cases were not so straightforward: 'It sometimes happens that some cases arise which are so obscure that you cannot know right away whether it is a case pertaining to high justice or to low', for example when it was uncertain whether a victim would die from their wounds. In that case, the person inflicting the wound would be detained for forty days to see whether the victim would die, and so whether the case was one of high justice (Beaumanoir, *Coutumes de Beauvaisis*, ed. Salmon, LVIII.1646).

Beamanoir's approach clearly departs from court proceedings and their presentation of information. *Coutumier* authors were creating a conceptual law by mentally grouping types of information and forming and distilling concepts out of particular instances. The similarities between the *Établissements* and Beaumanoir show where ideas on high justice were firmly established, and the differences show where opinions were unsettled or diverged.

The *coutumiers* and records of lawsuits covered similar subjects but were separated by a 'zone of silence' because these sources tell very different stories about law.[40] Judicial proceedings are records of attempts to resolve ambiguity or controversy in law, either where normal rules and customs could not sufficiently decide an issue, or where these were contested and required formal institutional resolution. Because of this, statements about law in records of court proceedings were not factual statements that embodied a consensus about law but acts 'of aggression, a way of claiming rights or of asserting authority'.[41] They do not reflect 'how law works when it works'.[42] They are events that permit the definition, or contestation and redefinition, of law.[43] The *coutumiers* likewise do not contain factual statements of law that embody an obvious consensus. Rather, they provided something unavailable elsewhere: an image of customary law presented as a coherent system constituted by enunciated principles. On the surface, the *coutumier* descriptions of high justice examined above might seem like mundane explanations of an obvious legal category. But their contrast to court records reveals that their work was both an imaginative and an intellectual act: they were drawing connections between disparate types of crimes or trying

---

[40] Wormald, *The Making of English Law*, p. 160.

[41] Hartog, 'Pigs and Positivism,' 930. As Hartog noted, 'The point is not that participants could make the law into anything they chose. Of course that was not the case. Parts of the law belonged to one's antagonist. Parts (perhaps the most important parts) were constituted out of the conflict between competing groups, and belonged to no one in particular' (*ibid.*).

[42] Sarat, 'Legal Effectiveness and Social Studies of Law', 29.

[43] In the words of Hendrik Hartog: 'The idea of a gap only makes sense where there is some shared consciousness [...] that law was law' (Hartog, 'Pigs and Positivism', 925). Being upheld by the court in view of claims to the contrary, as we have seen, also created custom. The effect of the judicial process was to create a firm rule from a contestable one. So, a case existed in which there was no such 'shared consciousness', and its goal was to create it.

to understand the taxonomy by which certain crimes had been grouped together. Even such mundane descriptions of terminology or procedure were interpretative acts of abstraction.

More than that, in performing these acts of abstraction *coutumier* authors were shaping particular instances into norms and presenting those norms as a gestalt. They created a coherent image of customary law, and this image lies at the heart of our understanding of customary law as something normative and based on coherent rules.

Charters and Norms

Charters, the most voluminous records produced and conserved throughout the medieval period, were also largely not descriptive of conceptual law as the *coutumiers* were.[44] Many charters were brief administrative documents, 'a workaday artefact, written on a scrap of parchment'.[45] The vast majority were records of various types of agreements. They offered testimony to basic transactions on a specific individual level, such as lease, sale, debt, or donation. In general, they were products of the effort to arrange one's affairs in advance with an eye to the prevention of future disputes.[46] Some charters survived as originals, but many survived in cartulary copies.[47] While many charters

---

[44] On charters, see Raymond Clemens and Timothy Graham, *Introduction to Manuscript Studies*, p. 222. The study of charters in the last decades has fundamentally changed our understanding of lay legal life in the period before the *coutumiers* by broadening our source base from a focus on legislation and lawbooks to include transactional documents. Lay legal life may not have been articulated legislatively or theoretically explicitly or at length but was articulated at the level of individual experience, at the very least tacitly in the structure and contents of their contractual relationships.

[45] Koziol, *Begging Pardon and Favor*, p. 87.

[46] Hyams, 'The Charter as a Source for the Early Common Law', 173–4.

[47] The massive expansion of documentary practices of lay lordship can be seen in the growth of the archive of the counts of Champagne: it included around 200 sealed letters (letters patent) in 1211, and by 1271 there were several thousand letters in the archive (*Littere Baronum*, ed. Evergates, p. 3). Many of these originals disappeared, and the cartularies are the only source for many of them (*ibid.*). However, we should be wary of talking about originals when we are receiving them though modulated copies: 'Because strict duplication seems to have been eschewed in producing the various versions of a single deed, it may be that the so-called archetype was never an original document in our modern sense, but truly an "act" by which actions, transactions, or judgments were accomplished. In that sense, every surviving document reporting such events may be best understood as a copy' (Bedos-Rezak, 'Towards an Archaeology of the Medieval Charter', p. 43).

FIGURE 6.1 Sample charter granting property rights. Charter composed on 9 March 1172 by Bernat Pasqual granting rights to Raimund Berengarius and his wife Dulcia in various properties in the county of Barcelona, in exchange for Raimund's holding the post of bailiff in those properties. The charter includes a list of witnesses and the name of the scribe, Gerallus. The document is dated to the reign of the French king Louis VII 'The Younger' (r. 1137–80) and is written on a small piece of parchment measuring 9 x 22 cm. Kislak Center for Special Collections, Rare Books and Manuscripts University of Pennsylvania Ms. Coll. 85.

that survived were monastic, some of these also testified to lay activity, such as that depicted in Figure 6.1.[48]

Charters are our main source for dispute resolution in northern France before the thirteenth century. A small proportion of these documents provided accounts of dispute that led to a specific truce agreement or resolution to a property issue. The accounts of dispute provided might include feud, mediation, arbitration, court process, or a combination of these. Presumably some sort of norm, procedure, or form had to be respected, in some way.[49]

---

[48] While the survival of charters before the twelfth century owed a lot to monasteries and certainly revealed the interests of those monasteries, their existence also reflected the commemorative bent of lay aristocracy and offer testimony of the extent of lay literacy and record-keeping (see Warren Brown et al. (eds.), *Documentary Culture and the Laity in the Early Middle Ages*; Adam Kosto, 'Laymen, Clerics, and Documentary Practices in the Early Middle Ages'). Some, notably the royal diploma – a charter issued by a king – evinced an implicit political and normative order through ritual gesture despite seeming singular (see Koziol, *Begging Pardon and Favor*).

[49] As Hyams has noted of charters, the parties 'were minimally affected by direction from above, from public institutions and royal law. Yet they were very conscious of forces beyond the needs of the immediate moment, norms they had, willy-nilly, to respect. [...] The more acute among them undoubtedly sensed that they were by their

Evaluated closely and carefully by modern historians, charters did suggest some procedures and norms, albeit often indirectly and obliquely. Individuals bargained and strategized 'in the shadow of the law', observes Caroline Humfress for the context of late antique Rome and its codifications.[50] But what could this mean when the law was largely an unwritten, unlegislated customary one and there was no code or significant corpus of legislation and no specific normative text 'in the shadow'?

In the late eleventh and early twelfth centuries, judicial battles and other ordeals were used to resolve cases on some rare occasions, but most of the time they were resolved through other means, although our sources rarely elaborate or describe them.[51] Aside from the pervasive use of compromise and the occasional use of war, we sometimes also see the logical evaluation of claims, use of witness testimony, evaluation of documents, the use of courts or other gatherings, or determinations of what seems right or just in a particular situation.[52] There was some notion of rights and an understanding of various ways one could make a good claim:

Even though the arguments and norms that litigants and third parties explicitly or implicitly used did not constitute a coherent legal system of the kind that later came into existence, participants in *placita* [i.e., discussions] evidently acknowledged the existence of a common body of argumentative 'officializing strategies' by means of which claims to property could be legitimated or undermined. [53]

Even without a bureaucratic sovereign authority to enforce rights or claims according to an overtly enunciated set of rules, society has a range of methods to legitimate claims.[54] It sometimes even had 'principles' – this is evident in the principle of hereditary succession, which was consistently seen as a right throughout charters and imaginative literature, even though notions varied about how to claim or enforce that right.[55] While we evaluate these sorts of claims of right or principles, we must always keep in mind these important

---

specific acts renewing custom' (Hyams, 'The Charter as a Source for the Early Common Law', p. 174).

[50] Humfress, 'Law's Empire', p. 92. Humfress said the latter for late-antique Roman law and its codifications.

[51] Stephen D. White, 'Inheritances and Legal Arguments in Western France', 97.   [52] *Ibid.*

[53] *Ibid.*, 96–7.   [54] *Ibid.*

[55] See generally, White, 'Inheritances and Legal Arguments in Western France'.

questions: what it means to draw on written Latin-language evidence of judicial proceedings made within a predominantly oral and vernacular culture, how to use records that favoured unusual and sensational cases over the mundane ones, and storytelling over details about legal reasoning.[56]

One might even say that assumptions underlying claims of right could sometimes resemble 'substantive law' even if the 'procedural law' of how these claims of right were handled could vary widely. This raises the question of whether normative thinking might lurk unnoticed in charters and, if so, how much.

A sense of legality can sometimes be hidden by language that is unfamiliar or that does not signify 'law' to modern readers. For instance, Matthew McHaffie asserts that scholars have assumed eleventh-century society to be lawless and centred on self-help because there was no public monopoly on the use of force, an assumption based on common assertions of violence in contemporary sources.[57] However, McHaffie's close study of these sources, where he suspends *étatiste* assumptions about courts as institutions that aim specifically to assert authority over and suppress violence, shows that violence in itself does not automatically imply chaos: violence here was a concept of legal utility harnessed in the courts for the purpose of legal decision-making in cases that concerned politically problematic land claims.[58]

Indeed, accounts that look like chains of facts may have a 'strong normative underpinning' in that they are responding to ideas about law.[59] Legal historians have made much of the distinction between facts and law, but it may be more helpful, especially for earlier periods, to think of 'legally charged facts'.[60] Scholars of the period of the 'feudal revolution' – a period with especially scattered, piecemeal, and often silent sources – have had to approach these questions with singular nuance, analytical depth, and a unique level of imagination. This bears witness to the utility of the charter as evidence and also shows that the charter was not a primary space

---

[56] Hudson, 'Court Cases and Legal Arguments in England', 93–5.
[57] McHaffie, 'Law and Violence in Eleventh-Century France', 8.   [58] *Ibid.*, 9ff.
[59] Hudson, 'Court Cases and Legal Arguments in England', 100.
[60] Hudson, 'Court Cases and Legal Arguments in England', 104.

for the overt articulation of explicitly normative thought for medieval contemporaries.

Charters of course reveal many fundamental aspects of legal history that other sources cannot.[61] The Cartulary of Nesle, for instance, made many references to usages and customs and so illuminates a number of legal practices and shows the importance of affirming these labels as justification of practice as well. That the chancery of the Lords of Nesle would evince a greater legal consciousness is perhaps unsurprising as the lords of Nesle and their cousin the count of Soissons are well known for their pivotal roles in the transformation of Capetian administrative and judicial institutions.[62] Perhaps the best known among these for participation in matters of justice was Simon of Nesle, who had high justice in his own fief, regularly attended the great occasions of Louis IX's reign, was called upon by the king for his opinion on matters of justice, and served as co-regent for the king when he embarked on his second crusading venture and then again under Philip III.[63] The cartulary nonetheless only mentioned customs relevant to the individual transaction in question, sometimes with an explanation and sometimes only with an affirmation that custom was followed but without any information about the custom itself.[64]

Conceptualizing, expository, and analytical forms of legal thought that related to the lay courts thus found a unique form of expression in the *coutumiers*. An example is a charter where Robert Count of Clermont and Amaury de Montfort granted lands to our jurist Philippe de Beaumanoir. The charter granted Beaumanoir lands from

---

[61] Hyams, Paul, 'The Charter as a Source for the Early Common Law'; Taylor, 'Formalising Aristocratic Power in Royal Acta in Late Twelfth- and Early Thirteenth-Century France and Scotland'.

[62] Griffiths, 'Royal Counselors and Trouvères in the Houses of Nesle and Soissons', 123.

[63] Jordan, *Men at the Center*, p. 78ff.

[64] For instance, a charter of 1269 notes an unexplained custom when it describes a donation made by the knight Etienne Boujon to his daughter according to the good usages and good customs of Bourgogne: 'Toutes ces choses cil Esteines at outroiiés et donées a sa fille heritaublement as bons us et as bones costumes de Borgoigne si cum il at reconeu devant nos' (Hélary, ed., 'Le cartulaire de la seigneurie de Nesle', www.cn-telma.fr/nesle/acte6 (accessed 16 October 2020)). This contrasts with another act from the same year: in a concord between Jean de Nesle and the men of Coulmier, presided over by Hugh, the duke of Bourgogne, three specific customs are described and labelled the 'customs of Bourgogne' (Hélary, ed., 'Le cartulaire de la seigneurie de Nesle', www.cn-telma.fr/nesle/acte13/ (accessed 16 October 2020)).

which he had earlier had the rents but did not fully hold.[65] The charter
noted the grant was given 'for love of him and for his good service'
though does not explain the nature of the services rendered.[66] The date
of the charter – 1283 – is rather suggestive, as this is the same year that
Beaumanoir completed his *Coutumes de Beauvaisis*. Of course, this
does not allow us to infer causality, and the land grant could have been
for his service as *bailli* of Clermont for Robert, for both the book and
the service together, or for something else entirely.

We thus have a charter concerning a *coutumier* author issued at the
time he wrote his book that turned on an issue discussed therein. The
charter specified that Count Robert 'retained high justice and all the
cases that belong to high justice; and low justice of the lands above will
be held by the aforesaid Philip and his heirs'.[67] It did not explain the
nature of the categories or division. From the description in his
Coutumes, evaluated above, we can assume what Philippe would have
understood these categories to mean. He likely would have
grouped the uncertain issue of larceny, for instance, as low justice
and thus under his jurisdiction for this land grant.

The charters involving our two known *coutumier* authors Pierre de
Fontaines and Philippe de Beaumanoir are not as revealing of the sorts
of legal thought found in their *coutumiers* as one might hope. They do
not have more substantive discussion or substantive discussion that is
more complex, nor do they offer meaningful glimpses into the
analytical forms behind customary law as their books do.

Instead, we see a true contrast in the forms of information provided by
different types of sources. This can be seen if we compare Beaumanoir's
mentions of cases in his *coutumier* to the charters associated with him
before 1284; in other words, his own description of what he saw
compared to outside records that testify to him around the same time.
He mentions tens of cases, which he reports with varying amounts of
detail.[68] In contrast, we have three known records associated with him

---

[65] Henri Léonard Bordier, *Philippe de Remi*, pp. 107–9.

[66] 'pour amour de li et pour son bon service' (*ibid.*, p. 108).

[67] 'sauf che que nous y retenons le haute justiche et tous les cas qui a haute justiche
apartienent; et la basses justiche o tous les heritagez dessus dis li dis Phelippez et si hoir
tenront ...' (*ibid.*).

[68] The way he talked about cases had a lot of range. He includes the parties, issue, and
court for some, while for others, he notes that he saw the case and describes it but
without specifying the parties or using generic names instead.

that date to the same period of time; namely 1283 or earlier.[69] In itself, this shows a man who had seen many cases and wrote a large book about all aspects of law, ranging from court process to everyday transactions, but who appears in two (known) charters in the same period of his life. That there are more for his subsequent career is likely related to the fact that he became a royal justice. He might have seen more, and more important, cases as a royal justice, or the greater number of cases might also reflect a rapidly professionalizing practice in his own lifetime (1247–1296) with ever-increasing numbers of records and, by the latter part of the century, with a greater amount of detail.

This example underscores how much form conditioned how information was selected and presented. One charter issued by Robert of Clermont mentions Beaumanoir as a negotiator on behalf of the count in an agreement made with the abbey of Saint Lucien.[70] Another, more revealing, charter from Beaumanoir's time as *bailli* was issued by Beaumanoir himself. It concerned a dispute between the prior of Breuil and the cloth merchants of Clermont over seisin of rents at the fair in Breuil during the feast of St Martin.[71] Each party claimed to have 'good seisin', and witness testimony was heard 'for a long time', though not recounted in the charter, and on its basis the judgment was in favour of the prior.[72] The goal of the charter, we can assume from the information presented, was to record the issue and parties of this specific dispute and its particular resolution. It does not relate – nor was it meant to – what constituted 'good seisin' or how long was 'a long time', how these factors were known, how the arguments were weighed, and why it was that the prior of Breuil had the better claim. This is just one example, but it illustrates the impact of form. The third charter was the one examined in Chapter 4 concerning reparations made by Beaumanoir as *bailli* of Clermont and his sergeants for abusing their power by violating the church's privilege to offer sanctuary. The charters produced by or mentioning Beaumanoir do not reveal the great jurist – this is accomplished instead by his *coutumier*.

---

[69] See 'Pièces justificatives' in Bordier, *Philippe de Remi*, pp. 127–32. For later in his career, some records have been found in addition to those listed by Bordier: Paul Collinet, 'Deux chartes inédites de Philippe de Beaumanoir (1290–1291)'; Carolus-Barré, 'Charte de Philippe de Beaumanoir', p. 264. The latter preserves Beaumanoir's seal.

[70] Bordier, *Philippe de Remi*, p. 127–29.   [71] *Ibid.*, xxiii, pp. 129–130.

[72] *Ibid.*, p. 130.

By the thirteenth century, because they were getting so numerous, charters provide an evocative and unmediated view for scholars of the matters that generally preoccupied a lordship.[73] This is true for the charters assembled in the cartulary of Countess Blanche de Champagne.[74] This corpus included 443 letters, the majority of which were authored by lay people.[75] According to these letters, governance of the county was comprised of property transactions (178 letters), 'grants (35 letters), sales, mortgages, debts, and exchanges (63 letters), quittances and receipts (20 letters), co-lordships contracts (23 letters), inquests (11 letters), and the resolution of disputes (26 letters)'.[76]

The cartulary of Champagne sketches the nature of customary law: it was comprised in part of property transactions, various sorts of contracts, matters of mediation or arbitration, and actions taken when a problem escalated and required the courts for a formal mechanism of resolution. Not coincidentally, these issues are mirrored in the contents of the *coutumiers* in their treatment of lay legal life.[77]

From Record of Practice to Abstract Rule

The *coutumiers* complemented thought about secular law and its practice through their synthesis, generalization, and abstraction, but their connection to court practice was stronger than that. Authors

[73] The earliest baronial letters patent were personal conveyances and confirmations of donations to monastic institutions and appear to have been written by monastic beneficiaries (*Littere Baronum*, ed. Evergates, p. 7). In contrast, 64 per cent of authors of the Cartulary of Blanche, who ruled Champagne as regent from 1201 to 1222, were lay persons (*The Cartulary of Countess Blanche of Champagne*, ed. Evergates, p. 12). The first in-house chancery, in the sense of stationary writing bureau, was founded by Henry the Liberal at Troyes, where the chapter of St Etienne served as chancery, treasury, chapel, and necropolis (p. 8).

[74] This was one of eight cartularies produced by the chancery of the Counts of Champagne during the thirteenth century and was unique in its commemorative focus on Blanche's achievements during her twenty-one years as regent for the county, notably her weathering of the succession crisis that followed the death of her husband, Thibaut III (*Littere Baronum*, ed. Evergates, p. 3; *The Cartulary of Countess Blanche of Champagne*, ed. Evergates, p. 3).

[75] *The Cartulary of Countess Blanche of Champagne*, ed. Evergates, p. 12.

[76] *Ibid.*, p. 13.

[77] *Demenées el Chastelet de Paris* and the *Ancien coutumier de Bourgogne* were exceptions in their more narrow focus on court procedure and pleading.

invoked custom without explaining their source of knowledge, but some of the *coutumier* authors also show us how they used specific cases to build abstract rules. When a *coutumier* author made a point of referring to cases and explaining the resulting norm, we can conclude this with certainty; in other cases, we can only surmise.

One example from Beaumanoir, typical of his approach, shows how he created norms from particular instances.[78] A gentlewoman named Marie had sued her younger sister Jehane, saying she should receive her sister's homage for land they inherited from their parents, to which Jehane replied that 'between sisters there was no right of firstborn'.[79] Beaumanoir then explained how the case was judged and himself formulated a rule about the right of firstborn between sisters by abstracting from the judgment:

> It was judged that Marie, the older sister, would take the dwelling before partition, and for half of the rest of the estate she would receive the homage of her younger sister, from which it appears that a sister has a right of firstborn only through dwelling.[80]

The norm enunciated by Beaumanoir was specifically based on the facts of the case. The fact that Marie was made to take the dwelling before partition led Beaumanoir to extrapolate the norm that the right of firstborn between sisters does exist and that it is based on being in control of the dwelling. The way he writes shows that the substantive rule was not expressly formulated by the parties or in the judgment. He himself was creating inferentially from the case's facts.

The *Coutumier de Champagne*, however, provides the clearest example of how a *coutumier* author could use records of judicial proceedings to formulate principles of customary law. This *coutumier* is unique for how it matched court practice and principles of law. While this text begins with an *ordinance* issued by the count of Champagne Thibault IV in 1224, the rest of the text is devoted to

---

[78] We see this form of reasoning in different ways throughout his text, sometimes in more or less detail. A couple more examples: 'a council of wise men convened to decide an issue "and by this it can be seen that ..."' (Beaumanoir, *Coutumes de Beauvaisis*, ed. Salmon, XV.524); 'and by this judgement you can see that ...' (*ibid.*, XXIV.689–690).

[79] *Ibid.*, XIV.472.   [80] *Ibid.*, XIV.473.

statements that declare custom and usage. Of fifty-nine provisions containing statements of custom, twenty-four were tied to court judgments, spanning nearly three decades and dated between 1270 and 1295.[81] The cases are drawn from different courts – from the court of the *bailli* of Chaumont to judgments of the Parlement of Paris – although the majority are from the Grands Jours de Troyes (both before and after the accession of Philip the Fair).[82]

A closer look at one section of the text illustrates how the author of this *coutumier* coaxed substantive statements of custom out of court judgments. This custom concerned the correct procedure for a widow to follow upon the death of her husband in order to secure his fief for their children if they are not yet of age:

It is the custom of Champagne that if a lady remains a widow [i.e. does not remarry] and has young children, that she must have custody and guardianship over them and she must take on their movables and debts if she wants to take them, and she must reclaim [the property] from the lord from whom they hold for the rightful claim of the children. And if there is a male heir, as soon as he reaches his fifteenth year, he must reclaim it from the lord. And if there is only a daughter, as soon as she is eleven years of age, she must reclaim it from the lord. And if they do not reclaim it, the lord can take the fief into his own hands until the time that they do reclaim it: indeed, a man is out of wardship in his fifteenth year and a woman at eleven years of age. This was judged by Lord John of Acre, who was then in charge of Champagne for count Haymon, in Troyes in the year 1278 in favour of the Lady of Moulin. Those present to make this judgment were Master Anselm of Montague, Florent of Roye (the lord of Broyes), Master Vincent of Pierrechatel (the chancellor of Champagne), Guillaume of the

---

[81] Two were sentences of the *bailli* of Chaumont, seven from the Grands Jours de Troyes before Philip the Fair acceded to the throne, eleven from the Grands Jours de Troyes in the reign of Philip the Fair (Portejoie, introduction to *Coutumier de Champagne*, ed. Portejoie, pp. 7ff).

[82] We have significant information on a number of the specific individuals in these cases, many of whom were important political, judicial, or administrative figures of the later thirteenth century. It is difficult to corroborate the cases here in other judicial records, but that is generally the case. Records of court judgments kept by *baillis* were still extremely 'meagre' in this period, as Poretjoie has said, while the original register of the Grands Jours de Troyes burned in a fire in 1737 (*ibid.*, p. 8). The four judgments of the Parlement of Paris here do not appear in the *Olim*, which contain a selective record and not every judgment of the Parlement (*ibid.*). There is no reason to doubt that the cases here are from archival record or the author's knowledge or experience. Here, these cases show how at least one *coutumier* author understood the relationship between the rules of custom he described and specific court cases.

Châtelet, Hugues of Chaumont, and Guillaume Puzvillains who was *bailli* of Champagne at the time. This is the usage we follow generally. [83]

Like nearly all sections of this *coutumier*, this one began by labelling the information as the custom of Champagne. The author then explained the specific procedure, stated a substantive rule concerning the age of majority in the country of Champagne, and supported this explanation of custom with a court judgment. The *coutumier* was constructed with and from records of court practice, here with significant detail about the particular case that proves the point. The rule of custom is linked to a case, even proved by it, but it is independent from the facts of the case. The case is subsumed under the rule of custom and not the other way around. Much of the *Coutumier de Champagne* follows this pattern of stating a norm with a corroborating case.

On rare occasions we can find a case referenced by a *coutumier* author corroborated by another source. For instance, Beaumanoir explained, 'Nevertheless as soon as the lord of a castle dies, the widow should remain in possession of the castle residence until the heir has provided her with an adequate dwelling according to the dower of the land and the place where the dower is situated, even though the widow has other residences on her land. And we saw a judgment on this matter for the lady of Milly in the king's court.'[84] There is a record of this judgment in the *Olim*.[85] This terse one-sentence record provides little information other than that the Lady of Milly won in a *causa dotalii* and retained dower rights in her castle.

---

[83] 'Il est coustume en Champagne que se une dame demore veuve et elle a petiz enfanz, qu'elle en doit avoir le bail et l'avouerie et en doit pourter les meubles et les debz si elle les veut panre, et doit repanre dou signour de cui il tiennent pour le droit des enfanz. Et se il y a hoirs male, si tost comme il est au quinsieme an, il doit repanre dou signour. Et si n'y avoit que files, si tost comme elles auroient XI anz, elle doit repanre dou signour. Et si ne repeannent, li sire puet asseoir sa main au fié jusques a tant qu'il reprannent: quar hons est hors d'avoerie au quinzainme an et fenme a XI anz. Ce fut jugié à Troies l'an M CC LXXVIII pour la dame de Moulin, par Monseigneur Jehan d'Acre qui lors gardoit Champagne pour lou conte Haimon. A ce faire furent Maistres Anceaux de Montagu, Florans de Roye, li sire de Broies, Maistres Vincens de Pierrechatel, chancelierz de Champagne, Guillaume dou Chatelet, Hugues de Chaumont, Guillaumes Puzvillains qui lors estoit bailli de Champagne. Ensinc en us'on generalmant' (*Coutumier de Champagne*, ed. Portejoie, s. V). See Evergates, *Feudal Society in Medieval France*, pp. 53–4.

[84] Beaumanoir, *Coutumes de Beauvaisis*, ed. Salmon, XIII.454.

[85] *Olim*, vol. 2, p. 208, no. 16.

Beaumanoir, on the other hand, explained the facts of the case, how it was resolved, and his reasoning for why the case gave rise to the rule above. Here, Beaumanoir speaks of a case that he says he saw in royal court; the truth of it is confirmed although nothing new is learned from the sparse record, and he uses this case to create an abstract rule.

Beaumanoir himself also hints at the discrepancy between the *coutumier* description and the record of the judicial proceeding. While there were certainly exceptions – notably in some of the records of judicial proceedings in royal court and the Norman Exchequer, especially near the close of the thirteenth century – records of judicial proceedings generally did not include especially detailed accounts of arguments made by parties and even less jury deliberations and reasoning.

This omission may actually have been a deliberate and practical choice: when delivering a judgment, Beaumanoir explained, it was better *not* to repeat the arguments the parties had made:

> When you give a judgment, there is no need to repeat the arguments of the two parties on which they request a judgment, indeed it is dangerous to repeat it all, for when the person giving the judgment repeats the substance [*procès*] of the trial, we have seen the party who was afraid of losing the decision say that the pleadings were not as stated, but were different, and he said what they were; and because of this disagreement the judgment had to be delayed until the recall from memory of the trial had been made: and some judgments have been delayed this way. [86]

Repeating the substance of the trial could lead the parties to contest that account of what had happened. This would create delays because witnesses to the trial would have to be convened to formally state what they recalled; this court 'record' (*recort*) was an oral recounting of the proceeding that consisted of the testimony of those who had judged the case as to what had taken place in the proceedings.[87] More information meant more problems. So, instead, Beaumanoir recommended terse judgments expressed in the following form:

> Therefore, you should not repeat everything; instead, it is enough for the person announcing the judgment to speak in this manner: 'Pierre and Jehan pleaded against each other on the seisin of such-and-such a piece of real property or concerning such-and-such a thing, and he should say what the thing is that is the subject of the suit. Each party has raised arguments in

[86] Beaumanoir, *Coutumes de Beauvaisis*, ed. Salmon, LXVII.1916.
[87] See Beaumanoir, *Coutumes de Beauvaisis*, ed. Salmon, XXXIV.1150-1.

support of his position; their arguments have been heard and declared ready for judgment, we find by law [*par droit*] that Jehan will take the seisin – or the ownership – of the subject of this suit.'[88]

The judgment should explain the final resolution of the case between the two parties; namely, in whose favour the issue was decided. We see this form in record after record – the parties involved and the issue at stake are described, but the arguments made are not. Or, if they are, then the weight assigned to those arguments, or the logic for the choice of one over the other, is largely if not completely absent.

Beaumanoir emphasized that this was an issue specifically for secular courts, which did not have the robust and consistent record-keeping practices of the ecclesiastical courts:

In the ecclesiastical courts, when the sentence is given they always repeat the pleadings; but there is no danger because the pleadings are written down and sealed by the court, so that the parties cannot say they were different, and for this reason the judge can repeat the pleadings without danger when the sentence is given. [89]

Pleadings were recorded in writing in ecclesiastical courts and could easily be read out if challenged. This provides crucial insight into why key information was so often absent from the very sorts of sources that modern historians would expect to include it.

Coherence and Incoherence

It is important to think about instances when a *coutumier* provides information that differs from records of practice. Some of the *coutumiers* show us that they were partially drawn from practice or, more specifically, the author's experience of practice. We can say that these *coutumiers* were made from practice and reflected practice. In turn, should we expect these *coutumiers* to provide an 'accurate' representation of practice, in the sense that details in a *coutumier* should precisely mirror practice as described in charters or records of courtroom practice?

This would only be the expectation if we saw the *coutumiers'* purpose to be a direct representation of practice rather than, as this book argues, to build a gestalt – a story of coherence – for customary

---

[88] Beaumanoir, *Coutumes de Beauvaisis*, ed. Salmon, LXVII.1916.   [89] *Ibid.*

law from practice and other sources. Beyond that, we would also need
to have an objectively correct practice, one that would be perceived the
same way by any individual.

That the latter was not the case is suggested by the descriptions of
high justice we examined in the *Établissements* and Beaumanoir's
Coutumes de Beauvaisis, which overlapped but did not match
perfectly. They differed as to the severity of the punishment: was the
loss of a limb enough, as the *Établissements* held, or did it have to be
death to qualify as an instance of high justice, as Beaumanoir asserted?
They also described categories of crime a bit differently. Was larceny
an issue of high justice as the *Établissements* explained or an issue of
low justice, as per Beaumanoir?

Perhaps the author of one text was mistaken, or perhaps that
practice had changed in the few years between the two texts. The
contrast shows at the very least that it was possible to notice or
emphasize various elements, or not to interpret them in the same
manner. Different individuals could thus see high justice in slightly
different ways in the 1270s and 1280s. It is also possible that,
while there was general agreement about the parameters of high
justice, some of its aspects were still hazy and not completely
settled.

The records of judicial proceedings in royal court show how often
custom was mentioned in contradictory terms or constituted proof
for contrary propositions and solutions.[90] In this sense, arguments
based on contrary customs or different presentations of custom in
judicial proceedings imply the co-existence of different, pre-existing
understandings of custom. These could co-exist and live in
contradiction peacefully enough, until a conflict arose that
provoked a contest between them. The *Olim*, records of the
Parlement of Paris, record many cases where contradictory visions
of custom had reached an impasse and required formal resolution.

---

[90] For instance, these contradictory allegations of custom in a case of high justice from
1260 show the co-existence of different visions of custom: '*predicti homines dicebant
quod per consuetudinem ipsius terre non tenebantur venire ad istam banniam eo
modo quo est proposita, cum ipsa consuetudo talis sit, quod nullus habeat talem
banniam nisi habeat totam altam justiciam (63). Capitulum negavit istam consuetudinem. Item dicebant ipsi homines quod dominus Rex est in saisina alte justicie in
Castro-Novo predicto*' (*Olim*, vol. 1, p. 117, no. 1).

This can be seen in the frequent phrase of customs alleged but not upheld: '*Non est probata ista consuetudo*'.[91] Different versions were valid and significant enough to be alleged in court, where they would be considered and declared acceptable or unacceptable by judgment of the court.

Coutumier authors were writing based on their impressions of practice, some of them without overt references to cases or records of practice at all. Because the texts are individual, and hence subjective, some incoherence is to be expected. Impressions of practice vary with different individuals: human perception varies based on their unique collection of experiences. Authors had their own personalities, training, knowledge, experience, education, personal history, community, external pressures, opinion, preferences, and interests. Impressions of practice also varied because the practice that they observed could itself be incoherent. This was certainly the case before the thirteenth century: the prevalence of compromise could attest not only to a desire for expedient resolution but also to the number of issues with no obvious custom to provide a clear solution.[92] The judicial ideal was not one that necessarily or consistently rested specifically on the consistent application of legal norms, nor was it identified with a fixed body of rules.[93]

The thirteenth century saw the development of new modes and spaces for thinking about and doing law in conjunction with an expansion of earlier practices. For instance, courts began to keep records of their judicial proceedings and also kept increasing numbers of transactional records and cartularies. Legal culture transformed rapidly, especially in the second half of the thirteenth century, and certainly looked very different by the end of the reign of Philip the Fair (r. 1285–1314).

---

[91] *Olim* vol. 1, p. 73, no. 24. For other examples of customs alleged in court but that were declared unproven: *Olim*, vol. 1, p. 100, no. 1; *Olim*, vol. 1, p. 139, no. 3; *Olim*, vol. 1, p. 150, no. 4. Other cases of parties asserting contradictory customs: '*preposito Silvanectensi asserente in contrarium quod consuetudo est ...*' (*Olim*, vol. 1, p. 108, no. 12). Or here, as in other cases, where one version of custom is chosen over another but without explanation of why that one won out: '*ad probandam hanc consuetudi-nem, quam dictus Theobaldus negabat, testes produceret* [...] *Per cujus inquestam inde factam inventum fuit quod consuetudo talis erat qualem proposuerat dictus Johannes*' (*Olim*, vol. 1, p. 351, no. 4).

[92] Stephen D. White, 'Inheritances and Legal Arguments in Western France', 94–5.

[93] Koziol, *Begging Pardon and Favor*, pp. 214–17.

Nonetheless, we should think about how quickly or completely we can reasonably expect custom to gain consistency or coherence.

Fundamentally, the attempt to create coherence out of what people do is inherent to the notion of custom itself. It is evident in the *coutumiers*, court proceedings, and the growing effort to ground procedures and rules mentioned in charters in the usage or custom of a specific jurisdiction.

We also see this effort at creating coherence in the evolving language of custom. By the last decades of the thirteenth century, we increasingly see references to settled custom – the sort that was unlikely to be contradicted. This was described as 'general custom' (*coutume generale*) and approved custom (*coutume approvée*) or, borrowing the language of canonists, 'notorious custom' (*coutume notoire*), and even 'common custom' (*comune costume*). These adjectives are in contrast to the notion of 'local' custom and to inchoate, undefined, and nebulous custom. Beaumanoir made a point of noting that his *Coutumes* would partially consist of 'clear usages and [. . .] clear customs that have been used and accustomed peaceably for a long time; and on the other hand, doubtful cases within the said county'.[94]

Beaumanoir had a panoply of adjectives and descriptors to distinguish different kinds of customs and the extent of their validity that went beyond those listed above. Customs could also be ancient, new, special, commonly used, or false.[95] That these adjectives were necessary tells us a lot about the status of custom. Customs not specified by an adjective or descriptor to indicate that they were established or commonly accepted might not have been so prevalent

---

[94] 'par clers usages et par cleres coustumes usees et acoustumees de lonc tans pesible-ment; et l'autre partie, des cas douteus en ladite contée' (Beaumanoir, *Coutumes de Beauvaisis*, ed. Salmon, prologue s. 6). He describes these and other sources of law in this section, which he says will 'confirm a large part of this book' (s. 6).

[95] *Coustumes* (prologue s. 1), *clers usage* (prologue s. 6), *cleres coutumes* (prologue s. 6), *le droit qui est communs a tous ou roiaume de France* (prologue s. 6), *coustumes des terres* (prologue s. 7), *coustume du païs* (I.26), *nostre coustume* (II.72), *la coustume de Beauvais* (IV.137), *coustume general* (VI.214), *droit commun* (VI.214), *ancienne coutume* (VI.227), *les coustumes des chasteleries le ou il manient* (VII.262), *coutume especial* (XI.314), *coustume bien approvee* (XII.366), *usé communément* (XV.536), *la coustume qui maintenant queurt* (XXOV.704), *droit commun de Beauvoisins* (XXV.724), *fausse coustume* (XXV.731), *coustume nouvele* (XXV.731), *coustume ou roiaume de France* (XLV.1434).

or generally accepted. As Beaumanoir noted, in some cases, 'the custom is so clear that it proves itself', but in others, where doubt arises about the custom, proof of the alleged custom might be required.[96] The challenge in thirteenth-century courts as well as in the *coutumiers* was to navigate between the certain and uncertain.

This can be seen in glimpses when the *coutumiers* mention divergent options around a custom. Only the *Usages de Bourgogne* overtly treats the issue of how to judge a case when the judges disagree: if the matter comes to judgment and they cannot agree, they should ask their lord to give them another day or to add another judge to help decide the case.[97] Otherwise, the *coutumiers* do not treat judicial deliberations. Deliberations generally do not feature in records of cases where judgments are simply given. Where the *coutumiers* tended to emphasize coherence, records of legal proceedings tended to emphasize resolution in the particular instance. Nonetheless, both coherence and incoherence were inherent to custom, and this was reflected, albeit in different ways, in the sources that discussed custom.

**

One of the challenges presented by the *coutumiers* is how this new form of legal literature linked to social and legal practice. *Coutumiers* were not just describing practice as it was, which means that gap analysis can only provide limited insight. Those *coutumier* authors who show us how they used records, experience, or knowledge drawn from practice show us that they were transforming that practice by writing about it in a unique fashion. Most obviously, they were transforming it into a coherent body of rules and practices that could be learned as a 'system'.

The creation of coherence in the *coutumiers* complemented the recognition of stable social practices and the work of the courts in choosing which custom to uphold, at the expense of others. Practice was in part stable, coherent, and generally accepted and, in part, unstable, incoherent, and the subject of disagreement. The *coutumiers* may not be perfect reflections of practice, and practice itself was not always easily discernible or the subject of consensus.

---

[96] Beaumanoir, *Coutumes de Beauvaisis*, ed. Salmon, XXXIX.1155.
[97] *Ancien Coutumier de Bourgogne*, ed. Marnier and Marnier, s. 8.

The contribution of the *coutumiers* was not that they perfectly reflected practice but that they created coherence and theorized custom. They took the impressionistic landscape of custom in court practice, transactions, and human behaviour and transformed it into a knowable, holistic customary law.

7

Dynamic Text: Dialectic, Manuscript Culture, and Customary Law

That *coutumier* authors saw their texts as written, but not fixed, aligns uneasily with our modern narratives of writtenness. The *coutumiers* stand Janus-like at a juncture in history that saw the 'transition from orality to literacy', when 'the first written codes began appearing'.[1] Traditionally scholars have interpreted the texts as the culmination of society's recognition that it operated according to normative patterns, ones that began to seem obligatory. This dawning consciousness that custom 'existed' resulted in the 'crystallization' of oral and personal custom and the 'transfer' of these crystallized rules into writing, which inaugurated territorial and written law.[2]

Scholars describe a purely oral customary law as flexible and its content as constantly changing and relatively recent.[3] Though it

---

[1] Cohen, *Crossroads of Justice*, pp. 28–29. See also Clanchy, *From Memory to Written Record*; Ong, *Orality and Literacy*; Havelock, *The Muse Learns to Write*; Goody, *The Logic of Writing*; Stock, *The Implications of Literacy*; Danet and Bogoch, 'From Oral Ceremony to Written Document'; Matthew Innes, 'Memory, Orality and Literacy in an Early Medieval Society'; Dobozy, 'From Oral Custom to Written Law'; Geary, 'Oblivion Between Orality and Textuality'.

[2] 'Il fallut sans doute quelques années pour que l'on prenne conscience qu'il existait des coutumes. La redaction des coutumiers allait être le résultat de cette prise de conscience' (Ourliac, 'Législation, coutumes et coutumiers', p. 482).

[3] Clanchy, 'Remembering the Past and the Good Old Law', p. 172. The modern tendency to think in terms of rules and enacted law has led scholars and jurists to 'force custom to look like what they have been trained to believe law is', namely rules in statute books, even though 'natural' custom is defined by its malleability (Kadens, 'Custom's Past', pp. 11, 16).

operated within a mythology of timelessness, its consistency lay 'in the living legal sense of the people, not in specific provisions'.[4] Scholars contrast these meanings to written custom – writing froze custom in place and made it difficult to change.[5] The language of transfer, codification, and the common phrase of 'the setting of custom in writing' (*la mise par écrit*) have all framed our understanding of the *coutumiers*.[6] These common descriptors imply a known and obvious body of rules that were inscribed from life into text and then became fixed in that text, no longer flexible or adaptable.[7] These accounts are striking for their lack of individual actors and lack of human agency: as they describe it, the history of the *coutumiers* is an account of impersonal social forces that led to the petrification of custom through its inscription.

These interpretations of the *coutumiers'* utility hold that they were instructions for judges, analysed for their 'correct' description of specific rules and critiqued when they did not include rules scholars deem significant.[8] Or they are described more generally as manuals for laymen, necessary in a society where the wrong form of plea could lose a case.[9] In both interpretations, the *coutumiers* have been framed as pedagogical because they teach the content of specific rules of customary law and the correct specific forms of speech to use in court.

These interpretations situate the *coutumiers* in a formalist legal culture. Formalism in the medieval legal context is usually taken to mean that the wrong form of plea could lose a case and that trials

---

[4] *Ibid.*   [5] Goody, *The Logic of Writing*, chap. 5.

[6] '*la mise par écrit ... cristallise cet instant ...* ' (Gouron, 'La coutume en France au Moyen Âge', p. 207).

[7] 'the only way to preserve custom and the practical knowledge of custom was by locking it into written mold' (Cohen, *Crossroads of Justice*, p. 32). Cohen goes on to explain the *coutumiers* authors were not conservatives who did not want custom to change, and they welcomed increasing centralization, but she nonetheless links writtenness to the preservation of custom and attempts at fixity (*ibid.*, p.33).

[8] Van Dievoet, *Les coutumiers, les styles, les formulaires*, pp. 64, 47. Van Dievoet describes them as aiming to instruct judges specifically (*ibid.*, p. 64). Robert Jacob also noted the pedagogical purpose of Beaumanoir's *Coutumes de Beauvaisis* (Jacob, 'Beaumanoir versus Revigny', p. 235).

[9] Ong, 'Orality, Literacy, and Medieval Textualization', 7. Cohen describes the *coutumiers* as manuals for laymen, 'in the nature of memoranda, a text to be referred to for information concerning material that carried its own immanent authority' and that were extremely necessary in a society 'in which the wrong form of plea could lose a case' (Cohen, *Crossroads of Justice*, p. 31).

followed precise formulae, the slightest departure from which could invalidate an entire proceeding.[10] The *coutumiers* have been an important source for the scholarly depiction and creation of the formalist nature of customary law.[11] The formalist view of procedure in legal practice was first critiqued by Yvonne Bongert, and Fredric Cheyette and Susan Reynolds reinforced this critique.[12] While the legal practice of thirteenth-century northern France is no longer viewed as formalist, the formalist story for the *coutumiers* has not been replaced by a new story.

The first *coutumiers* permit us to tell a different story about the descriptions of procedure and form of speech in these texts: they capture a fundamental change in legal culture by which holistic and systematized text began to complement an oral legal culture. This oral culture already had record-keeping practices, to which the *coutumier*

[10] Bloch, R. Howard, *Medieval French Literature and Law*, p. 23. Legal formalism in modern law, also described as a 'mechanical jurisprudence', means a method of interpretation with a focus on technicality, method, and 'correct' application of law rather than a correct or just result (Roscoe Pound, 'Mechanical Jurisprudence', pp. 607–608). For the medieval context, it is more commonly taken to mean strict adherence to form in the sense of correct procedure or correct form of plea.

[11] Bongert showed the flexibility of French law based on charter evidence in order to make the point that the formalist impression of high medieval French law built by scholars – on the basis of the *coutumiers* – was wrong. She thus made an argument about how we view practice but not how we view the *coutumiers*. That records of practice showed flexibility rather formalism left the impression that the *coutumiers* were out of touch with live customary law ('... encore que le formalisme apparaisse moin accentué dans les actes de la pratique que ne tendraient à faire croire les coutumiers' (Bongert, *Recherches sur les cours laïques*, pp. 183ff)). Ultimately, this leaves the impression that the *coutumiers* are formalist texts.

[12] Bongert used charter evidence to show that judicial procedure – outside of the ordeal and trial by battle – lacked the formalism attributed to it (*ibid.*, p. 183). Usage (*usages*), as she showed, was still variable and had not yet acquired the character of 'obligatory' custom (*ibid.*). Cheyette echoed her findings, noting that historians 'had generally assumed without evidence that the formalism of thirteenth-century custom was but a mitigated form of an even greater formalism during the dark centuries that preceded. But the opposite seems to have been the case. Not only did courts scarcely survive, but when they did function, there was hardly any consistency, still less formalism, to their procedure', and this only changed with the new class of legal professionals who brought in novel procedures and methods of proof (Cheyette, 'Custom, Case Law and Medieval "Constitutionalism"', 374). Being sceptical about the formalism of feudal procedure was still an exceptional view in the late 1970s (Bloch, *Medieval French Literature and Law*, p. 23). Susan Reynolds provided further support, emphasizing that the view of a formal and ritualized medieval law was created by our own assumptions that these were the characteristics of 'primitive law', which guided the interpretation of information and created the assumed results (Reynolds, *Kingdoms and Communities*, pp. 37–8).

authors added a new textual form. These texts are part of a continuum of oral and literate cultures rather than markers of transition from one to the other and reveal different styles of interaction with written text.[13] The *coutumiers* expanded the literary forms relating to secular law and, because of the choice of the vernacular language, also expanded the audience that could interact with written aspects of secular law.

This chapter makes two arguments about the continuum of oral and literate cultures. First, I argue that the heart of orality is not just the spoken word and verbal communication but interaction, conversation, and communication. In the case of law, it is often also dialectical, part of a process of reasoning and argumentation. The authors of the *coutumiers* were showing readers and listeners how to successfully participate in the courtroom dialectic, one that was becoming specialized and not easily known or intuitive but that had to be learned. This task went beyond textualizing oral forms and providing scripts for court elocution. *Coutumier* authors were teaching their audience how to think in terms of law and its categories. They made the subject teachable by making it coherent, as we have seen; by explaining the meaning of specialized or unfamiliar terminology in ordinary language; and by showing how to identify a legal issue. They taught how a strong legal argument sounded, in which claims were not made subjectively in terms of anger or sorrow but in terms relevant to law. I do not interpret this as a sign of formalism but of a specializing practice.

Second, I argue that the modes of thought that constituted customary law were conditioned by manuscript culture. It is well known that texts varied between manuscripts – every modern critical edition of the *coutumiers* has a discussion of the manuscripts in the frontmatter, and the authors of those editions laboured hard to examine the different manuscript versions of texts in order to provide the modern reader with a relatively representative version. While invaluable, we must remember that the *coutumiers* did not circulate in the medieval period in this standardized form but in manuscripts

---

[13] Simon Teuscher makes this important insight when he describes different 'styles of interacting with legal records' which did not neatly stand at the transition between oral and literate cultures but within a continuum between the two (Teuscher, *Lords' Rights and Peasant Stories*, p. 195). This continuum was bookended by the material aspect of writing used for public display on one end and textualized chancery practices oriented towards specific written content at the other end (*ibid.*).

that differed from one another. Readers and listeners would have had a slightly or significantly different understanding of the customs of a certain area depending on the particular manuscript at hand.

This says something important about how written texts were assimilated into a predominately oral legal culture. It also says something important about the nature of textualized customary law. For one, the *coutumiers* and their manuscript cultures show that custom was not simply a set of legal data to be recognized but was also something composed and re-composed.[14] As we will see, the manuscript culture of customary law complicates modern understandings of medieval ideas and assumptions about the fixity of legal texts. Whether the changes made to the text were small or large, each manuscript constituted one voice in a conversation about the meaning of custom, both as a whole and in its specific provisions. The changes generally evince a continuing dialectic, a living law that was not pinned down through text.

Montesquieu once remarked in passing the forgotten sentiment that the goal of the *coutumiers* 'was rather to transmit a judicial practice than contemporary usages on the disposition of goods'.[15] That the *coutumiers* transmitted a framework for how to think and do law made the texts valuable throughout the fourteenth and fifteenth centuries, when they continued to be copied. While some of the specific rules therein might have changed, the *coutumier* authors' purpose in writing custom, ultimately, was to change patterns of thought and therefore teach the audience a set of ideas and skills that would permit them to perform convincingly in lay court.

The Dialectic of Custom

Narrative reconstructions of the court process can help us imagine thirteenth-century northern French customary culture, especially when they provide detail about substantive deliberations that are

---

[14] The writing of custom did mirror a legal culture and practice that was changing, and it was true, in some ways, that 'the ever-changing nature of custom made it very difficult to know what it was' (Cohen, *Crossroads of Justice*, p. 32). At the same time, the court process as well as the *coutumiers* both constituted mechanisms that produced knowledge of custom. Notions of 'notorious' custom and 'general' custom indicated some customs were well known and largely unquestioned.

[15] Charles-Louis de Secondat, Baron de Montesquieu, *Œuvres de Montesquieu*, p.493.

often missing or sparse in court records before the fourteenth century. Unlike records of court proceedings, the *Roman de Renart* provides an unusually long and detailed account of deliberations and thus provides a glimpse of the sorts of deliberation and discussion that must have animated the decision making of the courts.[16]

To recall the tale (see Chapter 4), the wolf Isangrin had accused Renart the fox of raping his wife Hersent and demanded justice in the court of the lion king, Noble.[17] The king granted Isangrin his trial, mostly so that the wolf would not take private vengeance, and reminded the court that Renart's love for Hersent was a mitigating factor as he promised a judgment according to the practice of his court.[18] The king then turned to the camel, the great jurist sitting next to him, and asked him whether he had heard such a complaint in his land and how it should be resolved.[19] The erudite camel provided a considered opinion based on canon law and continued with a forceful speech reminding the king of his role in upholding justice. After this speech, which the barons received with a mixture of joy and irritation, the king called on the animals at court to judge the case.[20]

The events that followed illustrate the conversational dialectic that constituted customary law. The king turned to the peers and framed the legal question for them: if one was overwhelmed with passion, must one be culpable of having cuckolded the other?[21] The jury-member barons on the council of peers, 'the most valiant and greater of the beasts', moved away from the royal tent, retreating in typical form to deliberate, express their opinions, and decide how to judge Isangrin's initial plaint.[22]

---

[16] This is, of course, an animal tale and does not replicate practice directly. But it does provide a view of the sorts of arguments and approaches that made sense in thinking through legal problems and to discuss in judicial deliberations.

[17] *Le Roman de Renart*, ed. Fukumoto, Harano, and Suzuki, trans. Bianciotto, vol. 9, pp. 1–124.

[18] 'Selonc l'esgart de ma meson' (*ibid.*, vol. 9, pp. 167–70, 178–81).

[19] *Ibid.*, vol. 9, pp. 182ff.

[20] 'Si jugiez de ceste clamor' (*ibid.*, vol. 9, p. 239).

[21] 'Les plus vaillans, les graignors bestes / Si jugiez de ceste clamor / Se cil qui est sorpris d'' *Ibid.*, vol. 9, pp. 235.

[22] *Ibid.*, vol. 9, pp. 243–5. The text describes an enormous group of over one thousand people (*ibid.*, vol. 9, p. 246).

The jurors were also parodied but for different reasons from the camel. In the many pages of deliberations that follow, most jurors are exposed for having unseemly, crude motives such as greed, spite, fear, and concern for family connections.[23] Nonetheless, they expressed opinions that were both reasoned and sophisticated and give us a unique view about legal reasoning in the lay courts of the first part of the thirteenth century. As Mary Jane Schenck writes, the scene provides a 'serious discussion' about proving the truth through witness testimony as well as issues of fairness.[24]

The first animal to speak is Brichemer the deer, who gives an opinion based on the sort of reasoning appropriate to the forum:

Lords, he said, listen now,	Seignors, fait il, ore escoutez,[25]
You have heard from Ysangrin,	Vos avez oï d'Ysangrin,
Our friend and neighbour,	Nostre ami et nostre voisin,
How he has accused Renart.	Con il a Renart accusé.
But [by] our usage in court,	Mes nous avons en cort usé,
When one complains of a wrong	Quant l'en se plaint de forfeiture
And one seeks to have Justice	Et l'en en velt avoir droiture,[26]
It is necessarily to prove it by a third party,	Prover l'estuet par tierce main,
Since anyone could from one day to another	Que tiex porroit d'ui a demain
Make a complaint at will	Fere clamor a son voloir
Which could cause harm to another.	Dont autre se porroit doloir.

Brichemer opened by noting Isangrin's close ties with the other lords and his strong social standing. Brichemer empathized with Isangrin and was even angry (*s'aïra*) on his behalf. At the same time, he would not manipulate the process for him. He explained that a man's wife was under his power, and he could have her lie for him, so a wife's support of her husband's statement was not a reliable form of

---

[23] Gravdal, *Ravishing Maidens*, p. 74.

[24] Schenck, 'Paulin Paris' Influence', 127, 128.

[25] The typical opening for any romance or epic should be recognized here. For more on how the procedures of feudal courts, based on formula, ritual, and communal forms, mirrored those of literary performances, see Bloch, *Medieval French Literature and Law*.

[26] I have translated *droiture* as 'Justice' because the text is referring to justice in terms of archetypal ideal justice in the sense of 'what is right' or 'right, righteousness, equity, due, or what is straight'. *Droiture* is what people seek at court, to have their right proclaimed or restored. In the *coutumiers* as well as in vernacular literature, *droiture* seems to express this ideal much more often than *justice*, which is more specifically related to the powers of justice, such as jurisdiction, holding court, and enforcement.

proof.²⁷ Brichemer explained court usage and then noted the rationale behind it, which established the usage as reasonable. His conclusion was that another witness had to be found. Brichemer's reasoning, then, was one based on procedural fairness – his feelings of anger were subordinate to upholding a customary procedural requirement that protects parties from the possible collusion within married couples.

With customary usage established, other parties brought up other arguments that weighed on the matter. Brun the bear reminded the jurors of Isangrin's position as constable and his excellent reputation.²⁸ Baucent the boar replied that such arguments could also be made on behalf of Renart, the only difference being that other people would be making them, and that the ties between husband and wife were such that she would support him in anything, which could be used to defraud people – and thus he supported Brichemer's opinion.²⁹ Plateau the fallow deer spoke next, reminding the jurors of other claims in the plaint: Renart took meat from Isangrin's house wrongfully and by force; Renart urinated on Isangrin's children to denigrate him; he beat them, tore out their hair, and called them bastards.³⁰ This, Plateau noted, called for great compensation because if Renart got away with doing this once, he would do it again.³¹

Brun the bear supported this argument, outraged that a good man could be dishonoured and wronged without getting reparation for it, and pointed his finger at the king, whom he felt should avenge his barons against such injustice.³² He then told a story about an outrage Renart had committed towards him, not in the spirit of a formal complaint, but to show what Renart was capable of.³³ Baucent the boar then reminded everyone about proper procedure: this was merely

---

²⁷ The text points to a shift in public opinion about expert testimony and explains that this testimony cannot be proved as that of a physician: wives 'ne sont mie fuisicïent / Itel tesmoing a esprover / Autre li covendra trouver' (*Le Roman de Renart*, ed. Fukumoto, Harano, and Suzuki, vol. 9, pp. 273–6).

²⁸ *Ibid.*, vol. 9, pp. 277–89.   ²⁹ *Ibid.*, vol. 9, pp. 290–312.

³⁰ *Ibid.*, vol. 9, pp. 313–23. For more on the importance of reputation in the Middle Ages, see T. S. Fenster and and Daniel Lord Smail, *Fama*.

³¹ *Le Roman de Renart*, ed. Fukumoto, Harano, and Suzuki, vol. 9, pp. 324–6.

³² *Ibid.*, vol. 9, pp. 334–43. The king in this narrative is not a strong, good king.

³³ *Ibid.*, vol. 9, pp. 489–90.

the first part of the process and the arguments of the adverse party had to be examined before right could be determined.[34] As Baucent noted, once the accusation was heard, the defence then had to be heard, and afterwards the respective rights of both parties had to be examined before reaching a conclusion – only then can the nature of the penalty be decided, by the judgment of the court.[35] Only the monkey Cointereau sided with Renart, irritating Brun the bear, who declared that Renart should be seized, bound, and thrown into jail so an example would be made out of him.[36] Instead, the assembled peers decided on mediation, a settlement that would bring peace between the parties. Brichemer the deer, whom the narrator considered wiser than the others, noted that when wrongful actions or words are neither manifest nor confessed, the judicial proceedings that lead to the maiming or death of a man should be avoided, and instead peace must be made.[37]

This tale gives us insight into different ideas of cultural legitimacy, legal thought, and conceptions of justice in the world that directly preceded the lay jurists who wrote the *coutumiers*. The narrator had defined views about the forms of authority, legal reasoning, and language that were appropriate and inappropriate in a court of law. The camel's learned pedigree was recognizably of the highest level. The mockery of the camel demonstrates the narrator's preference for one sort of legal knowledge over another, and presumably the audience would be laughing along, as this was their view as well.

The jury's mode of reasoning was quite different from that of the polyglot camel (examined in Chapter 4), who began his legal opinion by citing the textual authority of the *Decretum*, explaining how canon law dealt with the violation of matrimony. The peers, on the other hand, were concerned with how rape was dealt with in the secular courts, and the first opinion voiced explained the proper usage of the court.

---

[34] *Ibid.*, vol. 9, pp. 507–13.
[35] 'Mout seroit sages qui savroit / Jugier d'un droit, et il n'avroit / l'autre partie encore atainte. / Et un droit après l'autre render / Tant que l'en viengne a la parsonme [. . .] Conment sera de l'amendise / Par le jugement de justice' (*ibid.*, vol. 9, pp. 511–17, 529–30).
[36] *Ibid.*, vol. 9, pp. 531–70.   [37] *Ibid.*, vol. 9, pp. 601–6.

Their discussion continued with matters of proof and the sorts of
precedents that might ensue, depending on their decision, vacillating
between the various options they had and different views of the
ultimate policy goal: some animals were more interested in
retributive justice and wanted to see the scoundrel Renart pay for his
misdeeds; others highlighted the importance of procedural justice and
placed the process above what they clearly viewed to be substantive
justice; still others focused on the restorative justice that would
compensate Isangrin for the harm done to him, his family, and his
honour.[38]

The *Roman de Renart* offers a glimpse into a spectrum of opinion
about how to properly resolve a case and the inherent uncertainty of
law that animates court cases until the moment of resolution.[39]
Discussion was the mechanism for grappling with this uncertainty.
The forms of knowledge and reasoning displayed by the jury-member
peers – citing court usage, discussing manner of proof, considering
precedent, thinking about the social consequences of various
approaches – illustrate how potentially expansive the discussion at
the heart of customary law could be. Generally, this suggests the
important place of conversation, deliberation, and dialectic to the
court process and thus in the production of custom. This discursive
view of customary law is supported by a manuscript of the *Coutumier
d'Artois*, as can be seen in Figures 7.1 and 7.2. Custom was approved
or disapproved as part of a court performance where different ideas
confronted each other. It was a conversation between 'the way we
did things in the past', 'how we do things now', and 'the manner in
which we ought to do things'. The *coutumier* texts were outgrowths of
this legal culture. Dynamic oral conversation did not end with text but
continued, albeit differently, within the inherently dynamic context of
medieval manuscript culture.

---

[38] One of the basic critiques of the narrator seems to be that these all fail in different
ways – the first necessitates a willingness to play beyond the rules, the other is overly
rule-bound and permits the guilty to walk away unpunished because of problems of
proof, and the last puts all the power into the hands of the person who committed the
wrong in the first place. Ultimately, they decide on a peace agreement, which later
fails, but it would have addressed the needs of the victim without running into the
problems of proof that a trial would require.

[39] This uncertainty is there throughout the debate that constitutes the trial as well as
judicial and jury deliberations.

FIGURE 7.1 Customary law as conversation. This image from a fourteenth-century manuscript of the *Coutumier d'Artois*, like other illuminations in this manuscript, emphasizes the centrality of conversation, deliberation, and dialectic in the visual culture of customary law. It features a discussion between teacher and student, a part within the text that the author of the text drew from Pierre de Fontaines. *Coutumier d'Artois*, Bibliothèque nationale de France, ms. fr. 5249, fol. 2v.

FIGURE 7.2 The lively nature of conversation in the courtroom. The dynamism of speech is emphasized in gestures of communication in this courtroom scene, from the same manuscript as above. Speech is also stressed in the incipit of the text, which states that 'this book speaks of the customs and usages of Artois' (Cis livres parole de coustumes et des usages d'Artoys). *Coutumier d'Artois*, Bibliothèque nationale de France, ms. fr. 5249, fol. 12v.

Manuscript Culture and a Dynamic Written Custom

The *coutumiers* were largely vernacular compositions and as such vernacular authorial culture and manuscript culture is integral to understanding them. The *coutumiers* circulated freely in handwritten copies: after medieval authors produced a work and were paid by their patrons, any claim to authorial ownership or control ended.[40] Just as these authors might incorporate the text of others into their own, often without attribution, later manuscript versions of their own texts were comprised of variant readings that ranged from dialect changes and small changes in lettering or word choice to more significant alterations such as the excision or addition of sections.[41] This context is essential to understanding any information presented by a manuscript text and must inform our broader understanding of customary law.

Authors of critical editions have long introductory sections that describe each manuscript or, if there are many, different family branches of the text. This work has involved a gargantuan effort of locating manuscripts and identifying their differences, a great service to the field that has made the texts accessible and easier to work with and discuss. The goal of the critical edition was to establish an original or accurate version – a correct text – and then to note its deviations or misunderstandings.[42]

The effect of this method has been to conform a medieval customary law that did not have fully stable texts into a modern mould whereby law is captured in unitary texts that reflect one correct and invariable version. Legal scholars are thus well aware of textual variation but have treated it as a problem to be resolved by scholarly method in order to arrive at a correct

---

[40] David F. Hult, 'Manuscripts and Manuscript Culture', p. 15.
[41] *Ibid.*, p. 18. Historically, the textual changes were not viewed positively: from the later fourteenth century, Renaissance philologists specifically sought out older exemplars of Latin texts to come closest to an original free of 'gothic' corruptions (Michael G. Sargent, 'Manuscript Textuality', p. 228).
[42] Most critical editions of the first *coutumiers* are from the nineteenth century. In the 1920s, Joseph Bédier argued that editorial work should instead focus on a 'best text' edition, one based on a manuscript that seems to be the best representative of an author's original rather than a version reconstructed by a modern editor (*ibid.*, p. 231). This way, the edited text at least corresponds directly to one manuscript of the medieval period rather than being a composite text that corresponds directly to no actual medieval manuscript. This method of textual research has characterized editorial work in the Romance language tradition throughout the twentieth century (*ibid.*).

(unitary) customary law, rather than as an important aspect of legal ideas in the Middle Ages that has larger implications for customary law.

Literary scholars have engaged in rich discussions about manuscript variation, especially with respect to vernacular writing. In his examination of vernacular literature, Paul Zumthor observes how frequently authorial anonymity was accompanied by textual variation that involved changes ranging from dialect and word edits to large-scale rewriting, rearrangement, and loss. He termed this aspect of vernacular literature *mouvance*, which he saw as a specific characteristic of an oral culture that co-existed with a nascent culture of writing.[43] Bernard Cerquiglini further developed these ideas by shifting his analysis away from the interaction between the oral and the written and towards *variance*, the relationship between different written instantiations of a medieval work.[44] For Cerquiglini, *variance* defined medieval textual culture and was not only an artefact of anonymity or orality. He saw the differentiation between the author and the scribe of medieval text as arbitrary and artificial, as each variant version provided an authoritative version of the text.[45]

These ideas have had a fundamental impact on the study of vernacular literature and are fundamental to understanding how medieval texts worked and were received. They must thus also be vital to the understanding of texts of customary law and must inform our interpretation of custom, as it comes to us, in written text.[46]

---

[43] See Zumthor, *Essai de poétique médiévale.*   [44] See Cerquiglini, *Éloge de la variante.*

[45] *Ibid.*, p. 57. As David Hult noted, 'in a certain way, the very notion of an edition of a medieval work runs counter to the nature of medieval textuality. The essential variability of manuscript copies is analogous to, but less dramatic than, the variability of texts produced by oral tellers of tales who, individually, recount a different version of a given story at each performance and, collectively, through tales being passed down through generations of storytellers, produce radically different versions that can scarcely be considered the same "text"' (Hult, 'Manuscripts and Manuscript Culture', p.16).

[46] While manuscript variance has been studied more significantly with respect to vernacular literature, and while I largely focus on variance in vernacular customary law because of the nature of my source base, it is important to emphasize that Latin texts could and did vary as well. Variation between manuscripts has been scrupulously theorized for vernacular literature, and I draw on these studies to understand the *coutumiers*. However, it must be significant that Latin texts of custom varied as well – this is the case for the Norman *coutumiers*, as well as *Glanvill* and *Bracton*. This may point less to a distinction between Latin and the vernacular than one between lay courts and learned circles (scholastic or university). However, nothing conclusive can be said without a study of variation among Latin legal texts, written both for court and learned contexts. While aspects of variance discussed here certainly resonate with Latin texts of customary law, these Latin texts were written for a different sort of

The importance of textual uniformity to university legal studies can be seen in new ways of maintaining textual integrity across copies developed in that milieu in the thirteenth century. Known as the *pecia* system, this system permitted consistent copying and also accelerated the supply of texts, permitting a number of people to copy the same text and standardize it so that students would be reading the same version of a given text.[47] This system was restricted to specific fields and available only at some universities.[48] This, in addition to scribal emendations that aimed to present a correct text, went some way towards ensuring a uniform Roman law, at least for the texts that formed its basis.

Meanwhile, some manuscripts of the thirteenth-century *coutumiers* have small annotations in the margins and the occasional emendation, but generally commentary existed as textual variation. This variation was incorporated into the text, and there was no differentiation – visually or intellectually – between an original text and later commentary. Some northern French *coutumiers* do appear in the fourteenth-century manuscripts glossed, but this is not a general or common approach to these texts. The first *coutumiers* have no standard or ordinary gloss.

Written custom was a live practice instantiated in different versions of *coutumier* texts. Universities and lay courts involved different

---

audience and existed within a different cultural spectrum of Latinate learning and written production, a significant part of which was linked to universities that prized the urtext and textual uniformity. A study of the forms of variation and uniformity across Latinate legal writing would be most welcome.

[47] Graham Pollard, 'The *Pecia* System in Medieval Universities', pp. 145–6. The first reference to the system occurred in a contract in 1228, between the commune of Vercelli and some masters of the of the university of Padua, where the community promised to create a system that made copies of text available 'complete and correct as much in text as in gloss' (*competentia et correctam tam in textu quam in gloxa*) (*ibid.*, p. 146–8). The *pecia* system worked in the following manner: stationers affiliated with the universities would take an official copy of a text and its gloss (called an *exemplar*) and had it copied into the *pecia* format, a pamphlet-type section of the text (four to twelve sheets), the accuracy of which was carefully monitored by the university (L'Engle, 'Production and Purchase', p. 41). Then, professional scribes or students who were copying books for themselves could rent the copied *exemplar*, *pecia* by *pecia*, picking up the next after returning the previous (*ibid.*, p. 46).

[48] At least eleven universities had this system, and in France, it existed both in the universities of Paris and Toulouse. No trace of the *pecia* has been found in Montpellier, Orleans, Angers, and Avignon, even though the university statutes did provide for *pecia* systems (Pollard, 'The *Pecia* System in Medieval Universities', p. 148). It was generally restricted to the service of the higher faculties: Theology, Canon law, and Civil law (*ibid.*, p. 150).

cultures of scribal practice, textual ideology, and intellectual philosophy. Even Beaumanoir, who invoked the idea of fixity against change, intimated that fixity did not seem possible and that customs were always open to the potential of change.

The copying of a *coutumier* involved the reproduction of a text, but the reproduction was not an exact replica of the model text: every version reflected some balance of variance and invariance. I focus on a discussion of variance here not because invariance does not merit study. The *coutumiers* indeed had stable aspects to their texts, and the copies were recognizably those of the earlier text. Both the parts of the text that varied and those that did not could be the product of scribal intent, though variation could also be accidental.[49]

Some *coutumiers* survive in one manuscript copy – *Le livre des constitutions demenées el Chastelet de Paris* and *Li Usages de Bourgogne* – and obviously have a unitary text. *Li livre de jostice et de plet* survives in one copy as well. The more manuscripts of a *coutumier*, the more they tell a story about legal variance.

On a minor level, spelling and dialect could vary between texts, as there was no set spelling for the vernacular. Occasionally words are adjusted but do not significantly have an impact on the meaning of the text.[50] Sometimes words are removed, apparently in the interest of economy and elegance.[51] Correction, as Daniel Wakelin has shown, 'although it reflects external pressures – cultural expectations; institutional habits of work – is not an automatic or unreflexive thing to do; it witnesses processes of thinking consciously about language and text'.[52] Variants were often minor changes made by scribes, but

---

[49] Daniel Wakelin notes that faithful and accurate copying must have been the intentional result of significant effort and cannot have been accidental; meanwhile, variance could have been either intentional or accidental and we should beware of interpreting unintentional changes, slips, misreadings, or misunderstandings as being manifestations of scribal intention (Wakelin, *Scribal Correction and Literary Craft*, pp. 55ff (chap. 3 generally)).

[50] For instance, 'les mesfesans' appears as 'les maufaiteurs' and 'les malfesteurs' in different manuscripts of Beaumanoir's *Coutumes de Beauvaisis* (Beaumanoir, *Coutumes de Beauvaisis*, ed. Salmon, I.14).

[51] Some manuscripts of the *Coutumes de Beauvaisis* refer the reader to 'the chapter which speaks of recusing judges' (il est dit ou chapitre qui parole de refuser juges) while others refer to 'the chapter on recusing judges' (ou chapitre de refuser juges), omitting words that are not necessary to sustain the meaning of the text (*ibid.*, I.40).

[52] Wakelin, *Scribal Correction and Literary Craft*, p. 4.

even these are not devoid of meaning. One word was preferred over another likely because scribes were paying close attention to textual detail and saw their adjustments as more accurate transcriptions.[53] These adjustments should be seen as signs of respect for and deference to the earlier source and are very common.[54]

On other occasions, a few words were changed but less innocuously, as they transformed the meaning in the earlier version. Certainly, scribes could make mistakes, and not every variation was intentional. It is difficult, however, not to see intention behind the addition or subtraction of words that change the legal substance of the text. A passage concerning dowries in the *Ancien Coutumier de Champagne* shows how the emendation of only a few words effectively transformed the law conveyed in the earlier text. One manuscript described a rule about women receiving their dowries when there were no conditions to the dowry.[55] Another stipulated that the rules expressed applied only to noble women.[56] Still another specified that the rules in this section also applied to movables and debts.[57] These were not massive textual changes, but each version actually presented a substantively different version of custom.

Another example of the implications of *variance* in the legal context where only a few words were changed can be seen in the *Établissements de Saint Louis*, whose different manuscripts describe slightly different rules about what happens to the property of a suicide. One manuscript said that the moveable property of a person who hanged, drowned, or otherwise killed themselves belonged to the baron.[58] Another specified that this sanction applied only if the person died without confession, unshriven.[59] Yet another noted that the baron obtained both the movables *and* the inheritance (so the immovables, or real property).[60] The different manuscripts of the *Établissements* change a few words or partial sentences fairly often, and sometimes, as in this example, the changes consequentially amend the rule or procedure described.

---

[53] *Ibid.*   [54] *Ibid.*, p. 41.
[55] 'Conmant femme est douaie s'il n'i a condicion' (*L'ancien coutumier*, ed. Portejoie, IX, see p. 154n.a).
[56] 'De douaire de noble fame', m.s. DH (*ibid.*, IX).
[57] 'Des douaires des nobles et des meubles et debtes', m.s. I (*ibid.*, IX).
[58] *Établissements*, ed. Viollet, I.XCII, see p. 150n.38.
[59] *Ibid.* Five manuscripts contain this version.
[60] *Ibid.* One manuscript contains this version.

Textual variants thus mean different manuscripts presented different ideas about what constituted law and custom. Chapter 8 illustrates how subtle changes of a few words can have a meaningful impact: changing titles, regional designations, and word changes in the *coutumiers* permit us to see developing notions of a French 'common law'.

More significant changes came in portions of text added or excised – from a few sentences to larger sections added or removed, in part of a text or throughout – and abridged versions of texts. For example, Beaumanoir's *Coutumes de Beauvaisis* manuscript tradition includes manuscripts the earliest of which dates from the late thirteenth or fourteenth century (A, B, E, F, H, M in Amédée Salmon's critical edition).[61] A is considered the best manuscript.[62] It is closely followed by B, which only omits three and a half sections. Manuscript E has only a few sections excised – sections 1637–1640 and 1644. Manuscript F resembles E closely but has additional sections removed – it does not contain sections 114, 633, 1098, 1113–1127, 1412–1451, in addition to those absent in manuscript E. Meanwhile, manuscript M ends its copy at section 1343, omitting sections 1344–1981 and the conclusion entirely. While the copying of the latter seems to have been discontinued for reasons unknown, the text circulated and was received in this partial version.

Later manuscripts of the *Coutumes de Beauvaisis* tended to drop the contextual and authorial material. Some eliminate the title, where Beaumanoir notes the subject of the book as the customs and usages

---

[61] A (Paris, Bibliothèque nationale de France, ms. fr. 11652), B (Berlin, Staatsbibliothek und Preussischer Kulturbesitz, Hamilton 193), E (Vatican, Biblioteca Apostolica Vaticana, Reginensi latini, 1055), F (Vatican, Biblioteca Apostolica Vaticana, Ottoboniani latini 1155), H (Paris, Bibliothèque nationale de France, ms. fr. 18761), and M (Troyes, Médiathèque de Troyes Champagne Métropole, 615). The seven other extant manuscripts used by Salmon date between the fifteenth and seventeenth century (Salmon's C, D, G, I, J, K, L). He also knew of two abridged versions, one from the fifteenth century and the other potentially from the sixteenth, and also lists manuscripts quoted in the work of sixteenth- and seventeenth-century jurists that have since then been lost (*Coutumes de Beauvaisis*, ed. Salmon, pp. xviii–xxxii).

[62] *Ibid.*, p. xxi. Manuscript A was used both by Arthur Beugnot and Amédée Salmon in their editions. Salmon considered it closest to the original because it was written with care with attention to corrections, contains few lacunas, does not entirely remove any complete paragraph, and interpolates only two sections, 865 and 987 (*ibid.*, p. xix). Beugnot also primarily used manuscript H, which Salmon saw as containing numerous omissions and false information and as not being executed with care (*ibid.*, p. xxv).

of Beauvaisis according to practice in the year 1283.[63] Three
manuscripts eliminate the prologue completely, and thereby remove
the information that Beaumanoir was in the service of count Robert of
Clermont, the purpose of the text, the description of sources, and the
invocation of divine support.[64]

These are only a few examples, but they do show that the text might
potentially change with each scribe. Those who made these textual
innovations generally did not explain why – was this a more accurate
description of an old rule, had the rule changed or narrowed, or was
this simply one author's view of how things should be? The nature of
the changes across manuscript versions of the *coutumiers* suggest that
they were very often deliberate. Like Cerquiglini, we should accept
them as authoritative versions, each expressing an authoritative vision
of the custom in question. Multiplicity of opinion was inherent to
custom, and this was captured in its early written tradition.

Pierre invited readers to change the text and embraced future
rewriting, while Philippe de Beaumanoir lamented its inevitability.
Either way, change was a fact of the transmission of these texts. Not
only was this heterogeneity apparently unproblematic; it was also a key
aspect of vernacular legal culture.

There is no reason to think that different manuscript versions of
coutumier texts were perceived as hierarchically ordered during the
medieval period, and no reason to privilege one manuscript as
presenting a better or more accurate view of law. Each manuscript
was an authoritative text, as Bernard Cerquiglini shows for manuscript
versions of vernacular literature. These variants, in fact, are proof of
the continued, conscious development of a living customary law that
was not petrified by and with written text. Instead, the texts were part
of the performative practice of lay jurists – a practice that increasingly
encompassed the written word. The emendation of texts as they were
copied mimicked the practicum of vernacular literature.

The thought process behind the creation of a new, more
authoritative, better version of a text was well illustrated by an
anecdote from Lawman's *Brut* (1190s), as emphasized by Michael

---

[63] Salmon's manuscripts E, G, J, K, L. Manuscript E is from the fourteenth century, the
others are posterior.
[64] Salmon's manuscripts J, K, L.

Clanchy. Though the passage in question did not describe the composition of a lawbook but a text of Arthurian legend, *Brut* illustrated the *techne* involved in improvement. Lawman was a priest who wanted to write his own book, so he travelled far and 'procured those noble books which he procured as exemplars'. He had one book in French, one in Latin, and one in English. He then 'laid these books out and turned over their leaves. He beheld them lovingly [. . .]. He took quills in his fingers and applied them to parchment and he set down together truer words and he compressed those three books into one.'[65]

Clanchy notes that the description of Lawman conforms to the stereotype of a scribe-copyist working from an exemplar and asks why Lawman would not have wanted to be portrayed as a creative writer. But wasn't he portrayed as exactly that? Lawman had sources in three languages and distilled these into the English vernacular. He significantly modified his sources in order to condense these three books into one volume. Finally, he also wrote a better version – 'he set down together truer words'. An almost mystical reverence for the ideas and texts of the past did not stop him from shortening, adapting, and writing a different version of these ideas and texts.

When not ignoring them, legal scholars have often treated variants between vernacular legal texts as mistakes or problems – scribal flourishes that have to be resolved and smoothed over to create the critical edition – the scholarly dream of an authoritative original version and the legal positivist's mainstay. Critical editions of the *coutumiers* have thus buttressed an illusion that there was one legitimate version of the text and therefore an always clear and knowable customary law.

Pragmatically, tracking the variation between *coutumier* manuscripts can be an invaluable source for understanding settled versus contested practice. For instance, the custom that there were three continuances in secular courts seems to have been well accepted because we can see it repeated, without alternation, throughout manuscripts. However, the custom concerning who acquired the property of a suicide was still unsettled enough to be subject to different opinions and thus the subject of variation within the manuscript tradition.

The elasticity of the text of customary law and the common practice of change and alteration reveal something about the nature of

---

[65] Lawman in Clanchy, *From Memory to Written Record*, p. 127.

customary law. I argue that customary law was a mode of thought conditioned by vernacular culture. This culture did not have the same reverence for original or authoritative texts that were so important to university approaches to law. The medieval period did have tools for creating uniformity; for instance, the *pecia* system for creating standardized university texts or the chirograph for uniform charter versions of the same transaction. But those who copied the *coutumiers* amended them in larger and smaller ways, akin to other forms of vernacular literature. This approach to text in the first decades of writing custom as bodies of law makes sense in an oral and performative legal culture with a dynamic approach to law.

The creative energy and performative aspect of customary law continued with writing, as the manuscript tradition of each *coutumier* reveals. An 'oral' and 'written' binary fits only awkwardly at best with the *coutumiers*. These texts extended oral culture even as they inaugurated a written culture. This written culture was not one that thought in terms of rigid formalism, either verbal or textual.

Some customs of course were so well accepted in practice that they might rarely, if ever, be disputed.[66] However, as Emily Kadens writes, we should not assume that the lack of challenge implies universal agreement on a particular custom: one might be convinced one held orthodox views of custom and act according to these until a dispute or accusation of nonconformity.[67] This fluctuating quality of custom described by Kadens for an oral legal culture was also, I argue, a feature of customary law as it was being set in writing in the first *coutumiers*.[68]

I am not arguing that every custom was constantly subject to contestation by rewriting – many customs were considered established, well known, or general – but that many were and any potentially *could* be contested through rewriting. Customary legal culture was not restrictive, traditionalist, or formalistic but expansive. If we take into account the composition of the text, changes made by copyist-authors in the manuscript tradition, and sections of text reused in different texts, then we get quite a different view of customary legal culture, its modes of thought, the relationship between orality and writing, and the nature of custom itself.

---

[66] Kadens, 'Custom's Past', p. 18.   [67] *Ibid.*   [68] See *ibid.*, pp. 17–19.

Indeed, this accords with a society that was comfortable with resolving disputes without the direct application of rules and instead found equitable solutions that were generally acceptable to the community.[69] Peace procedures, especially mediation and arbitration, were commonly used to resolve disputes recorded in cartularies.[70] Common wisdom, such as the proverb 'better a bad compromise than a good trial', encoded this approach.[71] Disputes over property until about 1250 were usually settled by arbitration and compromise in southern and north-western France.[72] The *coutumier* authors included mediation as an important part of judges' duties. It is difficult to imagine that the results of these mediations did not inform ideas of appropriate resolution of specific issues or that the fact of negotiation was not inherent to the activity of customary law, unsettled as it often was.

Copying a *coutumier* certainly involved the reproduction of a text, but the variants show how copyists were not simple rote transcribers but brought something of themselves to their text of customary law. The manuscript tradition reveals that the content of custom could be unstable and at its heart entailed the negotiation of a plurality of opinions.

To think about custom – even in text – meant to join an ongoing dialectic. This dialectic can be seen in previous norms repeated and upheld, as well as the amendment or rejection of earlier rules, discarded as 'evil customs' or 'contrary to reason', or in questions as to whether something was actually a custom – or, indeed, by the revision of smaller or larger parts of lawbooks. The *coutumiers* and their manuscript

---

[69] *Ibid.*

[70] Bongert, *Recherches sur les cours laïques*, pp. 103–11. In twelfth-century charters, the word *judicium* does not yet imply 'judgment' (*ibid.*, p. 196).

[71] Cohen, *Crossroads of Justice*, p. 43.

[72] Cheyette, 'Suum Cuique Tribuere', and Stephen D. White, '"Pactum … Legem Vincit et Amor Judicium"'. Compromise was the prevalent mode of settlement even when there was a clear winner, and the clear loser rarely went empty handed (Cheyette, 'Suum Cuique Tribuere', p. 293). The goal of dispute resolution, and the role of arbiters, was not to 'do justice' but to satisfy both parties so that they would both be assuaged and the dispute would end. A judgment was difficult to enforce, could leave one party resentful, and could mean that the peace would not last. Compromise, on the other hand, generally meant reconciliation and an incentive to keep the peace, and the witnesses involved were usually people close to the parties able to pressure them to honor the compromise (Stephen D. White, 'Pactum … Legem Vincit et Amor Judicum', 300–1). Cheyette argues that this changed from around 1250 onward, when courts began making 'normative judgments' (Cheyette, 'Suum Cuique Tribuere', 296). White also ends his study in 1250.

cultures show that custom was not simply a set of legal data to be
recognized but was also something composed and re-composed.

Manuscripts in Conversation

Not only did individual manuscripts participate in a discussion about
custom, but this discussion also featured within the texts' narratives;
notably in the adversarial procedure highlighted in cases and exempla,
as well as in jurists' comments about their own agreement or disagreement
with other opinions on custom. In these instances, we can see how the
textualization of custom co-existed in the culture of written customary
law with a creative, spoken, and performed customary culture.

Set or confirmed custom was as clear in memory or in action as it was
in writing, but when people did not agree or there was no precedent to
invoke, custom had to be found or, in other words, generated.[73] In this
sense, custom was embedded in the medieval culture of claims. In these
moments, the texts feature as a process that involves various steps and
consultations and negotiations between parties.

The question and (reasoned) answer format had long been a classic
feature of learning.[74] Pierre de Fontaines' *Conseil à un ami* clearly saw
custom as part of a practice that included well-known and accepted
rules as well as unsettled ones. The text had a naturally conversational
tone because it dispensed advice and was styled as a personal
conversation between teacher and student.[75] In teaching his student,
who was or would be a regular attendee of the lay courts but was not
a *légistre* (law expert) about custom and customary practice, Pierre
also gives us his view of these practices – the view of a man who clearly
had some advanced education that included some Roman and canon

---

[73] There is a deeper philosophical question underlying this statement about whether
ideas can be said to exist before they are articulated (or for historians of the Middle
Ages, before their first known articulation).

[74] The question-and-answer format of teaching and learning was a regular part of
medieval education. On the breadth that debate and dialogue could have in the
culture of high medieval scholasticism, see generally Alex J. Novikoff, *The
Medieval Culture of Disputation*. Where it came from is a different question.
However, it cannot be purely learned influence since this aspect of negotiation is so
fundamental to customary practice generally.

[75] See, for instance, Pierre de Fontaines, *Conseil*, ed. Marnier, XXII.32. Note this
conversation is stylized and conventional, not a representation of regular people in
an everyday conversation.

law in translation but who had a long career in the lay courts, first in comital courts and then in the highest echelons of the royal courts as a counsellor close to the king.

For Pierre, practice was composed of things known and things uncertain, and, within the latter, custom became a matter of opinion and discussion. This was the case when a custom has not been firmly established on a certain matter, and Pierre gives his opinions about what he thinks custom might be: 'You are asking something I never saw brought to judgment, nor saw a suit on: whether serfs also lose their right to answer one another in court, like gentlemen? And certainly I will give you my opinion'.[76] Lay jurists supplied opinions in the absence of precedent. These did not necessarily represent community consensus, but they did present one authoritative voice in the discussion of what custom is.

Indeed, Pierre occasionally notes that his interlocutor had been wrongly informed in a certain case. Pierre once told him: 'You were not rightly informed by whoever told you that Robert had lost his right to an answer in court.'[77] Although Pierre disagreed with it, this wrong opinion was clearly circulating, and different opinions about customs would confront each other should a dispute end up in court. It was this confrontation that established custom, and even absurd or wrong ideas were part of the conversation:

The person who told you that you had begun a proceeding merely because you had asked for a counsel day was not a good law expert [*légistres*] nor was he knowledgeable about the customs of the area. For I believe that all written law that exists, and all the good customs whose practice is followed, are against such a ruling, even the law of La Bassée.[78]

In Pierre's opinion two types of people properly understood the rules of procedure in secular court: law experts by virtue of some form of study and those who had knowledge of local custom from practice. However, that did not mean that others lacked opinions about custom or that they withheld their counsel. Claims that were misinformed had to be proved wrong. Claims of misinformation could also be used to try to discredit

---

[76] *Ibid.*, XIII.22.

[77] 'You were not rightly informed by whoever told you that Robert had lost his right to an answer in court, because of a theft he was accused of, but which was never proved, but was put in prison at the will of the judge' (*ibid.*, XIII.16).

[78] *Ibid.*, XVII.37.

other assertions of custom. Whether or not they were actually misinformed was less relevant than whether the claim could be proved or disproved.

Even custom that seemed approved, established, and agreed upon by people with different sources and approaches could be subject to different opinions. Confirmation by the courts certainly lent greater authority to a custom, but even then, jurists thought about them critically. A judgment, that is, was not the final word, as Cheyette argued, because in practice the possibility of future contestation always existed. This aspect of practice was apparent in the *coutumiers*: their authors worked to articulate coherent rules but did not go so far as to present a false illusion that there was necessarily uniform thought on customary law. For instance, Pierre described one judgment he felt was wrong:

> It is not my opinion that a right judgment was given by [the judge] who asked the parties if they were ready to hear judgment according to the arguments they had made, and then in his judgment paid attention only to the last arguments which had been made, without the parties having renounced in any way what they had said earlier.[79]

Judgments were not the last word, they could be subject to disagreement and contestation, and a rule 'established' by a court ruling may not stand the test of time. Pierre also intimated that proceedings were not as formal, or *legal*, as he wished; in this case, the judge was not paying attention to the actual arguments made throughout the proceeding and was judging according to partial information.

Incidentally, this passage shows that Pierre believed that parties' arguments should be judged, rather than the right or wrong 'feel' of a claim. Pierre was making a case for a true adversarial legal system where two sides present arguments before a judge or jury, whose role is to weigh the full arguments, find truth, and make a decision. Pierre, at the vanguard of a professional legal culture, shows in this passage that some justices had low professional standards while some, like him, were trying to construct a professionalized law that at least aspired to judgment according to the facts and arguments of a case.[80]

This negotiated custom, produced by allegations and dialogue, also appeared in other guises in Pierre's text. Neither he nor his interlocutor

---

[79] Pierre de Fontaines, *Conseil*, ed. Marnier, XVII.54.
[80] See more in the following section.

seem to have believed that a font of old law could answer all questions and settle all matters, or at least, they did not turn to this belief when in doubt. Instead, they would generate discussion and questioning when confronted with confusing or pressing issues. For instance, Pierre noted on one occasion that 'this question has often been asked about a man who is appealed against for a crime and who settles [*en fait pes*]; namely whether he loses his right to an answer in court. And certainly he does'.[81]

These texts do not indicate a body of custom well known and agreed upon by the community or a pool of ancestral knowledge from which to source custom. We are left, in this case, with wise men who were learned in the practices of the lay courts whose opinions carried authoritative weight. Pierre presents himself as one of these wise men when he comments that people often ask his opinion on points of proper customary practice. For instance, on the nature of the tenure of land inherited by a minor, Pierre said that those who are under fifteen years of age must continue to hold their property in the same type of tenancy in which their parents held it.[82] Pierre noted that 'I have been asked many times how I interpret this assertion', and proceeds to explain how one should understand it in different situations and circumstances.[83] If Pierre was asked about it many times, then we can infer that the question arose often but remained unsettled. The customary rule was not obvious within the community and required interpretation.

Occasionally, Pierre responded directly to his young student's questions about whether certain types of customary practice were *good* customary practice:

You are telling me there was a gentleman in the Vermandois who had brothers and sisters, and who married under an agreement that his widow would get a half of his land in dower, and from the other half, if he died without heirs of his body, she would get back what she brought to him as a dowry: now you are asking me if such an agreement is valid according to our practice. And certainly it is, as long as maintenance is provided for children existing before the marriage, and [dowry] provided for the sisters, if their father had left these instructions.[84]

The facts are recounted without names and dates. The important matter is instead the facts of the situation, a notably conceptual way of approaching

[81] *Ibid.*, XIII.24.   [82] *Ibid.*, XIV.1.   [83] *Ibid.*, XIV.2.   [84] *Ibid.*, XV. 8.

information pertinent to a conflict or dispute. Passages such as this one provide insight into the conversations at the heart of customary thinking in the mid-thirteenth century: one young jurist heard of a chain of events and asked an experienced jurist his opinion on the legal issue.

Philippe de Beaumanoir, like Pierre de Fontaines, noted a number of occasions where practices contradicted 'law or custom'.[85] However, he went one step further than Pierre – not only did he note when he disagreed with a certain common custom, but he also explained that a rule might be contested if a custom defied reason.[86]

Beaumanoir encouraged the reader to do just this. In one instance, he noted that both custom and court practice were clear and consistent in their approach to upholding wills, even when heirs were cut out without known or obvious cause. However, he disagreed with this approach and seems to encourage his readers to contest custom through the proper channels:

> and certainly all is such that our custom and the court of Beauvais follows this, we do not believe that this accords with reason and we believe that it would be good and charitable to contest such wills and to make them invalid, especially when they exclude heirs without cause; and we believe that whoever would go to the point of definitive sentence, appealing either from the bishop to the pope or from the barons to the king, that such a will would not be upheld.[87]

A clash of opinions about certain customs appears on a number of occasions in Beaumanoir's text, where Beaumanoir explained that 'we say that ... [...] And people have sometimes said that [...] but it is not so'.[88]

---

[85] For instance, a 'will which was made contrary to law or custom [*qui a fu fes contre droit ou contre coustume*]' (Beaumanoir, *Coutumes de Beauvaisis*, ed. Salmon, XII.382, see also XII.383).

[86] Reason as a way of validating or invalidating custom grew out of canon law approaches to custom, as we saw in Chapter 1.

[87] 'et certes tout soit il ainsi que nostre coustume le sueire et la court de Beauvais, nous ne creons pas que ce soit resons et creons que biens et aumosneseroit de contester a teus testamens et de fere les de nule valeur, meismement quant ele en oste ses oirs sans cause; et creons que qui en iroit a sentence disfinitive, en apelant de l'evesque dusques a l'apostoile, ou des barons dusques au roi, que teus testament ne seroient pas tenu' (*ibid.*, XII.387). Note that a judgment at these highest levels would provide some degree of certainty about how the type of case would be judged again.

[88] 'Nous disons qu'il convient qu'il soit mis en trois pures defautes, tout sans les jours qu'il puet contremander et essoinier par coustume. Et ont aucune fois dit li aucun qu'il convenoit que teus defautes soient fetes pres a pres, mes non fet' (*ibid.*, II.64).

The role of consensus in custom is so often emphasized as its generative factor. The inquest is sometimes romanticized as a context where clear and known customs are harvested from a community that knows rather than decides the meaning of custom. This is especially true of the *enquête par turbe*.[89] While those who have examined the *enquête par turbe* closely disagree on a number of points, they do agree that it was a procedure used when there was controversy about custom.[90]

The ordinance which gives us the *enquête par turbe* explained that inquiries into custom ought to be made in the following manner.[91] Wise men were to be gathered and a custom was to be put to them both orally and in writing. They would then take an oath to speak loyally about what they know and believe and have seen in reference to that custom. Now under oath, they would remove themselves to deliberate

[89] For descriptions of the *enquête par turbe*, see Stein, *Roman Law in European History*, p. 83; Cohen, *Crossroads of Justice*, p. 30; Waelkens, 'L'origine de *l'enquête par turbe*', 337; Gilissen, *La coutume*, p. 66; Dawson, *A History of Lay Judges*, p. 46.

[90] Brief treatments of the *enquête par turbe* abound, but a new detailed study would be welcome because there is disagreement on basic aspects such as what exactly counted as an *enquête par turbe*. If one defines it as any group inquest into *consuetudines*, no matter whether an exaction, jurisdictional issue, or substantive custom, then the procedure does indeed seem common – this was the approach of Pissard, whose study was highly influential (Pissard, *Essai sur la connaissance et la preuve*, pp. 107ff). If one defines it as any inquest into custom as a substantive rule, then the *Olim* do provide tens of examples of inquiries into the specific custom of a place. This was the approach of Poudret, who made a distinction between *consuetudo* as an exaction or seigneurial right and *consuetudo* as a substantive custom, which made a very big difference: while Pissard finds inquests into custom as early as 1116, Poudret finds the first incontrovertible example in 1255 (Poudret, 'Réflexions sur la preuve de la coutume', 74). If one looks for the actual use of the term *turba* in this context, then the first is in the ordinance above; it is more common in the work of Roman jurists than in cases, and most of the few date to the fourteenth century (Waelkens, 'L'origine de *l'enquête par turbe*', 340ff, esp. 346; Waelkens, *La théorie de la coutume chez Jacques de Révigny*, p. 354). These descriptions of *enquête par turbe* differ significantly: Pissard's was basically the regular inquest, Poudret's is specific to substantive law, while Waelkens' is even more specific to the procedure outlined in the ordinance.

[91] Boutaric places the ordinance under the heading of those without a date under the reign of Philip the Bold (r. 1270–85) (*ibid.*), but other authors generally place it in the reign of Louis IX in 1270 (see Waelkens, 'L'origine de *l'enquête par turbe*', 338). The text itself is an undated act from a royal register that contains documents that range in date and content. The documents before and after this one that are written in the same hand have dates that range from 1224 to 1290 (*Coutumes de l'Anjou et du Maine*, ed. Beautemps-Beaupré, pp. 26–7). Beautemps-Beaupré, for one, saw it as arbitrary to choose a precise date between 1224 and 1290 for this text (*ibid.*, p. 27).

what they had seen concerning that custom, the parties involved, the
nature of the dispute, where it happened, the judgment in the case, and
the circumstances surrounding it. These deliberations were to be
recorded in writing and delivered to the court with the seals of these
members of the inquest, who would deliver the case *as a group*.[92]

This was thus a procedure that took multifarious and dissenting
views about a customary rule and made custom by generating a unified
view.[93] Laurent Waelkens notes that *turba* in Latin connotes turmoil,
disorder, tumult, and uproar.[94] *Turbacion* in Old French also meant
trouble and confusion, while *turber* as a verb meant to trouble, impede,
and torment. *Turbe* meant the crowd or multitude often in a way that

---

[92] 'Inquiretur de consuetudinis in hunc modum. Vocabuntur pluers sapientes carentes
    suspicione. Ipsis vocatis proponetur eis consuetudo per os unius ex ipsis [et dabitur eis
    in scripto]. Qua proposita iurabunt quod ipsi dicent et fideliter referent illud quod
    sciunt et credunt {per os unius ex ipsis} et viderunt usitari super illa consuetudine.
    Quo iuramento praestito, trahent se ad partem et deliberabunt et referent deliber-
    ationem illam, et dicent inter quos viderunt illam consuetudinem, et qui in quo casu et
    quo loco, et si fuerit iudicatum et de circumstanciis et omnia redigentur in scriptis et
    mittantur in curiam clausa sub sigillis inquisitorum [et reddent omnes causam dicti
    sui, eciam in turba]' Boutaric, ed., *Actes du Parlement de Paris*, vol. 1, p. 242, entry
    2547B. The brackets do not appear in Boutaric but were included by Beautemps-
    Beaupré to indicate additions to the original text made in a different hand but around
    a similar time to the original text. These three additions are in the same hand; the first
    square bracket contains text in the margin that Boutaric incorporated into the text,
    the curly bracket containing text inserted between the lines appears earlier in
    Boutaric's text, and the last square bracket contains words added to the end of the
    text and included by Boutaric (*Coutumes et institutions de l'Anjou et du Maine*, ed.
    Beautemps-Beaupré, pp. 25–6). The first and third additions are interesting, the first
    because it adds the requirement of putting the custom in question in writing for the
    wise men and the third because it adds the key word *turba*. Beautemps-Beaupré sees
    these changes as corrections made because the copyist omitted those portions from
    the text (*ibid.*, p. 26n.4). The corrections add elements that could equally be the result
    of a difference of emphasis, opinion, or indeed experiential knowledge between
    scribes. They could also indicate changes in practice within the decades of the later
    thirteenth century. Importantly, while our editions of ordinances provide a unitary
    view of legislation, as one might expect in modern law, we can see from this that
    ordinances could be, and were, amended. This means legislation too was not neces-
    sarily a stable text. How much and in what ways certainly merits further study.
[93] Waelkens, 'L'origine de l'*enquête par turbe*', 346; Poudret, 'Réflexions sur la preuve
    de la coutume', 6. Other points of disagreement between Waelkens and Poudret
    include whether the *enquête par turbe* descends from the Carolingian inquest or
    was a novel procedure developed because of the influence of Roman law and some
    procedural elements concerning the nature of 'crowd' decision-making about custom
    (e.g. Was there a condition of notoriety? Did it have to be unanimous?).
[94] Waelkens, 'L'origine de l'*enquête par turbe*', 339.

included these tumultuous connotations.[95] While the *enquête par turbe* is commonly taken by modern scholars to represent community agreement and a united popular voice, it is likely that contemporaries linked it to deep community dissention and conflict. That this is muted in records of proceedings is not surprising because, as we saw in the previous chapter, these do not usually contain deliberations but the resulting group consensus that followed.

Certainly, as we have seen, some customs were indeed well known and agreed upon. Disagreement also propelled discussion that, in turn, formulated or pronounced custom. The lack of consensus also had an essential and formative role in the creation of custom.[96]

This aspect of disagreement about custom is sometimes apparent in the *coutumiers*. Beaumanoir, for instance, disapproved of some specific customs to the extent that he openly disregarded them. For instance, he explained that he felt that the penalties for commoners who strike noblemen were too light: 'It is an annoying thing that our custom permits a commoner [*petis hons de poosté*, lit. little men subjected to other people's power] to strike a valiant man [*homme vaillant*] and only pay five sous as a penalty; and for this reason I agree that he can be given a long prison term, so that for fear of prison the miscreant will refrain from such mad acts.'[97]

Beaumanoir's *Coutumes de Beauvaisis* thus openly asserted penalties contrary to accepted custom in the area, with very different results for the person involved – a five-sou fine became a prison sentence. It may have been easier to do so in this particular case, since the people whose traditional rights were circumvented were 'little men subjected to other people's power'. Whatever the case, Beaumanoir indicates that if one disagreed with custom, one would just act in contravention to it, presumably until there was some complaint or contestation.[98] This

---

[95] See *turbacion, turbe, turber* in Godfroy's Dictionary.

[96] The notion of 'contrary judgment' developed by the schools acknowledges this. However, I mean this more expansively here to include not only the resolution provided by the judicial process but also the sorts of discussions this section has been examining.

[97] 'C'est anieuse chose quant nostre coustume suefre qu'un petis hons de poosté puet ferir un homme vaillant et si n'en paiers que .v.s. d'amende, et pour ce je m'acort que longue prisons li musart se chastient de fere teus folies' (*ibid.*, XXX.842).

[98] Beaumanoir's violation of sanctuary discussed in Chapter 4 provides one example of such pushback.

was true even for Beaumanoir, a complex thinker who worked officially as a comital justice and whose *Coutumes de Beauvaisis* expresses a great desire for order and consistency.

The *coutumiers*, then, assumed the importance of the negotiation of ideas and its constitutive power in various stages of the customary legal process. This was significant on one level because it says something about formalism or formalistic practices – without a doubt many *coutumier* authors and creative copyists envisioned conversation, mediation, and change as fundamental aspects of the practice of custom in lay courts. They knew that time, opinions, challenges, discussions, allegations of unreasonableness or reasonlessness, and desuetude all might change the rules and they operated in this environment. Indeed, the malleability of rules within customary law, even when written, meshes with studies of other facets of the legal process, including Susan McDonough's work on the role of witnesses in shaping the discussion and legal framework of court proceedings.[99] It also shows that the popular *Roman de Renart*'s account of a quintessentially deliberative rather than formalistic customary legal culture remained illustrative of the modalities of customary law at the same time that legal practice was becoming professionalized and beginning to have a relationship with the written culture.

The *coutumiers* do not showcase a legal practice in transition from orality to writtenness or from flexible memory to fixed text. Instead, they show that written text had a voice in the various conversations that formed the foundation of customary legal culture. Written text was a space for thinking through and working out notions of customary law.

Written text permitted a Pierre de Fontaines or the compiler of the *Établissements* to extend and generalize the conversation beyond their own person, region, and lifetime. To some lay jurists, these texts would be authoritative. After all, this is why they were copied and adapted by critical thinkers who also sought to be part of the conversation. To others, text was simply not the place of custom, and they might not

---

[99] Susan McDonough, 'Poor Widows and Impoverished Mothers', 'She Said, He Said, They Said'. For an earlier study of the active role of witnesses in giving shape to the nature of legal discussion within proceedings, see Sally Humphreys, 'Social Relations on Stage'.

think of written custom at all, either negatively or positively, because for them custom was an inherently performative practice. This does not change the fact that the written was part of the general conversation that constituted custom in practice, which was forged out of discussion, negotiation, disagreement, challenge, and consensus.

If the voices that participated in the customary discussion converged to form a chorus on a particular subject, then they might become a prevailing view and thus might constitute proper practice and custom. Even established custom could change through an ongoing conversation.

Written text and spoken word were thus both part of a greater conversation about the proper forms of normativity in lay courts, the proper presentation of arguments and ideas, about the kinds of claims that would have adjudicable legal meaning, as opposed to opinion, emotion, prejudice and so on. This is perhaps nowhere better captured than in Figure 7.3, which shows the *coutumier* book being presented

FIGURE 7.3 The many voices of customary law. This manuscript of the *Établissments de Saint Louis* from the end of the thirteenth century shows the many voices that together created customary law, including the author and his book, various people making competing claims of custom, rights, and justice in the lay courts, as well as the judge as the arbiter of these voices. *Établissments de Saint Louis*, Bibliothèque nationale de France, ms. fr. 5899, fol. 1r.

amidst a cacophony of voices. Each *coutumier* presented one way of speaking and was itself part of the deliberative conversation that constituted custom.

Learning to Think through a Legal Framework

If unstable texts were part of a practice that itself had elements of instability, then what was the purpose of writing custom? In other words, how and to what extent did *coutumier* authors intend their writing to shape practice, especially when the authors of the texts clearly knew that practice changed and, indeed, sometimes encouraged it to change themselves? *Coutumier* authors and copyists not only recorded an extended conversation about customary law over time but also tried to shape that conversation by moulding the practice and thinking of their audience.

Scholars describe the *coutumiers* as pedagogical texts, but what exactly they believe they were teaching is left unexplained. However, based on context, the pedagogy of the texts is assumed to turn around the transmission of specific information, a particular list of rules and procedures.[100] At a basic level, the *coutumiers* do provide specific content about inheritance, dowry, excusable trial delays, land law, and other topics. But *coutumier* authors did not perceive this information, or for that matter, legal culture, to be fundamentally static. Their receptivity to change is evident in overt exhortations to change as well as the fact that emendation with copying was a fundamental characteristic of medieval manuscript culture. Textual variation was the norm and textual stasis an aberration, one achieved with much effort.[101] Nonetheless, the composition of custom into written text was offering something valuable enough, across time and space, that the first *coutumiers* continued to be copied for at least two centuries.[102]

---

[100] Van Dievoet implied this when he turned from mentioning that the *coutumier* authors sought to instruct judges and local inhabitants to a discussion of how well they knew local law (van Dievoet, *Les coutumiers, les styles, les formulaires*, 47).

[101] See generally, Wakelin, *Scribal Correction and Literary Craft*; and on the *pecia* system, Mary A. Rouse and Richard H. Rouse, *Manuscripts and Their Makers*.

[102] With the exception of those that only come in one manuscript, namely the *Usaiges de Bourgogne* and the *Demenees el Chastel de Paris*. The *Livre de justice et de plet*, which I do not consider a *coutumier* for reasons outlined earlier, also exists in one manuscript.

Emily Kadens shows how the mentalities of those who learned custom within community practice differed from those who went to university to study Roman law, and how a training in Roman law fundamentally altered perceptions of custom and how it functioned.[103] The *coutumiers* likewise fundamentally transformed the concept of custom for their audience, an audience that did not have years to attend university but that did need the ability to argue convincingly – with the right language, categories, and relevant facts.

Legal culture, even when textualized, always also has some aspect of performance.[104] A convincing or unconvincing performance could result in either good or bad law, in victory or loss. Various legal actors – judges, lawyers, litigants, juries – were responsible to their audience, which had to be persuaded that theirs was the just, correct, and authoritative conception of the law.[105]

The *coutumier* authors were trying to help their audience with exactly this task. *Coutumiers* participated in the making of a 'common stage and the shaping of a public sphere', as Carol Symes describes, that 'relied on performance to delineate' spaces.[106] For the legal sphere, this meant that the performance of customary culture itself – the discussion, contestation, rejection, and approval of custom – contoured custom. The *coutumiers* were not texts to be used in practice like codes and might be likened to scripts. They were the basis of performance but from which actors could extemporize and innovate. They contained rules, procedures, and arguments that their authors felt would aid the enactment of law in court. In short, *coutumiers* contained the medieval secular court equivalent of what Elizabeth Mertz has described for modern society as 'learning to think like a lawyer', a process of intellectual transformation that entailed new attitudes towards spoken and written language.[107] The *coutumier*

---

[103] Kadens, 'Convergence and the Colonization of Custom in Pre-Modern Europe.'
[104] To read more about performance in legal culture, see for instance Johan Huizinga, 'Play and Law'; J. M. Balkin and Sanford Levinson, 'Law as Performance'; Julie Stone Peters, 'Legal Performance Good and Bad'; Pierre Legendre, *Le désir politique de Dieu*; Jacques Derrida, 'The Force of Law'; Nicole Rogers, 'The Play of Law'.
[105] See Balkin and Levinson, 'Law as Performance', pp. 729ff.
[106] Symes, *A Common Stage*, p. 135.
[107] See Elizabeth Mertz, *The Language of Law*. The phrase was originally coined in the 1973 film *The Paper Chase*, where the law professor tells his students, 'You teach

authors tried to shape a listener or reader into a legal actor and a legal reader.

That *coutumier* authors intended to change habits of mind can be seen even in the *coutumiers* that do not explicitly state this aim. The earliest vernacular *coutumier*, *Coutumes d'Anjou et du Maine* (1246), has no introduction that explains the spirit or goal of the text but simply begins by describing what should or should not be done in specific situations.[108] The text, however, also indicated the types of things that could be said in certain types of situations. For instance, it gave advice on how to navigate properly an accusation of false judgment against one's lord: 'If any gentleman hears that his lord gave him a bad judgment [*mauves jugement*], he may well say: "This judgment is false [*faux*], and I will not plead about this before you anymore."'[109] Without this type of protest, the gentleman might be seen as implicitly acknowledging the authority of the lord or the legitimacy of the judgment. The text showed how to avoid potential unintended legal consequences and how to indicate a change in jurisdictions – to turn a perceived bad or wrong judgment into a legal claim of false judgment, which was grounds for appeal to a higher court. They had to do this when the judgment was given, and if they did, they could then go to the court of his lord's lord to make a complaint against their lord:

and he can say: 'Sire, this man gave me a false judgment [*faux jugement*] and I do not want to hold from him, and I shall hold from you who are the chief lord.' And if the other says: 'I defend myself of this [accusation],' the other says: 'Sire, I do not want for him to be able to defend himself, because he gave me this false judgment [*faux jugement*] in the sight and knowledge of me, who owes faith to him, I am ready to show him if he wants to deny it with his body [i.e. in a trial by battle].'[110]

The elements of speech here are not ritualized forms but meaningful legal points or procedures, or proof with legal consequences. Next, the

---

yourselves the law, but I train your minds. You come in here with a skull full of mush; you leave thinking like a lawyer.'

[108] The text begins with: 'A gentleman cannot give but a third of his land to his young children. But he can well give his purchases and things he acquired [*conquetes*] to whichever of his children that he wants ... ' (*Coutumes d'Anjou et du Maine*, ed. Beautemps-Beaupré, p. 1).

[109] *Ibid.*, p. 90.   [110] *Ibid.*, p. 90.

text turned to what the judge should make of these points of legal information:

Thus we can adjudge one battle from this. And if the one who appealed against his lord for false judgment wins, he will never again hold from him, but will hold from the overlord. And if he was vanquished, he would lose his fief.

The text thus taught the judge the set of factors that constituted grounds for a trial by battle and the legal consequences that followed. The text turned individuals into legal actors, showing them how to speak in recognizable legal terms rather than the moral or emotional language that might have come more naturally to a person wronged or on the defensive.

This sort of court pedagogy appeared throughout the *coutumiers*. The *Établissements de Saint Louis* naturally did this as well, since it incorporated the text of the *Coutumes d'Anjou et du Maine*. While the texts do refer to words that 'must be said' by the litigants or the justices, these are not necessarily the only words that could be said when a dispute went to trial. A person requesting seisin, for instance, was told the manner in which he was to do so ('he must ask in this way'), but the *coutumier* also informed its audience that 'he should reserve the right to do or say more, if he needs to'.[111]

The *coutumiers* do not evince the Medusa effect commonly attributed to them – the ossification of court language and performance through its inscription in text. Different manuscript versions of the texts only underscore this point. For instance, the *Coutumes de Champagne* explained what various parties should say in specific situations. When an accusing party neglected to appear at court, the defendant said that since the accusing party was not present, he did not have to answer to the missing accuser's accusation, and nor could he be constrained by the court.[112] Tellingly, the wording of this exchange did not remain stable throughout the manuscript versions. This suggests that meaning was valued over exact wording.[113]

---

[111] 'il doit demander en tele maniere [...] Et si doit faire retenue de plus faire et de plus dire, se mestiers li en est' (*Établissements*, ed. Viollet, II.4).

[112] 'se li defanderres se deffant et die ensinc: "Sire, il me fait demande qui tuiche a partie ou a persone qui n'est pas presenz je ne vuil respondre se cil n'est presenz" et n'i doit respondre ne ne l'en doit on contraindre. Ensinc en us'on generalment' (*Coutumes de Champagne*, XXXIV).

[113] *Coutumes de Champagne*, p. 189nn.p–w.

These rights had to be claimed aloud but substantively rather than through a strict adherence to a form. Yvonne Bongert notes that, in juridical practice, usages varied and had not yet acquired the character of 'obligatory' custom.[114] The *coutumiers* actually corroborate this view rather than the formalist claims about them. In the examples above, we can see that the *coutumier* authors were not thinking in terms of a 'coercive textuality' – a kind of obtuse formalism that bound ideas and actions directly to text.[115]

Rather, ideas and actions were in conversation with text. These passages should be seen as examples of using text to shape practice rather than as examples of formalism. Formalism, in the sense that exact words must be replicated in court, does not seem to have been a concern for *coutumier* authors.[116] The purpose of the conversational oral passages was to train audiences to shape their responses at court so that they would have a legal meaning and resonance.

Pierre de Fontaines was even more explicit about trying to shape good legal practitioners, as he explained in his preface: his text instructed on how to do justice to subjects, how to keep land according to the laws and customs of the country, and give advice to friends when needed.[117] What followed in the texts was quite a mixed bag of advice, but it was clear that Pierre was trying to mould the hearer or reader into understanding the legal sphere and his role in it.

Indeed, he notably advised his audience on judicial techniques, the right and wrong way to judge. Medieval legal texts often had exhortations to judge justly and disapproved of those who did not. Pierre went further and provided very specific advice in a long section on judgment. Apparently, parties tried to sway judges with dramatic displays of tears and sorrows. This is unsurprising considering the emphasis placed by rhetorical learning on the role of emotion in persuasive discourse.[118] Pierre, however, counselled that a judge should steel himself against these emotional appeals.[119] Pierre was

---

[114] Bongert, *Recherches sur les cours laïques*, p. 183.
[115] Julie Stone Peters, 'Legal Performance Good and Bad', 194.
[116] Oaths and rituals were probably different, the wording of these obviously mattered more.
[117] Pierre de Fontaines, *Conseil*, ed. Marnier, I.2.
[118] See generally Copeland, *Emotion and the History of Rhetoric in the Middle Ages.*
[119] 'and do not pay any attention to tears nor to wailing that the parties put on before you, but do pay attention to making right judgments [*ne ne pren mie garde as larmes*

overtly trying to professionalize those who judge by teaching them to focus on words and arguments rather than the illusory stuff of emotional appeals:

> Be attentive to all the words that will be said in court where you are going to have to give a judgment, and do not do at all what many people do, who talk two by two while the parties are pleading, and do not hear any of the words that they will then have to give judgment on; and thus it often happens that the party who is not well heard loses when they should have won if they had properly been heard.[120]

Pierre was convinced that the act of judging had to be taken seriously, that it was hard work and it demanded proper attentiveness. It was only through careful listening and decision-making based on allegations and arguments that cases would arrive at their proper conclusions.

Judges had to ensure they had the right information and were doing their jobs properly. Indeed, they had to fact-check if they felt they had forgotten important information. As Pierre advised, 'even those who do their best to hear and retain, if they have not remembered things well, should have them repeated [*recorder*, an official court recounting done orally] so often as it takes until they have heard them properly; for otherwise they would not be without guilt according to God'.[121]

The passage discussed above reappeared in the prologue to the *Coutumier d'Artois*, as the prologue was largely copied from Pierre de Fontaines'. Hence it repeated the exhortation about good rulership and the proper delivery of justice to one's subjects.[122] The author of the *Coutumier d'Artois* also displayed his concern for pleaders, noting that 'because many cases perish very often because people rashly [*folement,*

---

    ne as plors que les parties font par devant toi, mès pren-toi garde à fère droit jugement]' (ibid., XXI.1).

[120] 'Soies ententiz à totes les paroles qu'en dira en cort là où il te covendra juger, et ne fai mie si come molt de gens font, qui dui et dui conseillent quanque les parties pleident, ne rien n'entendent des paroles qu'il lor covendra jugier: et einsi en avient-il sovent que la partie que n'est pas bien entendue pert là où ele deust gaaignier s'ele fust bien entendue' *(ibid., XXI.4).*

[121] 'Et cil meismes qui lor pooir font de bien oïr et retenir, s'il ne l'ont bien retenu, facent le tant bien recorder as parties qu'il aient bien entendu; car autrement ne sauroient il mie sanz colpe selon Deu' *(ibid., XXI.5).*

[122] *Coutumier d'Artois*, ed. Tardif, Prologue.2.

madly] respond to many accusations that are made in court, I want to show you something very profitable and necessary to avoid [*a eschiever*] the bad causes that may arise'.[123] Parties that considered anger to be part of the juristic process were now seen to lack an understanding of proper habits and behaviours in the courts. The place of outrage and emotion in law was changing, and the author of the *Coutumier d'Artois* taught his audience to turn a reflex response to a personal attack into a legal response to an accusation.

The author of *Le livre des constitutions demenées el Chastelet de Paris* said explicitly that he aimed to shape legal practitioners and focused on the parties appearing at court, beginning his text with: 'Here begins the book which teaches how one must propose to speak before all judges and especially those in lay court: first, how the plaintiff must form his complaint and how he must plead; and after how the defendant should defend himself'.[124] This was more than an introduction to the lay courts, a simple description of procedure, or a collection of verbal formulae to repeat by rote. Rather, the author was using the text to produce lay 'jurists' – to sharpen, reinforce, and reproduce some of the forms and patterns of thought solidifying in lay courts.

Some *coutumier* authors sought to further refine their audiences into legal thinkers by training them in legal thinking around specific subjects. Beaumanoir explained how to employ a thinking tool he does not name, now called a table of contents:

Since it would be hard for those who want to consult this book on some matter which is relevant to what they want to do for themselves and for their families to have to search through this book from end to end, in this section we will set out briefly and give a name to all the chapters which will be contained in this book, in the order in which they will appear, and designate them by a number in this division and each chapter when it appears by the same number, so that in this way you can easily find the material you want to study.[125]

---

[123] 'Pour ce que mout de causes sont peries mout souvent par folement respondre a plusieurs demandes qui sont faites en court, te voel je monstrer chose pourfitable et necessaire a eschiever les mauvaises coses qui avenir en pueent' (*ibid.*, II.1).

[124] 'Ci commence li livres qui enseigne comment l'en doit proposer à parler devant tous juges et especiaument en court laie: premierement, comment li demanderres doit former sa demande et comment il doit plaidoier; et apres, comment li defenderres se doit desfendre ... ' (*Le livre des constitutions demenées*, ed. Mortet, Prologue).

[125] Beaumanoir, *Coutumes de Beauvaisis*, ed. Salmon, prologue s. 9.

This passage envisions that some in the *coutumier* audience will not want to read through the entire lawbook but would have an interest in searching for specific topics in times of need.

Since the work of Mary and Richard Rouse, scholars have seen the widespread use of the table of contents as a thirteenth-century development, one associated with the formalization of education and preaching that led to a more practical approach to books.[126] However, Adam Kosto shows that such research tools and finding aids were quite common in legal and administrative works before the scholastic period, including secular law and canon law lawbooks, estate surveys, fiscal records, and cartularies.[127] This new evidence tells a different story about the development of these intellectual techniques: clerics were administrators throughout the preceding centuries, they developed appropriate working tools for their administrative needs, and these tools were adapted to new contexts and on a wider scale in the thirteenth century.[128]

Beaumanoir's description of the benefits of and ways to use a table of contents is thus less suggestive of the development of new tools for legal thinking and more suggestive of the popularization of these tools outside of their administrative origins, and later clerical and university ambits. It also says something about the readership he envisioned. Some would not be familiar with this research tool geared to utilitarian reading – they might have assumed that texts were read consecutively from beginning to end – so Beaumanoir had to explain how to read his *coutumier* as a source for relevant law. The purpose of the table of contents was explained in terms of the acquisition of subject-specific knowledge. Like the earlier sources studied by Kosto, the *Coutumes de Beauvaisis* was consciously designed to be simply and conveniently usable.[129]

Beaumanoir was the *coutumier* author who gave the most detailed description of how to use his text but not the only one to do so. The author of the *Coutumier d'Artois* wrote in his prologue that 'the titles of this book are written out at the beginning, and they were ordered so to better find what is needed, in case that counsel shall be

---

[126] Rouse and Rouse, 'The Development of Research Tools in the Thirteenth Century', *Manuscripts and their Makers.*
[127] Kosto, Adam, 'Statim invenire ante'.   [128] *Ibid.*, 309.   [129] *Ibid.*, 291ff.

required'.[130] This author perceived the same need as Beaumanoir: texts were not just general statements of law in the secular courts but also needed to be accessible by subject matter and specific legal issue. It is noteworthy, in this consideration of custom as conversation, that the *Coutumier d'Artois* regarded the text as 'counsel'.

A general understanding of custom remained fundamental, and subject-specific searches were only to be used 'in case that counsel shall be required' and thus clearly remained secondary. Later manuscripts of the *Coutumier de Champagne* also indicate the expansion of subject-specific access to information for lay thinkers and participants in secular courts. Though not originally equipped with a table of contents, one was introduced into its manuscript tradition in the fourteenth century.[131] The same was also true for later manuscript versions of the *Établissements de Saint Louis*.

Lay jurists were changing the shape of legal knowledge from one defined by experienced and instinctive knowledge of right and wrong to one that was specific and processual. Pierre de Fontaines, for instance, occasionally pointed out when his interlocutor (the audience for his advice, whether real or imagined) noticed complicated or tricky legal issues and asked about them. For instance, Pierre commended him on a question he asked about the matter of minors who sold land or goods, namely, 'You are asking a very good question about whether a minor who had made some transaction clearly to his credit, and then asked for restitution by his own will, would obtain it. And certainly not'.[132]

This effort to shape authoritative legal actors was obviously distinct from the construction of law in the ecclesiastical courts or in Roman law courses. Nonetheless, it required that various parties involved in the court process participate in a conversation with an internal logic, and one that had legal implications. The *coutumier* authors wrote their texts, and later lay jurists copied and reshaped them, with the purpose of commenting on and conditioning practice in the lay courts. The *coutumiers* partially reflected an extended conversation while also

---

[130] 'Dont le titre de ce livre sont escrit ou commencement, et les ordena ensi pour mieus trouver ce que mestier [besoin] seroit, au cas dont consaus li seroit requis' (*Coutumier d'Artois*, ed. Tardif, Prologue).
[131] *Coutumes de Champagne*, BnF ms. fr. 25546.
[132] Pierre de Fontaines, *Conseil*, ed. Marnier, XIV.24.

aiming to shape that conversation by trying to mould how their audience thought about law, text, and legal argument and to show them how to think like a lay jurist – a legal practitioner specializing in the practice of the lay courts.

Writing and Orality

While this discussion has centred on the written and textual culture of the *coutumiers*, these texts have larger implications. They mark a key moment in legal thought, when the *coutumiers* provided a written expression of customary law in the language of rules and procedures and in the shape of bodies of rules. The oral and performative aspects of these texts generally advance these goals and purposes.

First, the *coutumiers* did not necessarily reflect a 'transition' from orality to writing. This is partially because they added a new form of writing to a legal culture that already balanced oral and written aspects, the latter in transactional documents and other records. And vernacular writing did not have the same association with textual tradition as Latin. Medieval vernacular literature, writes Simon Gaunt, did not have a 'straightforward opposition of orality to writing: written texts are always to a certain extent conceived as "voiced" in the Middle Ages because they were usually read aloud'.[133]

Importantly, the *coutumiers* do not describe pre-inscription traditions of oral recitation of a body of law. This differentiates *coutumiers* from legal origin stories in Ireland, where law was depicted in lawbooks as having been transmitted orally by many successive generations of poet-jurists before it took written form.[134] It also differentiates them from the role of the lawspeaker in Iceland, the subject of a chapter of the *Grágás*, which describes him as a man appointed 'to recite all the sections of the law over three summers'.[135] There is no conceptualization in the *coutumiers*

---

[133] See Gaunt, *Retelling the Tale*, p. 23.
[134] Robin Chapman Stacey, *Dark Speech*, p. 55.
[135] *Laws of Early Iceland*, trans. Andrew Dennis, Peter Godfrey Foote, and Richard M Perkins. p. 187. The *Grágás* are Icelandic lawbooks of which the earliest manuscripts date to the second half of the thirteenth century, and, although they contain older material, distinguishing what is contemporary thirteenth-century material and what is older can be difficult. They describe the lawspeaker's recitation as a complete

themselves, mythologized or real, of a pre-existing body of oral law being transmitted and transferred into written form.

The *coutumiers* utilized and exhibited orality in a different way, and with different approaches. One approach was dialogue form.[136] Pierre de Fontaines' *Conseil à un ami* and the *Coutumier d'Artois* were both structured as dialogues. One manuscript of Pierre de Fontaines' *Conseil à un ami* refers to the text as Pierre's words (*paroles*), and so a speech rather than advice.[137] The text itself does not cite the written text of Justinian's *Code* but refers to the words of various late-antique emperors.

Another approach referred to text as speech. When the poetic introduction to the *Établissements'* manuscript N ended, the compiler explained he would now 'speak of justice'.[138] The addition of this introductory poem and references to speech are themselves suggestive of performance – reading aloud or recitation. The power to speak the law, to create law by speech, is itself the essence of *jurisdiction*. In the *Établissements*, *ius* or *droit* speaks. The phrase 'law/ right says' which opened every line of the poem recurred commonly in the *Établissements*.[139] This spoken aspect of text generally differentiated vernacular written custom from Roman and canon law, which are distinguished by their writtenness and for which the term 'written law' had become a term of art.[140]

Many *coutumier* authors also described modes of direct speech in their texts. Though lawbooks like the *coutumiers* were once taken as troves of information for an illiterate oral culture, Simon Teuscher is

---

presentation of all law: 'the Lawspeaker shall recite all the sections so extensively that no one knows them much more extensively' (*ibid.*, p. 188).

[136] Dialogue form was, of course, common in Latin texts and not at all specific to vernacular writing.

[137] 'Chi parole mon sires Pieres de Fontaines ... ' (the description of the auction house Lafon: www.auctionstories.net/manuscript.html). This manuscript was sold at auction to a private purchaser. The *Coutumier d'Artois*, which incorporates sections of Pierre's text, is also packaged as a dialogue.

[138] 'Por ce, veuil de joutise presentement *parler*', *Établissements*, ed. Viollet, II.I [emphasis added].

[139] 'droit dit'. See for instance *ibid.*, II.4, II.6.

[140] In the rule on requesting seisin, the *Établissements de Saint Louis* notes 'Right/law *says* ("droiz dit") that the heir should be in possession; and it is written in the Code, *De edicto divi Adriani tollendo*' ('*Droiz dit que* li oirs doit estre en possession; et est escrit ou Code, De edicto divi Adriani tollendo, l. Quamvis quis se filium defunct, etc.') (*ibid.*, II.4).

certainly right that the modes of direct speech therein were the products of a written culture rather than an oral tradition; they are best understood as part of the history of written practices.[141] This does not change the fact that, in the era of the first *coutumiers,* orality was at the core of customary legal practice and the 'spoken word was the main vehicle of law'.[142] Aspects of orality and modes of verbal expression within the textual world of the *coutumiers* are not straightforward transcriptions of natural speech but are conditioned by the goals of the texts that include them.

The spoken appears to varying extents in the *coutumiers.* The *Coutumes d'Anjou et du Maine* and *Établissements de Saint Louis* have it scattered throughout, and direct speech and verbal exchanges are included in approximately one-third of the provisions in these texts.[143] Beaumanoir's *Coutumes de Beauvaisis* and the *Coutumier d'Artois* also disperse the spoken throughout the text, although to

---

[141] Teuscher, *Lords' Rights and Peasant Stories*, p. 133, see chap. 4 generally.

[142] Cohen, *Crossroads of Justice*, p. 29.

[143] For example, in *Etablissements* book I (I.10–175) the following sections include direct speech: on giving a guaranteed peace (I.31, I.41), showing your fief to your liege lord (I.50), summoning a vassal to make war on the king (I. 53), inspections made by a judge (I. 60), ladies providing liege lords with security that they will not marry off their daughter without their advice (I. 67), claims of novel disseisin (I. 69), the assignment of court dates by judges (I. 71), on vassals avoiding default when summoned (I.72), on paying penalties adjudged by the courts (I.73), on a baron's right to be judged by his peers (I.75), on delays so a gentleman can receive knight's privileges (I.77), on calculating kinship (I.79), issues concerning service horses (I.80), having children in custodianship (I.82), on seeking a hearing from the king (I.84), how to request the amendment of a judgment (I.85), on appeals for false judgment (I.86), on finding buried treasure (I.94), on vouching warrantors for stolen things (I.95), reimbursements of adversary's costs (I.95), breaches of seisin (I.97), failure to pay service dues (I.105), legal excuses for delays (I.106), offences before court date (I.107), appealing against a man for murder or treachery (I.108), on dividing land by judgment (I. 110), on millers and mills (I.111), co-holders of mills (I.112), the lack of dower rights of women to king's gifts given to a man and his heir by his wedded wife (I. 117), marriage gifts (I. 119), on discharging sureties (I.122), on legal excuses in royal court (I.124), reimbursements for damages caused by animals (I.125), on paying debts to a dead man's son (I.126), contracts in contemplation of marriage (I.128), gifts to the church (I.129), warranting as co-holders (I.130), on giving a service horse to one's lord (I.135), on dividing inheritance among brothers (I.136), on appealing for false judgment (I.142), when merchants avoid tolls and are arrested (I.149), on slander (I.154), seizure by lords of commoners' property (I.159), redemption of purchases (I.161–2), swearing to honest expenses in a redemption (I.166), on lost bees (I.172), on women's dower rights (I.173), on fighting judicial battles by champion because of infirmity (I.175).

a lesser extent than the previous two texts; the spoken form is occasional in the *Summa de legibus Normanniae* and infrequent in the *Ancien coutumier de Normandie* and the *Coutumier de Champagne*. Meanwhile, *Le livre des constitutions demenées el Chastelet de Paris* and *Li usages de Bourgogne* were guides to speaking in court predominantly composed of recommended oral claims and responses, and specifically written in the service of legal speech. Descriptions or suggestions of forms of direct speech in the *coutumiers* appear in a wide variety of ways, from very little to texts completely geared towards verbal expression as a purpose.

These sorts of passages that provided descriptions or instructions on how to speak, once seen as evidence of formalism, have recently been compared to dialogues in romances, stage scripts, conversation primers, and 'blueprints for public performance'.[144] Underlying these suggestions is the recognition that performance was the important pivot of medieval legal culture.[145] Indeed, Jody Enders argues that legal rhetoric was one of the origins of medieval drama, characterized as it was by 'such crucial protodramatic components as theatrical space, costume, staging, ritual conflict, audience participation, spectacle, dialogue, "imitation of action," and, most of all, impersonation'.[146] Performance 'was the unspoken assumption that lay behind all the various procedures, partnerships and *politesses* by which public order was defined'.[147]

Performance brought law and order together with legal drama, rhetoric, orality, ritual, procedure, and language, both unwritten and

---

[144] As noted earlier, Bernard Ribémont explored this in the French context and showed how linguistic and narrative elements of the *fabliaux*, French vernacular poems distinguished by their bawdy humor, appeared in the case descriptions in the *Livre de Jostice et de Plet* (Ribémont, 'Compiling and Writing a Legal Treatise in French', pp. 139–140). Michael Clanchy described dialogues such as those in the *Court Baron* as stage scripts or modern conversation primers for learning foreign languages (Clanchy, *From Memory to Written Record*, pp. 278–80). Carols Symes described them as a 'blueprint for public performance' (Symes, *A Common Stage*, p. 176).

[145] For an important intellectual precursor to the idea of legal performance, see Huizinga, *Homo Ludens*, pp. 76ff. For general studies, see for instance, Julie Stone Peters, 'Legal Performance Good and Bad', 'Law as Performance'; Marianne Constable, *Our Word is Our Bond*. For the crucial medieval study, see Jody Enders, *Rhetoric and the Origins of Medieval Drama*.

[146] Enders, *Rhetoric and the Origins of Medieval Drama*, p. 4.

[147] Stacey states this for early Irish culture, but it also elegantly captures the nature of legal culture of thirteenth-century northern France and probably beyond (Stacey, *Dark Speech*, p. 16).

written.[148] I will only address a small aspect of how this relates to the
coutumiers. Carol Symes emphasizes the theatricality of the
coutumiers, which she notes offered a 'blueprint for public
performance' that showed how particular pleas should be enacted.[149]
At the same time, the idea of 'adhering to a set part written down
verbatim' was not familiar to thirteenth-century culture, and script was
more geared to teaching the manner in which to speak with subtlety.[150]
This important notion of script, blueprint, and subtle speech in the
coutumiers can be unpacked yet further to understand how exactly
their authors taught readers to 'enact' a plea and what subtle speech
meant in the context of the customary law of the lay courts. Direct
speech in the *coutumiers* was generally descriptive or advisory. It
included the sorts of things that were said or might be said, or the
sorts of things that a *coutumier* author advised could or should be said,
in particular situations. The author of the *Établissements de Saint
Louis*, for instance, commonly described claims and counterclaims
made in court and then explained the nature of their legal
consequences. This was meant to instruct both parties as well as judges.

[148] There is a difference between performative utterances and the general notion of
performance. The former can best be seen in Geoffrey Koziol's deployment of John
Austin's theory of performative utterance to understand how medieval diplomas
were used in political performances to create new realities. John Austin's renowned
study on 'doing things with words' showed the world of law to be a world of
performative utterance, where words don't merely constitute saying something but
are performing an action where, for instance, an 'I do' is an act of creating a marriage
(Austin, *How to Do Things with Words*). Emily Steiner shows how 'act and will are
inseparable within documentary rhetoric,' whereby charters gain agency as primary
sites of legal action, not only in *Bracton* but also in wider literary culture (Emily
Steiner, *Documentary Culture and the Making of Medieval English Literature*,
pp. 21–8). As Koziol noted, 'in the moment of their issuance, diplomas were
therefore artifacts (props) used in political performances, and many of their most
distinctive characteristics stemmed from their uses in these performances' (Koziol,
The Politics of Memory and Identity, p. 39). The importance of these 'performa-
tives', he explained, 'is contained not in what they state but in what they do' and the
new realities they initiate, such as becoming king (*ibid.*, pp. 40–1). This form of
performative utterance overlaps but is not equivalent to the notion of performance
as constitutive legal culture, both in terms of what it is and how it changes (Stacey,
Dark Speech, p. 4). Marco Mostert provides a nice introduction to law from the
angle of performance, 'the (written and unwritten) rules of social behavior we call
"law" [that] are in a sense performed as a set of symbolic acts' (Mostert and
Barnwell, *Medieval Legal Process*).
[149] Symes, *A Common Stage*, p. 176.
[150] Clanchy, *From Memory to Written Record*, p. 280.

For instance, if a man had a swarm of bees and they swarmed,

And the person on whose grounds they alight collects them before the first man arrives, and the latter says afterwards: 'These bees are mine', and the other party says: 'I don't believe you', and the [first] party goes before the judge in whose jurisdiction this is, and says to him: 'Sir, such-and-such a man captured my bees', the lord must send for him to appear before him, and the plaintiff must say to him: 'Sir, I had some bees that swarmed out of my swarm and I followed them until I saw them light in this man's land who collected them and will not give them back to me; and I am ready to do whatever the court rules, for they are mine and I followed them by sight and without losing sight of them'; and if the other party says: 'I don't believe him, and I want him to do whatever he has to do to be believed', then it may be ruled that he must swear with his hand on the saints that the bees are his, and that they left his swarm, in his sight and knowledge, without his losing sight of them, and [went] as far as the place where the other party collected them. And upon this, he can have his bees; and he must give the other party the value of the container he collected them in. [151]

In this passage from the *Établissements de Saint Louis*, a claim of ownership and a denial of that claim created grounds for a suit. The claim had to contain the following elements: I owned bees, my bees swarmed, I followed them to another man's land, this other man collected them, he refused to return them, there is no doubt that these are my bees because I never lost sight of them as they moved to their new location, and I request a court ruling on the issue. Without one of these elements, the issue could not simply be resolved by oath because the claim would be weaker: if the first party had lost sight of the bees, the claim that the swarm in question was actually his would become uncertain.

The *Établissements* did refer to words that 'must be said' in the above passage, but not because different wording would lose the case. The point was to ensure that the necessary facts of the disputed ownership were established, and that the oath testified to those same facts and established some certainty about the plaintiff's ownership. [152]

---

[151] *Établissements de Saint Louis*, I.172. While I use this text to examine how the *Établissements* constructs verbal exchanges, Roman law provided the substantive background of the law of bees (see Bruce W. Frier, 'Bees and Lawyers'). The passage could thus also be examined to see how Roman law was used by *coutumier* authors.

[152] The words mattered because of their legal implications. The plaintiff could have said the other man stole his bees and thereby initiated a claim of theft rather than a suit turning around his own ownership.

These legal elements then dictated how a judge should rule on the matter.[153]

In fact, the author of the *Établissements* also described direct speech in terms of possibilities rather than requirements:

If some gentleman hears his lord giving him an incorrect judgement, he can very well say: 'This judgment is wrong, and I will no longer litigate this matter before you'. And if the lord is a baron, he should appeal to the court of the king or the court of the person from whom he held [... and the person making the appeal] can speak in this manner: 'Sir, this person has given me a false judgment, for which reason I no longer wish to hold [my fief] from him, instead I will hold [directly] from you, who are my overlord'. And the lower lord can say: 'Sir, I am ready to deny it', the other man can say: 'Sir, I do not want him to be able to deny it'.[154]

The *coutumier* author was expressing the types of things that *could* be said to make legal claims. When the same author explained how a person requesting seisin should do so ('he must ask in this way'), he noted that 'he should reserve the right to do or say more, if he needs to', as mentioned earlier.[155] The *coutumier* offered sample statements that individual actors could then customize and expand.

The sample statements presented the basic scaffolding of legal claims, counterclaims, and judicial responses and judgments. The nature of the script was rather flexible and, in the words of Enders, geared towards 'forensic delivery'.[156] Every section concerning a claim of desseised land, false judgement, arson, or a dowry issue connected to the lived drama of the law. Though a sense of drama can be excavated from these texts, the *coutumiers* do not dwell on the dramatic narrative of backstory, the feeling of being wronged, the fear of being accused, or

---

[153] There are many examples of this: 'If one person makes complaint about another concerning money, and the latter appears in court, and the plaintiff says: "You owe me this much money", and the debtor says: "I have never before heard this complaint; for which reason I request an appropriate court date; and on that day I will make a proper answer, as a defendant who never did you wrong"; and if the other party says: "I am not willing to have another date assigned, but I want you to admit or deny your debt to me, and I will await a ruling", then the ruling should be that he must admit or deny' (*Établissements de Saint Louis*, I.73).

[154] *Établissements de Saint Louis*, I.86.

[155] 'il doit demander en tele maniere [...] Et si doit faire retenue de plus faire et de plus dire, se mestiers li en est' (*Établissements*, ed. Viollet, II.4).

[156] Enders, *Rhetoric and the Origins of Medieval Drama*, p. 14.

the shame of public judgment. In this regard they resembled records of judicial proceedings, which were designed to present logics of argumentation rather than the dramatic immediacy of performance, though judicial proceedings were more revealing in this regard than the *coutumiers*.[157] This was purposeful: 'Since part of the very nature of forensic delivery was its tendency to become increasingly theatrical, the reproduction of the bare bones of legal argumentation discouraged the perception that [legal] rhetoric was a form of spectacle'.[158]

Absent from the first *coutumiers* were suggestions of professional etiquette and physical aspects of gesture and performance found in contemporary texts of canon law such as William Durand's *Speculum iudicale*, composed in 1271 and revised twice before his death in 1296. This text commented on the proper dress of advocates as well as on movements and gestures such as rising and walking to the right place to speak, doffing their caps, and bowing.[159] Durand also suggested especially effective rhetorical performances, such as overweening praise of the judges, and described how to craft them.[160] The *coutumiers*, in contrast, tended to emphasize clarity, simplicity of meaning, brevity, and expediency.

Depictions or suggestions of verbal expression – the scripts – were but one part of each *coutumier*, which in most cases contained descriptive matter in larger proportion. *Coutumier* authors as a group used direct speech as one technique to shape actors in a variety of actions and roles. The idea of transition from oral to written connotes a full shift from the primitive to the modern, or from the romantic to the bureaucratic, and suggests that the oral and written were separate states.[161] However, the shift in literacy is better stated, in the words of Adam Kosto, 'as not one from memory to written record, but from memory to imagination, from the use of

---

[157] *Ibid.*, p.38. As Guillaume DuBreuil noted in around 1330, 'in writing, one finds little of the parliamentary style of the noble court of France, which sometimes changes and varies' (*ibid.*, p.39).

[158] *Ibid.*   [159] Brundage, *The Medieval Origins of the Legal Profession*, pp. 425–6.

[160] *Ibid.*, p. 426.

[161] Despite this connotation, even today, law happens in the argument or in judicial pronouncement, also a form of speech (records are then evidence for these). The debates over the multiple and occasionally contradictory, interpretations of the American Constitution are one example. Adversarial procedure itself is another.

writing to reconstruct the past to the use of writing to construct the future'.[162]

**

The texts and manuscript traditions of the *coutumiers* were remarkable repositories of the thinking that animated 'vernacular law' – the different forms and articulations of custom and the fundamentally dialectical nature of customary legal culture, even as it was beginning to textualize. Each *coutumier* manuscript presented a legitimate version of custom and was part of the constant conversation and negotiation of authority that defined customary law. The customs we find in the *coutumiers* were those of jurists who attended the secular courts, who were knowledgeable about the practices of these courts, and who felt that their customs were important enough to set in writing. The authors of the text were conscious of the rapid legal change that was occurring around them: they were reacting to these changes just as they were contributing to them.

To be sure, not every custom was relentlessly contested through rewriting – many customs were considered established, well-known, or general – but every custom could have been. The larger implication of this rewriting is that there was no swift or complete transition to a textualized practice. This law 'in the books' was a type of 'law in action'.[163] Moreover, law in the books was constituting and trying to shape various types of law in action. While the practice of the lay courts was not rigidly formalized, in the sense of court-enforced rules indexed to and proven by written law, it did have its own customs, usages, and forms of practice that were perceived as good or bad, successful or weak, convincing or not. The *coutumier* authors tried to groom professionalized court performers who would convince judges and members of juries that theirs was the winning legal argument.

The manuscript traditions around these texts demonstrate the birth of textual communities as well as real communities around them. The different manuscript versions of these texts were, some to a lesser and some to a greater extent, written by people who were thinking about the

---

[162] Kosto, *Making Agreements in Medieval Catalonia*, p. 294.
[163] I would like to thank Marianne Constable for our conversation on this subject years ago.

texts they copied and customizing them to their own needs.[164] The variation between manuscripts was a testament to the juridical communities that formed around these texts as well as the continued conscious development of a living customary law that was not, as has been assumed, petrified in written text. Each *coutumier* created and provided an authoritative text, and each text, read or heard, taught its audience to think like a lawyer, to participate in the dialectic of custom effectively. In turn, this permitted them to play with the theatricality of a convincing court performance and to efficaciously enact certain rituals.

The *coutumier* authors sought to help lay people become lay practitioners by developing their ability to participate properly in the conversations that constituted the affirmation, delineation, contestation, and reconstitution of custom. They shaped the conversation at the basis of customary legal culture and placed this conversation within an increasingly professionalized framework based on specific processes of thought. The variations between manuscripts, even in the suggested words to be spoken at court, showed that texts co-existed with a live, critical, engaged customary legal culture.

---

[164] Scholars are using new media platforms to present manuscripts as complete documents in their own right, their intertextual nature, and their place as part of one textual tradition (Martin Foys, 'Medieval Manuscripts: Media Archaeology and the Digital Incunable', pp. 133ff).

8

Implications of Circulating Text: Crafting a French Common Law

The language of geography and images of maps have long dominated our understanding of French law in the high Middle Ages. While medieval English law is typically characterized by a nascent 'common law', medieval French law is typically characterized by a mosaic of different legal identities. Henri Klimrath had already established the first cartography of French medieval custom in 1837.[1] The most important feature of this map was the famed fault line that ran more or less from La Rochelle to Lake Geneva and divided the *pays de coutumes*, the areas of northern France governed by custom, from the *pays de droit écrit*, the areas of southern France with a Roman-influenced law.[2]

This chapter significantly reproduces my article 'Inventing Legal Space: From Regional Custom to Common Law in the *Coutumiers* of Medieval France' in *Space in the Medieval West Places, Territories, and Imagined Geographies*, ed. Meredith Cohen and Fanny Madeleine (Ashgate, June 2014), pp. 133–155, with some revisions.

[1] Klimrath, *Études sur les coutumes*.

[2] Hilaire, *La vie du droit*, p. 157. For a good introduction to the 'two zones' of France's juridical map and their relationship to Roman law and to custom, see Guillot, Rigaudière, and Sassier, *Pouvoirs et institutions*) pp. 139ff. This line between the two zones is now understood to have been rather blurry and uneven in the thirteenth century and into the fourteenth, with enclaves of the other 'system' on either side (*ibid.*, p. 140). Jean Hilaire has also critiqued this map for being essentially judicial. He notes that the ambit of custom may better be seen by looking at notarial practice which, at least in the South, is an awkward match for Klimrath's map (see Hilaire, *La vie du droit*, p. 159). The disjunction between judicial and notarial maps should, in itself, lead us to question a unified customary law indexed to specific territory.

These cartographers of medieval custom found an essential source in the *coutumiers*. These *coutumiers* are commonly defined geographically as private works that set the customs and usages of a specific region in writing, and this area, ruled by a specific *coutume*, could be as small as a particular castellany or as large as entire duchy.[3] These texts are seen as artefacts of the shift to the territoriality of law; they represent the culmination of the story of an oral and personal custom that 'crystallized', was tied to a specific territory, and was eventually designated by that territory.[4] The notion of the region thus dominates current understandings of the *coutumiers*.

Klimrath had worked deductively from geographic indicators in the *coutumiers* and from the limits of the regional Parlements in pre-revolutionary France. However, custom, legal practice, and geographic boundaries had undergone some notable changes between the thirteenth and eighteenth centuries.[5] In the 1960s, Jean Yver adjusted Klimrath's customary map for northern France in his *Géographie coutumière*, where he amended the territorial delimitation of the customs and gathered them into affiliated groups.[6]

John Hudson notes that much of the scholarly attention paid to medieval secular law in France has focused on these geographical aspects because of the later importance of regional custom in the development of French law.[7] Notions of what 'common law' means and has meant have also contributed to this focus on geography. It is

---

[3] Gilissen, *La coutume*, p. 86; van Dievoet, *Les coutumiers, les styles, les formulaires*, p. 13; Cohen, *Crossroads of Justice*, p. 28.

[4] Gilissen, *La coutume*, p. 33. Also see generally Simeon Guterman, *From Personal to Territorial Law*.

[5] An excellent case study of these geographic changes may be found in Daniel Power's analysis of Normandy, see Power, *The Norman Frontier in the Twelfth and Thirteenth Centuries*, pp. 148–51.

[6] Yver, *Égalité entre héritiers et exclusion des enfants dotés*. Yver's method was to follow a specific rule of inheritance – the equality of heirs in inheritance, and the exception that dowered children were excluded from inheritance – and then to see to what extent it made a mark on the various regions of the *pays de coutumes*. Yver has also argued that instead of discussing individual customs, we need to see them as part of customary groupings. See also Yver, 'Les caractères originaux'. Paul Ourliac and Jean-Louis Gazzaniga offer a useful updated summary in their discussion of the 'juridical map' of these customary grouping ('Essai de géographie juridique', in Ourliac and Gazzaniga, *Histoire de droit privé français*, pp. 81–120).

[7] Hudson, 'Customs, Laws and the Interpretation of Medieval Law', p. 9.

still widely thought that if there was a 'common law' in France in the Middle Ages, then it was the pan-European *ius commune* composed of Roman and canon law. While this has been challenged, and the existence of a 'common customary law' has been acknowledged by many scholars, scholarship has focused on the particular instances of the term 'common law' (*droit commun/ius commune*) in legal treatises and court records.[8] H. Patrick Glenn, in his comprehensive study of the concept of common law, also argues that the notion of 'common law' historically extended beyond the *ius commune* and the English common law.[9] However, the implications of a French common law for other orthodoxies of French legal history have not yet received significant attention. For instance, where did this 'common law' come from? What does it mean for the narrative of regional custom?

This chapter discusses the circulation of legal ideas among the lay jurists who wrote about laws and customs of the secular courts of thirteenth-century France and how, in writing 'regional' customs, they participated in the creation of the idea of a French common law. My focus will be on similarities rather than differences in order to illuminate ideas of common law in these texts, generally described as containing local or regional customary laws.[10]

While at first glance the *coutumiers* may seem like the quintessential representatives of an inward-looking, local legal identity, the textual practices of lay jurists who composed these texts reveal that the *coutumiers*, as a group, were seen and used as a common – one might say generic – pool of legal knowledge that transcended regional boundaries. Together, these texts formed a pool of knowledge from which to draw in the composition of subsequent *coutumiers*. One might say that they formed a sort of *ius commune* for the lay courts.

---

[8] See the section below titled 'The *Droit Commun* Debate'.

[9] H. P. Glenn, *On Common Laws*, p. vii.

[10] This chapter examines how references to common law in the *coutumiers* and the textual practices of authors and copyists of these texts revealed assumptions about notions of common law and showed its increasing importance in northern France as the thirteenth century progressed. While it does not aim to provide a comprehensive description of French notions of common law in the *coutumiers* that includes a full survey of the substantive and procedural laws, such a full survey is the necessary next step in further developing our understanding of French notions of common law and how these compared to the range of uses and meanings of the term in other kingdoms.

The Language of Custom

The *coutumiers* departed from legal writing that preceded them because they were written in the vernacular and accessible to an audience beyond the Latin literate.[11] For the first time, the *coutumiers* presented the voice of the lay practitioner describing and even theorizing the practice of the customary law of the secular courts in the vernacular, and one of the clues that they did, in fact, exercise these new abilities can be found in the language of the texts.

Not everyone spoke the same French in the thirteenth century. The various dialects included Picard, Champenois, Orléanais, Tourangeau, Poitevin, Normand, and Francien, to name a few. Even before the expansion of the French crown in the thirteenth century, however, the French from the royal domain and especially from the Paris region (Francien) was understood by many to be superior to other dialects.[12]

The affinity between law, language, and geography popularized in the nationalisms of the late-eighteenth and nineteenth centuries does not map neatly onto these medieval texts. Though they are supposed to be regional customary texts, many *coutumier* manuscripts were written in the Francien dialect.[13] This is actually the most common one in the thirteenth-century *coutumiers*, which all have at least one manuscript in Francien. The use of this dialect can mean different

---

[11] There were some cases of texts being written in Latin and then translated into the vernacular, such as the *Sachsenspiegel* (1235) or *the Très ancien coutumier de Normandie* (ca. 1200).

[12] For more on dialects, see Lusignan, *La langue des rois au Moyen Âge*, pp. 62ff. Until the twelfth century, the vernacular is referred to as 'romana lingua' or 'roman', but during the twelfth century 'franceis' and later 'françois' begin to overtake it (*ibid.*, pp. 221–2). Lusignan recounts an episode from the miracles of Saint Louis collected by Guillaume de Chartres soon after 1290, where a deaf and dumb man from Bourgogne went to pray at Saint Louis' grave in Saint Denis to recover these senses. Then a miracle occurred. He recovered the ability to speak, and Saint Louis added the perk of speaking properly – instead of recovering the Bourguignon dialect, he recovered good Parisian French! (*ibid.*, p. 21). Other than Francien, Picard was the most widespread rival dialect (*ibid.*, p. 225).

[13] The oldest translation of the *Statua et consuetudines Normannie* into French that we have was written in the Ile-de-France dialect and not the Norman dialect (introduction to *Coutumiers de Normandie*, ed. Tardif, vol. 1, part II, xl, l). The earliest extant version of Pierre de Fontaines' text, copied between 1260 and 1280, is also in the language of the Ile-de-France (introduction to Pierre de Fontaines, *Conseil*, ed. Marnier, p. xxxi). Philippe de Beaumanoir's text is written in both the Ile-de-France dialect and in Picard.

things: perhaps the authors or copyists in the regions wanted to ennoble their texts by using 'superior' Ile-de-France French, or the copyist was a native Francien speaker. Both possibilities prove the extra-regional appeal of the *coutumiers* – the first because use of an outside or prestigious dialect implies an audience outside the region, and the second because the text had already passed into an outsider's hands.

Francien is not the only extra-regional dialect in which the *coutumiers* appear. Most *coutumiers* have manuscripts in dialects that are unrelated to their affiliated region and even include some southern dialects.[14] This mixture of languages would be impossible if these texts were of purely local interest. It indicates a community practice – texts, jurists, and copyists must all have been mobile, and the *coutumiers* must have had appeal beyond their own region.

Shifting Territoriality

In fact, lay jurists were treating these texts of customary law as a creative commons from which they could draw as they wanted or needed. The practice of copying from one *coutumier* to another began soon after the first few *coutumiers* were written in the mid-thirteenth century and continued with vigour well beyond that time. While each *coutumier* is conventionally linked to a specific territorial unit, the manuscript tradition indicates that the texts were subject to a shifting territoriality. It was common practice among the *coutumier* authors to copy portions of earlier customary texts, often with other regional labels, in the composition of their own *coutumier*. This suggests that the *coutumiers*, and the customs within, were transplanted and cross-pollinated, and further suggests they were part of an organic circulation of ideas that were understood to have a more general application.

Alan Watson notes that even customary law may be the subject of 'legal transplant'.[15] Some instances are well known, such as the movement of the *Sachsenspiegel* and the laws of some cities, such as

---

[14] Manuscript M of Pierre de Fontaines' work is written in a southern dialect (Pierre de Fontaines, *Conseil*, ed. Marnier, p. xxxvii). The *Coutumier d'Artois* is the only one written in dialects not connected to the Ile-de-France, but in the Artois and Picard dialects (introduction to *Coutumier d'Artois*, ed. Tardif, p. xvi). The difference is visually significant – gages and waiges, manaces and manaiches, suer and sereurs, etc.

[15] In the appendix to the second edition (Alan Watson, *Legal Transplants*, p. 114).

Magdeburg, beyond their original geographic ambit.[16] Nonetheless, modern commentators tend to react to this practice largely with disdain. Unlike the citation of Roman and canon law, which is regarded as a reverent citation of authority – whether attributed or not– the practice of copying portions of one *coutumier* into another has largely been handled with vague notions of intellectual hypocrisy and cultural plagiarism. After all, how can you take the customs of one region and say they are another's?

According to Peter Edwards, Philip of Novara's work was 'plagiarized' by later authors.[17] Guido van Dievoet, in turn, claimed that the *Livre des droiz et des commendemens d'office de justice* of Poitou 'shamelessly pillages' the *Établissements de Saint Louis* to compose its text, and both Jean Boutillier's *Somme rural* and the *Coutumier d'Artois* also take selections from the *Établissements* and copy them into their own texts.[18] The *Demenées el Chastelet de Paris* was also used by the redactor of the *Grand coutumier de France*.[19] As van Dievoet notes, all of these texts use the work of their predecessors without citing them.[20] The 'harm' (*mal*) would not be so great, he suggests, if these *coutumiers* had contented themselves with using the customs from their own regions – but they did not.[21]

Thus, the author who copied from texts of Roman and canon law is praised as appealing to an authority and aspiring to something better, as legitimately drawing on a common law. Meanwhile, the author copying from a *coutumier* is criticized as uninventive at best and disingenuous at worst – a thief of custom and identity. This understanding of the medieval lay jurist's approach to custom seems to be related to modern, almost instinctual feelings about customary law as *volksgeist* as well as a prescriptive and particular notion of authenticity. As this section will demonstrate, the medieval lay jurists writing the *coutumiers* did not share this anxiety about the regional authenticity of custom.

---

[16] Glenn, *On Common Laws*, p. 38.
[17] Philip of Novara, *Le livre de forme de plait*, trans. Edbury, p. 6.
[18] Van Dievoet, *Les coutumiers, les styles, les formulaires*, p. 43. See Van Dievoet for more examples of the practice outside of France (*ibid.*, p. 44).
[19] Mortet, 'Seconde partie: Étude du texte' in *Le livre des constitutions demenées*, ed. Mortet, p. 19.
[20] Van Dievoet, *Les coutumiers, les styles, les formulaires*, p. 43.
[21] 'S'ils s'étaient limités aux coutumiers ou aux styles de leur region, le mal ne serait pas grand' (*ibid.*).

To be sure, the *coutumiers* do give the impression of fixity of place, to some extent. The texts do not have titles in the modern sense but generally begin by defining the nature of the text. For example, the text that describes the customs of Champagne opens by explaining, 'This is the book of rights and customs of Champagne'; throughout the text the author attributes rules to that region by saying that 'it is custom in Champagne', and one of the manuscripts ends by saying, 'Here end the customs of Champagne.'[22] Generally, a *coutumier* will include this form of regional attribution either at the beginning of the text, in its discussion of specific rules, or in the last few sentences. Based on such geographic clues, each *coutumier* is understood to overlay a specific regional delimitation: Pierre de Fontaines' *coutumier* concerns the Vermandois; Philippe de Beaumanoir's *Coutumes de Beauvaisis* discusses the custom of the Beauvaisis; the *Établissements de Saint Louis* contain the customs of Touraine and Anjou in Book I and the customs of Orleans in Book II; and the various anonymous texts are specific to Artois, Normandy, Champagne, Touraine, and Maine.

The manuscript tradition of these texts, however, tells a different story about regions. In fact, different manuscripts do not always agree about the identity of the region to which a specific set of customs is attached. This can clearly be seen by looking at the manuscript tradition of the *Établissements de Saint Louis*. Paul Viollet's critical edition of the *Établissements* is divided into two parts. Part I contains the customs of Touraine and Anjou (*Usages de Touraine et d'Anjou*), while Part II contains the customs of the Orleans region (*Li usages d'Orlenois*).[23] However, some manuscripts tie the same text to different territory.

Book I of the *Établissements* is commonly known as the *Usages de Touraine et d'Anjou*.[24] Some manuscripts, however, do not designate

---

[22] 'C'est li livre de drois et des costumes de Champegne' (*L'ancien coutumier de Champagne*, ed. Portejoie, p. 131); 'il est coustume en Champane' (*ibid.*, II, V, etc.); this explicit occurs only in Portejoie's manuscript A where it says 'ci faillent les coustumes de Champaigne' (*ibid.*, p. 230).

[23] Viollet does not break up the two parts of Book I, while F. R. P. Akehurst separates the royal ordinances from the Customs of Touraine and Anjou in his translation (*Établissements*, ed. Viollet; *Établissements*, trans. Akehurst).

[24] Book II is pretty uncontroversial – the customs of Orléans are sometimes attributed to Orleans alone, sometimes to both Orleans and Paris: '*L'usage dou Chatelet d'Orliens en cort de baronnie*', '*L'usage d'Orlenois et de Paris*', and '*L'usage dou chatelet de*

them as the customs of Touraine-Anjou at all and, instead, they present Book I as the first part of the king's *établissements* according to the usage of Paris and Orleans.[25] This means that the regional customs of Touraine and Anjou, a cultural and geographic space distinctly separate from the royal domain, were being passed off as the customs of the royal domain. If regional customs were indeed so distinct, then this would be disorienting to any contemporary. Would such a book not be useless to litigants, lawyers, and judges? If we conceive of custom, as recorded in the *coutumiers*, as deeply embedded in territorial identity, it is notable that the same rules that could be attributed to such culturally different areas as Touraine and Anjou were from Paris and Orleans.

This sort of shifting and unstable territoriality also occurs elsewhere. The first nine provisions of Book I were actually royal ordinances.[26] We know this from unrelated works, not from the *Établissements*. The *Établissements* incorporates the royal ordinances into the customs of Book I without ever mentioning that they were royal ordinances.[27] Here, royal decree was presented as regional custom.

Viollet's investigations led him to detect yet another extraterritorial connection. He found that the contents of the customs of Touraine-Anjou in the *Établissements* largely correspond to the Customs of Anjou and Maine (*Coutumes d'Anjou et du Maine*), which was

Paris et d'Orliens' (*Établissements*, trans. Akehurst, p. 327n.7). That the same customs might be attributed sometimes to Orleans, and sometimes to Orleans and Paris is not very startling as both of these cities had long been part of the royal domain.

[25] The title of the customs of Touraine-Anjou are drawn from the explicit. The text that Viollet chose is from the manuscripts that end with: 'The usages of Touraine and Anjou finish here (*Ci fenist li Usages de Touraine et d'Anjou*)' (*Établissements*, ed. Viollet, I.175). Other manuscripts, however, close Book I with 'The first books of the Establishments of the king of France according to the usage of Paris and Orléans and baronial court end here (*Ci fenist li premiers livres des Establissemenz le roi de France selon l'Usage de Paris et d'Orliens et de cort de baronie*)' (*Établissements*, trans. Akehurst, p. 325 and n.7).

[26] See *Établissements*, ed. Viollet, I.5–8.

[27] Viollet points this out in his introduction (*Établissements*, ed. Viollet, vol. 1), but does not separate the first nine provisions from the text that follows and kept the text united, as presented in the manuscripts (see *Établissements*, ed. Viollet, II.19). Akehurst opens Book I with the first nine provisions under the title 'The Rules of Procedures in the Châtelet', and provisions from ten onwards are separated and placed under the title 'The Customs of Touraine and Anjou' (*Établissements*, trans. Akehurst, pp. 7, 15).

about thirty years older.[28] Actually, the *Coutumes d'Anjou et du Maine* basically became Book I of the *Établissements* (or the customs of Touraine-Anjou, depending on the manuscript). Beyond the addition of citation discussed in Chapter 5, the changes between the two texts are not so vast – twenty-four insertions are made in approximately 150 chapters – that Beautemps-Beaupré's statement that the *Usages de Touraine et d'Anjou* in the *Établissements* is in fact the glossed version of the *Coutumes d'Anjou et du Maine* is not a rhetorical flourish.[29] Yet, in this process, the identity of the text changed. While the attribution to Anjou remained, the earlier customs of Maine were transposed to Touraine.

Viollet dismisses this by saying that the juridical nuances that separated Touraine and Maine were probably so trivial that this fuzzy territoriality did not create a problem.[30] This may be true, but it does not explain why so many authors of subsequent *coutumiers* used the *Établissements* – the customs of Touraine, Anjou, and Orleans – in their own works.

Historians have often dismissed the *Établissements* for its crudeness and lack of sophistication, paying little attention to the text in comparison to Beaumanoir's refined work. However, as the copying practices attest, the *Établissements* was possibly the most popular French *coutumier* of the thirteenth century. We can see the influence of this text on the customs of Brittany, Champagne, Artois, Picardy, and even in Beaumanoir's erudite *Coutumes de Beauvaisis*.[31] Tellingly, an abridged version of the *Établissements* pops up in Champagne, and this new abridged version of the customs of Touraine-Anjou-Orleans holds itself out to be the customs of both France (in the sense of the royal domain) and Champagne.[32] In the first years of the fourteenth century, the *Établissements* even makes its mark on the South, in Poitou, where a jurist glosses the text.[33]

---

[28] *Établissements*, ed. Viollet, I.8–33. See *Coutumes d'Anjou et du Maine*, ed. Beautemps-Beaupré, vol. 1, pp. 64–176. The *Coutumues d'Anjou et Maine* correspond to provision ten onwards of Book I, and pre-date the royal ordinances mentioned above.

[29] Beautemps-Beaupré, 'Observations sur les texts A, B et C', in *Coutumes d'Anjou et du Maine*, vol. 1, p. 15.

[30] *Établissements*, ed. Viollet, I.23.   [31] *Établissements*, ed. Viollet, I.280–394.

[32] See *Abrégé Champenois* in *Établissements*, ed. Viollet, IV.141–87.

[33] Hasenohr and Zink (eds.), *Dictionnaire des lettres françaises*, p. 418.

The text we call the *Établissements de Saint Louis*, then, was a composite work composed by interleaving two royal ordinances and larger works on custom written by earlier jurists, and partially reassigning the customs of one location to another. Not only did the lay jurist who compiled the *Établissements* reorient the customs of Anjou and Maine as those of Anjou and Touraine, but afterwards other lay jurists spread his text far beyond its original ambit of Anjou, Touraine, and Orleans.

Coutumiers, Textual Communities, and Dialogues between Lay Jurists

The compiler of the *Établissements* used the entire texts of earlier *coutumiers* wholesale, but the more common practice among lay jurists composing a customary treatise was to use selections from the *coutumiers* from which they copied. This was the case for the *Coutumier d'Artois*, composed sometime between 1283 and 1302.[34] The two major sources for this text are Pierre de Fontaines' *Conseil à un ami*, a *coutumier* based on the Vermandois written in 1253, and the *Établissements de Saint Louis*. The majority of the text is of the author's own composition, with intermittent sections from Pierre's *Conseil* or the *Établissements*.

The prologue of the *Coutumier d'Artois* is the part of the text most indebted to others. In fact, with the exception of one paragraph, the entire, fairly long prologue is lifted directly from Pierre de Fontaines' *coutumier*, ostensibly based on the region of Vermandois. It is not quoted or cited; the text is incorporated as if it had been written originally for this *coutumier*. The portion of Pierre's *Conseil* used in the *Coutumier d'Artois* included the prologue where Pierre invited future readers of his work to amend the text as they see fit:

And it would be very pleasing to me that they make their amendments, if they see that it will be useful. And let them well know that where they make amendments, they will make something *more* worthy of praise than I did. For, as the law says, he who skilfully amends a previous work does something more praiseworthy than the one who created it. [35]

---

[34] *Coutumier d'Artois*, ed. Tardif.   [35] *Ibid.*

Pierre encouraged future changes, as long as they constituted an improvement – and praised skilful amendments and emendations above the actual original writing of the text. The notion of using a customary text and changing it was present in one of the sources that the author of the *Coutumier d'Artois* used to construct his own text.

In fact, the author of the *Coutumier d'Artois* seemed to respond directly to Pierre's invitation to amend and improve. The one section of the prologue that the author wrote himself is a defence of brevity: he explains that he put the laws and customs of the lay courts of the region in writing but that he did so with brevity because 'memory is fleeting and things soon forgotten, and it is not enough to try to remember many things, because new things take away the memory of old ones'.[36] People remember better what is short than what is long so, he explained, it 'profits my book to speak briefly instead of at length'.[37] The author of the *Coutumier d'Artois* must have been replying directly to Pierre de Fontaines' words here. This one-paragraph addition to the prologue is an explanation for the changes he made and an argument for why they constitute an improvement.

The technique used by the author of the *Coutumier d'Artois* echoes those employed by the compiler of the *Établissements de Saint Louis*. Both of these lay jurists adopted, and adapted, portions of other *coutumiers* into their own text. The author of the *Coutumier d'Artois*, however, did not simply use the text of another lay jurist. He was clearly in conversation with Pierre de Fontaines, and his use of the text was a living exchange of ideas. He was consciously building upon Pierre's work, claiming, reusing, and transforming it as part of a common endeavour and practice, and a continuing dialogue.

By circulating individual *coutumiers* beyond the ambit of one region, these jurists were creating dialogue between local laws and customs. In this sense they were building juristic communities based on common textual practices and, one might even say, on a coherent methodological approach. In effect, they were treating the *coutumiers* as though they formed a common pool of legal knowledge from which to compose texts of customary law.

---

[36] *Coutumier d'Artois*, ed. Tardif, prologue.4. [37] *Coutumier d'Artois*, ed. Tardif.

Judicial Abstraction and a Royal Connection

This use of texts of customary law as a pool of common customary legal knowledge is closely connected to a movement towards judicial abstraction during this period. Alain Boureau coined the term 'judicial abstraction' to describe the dynamic process whereby the complex and diverse situations that give rise to conflicts are generalized and formalized.[38]

The *coutumiers* provide evidence of two main factors that contributed to the movement to judicial abstraction. One factor, at least partially, must be a context of expanding royal power and territorial state. The intense secular legal activity of the thirteenth century seems to have been a second factor in the development of the generalizable norm.

The writing of the first *coutumiers* in the second half of the thirteenth century occurs simultaneously with the cementing of the links between royal power and the territory with which it is identified – the king shifts from *rex Francorum* to *rex Franciae*, and 'France' is constituted as a space.[39] The swift establishment of royal sovereignty no doubt went hand in hand with the expansion of jurists in the royal service and of juridical study generally.[40] Jacques Krynen notes that royal power was consolidated in the kingdom primarily through justice and by insistence on the judicial sovereignty of the king.[41]

The *Établissements* are the only thirteenth-century French *coutumier* specifically attributed to a king. There is good reason to think that this royal attribution might be linked to the shifting regional affiliations in the different manuscripts. Louis IX (1226–70) was not just any king – he had a now legendary concern for justice. Canonized soon after his death, he became Saint Louis, whose words and deeds were to be revered and emulated as a sort of informal constitution.[42] This *coutumier*, it is true, was the work of a redactor who copied and pasted previous texts to create the patchwork known as the *Établissements*. A later copyist probably attributed the text to this king himself. Only three manuscripts – such as

---

[38] Boureau, *La loi du royaume*, pp. 18–19.

[39] Daniel Nordman and Jacques Revel, 'La formation de l'espace français', pp. 71, 72. By 1254 the king has shifted from *rex Francorum* to *rex Franciae* in the acts of the royal chancellery, and this evolution seems to be complete by 1300 (*ibid.*, p. 71).

[40] Krynen, *L'empire du roi*, pp. 69ff.   [41] *Ibid.*, p. 252.

[42] William Chester Jordan has noted that Saint Louis' life in fact became the unwritten constitution of medieval France in his concluding words (Jordan, 'Closing remarks').

the one in Figure 8.1 – contain the prologue that described the text as legislation issued by the king (rather than an anonymous description of the practices of the royal courts in Paris and/or Orleans), but it was the one that captured popular imagination, and even inspired a poem.[43]

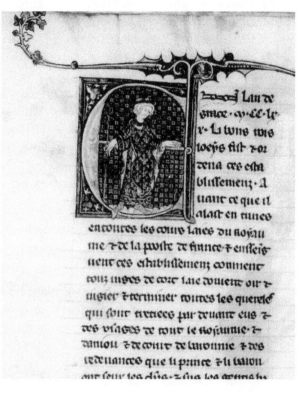

FIGURE 8.1 Added prologue that presents the *Établissements de Saint Louis* as a 'common law' for the kingdom of France. This prologue, contained in three manuscripts, made the *Établissements* into legislation composed for Louis IX by 'wise men and good clerks' after great consultation and issued by the king before he went on crusade in 1270. This prologue claims that these 'laws' were imposed in all the lay courts in the kingdom of France and that they confirm 'good practices and ancient customs' adhered to in the kingdom of France through a concordance of laws, canons, and decretals. *Établissements de Saint Louis*, Bibliothèque nationale de France, ms. fr. 18096, fol. 3v.

---

[43] 'Chanson sur les Établissements du roi Saint Louis' in Antoine Leroux de Lincy, 'Chansons historiques des XIIIe, XIVe et XVe siècles'. This poem was a lament about the legal changes brought in by Louis IX.

It was only in the nineteenth century that scholars began doubting the royal authorship of this text.[44] For centuries, then, it was generally considered as a representation of Saint Louis' will, if not authorship.

The *Établissements* seems to have been the best-travelled *coutumier*, as demonstrated by its geographic dispersion. The remarkable shifting territoriality of this text must largely be due to its acquisition of a royal attribution. In the manuscripts attributing the text to Louis IX, the personal charisma of this unique king as well as the powerful *post mortem* mythology surrounding him undoubtedly played a part.[45] In those manuscripts that did not share this royal attribution, the traditional bastions of royal power – Paris and Orleans – were mentioned often enough to give the text the support of royal authority.

Other texts also illustrate this kind of generalization. Manuscript M of Pierre de Fontaines' *Conseil à un ami*, copied between 1280 and 1300, is one example.[46] It states that the text records 'the customs of France and of Champagne and of Vermandois and of other lay courts'.[47] This attribution generalizes the customs from Vermandois to other lay courts and also makes the particular customs of Vermandois those of the royal domain and of Champagne.

It is tempting to see a direct correlation between the expansion of royal power and the extra-territorial turn of these texts. However, some *coutumiers* show that this shifting territoriality could also occur with no discernible royal connection. Thus, the expansion of royal power and the territorialization of the French kingdom could explain partially the movement of custom and customary text, but absent a royal connection, this shifting territoriality was due to the increasingly abstract thinking of jurists who participated in, wrote about, and theorized lay court activity.

Pierre de Fontaines' *Conseil à un ami* was also subject to this sort of judicial redrawing or blurring of legal ideas, though in this case the

---

[44] *Établissements*, ed. Viollet, I:1.
[45] After his death, different parties constructed Louis IX's memory in ways that led to the development of his sanctity, canonization, and cult, see Gaposchkin, *The Making of Saint Louis: Kingship, Sanctity, and Crusade in the Later Middle Ages*.
[46] For more on manuscript M, see Marnier's introduction to Pierre de Fontaines, *Conseil*, ed. Marnier, p. xxxvii.
[47] 'les costumes de France et de Champaingne et de Vermandois et d'autres corz laies' (Pierre de Fontaines, *Conseil*, ed. Marnier, p. 4n.1).

movement did not seem related to a royal connection. Philip of Novara appears to have used it for his lawbook written for the crusader kingdoms in Cyprus and Jerusalem, *Livre à un sien ami en forme de plais* (ca. 1264), which he also styled as advice to a friend. The *Coutumier d'Artois*, as we have seen, copies extensively from Pierre's *Conseil*, replicating entire passages verbatim, including the section in the prologue where Pierre claims to be doing something that no one has done before. The *Conseil* continued to be used for other works in the fourteenth century – passages are quoted in the *Somme rurale* and in the *Coutumier de Charles VI*.[48] Another version of the *Conseil*, probably a little later, appears translated into Dutch.[49]

This shifting territoriality also manifests itself in the manuscript tradition of the *Coutumes de Beauvaisis*. Robert Jacob remarked that the prologue and the conclusion to Beaumanoir's work announce slightly different goals – customs of the Beauvais region, and customs of the county of Clermont.[50] Beaumanoir states that he is writing his book on the customs of Beauvaisis so that Robert the count of Clermont can know how he should keep the customs of the county of Clermont, and Jacob is certainly correct that the text seems to vacillate between the two.[51] This may indicate the difficulty of writing a purely regional custom without drawing on outside customs. This difficulty is evident from Beaumanoir's prologue, where he explains that in order to write his *Coutumes de Beauvaisis*, he will draw from the judgments of neighbouring castellanies as well as the law common to the kingdom of France.[52] This indicates, in turn, the composite nature of written custom and the generative role of the *coutumier* authors.

[48] Marnier, introduction to Pierre de Fontaines, *Conseil*, ed. Marnier, p. xliii.
[49] Collinet, 'Une traduction néerlandaise inédite du Conseil de Pierre de Fontaines'. The manuscript (Bibliothèque royale de Bruxelles, ms. 16775) is from the fifteenth century and contains various texts relating to the political history of Flemish cities in the thirteenth and fourteenth centuries (*ibid.*, 409–10). Paul Collinet does not give a potential date for the translation itself, though he says the manuscript is undoubtedly a copy of an earlier one (*ibid.*, 413).
[50] Jacob, 'Beaumanoir versus Révigny, p. 271.
[51] 'par cest livre pourra il estre enseignié comment il devra garder et fere garder les coustumes de sa terre de la conteé de Clermont' (Beaumanoir, *Coutumes de Beauvaisis*, ed. Salmon, prologue s. 3).
[52] *Ibid.*, prologue s. 6.

A more interesting case of shifting territory concerning Beaumanoir shows up in a fourteenth-century abridged version of his text.[53] This abridged version removes the prologue, Beaumanoir's name from the text, and passages that refer to the Beauvaisis; it changes references to the count of Clermont to 'the sovereign' and in so doing removes any information that identifies the original text, its author, and its geographical ambit.[54] Only one geographic indicator remains in the text, in the chapter on inheritance, where the redactor inserts two paragraphs mid-text that refer to the region of Champagne.[55] Champagne, as a region, does not seem to be the particular focus of the text. This abridged version takes the customs of Beauvais/Clermont as outlined by Beaumanoir and not only deracinates them but makes them virtually placeless.

This demonstrates the creative work of *coutumier* authors and those who amended them later. Beyond that, it also shows the changing conception of custom from territorialized rule to abstract and generally applicable norms. In fact, this movement towards extraterritoriality and judicial abstraction, evident in the *coutumiers*, can be linked to a nascent concept of *droit commun* developing contemporaneously in France.

The *Droit Commun* Debate

Delimiting these texts to their specific regions disguises the important role they played in the creation of something common and, in fact, the formation of a common law, *à la française*, comparable to parallel initiatives of the Crown and jurists in England. The term common law today may seem to describe a quintessentially Anglo-American form of legal culture, inimical to both the narrative of regional custom of *Ancien Régime* France and the codal culture that replaced it.[56]

---

[53] This is manuscript Bibliothèque nationale de France, ms.fr. 5332 (André Giffard, 'Un troisième abrégé de Beaumanoir', 626). Giffard says it is a fourteenth-century text.
[54] *Ibid.*, 627.   [55] *Ibid.*
[56] Modern sensitivity about this term, and worries about the spread of Anglo-American legal dominance, can be seen, for instance, in the preliminary provision of the Quebec Civil Code. This bilingual text states, in the French language version that the code constitutes 'le droit commun' of Quebec. However, in order to avoid saying in the English language that the text is 'common law', and the baggage of Anglo-American legal culture it carries, drafters chose instead to use the Latin term 'ius commune'.

However, the term 'common law' flourished in thirteenth-century legal sources – both in England and in France.

References to 'common law' in the *coutumiers* are not a rare occurrence. The meaning of this term has elicited much debate and, indeed, has monopolized analysis of the subject. Scholarly treatment of this 'common law' has been caught in a tug-of-war between those who believe that it refers to the learned laws of the *ius commune* and those who believe it refers in some sense to a customary law. The debate initially focused on Philippe de Beaumanoir's use of the term '*droit commun*' in his *Coutumes de Beauvaisis*. In 1908, Polynice van Wetter argued that the 'common law' in Beaumanoir's work was primarily the Roman law as it had been incorporated into custom, canon law in lesser part, and also the ordinances of the kings of France, feudal law, and custom that had no connection to learned law.[57] This view was challenged in 1960, when Pierre Petot argued that the term *droit commun* in Philippe de Beaumanoir's work referred to a notion, albeit blurry, of general rules common to the various customary regions of France and upheld by judgments of the Parlement in Paris.[58]

Various scholars have since contributed to the debate.[59] Most recently, the two proponents of the learned-law view have been Gérard Giordanengo and Jacques Krynen. Giordanengo argues that only in a few cases can references to 'common law' be shown to designate a general custom, and then only in texts that were not very learned and where terminological fluctuations are unsurprising.[60] Krynen has argued that 'common law' was Roman law and that the

---

[57] P. van Wetter, 'Le droit romain et Beaumanoir', vol. 2, pp. 538–9.
[58] See Petot, 'Le droit commun en France selon les coutumiers'.
[59] J. P. Lévy said that the 'common law' was the learned law, and custom was only its application, its complement (Lévy, 'La pénétration du droit savant', 17). Jean Gaudemet also stated that Roman law was more 'realistic' because he felt that the notion of a common customary law was scarcely outlined by the end of the thirteenth century, and legislation via royal ordinances was still very limited (Gaudemet, 'L'influence des droit savants', p. 181). As Castaldo has noted, van Wetter's view seems to have been remembered as a claim only for Roman law, instead of a claim *primarily* for Roman law (Castaldo, 'Pouvoir royal, droit savant et droit commun coutumier dans la France du Moyen Âge', 187).
[60] Giordanengo, '*Jus commune* et "droit commun"', esp. p. 232. Giordanengo gives a cursory glance to a few of the thirteenth-century *coutumiers* but focuses his analysis on Beaumanoir and the fourteenth-century *coutumiers*. The latter say more about the later development of learned laws as 'common law' than about the 'common law' in the *coutumiers* of the thirteenth century.

French kings had allied with Roman law because of its imperial stature in their attempt to bolster the state.[61]

Many scholars have also supported a customary common law thesis.[62] André Castaldo made a strong case for this in a long article that systematically challenges and unravels arguments presented for Roman law.[63] He shows how mentions of 'common law' in the thirteenth-century *coutumiers* can all be linked to general customs.[64] He examines Beaumanoir's work in detail, noting that although this author was clearly inspired by learned law in his writing, each reference to the expression *'droit commun'* concerns issues of customary law, such as roads.[65] He also examines the records of Parlement of Paris that refer to *ius commune* and argues that they do not refer to Roman law, either explicitly or implicitly.[66] Castaldo has proven that *droit commun* in the *coutumiers* is customary in nature.[67]

---

[61] See Krynen, 'Le droit romain, droit commun de France' and his '*Voluntas domini regis in suo regno facit ius*'.

[62] Paul Ourliac supported Petot's argument, adding that the 'common law' was an imprecise notion that was composed of the adages that circulated in the *pays de coutumes* among people involved in the law and that were most often taken up in the judgments of the Parlement of Paris (Ourliac, 'Beaumanoir et les Coutumes de Beauvaisis', p. 77). André Gouron goes a little further than Ourliac, noting that references to *comun droit* in the *coutumiers* refer to the whole of customary and jurisprudential rules (Gouron, 'Le droit commun a-t-il été l'héritier du droit romain?', 290). Gouron also notes that during the thirteenth century royal ordinances are devoid of any reference to the *ius commune* as learned law, which is rather interesting since *jura scripta* are mentioned (though with distrust), and it is actually difficult to find the term *jus commune* referring to Roman law even in the consciously Romanizing South (*ibid.*). Robert Jacob has also said Beaumanoir's *droit commun* is customary law and not the *ius commune* of scholars (Jacob, 'Beaumanoir versus Révigny', p. 243).

[63] Castaldo, 'Pouvoir royal, droit savant et droit commun coutumier dans la France du Moyen Âge', 173–247. This article is essentially a mini-treatise on the term 'common law' in France.

[64] *Ibid.*   [65] *Ibid.*, 190–204.   [66] *Ibid.*, 221.

[67] This does not take away from the pivotal importance of Roman law for the development of French legal practice and its ever-increasing use especially in the royal courts, as well as its significant use by *coutumier* authors, as most recently thoroughly demonstrated in Giordanengo's response to Castaldo (see Giordanengo, 'Roma nobilis, orbis et domina: Réponse à un contradicteur'). This response proves that Roman law was common and commonly used, which is indeed true, but not that the term 'common law' was a term of art that specifically designated Roman law to the exclusion of customary law. Indeed, the thirteenth-century sources cited in this response tend to refer to Roman law as *ius scriptum*, which they differentiate from *ius non scriptum* and *consuetudo* (see Chapter 3 on this terminology).

The study of the terminology of French common law has been quite exhaustive. Nonetheless, a couple of contextual notes can be added. Scholars agree that the term originated in Roman law – references to the *ius commune* are sprinkled across the *Corpus iuris civilis*.[68] However, as André Gouron noted, the term '*ius commune*' in the works of Romanists was opposed to privileges or exceptions until the middle of the thirteenth century, and only then did it start to be opposed to custom and territorial law.[69] The *coutumiers*, as we have seen, referred to the learned laws as 'written law'. The concept of the learned laws as *ius commune* in its modern instantiation was really formed in the late thirteenth and fourteenth centuries.[70]

The references to 'common law' that indicate overarching laws and customs of the secular courts seem to appear in earnest at a similar time in both French and English texts. Surprisingly, for all the many volumes of work devoted to the origins of the common law and its operation as a system, relatively little work seems to have been done on the development of the use of 'common law' terms, while the opposite holds true in French historiography. As Pollock and Maitland have noted, the term 'common law' is not often used in the early thirteenth century.[71] When the term appears in the Dialogue of the Exchequer and in Bracton it is in reference to a privilege, a special contract, or a donation.[72] John Hudson points to a writ of 1246 that referred to common law 'to indicate the normal law of England, enforced by the

---

[68] Petot, 'Le droit commun en France selon les coutumiers', 414; Gouron, 'Le droit commun a-t-il été l'héritier du droit romain?', 284; Rigaudière, *Penser et construire l'État*, p. 83.

[69] Gouron, 'Le droit commun a-t-il été l'héritier du droit romain?', 286–8. The only earlier instance of the use of *ius commune* in the latter sense, according to F. Calasso, was made by a Lombard jurist at the end of the twelfth century – Gouron doubts this interpretation while Glenn accepts it (Gouron, 'Le droit commun a-t-il été l'héritier du droit romain?', 287; Glenn, *On Common Laws*, p. 11).

[70] Glenn, *On Common Law*, p. 11.

[71] Frederick Pollock and F. W. Maitland, *The History of English Law*, pp. 176–7.

[72] *Ibid.*, p. 177. In the *Dialogue of the Exchequer*, it is used to contrast the writer's disapproval of the king's bad forest laws with the common law of the realm. Glenn, however, sees more in this and feels this is a first instance of 'the common law tradition to identify a distinct and overarching source of common law' (Glenn, *On Common Law*, p. 11).

king's court, above local custom'.[73] Charles McIlwain found several
later instances of the term in connection to the confirmation of Magna
Carta by Edward I in 1297, for instance the reference to treating the
'great charter of liberties as common law' (*la grande charte des
franchises cume lay commune*).[74]

This subject would greatly benefit from a comprehensive study, not
only for England but also for other areas. Hector MacQueen has
identified the use of the term in Scotland in a royal brief from 1264
that referred to 'the usage throughout the kingdom of Scotland
according to ancient approved custom and by common law [*ius
commune*]'.[75] This provokes questions about the pervasiveness of
a notion of the laws of a realm as 'common law' throughout Europe.

In any case, these few examples do indicate that terminological
allusions to 'common law' in England were fairly contemporaneous
with those in France. In the French *coutumiers*, *droit commun* appears
in Pierre de Fontaines' *Conseil à un ami*, finished in 1253, in two ways:
it is part of the Roman law quotations in the text and refers to the
corpus of rules that were valid in Vermandois.[76] Beaumanoir's use of
droit commun in his *Coutumes de Beauvaisis* of 1283 includes the
'common law according to the custom of the county', 'the law that is
common to all in the kingdom of France', 'general custom', 'common
custom', and 'common law' (*commune loy*).[77] Castaldo's article
contains a comprehensive analysis of these terms.

---

[73] Hudson, *The Formation of the English Common Law*, p. 18. Hudson focuses on
institutional factors that contributed to the development of common law and only
looks at this term briefly, in a little over half a page (*ibid.*, pp. 18–19).

[74] Charles McIlwain, 'Magna Carta and Common Law', p. 123.

[75] MacQueen, *Common Law and Feudal Society in Medieval Scotland*, p. 2.

[76] Gouron, 'Le droit commun a-t-il été l'héritier du droit romain?', 290. We do not
know the source Pierre used for his lengthy Roman law quotations, but it is likely that
he used a vernacular translation. It should also be noted that the *jura publica* of
Roman law gets translated as 'droit commun' (Pierre de Fontaines, *Conseil*, ed.
Marnier, XVII.16 and 174n.e), and *publicum judicium* is translated as 'commun
jugement' (*ibid.*, XIX.53 and 202n.p), which means that both *commune* and *publicum* were translated into French as 'commun'.

[77] 'par droit commun selonc la coustume de la contreé' (Beaumanoir, *Coutumes de
Beauvaisis*, ed. Salmon, XVII.571); 'le droit qui est communs a tous ou roiaume de
France' (*ibid.*, prologue 6); 'coustume general' (*ibid.* VI.214, XIII.430, XXIV.697);
'commune costume' (Pierre de Fontaines, *Conseil*, ed. Marnier, XXII.24;
Beaumanoir, *Coutumes de Beauvaisis*, ed. Salmon, XXVII.773); for 'commune loy'
(Pierre de Fontaines, *Conseil*, ed. Marnier, XXII.24 and 315n.10; *Coutumier*

The 'common law' debate largely passed over the *Établissements de Saint Louis*. That it was overlooked is not altogether surprising as 'common law' is mentioned only once, and then only in one manuscript. After explaining that those who are judged guilty of disavowing their lord lose their land, manuscript N (copied in the first years of the fourteenth century) explains that 'practice and general, tested, and ancient custom, and the common law, are in agreement; for by his laws our lord the king forbids arms and excursions, and claiming to hold your land from a new lord, and [private] wars'.[78] A reference to common law is also present in a slightly different guise in other manuscripts of the *Établissements* that were also copied between the end of the thirteenth and fourteenth century: manuscript T states 'custom generally', manuscript U has 'approved and general custom', and K had 'proven and general custom'.[79] This indicates that 'common law' was becoming a concept sufficiently important and widespread for copyists to insert 'common law' and 'general custom' into a text whose manuscript tradition had previously contained no mention of it.

Coutumier Authors and French Common Law

France, then, was not simply divided into a multitude of independent regions with their own legal customs but, like England at the same time, was also developing legal commonality based on custom.[80] Of course, this development was not identical on both sides of the Channel, and there are still many questions about the nature of the

d'*Artois*, ed. Tardif, XXVII.12, XXVII.14). See also Castaldo, 'Pouvoir royal, droit savant et droit commun coutumier dans la France du Moyen Âge', 198. The common law of the kingdom of France is the outer limit of the *coutumiers*' assertions of commonality. As the variety of uses of '*droit commun*' show, there were layers upon layers of common law – there were laws common to a county, a region, a kingdom. As Robert Jacob notes for the *Coutumes de Beauvaisis*, 'customs are not all equal; they rise in tiers of decreasing order of generality, forming a kind of pyramid' (Jacob, 'Beaumanoir versus Révigny', p. 243).
[78] 'Et usage et costume generaus esprovée et ancienne, et drois communs s'i acorde; car mes sires li roi deffant les armes et les chevauchiées, par ses establissemenz, et les novels avoeries, et les guerres' (*Établissements*, ed. Viollet, II.38, II:470n.23).
[79] *Établissements*, ed. Viollet, II:468n.21.
[80] This makes the English Common Law an interesting parallel for comparison, rather than an exception to continental legal developments.

French *droit commun* and its exact legal implications. This section examines one small aspect of this vast subject – the extra-regional juristic practices of the *coutumier* authors and how these connect to the contemporary development of common law in France. The movement towards abstraction in the thought of the lay jurists of northern France, and the concomitant understanding of rules and procedures in generalizable terms, created the conceptual space for thinking of legal homogeneity – legal commonality – within the largest jurisdictional domain; namely the kingdom. This conception of custom, normativity, and legal territoriality best explains why customs could be transferred from one region to another unproblematically by simply renaming the region in a different manuscript.

It also explains why the *coutumiers* refer to areas beyond their region, as is evident even in the earliest text in our group. While Pierre de Fontaines' text is taken to represent the customs of Vermandois, Pierre is clear in his prologue that he has been asked 'to write a text according to the usages and customs of Vermandois *and other lay courts*'.[81] There is some variation on the wording in different manuscripts, but they do agree about the text's extra-regional scope. According to Manuscript A, Pierre de Fontaines writes about 'the customs of the region and *all* lay courts'.[82] Manuscript P elides the region and simply states that the text concerns the 'customs of *all* lay courts'.[83]

The emphasis here was a jurisdictional claim for the lay, secular, courts as opposed to the church courts and their jurisdiction, procedure, and rules. The different manuscripts do not seem to be concerned with opposing the Vermandois to other regions. If anything, they assume similarities between different regions.

Manuscript M emphasizes this point. As M. Marnier notes, all references to rules normally made 'according to our usage' (*selon notre usage*) are instead made 'according to right usage' (*selonc droit usage*).[84] In one case, 'our usage' (*nostres usages*) becomes 'usages that

---

[81] 'que je li face un escrit selonc les us et les costumes de Vermandois et d'autres corz laies' (Pierre de Fontaines, *Conseil*, ed. Marnier, I.2; emphasis added).

[82] 'les coustumes du païs et de toutes cours laies' (*ibid.*, 4n.2; emphasis added).

[83] 'les costumes de toutes cors laies' (*ibid.*; emphasis added).

[84] Marnier, introduction, *ibid.*, p xxxvii.

exist generally everywhere' (usages qui s'estent généraument partout).[85] In effect, manuscript M has written out specific geographic attribution in the text in order to emphasize the general application of the rules to lay courts.

This belief is echoed in the coutumiers that followed. The Établissements de Saint Louis also has rules that were upheld both by regional custom and by the usage of lay courts.[86] For instance, there is a rule that after the death of a spouse, the live spouse may not give an unequal inheritance to their children unless all the children agree to it.[87] The main text of the critical edition attributes this to the practice of the Orleans district.[88] Manuscript E attributes it to both Paris and Orleans, while manuscript J goes beyond this and attributes the rule to the practice of lay courts.[89] Eleven other manuscripts, about half of those we have, attribute the rule to the practice of many regions, l'usage de divers païs.[90]

The authors of critical editions of some coutumiers did entertain the idea that rules repeated in the coutumiers may express general principles. Tardif mentioned that many of the rules that the author of the Coutumier d'Artois borrowed from Pierre de Fontaines and the Établissements were general principles.[91] Mortet has similarly noted that the rules in the Demenées el Chastelet de Paris could not be construed as unique to the jurisprudence of the Châtelet in Paris.[92] This led him to wonder if the rules discussed could be of general application and suited the pays de droit coutumier generally. Ultimately, Mortet talked himself out of the idea – the well-known

[85] Ibid., p. 103n.10.
[86] 'And the tested custom of the area and the practice of the secular court are in agreement' ['Et coustume de païs esprouvée et usages de cort laie s'i acorde'] – I think that it is quite clear that the coustume de païs esprouvée and the usages de cort laie do not constitute a repetition for emphasis but refer to different things, otherwise, there would be no need to state whether they are in agreement (Établissements, ed. Viollet, II.34).
[87] Ibid., II.26.
[88] 'established according to the usage of the Orléanais' [estable selonc l'usage d'Orlenois] (ibid.; my translation).
[89] 'l'usage de Paris et d'Olliens' (Établissements, ed. Viollet, II:419n.42); 'l'usage de la curt laie' (ibid.).
[90] These are manuscripts A, B, C, D, O, P, Q, R, S, T, V (ibid.).
[91] Tardif, introduction to Coutumier d'Artois, ed. Tardif, p. xiii.
[92] Mortet, 'Seconde Partie: Étude du texte', in Le livre des constitutions demenées, ed. Mortet, p. 9.

'essentially local character' of the *coutumiers* made this conclusion impossible.[93] For this reason, he decided that the locality described by the text was the local practice of the royal domain.[94]

The authors of critical editions, then, seem to have privileged the manuscripts that gave a regional or local provenance to a rule, as opposed to a more general attribution. This interpretive bias can also be seen in Paul Viollet's work on the *Établissements*.[95] For instance, in his choice of attribution for a rule that those accused of murder, treachery, or rape must respond to the accusation immediately, without any delay provided for counsel, he chooses to attribute this to practice in Orleans in the main text of the critical edition, but this attribution only appears in four manuscripts.[96] Two manuscripts give no geographic attribution, manuscript J alone designates the lay courts specifically, but all the other manuscripts – the majority – explain that this rule accords with the practice of *divers païs*, or various regions.[97] Again, Viollet decides to privilege the manuscripts with the regional attribution of a rule concerning the proper summons of a baron to court.[98]

The rules in the *Établissements* are not all attributed to a geographic space, however small or large, but they are very often simply attributed to the practice of lay courts. The text occasionally specifies that it is referring to the practice of the lay court of Orleans, but the majority of references to lay court are unspecified by region.[99] The same is true for Philippe de Beaumanoir, who mentions the customs of the lay courts

---

[93] *Ibid.*, pp. 9–10.

[94] The examples he cites focus on the few local references in the text (see *ibid.*).

[95] This is not to detract from Viollet's critical edition, which is masterful and has the most detailed and helpful of notes, explaining the minutia of variation between the manuscripts in detail. Modern historians owe him great thanks.

[96] *Établissements*, ed. Viollet, II.21; these are manuscripts N, G, F, I (*ibid.*, 408n.33).

[97] Manuscripts T and V give no geographic attribution, J states it is 'selcon l'usage de cort laie,' and all the others have 'selonc l'usage de divers païs' (*Établissements*, incipit).

[98] The main text of his critical edition makes it a regional custom from Orleans [selonc l'usage d'Orlenois] (*Établissements*, ed. Viollet, II.33), which is true for some manuscripts. But many other manuscripts (C D E P Q R S T J V) clearly indicate that this rule is used in diverse regions [*selonc l'usage de divers païs*] (*ibid.*).

[99] 'selonc l'usage d'Orlenois, en cort laie' (*ibid.*, II.4). On the other hand, there are many references to lay court. A few examples are: 'accostumé en cort laie' (*ibid.* I.3), 'l'usage de la cort laie' (*ibid.*, I.85); 'Tele est la costume en cort laie que' (*ibid.*, I.96), 'selonc l'usage de la cort laie' (*ibid.*, I.136, II.5, II.7, II.28, etc.).

many times throughout his *Coutumes de Beauvaisis*.[100] The question is whether the *Établissements* and the *Coutumes de Beauvaisis* refer to regional lay courts or whether they refer to lay courts generically.

The meticulous Beaumanoir provides some clues. When Beaumanoir refers to lay courts, he refers to the general practice in lay courts and not exclusively to the lay courts in Beauvaisis. He mentions lay courts when he is trying to differentiate their customs from those of the church courts.[101] He makes clear that he is only interested in discussing the lay courts, not the ecclesiastical courts.[102] He does devote an entire chapter to the jurisdiction of the lay court and that of the ecclesiastical court, to avoid jurisdictional confusion.[103] He is quite clear about the cases where 'the secular courts should be in control, and Holy Church should not get involved'.[104] There is no such discussion of the respective jurisdictions of different regions, or choice of law rules in cases of disagreement about 'regional' jurisdiction.

Beaumanoir's references to lay courts, then, do not designate how these courts function in his specific region, but designate the general practice of the secular courts as opposed to ecclesiastical courts. That is why he can assimilate them to general popular wisdom, for instance, that 'it is said that in the secular courts you only argue once'.[105] A little earlier, the *Établissements* similarly quoted some proverbial wisdom from the lay courts: 'for according to the custom in secular courts, "a commoner's purse is his patrimony"'.[106]

Our other texts confirm the trans-regional tendency. The *Ancien coutumier de Champagne* implies that there is little difference between

[100] See for instance Beaumanoir, *Coutumes de Beauvaisis*, ed. Salmon, II.92, VII.246, VII.248, VII.257, XI.357, XXXI.946, XXXIX.1211.
[101] For instance, *ibid.*, II.91–92, VI.221, VII.248, XI.357.
[102] 'But when they plead against each other in an ecclesiastical court – we should not speak of that since we intend to speak only of the customs of secular courts' ['Mes quant il pledent li uns a l'autre en court de crestienté, il ne convient ja que nous en parlons pour ce que nous n'entendons a parler fors que des coustumes de la court laie'] (*ibid.*, XXIX.1211).
[103] *Ibid.*, chapter XI.   [104] *Ibid.*, II.340.
[105] 'dit on que l'en ne barroie qu'une fois en court laie' (*ibid.*, VII.248). This is said because while in church courts you can make your arguments and then reserve the right to make more arguments, in secular court you cannot make such a reservation and so cannot make additional arguments at a later time (*ibid.*).
[106] 'car borse à vilain si est partimoines, selonc l'usage de la cort laie' (*Établissements*, ed. Viollet, I.136).

the practice of the regional courts of the lord or Prince and the royal court of the king.[107] The *Demenées el Chastelet de Paris* claims to describe the 'custom of France and especially of the Châtelet in Paris'.[108] This reference to 'France' may be to the king's domain rather than the kingdom (though this was approaching something significantly close to the kingdom by the end of the thirteenth century), but it nonetheless shows that a text can simultaneously claim a specific place and general application. In any case, the text opens with a clear and overt statement of its *general* application: 'Here begins the book which teaches how we ought to undertake to speak before all judges, especially in lay courts.'[109] The *Coutumier d'Artois*, as other texts before it, also refers to the general practice of lay court as well as 'the customs of Artois and other places'.[110] For instance, 'by the general custom of lay courts' people caught red-handed committing a crime are judged by the *lex loci*.[111] Such a rule would be useless if it were not generally applied.

In fact, some rules are repeated across several *coutumiers*. For instance, the rule that the parties may each ask for up to three continuances (*contremands*) during the course of a particular case appears in several texts.[112] Pierre de Fontaines explains that 'according to current practice parties can make three continuances' in Vermandois; the *Demenées el Chastelet de Paris* claims that three

---

[107] 'Encor use on en Champaigne que se uns hons aseure un autre *en cort de Roy ou Prince ou d'autre signour* ... ' (*L'ancien coutumier de Champagne*, ed. Portejoie, XXX; emphasis added). This clause explains a rule on warranty that applies in the any court – be it that of the king, prince, or another lord.

[108] 'selonc la coustume de France et especiaument de la court de Chastelet de Paris' (*Le livre des constitutions demenées*, ed. Mortet, 44).

[109] 'Ci commence li livres, qui enseigne comment l'en doit proposer à parler devant tous juges, et especiaument en cort laie' (*ibid.*, prologue). Also, the text later refers to rules applicable 'before all the judges in the lay courts' [*par devant tous les juges de la court laie*] (*ibid.*, 50).

[110] 'par l'usaige de court laie' (*Coutumier d'Artois*, ed. Tardif, II.9); 'Je te di generaument que par l'usage de court laie' (*ibid.*, III.1). And, 'par la coustume d'Artois et d'autres lieus' (*ibid.*, V.1); 'si conme il est de coustume en Artois et ailleurs' (*ibid.*, LIII.12).

[111] 'La ou li criesme sont fait, doivent li malfaiteur iestre jugiet par general coustume de court laie, s'il est pris en present meffait' (*ibid.*, XI.10).

[112] This is a type of delay given for a specific period of time, for instance, fifteen days. The other type of delay is an *essoine*, which is a delay given for an indefinite amount of time that would be used in cases of illness and such.

continuances can be made according to the custom of the royal domain; Philippe de Beaumanoir also notes the possibility of three continuances in Beauvaisis; and the *Coutumier d'Artois* also states generally that 'by the usage of the lay courts, parties can make three continuances'.[113] Though only the author of the *Coutumier d'Artois* explicitly claimed this rule for the lay courts generally, its appearance in so many texts clearly situates it as a general custom.

Among other examples several *coutumiers* refer to a rule that minors may request seisin when they come of age, and until then the case waits for them to reach the age of majority.[114] The same is also true for the rule that agreements trump law, (*convenance loi veint*), which appears in a number of *coutumiers*.[115] This last rule was of Roman origin – the *Digest* instructs that *conventio vincit legem*.[116] This origin, however, was unacknowledged even by Pierre de Fontaines, who was not at all shy about attributing ideas and quotations to Roman law, and it seems *coutumier* authors saw it as part of general knowledge. The authors of these texts, attributed to regions, clearly saw many of the customs they described as existing in lay courts generally.

Robert Jacob notes that Beaumanoir saw his work as a pedagogical tool – the reader would learn other bodies of rules more easily after learning how a trial worked in the Beauvaisis.[117] If the *coutumiers* were learning tools with utility outside their particular region, the extent of regional diversity of customary law has likely been overemphasized by modern scholars.

Beaumanoir famously states in his prologue that 'the customs of France are so varied that you could not find in the kingdom of France

---

[113] 'Par l'usage qui cort, puet l'en fère III contremaz' (Pierre de Fontaines, *Conseil*, ed. Marnier, VI.18); 'il puet faire trios contremans par la coustume de France' (*Le livre des constitutions demenées*, ed. Mortet, 49, see also 86); 'puet li hons .III. fois contremander' (Beaumanoir, *Coutumes de Beauvaisis*, ed. Salmon, II.59); 'Je te di generaument que par l'usage de court laie, puet on faire .iij. contremans' (*Coutumier d'Artois*, ed. Tardif, III.1).

[114] See Pierre de Fontaines, *Conseil*, ed. Marnier, XIV.5; Beaumanoir, *Coutumes de Beauvaisis*, ed. Salmon, III.118; *Établissements*, ed. Viollet, I.71; *Ancien coutumier de Champagne*, V.

[115] 'une parole que on seult dire selonc nostre usage, que convenance loi veint' (Pierre de Fontaines, *Conseil*, ed. Marnier, XV.6); see also *Coutumier d'Artois*, ed. Tardif, VII.5; Beaumanoir, *Coutumes de Beauvaisis*, ed. Salmon, XXXIV.999.

[116] Justinian, *Digest* 16.3.1.6.   [117] Jacob, 'Beaumanoir versus Révigny', p. 235.

two castellanies which in all cases use one same custom'.[118] Less noted is
that he follows his emblematic statement on the regional diversity of
customary law with an addendum that indicated nearly the converse:
'But you should not for this reason fail to learn and remember customs
of the district where you are resident, for from there you more easily
learn and remember the others, and in any case in several instances they
are identical in several castellanies.'[119]

When Beaumanoir noted endless variation, he could have been
saying either that no two castellanies have the exact same set of
customs or that there was no legal issue that was treated uniformly
in all cases throughout the kingdom. Either way, his comment on
diversity is tempered by his statement on the notable similarity of
custom. Beaumanoir was incentivizing readers to learn the customs
of their region because this has the additional utility of being
a springboard for the knowledge of others. Though there was
not complete uniformity throughout the kingdom of France,
there must have been significant commonality indeed if learning
the customs of one place made it easier – not more difficult – to
learn the customs of another.

Underlying the extra-regional movement and commoning of
custom were communities. While the identities of the authors of
many *coutumiers* are not known, those names we do have point to
extra-regional networks and communities among lay jurists. One
future avenue of inquiry would be to identify some lay legal
centres. For instance, there is reason to believe that Artois was
such a hub. It was a county very close to the heart of the Capetian
monarchy: the future Louis IX was count of Artois from 1226 to
1237, when it became an appanage for his brother Robert. Philippe
de Remy, father of Philippe de Beaumanoir, was *bailli* for Robert
d'Artois, probably from 1239 until 1250, and when Robert died in
1250, Philippe continued to work for his widow Mahaut throughout

---

[118] 'Et bien i pert a ce que les coustumes sont si diverses que l'en ne pourroit pas trouver
ou roiaume de France dues chasteleries qui de tous cas usassent d'une meisme
coustume' (Beaumanoir, *Coutumes de Beauvaisis*, ed. Salmon, prologue s. 7).

[119] 'Mes pour ce ne doit on pas lessier a aprendre et a retenir les coustumes de païs ou
l'en est estans et demourans, car plus legierement en aprent on et reticent on les
autres, et meismement de pleusers cas eles s'entresievent en pleusers chasteleries'
(Beaumanoir, *Coutumes de Beauvaisis*, ed. Salmon, prologue s. 7).

the 1250s.[120] Pierre de Fontaines was in Mahaut's service until 1253, and it is likely that the two knew each other. It is possible that Pierre had met a very young Philippe de Beaumanoir, who actually became *bailli* of Pierre's Vermandois from 1289 to 1291, a few years after he had written his own *coutumier*.[121] In any event, they did not need to meet for Beaumanoir to know of Pierre's *Conseil*. Later, the author of the *Coutumier d'Artois* composed a *coutumier* for this area that was already linked to two earlier great lay juristic compositions of the era. We only know the identities of two *coutumier* authors, but we can identify them as navigating similar regions and conducting their judicial business for a closely related aristocracy.

This generalizing, or 'commoning', tradition continued long after these early developments. Jacques d'Ableiges' *Grand coutumier de France* (1389) was a *coutumier* for France as the royal demesne rather than a 'national' *coutumier*, yet like his predecessors, d'Ableiges considered it applicable to other areas. In the *explicit*, he stated that the *Grand coutumier de France* provided 'instruction as to practice and the manner of procedure and practice in the sovereign court of the Parlement, provostship and viscountship of Paris and other jurisdictions of the kingdom of France'.[122] While the sixteenth century saw the vast expansion of the idea of a French common law in political discourse, notably from Charles Dumoulin, we can see that there existed an earlier tradition to draw upon and amplified later.[123] This was to be a longstanding part of French legal history – in the later eighteenth century, French jurists were still speaking of French law in terms of common law.[124]

---

[120] Carolus-Barré, 'Origines, milieu familial et carrière de Philippe de Beaumanoir', pp. 23–5.

[121] Griffiths, 'Les origines et la carrière de Pierre de Fontaines', 553. Griffiths did not know of the earlier cases that place Philippe de Remy in Artois long before 1257. Pierre, who died in 1267, had at this point become a counsellor to Louis IX and was a member of his Parlement, but it is possible that Philippe met him as a young man. As Griffiths has noted, it was not improbable that Philippe had some direct juridical formation from Pierre or was influenced by Pierre via his father Philippe de Rémy.

[122] 'Cy finist le grant Coustumier de France, instruction de practique et manière de procéder et practiquer ès souveraines Cours de parlement, prévosté et viconté de Paris et aultres jurisdictions du royaulme de France' (Jacques d'Ableiges, *Le grand coutumier de France*, ed. Laboulaye and Dareste, *explicit*, p. 841).

[123] For more on Dumoulin, see Thireau, *Charles du Moulin*.

[124] François Bourjon, *Le droit commun de la France*.

Lay Jurists and a Customary Creative Commons

Comparison to areas beyond northern France shows that lay juristic attitudes and practices discussed were not localized and particular to that area, but a widespread lay juristic practice. The crusader laws, arguably an early European colonial law, provide a useful counterpoint because there is no later national legal tradition explicitly attached to these texts, and thus they are more or less a historiographical *tabula rasa*. Also, like the northern French *coutumiers*, these texts were composed in the French vernacular, marking the rise of the French vernacular as a trans-regional language of law that also stretched through the Mediterranean.[125] Finally, as discussed in this section, while geographically distant, the lay jurists of northern France and of the crusader states shared important similarities in attitudes and practice. These suggest a wider understanding within lay legal culture that while some of the value of texts of customary law lay in revealing aspects of local law, it was not restricted to this and extended outside specified territorial ambits.

The crusader texts add to our insight about the textual communities of lay jurists, as the following entangled textual relationships attest. Philip of Novara styled his *Livre en forme de plet* (1250s) as advice to a friend, possibly following Pierre de Fontaines. According to Peter Edbury, he wrote this text for his friend, John II of Ibelin – a relative of another great Levantine jurist who finished a text called the *Assises de Jerusalem* in 1265.[126] Subsequent jurists who copied John of Ibelin's text found it profitable to add sections taken from the text of Philip of Novara. Later in the thirteenth century, selections from John of Ibelin's *Assises of Jerusalem* appear in the *Assises of Romania*, a text written by an unknown author for the kingdom of Morea, the Greek part of the crusader kingdom formed after the conquest of Constantinople in 1204.

The author of the *Assises of Romania* gives a rather detailed explanation of the textual link between his own text and that of the *Assises of Jerusalem*. As he explained, out of a desire for justice, right, and reason, and because of the various types of peoples within this new

---

[125] Kuskowski, 'Lingua Franca Legalis?', 141, 155.
[126] Peter Edbury, introduction to Philip of Novara, *Livre de forme de plait*, trans. Edbury, pp. 19ff, esp. 21.

state, 'and since [the emperor and the barons] could not rule the empire well except with the usages and assises which exist in the land of the West, it was agreed to send to Jerusalem, to the king and the patriarch, asking them to send their usages and assizes, for they wished to be ruled by them since they were usages of conquest'.[127] When the *Assises of Jerusalem* arrived, the author explained, it was read before all the barons; the most necessary articles for the new kingdom of Romania were retained in the *Assises of Romania*, and an oath was sworn by the magnates to follow these laws.

This was probably more of a literary device than a faithful account, and the author only took two somewhat large sections from John of Ibelin's text, apparently having composed the remainder of the text himself. This account of origins was likely invented but nonetheless indicates the importance placed on written custom, as well as the assumption that these written customs could be adopted from one place to another, and, indeed, that they should be. The author emphasized that he was creating a textual link to the *Assises of Jerusalem* – this was not a reception of custom from practice, imported through habit or *habitus*, but specifically a textual import. The author clearly thought that the textual import enhanced the authority of his own text. While he justifies his selection of the customs of Jerusalem as the source for this text, his unapologetic textual borrowing intimates that it was a common practice and did not require comment or justification.

We can see the dialogic relationship between juristic works in another crusader text, Sempad the Constable's translation of the *Assises of Antioch* for the Kingdom of Armenia. At the beginning of this text, Sempad explained that he requested the text of the Assises of the Barony of Antioch from his kinsman Lord Simon, Constable of Antioch, who had received them from his father, Lord Mancel, who had been Constable of Antioch before him.[128] As Sempad described,

Simon then gave it to me, out of love and upon my request, and I took the trouble to translate it into Armenian. [...] Once the translation was finished, I sent the original and the translation to the Court in Antioch, so that they

---

[127] *Les Assises de Roumanie*, ed. Recoura, p. 258; Topping, *Feudal Institutions as Revealed in the 'Assizes of Romania'*, prologue.
[128] *Assises d'Antioche*, prologue.

could be compared. And they affirmed by their signatures and attestations that the translation is just and corresponds word for word. So, for those who want to conduct themselves according to this Assises and law, it is the true Assise of Antioch.[129]

Sempad's text differs from the ones discussed earlier because it is a translation, but it gives us a clear indication of one way that the *coutumiers* circulated. The *Assises of Antioch* took the following path: Lord Mancel, Constable of Antioch, gave the text to his son Simon, who became Constable of Antioch after him, and Simon then sent the text to his kinsman Sempad, who was Constable of Armenia.[130] Here, we see the texts circulating through the hands of the members of a juristic family. Again, Sempad offers no explanation as to why someone in Armenia would find a set of Antiochene customs useful – their relevance and legitimacy is assumed.

The crusader texts demonstrate that lay jurists of the thirteenth century clearly had some common attitudes and practices, which derived from the sharing of legal ideas through circulating texts. Notably, the customary texts of both northern France and the crusader kingdoms display the remarkable transferability of legal ideas among lay jurists who wrote about the laws and customs of the secular courts. In both cases, texts of purportedly regional custom participated in a 'commoning' of legal ideas. These texts were not the embodiment of an inward-looking, locally idiosyncratic legal identity but a common pool of trans-regional legal knowledge.

**

Undoubtedly, regional custom and differences between the customs of various areas in thirteenth-century France did exist. But this study argues that thirteenth-century customary law in France is more than a map of regional custom. The lay jurists who composed the *coutumiers* not only recognized similarities across regions but also

---

[129] *Assises d'Antioche.*

[130] Simon was not Sempad's only juristic family connection. In fact, his sister had married John of Ibelin, author of the *Assises of Jerusalem* mentioned earlier. Sempad himself later also became author of his own *coutumier* for Armenia. Sempad, then, was also operating within juristic circles that were connected through family networks and textual communities, and in this case, the textual communities were also mapped onto family connections.

created them as the *coutumiers* were read and even adopted outside of their original regions and affiliation. In fact, these jurists participated in the nascent idea of a French 'common law' in the thirteenth century.

Common law and customary law, and the *ius commune* and the *iura propria*, have long been understood as antagonists, and their traditional enmities have played out over pages of historical, legal, and political work. H. Patrick Glenn emphasized that 'common law' is a fundamentally relational concept born of a plural context: it exists in relation to particular law and is in constant conversation with it.[131] Additionally, as we have seen, the development of written custom is not necessarily indicative of fractured regionalism and can also be part of the consolidation of central power and a vehicle for legal harmonization.

Thirteenth-century lay jurists were forming communities based on common textual practices and methods of thinking, and in so doing they were developing a common pool of customary legal knowledge. The *coutumiers* have long been seen as discrete texts that all but sprung from the ground of the region whose customs they purported to describe. Where Roman law was a product of the intellect, *coutumiers* were rustic products of the soil. However, the practice of copying, excising, and appropriating formed part of a common juristic endeavour that went some way to creating a common pool of legal knowledge – a creative commons – that could be drawn upon to build other *coutumiers* and constituted a sort of lay vernacular *ius commune* for the lay courts and the jurists connected to them.

---

[131] Glenn, *On Common Laws*, p. vii. This book argues that the concept of 'common law' can reconcile national and transnational laws.

CONCLUSION

Lasting Model and Professional Community

'No one before me ever undertook this thing, such that I have a model,' noted the author of the *Coutumier d'Artois* sometime between 1283 and 1302.[1] This, of course, was untrue. Unlike Pierre de Fontaines, this *coutumier* author must have been well aware that this claim from him was untrue: he copied those words directly from Pierre's *Conseil* and also incorporated other parts of Pierre's text into his own. The truth of the claim was less important than building upon an earlier model, being part of a common textual tradition, and establishing links with a professional community of lay jurists.

Fourteenth-century jurists built upon the texts and communities developed by the first *coutumier* authors. The author of the *Coutumier d'Artois* noted that he 'put those who treated this subject in his book, a little bit from all of them'.[2] Jacques d'Ableiges, the author of the *Grand coutumier de France* (ca. 1388), said a similar thing: he assembled his work 'over a long period of time and from many other books and opinions of wise patricians, and from many other things concerning and regarding the actual nature of practice (*le faict de ladicte praticque*)'.[3] This was not 'plagiarism' but a statement

---

[1] 'nus n'enprist onques devant moi ceste chose, dont je aie exemplaire' (*Coutumier d'Artois*, ed. Tardif, prologue 2).

[2] 'et en a mis cieus qui ce traita en ce livre, de chascun un pau' (*Coutumier d'Artois*, ed. Tardif, prologue).

[3] 'Lequel traictié j'ay prins et assemblé dès longtems sur plusieurs aultres livres et opinions des saiges praticiens, et sur plusieurs aultres choses concernans et regardans

on how one composed the custom of the lay courts. It was a statement on the sources and authorities of customary law.

Fourteenth-century authors were building on earlier developments and intellectual and professional community mores that defined how lay jurists assessed practice and sources as part of their *techne*. Indeed, just as the author of the *Coutumier d'Artois* retained Pierre de Fontaines' claim of being the first to undertake the task, Jean Boutillier copied several cases from the *Coutumier d'Artois* into his *coutumier* of the late fourteenth century and repeated the earlier author's claims of being present at court. 'I saw a daughter of Madame de Seles' said the author of the *Coutumier d'Artois*.[4] Jean Boutillier repeated the exact same thing.[5] Our modern discomfort with the fact that Jean's statement was not true contrasts with medieval practice of – and therefore comfort with – the reuse of text and indeed the reuse of experience and even witnessing.

New *coutumiers* continued to be composed, either for regions that did not yet have one or new texts for regions that already did. Anonymous authors composed the *Coutume de Picardie* (early fourteenth century), the *Très ancienne coutume de Bretagne* (ca. 1341), *Le vieux coutumier de Poitou* (1417), as well as different versions of the customs of Anjou et Maine.[6]

In the generation of Pierre de Fontaines and Philippe de Remi, Philippe de Beaumanoir's father, lay jurists included great lords who were active in court, especially as judges, and petty nobles who made their careers in the administration of justice. By the fourteenth century, this was shifting significantly to include more university-trained men of law steeped in the study of the *ius commune*.[7] More Latin concepts,

---

le faict de ladicte praticque, selon ma possibilité, faculté et puissance, laquelle j'ay réputé estre petite et foible' (Jacques d'Ableiges, *Grand coutumier de France*, ed. Laboulaye and R. Dareste, prologue).

[4] *Coutumier d'Artois*, 35.2.

[5] Van Dievoet, *Les coutumiers les styles, les formulaires*, p. 45. He also copied cases from Guillaume du Breuil's *Stylus*, and further describes tens of cases he saw himself as *bailli*.

[6] *Ancien coutumier inédit de Picardie*, ed. Marnier; *La très ancienne coutume de Bretagne*, ed. Planiol; *Le vieux coutumier de Poictou*, ed. Filhol. The *Très ancienne coutume de Bretagne* was finished by 1341 but may have been composed a couple of decades earlier.

[7] See Griffiths, 'New Men among the Lay Counselors of Saint Louis' Parlement', 241, 243.

definitions, and modes of commentary from Roman law and canon law were incorporated into customary law and its practice. Not only that, but the texts became the subject of study methods associated with learned laws: the comments and glosses added to some *coutumier* manuscripts displayed an increasing Roman-law influence on the writing and intellectual assessment of custom.[8]

The custom of royal courts also acquired its own literature at this time. Guillaume de Breuil composed his *Style du Parlement de Paris* (around 1330), the Macreux brothers combined their efforts to write the *Ordonnances de plaidoier de bouche et par escript*, Jean Boutillier wrote the *Somme rural* (ca. 1393–6), and Jacques d'Ableiges wrote the *Grand coutumier de France* (around 1388).[9] Many of the manuscripts of the thirteenth-century *coutumiers* that we preserve today are, in fact, copies written in the fourteenth century. In addition to copies, which did not necessarily replicate the entirety of the text, we also find abridgements and glossed or annotated versions, as well as translations.

The fourteenth century thus saw the development of legal literatures relating to royal law. Lawbooks were composed about the workings of the Parlement of Paris, and authors began to write lawbooks that addressed the entire kingdom of France.[10] Roman law has a much more important place in these texts, which reflected the changing membership of Parlement with the influx of university-trained jurists.[11] Jean Boutillier, in his *Somme rural*, shows the increasing tension between custom and Roman law and greater stridency of opinion.[12] Custom, he

---

[8] Van Dievoet, *Les coutumiers, les styles, les formulaires*, p. 39.

[9] Guillaume du Breuil, *Style de Parlement de Paris*; Stéphane Pillet (ed.), '"Les Ordonnances de Plaidoyer de Bouche et Par Escript"'; Jacques d'Ableiges, *Grand coutumier de France*, ed. Leboulaye and Dareste There is no modern edition of Jean Boutillier's *Somme rural*. The many print editions made between the fifteenth and seventeenth centuries testify to its popularity in that period.

[10] Guillaume du Breuil composed a procedural guide to the Parlement around 1330. The brothers Pierre and Guillaume Maucreux de Montaigu did as well but also described procedures outside its ambit (Peralba, 'Des coutumiers aux styles', s. 1). See generally, Guilhiermoz, *Enquêtes et procès*.

[11] The Parlement developed its judicial function between the reigns of Louis IX and Philip IV and by 1314 was composed mostly of jurists (Peralba, 'Des coutumiers aux styles', s. 1).

[12] Despite the title, the text was not 'popular' in any sense. The title indicates the text is a learned *summa*, and its subject was the usages and customs of northern France, but its exposition was very heavily inflected with Roman law (Steiner, 'La Somme rural de Jean Boutillier', 122).

explained, could not be tolerated unless it accorded with Roman law, and if it did not, it should be considered a *jus odiosum*, an odious law.[13] This tension continued long afterwards.

Despite this change, the thinking about and study of the practice of secular courts remained vernacular in many ways. The thirteenth-century *coutumiers* were often packaged alone or with other legal works. They were thus often stand-alone legal texts or part of a legal corpus. On occasion, they were coupled with moralistic tracts – for instance, one text of Pierre's *Conseil* is packaged within a manuscript that also includes the lives of saints Brendan, Hispan, Hervei, and Alcuin.[14] Sometimes they were coupled with other legal texts, and in this case, they were coupled with texts written in the vernacular, even if we know the original to have been in Latin. At the beginning of the fourteenth century, one manuscript containing the *Établissements* also contained a compendium of customary knowledge, including a series of legal maxims, the *Coutumier d'Artois*, and the customs of Ponthieu, Vimeux, and Amiens.[15] One manuscript of Pierre's *Conseil* from the first decades of the fourteenth century, for instance, also contained the French translation of the *Grand coutumier de Normandie* as well as a selection of Roman-law texts in French translation.[16] A mid-fourteenth-century manuscript contained both the *Établissements* and Tancred's *Ordo* in French translation.[17] The authors of the vernacular *coutumiers* had invented and shaped the form and discourse that framed the practices of the lay jurists into the fourteenth and even the fifteenth centuries.

Coutumiers from the Fifteenth to Nineteenth Century

The *coutumier* was a cornerstone upon which French legal culture was erected until the early nineteenth century. The legal life of the *coutumiers* only ended several centuries after it began, later, with the French Revolution, when the multiplicity of custom was replaced with the unity of the Code in 1804.[18] The place of custom and the *coutumier*

---

[13] Krynen 'Entre science juridique et dirigisme', s. 32.
[14] Introduction to Pierre de Fontaines, *Conseil*, ed. Marnier, xxxi. BnF, ms.fr.9822.
[15] Manuscript P.   [16] BnF, ms.fr. 9822.   [17] Manuscript E.
[18] This is true for mainland France. In French colonies and former French colonies, their life often extended beyond that.

in legal culture transformed fundamentally over this long period. After reaching their apogee and enjoying widespread use, custom and the *coutumiers* came to be perceived as emblems of an archaic past and were ultimately overthrown in the era of Revolution.

The French king determined to reform custom in the aftermath of the Hundred Years' War. In the ordinance of Montils-lès-Tours of April 1454, Charles VII ordered that official versions of the customs of each region of France be made in order to 'eliminate variation and contradiction'.[19] This language, familiar from the prefatory materials of the *Corpus Iuris Civilis*, was the language of reform. And indeed, the commissioners composing official reformed versions of custom were charged with proposing modifications in order to clarify and ameliorate written custom.

This was an affirmation of custom as the central norm of French legal culture and the *coutumier* as its vehicle of expression. Yet this custom was to be codified into a stable and fixed text, and the *coutumier* was to become legislation. The production of official versions of French customs would be neither immediate nor swift.

Some earlier *coutumiers* continued to be copied and printed, such as Jean Boutillier's *Somme rural* shown in Figures 9.1 and 9.2.[20] While Jean Boutillier's *Somme rural* from 1537 (Figure 9.1) did not have Boutillier's name on the title page, it retained the preface, where the author introduced himself and his work. The text was later edited and commented by the great humanist jurist Louis Charondas le Caron (1536–1614).[21] Le Caron's edition credited Boutillier on the title page

---

[19] 'voulans abréger les procez et litiges d'entre nos subjects et les relever de mises et despens et oster toutes matières de variations et contrariétez' (Art. 125, ordinance of Montils-lès-Tours (1454) in Anette Smedley-Weill and Simone Geoffroy-Poisson, 'Les assemblées d'états et la mise en forme du droit', 6). The commissioners appointed to draft the customs were 'Parliamentarians, local officials of the bailli, not yeoman farmers' (*ibid.*, 14). For more on this process, see also Dawson, 'The Codification of the French Customs'; Martine Grinberg, *Écrire les coutumes*, pp. 63ff.

[20] Also note these examples of fifteenth-century texts of the thirteenth-century *coutumiers*: Philippe de Beaumanoir's *Coutumes de Beauvaisis* BnF ms.fr. 24060; the *Grand Coutumier de Normandie* BnF ms.fr. 5336; *Cy commencent les coustumes des pays Danjou et du Maine contenans seize parties* (Paris: par Le Petit Laurens pour Jehan Petit, ca. 1495).

[21] Le Caron's title emphasizes the authenticity of the text, which he based on a manuscript and not an earlier print edition. At the same time, it highlights his own changes – commentary, annotation, enrichment by adding many other sources – to the text: Louis Charondas le Caron, *Somme rural, ou le grand coustumier general de practique civil et canon: composé par M. Jean Bouteiller, conseiller du roy en sa cour de*

FIGURE 9.1 Jean Bouteiller, *Somme rural*. Jean Boutillier composed his *Somme rural*, a text describing the 'style' of the lay courts that drew very heavily on Roman and canon law, around 1393. This manuscript of the text from 1471 was copied for John of Bruges (Jean Bouteiller, *Somme rural*, Bibliothèque nationale de France, ms. fr. 201, fol. 9v). Note the continued iconography of the *coutumier* book presented by the author or copyist to the patron. The text was also translated into Dutch near the end of the fifteenth century.

FIGURE 9.2 An early printed version of Jean Bouteiller's *Somme rural* from 1537, with the title now 'The Great General Coutumier on Practice, Otherwise Called Somme Rural...' (*Le grand coustumier general de practique aultrement appellé Somme rural...* Paris: Galliot du Pré, 1537). The text was later edited and commented by the great humanist jurist Louis Charondas le Caron (1536–1614).

but removed the preface where the author introduced himself and the work, beginning instead with the second preface that describes the Aristotelian division of knowledge and the place of law within it. From manuscript to print, and between different print versions, we can see the long history of this text, its continued updating as well as its progressive generalization – processes, as we have seen, that were characteristic of the *coutumier* tradition from the beginning.

It took a century and additional orders from several kings to get the customs of the various regions in writing.[22] These were published when composed and continued to be reissued in different updated editions afterwards.

That custom was unclear, confused, or inchoate was an old accusation of Roman-law devotees, and these grew louder in the later Middle Ages and after. Calls for greater clarity of custom became particularly acute in the sixteenth century. This was partially rooted in a fact so mundane that it flies under the radar of the great transition of custom to law: the fact that, along with printed editions, sixteenth-century lawyers continued to use lawbooks from the thirteenth, fourteenth, and fifteenth centuries still in their original manuscripts, with their written scripts and languages that now looked archaic.[23]

---

parlement. *Reveu, corrigé sur l'exemplaire manuscrit, illustré de commentaires et annotations, enrichies de plusieurs ordonnances royaux, arrests des cours souveraines, singulieres antiquitez et notables decisions du droict roman, et autres observations* (Paris: Barthelemy Macé, 1603).

[22] The new official version of the customs of Touraine was completed in 1461 and that of Anjou in 1463, though most were composed between 1506 and 1540 (Grinberg, 'La rédaction des coutumes et les droits seigneuriaux', 1017). For more on the process of creation of these official *coutumiers*, see Grinberg, *Écrire les coutumes*. Marie Seong-Hak Kim's new book on law, custom and kings in early modern France, which I learned of after I had completed final revisions on this book, promises to illuminate how the official reform and codification of custom at the behest of French kings enhanced royal legislative power and paved the way for a unified French law, whose ultimate culmination was the French Civil Code of 1804 (Kim, *Custom, Law, and Monarchy: A Legal History of Early Modern France*).

[23] The question of script has not received much attention. The text in manuscripts of the *coutumiers* was partially written in gothic script (also known as *textualis, textura*, or Gothic bookhand), and partially in what is known as '*lettre bâtarde*', a mixture of formal blackletter and more informal cursive scripts, which spread in the late fourteenth and fifteenth centuries and appears in later medieval manuscripts of the *coutumiers*. The latter script emerged in vernacular and Latin texts at the same time, significant because with the *lettre bâtarde*, the vernacular was not written in a script that had evolved for the transcription of another language (Paul Saenger,

These medieval manuscripts are inscribed with their names and their annotations. And so, as new 'official' versions of the *coutumiers* were produced, not only rules and procedures but also vocabulary, orthography and punctuation were updated and regionalisms were written out of texts.[24] It was in 1539 that the *ordonnance* of Villers-Cotterêts (1539) dictated that court documents and records be written in French.[25] The language of royal justice was now *françois*, but between the humanist movement and university education, Latin remained an important language of law.

In the background were also the epic debates between 'Romanists' and 'Germanists' over the soul of French law that occupied the great jurists, parliamentarians, and potentates of the sixteenth century. The 'Romanist' jurists, notably Pierre Lizet, Jean Bouhier, and Jacques Cujas, argued that the provenance and 'spirit' of French custom was actually Roman and that Roman law was 'common law'.[26] The 'Germanist' jurists, most famously Christophe de Thou and Charles Dumoulin (1500–66), argued that French custom and law was 'our common law'.[27] The notion of French common law, familiar to

'Reading in the Later Middle Ages', p. 143). By the mid-fifteenth century, Gothic *textualis* was considered less legible and was restricted to Latin Bibles, books of hours, and some liturgical books, while *lettre bâtarde* became the standard script for books made for secular patrons, whether Latin or vernacular (*ibid.*). A copy of the *Grand coutumier de Normandie* copied between 1392 and 1420 provides a nice example of *lettre bâtarde* (*Grand coutumier de Normandie*, Bibl. nat. ms. fr. 5959).

[24] Grinberg, 'La rédaction des coutumes et les droits seigneuriaux,' 1030. By the later sixteenth century, the medieval *coutumiers* were seen to be written in a language now considered archaic: in 1577, the old *coutumier* of Normandy was described as 'a very ancient book composed in a language and with words that were not very intelligible, being out of use for the most part, and rarely if at all heard among those living in the region' (*ibid.*).

[25] Already under Philip VI there was an expansion of the use of French in the royal chancery, but it was really from the reign of Charles V (1364–80) onward that French kings began to champion French as the language of their court (Lusignan, *La langue des rois*, p. 149). Latin was common in their chancery and among jurists until this ordinance; while a few examples of the use of Latin can be found afterwards, royal justice now functioned in French.

[26] Kelley, '"Second Nature"', p. 150. Lizet was president of the Parlement of Paris, and Bouhier was president of the Parlement of Burgundy (*ibid.*, p. 150). Jacques Cujas was an eminent scholar and professor of Roman law of international European reputation; a member of the Parlement de Grenoble, courted by Pope Gregory XIII to teach at Bologna, he ended his life as a professor at Bourges.

[27] Kelley, '"Second Nature"', pp. 150–1. Christophe de Thou was a prominent jurist, magistrate, and the president of the Parlement of Paris. Charles Dumoulin was an

sixteenth-century jurists from the thirteen-century *coutumiers*, which continued to be read, was central to the political and juridical debates of the day. Dumoulin saw the *Coutume de Paris* as the dominant custom in France and saw the other French *coutumes* as being in 'concord and union', which served as the theoretical basis for de Thou's reform of custom.[28] These were not purely intellectual legal debates, and, as Jean Louis Thireau noted, François Hotman's *Antitribonian* (1603) – precisely the invective against the Roman jurist that the title suggests – shows how anti-Romanism triangulated between the juridical, the political, and the religious.[29] The notion of a French 'common law', grounded in custom, was to have a long life (as can be seen in Figure 9.3) even while France was known for its mosaic of different customary laws.[30]

In the seventeenth century, custom came to be designated as 'second nature', a baser source of legal knowledge as contrasted with the 'reason' of Roman law.[31] This was especially powerful because the language of reason was gaining primacy as the discourse of authority with the flourishing scientific revolution. Practice still functioned according to custom through most of the eighteenth century. Some held romantic views of custom, as exemplified by a verse translation of the Custom of Paris.[32] Others commented on what they felt was an absurd legal culture, as Voltaire did in the entry on custom in his

advocate before the Parlement of Paris, vastly respected, and author of one of the most important commentaries on the *Coutume de Paris*. For studies of Dumoulin and other early modern jurists, see Descamps and Domingo, *Great Christian Jurists*.

[28] Kelley, '"Second Nature"', p. 151.

[29] Thireau, *Charles du Moulin*, vol. 1, p. 95. Legal Romanism and Germanism, especially around the time of the Wars of Religion, meant something beyond a preference for a certain set of base norms and was also a religio-political alignment with or against the papacy and, through it, the law of Rome.

[30] For Bourjon and Pothier as the two intellectual bases of codification, though Pothier to a greater extent, see Bart Wauters and Marco de Benito, *The History of Law in Europe*, pp. 124ff.

[31] Kelley, '"Second Nature"', p. 153.

[32] This rhymed version of the Custom of Paris was published by Edme-Hilaire Garnier-Deschênes (Garnier-Deschênes, *La Coutume de Paris mise en vers*). If he knew of medieval *coutumiers* translated into verse, he does not say so. Rather, he explained his choice to versify the Custom of Paris by saying that he composed it in his youth as a salve for the ennui cause by his studies, and that he only published it at the encouragement of friends who found it useful – an earlier topos, as we have seen, but not conclusive of a connection with our medieval texts. The author is better known for a treatise on the notariate that earned him the cross of the Legion of Honor.

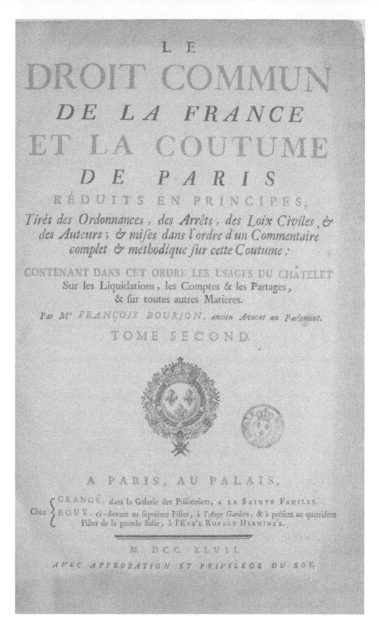

FIGURE 9.3 François Bourjon, *The Common Law of France and the Custom of Paris Reduced to Its Principles* (1747). Though thirteenth-century *coutumier* authors had a notion of 'common law' they did not link this notion to a specific text. It was Charles Dumoulin who saw the common law as grounded in the Custom of Paris. François Bourjon described the 'common law' of the kingdom as the 'exact explication' of the Custom of Paris and, though he acknowledged that there were many commentaries, his contribution was to bring together, simplify, and arrange all of the judicial decisions relevant to the common law of France and the Custom of Paris (Preface to the 'Dissertation' that precedes *The Common Law of France and the Custom of Paris Reduced to its Principles*, unpaginated). Bourjon's reworking of the Custom of Paris was, along with the vast writings of Robert Joseph Pothier, one of the intellectual bases for the French Civil Code.

Dictionnaire Philosophique (1764): 'There are, they say, 144 customs in France that have the force of law; these laws are almost all different. A man who travels in this country changes law almost as many times as he changes postal horses'.[33] Voltaire did not follow this with a comment on their similarity, as had Beaumanoir. For Voltaire, the great number of *coutumes*, and the variety of interpretation they engendered, was absurd.[34] For many at this time, custom had become associated with a confused primitive feudal culture and a corrupt judiciary that by the end of the eighteenth century was one of the many contributing factors to the French Revolution.

With the Revolution, French legal culture moved from one based on customary law to one based on codification. The reaction against 'custom' at the time was so strong that the commission composing the *Code Civil* entirely avoided the term 'custom', and, if the concept was necessary, the term 'usage' was employed instead.[35] Customary law, rejected in favour of the Code, had grown out of medieval developments, but it no longer resembled medieval law in fundamental ways: it was officially promulgated and fixed legal text; it was navigated by highly professionalized actors; it had become a subject of university study; and it had gone far beyond the region and the kingdom to become the law of empire. Nonetheless, the rhetoric of the time described a tangled, barbarous, 'medieval' custom displaced by a Code, founded in the principles of equality, rationality, and order and emblematic of modernity.[36]

---

[33] Voltaire, *Dictionnaire philosophique*, vol. 3, p. 229.
[34] The number of *coutumiers* and their commentaries had built up progressively over time. Commenting on his own day, Voltaire continued, but 'jurisprudence has so perfected itself, that there are few texts of custom without several commentators; and all of a different opinion. There are already twenty-six on the Custom of Paris. Judges do not know which one to follow; but to put their minds at ease, the Custom of Paris was just made into verse. This is how the priestess of Delphi used to deliver her oracles' (*ibid.*, p. 230). What was correct in one place was false in another, said Voltaire, finishing his entry with 'May God have pity on us!' (*ibid.*).
[35] Hilaire, *La vie du droit*.
[36] Of course, despite the Revolutionary rhetoric surrounding it, the French Code was composed by a rather conservative committee of *Ancien Régime* jurists, and it reinforced the preceding legal order in many areas of law (see, for instance, Jean-Louis Halperin, *L'impossible Code Civil*). According to Portalis, one of the main drafters, when the Code was drafted, complaints arose that it was only a reworking of Roman law, ancient customs, and old maxims (Gordley, 'Myths of the French Civil Code,' 505). The revolutionary principles of the *Code Civil* were ones that French

At the same time, the nineteenth-century romanticism that followed soon mythologized texts like the *coutumiers* as a form of folklore – a folk-law endowed with the spirit of its people. It was at this time that Friedrich Carl von Savigny (1779–1861) developed his idea of *Volksgeist*, composed of autochthonous primordial customs as developed from ancient Rome to his own contemporary times.[37] This was when Jacob Grimm (1785–1863) was collecting German *Rechtsbucher* and *Weistümer*.[38] It was also when most of the critical editions of the French *coutumiers* were published. On the whole, these are extremely careful scholarly works that brought the manuscript traditions of the *coutumier* together in order to establish one main text. This service to scholarship was invaluable. However, it also shaped medieval custom in the image of nineteenth-century law in ways that we continue to uncover.

Crafting Customary Law

From the Twelve Tables that define the earliest moments of Roman legal history to modern constitution-making, the story of law cannot be separated from the story of writing. Legal history is in many ways defined by great moments of law-making, legislative moments of inscription and promulgation, or by bureaucracy and its voluminous production of redundantly essential documentation. Custom has an uneasy place in all of this. It has often served as the foil to the behemoth of law: the oral, community-driven, informal counterpart to something centralized, authoritative, written, and enforced. Custom as commonly

treatise writers of the nineteenth century read into the text as they interpreted it (*ibid.*, 459).

[37] For more on this, see von Savigny, *The Vocation of Our Age*. Savigny, of course, identified the spirit of German law not with medieval custom but with Roman law as passed down and renegotiated from antiquity to his own present day. Roman law acquired a new political significance in sixteenth-century Germany that lasted into the nineteenth century, when it was reshaped again by professors like Savigny as part of an ancient constitutionalism that linked their own time to Roman antiquity (Whitman, *The Legacy of Roman Law in the German Romantic Era*, pp. 98ff). This was also part of a debate between Romanists and Germanists; both believed law should represent a *Volksgeist*, but the latter – based on the romantic medievalism of the day – saw the *Volk* in question as German peasants (*ibid.*, pp. 122ff).

[38] For more on Grimm and the effect of his legacy for our contemporary understanding of late medieval *Weistümer*, see Teuscher, *Lord's Rights and Peasant Stories*, pp. 3ff.

defined thus floats in a not-law, almost-law space. However, unpacking custom's medieval history illuminates the stories that medieval actors told themselves about law, how they created the norms by which they felt their societies should function, the language they used to express these norms, and how these have permeated the language we still use to think about and express basic legal categories.

This evaluation of written custom offers fruitful comparison with the development of customary law in other times and places, from autochthonous textualizations of customary law by various peoples to the treatment of custom in colonial law, and even to the contemporary recognition of norms in developing legal fields. I have approached these lay jurists from the vantage point of a cultural history of knowledge. However, my emphasis has been on active creation and on how thought-worlds constitute a certain culture while also trying to shape other cultural spheres: the social context of *coutumier* authors, their interest in shaping their audience and teaching them to 'think like a lawyer', and their articulation of a French common law.

Taking the *coutumiers* on their own terms permits us to evaluate their role in the professionalization, production, and dissemination of knowledge. Through this, we can see professionalization in its intellectual and cultural context. We can see not only how authors acquire the intellectual capital to be able to compose these texts but also the sort of intellectual capital they aimed to transfer to their audience. This allows us to track how abstract knowledge develops in the more modest practices of readers and copyists as well as through major texts and shifts in ideas.

The history of the *coutumiers*, as part of a new legal movement associated with the vernacularization of law, the rise of the lay jurist, and the professionalization of the lay courts, has wider implications for our understanding of custom and how custom is transformed into law. Notably, it shows how cultural changes can affect practitioners' approaches to normativity, which in turn make rules into either usages, customs, or laws. As well, it shows custom and law to be cultural constructions rather than a fact, a construction deeply related to changes in technology such as writing, in changing methods of reasoning and proving authority, and in developing communities that crafted new spheres of knowledge.

Medieval lay jurists constructed custom. They invented how it was packaged and articulated when they wrote the *coutumiers*; they decided what was included and what was excluded within that category; and they developed its ambit as a category of rule in the spectrum of obligatory norms. The thirteenth-century *coutumiers* capture a moment of intellectual ebullience. They were part of the formative moments of the lay courts and the theorization of 'law in practice', and in this sense the *coutumiers* were the linchpin of French legal thinking until the Revolution and beyond in some French colonies. They created something powerful in the French legal imagination, so powerful that their use only increased with time and eventually became official law when the kings demanded *coutumiers* to be written for all the regions of France in the fifteenth and sixteenth centuries. This was all due to the ingenuity and intellectual creativity of the thirteenth-century lay jurists who borrowed, constructed, and effectively created a field of knowledge known as 'customary law'.

Bibliography

Primary Sources

L'ancien coutumier de Champagne (XIIIe siècle), ed. Émile Chénon (Paris: Larose et Tenin, 1907)

L'ancien coutumier de Champagne (XIIIe siècle), ed. Paulette Portejoie (Poitiers: P. Oudin, 1956)

Ancien coutumier de Bourgogne, ed. A.-J. Marnier and N. Marnier, *Revue historique de droit français et étranger*, 3 (1857), 525–60

Ancien coutumier en vers in David Hoüard, *Dictionnaire analytique, historique, étymologique, critique et interprétatif de la coutume de Normandie*, vol. 4, *Supplément* (Rouen: Le Boucher, 1782), pp. 49–108

Ancien coutumier inédit de Picardie, ed. M. A. J. Marnier (Paris: Techner, 1840)

Arresta communia scacarii: Deux collections d'arrêts notables de l'Échiquier de Normandie de la fin du XIII siècle (1276–1290, 1291–1294), ed. Ernest Perrot (Caen: L. Jouan, 1910)

Assises d'Antioche: Reproduites en français et publiées au sixième centenaire de la mort de Sempad le connétable, leur ancien traducteur arménien dédiées á l'Académie des inscriptions et belles-lettres de France par la Société mekhitariste de Saint-Lazare (Venice: Imprimerie arménienne médaillée, 1876)

Les Assises de Roumanie, ed. Georges Recoura (Paris: Bibliothèque de l'École des Hautes Études, 1930)

The Cartulary of Countess Blanche of Champagne, ed. Theodore Evergates (Toronto: University of Toronto Press, 2010)

La chanson de Girart de Rousillion, trans. Gerard Gouiran (Paris: Lettres Gothiques, 1993)

The Code of Cuenca: Municipal Law on the Twelfth-Century Castilian Frontier, trans. James F. Powers (Philadelphia: University of Pennsylvania Press, 2000)

Codex Theodosianus, https://droitromain.univ-grenoble-alpes.fr/Codex_Theod .htm (accessed 30 March 2020)

Corpus iuris civilis, ed. Paul Krueger, Theodor Mommsen, Rudolf Schöll, and Wilhelm Kroll, 3 vols, *Codex Iustinianus, Iustiniani Digesta, Iustiniani Institutiones* (Berlin: Weidmann, 1872–95)

Corpus iuris civilis: The Digest of Justinian, text ed. Krueger, Paul, Theodor Mommsen, Rudolf Schöll, and Wilhelm Kroll, trans. and ed. Alan Watson, 4 vols. (Philadelphia: University of Pennsylvania Press, 1998)

Corpus iuris civilis: Justinian's Institutes, text ed. Krueger, Paul, Theodor Mommsen, Rudolf Schöll, and Wilhelm Kroll, trans. Peter Birks and Grant McLoed (Ithaca, NY: Cornell University Press, 1987)

The Court Baron: Being Precedents for Use in Seignorial and Other Local Courts, Together with Select Pleas from the Bishop of Ely's Court of Littleport, ed. and trans. Frederic William Maitland and W. Paley Baildon (London: B. Quaritch, 1891)

Coutumes d'Anyou et dou Maigne, in M. C.-J. Beautemps-Beaupré (ed.), *Coutumes et institutions de l'Anjou et du Maine antérieurs au XVIe siècle* (Paris: Durand et Pedone-Lauriel, 1877), vol. 1, pp. 63–176

Les Coutumes de Saint-Gilles (XIIe-XIVe siècles), texte latin critique, avec traduction, notes, introduction et tables, ed. E. Bligny-Bondurand (Paris: Picard, 1915)

Coutumier d'Artois, ed. Adolphe Tardif (Paris: Picard, 1883)

Coutumiers de Normandie: Textes critiques, vol. 1, *Le très ancien coutumier de Normandie*, ed. Ernest-Joseph Tardif (Rouen: E. Cagniard, 1881)

Coutumiers de Normandie: Textes critiques, vol. 2, *La Summa de legibus in curia laicali*, ed. Ernest-Joseph Tardif (Rouen: Lestringant, 1896)

The Danish Medieval Laws: The Laws of Scania, Zealand and Jutland, ed. Ditlev Tamm and Helle Vogt (London: Routledge, 2016)

Les établissements de Saint Louis, ed. Paul Viollet, 4 vols. (Paris: Renouard, 1881)

The Établissements de Saint Louis: Thirteenth-Century Law Texts from Tours, Orléans, and Paris, trans. F. R. P. Akehurst (Philadelphia: University of Pennsylvania Press, 1996)

Établissements et coutumes, assises et arrêts de l'Échiquier de Normandie, au treisième siècle (1207–1245), ed. M. A. J. Marnier (Paris: Techener, 1839)

Fet Assaver in *Four Thirteenth Century Law Tracts*, ed. and trans. George Edward Woodbine (New Haven, CT: Yale University Press, 1910)

Four Thirteenth Century Law Tracts, ed. and trans. George Edward Woodbine (New Haven, CT: Yale University Press, 1910)

Le grand coustumier général de practique, aultrement appellé Somme rural, contenant la forme commune de procéder et practiquer en toutes courts et jurisdictions. Nouvellement oultre les précédentes impressions reveu et corrigé, hors mys et osté le superflu qui de présent n'est observé en practique, restituées les allégations et raisons de droit, adjousté plusieurs décisions, coustumes, ordonnances et arretz de la cour, selon les matières occurrentes, ainsi que l'on pourra veoir marquées en tel signe ... (Paris : Galliot du Pré, 1537)

Le grand coutumier de Normandie, ed. William Laurence de Gruchy, trans. Judith Anne Everard (St Helier: Jersey and Guernsey Law Review, 2009)

Laws of the Alamans and Bavarians, trans. Theodore John Rivers (Philadelphia: University of Pennsylvania Press, 1977)

Laws of Early Iceland: Grágás, the Codex Regius of Grágás, with Material from Other Manuscripts, trans. Andrew Dennis, Peter Godfrey Foote, and Richard M Perkins. (Winnipeg: University of Manitoba Press, 1980)

The Laws of the Kings of England from Edmund to Henry I. Part Two: William I to Henry I, ed. and trans. A. J. Robertson (Cambridge: Cambridge University Press, 1925)

Leges Baiwariorum, ed. Ernst von Schwind, MGH, Leges 2.1, Tom. 5.1 (Hannover: Hahn, 1926), preface, www.dmgh.de/mgh_ll_nat_germ_5_2/index.htm#page/(197)/mode/1up (accessed 28 April 2020)

Littere Baronum: The Earliest Cartulary of the Counts of Champagne, ed. Theodore Evergates (Toronto, ON: University of Toronto Press, 2003)

Li livre de jostice et de plet, ed. Pierre-Nicolas Rapetti (Paris: Firmin Didot, 1850)

Le livre des constitutions demenées el Chastelet de Paris, ed. Charles Mortet, *Mémoires de la Société de l'Histoire de l'Ile-de-Paris*, 10 (1883), 1–99

Les olim, ou, Registres des arrêts rendus par la Cour du roi sous les règnes de Saint Louis, de Philippe le Hardi, de Philippe le Bel, de Louis le Hutin et de Philippe le Long, ed. Le comte Bougnot, 4 vols. (Paris: Imprimerie royale, 1839–1848)

Recueil des actes de Philippe-Auguste, roi de France, ed. Élie Berger, vol. 2 (Paris: Imprimerie Nationale, 1916)

Recueil de jugements de l'echiquier de Normandie au XIIIe siècle (1207–1270), ed. Léopold Delisle (Paris: Imprimerie imperiale, 1864)

Le roman de Renart, ed. Naoyuki Fukumoto, Noboru Harano, and Satoru Suzuki, trans. Gabriel Bianciotto (Paris: Librairie Générale Française, 2005)

Las siete partidas, ed. Robert I. Burns, SJ; trans. Samuel Parsons Scott, 5 vols. (Philadelphia: University of Pennsylvania Press, 2001)

Summa Azonis, locuples iuris civilis thesaurus (Venice: Gaspar Bindoni, 1584)

The Theodosian Code and Novels, and the Sirmondian Constitutions, trans. Clyde Pharr (Princeton, NJ: Princeton University Press, 1952)

La très ancienne coutume de Bretagne, ed. Marcel Planiol (Rennes: Plihorn et Hervé, 1896)

The Ustages of Barcelona: The Fundamental Law of Catalonia, trans. Donald J. Kagay (Philadelphia: University of Pennsylvania Press, 1994)

Le vieux coutumier de Poictou, ed. René Filhol (Bourges: Tardy, 1956)

d'Ableiges, Jacques, *Le grand coutumier de France*, ed. Édouard Laboulaye and Rodolphe Dareste (Paris: Durand et Pédone-Lauriel, 1868)

Augustine of Hippo, 'Letter 55 (A.D. 400)', trans. J.G. Cunningham in *Nicene and Post-Nicene Fathers, First Series*, vol. 1, ed. Philip Schaff, 18.34 (New York: Christian Literature Publishing, 1887.) Revised and edited for New Advent by Kevin Knight, www.newadvent.org/fathers/1102055.htm (accessed 30 April 2020)

de Beaumanoir, Philippe, *Coutumes de Beauvaisis*, ed. Amédée Salmon, 2 vols. (Paris: Picard, 1899–1900)

de Beaumanoir, Philippe, *The Coutumes de Beauvaisis of Philippe de Beaumanoir*, trans. F. R. P. Akehurst (Philadelphia: University of Pennsylvania Press, 1992)

Béroul, *Tristan et Iseut*, in *Tristan et Iseut: Les poèmes français, La saga norroise*, trans. Daniel Lacroix and Philippe Walter (Paris: Livre de Poche, 1989)

Beugnot, Auguste-Arthur, *Assises de Jérusalem ou Recueil des ouvrages de jurisprudence composés pendant le XIIIe siècle dans les royaumes de Jérusalem et de Chypre*, 2 vols. (Paris: Imprimerie Royale, 1841–3)

Boutaric, Edgar (ed.), *Actes du Parlement: Arrêts et enquêtes antérieurs aux olims, 1180–1254* (Paris: Henri Plon, 1803)

Bracton, *De legibus et consuetudinibus Angliæ*, ed. and trans. Samuel Thorne, 4 vols. (Oxford: Oxford University Press, 1968–77), Bracton Online, bracton.law.harvard.edu/Framed/mframe.htm (accessed 26 June 2022)

du Breuil, Guillaume, *Style de Parlement de Paris*, with introduction by Gerard Giordanengo (Paris: Dalloz, 2011)

Capellanus, Andreas, *On Love*, trans. P. G. Walsh (New York: Bloomsbury, 1993)

Charondas le Caron, Louis, *Somme rural, ou le grand coustumier general de practique civil et canon: Composé par M. Jean Bouteiller, conseiller du roy en sa cour de parlement. Reveu, corrigé sur l'exemplaire manuscript, illustré de commentaires et annotations, enrichies de plusieurs ordonnances royaux, arrests des cours souveraines, singulieres antiquitez et notables decisions du droict roman, et autres observations* (Paris: Barthelemy Macé, 1603)

Cicero, Marcus Tullius, *De inventione; De optimo genere oratorum; Topica*, trans. H. M. Hubbell, Loeb Classical Library 386 (Cambridge, MA: Harvard University Press, 1960)

Dante, Alighieri, *Literature in the Vernacular (De vulgari eloquentia)*, trans. Sally Purcell (Manchester: Carcanet New Press, 1981)

de Corbiac, Pierre, *Le trésor de Pierre de Corbiac en vers provençaux: Publie en entier avec une introduction et des extraits du Bréviaire d'amour de Matfre Ermengau de Beziers, de l'Image du monde De Gautier de Metz et du Trésor de Brunetto Latini*, ed. Karl Ernest August Sachs (Brandenburg: J. J. Wiesike, 1859)

de Fontaines, Pierre, *Le Conseil de Pierre de Fontaines*, ed. M. A. J. Marnier (Paris: Joubert, 1846)

Fourth Lateran Council, Papal Encyclicals Online, www.papalencyclicals.net /councils/ecum12-2.htm (accessed 16 June 2020)

Fulbert of Chartres, 'Ad Willelmum ducem Aquitanorum' in Léopold Delisle (ed.), *Recueil des historiens des Gaules et de la France*, vol. 10 (Paris: V. Palmé, 1904), p. 463

'Letter from Bishop Fulbert of Chartres, A.D. 1020', ed. E. P. Cheyney, *University of Pennsylvania Translations and Reprints* (Philadelphia: University of Pennsylvania Press, 1898), vol 4, no. 3, pp. 23–4

Galbert of Bruges, *The Murder of Charles the Good*, trans. James Bruce Ross (New York: Columbia University Press, 2005)

García y García, Antonio (ed.), *Constitutiones Concilii quarti Lateranensis una cum Commentariis glossatorum (Monumenta iuris canonici)*, Series A: Corpus Glossatorum 2 (Città del Vaticano: Biblioteca Apostolica Vaticana, 1981)

Garnier-Deschênes, Edme-Hilaire, *La Coutume de Paris mise en vers, avec le texte à côté* (Paris: Saugrain, jeune, 1768)

Gratian, *Decretum magistri Gratiani*, https://bit.ly/3mptc4d (accessed 30 March 2020)

The Treatise on Laws with the Ordinary Gloss, trans. Augustine Thompson and James Gordley (Washington, DC: Catholic University of America Press, 1993)

Hall, G. D. G. (trans.), *The Treatise on the Laws and Customs of the Realm of England Commonly Called Glanvill* (Oxford: Oxford University Press, 1983)

Hallinger, K. (ed.), *Corpus consuetudinum monasticarum* (Sieburg: Schmitt, 1967)

Hélary, Xavier (ed.), 'Le cartulaire de la seigneurie de Nesle (1269, Chantilly, 14 F 22)', in *Le cartulaire de la seigneurie de Nesle* (Orléans: Institut de Recherche et d'Histoire des Textes, 2006), www.cn-telma.fr/nesle/acte6/ and www.cn-telma.fr/nesle/acte13/ (accessed 16 October 2020)

Isidore of Seville, *The Etymologies (The Origins)*, ed. W. M. Lindsay (Oxford: Oxford University Press, 1911), https://bit.ly/3Mqfrww (accessed 7 June 2022)

de Joinville, Jean, *Vie de Saint Louis*, ed. and trans. Jacques Monfrin (Paris: Garnier, 1995)

Latini, Brunetto, *Li livre dou tresor*, ed. P. Chabaille (Paris: Imprimerie Impériale, 1863)

Löfstedt, Leena, *Gratiani decretum: La traduction en ancien français du Décret de Gratien*, vol. 2, *Causae 1–11* (Helsinki: Societas scientiarum fennica, 1993)

Musée des Archives nationales, *Documents originaux de l'histoire de France exposés dans l'Hôtel Soubise: Ouvrage enrichi de 1200 fac-simile des autographes les plus importants depuis l'époque mérovingienne jusqu'à révolution française* (Paris: Henri Plon, 1872)

Philip of Novara, *Le livre de forme de plait*, trans. Peter Edbury (Nicosia: Theopress, 2009)

Pierre de Fontaines, *Le Conseil de Pierre de Fontaines*, ed. M. A. J. Marnier (Paris: Joubert, 1846)

Pillet, Stéphane (ed.), '"Les ordonnances de plaidoyer de bouche et par escript" des frères Maucreux (BnF. ms. fr. 19832)', *Revue Historique de Droit Français et Étranger (1922-)*, 84:2 (2006), 177–228

Renart, Jean, *Roman de la rose, ou Guillaume de Dole*, trans. Jean Dufournet (Paris: Champions Classiques, 2008)

Richebourg, Bourdot de (ed.), *Nouveau coutumier général*, 4 vols. (Paris. M. Brunet, 1724)

Philip Schaff (ed.), *Nicene and Post-Nicene Fathers*, First Series, vol. 1 (Buffalo, NY: Christian Literature Publishing Co., 1887. Revised and edited for New Advent by Kevin Knight, www.newadvent.org/fathers/ 1102055.htm (accessed 30 April 2020)

The Third Lateran Council, Papal Encyclicals Online, www .papalencyclicals.net/councils/ecum11.htm (accessed 27 May 2020).

Zecchino, Ortensio (ed.), *Le Assise di Ruggiero II* (Naples: Casa Editrice Dott. Eugenio Jovene, 1984)

Secondary Sources

The Law Dictionary, https://thelawdictionary.org/precendent/ (accessed 11 June 2020)

Abulafia, David (ed.), *The New Cambridge Medieval History*, vol. 5, *c. 1198–1300* (Cambridge: Cambridge University Press, 1999)

Alonso, José Luis, 'The Status of Peregrine Law in Egypt: "Customary Law" and Legal Pluralism in the Roman Empire', *Journal of Juristic Papyrology*, 43 (2013), 351–404

Andersen, Per, and Mia Münster-Swendsen (eds.), *Custom: The Development and Use of a Legal Concept in the Middle Ages* (Copenhagen: Djøf, 2009)

Andersen, Per, Mia Münster-Swendsen, and Helle Vogt (eds.), *Law before Gratian: Law in Western Europe c. 500–1100; Proceedings of the Third Carlsberg Academy Conference on Medieval Legal History, 2006* (Copenhagen: Djøf, 2007)

Ando, Clifford, *Law, Language, and Empire in the Roman Tradition* (Philadelphia: University of Pennsylvania Press, 2011)

Anker, Elizabeth S., and Bernadette Meyler (eds.), *New Directions in Law and Literature* (New York, NY: Oxford University Press, 2017)

Arabeyre, Philippe, Jean-Louis Halpérin, and Jacques Krynen (eds.), *Dictionnaire historique des juristes français (XIIe–XXe siècle)* (Paris: Presses Universitaires de France, 2008)

Aubertin, Charles, *Histoire de la langue et de la littérature au Moyen Âge*, vol. 2 (Paris: E. Belin, 1883)

Aurell, Martin, *Le chevalier lettré: Savoir et conduite de l'aristocratie aux XIIe et XIIIe siècles* (Paris: Fayard, 2011)

Austin, Greta, 'Jurisprudence in the Service of Pastoral Care: The "Decretum" of Burchard of Worms', *Speculum* 79:4 (2004), 929–59

Shaping Church Law Around the Year 1000: The Decretum of Burchard of Worms (Farnham: Ashgate, 2009)

Austin, John L., *How to Do Things with Words*, 2nd ed. (Cambridge, MA: Harvard University Press, 1975)

Baldwin, John, *The Government of Philip Augustus: Foundations of French Royal Power in the Middle Ages* (Berkeley: University of California Press, 1986)

Knights, Lords, and Ladies in Search of Aristocrats in the Paris Region, 1180-1220, (Philadelphia: University of Pennsylvania Press, 2020)

Balkin, J. M., and Sanford Levinson, 'Law as Performance' in Michael Freeman and Andrew D. E. Lewis (eds.), *Law and Literature* (Oxford: Oxford University Press, 1999), pp. 729–51

Bartlett, Robert, *Trial by Fire and Water: The Medieval Judicial Ordeal* (Oxford: Clarendon Press, 1986)

Bautier, Robert-Henri (ed.), *La France de Philippe Auguste: Le temps des mutations (Colloques internationaux CNRS no. 602)* (Paris: CNRS, 1982)

'Philippe de Beaumanoir: Rapport Général au Colloque' in Philippe Bonnet-La Borderie (ed.), *Actes du colloque international Philippe de Beaumanoir et les Coutumes de Beauvaisis (1283–1983)* (Beauvais: GEMOB, 1984), pp. 5–17

'Typologie diplomatique des actes royaux français (XIIIe–XVe siècles)' in José Marques (ed.), *Actes du colloque diplomatique royale du Moyen Âge, XIII–XIVe siècles* (Universidade do Porto, 1996), pp. 25–68, https://bit.ly /3buNsis (accessed 26 June 2022)

Bederman, David J., *Custom as a Source of Law* (Cambridge: Cambridge University Press, 2010)

Bedos-Rezak, Brigitte, 'French Medieval Regions: A Concept in History', *Historical Reflections/Réflexions Historiques*, 19:2 (1993), 152–66

'Medieval Identity: A Sign and a Concept', *The American Historical Review*, 105 (2000), 1489–533

'Towards an Archaeology of the Medieval Charter: Textual Production and Reproduction in Northern French *Chartriers*' in Adam J. Kosto and

Anders Winroth (eds.), *Charters, Cartularies and Archives: The Preservation and Transmission of Documents in the Medieval West: Proceedings of a Colloquium of the Commission Internationale de Diplomatique (Princeton and New York, 16–18 September 1999)* (Toronto: Pontifical Institute of Mediaeval Studies, 2002), pp. 37–54

When Ego Was Imago: Signs of Identity in the Middle Ages (Leiden: Brill, 2011)

Bedos-Rezak, Brigitte, and Dominique Iogna-Prat (eds.), *L'individu au moyen âge: Individuation et individualisation avant la modernité*, (Paris: Aubier, 2005)

Beer, Jeanette, 'Medieval Translations: Latin and the Vernacular Languages' in F. A. C. Mantello and A. G. Rigg (eds.), *Medieval Latin: An Introduction and Bibliographical Guide* (Washington, DC: Catholic University of America Press, 1996), pp. 728–34

Bellomo, Manlio, *The Common Legal Past of Europe*, trans. Lydia G. Cochrane (Washington, DC: Catholic University of America Press, 1995)

Benham, Jenny, Matthew McHaffie, and Helle Vogt (eds.), *Law and Language in the Middle Ages*, Medieval Law and Its Practice 25 (Leiden: Brill, 2018)

Bercé, Yves Marie, and Alfred Soman (eds.), *La justice royale et le parlement de Paris (XIVe–XVIIe siècle)* (Paris: Librairie Droz, 1995)

Berman, Harold, *Law and Language: Effective Symbols of Community*, ed. John Witte, Jr. (Cambridge: Cambridge University Press, 2013)

Law and Revolution: The Formation of the Western Legal Tradition (Cambridge, MA: Harvard University Press, 1983)

Besnier, Robert, *La Coutume de Normandie: Histoire Externe* (Paris: Sirey, 1935)

Bevan, Kitrina, 'English Legal Culture and the Language of the Law: Rethinking the Statute of Pleading (1362)', unpublished Master's thesis, University of Ottawa (2008), www.ruor.uottawa.ca/bitstream/10393/27795/1/MR48633.PDF (accessed 30 May 2016)

Bezemer, Kees, *What Jacques Saw: Thirteenth-Century France Through the Eyes of Jacques de Revigny, Professor of Law at Orleans* (Frankfurt am Main: Vittorio Klostermann, 1997)

Binder, Guyora, and Robert Weisberg, *Literary Criticisms of Law* (Princeton, NJ: Princeton University Press, 2000)

Bisson, Thomas N. *The Crisis of the Twelfth Century: Power, Lordship, and the Origins of European Government* (Princeton, NJ: Princeton University Press, 2009).

Biu, Hélène, 'La *Somme Acé*: Prolégomènes à une étude de la traduction française de la *Summa Azonis* d'après le manuscrit Bibl. Vat., Reg. lat. 1063', *Bibliothèque de l'École des Chartes*, 167 (2009), 417–64

Bloch, R. Howard, *Medieval French Literature and Law* (Berkeley: University of California Press, 1977)

Bloom, Harold, *The Anxiety of Influence: A Theory of Poetry* (Oxford: Oxford University Press, 1973)

Bongert, Yvonne, *Recherches sur les cours laïques de Xe au XIIIe siècle* (Paris: Éditions A. et J. Picard, 1949)

Bonnet-La Borderie, Philippe (ed.), *Actes du colloque international Philippe de Beaumanoir et les Coutumes de Beauvaisis (1283–1983)* (Beauvais: GEMOB, 1984)

Bordier, Henri Léonard, *Philippe de Remi, sire de Beaumanoir, jurisconsulte et poète national du Beauvaisis, 1246–1296* (Genève: Slatkine, 1869)

Bouchard, Constance, 'Community: Society and the Church in Medieval France', *French Historical Studies*, 17:4 (1992), 1035–47

Boucher, Caroline, 'De la *subtilité* en français: Vulgarisation et savoir dans les traductions d'*auctoritates* des XIIIe–XIVe siècles' in R. Voaden et al. (eds.), *The Theory and Practice of Translation in the Middle Ages*, The Medieval Translator 8 (Turnhout: Brepols, 2003), pp. 89–99

Bougard, François, 'Écrire le procès: Le compte rendu judiciaire entre VIIIe et XIe siècle', *Médiévales*, 56 (2009), 23–40

'Genèse et réception du *Mâconnais* de Georges Duby', Special ed., *Bulletin du centre d'études médiévales d'Auxerre*, 1 (2008), 1–22, https://doi.org /10.4000/cem.4183 (accessed 27 June 2022)

Boulet-Sautel, Marguerite, 'Le droit romain et Philippe Auguste' in Robert-Henri Bautier (ed.), *La France de Philippe Auguste: Le temps des mutations (Colloques Internationaux CNRS no. 602)* (Paris: CNRS, 1980), pp. 489–502

'Le notaire contre le *Jus civile* au Moyen Âge en région parisienne' in Bernard Durand and Laurent Mayali (eds.), *Excerptiones iuris: Studies in Honor of André Gouron* (Berkeley, CA: Robbins Collection Publications, 2000), pp. 71–81

Bourdieu, Pierre, *Language and Symbolic Power*, trans. Gino Raymond and Matthew Adamson (Cambridge, MA: Harvard University Press, 1991)

Boureau, Alain, 'Droit naturel et abstraction judiciare: Hypothèse sur la nature du droit medieval', *Annales, Histoire, Sciences Sociales*, 57:6 (2002), 1463–88

La loi du royaume: Les moines, le droit et la construction de la nation anglaise (Xie–XIIIe siècles) (Paris: Belles Lettres, 2004)

Bourjon, François, *Le droit commun de la France et la coutume de Paris réduits en principes* (Paris: Grangé et Cellot, 1770)

Brand, Paul, 'The Age of Bracton', *Proceedings of the British Academy* 89 (1996), 65–89

'The Date and Authorship of Bracton: A Response', *The Journal of Legal History*, 31:3 (2010), 217–44

'The English Difference: The Application of Bureaucratic Norms within a Legal System', *Law and History Review*, 21 (2003), 383–8

'The Languages of the Law in Late Medieval England' in D. A. Trotter (ed.), *Multiculturalism in Later Medieval Britain* (Cambridge: D. S. Brewer, 2000), pp. 63–76

Brasington, Bruce C., 'Canon law in the Leges Henrici Primi', *Zeitschrift der Savigny-Stiftung der Rechtsgeschichte: Kanonistische Abteilung*, 92 (2006), 288–305

'Collections of Bishops' Letters as Legal Florilegia' in Per Andersen, Mia Münster-Swendsen, and Helle Vogt (eds.), *Law Before Gratian: Law in Western Europe c. 500–1000; Proceedings of the Carlsberg Academy Conference on Medieval Legal History, 2006* (Copenhagen: Djøf, 2007), pp. 81–106

Order In the Court: Medieval Procedural Treatises in Translation, Medieval Law and Its Practice 21 (Leiden: Brill, 2016)

Broche, Lucien, 'Trois chartes inédites de Philippe de Beaumanoir, bailli de Vermandois (1289–1291)', *Nouvelle revue historique de droit français étranger*, 28 (1904), 755–65

Brooks, Peter, and Paul Gewirtz (eds.), *Law's Stories: Narratives and Rhetoric in the Law* (New Haven, CT: Yale University Press, 1996)

Brown, Cynthia Jane, *Poets, Patrons, and Printers: Crisis of Authority in Late Medieval France* (Ithaca, NY: Cornell University Press, 1995)

Brown, Elizabeth A. R., *Customary Aids and Royal Finance in Capetian France: The Marriage Aid of Philip the Fair* (Cambridge, MA: Medieval Academy of America, 1992)

'The Tyranny of a Construct: Feudalism and Historians of Medieval Europe', *The American Historical Review*, 79:4 (1974), 1063–88

Brown, Gary, and Keira Poellet, 'Traditional and Modern Approaches to Customary International Law: A Reconciliation', *The American Journal of International Law*, 95:4 (2001), 757–91

Brown, Warren C., *Violence in Medieval Europe* (Routledge: London, 2011)

Brown, Warren, and Piotr Górecki (eds.), *Conflict in Medieval Europe: Changing Perspectives on Culture and Society* (Aldershot: Ashgate, 2003)

Brown, Warren, et al. (eds.), *Documentary Culture and the Laity in the Early Middle Ages* (Cambridge: Cambridge University Press, 2013)

Brundage, James A., *Medieval Canon Law* (New York: Longman, 1995)

The Medieval Origins of the Legal Profession: Canonists, Civilians, and Courts (Chicago, IL: University of Chicago Press, 2008)

Bruni, Francesco, *Testi e chierici del medioevo* (Genoa: Marietti, 1991)

Brunner, Thomas, 'Le passage aux langues vernaculaires dans les actes de la pratique en occident', *Le Moyen Âge*, 115:1 (2009), 29–72

Brynteson, William E., 'Roman Law and Legislation in the Middle Ages', *Speculum* 41:3 (1966), 420–37

Burgwinkle, William E., Nicholas Hammond, and Emma Wilson. *The Cambridge History of French Literature* (Cambridge: Cambridge University Press, 2011)

Burke, Peter, *A Social History of Knowledge: From Gutenberg to Diderot* (Cambridge: Polity Press, 2000)

Cabrillac, Rémy, *Les Codifications* (Paris: Presses Universitaires de France, 2002)

Cairns, John, and Paul du Plessis (eds.), *The Creation of the* Ius Commune*: From* Casus *to* Regula (Edinburgh University Press, 2010)

Cam, Helen, 'Suitors and Scabini', *Speculum*, 10:2 (1935), 189–200

Canning, Joseph, *The Political Thought of Baldus de Ubaldis* (Cambridge: Cambridge University Press, 2003)

Cardozo, Benjamin N., 'Law and Literature', *Yale Law Journal*, 14 (1925), 699–718

Carlyle, R. W., and A. J. Carlyle, *A History of Mediaeval Political Theory in the West*, vol. 2, *The Political Theory of the Roman Lawyers and the Canonists, from the Tenth Century to the Thirteenth Century* (New York: G. P. Putnam's Sons, 1909)

Carolus-Barré, Louis, 'Charte de Philippe de Beaumanoir', *Bulletin de la Société nationale des Antiquaires de France*, 1945–1947 (1950), 264

'La Grande Ordonnance de Réformation de 1254', *Comptes rendus des séances de l'Académie des Inscriptions et Belles-Lettres* (1973), 181–86

'Origines, milieu familial et carrière de Philippe de Beaumanoir' in Philippe Bonnet-La Borderie (ed.), *Actes du colloque international Philippe de Beaumanoir et les Coutumes de Beauvaisis (1283–1983)* (Beauvais, France: GEMOB, 1984), pp. 19–37

Carruthers, Mary, *The Book of Memory: A Study of Memory in Medieval Culture* (Cambridge: Cambridge University Press, 2008)

Castaldo, André, 'Pouvoir royal, droit savant et droit commun coutumier dans la France du Moyen Âge: À propos de vues nouvelles I', *Droits*, 46:2 (2007), 117–58

'Pouvoir royal, droit savant et droit commun coutumier dans la France du Moyen Âge: À propos de vues nouvelles II: Le droit romain est-il le droit commun?', *Droits*, 47:1 (2008), 173–248

André Castaldo and Yves Mausen, *Introduction historique au droit*, 5th ed. (Paris: Dalloz, 2019)

Cerquiglini, Bernard, *Éloge de la variante: Histoire critique de la philologie* (Paris: Éditions du Seuil, 1989)

In Praise of the Variant: A Critical History of Philology, trans. Betsy Wing (Baltimore: Johns Hopkins University Press, 1999)

Champeaux, Ernest, *Essai sur la vestitura ou saisine, et l'introduction des actions possessoires dans l'ancien droit français* (Paris: A. Fontemoing, 1899)

Chénon, Émile, 'Quelques mots sur les deux manuscrits récemment découverts du coutumier de Champagne', *Nouvelle revue historique de droit français et étranger* 35 (1911), 66–74

Chevrier, G., 'L'originalité du droit franc-comtois', *Tijdschrift voor Rechtsgeschiedenis/ Legal History Review* 27:1 (1959), 1–35

Cheyette, Fredric L., 'Custom, Case Law, and Medieval "Constitutionalism": A Re-Examination', *Political Science Quarterly*, 78:3 (1963), 362–90

'La justice et le pouvoir royal à la fin du Moyen-Âge français', *Revue historique de droit français et étranger*, 40:3 (1962), 373–94

'*Suum Cuique Tribuere*', *French Historical Studies*, 6 (1970), 287–99

Chiffoleau, Jacques, 'Saint Louis, Frédéric II et les constructions institutionnelles du XIIIe siècle', *Médiévales*, 17:34 (1998), 13–23

Clanchy, Michael T., *From Memory to Written Record: England 1066–1307*, 3rd ed. (Oxford: Wiley-Blackwell, 2013)

'Remembering the Past and the Good Old Law', *History* 55:184 (1970), 165–76

Clark, Suzannah, and Elizabeth Eva Leach (eds.), *Citation and Authority in Medieval and Renaissance Musical Culture: Learning from the Learned* (Woodbridge: Boydell and Brewer, 2005)

'Learning, Citation and Authority in Musical Culture before 1600' in Suzannah Clark and Elizabeth Eva Leach (eds.), *Citation and Authority in Medieval and Renaissance Musical Culture: Learning from the Learned* (Woodbridge: Boydell and Brewer, 2005), pp. xxi–xxiv

Clemens, Raymond, and Timothy Graham, *Introduction to Manuscript Studies* (Ithaca, NY: Cornell University Press, 2007)

Cohen, Esther, *The Crossroads of Justice: Law and Culture in Late Medieval France*, Brill's Studies in Intellectual History 36 (Leiden: Brill, 1993)

Collinet, Paul, 'Deux chartes inédites de Philippe de Beaumanoir (1290–1291)', *Nouvelle revue historique de droit français étranger*, 18 (1894), 697–702

'Une traduction néerlandaise inédite du Conseil de Pierre de Fontaines', *Compte rendu des séances de la commission royale d'histoire*, 70 (1901), 408–19

Collins, Roger, *Early Medieval Spain: Unity in Diversity, 400–1000*, 2nd ed. (New York: St. Martin's Press, 1995)

Comaroff, J. L., and S. A. Roberts, *Rules and Processes: The Cultural Logic of Dispute in an African Context* (University of Chicago Press, 1981)

Connors, Robert J., 'The Rhetoric of Citation Systems, Part I: The Development of Annotation Structures from the Renaissance to 1900', *Rhetoric Review*, 17:1 (1998), 6–48

Constable, Marianne, *Our Word is Our Bond: How Legal Speech Acts* (Stanford University Press, 2014)

Conte, Emanuele, 'Roman Law *vs* Custom in a Changing Society: Italy in the Twelfth and Thirteenth Centuries' in Per Anderson and Mia Münster-Swendsen (eds.), *Custom: The Development and Use of a Legal Concept in the Middle Ages* (Copenhagen: Djøf, 2009), pp. 33–49

Copeland, Rita, *Emotion and the History of Rhetoric in the Middle Ages* (Oxford: Oxford University Press, 2021)

Rhetoric, Hermeneutics, and Translation in the Middle Ages (Cambridge: Cambridge University Press, 1991)

Corcoran, Simon, 'Roman Law in Ravenna' in Judith Herrin and Jinty Nelson (eds.), *Ravenna: Its Role in Earlier Medieval Change and Exchange* (London: University of London Press, 2016), pp. 163–98

Cormack, Bradin, *A Power to Do Justice: Jurisdiction, English Literature, and the Rise of Common Law, 1509–1625* (University of Chicago Press, 2007)

Cover, Robert, 'Nomos and Narrative' in Martha Minow, Michael Ryan, and Austin Sarat (eds.), *Narrative, Violence, and the Law: The Essays of Robert Cover* (Ann Arbor: University of Michigan Press, 1995), pp. 95–172

Danet, Brenda, and Bryna Bogoch, 'From Oral Ceremony to Written Document: The Transitional Language of Anglo-Saxon Wills', *Language & Communication*, 12:2 (1992), 95–122

Davis, Adam Jeffrey, *The Holy Bureaucrat: Eudes Rigaud and Religious Reform in Thirteenth-century Normandy* (Ithaca, NY: Cornell University Press, 2006)

Davis, Jennifer R., *Charlemagne's Practice of Empire* (Cambridge: Cambridge University Press, 2015)

Davis, Kathleen, 'Sovereign Subjects, Feudal Law, and the Writing of History', *Journal of Medieval and Early Modern Studies*, 36:2 (2006), 223–61

Davis, Natalie Zemon, *Fiction in the Archives: Pardon Tales and their Tellers in Sixteenth-Century France* (Stanford University Press, 1987)

Davy, Gilduin, 'Les chartes ducales, miroir du droit coutumier normand? Hypothèses sur les évocations de la coutume dans les actes des ducs de Normandie (fin XIe–fin XIIe siècles)', *Revue historique de droit français et étranger* (1922–), 85:2 (2007), 197–218

'La Normandie, terre de traditions juridiques: Les grandes tendances de l'historiographie du droit normand', *Cahiers historiques des Annales de droit*, 2 (2016) 11–24

Dawson, John P., 'The Codification of the French Customs', *Michigan Law Review*, 38 (1940), 765–800

A History of Lay Judges (Cambridge, MA: Harvard University Press, 1960)

de Germiny, Maxime, *Les lieutenants de Robert II, comte d'Artois, gardes et maitres de toutes ses terres, 1270–1299* (Arras: F. Guyot, 1898)

Dejoux, Marie, *Les enquêtes de Saint Louis: Gouverner et sauver son âme* (Paris: Presses Universitaires de France, 2014)

'Gouverner par l'enquête en France, de Philippe Auguste aux derniers Capétiens',*French Historical Studies*, 37:2 (2014), 271–302

Delisle, M. L., 'Mémoire sur les recueils de jugements rendus par l'échiquier de Normandie sous les règnes de Philippe-Auguste, de Louis VIII et de saint Louis', *Mémoires de l'institut impérial de France, Académie des inscriptions et belles-lettres*, 24: 2(1861), 343–85; also in *Recueil de*

Jugements de l'echiquier de Normandie au XIIIe siècle (1207–1270), ed. Léopold Delisle (Paris: Imprimerie imperiale, 1864), pp. 247–88

Derrida, Jacques, 'The Force of Law: The "Mystical Foundation of Authority"' in David G. Carlson, Drucilla Cornell and Michel Rosenfeld (eds.), *Deconstruction and the Possibility of Justice* (New York: Routledge, 1991), pp. 3–67

Descamps, Olivier, and Rafael Domingo, *Great Christian Jurists in French History* (Cambridge: Cambridge University Press, 2019)

Diamond, Stanley, 'The Rule of Law versus the Order of Custom', *Social Research*, 38:1 (1971), 42–72

Dobozy, Maria, 'From Oral Custom to Written Law: The German Sachsenspiegel' in Gerhard Jaritz (ed.), *Oral History of the Middle Ages: The Spoken Word in Context* (Budapest: Central European University, Department of Medieval Studies, 2001), pp. 154–63

du Plessis, Paul J. (ed.), *New Frontiers Law and Society in the Roman World* (Edinburgh University Press, 2013)

   'Jacques de Revigny' in Olivier Descamps and Rafael Domingo (eds)*Great Christian Jurists in French History* (Cambridge: Cambridge University Press, 2019), p. 71–84

Dufour, J., G. Giordanengo, and A. Gouron, 'L'attrait des *leges*: Note sur la lettre d'un moine victorin (vers 1124/1127)', *Studia et documenta historiae et iuris*, 45 (1979), 504–29

Dunbabin, Jean, 'The Political World of France, c. 1200–c. 1336', *France in the Later Middle Ages*, David Potter ed. (Oxford: Oxford University Press, 2003), pp. 24–27.

Ellul, Jacques, 'Le problème de l'émergence du droit', *Annales de la Faculté de droit de l'Université de Bordeaux*, 1 (1976), 5–15

Enders, Jody, 'Rhetoric and Theater' in William E. Burgwinkle, Nicholas Hammond, and Emma Wilson (eds.), *The Cambridge History of French Literature* (Cambridge: Cambridge University Press, 2011), pp. 164–71

   Rhetoric and the Origins of Medieval Drama (Ithaca: Cornell University Press, 1992)

Epurescu-Pascovici, Ionu, *Human Agency in Medieval Society, 1100-1450* (Woodbridge: Boydell and Brewer, 2021)

Eschbach, Prosper-Louis-Auguste, *Introduction générale à l'étude du droit* (Paris: Cotillon, 1856)

Esmein, Adhémar, *Cours élémentaire d'histoire du droit français: À l'usage des étudiants de première année* (Paris: Larose & Forsel, 1892)

   'Un passage de la Somme rural de Boutillier dans l'édition de Charondas le Caron de Paris (1603)', *Revue historique de droit français et étranger*, 19 (1895), 48–58

Estey, E. N., 'The Scabini and the Local Courts', *Speculum*, 26 (1951), 119–29

Everard, Judith, 'Sworn Testimony and Memory of the Past in Brittany' in Elisabeth van Houts (ed.), *Medieval Memories: Men, Women and the Past, 700–1300* (New York: Longman, 2001), pp. 72–91

Eves, William (ed. and trans.), The *Antiqua consuetudo Normannie*, or 'part one' of the so-called *Très ancien coutumier* of Normandy (St. Helier: Jersey and Guernsey Law Review, 2022) [forthcoming]

The Earliest Treatise within the Materials Comprising the So-Called Très Ancien Coutumier of Normandy, as found in Vatican Library ms. Ott. Lat. 2964, transcr. William Eves, in *Civil Law, Common Law, Customary Law Project Publications* (St Andrews, 2018), https://clicme.wp.st-andrews.ac.uk/tac-vatican2964/ (accessed 26 June 2022)

Evergates, Theodore, *Feudal Society in Medieval France: Documents from the County of Champagne* (Philadelphia: University of Pennsylvania Press, 1993)

The Aristocracy in the County of Champagne, 1100–1300 (Philadelphia: University of Pennsylvania Press, 2007)

Farrell, Joseph, *Latin Language and Latin Culture from Ancient to Modern Times* (Cambridge: Cambridge University Press, 2001)

Fensterand, T. S., and D. L. Smail, *Fama: The Politics of Talk and Reputation in Medieval Europe* (Ithaca, NY: Cornell University Press, 2003)

Fenster, Thelma S., and Carolyn P. Collette, *The French of Medieval England: Essays in Honour of Jocelyn Wogan-Browne* (Rochester, NY: D. S. Brewer, 2016)

Ferguson, Charles, 'Diglossia', *Word*, 15 (1959), 325–40

Field, Sean L., and M. Cecilia Gaposchkin, 'Questioning the Capetians, 1180–1328', *History Compass*, 12 (2014), 567–85

Firnhaber-Baker, Justine, *Violence and the State in Languedoc, 1250–1400* (Cambridge: Cambridge University Press, 2014)

Fishman, Talya, *Becoming the People of the Talmud: Oral Torah as Written Tradition in Medieval Jewish Cultures* (Philadelphia: University of Pennsylvania Press, 2011)

Föller, Carola, *Konigskinder: Erziehung Am Hof Ludwigs IX. Des Heiligen Von Frankreich* (Vienna: Böhlau, 2018)

Forcadet, Pierre-Anne, 'Les premiers juges de la cour du roi au XIIIe siècle', *Revue historique de droit français et étranger* (1922–) 94:2 (2016), 189–273

Fournier, Paul, *Les officialités au Moyen Âge: Étude sur l'organization, la compétence et la procédure des tribunaux ecclésiastiques ordinaires en France de 1180 à 1328* (Paris: Plon, 1880)

'Un tournant de l'histoire du droit, 1060–1140', *Nouvelle revue historique de droit français et étranger* 41 (1917), 129–80

Fowler-Magerl, Linda, *'Ordines iudiciarii' and 'Libelli de ordine iudiciorum': From the Middle of the Twelfth to the End of the Fifteenth Century* (Turnhout, Belgium: Brepols, 1994)

Foys, Martin, 'Medieval Manuscripts: Media Archaeology and the Digital Incunable', in M. Van Dussen and M. Johnston (eds.), *The Medieval Manuscript Book: Cultural Approaches* (Cambridge: Cambridge University Press, 2015), pp. 119–39

Fraher, Richard M., 'Conviction According to Conscience: The Medieval Jurists' Debate Concerning Judicial Discretion and the Law of Proof', *Law and History Review*, 7:1 (1989), 23–88

Friedman, Lawrence M., 'Law and Its Language', *George Washington Law Review*, 33 (1964–5), 563–79

Frier, Bruce W., 'Bees and Lawyers', *The Classical Journal*, 78 (1982), 105–14 http://www.jstor.org/stable/3297059 (accessed 1 October 2021)

Fudeman, Kirsten Anne, *Vernacular Voices: Language and Identity in Medieval French Jewish Communities* (Philadelphia: University of Pennsylvania Press, 2010)

Galanter, Marc, *Law and Society in Modern India*, ed. Rajeev Dhavan (New York: Oxford University Press, 1989)

Galgerisi, Claudio (ed.), *Translations médiévales: Cinq siècles de traductions en français au Moyen Âge (XIe–XVe siècles)*, 3 vols., Medieval Latin & Vernacular Literature: Studies (Turnhout: Brepols, 2011)

Ganshof, F. L., *Recherches sur les tribunaux de châtellenie en Flandre avant le milieu du XIIe siècle* (Paris: Édouard Champion, 1932)

Gaposchkin, M. Cecilia, *The Making of Saint Louis: Kingship, Sanctity, and Crusade in the Later Middle Ages* (Ithaca, NY: Cornell University Press, 2008)

García y García, Antonio, 'The Faculties of Law' in Hilde de Ridder-Symoens (ed.), *A History of the University in Europe*, vol. 1, *Universities in the Middle Ages* (Cambridge: Cambridge University Press, 1992), pp. 388–408

Gaudemet, Jean, 'La coutume en droit canonique' in Jacques Vanderlinden (ed.), *La Coutume = Custom*, vol. 2, *Europe occidentale médiévale et moderne*, Société Jean Bodin pour l'histoire comparative des institutions (Brussels: De Boeck, 1990), pp. 41–61

'Le droit romain dans la pratique et chez les docteurs aux Xie et XIIe siècles', *Cahiers de civilisation médiévale (Xe–XIIe siècles)*, 8 (1965), 365–80

'L'influence des droits savants (Romain et canonique) sur les texts de droit coutumier en occident avant le XVIe siècle' in *La norma en el derecho canonico: Actas del III congreso internacional de derecho canonico (Pamplona, 10–15 de octubre de 1976)* (Pamplona: Ediciones Universidad de Navarra, 1979), pp. 165–96

Gaunt, Simon, *Retelling the Tale: An Introduction to Medieval French Literature* (London: Duckworth, 2001)

Gaunt, Simon, and Sarah Kay, introduction to Simon Gaunt and Sarah Kay (eds.), *The Cambridge Companion to Medieval French Literature* (Cambridge: Cambridge University Press, 2008), pp. 1–18

Gauvard, Claude, *'De grace especial': Crime, État et société en France à la fin du Moyen Âge* (Paris: Publications de la Sorbonne, 1991)
'La justice du roi de France et le latin à la fin du Moyen Âge: Transparence ou opacité d'une pratique de la norme' in Monique Goullet and Michel Parisse (eds.), *Les historiens et le latin médiéval: Colloque tenu à la Sorbonne, les 9, 10 et 11 septembre 1999* (Paris: Publications de la Sorbonne, 2001), pp. 31–54
Violence et ordre public au Moyen Âge (Paris: Picard, 2005)
Gauvard, Claude, et al., 'Normes, droit, rituel et pouvoir' in Jean-Claude Schmitt and Otto Gerhard Oexle (eds.), *Les tendances actuelles de l'histoire du Moyen Âge en France et en Allemagne (Actes des colloques de Sèvres (1997) et Göttingen)* (Paris: Publications de la Sorbonne, 2002), pp. 461–82
Geary, Patrick J., *Language and Power in the Early Middle Ages* (Lebanon, NH: Brandeis University Press, 2013)
'Oblivion between Orality and Textuality in the Tenth Century' in Gerd Althoff (ed.), *Medieval Concepts of the Past: Ritual, Memory, Historiography* (Washington, DC: German Historical Institute, 2002), pp. 111–22
'What Happened to Latin?', *Speculum*, 84:4 (2009), 859–73
Génestal, R., 'La formation et le développement de la coutume de Normandie', *Travaux de la semaine d'histoire du droit normand* (1927), 37–55
Giffard, André, 'Un troisième abrégé de Beaumanoir', *Nouvelle revue historique de droit français et étranger*, 30 (1906), 626–9
Gilissen, John, *La coutume*, Typologie des sources du moyen âge occidental 41 (Turnhout: Brepols, 1982)
Gilissen, John (ed.), *La coutume = Custom*, vol. 2, *Europe occidentale médiévale et moderne (Société Jean Bodin pour l'histoire comparative des institutions)* (Brussels: De Boeck, 1992)
Ginoulhiac, C., 'Cours de droit coutumier français dans ses rapports avec notre droit actuel', *Revue historique de droit français et étranger*, 5 (1859), 66–79
Giordanengo, Gérard, 'Le droit romain au temps de la Reforme: Une étincelle? (1050–1130)', *Mélanges de l'école française de Rome*, 113:2 (2001), 869–911
'Les droit savants au Moyen Âge: Textes et doctrines, la recherche en France depuis 1968', *Bibliothèque de l'École des Chartes*, 148:2 (1990), 439–76
'Jus commune et "droit commun" en France du XIIIe au Xve siècle' in Jacques Krynen (ed.), *Droit romain, jus civile, et droit français* (Toulouse: Presses de l'Université des sciences sociales de Toulouse, 1999), pp. 220–47
'Le pouvoir législatif du roi de France (XI–XIIIe siècles). Travaux récents et hypothèses de recherche', *Bibliothèque de l'École des Chartes*, 147 (1989), 283–310

'Roma nobilis, orbis et domina: Réponse à un contradicteur', *Revue historique de droit français et étranger*, 88:1 (2010), 91–150

Given, James, 'Power and Fear in Philip IV's France', *Historein*, 6 (2006), 88–96

Glenn, H. P., *On Common Laws* (Oxford: Oxford University Press, 2005)

Goodrich, Peter, *Law in the Courts of Love: Literature and Other Minor Jurisprudences* (London: Routledge, 1996)

Goody, Jack, *The Logic of Writing and the Organisation of Society* (Cambridge: Cambridge University Press, 1986)

Gordley, James, '*Ius Quarens Intellectum*: The Method of the Medieval Civilians' in John Cairns and Paul du Plessis (eds.), *The Creation of the Ius Commune: From Casus to Regula* (Edinburgh: Edinburgh University Press, 2010), pp. 77–102

'Myths of the French Civil Code', *The American Journal of Comparative Law*, 42:3 (1994), 459–505

Górecki, Piotr, 'A View from a Distance', *Law and History Review*, 21 (2003), 367–76

Górecki, Piotr, Charles M. Radding, and Paul Brand, 'Forum: The Emergence of Professional Law', *Law and History Review*, 21 (2003), 247–391

Gouron, André, 'Aux origines de l'émergence du droit: Glossateurs et coutumes méridionales (XIIe–XIIIe siècle)' in Etienne Bravasa, Claude Emeri, and Jean-Louis Seurin (eds.), *Religion, société et politique: Mélanges en hommage à Jacques Ellul* (Paris: Presses Universitaires de France, 1983), pp. 255–70

'La coutume en France au Moyen Âge' in Jacques Vanderlinden (ed.), *La Coutume = Custom*, vol. 2, *Europe occidentale médiévale et moderne* (Brussels: De Boeck, 1990), pp. 193–217

'Le droit commun a-t-il été l'héritier du droit romain?', *Comptes-rendus des séances de l'Académie des Inscriptions et Belles-Lettres*, 142:1 (1998), 283–92

'Du nouveau sur Lo Codi', *Revue d'histoire du droit*, 43:2 (1975), 271–7

Grace-Heller, Sarah, and Michelle Reichert (eds.), *Essays on the Poetic and Legal Writings of Philippe de Rémy and His Son Philippe de Beaumanoir of Thirteenth-Century France* (Lewiston, NY: Edwin Mellen Press, 2001)

Grafton, Anthony, *The Footnote: A Curious History* (Cambridge, MA: Harvard University Press, 1997)

'Learning, Citation and Authority in Musical Culture before 1600' in Suzannah Clark and Elizabeth Eva Leach (eds.), *Citation and Authority in Medieval and Renaissance Musical Culture: Learning from the Learned* (Woodbridge: Boydell and Brewer, 2005), pp. xxi–xxiv

Gravdal, Katheryn, *Ravishing Maidens: Writing Rape in Medieval French Literature and Law* (Philadelphia: University of Pennsylvania Press, 1991)

Green, Michael S., 'Legal Realism as Theory of Law', *William & Mary Law Review*, 46 (2005), 1915–2000

Green, Thomas Andrew, *Verdict According to Conscience: Perspectives on the English Criminal Trial Jury, 1200–1800* (Chicago, IL: University of Chicago Press, 1985)

Greimas, Algirdas Julien, *Dictionnaire de l'ancien français* (Paris: Larousse, 2004)

Griffiths, Quentin, 'New Men among the Lay Counselors of Saint Louis' Parlement', *Mediaeval Studies*, 32:1 (1970), 234–72

'Les origines et la carrière de Pierre de Fontaines, Jurisconsulte de Saint Louis: Une reconsidération avec documents inédits', *Revue historique de droit français et étranger*, 48:4 (1970), 544–67

'Royal Counselors and Trouvères in the Houses of Nesle and Soissons', *Medieval Prosopography*, 18 (1997), 123–37

Grinberg, Martine, *Écrire les coutumes: Les droits seigneuraux en France* (Paris: Presses Universitaires de France, 2006)

'La rédaction des coutumes et les droits seigneuriaux: Nommer, classer, exclure', *Annales. Histoire, Sciences Sociales*, 52:5 (1997), 1017–38

Guenée, Bernard, *Tribunaux et gens de justice dans le baillage de Senlis à la fin du Moyen Âge (vers 1330–vers 1550)* (Paris: Belles Lettres, 1963)

Guilbert, Aristide, *Histoire des villes de France: Avec une introduction générale pour chaque province* (Paris: Furne, 1859)

Guilhiermoz, P., *Enquêtes et procès: Étude sur la procédure et le fonctionnement du Parlement au XIVe siècle* (Paris: Picard, 1902)

Guillot, Olivier, '*Consuetudines, consuetudo*: Quelques remarques sur l'apparition de ces termes dans les sources françaises des premiers temps Capétiens (à l'exception du Midi)', *Mémoires de la Société pour l'Histoire du Droit et des Institutions des anciens pays bourguignons, comtois et romands*, 40 (1983), 21–47

'Sur la naissance de la coutume en Anjou au XIe siècle', *Droit romain, 'jus civile' et droit français*, 3 (1999), 273–95

Guillot, Olivier, Albert Rigaudière, and Yves Sassier, *Pouvoirs et institutions dans la France médiévale: Des temps féodaux aux temps de l'État* (Paris: Armand Collin, 1994)

Guterman, Simeon L., *From Personal to Territorial Law: Aspects of the History and Structure of the Western Legal-Constitutional Tradition* (Metuchen, NJ: The Scarecrow Press, 1972)

Guzmán, Alejandro, *Ratio scripta* (Frankfurt am Main: Klostermann, 1981)

Hagger, Mark, 'Secular Law and Custom in Ducal Normandy c. 1000–1144', *Speculum*, 85:4 (2010), 827–68

Halperin, Jean-Louis, *L'impossible Code Civil* (Paris: Presses Universitaires de France, 1992)

'Law in Books and Law in Action: The Problem of Legal Change', *Maine Law Review*, 64 (2011), 45–76

Harding, Alan, *Medieval Law and the Foundations of the State* (Oxford: Oxford University Press, 2002)

'Political Liberty in the Middle Ages', *Speculum* 55:3 (1980), 423–43

Hart, H. L. A., *The Concept of Law* (Oxford: Oxford University Press, 1961)

Hartog, Hendrik, 'Pigs and Positivism', *Wisconsin Law Review*, 899 (1985), 899–935

Hasenohr, Geneviève, and Michel Zink (eds.), *Dictionnaire des lettres françaises, Le Moyen Âge* (Paris: Fayard, 1992)

Havelock, Eric A., *The Muse Learns to Write: Reflections on Orality and Literacy from Antiquity to the Present* (New Haven, CT: Yale University Press, 1986)

Heirbaut, Dirk, 'The Spokesmen in Medieval Courts: The Unknown Leading Judges of the Customary Law and Makers of the First Continental Law Reports' in Paul Brand and Joshua Getzler (eds.), *Judges and Judging in the History of the Common Law and Civil Law: From Antiquity to Modern Times* (Cambridge: Cambridge University Press, 2012), pp. 192–208

'Who Were the Makers of Customary Law in Medieval Europe? Some Answers Based on Sources about the Spokesmen of Flemish Feudal Courts', *The Legal History Review*, 75:3 (2007), 257–74

Helmholz, Richard, *The Ius Commune in England: Four Studies* (Oxford: Oxford University Press, 2001)

Herzog, Tamar, *A Short History of European Law: The Last Two and a Half Millennia* (Cambridge, MA: Harvard University Press, 2018)

Hilaire, Jean, 'Coutume et droit écrit au Parlement de Paris d'après les registres des *Olim* (1254–1318)' in Véronique Gazeau and Jean-Marie Augustin (eds.), *Coutumes, doctrine et droit savant: Actes du colloque des 20 et 21 octobre 2006* (Poitiers: LGDJ, 2007), pp. 65–88

'Coutumes et droit écrit: Recherche d'une limite', *Mémoires de la Société pour l'histoire du droit et des institutions des anciens pays bourguignons, comtois et romands*, 40 (1983), 153–75

La vie du droit (Paris: Presses Universitaires de France, 1995)

Hobsbawm, E. J., and T. O Ranger, *The Invention of Tradition* (Cambridge: Cambridge University Press, 1992)

Holsinger, Bruce, 'Vernacular Legality: The English Jurisdiction of *The Owl and the Nightingale*' in Emily Steiner and Candace Barrington (eds.), *The Letter of the Law: Legal Practice and Literary Production in Medieval England* (Ithaca, NY: Cornell University Press, 2002), pp. 154–84

Holzknecht, Karl, *Literary Patronage in the Middle Ages* (London: Frank Cass, 1923)

Hubrecht, Georges, 'Le droit canonique dans le coutumier de Beaumanoir' in *Mélanges offerts à Pierre Andrieu-Guitrancourt: L'Année Canonique*, vol. 17 (Paris: Faculté de Droit Canonique de Paris, 1973), pp. 579–88

Hudson, John G. H., 'Court Cases and Legal Arguments in England, c.1066–1166', *Transactions of the Royal Historical Society*, 10 (2000), 91–115

'Customs, Laws and the Interpretation of Medieval Law' in Per Anderson and Mia Münster-Swendsen (eds.), *Custom: The Development and Use of a Legal Concept in the Middle Ages* (Copenhagen: Djøf, 2009), pp. 1–16

The Formation of the English Common Law: Law and Society in England from the Norman Conquest to Magna Carta (London: Longman, 1996)

'From the Leges to Glanvill: Legal Expertise and Legal Reasoning' in Stefan Jurasinski, Lisi Oliver, and Andrew Rabin (eds.), *English Law Before Magna Carta: Felix Liebermann and Die Gesetze der Angelsachsen* (Leiden: Brill, 2010), pp. 221–49

The Oxford History of the Laws of England, vol 2, 871–1216 (Oxford: Oxford University Press, 2012)

Huizinga, Johan, *Homo Ludens: A Study of the Play-Element in Culture* (London: Routledge & Kegan Paul, 1949)

'Play and Law' in *Homo Ludens: A Study of the Play-Element in Culture* (Boston, MA: Beacon Press, 1955), pp. 76–88

Hulsebosch, Daniel J., 'Writs to Rights: "Navigability" and the Transformation of the Common Law in the Nineteenth Century', *Cardozo Law Review*, 23:3 (2002), 1049–1106

Hult, David F., 'Manuscripts and Manuscript Culture' in W. Burgwinkle, N. Hammond, and E. Wilson (eds.), *The Cambridge History of French Literature* (Cambridge: Cambridge University Press, 2011), pp. 11–19

Humfress, Caroline, 'Law and Custom under Rome' in Alice Rio (ed.), *Law, Custom, and Justice in Late Antiquity and the Early Middle Ages: Proceedings of the 2008 Byzantine Colloquium, Centre for Hellenic Studies Occasional Publications, King's College London* (London: Centre for Hellenic Studies, 2011), pp. 23–47

'Law's Empire: Roman Universalism and Legal Practice' in Paul J. du Plessis (ed.), *New Frontiers Law and Society in the Roman World* (Edinburgh: Edinburgh University Press, 2013), 73–101

Humphreys, Sally, 'Social Relations on Stage: Witnesses in Classical Athens', *History and Anthropology*, 1:2 (1985), 313–69

Hyams, Paul, 'The Charter as a Source for the Early Common Law', *The Journal of Legal History*, 12:3 (1991), 173–89

'The Common Law and the French Connection' in R. Allen Brown (ed.), *Proceedings of the Battle Conference* (Woodbridge: Boydell and Brewer, 1982), pp. 77–92

'Orality and Literacy in the Age of Angevin Law Reforms' in Richard Kaeuper, Paul Dingman and Peter Sposato (eds.), *Law, Governance, and Justice: New Views on Medieval Constitutionalism*, Medieval Law and Its Practice 14 (Leiden: Brill, 2013), pp. 27–71

'Review of *Fiefs and Vassals: The Medieval Evidence Reinterpreted*, by Susan Reynolds', *The Journal of Interdisciplinary History*, 27:4 (1997), 655–62

Ibbetson, David, 'Custom in Medieval Law' in Amanda Perreau-Saussine and James B. Murphy (eds.), *The Nature of Customary Law: Legal, Historical, and Philosophical Perspectives* (Cambridge: Cambridge University Press, 2007), pp. 151–75

Ingham, Patricia Clare, *The Medieval New: Ambivalence in an Age of Innovation* (Philadelphia: University of Pennsylvania Press, 2015)

Innes, Matthew, 'Memory, Orality and Literacy in an Early Medieval Society', *Past & Present*, 158 (1998), 3–36

Interencheres, 'Les Paroles de Pierre de Fontaines', *Magazine des enchères* (9 October 2009) https://bit.ly/3yay046 (accessed 22 June 2022)

Jacob, Robert, 'Beaumanoir versus Révigny: The Two Faces of Customary Law in Philip the Bold's France' in Sarah-Grace Heller and Michelle Reichert (eds.), *Essays on the Poetic and Legal Writings of Philippe de Rémy and His Son Philippe de Beaumanoir of Thirteenth-Century France* (Lewiston, NY: Edwin Mellen Press, 2001), pp. 221–76

'La coutume, les moeurs et le rite: Regards croisés sur les categories occidentals de la norme non écrite', *Extrême-Orient, Extrême-Occident*, 23 (2001), 145–66

'Les coutumiers du XIIIe siècle ont-ils connu la coutume?' in Mireille Mousnier and Jacques Poumarède (eds.), *La coutume au village dans l'Europe médiévale et moderne* (Toulouse: Presses Universitaires du Mirail, 2008), pp. 103–20

Images de la justice: Essai sur l'iconographie judiciare du Moyen Âge à l'âge classique (Paris: Le Léopard d'Or, 1994)

'Philippe De Beaumanoir et le savoir du juge (réponse à M. Giordanengo)', *Revue historique de droit français et étranger (1922–)* 92:4 (2014), 577–88

'Philippe de Beaumanoir et les clercs: Pour sortir de la controverse du "ius commune"', *Droits*, 50:2 (2009), 163–88

Jordan, William Chester, 'The Capetians from the Death of Philip II to Philip IV' in *The New Cambridge Medieval History*, vol. 5, c. 1198–c. 1300, ed. D. Abulafia (Cambridge: Cambridge University Press, 1999), pp 277–313

'Closing remarks', presented at the conference Law, Justice and Governance: New Views on Medieval Constitutionalism, Rochester, NY, April 2009

Louis IX and the Challenge of the Crusade: A Study in Rulership (Princeton, NJ: Princeton University Press, 1979)

Men at the Center: Redemptive Governance under Louis IX (New York: Central European University Press, 2012)

Servant of the Crown and Steward of the Church: The Career of Philippe of Cahors (Toronto, ON: University of Toronto Press, 2020)

Jurasinski, Stefan, and Lisi Oliver, *The Laws of Alfred: The Domboc and the Making of Anglo-Saxon Law* (Cambridge: Cambridge University Press, 2021)

Kadens, Emily, 'Convergence and the Colonization of Custom in Pre-Modern Europe' in Olivier Moreteau and Kjell Modeer (eds.), *Comparative Legal History* (London: Edward Elgar, 2019), pp. 167–85

'Custom's Past' in Curtis A. Bradley (ed.), *Custom's Future: International Law in a Changing World* (Cambridge: Cambridge University Press, 2016), pp. 11–33

'Custom's Two Bodies' in Katherin L. Jansen, G. Geltner and Anne E. Lester (eds.), *Center and Periphery: Studies on Power in the Medieval World in Honor of William Chester Jordan*, Later Medieval Europe 11 (Leiden: Brill, 2013), pp. 239–48

Kaeuper, Richard, 'The King and the Fox: Reactions to Kingship in Tales of Reynard the Fox' in Anthony Musson (ed.), *Expectations of the Law in the Middle Ages* (Woodbridge: Boydell and Brewer, 2001), pp. 9–22

Kaeuper, Richard W., Paul Dingman, and Peter Sposato (eds.), *Law, Governance, and Justice: New Views on Medieval Constitutionalism*, Medieval Law and Its Practice 14 (Leiden: Brill, 2013)

Kamali, Elizabeth Papp, *Felony and the Guilty Mind in Medieval England* (New York: Cambridge University Press, 2019)

Karras, Ruth Mazzo, *From Boys to Men: Formations of Masculinity in Late Medieval Europe* (Philadelphia: University of Pennsylvania Press, 2003)

Kelley, Donald R., 'De origine feudorum: The Beginnings of an Historical Problem', *Speculum* 39:2 (1964), 207–28

'"Second Nature": The Idea of Custom in European Law, Society and Culture' in Anthony Grafton and Ann Blair (eds.), *The Transmission of Culture in Early Modern Europe* (Philadelphia: University of Pennsylvania Press, 1998), pp. 131–72

Keyser, Richard, 'Peaceable Power: Civil Law and the Limitations of Lordship', paper presented at the 46th International Conference on Medieval Studies, Kalamazoo, MI, May 2011

Kim, Marie Seong-Hak, *Custom, Law, and Monarchy: A Legal History of Early Modern France* (Oxford: Oxford University Press, 2021)

Kinoshita, Sharon, *Medieval Boundaries: Rethinking Difference in Old French Literature* (Philadelphia: University of Pennsylvania Press, 2006)

Klimrath, Henri, *Études sur les coutumes* (Paris: Levrault, 1837)

Mémoire sur les monumens inédits de l'histoire du droit français au moyen âge. Paris: F. G. Levrault, 1835.

Koenigswarter, Jean Louis, *Sources et monuments du droit français antérieurs au quinzième siècle, ou, Bibliothèque de l'histoire du droit civil français depuis les premières origines jusqu'à la rédaction officielle des coutumes* (Paris: A. Durant, 1853)

Korpiola, Mia (ed.), *Regional Variations in Matrimonial Law and Custom in Europe, 1150–1600*, Medieval Law and Its Practice 12 (Leiden: Brill, 2011)

Kosto, Adam, 'Laymen, Clerics, and Documentary Practices in the Early Middle Ages: The Example of Catalonia', *Speculum*, 80:1 (2005), 44–74

Making Agreements in Medieval Catalonia: Power, Order, and the Written Word, 1000–1200 (Cambridge: Cambridge University Press, 2001)

'Statim invenire ante: Finding Aids and Research Tools in Pre-scholastic Legal and Administrative Manuscripts', *Scriptorium*, 70 (2016), 285–309

Kosto, Adam J., and Anders Winroth (eds.), *Charters, Cartularies and Archives: The Preservation and Transmission of Documents in the Medieval West: Proceedings of a Colloquium of the Commission Internationale de Diplomatique (Princeton and New York, 16–18 September 1999* (Toronto, ON: Pontifical Institute of Mediaeval Studies, 2002)

Kowaleski, Marianne, 'The French of England: A Maritime Lingua Franca?' in Jocelyn Wogan-Browne (ed.), *Language and Culture in Medieval Britain: The French of England, c. 1100–c. 1500* (York Medieval Press, 2009), pp. 103–17

Koziol, Geoffrey, *Begging Pardon and Favor: Ritual and Political Order in Early Medieval France* (Ithaca, NY: Cornell University Press, 1992)

The Politics of Memory and Identity in Carolingian Royal Diplomas: The West Frankish Kingdom (840–987), Utrecht Studies in Medieval Literacy 19 (Turnhout: Brepols, 2012)

Krynen, Jacques, 'Le droit romain, droit commun de France', *Droits*, 38 (2003), 21–35

L'empire du roi, idées et croyances politiques en France XIIIe–XVe siècle (Paris: Gallimard, 1993)

'Entre science juridique et dirigisme: Le glas médiéval de la coutume', *Cahier de recherches médiévales* 7 (2000), https://doi.org/10.4000/crm.892

Idéal du prince et pouvoir royal en France à la fin du Moyen Âge (1380–1440): Étude de la littérature politique du temps (Paris: A. et J. Picard, 1981)

'*Voluntas domini regis in suo regno facit ius*': El dret comú i Catalunya, 7 (1998), 59–89

Kullmann, Dorothea (ed.), *The Church and Vernacular Literature in Medieval France* (Toronto, ON: Pontifical Institute of Mediaeval Studies, 2009)

Kuskowski, Ada Maria, '*Lingua Franca Legalis*? A French Vernacular Legal Culture from England to the Levant', special issue, *Reading Medieval Studies*, 40 (2014), 140–58

'Inventing Legal Space: From Regional Custom to Common Law in the *Coutumiers* of Medieval France' in Meredith Cohen and Fanny Madeleine (eds.), *Space in the Medieval West Places, Territories, and Imagined Geographies* (Farnham: Ashgate, 2014), pp. 133–55

'The Time of Custom and the Medieval Myth of Old Customary Law', *Speculum* (in press)

'Translating Justinian: Transmitting and Transforming Roman Law in the Middle Ages' in Jenny Benham, Matthew McHaffie, and Helle Vogt (eds.), *Law and Language in the Middle Ages*, Medieval Law and Its Practice 25 (Leiden: Brill, 2018), pp. 30–51

Kuttner, Stephan, 'Sue les origines du terme "droit positif"', *Revue historique de droit français et étranger* 15 (1936), 728–40

Laferrière, Louis-Firmin-Julien, *Histoire du droit civil de Rome et du droit français*, vol. 6 (Paris: Joubert, 1858)

Lafosse, Aurore, 'La procedure de l'enquête testimoniale à la fin du Moyen Âge: L'example angevin', *Annales de Bretagne de des Pays de l'Ouest*, 112:1 (2005), 101–19, http://abpo.revues.org/1141?file=1 (accessed 21 February 2016)

Lalou, Élisabeth, 'Le comté d'Artois (xiiie–xive siècle)' in Alain Provost (ed.), *Les Comtes d'Artois et leurs archives. Histoire, mémoire et pouvoir au Moyen Âge* (Arras: Artois Presses Université, 2012)

Lambert, T. B., *Law and Order in Anglo-Saxon England* (Oxford: Oxford University Press, 2017)

Lamond, Grant, 'Precedent and Analogy in Legal Reasoning' in *The Stanford Encyclopedia of Philosophy* (Spring 2016 Edition), ed. Edward N. Zalta, https://plato.stanford.edu/archives/spr2016/entries/legal-reas-prec/ (accessed 16 October 2020)

Lauranson-Rosaz, Christian, 'Des "mauvaises coutumes" aux "bonnes coutumes": Essai de synthése pour le Midi (Ve–XIIe siècle)' in Mireille Mousnier and Jacques Poumarède (eds.), *La coutume au village dans l'Europe médiéval et modern* (Toulouse: Presses Universitaires du Mirail, 2008), pp. 19–52

Laurent-Bonne, Nicolas, *Aux origines de la liberté de disposer entre époux*, Bibliothèque d'Histoire du Droit et Droit Romain 28 (Paris: LGDJ, 2014)

Lavigne, Claire-Hélène, 'La traduction en vers des *Institutes* de Justinien 1er: Mythes, réalités et entreprise de versification', *Meta: Translator's Journal*, 49:3 (2004), 511–25

Le Goff, Jacques, *Intellectuals in the Middle Ages*, trans. Teresa Lavender Fagan (Cambridge, MA: Blackwell, 1993)
Les intellectuels au Moyen Âge (Paris: Édition du Seuil, 2000)

Lee, Daniel, *Popular Sovereignty in Early Modern Constitutional Thought* (Oxford: Oxford University Press, 2016)

Lefebvre-Teillard, Anne, *Autour de l'enfant: Du droit canonique et romain medieval au Code Civil de 1804*, Medieval Law and Its Practice 2 (Leiden: Brill, 2008)
'Recherches sur la pénétration du droit canonique dans le droit coutumier français (XIIIe–XVIe siècles)', *Mémoires de la Société pour l'histoire du*

droit et des institutions des anciens pays bourguignons, comtois et romands, 40 (1983), 59–76

Legendre, Pierre, *Le désir politique de Dieu: Étude sur les montagnes de l'état et du droit* (Paris: Fayard, 1988)

Lemarignier, J.-F., 'La dislocation du 'pagus' et le problème des 'consuetudines' (Xe–XIe siècles)' in *Mélanges L. Halphen* (Paris: Presses Universitaires de France, 1951), pp. 401–10

Lemesle, Bruno, *Conflits et justice au Moyen Âge: Normes, loi et résolution des conflits en Anjou aux XIe et XIIe siècles* (Paris: Presses Universitaires du France, 2008)

L'Engle, Susan, 'Production and Purchase: Scribes, Illuminators and Customers' in Susan L'Engle and Robert Gibbs, *Illuminating the Law: Legal Manuscripts in Cambridge Collections* (London: Harvey Miller Publishers, 2001), pp. 39–53

L'Engle, Susan and Gibbs, Robert. *Illuminating the Law: Legal Manuscripts in Cambridge Collections* (London: Harvey Miller Publishers, 2001)

Le Patourel, John, 'The Authorship of the *Grand Coutumier De Normandie*', *The English Historical Review* 56: 222 (1941), 292–300.

Lévi-Strauss, Claude, *The Savage Mind* (Chicago, IL: University of Chicago Press, 1966)

Lévy, Jean-Philippe, 'La pénétration du droit savant dans les coutumiers angevins et Bretons au Moyen Âge', *Tijdschrift voor Rechtsgeschidenis*, 25:1 (1957), 1–53.

de Lincy, Antoine Leroux, 'Chansons historiques des XIIIe, XIVe et XVe siècles', *Bibliothèque de l'École des Chartes*, 1:1 (1840), 359–88

Livelton, Trevor, *Archival Theory, Records and the Public* (Lanham, MD: Scarecrow Press (Society of American Archivists), 1996)

Löfstedt, Leena, *Gratiani decretum: La traduction en ancien français du Décret de Gratien*, vol. 2, *Causae 1–14* (Helsinki: Societas scientiarum fennica, 1993)

Lusignan, Serge, 'French Language and Contact with English: Social Context and Linguistic Change (mid-13th–14th centuries)' in Jocelyn Wogan-Browne (ed.), *Language and Culture in Medieval Britain: The French of England, c. 1100–c. 1500* (York Medieval Press, 2009), pp. 19–30

La langue des rois au Moyen Âge: Le français en France et en Angleterre (Paris: Presses Universitaires de France, 2004)

Parler vulgairement: Les intellectuels et la langue française aux XIIIe et XIVe siècles (Montreal: Les Presses de Université de Montréal, 1986)

MacQueen, Hector L., *Common Law and Feudal Society in Medieval Scotland* (Edinburgh: Edinburgh University Press, 1993)

Maddox, Donald, 'Yvain et le sens de la coutume', *Romania*, 109:433 (1988), 1–17

Main, Thomas O., 'The Procedural Foundation of Substantive Law', *Washington University Law Review*, 87:4 (2010), 801–41

Mattila, Heikki E. S., 'Legal Vocabulary' in Peter M. Tiersma and Lawrence M. Solan (eds.), *The Oxford Handbook of Language and Law* (Oxford: Oxford University Press, 2012), pp. 27–38

Mayali, Laurent, 'La coutume dans la doctrine romaniste au Moyen Âge' in Jacques Vanderlinden (ed.), *La Coutume* = Custom, vol. 2,*Europe occidentale médiévale et moderne* (Brussels: De Boeck, 1990), pp. 11–31

'Law and Time in Medieval Jurisprudence' in Richard R. Helmholz et al. (eds.), *Grundlagen des Rechts: Festschrift für Peter Landau zum 65. Geburtstag* (Paderborn: Schöningh, 2000), pp. 605–19

'The Legacy of Roman Law' in David Johnston (ed.), *The Cambridge Companion to Roman Law* (Cambridge: Cambridge University Press, 2015), pp. 374–95

Mayali, Laurent, and Pierre Mousseron (eds.), *Customary Law Today* (Cham: Springer, 2018)

McAuley, Finbarr, 'Canon Law and the End of the Ordeal', *Oxford Journal of Legal Studies* 26:3 (2006), 473–513

McDonough, Susan, 'Poor Widows and Impoverished Mothers: Negotiating Images of Poverty in Marseille's Courts', *Journal of Medieval History*, 34:1 (2008), 64–78

'She Said, He Said, They Said: Claims of Abuse and a Community's Response in Late-Medieval Marseille', *Journal of Women's History*, 19:4 (2007), 35–58

McDougall, Sara, *Bigamy and Christian Identity in Late Medieval Champagne* (Philadelphia: University of Pennsylvania Press, 2012)

Royal Bastards: The Birth of Illegitimacy, 800–1230 (Oxford: Oxford University Press, 2017)

McHaffie, Matthew W., 'Law and Violence in Eleventh-Century France', *Past & Present*, 238:1 (2018), 3–41

McIlwain, Charles, 'Magna Carta and Common Law' in Henry Elliot Malden (ed.), *Magna Carta Commemoration Essays* (London: Longman, 1917), pp. 122–79

McKitterick, Rosamond, *The Carolingians and the Written Word* (Cambridge: Cambridge University Press, 1989)

The Uses of Literacy in Early Mediaeval Europe (Cambridge: Cambridge University Press, 1990)

McLuhan, Marshall, *Understanding Media* (New York: Signet, 1964)

McSweeney, Thomas J., 'Between England and France: A Cross-Channel Legal Culture in the Late Thirteenth Century' in Richard W. Kaeuper, Paul Dingman and Peter Sposato (eds.), *Law, Governance, and Justice: New Views on Medieval Constitutionalism*, Medieval Law and Its Practice 14 (Leiden: Brill, 2013), 73–100

Priests of the Law: Roman Law and the Making of the Common Law's First Professionals (Oxford: Oxford University Press, 2019)

Meijers, E. M. 'L'Université d'Orléans au XIIIe siècle' in E. M. Meijers (ed.), *Études d'histoire du droit*, vol. 3 (Leiden: Leiden University Press, 1956), pp. 3–148

Mellinkoff, David, *The Language of the Law* (Boston, MA: Little, Brown, 1963)

Melville, Gert, *The World of Medieval Monasticism: Its History and Forms of Life* (Collegeville, MN: Liturgical Press, 2016)

Menegaldo, Silvère, and Bernard Ribémont (eds.), *Le roi fontaine de justice: Pouvoir justicier et pouvoir royal au Moyen Âge et à la Renaissance* (Paris: Klincksieck, 2012)

Mertz, Elizabeth, *The Language of Law: Learning to Think Like a Lawyer* (Oxford: Oxford University Press, 2007)

Monagle, Claire, *The Scholastic Project* (Kalamazoo, MI: Arc Humanities Press, 2017)

Montesquieu, Charles-Louis de Secondat, Baron de, *Œuvres de Montesquieu, contenant L'esprit des lois, Livres I–XXII* (Paris: A. Belin, 1817)

The Spirit of the Laws, trans. Tomas Nugent (New York: Hafner, 1949)

Mostert, Marco, *The Political Theology of Abbo of Fleury: A Study of the Ideas about Society and Law of the Tenth-century Monastic Reform Movement* (Hilversum: Uitgeverij Verloren, 1987)

Mostert, Marco, and P. S. Barnwell (eds.), *Medieval Legal Process: Physical, Spoken and Written Performance in the Middle Ages*, Utrecht Studies in Medieval Literacy 22 (Turnhout: Brepols, 2011)

Mousnier, Mireille, and Jacques Poumarède (eds.), *La coutume au village dans l'Europe médiéval et modern* (Toulouse: Presses Universitaires du Mirail, 2008)

Nelson, Janet, 'Dispute Settlement in Carolingian West Francia' in Wendy Davies and Paul Fouracre (eds.), *The Settlement of Disputes in Early Medieval Europe* (Cambridge: Cambridge University Press, 1992), pp. 45–64

The Frankish World, 750–900 (London: Hambledon Press, 1996)

Neveux, François, 'Le contexte historique de la rédaction des coutumiers normands', *Annales de Normandie*, 61 (2011), 11–22.

Niles, John D., 'Orality' in Neil Fraistat and Julia Flanders (eds.), *The Cambridge Companion to Textual Scholarship* (Cambridge: Cambridge University Press, 2013), pp. 205–23

Nordman, Daniel, and Jacques Revel, 'La formation de l'espace français' in André Burguière and Jacques Revel (eds.), *Histoire de la France*, vol. 1, *L'espace français* (Paris: Éditions du Seuil, 1989), pp. 33–174

Novikoff, Alex J., *The Medieval Culture of Disputation: Pedagogy, Practice, and Performance* (Philadelphia: University of Pennsylvania Press, 2013)

O'Brien, Bruce, *Reversing Babel: Translation among the English during an Age of Conquests, c. 800 to c. 1200* (Newark: University of Delaware Press, 2011)

'Translating Technical Terms in Law-Codes from Alfred to the Angevins' in Elizabeth M. Tyler (ed.), *Conceptualizing Multilingualism in England, c. 800–c. 1250*, Studies in the Early Middle Ages 27 (Turnhout: Brepols, 2011), pp. 57–76

Olivier-Martin, Félix, *Les institutes de Justinien en français* (Paris: Sirey, 1935)

Ong, Walter J., *Orality and Literacy: The Technologizing of the Word* (London: Routledge, 1988)

'Orality, Literacy, and Medieval Textualization', *New Literary History*, 16:1 (1984), 1–12

'Writing is a Technology that Restructures Thought' in Ellen Cushman et al. (eds.), *Literacy: A Critical Sourcebook* (Boston, MA: Bedford/St. Martin's, 2001), pp. 19–31

Ormrod, W. M., 'The Use of English Language, Law, and Political Culture in Fourteenth-Century England', *Speculum*, 78:3 (2003), 750–87

Ost, François, *Lettres et lois: Le droit au miroir de la littérature* (Brussels: Publications des facultés universitaires Saint-Louis, 2001)

Ourliac, Paul, 'Beaumanoir et les Coutumes de Beauvaisis' in Philippe Bonnet-La Borderie (ed.), *Actes du colloque international Philippe de Beaumanoir et les Coutumes de Beauvaisis (1283–1983)* (Beauvais: GEMOB, 1984), pp. 75–9

'Législation, coutumes et coutumiers au temps de Philippe Auguste' in Robert-Henri Bautier (ed.), *La France de Philippe Auguste: Le temps des mutations (Colloques Internationaux CNRS no. 602)* (Paris: CNRS, 1980), pp. 471–88

'Réflexions sur l'origine de la coutume' in *Les pays de Garonne vers l'an mil* (Toulouse: Privat, 1993), pp. 271–84

'Un nouveau style du Parlement de Paris', *Mélanges de l'école française de Rome*, 54 (1937), 301–43

Ourliac, Paul, and Jean-Louis Gazzaniga, *Histoire de droit privé français, de l'an mil au Code Civil* (Paris: Albin Michel, 1985)

Padoa Schioppa, Antonio, *A History of Law in Europe: From the Early Middle Ages to the Twentieth Century* (Cambridge: Cambridge University Press, 2017)

Paris, Gaston, *La française au Moyen Âge (Xie–XIVe siècle)* (Paris: Hachette, 1888)

Pastore, Graziella, and Frédéric Duval, 'La tradition française de l'infortiat et le Livre de jostice et de plet', *Bibliothèque de l'école des chartes* 171:1 (2013), 199–225

Pegues, Franklin J., *The Lawyers of the Last Capetians* (Princeton, NJ: Princeton University Press, 1962)

Pennington, Kenneth, 'The Birth of the *Ius Commune*: King Roger II's Legislation', *Rivista internazionale di diritto commune*, 17 (2006), 1–40

'Feudal Oath of Fidelity and Homage' in Kenneth Pennington and Melodie Harris Eichbauer (eds.), *Law as Profession and Practice in Medieval*

Europe: Essays in Honor of James A. Brundage (New York: Routledge, 2011), pp. 93–116

'The Fourth Lateran Council, its Legislation, and the Development of Legal Procedure' in Gert Melville and Johannes Helmrath (eds.), *The Fourth Lateran Council: Institutional Reform and Spiritual Renewal* (Affalterbach: Didymos Verlag, 2017), pp. 41–54

'Learned Law, *Droit Savant, Gelehrtes Recht*: The Tyranny of a Concept', *Rivista internazionale di diritto commune*, 5 (1994), 197–209

The Prince and the Law, 1200–1600: Sovereignty and Rights in the Western Legal Tradition (Berkeley: University of California Press)

Peralba, Sophie, 'Des coutumiers aux styles: L'isolement de la matière procéduraleaux XIIIe et XIVe siècles', *Cahiers de recherches médiévales*, 7 (2000), https://doi.org/10.4000/crm.887 (accessed 30 September 2020)

Perreau-Saussine, Amanda, and James B. Murphy (eds.), *The Nature of Customary Law* (Cambridge: Cambridge University Press, 2007)

Peters, Edward, 'Death of the Subdean: Ecclesiastical Order and Disorder in Eleventh-Century Francia' in *Law, Custom, and the Social Fabric in Medieval Europe: Essays in Honor of Bryce Lyon*, Studies in Medieval Culture 28 (Kalamazoo: Medieval Institute Publications, Western Michigan University, 1990), pp. 51–71

introduction to Philip of Novara, *Le livre de forme de plait*, trans. Peter Edbury (Nicosia: Theopress, 2009)

Peters, Julie Stone, 'Law as Performance: Historical Interpretation, Objects, Lexicons, and Other Methodological Problems' in Elizabeth S. Anker and Bernadette Meyler (eds.), *New Directions in Law and Literature* (Oxford: Oxford University Press, 2017), pp. 193–209

'Legal Performance Good and Bad', *Law, Culture, and the Humanities*, 4:2 (2008), 179–200

M. Petitjean, 'La coutume de Bourgogne. Des coutumiers officieux à la coutume officielle', *Mémoires de la société pour l'histoire du droit et des institutions des anciens pays bourguignons, comtois et romands*, 42 (1985), 13–20

Petot, Pierre, 'Le droit commun en France selon les coutumiers', *Revue historique de droit français et étranger*, 38 (1960), 412–29

'Pierre de Fontaines et le droit romain' *in Études d'histoire du droit canonique dédiées à Gabriel Le Bras*, vol. 2 (Paris: Sirey, 1965), pp. 955–64

Pirie, Fernanda, *The Anthropology of Law* (Oxford: Oxford University Press, 2013)

Pissard, Hippolyte, *Essai sur la connaissance et la preuve des coutumes en justice dans l'ancien droit français et dans le système romano-canonique* (Paris: Rousseau, 1910)

Pollock, Frederick, and F. W. Maitland, *The History of English Law*, 2nd ed. (Cambridge: Cambridge University Press, 1952)

Pollard, Graham, 'The *Pecia* System in Medieval Universities' in M. B. Parkes and Andrew G. Watson (eds.), *Medieval Scribes, Manuscripts and*

Libraries: Essays Presented to N.R. Ker (London: Scholar Press, 1978), pp. 145–6

Posner, Richard A., *Law and Literature: A Misunderstood Relation* (Cambridge, MA: Harvard University Press, 1988)

Potter, David (ed.), *France in the Later Middle Ages* (Oxford: Oxford University Press, 2002)

Poudret, J.-Fr., 'Réflexions sur la preuve de la coutume devant les juridictions royales françaises aux XIIIe et XIVe siècles, notamment le rôle de l'enquête par turbe', *Revue historique du droit français et étranger*, 65:1 (1987), 71–86

Pound, Roscoe, 'Law in Books and Law in Action', *American Law Review*, 44:1 (1910), 12–36

'Mechanical Jurisprudence', *Columbia Law Review* 8:8 (1908), 605–23

Power, Daniel, *The Norman Frontier in the Twelfth and Thirteenth Centuries* (Cambridge: Cambridge University Press, 2004)

Provost, Alain (ed.), *Les Comtes d'Artois et leurs archives. Histoire, mémoire et pouvoir au Moyen Âge* (Arras: Artois Presses Université, 2012)

Radding, Charles M., 'Legal Theory and Practice in Eleventh-Century Italy', *Law and History Review*, 21 (2003), 377–82

The Origins of Medieval Jurisprudence: Pavia and Bologna, 850–1150 (New Haven, CT: Yale University Press, 1988)

'Reviving Justinian's *Corpus*: The Case of the Code' in Per Andersen, Mia Münster-Swendsen and Helle Vogt (eds.), *Law before Gratian: Law in Western Europe c. 500–1000; Proceedings of the Carlsberg Academy Conference on Medieval Legal History, 2006* (Copenhagen: Djøf, 2007), pp. 35–50

Rains, Robert E., 'To Rhyme or Not to Rhyme: An Appraisal', *Law and Literature*, 16:1 (2004), 1–10

Rait, Robert S., *Life in the Medieval University* (Cambridge: Cambridge University Press, 1912)

Reimitz, Helmut, *History, Frankish Identity and the Framing of Western Ethnicity, 550–850* (Cambridge: Cambridge University Press, 2015)

Reynolds, Susan, 'The Emergence of Professional Law in the Long Twelfth Century', *Law and History Review*, 21:2 (2003), 347–66

Fiefs and Vassals: The Medieval Evidence Reinterpreted (Oxford: Clarendon Press, 1994)

Kingdoms and Communities in Western Europe, 900–1300 (Oxford: Clarendon Press, 1984)

'Law and Communities in Western Christendom c. 900-1140', *The American Journal of Legal History*, 25 (1981), 205–24

'Social Mentalities and the Case of Medieval Skepticism', *Transactions of the Royal Historical Society*, 6:1 (1991), 21–41

Ribémont, Bernard, 'La chanson de geste, une "machine judiciaire"? (en guise d'avant-propos)' in Bernard Ribémont (ed.), *Crimes et châtiments dans la chanson de geste* (Paris: Klincksieck, 2008), pp. vii–xxv

'Compiling and Writing a Legal Treatise in French: *The Livre de Jostice et de Plet*' in Darci N. Hill (ed.), *News from the Raven: Essays from Sam Houston State University on Medieval and Renaissance Thought* (Newcastle upon Tyne: Cambridge Scholars Publishing, 2014), pp. 133–42

'Le 'crime épique' et sa punition: quelques exemples (XIIe-XIIIe siècles)' in Albrecht Classen and Connie Scarborough (eds.), *Crime and Punishment in the Middle Ages and Early Modern Age* (Berlin: De Gruyter, 2012), pp. 29–42

'Justice et procédure dans le Tristan de Béroul', *Méthode!* 20 (2012), 55–68

Rico, Gilles, '"Auctoritas cereum habet nasum": Boethius, Aristotle, and the Music of the Spheres in the Thirteenth and Early Fourteenth Centuries' in Suzannah Clark and Elizabeth Eva Leach (eds.), *Citation and Authority in Medieval and Renaissance Musical Culture: Learning from the Learned* (Woodbridge: Boydell and Brewer, 2005), pp. 20–8

Rigaudière, Albert, 'Législation royale et construction de l'État dans la France du XIIIe siècle' in A. Gouron and A. Rigaudière (eds.), *Renaissance du pouvoir législatif et genèse de l'État* (Montpellier: État Socapress, 1988), pp. 203–36

Penser et construire l'État dans la France du Moyen Âge (XIIIe–Xve siècle) (Paris: Comité pour l'histoire économique et financière de la France, 2003)

'La royauté, le Parlement et le droit écrit aux alentours des années 1300', *Académie des inscriptions et belles lettres*, 140:3 (1996), 885–908

Rio, Alice, *The Formularies of Angers and Marculf: Two Merovingian Legal Handbooks* (Liverpool: Liverpool University Press, 2008)

Legal Practice and the Written Word in the Early Middle Ages: Frankish Formulae, c. 500–1000 (Cambridge: Cambridge University Press, 2009)

Rodríguez Velasco, Jesús D., *Dead Voice: Law, Philosophy, and Fiction in the Iberian Middle Ages* (Philadelphia: University of Pennsylvania Press, 2020)

Rogers, Nicole, 'The Play of Law: Comparing Performances in Law and Theatre', *Queensland University of Technology Law Journal*, 8:2 (2008), 429–43

Rolker, Christof, *Canon Law and the Letters of Ivo of Chartres* (Cambridge: Cambridge University Press, 2010)

Rosen, Lawrence, *Law as Culture: An Invitation* (Princeton, NJ: Princeton University Press, 2006)

Rothwell, William, 'The Trial Scene in "Lanval" and the Development in the Legal Register in Anglo-Norman', *Neuphilologische Mitteilungen*, 101:1 (2000), 17–36

Roumy, Franck, '*Lex consuetudinaria, Jus consuetudinarium*: Recherche sur la naissance du concept de droit coutumier aux Xie et XIIe siècles', *Revue historique de droit français et étranger*, 79:3 (2001), 257–91

Rouse, Mary A., and Richard H. Rouse, *Manuscripts and their Makers: Commercial Book Producers in Medieval Paris, 1200–1500*, vol. 1, *Illiterati et uxorati 1* (Turnhout: Harvey Miller, 2000)

'The Development of Research Tools in the Thirteenth Century' in Mary A. Rouse and Richard H. Rouse, *Authentic Witnesses: Approaches to Medieval Texts and Manuscripts* (Notre Dame, IN: University of Notre Dame Press, 1991), pp. 221–55

Ruff, Carin, 'Latin as an Acquired Language' in Ralph Turner and David Townsend (eds.), *The Oxford Handbook of Medieval Latin Literature* (Oxford: Oxford University Press, 2015), pp. 47–62, www.oxfordhandbooks.com (accessed 6 April 2016)

Ryan, Magnus, 'Succession to Fiefs: A *Ius Commune Feudorum*' in John Cairns and Paul du Plessis (eds.), *The Creation of the* Ius Commune: *From* Casus *to* Regula (Edinburgh University Press, 2010), pp. 143–58

Paul Saenger, 'Reading in the Later Middle Ages' in Guglielmo Cavallo, Roger Chartier, and Lydia G. Cochrane (eds.), *A History of Reading in the West* (Amherst: University of Massachusetts Press, 1999), pp. 120–48

Sarat, Austin, 'Legal Effectiveness and Social Studies of Law: On the Unfortunate Persistance of a Research Tradition', *Legal Studies Forum*, 9:1 (1985), 23–32

Sargent, Michael G., 'Manuscript Textuality' in Neil Fraistat and Julia Flanders (eds.), *The Cambridge Companion to Textual Scholarship* (Cambridge: Cambridge University Press, 2013), pp. 224–35

Schenck, Mary Jane, 'Paulin Paris' Influence on Writing about the Feudal Trial in the Roman de Renart', *Reinardus*, 18 (2005), 117–30

'Reading Law as Literature, Reading Literature as Law: A Pragmatist's Approach', *Cahiers de recherches médiévales et humanistes*, 25 (2013), 9–29

Sergène, A., 'Le précédent judiciaire au moyen âge', *Revue historique du droit français et étranger*, 39 (1961), 224–54

Shoemaker, Karl, '"I Have Asked for Nothing Except the *Ius Commune*": Legal Change in Thirteenth-Century France' in Elisheva Baumgarten and J. Galinsky (eds.), *Jews and Christians in Thirteenth-Century France* (New York: Palgrave Macmillan, 2–15), pp. 65–76

Sanctuary and Crime in the Middle Ages, 400–1500 (New York: Fordham University Press, 2011)

Small, Carola, 'Artois in the Late Thirteenth Century: A Region Discovering Its Identity?', *Historical Reflections / Réflexions Historiques* 19:2 (1993), 189–207

Smedley-Weill, Anette, and Simone Geoffroy-Poisson, 'Les assemblées d'états et la mise en forme du droit: Comparaisons et analyses formelles des coutumes rédigées et réformées d'Auxerre, de Sens et de Touraine', *Les Cahiers du Centre de Recherches Historiques*, 26 (2001), 1–62

Smith, Colin C., 'The Vernacular' in David Abulafia (ed.), *The New Cambridge Medieval History*, vol. 5, c. *1198–1300* (Cambridge: Cambridge University Press, 1999), pp. 71–83

Sobecki, Sebastian, *Unwritten Verities: The Making of England's Vernacular Legal Culture, 1463–1549* (University of Notre Dame Press, 2015)

Spiegel, Gabrielle M., *Romancing the Past: The Rise of Vernacular Prose Historiography in Thirteenth-Century France* (Berkeley: University of California Press, 1993)

Stacey, Robin Chapman, *Dark Speech: The Performance of Law in Early Ireland* (Philadelphia: University of Pennsylvania Press, 2007)

Stein, Henri, 'Conjectures sur l'auteur du "Livre de jostice et de plet"', *Nouvelle revue historique de droit français et étranger* 41 (1917), 346–82

Stein, Peter, 'Custom in Roman and Medieval Civil Law', *Continuity & Change*, 10:3 (1995), 337–44

   Roman Law in European History (Cambridge: Cambridge University Press, 1999)

Steiner, Emily, *Documentary Culture and the Making of Medieval English Literature* (Cambridge: Cambridge University Press, 2003)

Steiner, Sylvie-Marie, 'La Somme rural de Jean Boutillier: Un coutumier au carrefour du droit, de l'histoire et de la sociologie', *Revue de la BNF*, 1:58 (2019), 122–33

Stella, Attilio, 'Bringing the Feudal Law Back Home: Social Practice and the Law of Fiefs in Italy and Provence (1100–1250)', *Journal of Medieval History*, 46:4 (2020), 396–418

Stock, Brian, *The Implications of Literacy: Written Language and Models of Interpretations in the Eleventh and Twelfth Centuries* (Princeton, NJ: Princeton University Press, 1983)

Strayer, Joseph, *On the Medieval Origins of the Modern State* (Princeton, NJ: Princeton University Press, 1970)

   'Review of Yvonne Bongert, *Recherches sur les cours laïques du Xe au XIIIe siècle*, Paris, A. et J. Picard, 1949', *Traditio*, 7 (1951), 507–8

Symes, Carol, 'The Appearance of Early Vernacular Plays: Forms, Functions and the Future of Medieval Theatre', *Speculum*, 77:3 (2002), 778–831

   A Common Stage: Theatre and Public Life in Medieval Arras (Ithaca, NY: Cornell University Press, 2007)

Szpiech, Ryan, 'Latin as a Language of Authoritative Tradition' in Ralph Turner and David Townsend (eds.), *The Oxford Handbook of Medieval Latin Literature* (Oxford: Oxford University Press, 2015), pp. 63–85

Tardif, Ernest Josef, *Les auteurs présumés du Grand coutumier de Normandie* (Paris, L. Larose et Forcel, 1885)

Taylor, Alice, 'Formalising Aristocratic Power in Royal Acta in Late Twelfth-
and Early Thirteenth-Century France and Scotland', *Transactions of the
Royal Historical Society* 28 (2018), 33–64

'Lex Scripta and the Problem of Enforcement: Anglo-Saxon, Welsh and
Scottish law compared' in Fernanda Pirie and Judith Scheele (eds.),
Legalism: Justice and Community (Oxford: Oxford University Press,
2014), pp. 47–75

Teuscher, Simon, *Lords' Rights and Peasant Stories: Writing and the
Formation of Tradition in the Later Middle Ages*, trans. Philip Grace
(Philadelphia: University of Pennsylvania Press, 2012)

Thireau, Jean-Louis, *Charles du Moulin (1500–1566), Études sur les sources,
la méthode, les idées politiques et économiques d'un juriste de la
Renaissance*, vol. 1 (Paris: Droz, 1980)

'La territorialité des coutumes au Moyen Âge' in Giles Constable and
Michel Rouche (eds.), *Auctoritas: Mélanges offerts à Olivier Guillot*
(Paris: Presses Universitaires de la Sorbonne, 2006), pp. 453–65

Thomas, Rosalind, 'Written in Stone? Liberty, Equality, Orality and the
Codification of Law', *Bulletin of the Institute of Classical Studies*, 40
(1995), 59–74

Thompson, E. P., *Customs in Common* (London: Merlin Press, 1991)

Tiersma, Peter M., *Legal Language* (Chicago, IL: University of Chicago Press,
1999)

Tisset, Pierre, 'Mythes et réalités du droit écrit' in *Études d'histoire du
droit privé offertes à Pierre Petot* (Paris: Montchrestien, 1959), pp.
553–60

Topping, Peter W., *Feudal Institutions as Revealed in the 'Assizes of Romania',
the Law Code of Frankish Greece* (Philadelphia: University of
Pennsylvania Press, 1949)

Trubek, David M., 'Where the Action Is: Critical Legal Studies and
Empiricism', *Stanford Law Review*, 36:1/2 (1984), 575–622

Turner, Ralph, and David Townsend (eds.), *The Oxford Handbook of
Medieval Latin Literature* (Oxford: Oxford University Press, 2015)

Uelmen, Amelia J., 'A View of the Legal Profession from a Mid-Twelfth-
Century Monastery', *Fordham Law Review*, 71:4 (2003), 1517–41

Umiker-Sebeok, Jean, and Thomas Sebeok (eds.), *Monastic Sign Language*
(Berlin: de Gruyter, 1987)

Valliere, Paul, *Conciliarism: A History of Decision-Making in the Church*
(Cambridge: Cambridge University Press, 2012)

Van Caenegem, R. C., *An Historical Introduction to Private Law*, trans.
D. E. L. Johnston (Cambridge: Cambridge University Press, 1992)

van de Wouw, Hans, 'Quelques remarques sur les versions
françaises médiévales des textes de droit romain' in André Gouron and
Aquilino Iglesia Ferreirós (eds.), *El Dret Comú i Catalunya: Ius*

proprium–ius commune a Europa (Barcelona: Fundació Noguera, 1993), pp. 139–50

van Dievoet, Guido, *Les coutumiers, les styles, les formulaires et les 'artes notariae'*, Typologie des sources du Moyen Âge occidental 48 (Turnhout: Brepols, 1986)

van Hoecke, Willy, 'La "première réception" du droit romain et ses repercussions sur la structure lexicale des langues vernaculaires', *Medieval Antiquity* (1995), 197–217

van Wetter, P. 'Le droit romain et Beaumanoir' in *Mélanges Fitting* (Paris: Flammarion, 1908), vol. 2, pp. 532–82

Vanderlinden, Jacques, 'Here, there and everywhere ... or nowhere? Some comparative and historical afterthoughts about custom as a source of law' in Olivier Moréteau, Aniceto Masferrer, and Kjell A. Modéer (eds.), *Comparative Legal History* (Northampton, MA: Edward Elgar, 2019), pp. 140–66

Verger, Jacques, *Les gens de savoir en Europe à la fin du Moyen Âge* (Paris: Presses Universitaires Français, 1997)

'The Universities and Scholasticism' in David Abulafia (ed.), *The New Cambridge Medieval History*, vol. 5, *c. 1198–1300* (Cambridge: Cambridge University Press, 1999), pp. 256–78

Vincent, Nicholas, 'Magna carta (1215) and the Charte aux Normands (1315): Some Anglo-Norman Connections and Correspondences', *The Jersey and Guernsey Law Review* 2 (2015), 189–97, www.jerseylaw.je/publicaton/jglr/Pages/JLR1506_ShorterVincent.aspx (accessed 13 October 2020)

Vinogradoff, Paul *Roman Law in Medieval Europe* (Oxford: Clarendon Press, 1929)

Viollet, Paul, 'Les Coutumiers de Normandie', *Histoire littéraire de la France*, 33 (1906), 41–190

Vismann, Cornelia, *Files: Law and Media Technology*, trans. by Geoffrey Winthrop-Young (Palo Alto, CA: Stanford University Press, 2008)

Voltaire, *Dictionnaire philosophique*, vol. 3. Vol. 40 of*Oeuvres de Voltaire, avec préfaces, avertissements, notes, etc.*, ed. M. Beuchot (Paris: Lefèvre, Werdet et Lequien fils, 1829)

von Savigny, Friedrich Karl, *The Vocation of our Age for Legislation and Jurisprudence*, trans. Abraham Hayward (London: Littlewood, 1831)

Waelkens, Laurent, 'L'origine de l'*enquête par turbe*', *Tijdschrift voor Rechtsgeschiedenis*, 53 (1985), 337–46

'La théorie de la coutume à l'école de droit d'Orléans (XIIIe siècle)' in Jacques Vanderlinden (ed.), *La Coutume = Custom*, vol. 2, *Europe occidentale médiévale et moderne* (Brussels: De Boeck, 1990), 33–39

La théorie de la coutume chez Jacques de Révigny: Éditions et analyse de sa répétition sur la loi De quibus (D. 1, 3, 32), Rechtshistorische Studies 10 (Leiden: Brill, 1984)

Wakelin, Daniel, *Scribal Correction and Literary Craft: English Manuscripts 1375–1510* (Cambridge: Cambridge University Press, 2014)

Wangerin, Laura E., *Kingship and Justice in the Ottonian Empire* (Ann Arbor: University of Michigan Press, 2019)

Watson, Alan, *Legal Transplants: An Approach to Comparative Law*, 2nd ed. (Athens: University of Georgia Press, 1993)

Watson, Nicholas, 'The Idea of Latinity' in Ralph Turner and David Townsend (eds.), *The Oxford Handbook of Medieval Latin Literature* (Oxford: Oxford University Press, 2015), pp. 124–50, www.oxfordhandbooks.com (accessed 6 April 2016)

Wauters, Bart, and Marco de Benito, *The History of Law in Europe: An Introduction* (Cheltenham: Edward Elgar Publishing, 2017)

Wehrlé, René, *De la coutume dans le droit canonique: Essai historique s'étendant des origines de l'Église au pontificat de Pie XI* (Paris: Sirey, 1928)

Weinrich, Lorenz (ed.), *Quellen zur deutschen Verfassungs-, Wirtschafts- und Sozialgeschichte*, trans. Steve Lane (Darmstadt, Germany: Wissenschaftliche Buchgesellschaft, 1977), www.fordham.edu/halsall/source/lexworms.asp (accessed 26 June 2022)

Weisberg, Richard, *Poethics and Other Strategies of Law and Literature* (New York: Columbia University Press, 1992)

White, G. Edward, 'From Realism to Critical Legal Studies: A Truncated Intellectual History', *SMU Law Review*, 40:2 (1986), 819–43

White, Hayden, 'The Value of Narrativity in the Representation of Reality', *Critical Inquiry*, 7:1 (1980), 5–27, www.jstor.org/stable/1343174 (accessed 25 February 2020)

White, James B., *The Legal Imagination* (Chicago, IL: University of Chicago Press, 1985)

White, Stephen D., *Customs, Kinship and Gifts to Saints: The Laudatio Parentum in Western France (1050–1150)* (Chapel Hill: University of North Carolina Press, 1988)

  'The Discourse of Inheritance in Twelfth-Century France: Alternative Models of the Fief in *Raoul de Cambrai*' in *Law and Government in Medieval England and Normandy: Essays in Honour of Sir James Holt*, ed. G. S. Garnett and J. G. H. Hudson (Cambridge, 1994), pp. 173–97

  'Inheritances and Legal Arguments in Western France, 1050–1150', *Traditio*, 43 (1987), 55–103

  '"Pactum . . . Legem Vincit et Amor Judicium" – The Settlement of Disputes by Compromise in Eleventh-Century Western France', *The American Journal of Legal History*, 22:4 (1978), 281–308

  'Review of *Fiefs and Vassals: The Medieval Evidence Reinterpreted*, by Susan Reynolds', *Law and History Review*, 15 (1997), 349–55

Whitman, James Q., 'Law and the Pre-Modern Mind', *Stanford Law Review*,
    44:1 (1991), 205–17
    *The Legacy of Roman Law in the German Romantic Era: Historical Vision
    and Legal Change* (Princeton, NJ: Princeton University Press, 1990)
    The Origins of Reasonable Doubt: Theological Roots of the Criminal Trial
    (New Haven, CT: Yale University Press, 2008)
    'Why Did the Revolutionary Lawyers Confuse Custom and Reason?',
    University of Chicago Law Review, 58:4 (1991), 1321–68
Wickham, Chris, *Legge, pratiche e conflitti: Tribunali e risoluzione delle
    dispute nella Toscana del XII secolo*, ed. Antonio Sennis (Rome: Viella,
    2000)
Winroth, Anders, *The Making of Gratian's Decretum* (Cambridge: Cambridge
    University Press, 2000)
    'The Two Recensions of Gratian's Decretum', *Zeitschrift der Savigny-
    Siftung für Rechtsgeschichte: Kanonistische Abteilung*, 83 (1997),
    22–31
Wogan-Browne, Jocelyn, et al., Jocelyn 'General Introduction: What's in
    a Name: The "French" of "England"' in *Language and Culture in
    Medieval Britain: The French of England, c.1100–c.1500* (Woodbridge:
    York Medieval, 2009), pp. 1–13
    *The Idea of the Vernacular: An Anthology of Middle English Literary
    Theory, 1280–1520* (University Park: Pennsylvania State University
    Press, 1999)
    *Language and Culture in Medieval Britain: The French of England, c.1100–
    c.1500* (Woodbridge: York Medieval, 2009)
Woodbine, George, 'The Language of English Law', *Speculum*, 18 (1943),
    395–436
Wormald, Patrick, '*Lex Scripta* and *Verbum Regis*: Legislation and Germanic
    Kingship, from Euric to Cnut' in *Legal Culture in the Early Medieval West*
    (London: Hambledon Press, 1999), pp. 1–44
    The Making of English Law: King Alfred to the Twelfth Century, vol. 1,
    Legislation and Its Limits (Oxford: Blackwell, 1999)
    *Papers Preparatory to the Making of English Law: King Alfred to the
    Twelfth Century*, vol. 2, *From God's Law to Common Law*, ed.
    Stephen Baxter and John Hudson (University of London: Early English
    Laws, 2014), https://bit.ly/3OmGXgf (accessed 24 June 2022)
Yen, Alfred C., 'Western Frontier or Feudal Society?: Metaphors and
    Perceptions of Cyberspace', *Berkeley Technology Law Journal*, 17:4
    (2002), 1207–63
Yver, Jean, 'Les caractères originaux du groupe de coutumes de l'ouest de la
    France', *Revue historique de droit français et étranger*, 30 (1952), 18–79
    *Égalité entre héritiers et exclusion des enfants dotés, Essai de géographie
    coutumière* (Paris: Sirey, 1966)

'Le très ancien coutumier de Normandie: Miroir de la législation ducale? Contribution à l'étude de l'ordre public normand à la fin du XIe siècle', *Tijdschrift voor Rechtsgeschiedenis*, 39 (1971), 333–74

Ziolkowski, Jan M., 'Cultural Diglossia and the Nature of Medieval Latin Literature' in Joseph Harris (ed.), *The Ballad and Oral Literature* (Cambridge, MA: Harvard University Press, 1991), pp. 193–213

'Latin and Vernacular Literature' in David Luscombe (ed.), *The New Cambridge Medieval History*, vol. 4, *c. 1024–1198* (Cambridge: Cambridge University Press, 2004), pp. 658–92

Zumthor, Paul, *Essai de poétique médiévale* (Paris: Du Seuil, 1972)

Zwalve, W. J., *Law & Equity: Approaches in Roman Law and Common Law*, Legal History Library 20 (Leiden: Brill, 2013)

Index

Abbo of Fleury, *Collectio Canonum*, 42, 132
Ableiges, Jacques d', *Grand coutumier de France*, 320, 343, 348, 350
abstraction, judicial, 326–30
Accursius, *Glossa ordinaria*, 50–1, 134
Achilles, 105
advocates, 33, 62, 72, 80, 312
advowson, 75
Alain of Lille, 193, 194
Alaric, *Breviary*, 13, 56, 58, 223, 224
Alexander III, pope, 115
Alexander the Great, 105
Alfonso X, king of Castile, 181
alms, 164
Amiens, 84, 351
Ancien coutumier de Bourgogne, 5
Ancien coutumier de Champagne, 5, 105, 151
  citations, 202–3, 228
  court cases, 235
  description of, 83–4
  jurisdiction, 339
  manuscripts of, 83
  variation, textual, 280
Andreas Capellanus, *On Love*, 64
animals, customs concerning, 68, 86
Anjou, 181, 185, 321, 322, 323, 324, 349
Ansegisus of Fontanelle, 56
Anthemius, Western Roman emperor, 38
Antoninius, Roman emperor, 224

appeals, 18, 69, 72, 78, 80, 85, 178, 179, 184, 298
Aquinas, Thomas, 48
arbitration, 72, 82, 248, 254, 285
Aristotle, 197
  Rhetoric, 50
army summons, 68
Arras, 99
arrests, 80
ars memorativa, 143
arson, 164, 244, 245, 311
Artois, 181, 243, 321, 323
  legal centre, lay, 342–3
assault, 74
Assises de Normandie, 87–8, 103
Assises of Antioch, 345–6
Assises of Romania, 108, 344–5
Assizes of Ariano (Assizes of Roger II), 64, 65, 100
Athens, 128, 130
Augustine, saint, bishop of Hippo, 37
Azo, *Summa Codicis*, 49–51, 101, 145, 237

baillis, 13, 112, 113, 114, 116, 117, 118, 145, 177, 180, 181, 201, 236, 242, 252, 253, 256, 257, 342, 343
Baldus, 53–4
Bartholomaeus Brixiensis, *Glossa Ordinaria*, 195
Bartolus, 53
Basil of Caesarea, 37

402

For EU product safety concerns, contact us at Calle de José Abascal, 56–1°, 28003 Madrid, Spain or eugpsr@cambridge.org.